BUSINESS
MARKETING
MANAGEMENT
A Strategic View of
Industrial and Organizational Markets
Fourth Edition

ABOUT THE TITLE

Since the first edition of *Industrial Marketing Management* was released in 1981, a rich and growing body of literature and thought has been devoted to this special marketing area. Increasingly, this research has been extended to include the full range of strategic issues confronting business-to-business marketers. Clearly, industrial customers, although assuming a very prominent role, constitute but one component of the much broader business market. The term *business marketing* has been adopted by professional associations (e.g., American Marketing Association), by research centers (e.g., Pennsylvania State's Institute for the Study of Business Markets), by corporations (e.g., AT&T Business Markets Group), and by marketing scholars in the United States, Canada, and Europe. Reflecting this broadening perspective, the third edition adopted the title *Business Marketing Management: A Strategic View of Industrial and Organizational Markets.* As trends in marketing for the 1990s and beyond continue to support this choice, the fourth edition retains this title and, more importantly, this strategic focus.

BUSINESS MARKETING MANAGEMENT

A Strategic View of
Industrial and Organizational Markets

Fourth Edition

MICHAEL D. HUTT
Arizona State University

THOMAS W. SPEH
Miami University

The Dryden Press
A Harcourt Brace Jovanovich College Publisher

Fort Worth Philadelphia San Diego New York Orlando Austin San Antonio
Toronto Montreal London Sydney Tokyo

Acquisitions Editor: Rob Zwettler
Project Editor: Teresa Chartos
Art and Design Manager: Alan Wendt
Production Manager: Bob Lange
Director of Editing, Design, and Production: Jane Perkins

Text and Cover Designer: C. J. Petlick, Hunter Graphics
Copy Editor: Cathy Crow
Indexer: Marie Miller, Best Indexing Service
Text Type: 10/12 ITC Garamond Light

Library of Congress Cataloging-in-Publication Data

Hutt, Michael D.
    Business marketing management : a strategic view of industrial and
organizational markets / Michael D. Hutt, Thomas W. Speh — 4th ed.
        p.   cm.
    Includes bibliographical references and index.
    ISBN 0-03-054167-0
    1. Industrial marketing—Management—Case studies.   I. Speh,
Thomas W.   II. Title.
    HF5415.13.H87   1992
    658.8'04—dc20   91-8610
                                                                      CIP

Printed in the United States of America
123-039-987654321
Copyright © 1992, 1989, 1985, 1981 by The Dryden Press

Address orders:
The Dryden Press
Orlando, Florida 32887

Address editorial correspondence:
The Dryden Press
301 Commerce Street, Suite 3700
Fort Worth, TX 76102

The Dryden Press
Harcourt Brace Jovanovich

Cover Illustration by Warren Gebert.

To Rita
and
To Michele, Scott,
Michael, and Betsy

THE DRYDEN PRESS SERIES IN MARKETING

PREFACE

Special challenges and opportunities confront the marketer who intends to serve the needs of organizations rather than households. Commercial enterprises, institutions, and all levels of government constitute a lucrative and complex market worthy of separate analysis. A growing number of collegiate schools of business in the United States, Canada, and Europe have added industrial or business marketing to their curricula. In turn, the past several years have witnessed a rich and growing body of literature and thought in this special marketing area. Increasingly, this research has been extended to include the full range of strategic issues confronting business-to-business marketers. Industrial customers, although assuming a prominent role, constitute but one component of the much broader business market environment. Reflecting this broadening perspective, the third edition adopted the title *Business Marketing Management: A Strategic View of Industrial and Organizational Markets*. As trends in marketing for the 1990s and beyond continue to support this choice, the fourth edition retains this title and, more importantly, this strategic focus.

The growing acceptance of the term *business marketing* and the rising importance of the area can be demonstrated by several factors. First, the Institute for the Study of Business Markets (ISBM) at Pennsylvania State University has provided important impetus to research in the area. ISBM has become a major information resource for researchers and practitioners and has assumed an active role in stimulating and supporting research on substantive business marketing issues. Second, the titles of trade journals such as *Business Marketing,* as well as the name of the Business Marketing Division of the American Marketing Association, reflect recent changes from an industrial to a business designation. More importantly, the launching of the *Journal of Business-to-Business Marketing* under the editorship of David T. Wilson (Pennsylvania State University) provides an additional forum for quality research in the area. Third, because more than half of all business school graduates enter firms that compete in business markets, a comprehensive treatment of business marketing management appears to be particularly appropriate.

Three objectives guided the development of this edition:

1. *To highlight the similarities between consumer goods and business-to-business marketing and to explore the points of departure in depth.* Particular attention is given to market analysis, organizational buying behavior, relationship management, and the ensuing adjustments required in the marketing strategy elements used to reach organizational customers.

2. *To present a managerial rather than a descriptive treatment of business market-ing.* Whereas some descriptive material is required to convey the dynamic nature of the business marketing environment, the relevance of the material is linked to business marketing management decision making.

3. *To integrate the growing body of literature into an operational treatment of business marketing management.* In this text, relevant work is drawn from organizational buying behavior, procurement, organizational behavior, logistics, strategic management, and the behavioral sciences, as well as from specialized studies of business marketing strategy components.

The book is structured to provide a complete treatment of business marketing while minimizing the degree of overlap with other courses in the marketing curriculum. A basic marketing principles course (or relevant managerial experience) provides the needed background for this text.

NEW TO THIS EDITION

Although the basic objectives, approach, and style of the first three editions have been maintained, several changes and additions have been made that reflect both the growing body of literature and the emerging trends in business marketing management. Specifically, the following distinctive features are incorporated into the fourth edition:

- A new chapter, "Business Marketing Strategies for Global Markets" (Chapter 9).

- New and expanded coverage of the timely topics of relationship management, fast-cycle product development processes, product quality, competitive bench-marking, market-driven management processes, and strategic alliances.

- A streamlined and richly illustrated discussion of forecasting techniques for busi-ness markets.

- Contemporary business marketing strategies and challenges illustrated with three types of engaging vignettes, "Inside Business Marketing," "The Global Market-place," and—new to this edition—"Ethical Business Marketing."

ORGANIZATION OF THE FOURTH EDITION

The needs and interests of the reader provided the focus in the development of this volume. The authors' goal is to present a clear and interesting examination of business marketing management. To this end, each chapter provides an overview, highlights key concepts, and includes several carefully chosen examples of contemporary busi-ness marketing practices as well as a cogent summary and a set of provocative discussion questions.

The book is divided into six parts with a total of 18 chapters. Part I introduces the distinguishing features of the business marketing environment. Careful examination is given to each of the major types of customers that constitute the business market. Organizational buying behavior establishes the theme of Part II, in which the many forces encircling the organizational buying process are explored in depth. This edition has been updated to incorporate the substantial amount of research that has been conducted in this area since the third edition was published.

Once this important background is established in the area of organizational buying behavior, Part III centers on the intelligence function and on the techniques that can be employed in assessing market opportunities. Chapter-length attention is given to the topics of business marketing intelligence, market segmentation, and market potential and sales forecasting. This edition also provides expanded treatment of international market analysis.

Part IV centers on the planning process and on designing marketing strategy for business markets. Recent work drawn from the strategic management and strategic marketing areas provides the foundation for this section. Special emphasis is given to competitive analysis and to the interfacing of marketing with other key functional areas such as manufacturing, research and development, and customer service. This functionally integrated planning perspective serves as a focal point in the analysis of the strategy development process. Here at the core of the volume, a new chapter provides an integrated treatment of strategy formulation for the international market arena. Next, each component of the marketing mix is examined from a business marketing perspective. Adding further depth to this core section are the chapters on managing product innovation and managing services for business markets.

Part V examines techniques for evaluating business marketing strategy and performance. It provides comprehensive treatment of marketing control systems and presents an organizing framework for marketing profitability analysis. Special attention is given to the critical area of strategy implementation in the business marketing environment. Part VI includes a collection of cases tailored to the business marketing environment.

CASES

Part VI includes 18 cases, 8 of which are new to this edition. This section provides cases of varying lengths, each of which isolates one or more business marketing problems. A *Case Planning Guide,* which keys the cases to relevant text chapters, provides an organizing structure for Part VI.

TEACHING PACKAGE

A comprehensive and thoroughly updated *Instructor's Manual, Test Bank, and Transparency Masters* is available, which includes suggestions for course design, support materials for teaching each chapter, and 50 transparency masters. Guidelines are provided for end-of-chapter discussion questions, and suggestions are provided for case use and analysis. Several hundred objective test questions are provided in the manual, and a comprehensive set of essay questions is included to allow instructors to tailor exams to their particular needs.

A *computerized test bank* for the IBM PC is also available for the first time with this edition.

ACKNOWLEDGMENTS

The development of a textbook draws upon the contributions of many individuals. First, we would like to thank our students and former students at Arizona State University, Miami University, the University of Alabama, and the University of Vermont. They provided important input and feedback when selected concepts or chapters were class-tested. We would also like to thank our colleagues at each of these institutions for their assistance and support.

Second, we express our gratitude to several distinguished colleagues who carefully reviewed the manuscript at various stages of development and provided incisive comments and valuable suggestions that improved the fourth edition. They include:

Paul D. Boughton, *Saint Louis University*
Jay L. Laughlin, *Kansas State University*
Bernard A. Rausch, *Illinois Institute of Technology*
David A. Reid, *The University of Toledo*
Paul A. Roobol, *Western Michigan University*
James F. Wolter, *Grand Valley State University*
Lauren K. Wright, *California State University–Chico*
John M. Zerio, *American Graduate School of International Management*

We would also like to express our continuing appreciation to others who provided important suggestions that helped shape earlier editions: Paul F. Anderson, *Pennsylvania State University;* Joseph A. Bellizzi, *Arizona State University–West Campus;* Jon M. Hawes, *University of Akron;* Gary L. Lilien, *Pennsylvania State University;* and Lindsay N. Meredith, *Simon Fraser University.*

Third, we would like to thank the Institute for the Study of Business Markets at Pennsylvania State University for giving us access to their rich working paper series.

A number of business marketing practitioners, including several participants in past management development seminars, provided valuable suggestions and interesting examples. We are especially indebted to Jeffrey A. Coopersmith, *Directel, Inc.;* Gerry Daley, *The Black-Clawson Company, Shartle-Pandia Division;* Patrick W. Fitzgerald, *Cincinnati Electric Equipment Company;* Rod O'Connor, *Motorola, Inc., Government Electronics Group;* Edward Sauer, *Industrial Product Division, Procter & Gamble;* and Cap Stubbs, *Raychem Corporation.*

The talented staff of The Dryden Press displayed a high level of enthusiasm and professionalism throughout the project. In particular, Rob Zwettler assumed an instrumental role in helping us shape the past two editions. In turn, our project editor, Teresa Chartos, again displayed that she is among the best in the industry.

Finally, but most importantly, our overriding debt is to our wives, Rita and Michele, whose encouragement, understanding, and expertise were vital to the completion of this edition. Their involvement and dedication are deeply appreciated.

Michael D. Hutt
Thomas W. Speh
September 1991

ABOUT THE AUTHORS

Michael D. Hutt, Ph.D., is Professor of Marketing at Arizona State University. He has also held positions at Miami University (Ohio) and the University of Vermont.

Dr. Hutt's teaching and research interests are concentrated in the areas of business marketing and marketing strategy. His research has been published in the *Journal of Marketing, Journal of Marketing Research, Industrial Marketing Management, Journal of Retailing, Journal of Personal Selling & Sales Management,* and other scholarly publications. He is also the co-author of *Macro Marketing* (John Wiley & Sons, Inc.). In 1991, Dr. Hutt was the recipient of the Distinguished Faculty Researcher Award in Arizona State University's College of Business.

Dr. Hutt has served as co-chairperson of the American Marketing Association Faculty Consortium on Industrial Marketing and as a member of the Business Marketing Council of the American Marketing Association. He is currently a member of the editorial review board of the *Journal of Business-to-Business Marketing.* Dr. Hutt has consulted on marketing strategy issues for such firms as Motorola, Arvin Industries, ADT, Black Clawson, and for the food industry's Public Policy Subcommittee on the Universal Product Code.

Thomas W. Speh, Ph.D., is the Joseph C. Seibert Professor of Marketing and Director of the Warehousing Research Center at Miami University (Ohio). Prior to his tenure at Miami, Dr. Speh taught at the University of Alabama and Michigan State University.

Dr. Speh has been a regular participant in professional marketing and logistics meetings and has published articles in a number of academic and professional journals, including the *Journal of Marketing, Journal of Business Logistics, Journal of Retailing, Journal of Purchasing and Materials Management, I.C.C. Practitioner's Journal,* and *Industrial Marketing Management.* He was the recipient of the Beta Gamma Sigma Distinguished Faculty award for excellence in teaching at Miami University's School of Business and of the Miami University Alumni Association's Effective Educator award.

Dr. Speh has been active in both the Warehousing Education and Research Council (WERC) and the Council of Logistics Management (CLM). He has served as president of WERC and as a member of the executive committee for both WERC and CLM. Dr. Speh has been a consultant on strategy issues to such organizations as Xerox, Procter & Gamble, Burlington Northern Railroad, Itel Distribution Services, J. M. Smucker Co., L. M. Berry, Inc., and Excel Logistics.

CASE CONTRIBUTORS

Roger D. Blackwell, *The Ohio State University*
Christine Hunt Blouke, *KnowledgeEdge, Inc.*
Jan Willem Bol, *Miami University (Ohio)*
James W. Cagley, *University of Tulsa*
Harold Crookell, *University of Western Ontario*
Cornelius A. de Kluyver, *University of Virginia (Darden Graduate Business School)*
John B. Gifford, *Miami University (Ohio)*
George B. Glisan, *Illinois State University*
H. Michael Hayes, *University of Colorado at Denver*
Roger A. Kerin, *Southern Methodist University*
Thomas J. Kosnik, *Harvard Business School*
Dale A. Lunsford, *University of Tulsa*
David McConaughy, *University of Southern California*
Roger More, *University of Western Ontario*
Robert A. Peterson, *University of Texas–Austin*
Stuart U. Rich, *University of Oregon*
David W. Rosenthal, *Miami University (Ohio)*
Alan J. Stenger, *Pennsylvania State University*
Dan R. E. Thomas, *KnowledgeEdge, Inc.*

CONTENTS IN BRIEF

CONTENTS

Chapter 10   Managing the Product Line for Business Markets   *271*

Chapter 11   Managing Innovation and New Industrial Product Development   *299*

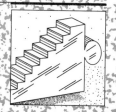

PART I

The Environment of Business Marketing

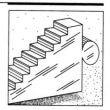

CHAPTER 1

A Business Marketing Perspective

The business market poses special challenges and significant opportunities for the marketing manager. This chapter introduces the complex forces that are unique to the business marketing environment. After reading this chapter, you will understand:

1. the dynamic nature of the business marketing environment as well as the basic similarities and differences between consumer-goods and business marketing.

2. the underlying factors that influence the demand for industrial goods.

3. the types of customers in this important market.

4. some important dimensions of the processes that customers use in buying products and services in the business market.

5. the basic characteristics of industrial products and services.

BUSINESS MARKETING

Business marketers serve the largest market of all; the dollar volume of transactions in the industrial or business market significantly exceeds that of the ultimate consumer market. In the business market, a single customer can account for an enormous level of purchasing activity. For example, General Motors' purchasing department spends more than $60 billion annually on industrial products and services—more than the gross national product of Ireland, Portugal, Turkey, or Greece. Others, such as General Electric, IBM, and AT&T, spend more than $50 million per day on purchases to support

3

their operations.[1] Indeed, all formal organizations, large or small, public or private, profit or not-for-profit, participate in the exchange of industrial products and services, thus constituting the business market.

Business markets are "markets for products and services, local to international, bought by businesses, government bodies, and institutions (such as hospitals) for incorporation (e.g., ingredient materials or components), for consumption (e.g., process materials, office supplies, consulting services), for use (e.g., installations or equipment), or for resale. . . . The only markets not of direct interest are those dealing with products or services which are principally directed at personal use or consumption, such as packaged grocery products, home appliances, or consumer banking."[2] The factors that distinguish business marketing from consumer marketing are the nature of the customer and how that customer uses the product. In business marketing, the customers are organizations (businesses, governments, institutions).

Business firms buy industrial goods to form or facilitate the production process or to be used as components for other goods and services. Government agencies and private institutions buy industrial goods to maintain and deliver services to their own market—the public. Industrial or business marketing (the terms can be used interchangeably) accounts for more than half the economic activity in the United States, Canada, and most other nations. More than 50 percent of all business school graduates enter firms that compete directly in the business market. The heightened interest in high-technology markets—and the sheer size of the business market—has spawned increased emphasis on business marketing management in universities and corporate executive training programs.[3]

This book is designed to provide an operational treatment of business marketing management by drawing on the literature of organizational buying behavior, procurement, organizational behavior, logistics, and strategic management, as well as by drawing on the specialized studies of business marketing strategy. The integrating questions are: What are the similarities and differences between consumer-goods marketing and business marketing? What customers constitute the business market? How can the multitude of industrial goods be classified into manageable categories? What forces influence the behavior of business market demand? These questions establish the theme of this first chapter.

---

[1] "Top 100: The Largest Purchasing Departments in U.S. Industry," *Purchasing,* 103 (November 23, 1989), pp. 51–72.

[2] Prospectus for The Institute for the Study of Business Markets, College of Business Administration, The Pennsylvania State University.

[3] Sue Kapp, "Education: Slowly on Course for '90s," *Business Marketing,* 75 (January 1990), p. 54; and Eugene J. Kelley and Lisa R. Hearne, "Management Education and the Broadening Role of Business-to-Business Marketing," Report #6-1986, Institute for the Study of Business Markets, College of Business Administration, The Pennsylvania State University.

BUSINESS MARKETING MANAGEMENT

Many large firms that produce goods such as steel, production equipment, or computer-memory chips cater exclusively to business market customers and never come into direct contact with ultimate consumers. Other firms participate in both the consumer-goods and the business markets. The introduction of personal computers brought IBM, historically a business-to-business marketer, into the consumer market.[4] Conversely, lagging consumer markets prompted Sony Corporation to expand to the business market by introducing office automation products. Both companies had to reorient their marketing strategies dramatically because of the significant differences between the buying behavior exhibited in the consumer market and that exhibited in the business market.

Products like calculators or personal computers are purchased in both the consumer and the business markets. What distinguishes business marketing from consumer-goods marketing is the *intended use of the product* and the *intended consumer.* Sometimes the products are identical, but a fundamentally different marketing approach is needed to reach the organizational buyer.

Business Markets versus Consumer-Goods Markets

The basic task of management cuts across both consumer-goods and business marketing.[5] Marketers serving both sectors can benefit by rooting their organizational plan in the **marketing concept**, which holds that the central aim of any organization is to define the needs of a target market and to adapt products or services to satisfy these needs more effectively than competitors.[6] Consumer-goods marketers seem to have embraced this concept more completely than have their business marketing counterparts.[7] Some business marketers are more concerned with the specifications of products than with how these specifications respond to customer needs.

Like consumer-goods marketers, business marketers must design a product or a service (including a communication program and a pricing and distribution system) that reaches and satisfies the needs of a targeted market segment. Philip Kotler's definition of **marketing management** captures the essence of the problem:

---

[4] John Markoff, "IBM Set to Re-enter PC Market," *The New York Times* (June 23, 1990), p. 17.

[5] For a discussion of the similarities between business and consumer marketing, see Edward F. Fern and James R. Brown, "The Industrial/Consumer Marketing Dichotomy: A Case of Insufficient Justification," *Journal of Marketing,* 48 (Spring 1984), pp. 68–77; and for the differences, see Gary L. Lilien, "Business Marketing: Present and Future," Report # 1-1986, Institute for the Study of Business Markets, College of Business Administration, The Pennsylvania State University.

[6] Ajay K. Kohli and Bernard J. Jaworski, "Market Orientation: The Construct, Research Propositions, and Managerial Implications," *Journal of Marketing,* 54 (April 1990), pp. 1–18.

[7] Frederick E. Webster, Jr., "Management Science in Industrial Marketing," *Journal of Marketing,* 42 (January 1978), p. 23; see also Franklin S. Houston, "The Marketing Concept: What It Is and What It Is Not," *Journal of Marketing,* 50 (April 1986), pp. 81–87.

Marketing management is the analysis, planning, implementation, and control of programs designed to create, build, and maintain mutually beneficial exchanges and relationships with target markets for the purpose of achieving organizational objectives.[8]

Industrial marketing and consumer-goods marketing are different. A common body of knowledge, principles, and theory applies to both consumer and business marketing, but because their buyers and markets function quite differently, they merit separate attention. The hope of capturing a share of a large but unfamiliar market leads many consumer-goods companies into the business market arena. Surprises often follow. Many of these firms are frustrated in their attempts to pinpoint specific markets; they are confused by the organizational buying process; many of their traditional marketing approaches turn out to be irrelevant in the business market. Between consumer and business marketing, there are differences in the nature of markets, market demand, buyer behavior, buyer–seller relationships, environmental influences (economic, political, legal), and market strategy. Yet the potential payoffs are high for the firm that can successfully penetrate the business market.

Business Market Demand

The nature of the demand for industrial products poses unique challenges—and opportunities—for the marketing manager.

Derived Demand

Demand for industrial products is derived from ultimate consumer demand. Customers in the business market, such as commercial firms, governments, and not-for-profit institutions, buy goods and services in order to produce other goods and services for their own customers. For example, Apple Computer spends more than 60 percent of each sales dollar on purchased materials.[9] Virtually all the parts and components that make up its computers are designed by Apple engineers, then produced to their specifications by other firms—a carefully chosen set of industrial suppliers. The size of orders that each of these suppliers receives from Apple depends on how well Apple's computers are selling. As this example illustrates, demand for an industrial product is derived from the buying organization's customers (computer buyers), not from the buying organization itself (Apple Computer).

Consider the materials and components used to make a dishwasher. Table 1.1 highlights the volume of materials needed to satisfy the annual U.S. demand of approximately 3.9 million units. At General Electric, for example, such purchased materials and components represent 58 percent of the manufacturing costs of a typical appliance and are provided by nearly 10,000 different suppliers.[10] In purchasing a

---

[8] Philip Kotler, *Marketing Management: Analysis, Planning, and Control,* 5th ed. (Englewood Cliffs, N.J.: Prentice-Hall, Inc., 1984), p. 22.

[9] J.William Semich, "How Apple Computer Buys for the 1990s," *Purchasing,* 103 (June 22, 1989), pp. 43–47.

[10] Shirley Cayer, "Special Report: Major Household Appliance Makers Are Winding Up 20 Years of Consolidation," *Purchasing,* 101 (January 15, 1987), pp. 42–49.

TABLE 1.1   Dishwasher Manufacturers' Annual Demand for Selected Materials and Components

Material	Demand	Material	Demand
Aluminum	7,334 tons	Hose, rubber	600 miles
Brass	189 tons	Valves, water	3.8 million
Plastic	9,025 tons	Connectors, electrical	60.2 million
Steel	106,375 tons	Timers	3.8 million
Insulation	22,755 tons	Paint	752,000 gallons
Motors	7.5 million	Porcelain enamel	3.5 sq. miles

Source: Shirley Cayer, "How the Appliance Industry Buys: Suppose There's a World 'White Goods' War!" *Purchasing,* 103 (March 9, 1989), p. 61.

particular General Electric or Whirlpool appliance, the customer is stimulating the demand for aluminum, brass, paint, and countless other products produced by business marketing firms.

Because demand is derived, the business marketing manager must carefully monitor demand patterns and changing buying preferences in the final consumer markets, often on a worldwide basis. If appliance producers forecast that sales will climb or fall next year, the business marketer must make corresponding changes in the forecast for this segment of the market. Any changes in styling, design, or composition dictated by appliance buyers, competitive pressure, economic conditions, or government agencies may create opportunities for some business marketers—and problems for others. To remain price competitive with Asian appliance producers, some U.S. firms have turned to foreign sources for selected items such as aluminum, electrical connectors, and compressors. As trade barriers have fallen and products have become standardized, U.S. appliance manufacturers have invested more than $1.2 billion to enter world markets, primarily in Europe.[11] For example, through a joint venture with Britain's largest appliance producer, General Electric's goal for the mid-1990s is for European sales of appliances to match the $5-billion-a-year level the firm generates in the United States. Astute business marketers monitor competition on a global basis.

Some business marketers must not only monitor final consumer markets but also develop a marketing program that reaches the ultimate consumer directly. Aluminum producers use television and magazine ads to point up the convenience and recycling opportunities that aluminum containers offer to the consumer—because the ultimate consumer influences aluminum demand by purchasing soft drinks in aluminum rather than in plastic containers. Nearly 5 billion pounds of aluminum are used annually in the production of beverage containers.[12] Du Pont and TRW also advertise to ultimate consumers to stimulate the sales of consumer goods that incorporate their products.

---

[11] Thomas A. Stewart, "A Heartland Industry Takes on the World," *Fortune* (March 12, 1990), pp. 110–112.

[12] Tom Stundza, "Metal Cans: Lusting for Market Share," *Purchasing,* 104 (February 22, 1990), pp. 61–64.

Price Sensitivity

Demand elasticity refers to the responsiveness of the quantity demanded to a change in price. Demand is elastic if a given percentage change in price brings about an even larger percentage change in the quantity demanded. Inelasticity results when demand is insensitive to price; for example, the percentage change in demand is less than the percentage change in price. Consider the demand for electronic components that is stimulated by companies making cellular telephones (car phones). As long as final consumers continue to purchase car phones and are generally insensitive to price, manufacturers of the equipment are relatively insensitive to the price of electronic components. At the opposite end of the spectrum, if consumers are price sensitive when purchasing soup and other canned grocery products, manufacturers of soup will be price sensitive when purchasing metal cans. Thus, the derived demand indicates that the demand for metal cans is price elastic.

Final consumer demand has a pervasive impact on the demand for products in the business market. By being sensitive to trends in the consumer market, the business marketer can often identify both impending problems and potential opportunities for growth and diversification.

Environmental Forces Influence Demand

In monitoring and forecasting demand, the business marketer must be alert to factors in the competitive, economic, political, and legal environment that directly or indirectly influence demand. A mild recession cuts deeply into some segments of the business market while leaving other segments unscathed. Rising interest rates alter the purchasing plans of both home buyers and commercial enterprises contemplating expansion. Federal legislation requiring improvements in gas mileage increases demand for lightweight materials like aluminum. Ecological concerns, which render some industrial products and processes obsolete, create challenging replacement opportunities. Du Pont, for example, has initiated plans to produce refrigeration chemicals for automotive air-conditioning and home refrigerators that do not endanger the earth's ozone layer.[13] To serve the global market, four plants will be built: two in the United States, one in the Netherlands, and another in Japan. Foreign markets that offer lucrative potential to some business marketers may pose a serious challenge to domestic producers such as the steel industry. Constant surveillance of these and other environmental forces is fundamental to accurate demand analysis in the business market.

A Global Market Perspective

"In international markets, innovations that yield competitive advantage anticipate both domestic and foreign needs."[14] Indeed the relevant unit of analysis in an increasing number of industries today is not the domestic but the worldwide market position. The accelerating demand for industrial goods in the international market and the dramatic

---

[13] John Holusha, "Du Pont to Construct Plants for Ozone-Safe Refrigerant," *The New York Times* (June 23, 1990), pp. 17–18.

[14] Michael E. Porter, "The Competitive Advantage of Nations," *Harvard Business Review,* 68 (March–April, 1990), p. 74.

"What country was it made in? Which part
of the car are you talking about?"

Source: From *The Wall Street Journal;* Permission, Cartoon Features Syndicate.

rise in competition—from Western Europe, from Japan, from the Pacific Rim (with Korea, Taiwan, Hong Kong, and Singapore becoming active players), and from nearly industrialized countries (notably India and Brazil)—necessitate a global perspective on competition. Meanwhile, Eastern Europe will likely evolve into an important customer and source of world industrial competition in the years ahead.[15]

Kotler and Singh contend that companies now have to choose markets whose needs they can satisfy and whose competitors they can handle.[16] A thorough competitive assessment must involve an analysis of formidable competitors in distant markets.

A global orientation is especially important to business marketers competing in rapidly changing industries like telecommunications and electronics or, at the other end of the continuum, in basic commodity industries such as steel and forest products. Japanese steelmakers are formidable competitors and enjoy cost and quality advantages over their major U.S. counterparts. In turn, many U.S.-based industrial firms such as IBM, Rockwell International, and Motorola have moved to establish a position

---

[15] Kate Bertrand, "Get Ready for Global Capitalism," *Business Marketing,* 75 (January 1990), pp. 42–54.

[16] Philip Kotler and Ravi Singh, "Marketing Warfare in the 1980s," *Journal of Business Strategy,* 1 (Winter 1981), reprinted in Richard Wendel, ed., *Marketing 83/84* (Guilford, CT: The Dushkin Publishing Group, Inc., 1983), pp. 12–22; see also Lindsay N. Meredith and Michael D. Hutt, "Toward an International Perspective of Market Analysis in Industrial Marketing," *Journal of Marketing Education,* 6 (Fall 1984), pp. 15–20.

of strength for selected products in Japan. For example, Motorola is the worldwide market leader in the rapidly growing cellular telephone industry.

John F. Welch, Jr., chairman and CEO of General Electric, spawned a strategic redirection that has provided G.E. with world market-share leadership in nearly all of its major businesses. He offers this challenging profile for competing successfully in the global market:

> The winners . . . will be those who can develop a culture that allows them to move faster, communicate more clearly, and involve everyone in a focused effort to serve ever more demanding customers. To move toward that winning culture, we've got to create what we call a "boundaryless" company. We no longer have the time to climb over barriers between functions like engineering and marketing . . . . Geographic barriers must evaporate. Our people must be as comfortable in Delhi and Seoul as they are in Louisville or Schenectady. The lines between the company and its vendors must be blurred into a smooth, fluid process with no other objective than satisfying the customer and winning in the marketplace.[17]

BUSINESS AND CONSUMER MARKETING: A CONTRAST

Many consumer products companies with a strong reputation in the consumer market decide to capitalize on perceived opportunities in the business market. The move is often prompted by a maturing product line, a desire to diversify operations, or the strategic opportunity to profitably apply research and development or production strength in a rapidly growing business market. Procter & Gamble Company (P&G), departing from its packaged consumer-goods tradition, is using its expertise in oils, fats, and pulps to diversify into fast-growing industries.[18]

The J. M. Smucker Company operates successfully in both the consumer and the business markets. Smucker, drawing upon its consumer product base (jellies and preserves), produces filling mixes used by manufacturers of yogurt and dessert items. Marketing strawberry preserves to ultimate consumers differs significantly from marketing a strawberry filling to a manufacturer of yogurt. Key differences are highlighted below.

ILLUSTRATION: Smucker: A Consumer and Business Marketer

Smucker reaches the consumer market with a line of products sold through a range of retail outlets. New products are carefully developed, tested, targeted, priced, and promoted for particular segments of the market. To secure distribution, the firm employs food brokers who call on both wholesale- and retail-buying units. The company's own sales force reaches selected larger accounts. Achieving a desired degree of market exposure and shelf space in key retail-food outlets is essential to any marketer of consumer food products. Promotional plans for the line include media advertising, coupons, special offers, and incentives for retailers. Pricing decisions must

---

[17] "Today's Leaders Look to Tomorrow," *Fortune* (March 26, 1990), p. 30.

[18] Zachary Schiller, "Procter & Gamble Goes on a Health Kick," *Business Week* (June 29, 1987), pp. 90–92.

reflect the nature of demand, costs, and the behavior of competitors. In sum, the marketer must manage each component of the marketing mix: product, price, promotion, and distribution.

The marketing mix takes on a different form in the business market. Attention centers on manufacturers that potentially could use Smucker products to produce other goods; the Smucker product will lose its identity as it is blended into yogurt, cakes, or cookies. Once all the potential users of the product are identified (e.g., large food processors, bakeries, yogurt producers), the business marketing manager attempts to identify meaningful market segments that Smucker can profitably serve. A specific marketing strategy is developed for each market segment.

When a potential organizational consumer is identified, the company's sales force calls directly on the account. The salesperson *may* begin by contacting a company president but, at first, generally spends a great deal of time with the research and development (R&D) director or the product development group leader. The salesperson is thus challenged to identify the **key buying influentials**—those who will have power in the buying process.

Armed with product specifications (e.g., desired taste, color, calories), the salesperson returns to the research and development department at Smucker to develop samples. Several months may pass before a mixture is finally approved. Next, attention turns to price, and the salesperson's contact point shifts to the purchasing department. Because large quantities (truckloads or drums rather than jars) are involved, a few cents per pound can be significant to both parties. Quality and service are also vitally important.

Once a transaction is agreed to, the product is shipped directly from the Smucker warehouse to the manufacturer's plant. The salesperson follows up frequently with the purchasing agent and the plant manager. How much business can Smucker expect from this account? The performance of the new consumer product in the marketplace will determine this: the demand for industrial goods is, as noted, derived from ultimate consumer demand. Note also the importance of (1) developing a close and continuing working relationship with business market customers, and (2) understanding the requirements of the total range of buying influentials in the target company.

Distinguishing Characteristics

This illustration spotlights some of the features that differentiate business marketing strategy from consumer-goods marketing strategy. The business marketer emphasizes personal selling rather than advertising (TV, newspaper) to reach potential buyers. Only a small portion of the business marketer's promotional budget is likely to be invested in advertising, most commonly through trade journals or direct mail. This advertising, however, often establishes the foundation for a successful sales call. The industrial salesperson must have a technical understanding of the organization's requirements and of how those requirements can be satisfied as well as having a detailed understanding of who influences the buying decision and why.

The business marketer's product also includes an important service component. The organizational consumer evaluates the quality of the physical entity and the quality of the attached services. Price negotiation is frequently an important part of the

TABLE 1.2 **Business Marketing versus Consumer-Goods Marketing: Selected Distinguishing Characteristics**

	Business Marketing	Consumer-Goods Marketing
Product	More technical in nature; exact form often variable; accompanying services very important	Standardized form; service important, but less so
Price	Competitive bidding for unique items; list prices for standard items	List prices
Promotion	Emphasis on personal selling	Emphasis on advertising
Distribution	Shorter, more direct channels to market	Passes through a number of intermediate links enroute to consumer
Customer Relations	More enduring and complex	Less frequent contact; relationship of a shorter duration
Consumer Decision-Making Process	Involvement of diverse group of organizational members in decision	Individual or household unit makes decision

industrial buying/selling process. Products made to particular quality or design specifications must be individually priced. Business marketers generally find that direct distribution to larger customers strengthens relationships between buyer and seller. Smaller accounts can be profitably served through intermediaries—manufacturers' representatives or industrial distributors.

As the Smucker example has illustrated, business marketing strategies differ from consumer-goods marketing strategies in the relative emphasis given to certain elements of the marketing mix. It is important to note that the example also highlights fundamental differences between the buyers in each market. In an organization, a variety of individuals influence the purchase decision. Several major questions confront Smucker's business marketing manager: Who are key participants in the purchasing process? What is their relative importance? What criteria does each apply to the decision? Thus, the business marketer must understand the *process* that an organization follows in purchasing a product and must know which organizational members have roles in this process. Depending on the complexity of the purchase, this process may span many weeks or months and may involve the participation of several members of the organization. The business marketer who becomes involved in the purchase process early may have the greatest chance for success.

Business marketing is fundamentally different from consumer marketing because of how organizations purchase products. The business marketer must respond not to a single consumer but to a much wider group of buying influentials, all of whom may bring different criteria to bear on the purchase decision.

While selected industrial-product and business market situations closely resemble those found in consumer-goods marketing, Table 1.2 emphasizes the common distinguishing characteristics of consumer-goods versus business marketing. Clearly, business

FIGURE 1.1   **The Supply Chain**

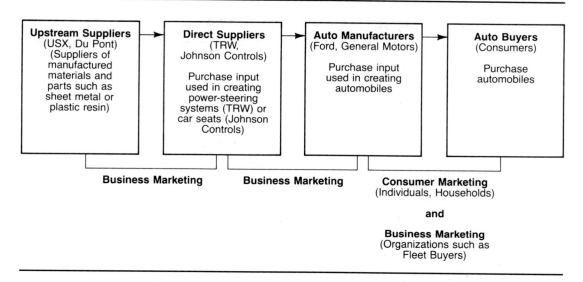

marketers can often benefit from using some of the creative marketing strategies found in consumer-goods marketing. Making sound marketing management decisions, however, requires knowledge of the fundamental traits that typify the business marketing environment.

The Supply Chain

Figure 1.1 further illuminates the differences between business and consumer marketing by considering the chain of suppliers involved in the creation of an automobile. Consider Honda and Ford. Honda, at its Marysville, Ohio, auto assembly plant, spends more than $2.2 billion annually for materials and components from some 175 U.S. suppliers.[19] Similarly, Ford relies on a vast supplier network, including firms such as TRW and Johnson Controls, to contribute half of the more than 10,000 parts of a typical Ford car.[20] The relationships between these auto producers and their suppliers fall squarely into the business marketing domain. Similarly, business marketers such as TRW rely on a host of others further back on the supply chain for raw materials, components, and other support. Each organization in this chain is involved in the creation of a product, marketing processes (including delivery), and support and service after the sale. In performing these value-creating activities, each also affects the

---

[19] Ernest Raia, "The Americanization of Honda," *Purchasing,* 104 (March 22, 1990), pp. 50–57.

[20] James B. Treece, "U.S. Parts Makers Just Won't Say 'Uncle,'" *Business Week* (August 10, 1987), pp. 76–78; and Somerby Dowst, "Quality in Design Means Quality in Production," *Purchasing,* 102 (January 28, 1988), pp. 80–82.

quality level of the Honda or Ford product. Michael Porter and Victor Millar observe: "To gain competitive advantage over its rivals, a company must either perform these activities at a lower cost or perform them in a way that leads to differentiation and a premium price (more value)."[21]

Buyer–Seller Interdependence

Some business marketers achieve a differentiated advantage by synchronizing their operations closely with those of their customers. Close coordination is vital to the efficiency and effectiveness of the supply chain. Johnson Controls, a producer of auto seats and trim, operates ten plants near its major customers, which include Ford, Toyota, Honda, and General Motors.[22] Each plant operates as a separate unit dedicated to the particular needs of a single customer. Likewise, Honda carefully nurtures the development of the supply chain.[23] Members of the purchasing staff make frequent visits to supplier plants and are on call 24 hours a day to address supplier problems. In turn, a "guest engineer" program gives the supplier's technical people the opportunity to observe first hand how their parts are brought into the production process at Honda. Developing and nurturing close, long-term relationships is an important goal for the business marketer. Built on trust and demonstrated performance, such strategic partnerships require open lines of communication between multiple layers of the buying and selling organizations.

Quality and the Supply Chain

Facing stiff competition from Japanese and other foreign producers, U.S. and Canadian producers are making fundamental adjustments to ensure better quality in their products and services.[24] Quality encompasses all dimensions of a business—products, services, and even the responsiveness of personnel to customer requests. Thus, quality means much more than precisely meeting customers' product requirements; it also involves the quality of supporting services (e.g., delivery) and the care with which the buyer–seller relationship is managed (see Figure 1.2). The Japanese, who emphasize quality in their business plans, have the lead, but the quality gap is closing. Ford made sweeping changes in manufacturing technology and management philosophy to reduce the number of product defects. For example, it began to emphasize statistical process control (SPC)—a technique to detect potential problems in the manufacturing process before they result in defective products. Likewise, Ford and other producers have carefully screened the supplier network to identify business marketers who can consistently provide quality products and who can certify that quality by employing SPC techniques themselves. Through this process, Ford has established a rigorous set

---

[21] Michael E. Porter and Victor E. Millar, "How Information Gives You Competitive Advantage," *Harvard Business Review,* 63 (July–August 1985), pp. 149–160; see also, Porter, *Competitive Advantage* (New York: Free Press, 1985).

[22] Treece, "U.S. Parts Makers Just Won't Say 'Uncle,'" pp. 76–78.

[23] Raia, "The Americanization of Honda," p. 55.

[24] See, for example, John M. Groocock, *The Chain of Quality* (New York: John Wiley and Sons, 1986).

FIGURE 1.2 **A Business Marketing Ad by Xerox, Winner of the Malcolm Baldrige National Quality Award**

Source: Courtesy, Xerox Corporation.

of quality standards, cut the size of its supplier list in half, and rewarded suppliers who consistently meet or surpass these standards with a preferred supplier status.[25] One such firm has supplied 1.6 million oil-pump parts to Ford without one rejected part—thus winning a long-term contract.[26]

Time and the Supply Chain [27]

The ways that leading companies manage time in the supply chain—in new product development and introduction, in production, in sales and distribution—are the most powerful new sources of competitive advantage. "Time as a source of competitive

---

[25] Nick Hunter, "Detroit Keys In on Quality," *Purchasing,* 104 (January 18, 1990), pp. 106–111.

[26] Treece, "U.S. Parts Makers Just Won't Say 'Uncle,'" pp. 76–78.

[27] George Stalk, Jr., and Thomas M. Hout, *Competing Against Time: How Time-based Competition is Re-shaping Global Markets* (New York: The Free Press, 1990).

advantage is relevant whenever customers have to wait to receive the value that they have decided they want." Successful time-based competitors have the ability to conceive, develop, and introduce new products and services much faster than their competitors, without sacrificing product quality or marketability. In the automobile industry, for example, firms such as Honda, Ford, and Toyota assume active leadership roles in managing time in their respective supply chains. Other successful time-based competitors include Compaq, Motorola, Canon, Intel, Sony, Merck, and Microsoft.

The following excerpt highlights some advantages of competitive time management.

> Consider the competitive advantages that speed provides: If both Honda and General Motors are designing an auto for the 1994 model year, and Honda needs two years to design the model while GM requires five, Honda has a number of advantages. It can use 1992-available technology, whereas GM must design in 1989 technology. Honda must forecast market demand just two years into the future, whereas GM requires a five-year time horizon—a much more difficult task. Finally, Honda's development teams acquire development experience 2.5 times more quickly than GM's.[28]

To compress time and enjoy these competitive advantages, supply-chain leaders can take three steps. First, they can provide each company in the chain with more complete and timely information concerning orders, new products, and special needs. To illustrate, accurate demand-based information saves time and money by reducing uncertainty and the amount of inventory that each member of the supply chain must hold. Second, supply-chain leaders shorten work cycles by removing the obstacles to compression that one company often unknowingly imposes on another. For example, a supplier may make engineering improvements in a power steering system and then alert the automobile manufacturer. The manufacturer in turn makes design changes in the car to accommodate the improved system. Earlier collaboration on these changes could have resulted in their new products being available in automobile showrooms months sooner. Third, supply-chain leaders can compress time by synchronizing lead times and capacities among the levels of the supply chain so that work can flow in a coordinated fashion through the chain. The goal here is to manage the chain so that each member can count on its suppliers to provide needed materials on a consistent schedule, regardless of which version of the final product is being made by the chain (e.g., Honda Accord or Honda Civic).

The quest for quality and the search for competitive advantage have spawned a quiet revolution in the business market. Business market customers are reducing the size of their supplier lists, forming strategic partnerships with "quality" suppliers, and emphasizing long-term contracts and speed to an unprecedented degree. Understanding the needs of business market customers is vital in this challenging environment.

---

[28] Gary Reiner, "Lessons from the World's Best Product Developers," *The Wall Street Journal* (August 6, 1990), p. A–12.

BUSINESS MARKET CUSTOMERS

Any attempt by the marketing strategist to isolate the similarities and differences among groups of customers in the business market must begin with a definition of customer type. These organizational customers can be broadly classified into three categories: (1) commercial enterprises, (2) governmental organizations, and (3) institutions. Each represents a sizable market with many diverse parts.

Commercial Enterprises as Consumers

Commercial enterprises can also be divided into three categories: (1) users, (2) original equipment manufacturers (OEMs), and (3) dealers and distributors.

Users
Users purchase industrial products or services to produce other goods or services that are, in turn, sold in the business or consumer markets. User customers purchase goods to set up or support the manufacturing process. To illustrate, user customers may purchase computers, photocopiers, or automated manufacturing systems. When purchasing machine tools from General Electric Company, an auto manufacturer is a user. These machine tools do not become part of the automobile but instead help to produce it.

Original Equipment Manufacturers
The OEM purchases industrial goods to incorporate into other products sold in the business or ultimate consumer market. For example, Intel Corporation produces the microprocessors that constitute the heart of IBM's personal computer. In purchasing these microprocessors, IBM would be classified as an OEM.[29]

Dealers and Distributors
Dealers and distributors include those commercial enterprises that purchase industrial goods for resale (in basically the same form) to users and OEMs. The distributor accumulates, stores, and sells a large assortment of goods to industrial users, taking title to the goods purchased. Handling billions of dollars worth of transactions each year, industrial distributors are growing in size and sophistication. The strategic role assumed by distributors in the business market is examined in detail later in the text.

Overlap of Categories
The three categories of commercial enterprises are not mutually exclusive. The classification of commercial enterprises rests upon the intended purpose that the product serves for the customer. American Honda Motor Company is a user when purchasing a machine tool for the manufacturing process, but the same company is an OEM when purchasing radios to be incorporated into the ultimate consumer product.

---

[29] "Tracking Quality Through the Supply Chain," *Purchasing,* 104 (January 18, 1990), pp. 99–108.

A marketer requires a good understanding of the diverse organizational consumers in the business market. Properly classifying commercial customers as users, OEMs, or dealers or distributors is an important first step to a sharpened understanding of the buying criteria that a particular commercial customer uses in evaluating an industrial product.

Understanding Buying Motivations

Figure 1.3 depicts the different types of commercial customers for a particular industrial product—electrical timing mechanisms. Each class of commercial customer views the product differently because each purchases the product for a different reason.

A food-processing firm such as Pillsbury buys electrical timers for use in a high-speed canning system. For this customer, quality, reliability, and prompt and predictable delivery are critical. The appliance manufacturer, an OEM who incorporates the industrial product directly into consumer appliances, is concerned with the effect of the timers on the quality and dependability of the final consumer product. Since the timers will be needed in large quantities, the appliance manufacturer is also concerned about the producer's production capacity and delivery reliability. Finally, the electrical supply dealer, an industrial distributor, is most interested in matching the capability of the timing mechanisms to the needs of customers (users and OEMs) in a specific geographical market.

Governmental Organizations as Consumers

The government, whether federal, state, or local, is the largest consumer in the United States—the federal government alone spends more than $300 billion on products and services annually.[30] Governmental units purchase from virtually every category of goods—office supplies, missiles, fire engines, fuel, desks, lumber, grease, concrete, furniture. Governmental units as consumers can be a lucrative market for the astute business marketer. Whereas some large defense contractors such as McDonnell Douglas derive a significant portion of their revenue from the government market, smaller business marketers now account for 25 to 35 percent of federal purchases.[31] The nondefense segments of the government market could expand in the future, if the reduced threat of Eastern-Bloc military power contributes to a reordering of federal spending priorities.[32] Indeed, some defense-oriented firms, such as Rockwell International Corporation, have begun aggressive expansion into nondefense areas like industrial automation and commercial aircraft avionics.[33]

Governmental buying procedures are highly specialized and sometimes frustrating. Typically, the government develops detailed specifications and invites bids from qualified suppliers. For more complex projects, the agency may negotiate directly with

[30] Timothy F. Regan, "Analyzing Government Markets," in Victor P. Buell, ed., *Handbook of Modern Marketing,* 2nd ed. (New York: McGraw-Hill Book Company, 1986), pp. 13–1 to 13–11.

[31] Regan, "Analyzing Government Markets," pp. 13–1 to 13–11.

[32] Carol Matlack, "Peace Dividend: Domestic Lobbies Trying to Cash In," *National Journal,* 22 (March 14, 1990), pp. 884–892.

[33] "Who Pays for Peace?" *Business Week* (July 2, 1990), p. 67.

FIGURE 1.3   **Tracing an Industrial Product to Commercial Customers**

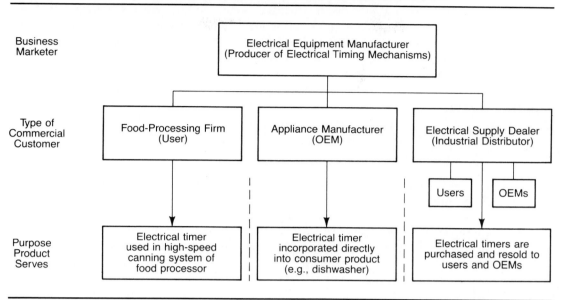

the few suppliers known to have the required knowledge or technical capability. Always, the emphasis is on competitive procurement. While some consideration may be given to the supplier's reputation or past performance, the low bidder usually has the edge.

To reach this important group, the marketer must understand government procurement procedures and locate the individuals who make or influence decisions. This market is explored in detail in Chapter 2.

Institutions as Consumers

Public and private institutions constitute another class of business market customers. Churches, hospitals, nursing homes, colleges, and universities all require goods and services. Some institutional customers, such as public universities, have specific purchasing procedures that are rigidly followed; others follow less standardized approaches. Business marketers often find it profitable to establish a separate division to respond to the unique needs of institutional buyers.

CLASSIFYING GOODS FOR THE BUSINESS MARKET

Having classified the customers that constitute the business market, we must now ask what types of goods they require, and how each type is marketed. One useful method of classifying industrial goods is to ask: How does the industrial good or service enter the production process, and how does it enter the cost structure of the firm?[34] The answer allows the marketer to find those who are influential in the organizational buying process and to understand how to design an effective business marketing strategy. In general, industrial goods can be divided into three broad categories: entering goods, foundation goods, and facilitating goods (see Table 1.3).

Entering Goods

Entering goods are those that become part of the finished product. This category of goods consists of raw materials and manufactured materials and parts. Their cost is an expense item that is assigned to the manufacturing process.

Raw Materials

Observe in Table 1.3 that raw materials include both farm products and natural products. Raw materials are processed only to the level required for economical handling and transport; they basically enter the production process of the buying organization in their natural state.

Shortages or rapid changes in the price of raw materials can trigger problems for producers who are heavily dependent on particular raw materials. To illustrate, each year AT&T spends $150 million on the open market to purchase copper and substantial quantities of gold and silver to be used in making telephone and communications equipment. Goodyear Tire and Rubber Company buys 10 percent of the world's production of natural rubber.[35] Unexpected surges in the prices of these materials will require swift changes in the pricing and product strategies of each firm.

Manufactured Materials and Parts

In contrast to raw materials, manufactured materials and parts undergo more initial processing. Component materials such as textiles or sheet steel have been processed before reaching a clothing manufacturer or automaker but must be processed further before becoming part of the finished product that the consumer buys. Component parts, on the other hand, include small motors, motorcycle tires, and automobile batteries; they can be installed directly into another product with little or no additional processing.

Foundation Goods

The distinguishing characteristic of foundation goods is that they are **capital items**. As capital goods are used up or worn out, a portion of their original cost is assigned to the production process as a depreciation expense. Foundation goods include installations and accessory equipment.

---

[34] Kotler, *Marketing Management*, p. 172.

[35] "Top 100: Corporate Profiles," *Purchasing*, 100 (November 6, 1986), p. 101.

TABLE 1.3   **Classification of Goods for the Business Market**

I. Entering Goods
  A. Raw materials
     1. Farm products (e.g., wheat, cotton, livestock, fruits, and vegetables)
     2. Natural products (e.g., fish, lumber, crude petroleum, iron ore)
  B. Manufactured materials and parts
     1. Component materials (e.g., steel, cement, wire, textiles)
     2. Component parts (e.g., small motors, tires, castings)
II. Foundation Goods
  A. Installations
     1. Buildings and land rights (e.g., factories, offices)
     2. Fixed equipment (e.g., generators, drill presses, computers, elevators)
  B. Accessory equipment
     1. Portable or light factory equipment and tools (e.g., hand tools, lift trucks)
     2. Office equipment (e.g., typewriters, desks)
III. Facilitating Goods
  A. Supplies
     1. Operating supplies (e.g., lubricants, coal, typing paper, pencils)
     2. Maintenance and repair items (e.g., paint, nails, brooms)
  B. Business services
     1. Maintenance and repair services (e.g., window cleaning, typewriter repair)
     2. Business advisory services (e.g., legal, management consulting, advertising)

Source: Adapted from Philip Kotler, *Marketing Management: Analysis, Planning and Control,* 4th ed. (Englewood Cliffs, N.J.: Prentice-Hall, Inc., 1980), p. 172, with permission of Prentice-Hall, Inc.

Installations

Installations include the major long-term investment items that underlie the manufacturing process, such as **buildings and land rights** and **fixed equipment**. Large computers and machine tools are examples of fixed equipment.

Accessory Equipment

Accessory equipment is generally less expensive and short-lived when compared to installations, and is not considered part of the fixed plant. This equipment can be found in the plant as well as in the office. Portable drills and typewriters illustrate this category.

Facilitating Goods

Facilitating goods are the supplies and services (see Table 1.3) that support organizational operations. Because these goods do not enter the production process or become part of the finished product, their costs are handled as **expense items**.

Supplies

Virtually every organization requires **operating supplies**, such as typing paper or business forms, and **maintenance and repair items**, such as paint and cleaning materials. These items generally reach a broad cross section of industrial users. In fact, they are very similar to the kinds of supplies that consumers might purchase at a hardware or discount store.

Services

As competitive pressure forces firms to reduce the size of the management staff and adopt more flexible structures, many firms are shifting selected service functions to outside suppliers. This opens up opportunities for firms who provide such services as computer support, payroll processing, mail distribution, food operations, and equipment maintenance. These specialists possess a level of expertise or efficiency that organizations can profitably tap. Business services include **maintenance and repair** support (e.g., machine repair) and **advisory support** (e.g., management consulting). Like supplies, services are considered expense items.

In the business market, services have experienced dramatic growth in such areas as computer repair and training, management consulting, engineering, and equipment leasing. For example, the market for computer services and software is growing twice as fast as the market for traditional computer hardware. To adapt to this growth pattern, IBM created a special unit to market its problem-solving skills and plans to derive a significant portion of its revenue from services throughout the 1990s.[36]

BUSINESS MARKETING STRATEGY

The significance of a goods classification system comes to light on examination of how marketing patterns differ by goods category. A marketing strategy appropriate for one category of goods may be entirely unsuitable for another. Often, entirely different promotional, pricing, and distribution strategies are required. The physical nature of the industrial good and its intended use by the organizational customer dictate to an important degree the requirements of the marketing program.

ILLUSTRATION: Manufactured Materials and Parts

Recall that manufactured materials and parts enter the buying organization's own product. Whether a part is standardized or customized will often dictate the nature of marketing strategy. For custom-made parts, personal selling activities assume an important role in marketing strategy. The salesperson must link the engineering departments of the buying and selling firms. Though the product is the critical factor in making a sale, once the account is sold, reliable delivery becomes primary. Standardized parts are typically purchased in larger quantities on a contractual basis, and the marketing strategy centers on providing a competitive price and reliable delivery. Frequently, industrial distributors are used to achieve responsive delivery service to smaller accounts.

---

[36] Paul B. Carrol, "IBM, Seeking a Source of Renewal, Markets Its Problem-Solving Skills," *The Wall Street Journal* (June 12, 1990), p. B-4.

Personal selling is pivotal for many customized materials and parts; advertising is more important for many standardized items. The role of the salesperson is to call not only on purchasing agents but also on other key buying influentials (engineers and production managers) who develop product specifications. Sometimes component marketers will utilize manufacturers' representatives—intermediaries who are independent salespersons representing a variety of suppliers of noncompeting products. The manufacturers' representative is paid a commission on sales and provides a cost-effective way of securing a quality selling effort in markets where demand is low. Advertising supplements personal selling activities. The basic advertising appeals focus on product quality, delivery reliability, price, and service. Many producers of component parts and materials attempt to gain a differential advantage based on their ability to design unique parts for specific applications as well as on their ability to provide the parts on a timely basis to meet production requirements.

To illustrate, Intel produces microprocessors that are used in diverse applications: automobiles, aircraft, communication equipment, and computers. Often, such sophisticated components are not visible to the prospective buyer or user. Observe in Figure 1.4 how the firm's advertising is geared toward enhancing the visibility of the Intel trademark and the "computer inside."

For manufactured materials and parts, the marketer's challenge is to locate and accurately define the unique needs of diverse customers, uncover key buying influences, and adjust the marketing program to serve these customers profitably.

ILLUSTRATION: Installations

Installations were classified earlier as foundation goods because they are capital assets that affect the buyer's scale of operations. Here the product itself is the central force in marketing strategy, and direct manufacturer-to-user channels of distribution are the norm. Less costly, more standardized installations such as lathes may be sold through marketing middlemen.

Once again, personal selling is the dominant promotional tool. The salesperson works closely with prospective organizational buyers. Negotiations can span several months and involve the top executives in the buying organization, especially for buildings or custom-made equipment. Multiple buying influences complicate the selling task. Each executive may be applying slightly different criteria to the decision process. Trade advertising and direct mail advertising supplement and reinforce personal selling.

Buying motives center on economic factors such as the projected performance of the capital asset and on emotional factors such as industry leadership. A buyer may be quite willing to select a higher-priced installation if the projected return on investment supports the decision. To illustrate, a packaging machine that saves the using organization one gram of plastic per unit produced would yield substantial cost savings over its productive life and would be preferred over lower-priced alternatives that did not offer such savings. In summary, the focal points for the marketing of installations include a strong personal selling effort, effective engineering and product design support, and the capability to offer a product that provides a higher return on

FIGURE 1.4   **A Business Marketing Ad that Highlights the
"Hidden" Intel Components for Prospective Buyers**

Source: Courtesy of Intel Corporation.

investment than competing products. Initial price, distribution, and advertising play lesser roles.

ILLUSTRATION: Supplies

The final illustration centers on a facilitating good—supplies. Again we find different marketing patterns. Most supply items reach a horizontal market of organizational customers from many different industries. Although some large users are serviced directly, a wide variety of marketing middlemen are required to cover this broad and diverse market adequately.

The purchasing agent plays the dominant role in the choice of suppliers and evaluates alternative suppliers on dependability, breadth of assortment, convenience, and price. While always searching for value, the purchasing agent lacks the time to carefully evaluate all available alternatives whenever a purchase requirement surfaces. Dependable sources have the edge.

INSIDE BUSINESS MARKETING
Nurturing a Relationship with Honda

At Honda of America's plant in Marysville, Ohio, the primary goal of the purchasing staff is to develop long-term relationships with business marketers who can supply quality component parts and materials in a timely and cost-effective manner. To become a member of Honda's supply network, a firm must be persistent and ready to demonstrate its capability. Consider the case of an Indiana-based company that wanted to supply the jack for the Honda Accord. After receiving little encouragement from Honda's purchasing staff, the president of the firm went to a Honda dealer and purchased jacks that were being supplied from Japan for the Accord. He took them back to his plant and studied every aspect of their design and function. In turn, he examined his company's capability to manufacture a jack of superior quality. Several months later he returned to Honda and placed a prototype of a new jack on a conference table at Honda's purchasing headquarters and declared that it was superior in every way to the competing product. Today his company is supplying the jack to every automobile produced at the Marysville plant, including those shipped to Japan.

Source: Ernest Raia, "The Americanization of Honda," *Purchasing,* 104 (March 22, 1990), pp. 50–57.

For supplies, the marketer's promotional mix includes catalog listings, advertising, and, to a lesser extent, personal selling. Advertising is directed to resellers (industrial distributors) and final users. Personal selling is less important for supplies than it is for other categories of goods having a high unit value, such as installations. Thus, personal selling efforts may be confined to resellers and large users of supplies. The degree of emphasis given to personal selling depends on the size of the company, the length of the firm's product line, and the amount of potential demand concentrated in large accounts or in particular geographic areas. For example, a large industrial firm that produces a wide assortment of supply items is better equipped to develop a direct sales force than are smaller firms with narrow product lines.

In general, then, the marketing strategy for supplies centers on developing the proper assortments of products to match the needs of diverse groups of customers. The selection of an effective group of industrial distributors is often fundamental to the marketing strategy. Price may be critical in the marketing strategy, since many supply items are undifferentiated. By providing the proper product assortment, timely and reliable delivery, and competitive prices, an industrial marketer of supply items may be able to develop a long-term contractual relationship with a customer.

The focus and direction of marketing strategy change from one category of industrial goods to another. Yet in every case, the marketer's ultimate concern must be about how potential organizational customers view a particular product. Views may be quite different from customer to customer; potential buyers have varying levels of experience with specific products, in addition to having distinct organizational objectives and requirements. The successful business marketer recognizes unique organizational needs and satisfies them.

A LOOK AHEAD

The chief components of the business marketing management process are shown in Figure 1.5. Business marketing strategy is formulated within the boundaries established by the corporate mission and objectives. A corporation determining its mission must define its business and purpose, assess environmental trends, and evaluate its strengths and weaknesses. Corporate objectives provide guidelines within which specific marketing objectives are formed. Business marketing planning must be coordinated and synchronized with corresponding planning efforts in R&D, procurement, finance, production, customer service, and other areas. Clearly, strategic plans emerge out of a bargaining process among functional areas. Managing conflict, promoting cooperation, and developing coordinated strategies are all fundamental to the business marketer's interdisciplinary role.

The business marketing management framework (Figure 1.5) provides an overview of the five major parts of this volume. This chapter introduced some of the features that distinguish industrial from consumer-goods marketing. The remaining chapter in Part I examines in more detail the nature of industrial market organizations. The major types of industrial customers—commercial enterprises, governmental units, and institutions—are examined closely.

Organizational buying behavior constitutes the theme of Part II, which first examines the organizational buying process and the myriad forces that affect the organizational decision maker. Part III turns to the measurement of business market opportunities, demonstrating specific techniques for measuring the relative attractiveness of alternative sectors of the market and for selecting target segments.

Part IV centers on designing business marketing strategy. Each component of the marketing mix is treated from a business marketing perspective. Special attention is also given to the marketing of services. Formulation of the business marketing mix (see Figure 1.5) requires careful coordination with such functional areas in the firm as R&D and production. The factors involved in monitoring and controlling the marketing program are analyzed in Part V. A central theme is how business marketing management seeks to minimize the discrepancy between planned and actual results in target markets by planning for and acquiring relevant and timely marketing information.

SUMMARY

The business market offers significant opportunities and special challenges for the marketing manager. Although a common body of knowledge and theory spans all of marketing, important differences exist between consumer and business marketing, among them the nature of markets, demand patterns, buyer behavior, and products. The accelerating demand for industrial goods in the international market, coupled with the dramatic rise in competition on a worldwide basis, requires a global perspective of markets. To secure a competitive advantage in this challenging environment, business market customers are developing closer, more collaborative ties with fewer suppliers

FIGURE 1.5   A Framework for Business Marketing Management

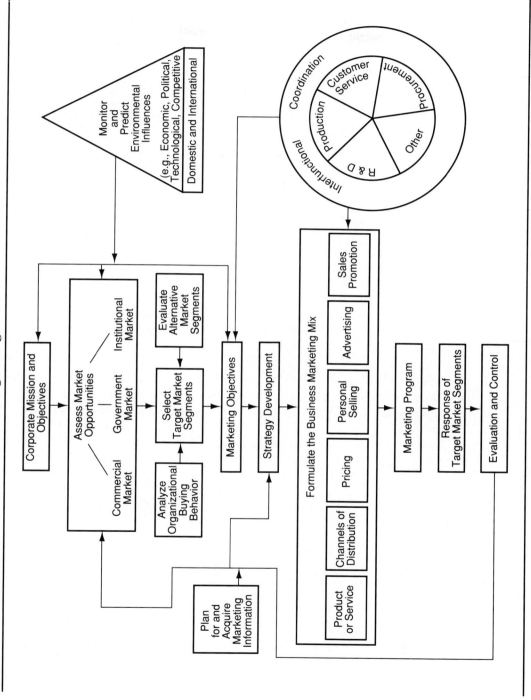

than they have used in the past, and are demanding quality and speed from their suppliers to an unprecedented degree.

The diverse organizations that make up the business market can be broadly divided into (1) commercial enterprises, (2) governmental organizations, and (3) institutions. Since purchases made by these organizational consumers are linked to goods and services that they generate in turn, derived demand is an important and often volatile force in the business market. Further, close buyer–seller relationships are required.

To penetrate the business market effectively, the marketer must understand the organizational buying process, which is affected by multiple buying influences, technical specifications, time lags, and complex buying motives. How the decision is made may vary with the type of industrial product under consideration. Industrial goods can be classified into three categories, based on how the product enters the cost structure and the production process of the buying organization: (1) entering goods, (2) foundation goods, and (3) facilitating goods. Specific categories of goods may require unique marketing programs.

Discussion Questions

1. Du Pont, one of the largest industrial producers of chemicals and synthetic fibers, spends millions of dollars annually on advertising its products to final consumers. For example, over one million dollars was invested in a TV advertising blitz that emphasized the comfort of jeans made of Du Pont's stretch polyester-cotton blend. Since Du Pont does not produce jeans or market them to final consumers, why are large expenditures made on consumer advertising?

2. What are the chief differences between consumer-goods marketing and business marketing? Use the following matrix as a guide in organizing your response:

	Consumer-Goods Marketing	Business Marketing
Customers		
Buying Behavior		
Buyer/Seller Relationship		
Product		
Price		
Promotion		
Channels		

3. Explain how a company such as General Electric might be classified by some business marketers as a user customer but by others as an OEM customer.

4. Using a product with which you are familiar, illustrate the concept of derived demand.

5. Consumer products are frequently classified as convenience, shopping, or specialty goods. This classification system is based on how consumers shop for particular products. Would this classification scheme apply equally well in the business marketing environment?

6. Ford Motor Company recently decided that it needed a single supplier of office systems to improve communications in its North American operations. Ford asked Digital Equipment Corporation, Wang Laboratories Inc., and IBM to bid on the $200 million contract. How would the marketing strategy patterns employed by these suppliers of foundation goods (office systems) differ from those employed by other business marketers who are selling entering goods (component parts) to Ford?

7. Evaluate this statement: "The ways that leading companies manage time in the supply chain—in new product development, in production, in sales and distribution—are the most powerful new sources of competitive advantage."

8. Evaluate this statement: "The demand for major equipment (a foundation good) is likely to be less responsive to shifts in price than that for materials, supplies, and components." Do you agree or disagree? Support your position.

CHAPTER 2

The Business Market: Perspectives on the Organizational Buyer

The business marketer requires an understanding of the needs of a diverse mix of organizational buyers drawn from three broad sectors of the business market—commercial enterprises, government (all levels), and institutions—as well as from an expanding array of international buyers. After reading this chapter, you will understand:

1. the nature and central characteristics of each of these market sectors.

2. how the purchasing function is organized in each of these components of the business market.

3. the importance and distinguishing characteristics of international organizational buyers.

4. the need to design a unique marketing program for each sector of the business market.

THE vast business market is characterized by tremendous diversity. In fact, many goods commonly viewed as final consumer products generate significant demand in the business market. To illustrate, all-vegetable deep-frying oil is a common grocery item that also enjoys a huge market in the business marketing arena. In fact, estimates place the total business market usage of deep-frying oil at somewhere close to 1.6 billion pounds annually. Deep-frying oil is bought by *commercial firms*—manufacturers of food products (frozen foods, breaded fish, etc.), fast-food restaurant chains, airline meal-preparation contractors, hotel restaurant operators, and business firms that furnish food for their employees; *institutions*—schools, hospitals and universities (in 1988 educational institutions, including schools, colleges and universities, had over $19 billion of food sales, whereas health-care institutions' food sales totaled more than $14.4 billion!); and *governments*—federal, state, and local (the U.S. Army is the single largest food-service organization in the world, and various officer and NCO clubs serve nearly $1 billion in food each year). The magnitude of the food-service market and its importance to manufacturers of deep-frying oil is illustrated by its sales volume in 1988—$250 billion![1]

The channels of distribution, as well as the product characteristics and packaging configurations for deep-frying oils, reflect the diversity of the business marketer's customers and of their requirements. For commercial firms in the food-processing industry, purchases of deep-frying oil are made directly from the manufacturer. A processor of frozen fish, who is a significant user of deep-frying oil, will buy standard grade oil in railroad-car quantities. Some large food processors utilize fryers that have the capacity for 1,000 pounds of oil.

In the restaurant market, oil is purchased directly from the manufacturer through the restaurant chain's own wholesaling company or through food-service distributors (wholesalers). Most company-owned Burger King franchises purchase deep-frying oil through Burger King's own subsidiary distributor, whereas the independent franchisees are free to buy from any manufacturer or distributor. For many school districts, on the other hand, deep-frying oil is purchased in much smaller quantities from a distributor. Universities, depending on the size of their food-service operation, will either purchase directly from the manufacturer (the University of Texas runs a sizable food-service operation and buys directly) or purchase through a food-service distributor (who also supplies hundreds of additional grocery and food-service products). Military purchases are made through a formal bidding process and usually provide the oil supplier with a six-month to one-year contract for supplying a stipulated quantity of oil. However, in some instances, the chef at a particular officers' club will specify that only a certain brand of deep-frying oil should be purchased. In this case, the bidding process is circumvented.

Requirements for product quality are as diverse as the types of buyers in the food-service market. A small, elegant restaurant will focus attention on quality; how long the deep-frying oil lasts and its impact on the taste of the food will be critical factors, so the highest-quality oil will be purchased. A school district will be responsive to cost and concentrate on finding the lowest-priced oil. The Marriott Corporation, which operates a major in-flight meal-preparation business for the airlines, will pay close attention to product availability (i.e., delivery service) as well as cost and quality.

Each of the three business market sectors—commercial firms, institutions, and governments—have identifiable and unique characteristics that must be understood by the business marketer. A significant first step in creating successful marketing strategy is to isolate the unique dimensions of each of the major sectors of the business

---

[1] "Food Service Industry Summary," *Restaurant Business* (September 20, 1989), pp. 81, 115.

market. How much market potential does each sector represent? Who makes the purchasing decision? The answers provide a foundation upon which the marketing manager can formulate marketing programs that respond to the specific needs and characteristics of each business market sector.

COMMERCIAL ENTERPRISES: UNIQUE CHARACTERISTICS

Commercial enterprises include manufacturers, construction companies, service firms (e.g., hotels), transportation companies, selected professional groups (e.g., dentists), and resellers (wholesalers and retailers purchasing equipment and supplies for use in their operations). Manufacturers are the most important commercial customers, spending $1.22 trillion on materials in 1986.[2]

Distribution by Size

A startling fact about the study of manufacturers is that there are so few of them. In 1986 there were only 355,000 manufacturing firms in the United States.[3] And though only 36,553 manufacturing firms (10 percent) employ more than 100 workers each, this handful of firms provides about 78 percent of all value added (i.e., economic value created) by manufacturing in the United States.[4] Clearly, these large buyers can be very important to the business marketer. Because each large firm has such vast sales potential, the business marketer will often tailor a marketing strategy for each customer. Smaller manufacturing firms also constitute an important segment for the business marketer. In fact, over half of all manufacturers in the United States have fewer than 20 employees. In smaller firms the organizational buyer has different needs and often a different orientation. Again, the astute marketer will adjust the marketing program to the particular needs of this market segment.

Geographical Concentration

Distribution of industrial firms by size is not the only form of concentration important to the business marketer: manufacturers are also concentrated geographically (Figure 2.1). Primary areas of industrial concentration include the Midwest (Ohio, Indiana, Illinois, and Michigan) and the Middle Atlantic states (New Jersey, Pennsylvania, and New York). However, significant industrial growth and concentration have occurred in the Southeast and Southwest over the past two decades. In 1973 the Southwest accounted for 5.8 percent of all shipments by manufacturers; by 1986 its share had risen

---

[2] *Annual Survey of Manufacturers,* U.S. Department of Commerce, Bureau of the Census, Washington, D.C., 1986, pp. 1–40.

[3] *Statistical Abstract of the United States,* U.S. Department of Commerce, Bureau of the Census, Washington, D.C., 1990, p. 528.

[4] *Census of Manufacturers, General Summary, Part 2,* U.S. Department of Commerce, Bureau of the Census, Washington, D.C., 1982, pp. 1–3.

FIGURE 2.1 **Geographic Concentration of Manufacturing Facilities in the United States**

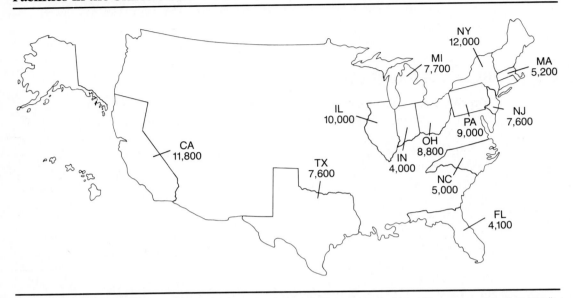

Source: Data from "SICBP: Your Manual on the Marketing Battlefield," *Sales & Marketing Management* (April 23, 1984), p. 22.

to 9.46 percent.[5] In 1988, the ten states of California, Illinois, Texas, Ohio, Pennsylvania, Michigan, New York, New Jersey, Indiana, and North Carolina accounted for 56 percent of all U.S. shipments; the 10 largest manufacturing counties accounted for 6.22 percent.[6] Most large metropolitan areas are lucrative business markets. Geographical concentration of industry, however, means only that a large potential volume exists in a given area; the requirements of each buyer may still vary significantly.

Geographic concentration has some important implications for the formulation of marketing strategy. First, firms can concentrate their marketing efforts in areas of high market potential and make effective use of a full-time personal sales force in these markets. Second, distribution centers in large-volume areas can ensure rapid delivery to a large proportion of customers. Finally, firms may not be able to tie their salespeople to specific geographic areas because many large buying organizations entrust to one individual the responsibility for purchasing certain products and materials for the entire company.

For example, the Kroger Company, a huge supermarket chain, has centralized purchasing in Cincinnati for store supplies and fixtures. Thus, everything from paper bags to display cases are purchased in Cincinnati for distribution to individual stores.

---

[5] "Survey of Industrial Purchasing Power," *Sales and Marketing Management,* 138 (April 27, 1987), p. 26.

[6] "Survey of Industrial Purchasing Power," *Sales and Marketing Management,* 140 (April 25, 1988), p. 12.

A paper-bag salesperson whose territory includes all retail stores in Tennessee and Arkansas cannot be very effective against a competitor who maintains a sales office in Cincinnati. The marketer requires an understanding of how a potential buyer's purchasing organization is structured.

The Purchasing Organization

Every firm, regardless of its organizational characteristics, must procure the materials, supplies, equipment, and services necessary to operate the business successfully. On an average, more than half of every dollar earned from sales of manufactured products is spent for the purchase of materials, supplies, and equipment needed to produce the goods.[7] For example, General Motors, Ford, and General Electric are the three largest industrial purchasers, spending $50 billion, $43 billion, and $18 billion, respectively, on goods and services in 1987.[8] How goods and services are purchased depends on such factors as the nature of the business, the size of the firm, and the volume, variety, and technical complexity of items purchased. Rarely do individual departments within a corporation do their own buying. Procurement is usually administered by an individual whose title is manager of purchasing, purchasing agent, director of purchasing, or materials manager.

Purchasing in Large Firms

In large firms purchasing has become quite specialized, with the work typically divided into five categories:

1. *Administrative.* Purchasing administration involves management tasks that emphasize the development of policies, procedures, controls, and mechanics for coordinating purchasing operations with operations of other departments.

2. *Buying.* Buying includes reviewing requisitions, analyzing specifications, doing informal research, investigating vendors, interviewing salespeople, studying costs and prices, and negotiating.

3. *Expediting.* Order follow-up involves vendor liaison work such as reviewing the status of orders, writing letters, telephoning and faxing vendors, and occasionally visiting vendors' plants.

4. *Special staff work.* Any well-developed purchasing operation has an unending number of projects and studies requiring specialized knowledge and uninterrupted effort, including economic and market studies, special cost studies, vendor investigations, and systems studies.

---

[7] Stuart F. Hainritz, Paul V. Farrel, and Clifton L. Smith, *Purchasing: Principles and Applications* (Englewood Cliffs, NJ: Prentice-Hall, Inc., 1986), p. 2.

[8] "The Top 100 Purchasing Organizations," *Purchasing,* 103 (November 24, 1988), p. 52.

5. *Clerical.* Every department must write orders and maintain not only working files but also catalog and library materials and records for commodities, vendors, and prices.[9]

The purchasing manager is responsible for administering the purchasing process and, on occasion, may be involved in the negotiations of a small number of important contracts.

The day-to-day purchasing function is carried out by buyers, each buyer responsible for a specific group of products. Organizing the purchasing function in this way permits buyers to acquire a high level of technical expertise on a limited number of items. As products and materials become more sophisticated, buyers must become more knowledgeable about material characteristics, manufacturing processes, and design specifications. In some cases, the salesperson requires enough knowledge of competing products to respond effectively to a buyer's probing questions.

The typical purchasing department is organized by type of product to be procured. If the firm is large, buyers will not report directly to the purchasing manager but to an intermediate-level manager, usually with the title of purchasing agent or buying department manager.[10] The buyers will be specialized by type of product and will concentrate all their attention on buying just a few items in their assigned product category. Frequently, a sizeable staff group will be employed to conduct research, evaluate materials, and perform cost studies.

The Marketer's Role

The nature and size of the purchasing department will have an important bearing on the formulation of marketing strategy. Considering the large number of small companies in the United States, most purchasing departments are one- or two-person operations. The purchasing agent may report to the president, general manager, controller, or production manager. The purchasing agent in the small firm may lack detailed knowledge and expertise. In this case, the industrial salesperson should be viewed as an extension of the customer's purchasing department, acting as a consultant and providing assistance wherever required.

When dealing with the large corporation, in which specialized buyers assigned to limited product categories have achieved sophistication in purchasing, the salesperson must be able to respond to specific questions about product quality, performance, and costs.[11] Purchasing units in large organizations are likely to use computer technology that significantly expands their ability to gather, process, and store information on the attributes and the performance history of alternative suppliers.

---

[9] Lamar Lee, Jr., and Donald W. Dobler, *Purchasing and Materials Management* (New York: McGraw-Hill Book Company, 1984), p. 440.

[10] Paul V. Farrell, coordinating ed., *Aljian's Purchasing Handbook,* 4th ed. (New York: McGraw-Hill Book Company, 1982), pp. 2–37.

[11] Dale C. Weisenstein, "Westinghouse Teams Up for Quality and Productivity," *Purchasing World,* 27 (May 1983), p. 48.

THE GLOBAL MARKETPLACE
Purchasing on an International Scale

To coordinate purchasing on a worldwide basis, Deere and Company created an international purchasing unit. The role of the unit is to act as a consultant or liaison to the various manufacturing operations, and to evaluate "the whole spectrum of what different countries have to offer."

To understand the supply capabilities of an individual country, the international purchasing unit develops a sourcing matrix that evaluates savings, lead time, delivery, quality, strengths, reliability, availability, technology, political stability, manufacturing expertise, infrastructure, exchange rate history, and economic stability.

Once the evaluations are completed, the purchasing staff creates a matrix listing required products on one axis and countries on the other. In each cell, the best suppliers in each location are identified. Finally, the top worldwide suppliers for each product line are selected.

The extensive information about worldwide suppliers of many products allows Deere to coordinate the needs of all company units and make significant inroads on reducing costs and improving quality. In addition, domestic suppliers are more willing to make changes in their own operations to remain competitive.

Source: Adapted from Shirley Cayer, "Low-key, But Savvy," *Purchasing,* 104 (October 12, 1989), p. 54.

Some large corporations that have geographically dispersed manufacturing facilities, with relatively similar requirements for supplies and materials, coordinate a significant volume of their purchases through a centralized procurement unit. Mead Corporation's Dayton, Ohio, headquarters directs the flow of equipment and materials to plant locations in Tennessee, Michigan, Wisconsin, and other locations. In response to centralized purchasing, many business marketers have developed a national accounts sales force, assigning one or more salespersons the responsibility of meeting the needs of a single large customer with sizable sales potential. The strategic implications of centralized buying and national accounts selling are explored in Chapter 4. Sales personnel and marketing managers who can effectively adapt to the purchasing conditions in each market segment are generally the leading marketers in their industry.

Materials Management: Integrating Purchasing into the Business Operation

Many manufacturers have adopted a more broad-based and integrated approach to the organization of purchasing activities. This organizational concept is referred to as **materials management**. All activities (including determination of manufacturing requirements; production scheduling; and procurement, storage, and disbursement of materials) are handled by a materials manager.[12] Table 2.1 presents a description of the array of tasks that are typically included under the materials management umbrella.

---

[12] Eberhard E. Scherring, *Purchasing Management* (Englewood Cliffs, NJ: Prentice-Hall, Inc., 1989), p. 85.

TABLE 2.1   **Tasks of Materials Management**

1. *Production planning:* To prepare the master production plan in support of the sales levels projected in the marketing plan.
2. *Requirements planning:* To translate planned production levels into materials requirements to establish the base for ordering.
3. *Scheduling:* To develop complete and detailed work schedules to determine production sequences and dates.
4. *Purchasing planning:* To establish materials budgets, ordering cycles, quantities, and dates as well as due dates for incoming materials.
5. *Order placement:* To execute purchasing plan by placing purchase orders with approved vendors and responding to emergency requests.
6. *Expediting:* To follow up on orders placed and shipments en route to make sure that materials are received on time.
7. *Traffic:* To select modes of transportation and carriers and to audit freight bills.
8. *Materials handling and storage:* To receive, inspect, move, store, and protect all incoming materials.
9. *Shipping:* To select, pack, and ship the finished product to the customer.
10. *Inventory control:* To manage inventory levels to minimize investment while avoiding stockouts.

Source: Eberhard E. Scherring, *Purchasing Management* (Englewood Cliffs, N.J.: Prentice-Hall, 1989), p. 85.

Note that the purchasing function is only one element of the entire materials management process. By giving the materials manager overall authority, the activities of various departments can be coordinated in order to ensure that the total cost of materials to the organization is minimized. Without this central authority, savings in one function, such as purchasing, may add cost in another, such as inventory control.

The materials management approach will be increasingly utilized in the coming years as a result of (1) its ability to increase efficiency, (2) professional development of trained materials managers, (3) computer systems, and (4) pressures exerted from worldwide competitors and economic events.[13] Large firms with geographically dispersed manufacturing facilities integrate their centralized and their operational materials management activities at plant and division levels. On-line computer systems combine and integrate all aspects of the materials management function.

Materials management has made purchasing personnel aware of the need to evaluate every element in the flow of purchased materials—including net delivered price, inventory control, traffic, receiving, and production control. The result places an extremely heavy burden on the business marketing strategist. Marketing managers must coordinate all activities that affect the materials management function of their customers—including sales management, credit, traffic, expediting, warehousing, and production—and must be able to secure the necessary distribution support from their own logistics department.

---

[13] John D. Davin, section editor, *Aljian's Purchasing Handbook*, 4th ed., pp. 19–21.

Just-in-Time Systems

A strategy of purchasing, production, and inventory which is spreading rapidly and is revolutionizing buyer–seller relationships is that of **just-in-time** or **JIT**. The essence of the concept is to deliver parts and materials to the production process just at the moment they are needed.

The JIT concept was originally introduced by the Toyota Motor Company nearly forty years ago and it has now taken hold in many manufacturing industries globally. In the United States, industries from automobiles to apparel have adopted the JIT concept. In the apparel industry's just-in-time inventory system, the distribution capability of fabric suppliers is critical. Suppliers that can synchronize their own production, inventory, and distribution systems with those of the apparel maker have the best chance of winning sizable, long-term contracts. The advent of the materials management concept and the associated JIT philosophy has stimulated a more systematic approach to business marketing strategy and a closer working relationship between buyers and sellers.

Just-in-time systems link purchasing, procurement, manufacturing, and logistics in such a way that the storage, movement, inspection, and production of all materials needed for the manufacturing of a given product are clearly specified. Inherent to such a system is a precise sequencing and scheduling of when these activities are to be completed. The goals of JIT are to minimize parts and materials inventories, improve product quality, maximize production efficiency, and provide optimal levels of customer service. At the core of any JIT system is the idea that parts and materials inventories are to be avoided; the goal is simply to eliminate inventory. NCR's Ithaca, New York, plant was able to do just that with the implementation of a JIT system. After implementing JIT, the plant was able to reduce the number of days of inventory it carried from 110 to 21. The firm hopes ultimately to reduce inventory to 9 days.[14]

It is instructive to compare a traditional manufacturing operation to one operating under the just-in-time philosophy. Table 2.2 provides such a comparison. The table strongly suggests that JIT, rather than being a narrow strategy for reducing inventory, is a much broader approach for operating a business. John Flanagan and James Morgan succinctly capture the essence of JIT:

> JIT is not just a system for keeping track of orders and schedules. It is a discipline that calls for continuous re-examination of how manufacturers go about making what they make—making the production cycle more and more functional, making it tighter from order to shipment—including interactions with suppliers. In short, it is a discipline that attacks waste at every level.[15]

Close Buyer–Seller Relationships

Companies that adopt the JIT approach typically change the way they do business with their suppliers. In most cases a JIT manufacturer will reduce the number of suppliers and enter into multiyear contracts with this smaller group of suppliers. A recent study

---

[14] Ernest Raia, "JIT in Purchasing: A Progress Report," *Purchasing,* 104 (February 23, 1989), p. 18.

[15] John Flanagan and James P. Morgan, *Just-in-Time for the '90s* (Washington, D.C.: DREF, 1989), p. 19.

TABLE 2.2   **Comparison of Traditional Manufacturing Operations to JIT Systems**

Elements	How the Elements Are Viewed in:	
	A Traditional Manufacturing System	**A JIT Manufacturing System**
Inventory	Viewed as an asset; an insurance policy against forecast errors and late delivery.	Viewed as a liability; it is an indicator of operational problems. To be eliminated.
Production setups	Reducing setup time is a low priority; key is maximum output.	A critical goal is to reduce setup time to the absolute minimum.
Suppliers	Use multiple sources (for "protection"); often viewed as adversaries.	Suppliers are partners; one or only a very few are used.
Quality	Tolerate a certain small percentage of rejects and scrap.	Emphasis on zero defects; quality expected to be 100%.
Equipment	Maintenance performed as needed; inventory available if a breakdown occurs.	No breakdowns are tolerated; strict routine maintenance schedules are followed.
Lead times	Are built into the process to compensate for problems in the system.	Short lead times are the objective; short lead times reduce the need for expediting.
Workers	Workers are supervised by management edict; standards are set up to assess whether workers are achieving management's directives.	Emphasis is on management by concensus; workers have a say and proprietary interest in the firm's operation.

Source: Adapted from John Flanagan and James P. Morgan, *Just-in-Time for the '90s* (Washington, D.C.: DREF, 1989), pp. 19–21.

indicates that a majority of firms are actively pursuing a strategy to reduce their supplier base. Almost 57 percent of the study's purchasing manager respondents indicated they will continue to reduce their supplier base in the coming year.[16] In return for the single-source, multiyear agreements, suppliers will be expected to deliver high-quality, defect-free materials on a just-in-time basis. General Motors, for example, looks to enter into a relationship of five to seven years with a limited number of machine-tool vendors.[17] These suppliers are required to deliver defect-free materials on time, every time, to accommodate GM's needs. The net impact of JIT is that customers and suppliers are communicating more freely, sharing what was once considered proprietary information, nurturing a close buyer–seller relationship. For JIT manufacturers the trend is definitely in the direction of a reduced supplier base, with single-sourcing of many components.

Many buyers today look at the relationship with their vendors as partnerships. Such relationships are often referred to as "strategic alliances," and they involve an enlightened view of the buyer–seller interaction. In these situations, buyers and sellers share sensitive business information, agree to work in a single-source mode, and work to totally integrate their operations so that the buyer's delivery and production requirements are

---

[16] Buyers Keep Trimming Supplier Base Despite Tight Supplies," *Purchasing,* 104 (February 23, 1989), p. 18

[17] Kate Bertrand, "Crafting 'Win-Win Situations' in Buyer–Seller Relationships," *Business Marketing,* 71 (June 1986), p. 46.

INSIDE BUSINESS MARKETING
Linkage: JIT in the Textiles Industry

A truck leaves a textile mill with a load of cloth destined for an apparel maker's plant. Through a computer hookup, the apparel maker is immediately notified as to what is on the truck—number of rolls of cloth, their width, color, and so forth. Once the goods arrive at the apparel maker's plant, they will bypass inspection and move directly to the company's cutting operation.

Such systems are the just-in-time approaches now being applied in the apparel industry. The electronic linking of cloth supplier to apparel maker has profound impacts: a reduction of cloth inventory, elimination of two to three weeks of warehousing cost, inspection reduction or elimination, and a significant reduction in production time.

Haggar Industries estimates that within the next 18 months 60 percent of its purchases will be sent directly to the cutting room floor. Burlington Industries, a supplier of fabrics, estimates that these linkages have the potential to save fabric buyers 12 to 20 cents per yard of fabric.

Source: Hannah Miller, "Just-in-Time: Some Textile Industries Call It 'Linkage'," *Purchasing,* 102 (April 9, 1987), pp. 58–61.

---

met. General Electric seeks out partnership arrangements with suppliers, but finds that "the most difficult task is convincing top management that multiple sourcing isn't necessary in running a business." Another key challenge for General Electric "is dealing with the mind-set among top managers and buyers who, in the past, were rewarded for beating up suppliers in price negotiations."[18] Buyers currently are taught to carefully evaluate long-term total costs associated with dealing with a particular supplier. As the adoption of JIT systems accelerates and global competitive pressures increase, the need to develop effective buyer–seller partnerships will be magnified. Such partnerships may prove to be the ingredient that ensures the long–term survival of both buyer and seller.

JIT: Strategy Implications

The implications of JIT to business marketers are far-reaching and perhaps severe. In those industries where JIT is being adopted, the ability to respond to JIT requirements is fundamental for survival. The ability to deliver defect-free components exactly when they are required provides the edge needed in this new competitive environment. The inability to develop consistent product quality is a major hindrance to the creation of a JIT relationship with a buyer.[19] The business marketer wishing to participate in JIT programs must focus careful attention on developing a quality-management program that ensures that products meet quality standards before they leave the plant. In addition, manufacturing flexibility, delivery capabilities, and responsiveness to customers'

---

[18] Bob Donath, "Partner Trend Might Cool From Hot Cycle," *Business Marketing,* 74 (January 1989), pp. 22, 24.

[19] A. Ansari and B. Modarress, "JIT Brings Problems and Solutions," *Purchasing World,* 34 (March 1990), p. 48.

requirements are critical elements in forging long-term relationships with customers. Information will play a pivotal role: supplier data on costs and pricing, supplier input to product design, and the electronic (computer) linkage of supplier and customer are all features of the buyer–seller relationship that are becoming more important. Some business marketers have been slow to respond to this new environment. If the business marketer can become an effective supplier to a JIT customer, the impact is significant: a possible single-source position in a long-term relationship in which the supplier is viewed as an extension of the customer's company.

GOVERNMENTS: UNIQUE CHARACTERISTICS

Like commercial enterprises, institutions and **government purchasers** are also enhancing the effectiveness of the purchasing function through the use of materials management and other methods. As indicated in Chapter 1, the federal government is the largest consumer in the United States; its buying procedures are highly specialized and often very confusing. To compete effectively in the government market, the business marketer must develop a thorough comprehension of this complex buying process. A first step is to understand the variety of governmental units and their characteristics.

In 1987, there were 83,166 governmental units in the United States (see Table 2.3). Note that a vast majority of these governmental units are local, providing the business marketer with a widely dispersed market. However, there is some market concentration; 10 states account for 49 percent of all governmental units in the United States.[20] The numbers in Table 2.3 are somewhat misleading, indicating the ratio of state and federal units to local units as 1 to 1,500. In reality, many functional areas within state government (education, state police, highway) and agencies within the federal government (defense, space, interior, transportation, postal service) are responsible for a sizable procurement volume. Thus, within federal and state governments, hundreds of people, agencies, and functional areas have direct and indirect influence on the purchasing process.

Federal, state, and local governments spent $969 billion on the purchase of goods and services in 1988. The federal government accounted for $382 billion of the total expenditure (state and local governments accounted for the other $587 billion) and over 77 percent of their total spending was for defense procurement.[21] Clearly, governmental units rival the commercial sector in terms of total market potential.

Influences on Government Buying

Another level of complexity is added to the governmental purchasing process by the array of influences on this process. In federal, state, and large city procurement, buyers will be responsible to or influenced by dozens of interested parties who specify,

---

[20] *Government Units in 1987,* U.S. Department of Commerce, Bureau of the Census, Preliminary Report, November 1987, p. 1.

[21] *Statistical Abstract of the United States,* U.S. Department of Commerce, Bureau of the Census, 1990, p. 425.

TABLE 2.3 **Types of Governmental Units**

Type of Unit		Number of Units
United States government		1
State government		50
Local government		83,166
County	3,042	
Cities and towns	35,896	
School districts	14,741	
Special districts	29,487	
Total		83,217

Source: *Government Units in 1987,* U.S. Department of Commerce, Bureau of the Census, Preliminary Report, November 1987, p. 1.

legislate, evaluate, and use the goods and services.[22] Clearly, the range of outside influences extends far beyond the originating agency.

Understanding Government Contracts

Government purchasing is also affected by goals and programs that have broad social overtones, including compliance, set-asides, and minority subcontracting. The **compliance program** requires that government contractors maintain affirmative action programs for minorities, women, and the handicapped. Firms failing to do so are barred from holding government contracts. In the **set-aside program**, a certain percentage of a given government contract is "set aside" for small or minority businesses; no others can participate in that proportion of the contract. The **minority subcontracting program** may require that major contractors subcontract a certain percentage of the total contract to minority firms. For example, Ohio law requires that 7 percent of all subcontractors on state construction projects be minorities. The potential government contractor must understand these programs and how they apply to the firm.

Most government procurement, at any level, is based on laws that establish contractual guidelines.[23] The federal government has set forth certain general contract provisions as part of the federal procurement regulations. These provisions include stipulations regarding product inspection, payment methods, actions as a result of default, and disputes, among many others.

Without a clear comprehension of the procurement laws, the vendor is in an unfavorable position during the negotiation phase. The vendor particularly needs to explore the advantages and disadvantages of the two basic types of contract:

1. *Fixed-price contracts.* A firm price is agreed to before the contract is awarded, and full payment is made when the product or service is delivered as agreed.

---

[22] Cecil Hynes and Noel Zabriskie, *Marketing to Governments* (Columbus, Ohio: Grid, 1974), p. 1.

[23] David E. Gumpert and Jeffery A. Timmons, "Penetrating the Government Procurement Maze," *Harvard Business Review,* 60 (May–June 1982), p. 15.

2. *Cost-reimbursement contracts.* The vendor is reimbursed for allowable costs incurred in performance of the contract and is sometimes allowed a certain number of dollars above cost as profit.

Each type of contract has built-in incentives to control costs or to cover future contingencies.

Generally, the fixed-price contract provides the greatest profit potential, but it also provides greater risks if unforeseen expenses are incurred, if inflation increases dramatically, or if conditions change. For example, inflation and unanticipated development problems resulted in a $60 million loss for a defense contractor producing the first 20 fighter planes for the Navy. However, if the seller can reduce costs significantly during the contract, profits may exceed those estimated when the contract was negotiated. Cost-reimbursement contracts are carefully administered by the government because of the minimal incentives for contractor efficiency. They are usually employed for contracts involving considerable developmental work for which it is difficult to estimate efforts and expenses.

To overcome the inefficiencies of both the cost-reimbursement contract, which often leads to cost overruns, and the fixed-price contract, which can discourage firms from bidding because project costs are uncertain, the government often employs incentive contracts. The incentive contract rewards firms when their actual costs on a project are below target costs, and it imposes a penalty when they exceed target costs.

Telling Vendors How to Sell: Useful Publications

Unlike most customers, governments often go to great lengths to explain to potential vendors exactly how to do business with them. For example, the federal government makes available such publications as *Doing Business with the Federal Government, Selling to the Military,* and *Selling to the U.S. Air Force.* Government agencies also hold periodic seminars to orient businesses to the buying procedures used by the agency. The objective is to encourage firms to seek government business.

Purchasing Organizations and Procedures: Government

Government and commercial purchasing are organized similarly. However, governments tend to emphasize clerical functions because of the detailed procedures the law requires. Although the federal government is the largest single industrial purchaser, it does not operate like a single company but like a combination of several large companies with overlapping responsibilities and thousands of small independent units.[24] The federal government has more than 15,000 purchasing authorities (departments, agencies, etc.). Figure 2.2 provides an example of the diversity of government buying. Every government agency possesses some degree of buying influence or authority. Federal government procurement is divided into two categories: defense and nondefense.

---

[24] Ibid., p. 16.

FIGURE 2.2   **The Diversity of Federal Government Procurement**

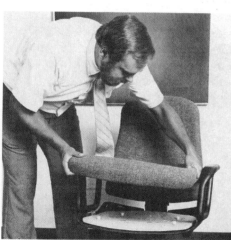

Source: *Doing Business With the Federal Government,* U.S. General Services Administration (Washington, D.C., 1986).

"Remember the guy who blew the whistle on
Pentagon waste? It seems the whistle cost
$875."

Source: From *The Wall Street Journal*; Permission, Cartoon Features Syndicate.

Defense Procurement

Each military division of the Department of Defense (DOD)—army, navy, and air force—is responsible for its own major purchases. However, the Defense Logistics Agency (DLA) procures billions of dollars worth of supplies used in common by all branches. In total the DLA manages about 1.5 million supply items for all the military services.[25] The purpose of the DLA is to obtain favorable prices through volume purchasing and to reduce duplication of purchasing within the military. Defense-related items may also be procured by other government agencies, such as the General Services Administration (GSA). In fact, DOD is GSA's largest customer. Under current agreements between GSA and DOD, the military purchases through GSA many items such as cars, desks, office machines, and hand tools.[26] Also, many supplies for military-base operations are procured locally.

Because of the many abuses in defense procurement, the Competition in Contracting Act was passed in 1986.[27] The act requires either competitive bids or justification of sole sourcing. Potential suppliers are required to follow detailed DOD rules and regulations in preparation of their bids. In addition, a sole-source relationship will be carefully reviewed and evaluated as to its conformance with applicable laws.

---

[25] John C. Franke, "Military Makes Its Own Purchasing Rules," *Marketing News* (October 9, 1989), p. 7.

[26] *Doing Business With the Federal Government,* U.S. General Services Administration, Washington, D.C., 1986, p. 5.

[27] Ansari and Modarress, "JIT Brings Problems and Solutions," p. 49.

ETHICAL BUSINESS MARKETING
Corporate Self-Governance in the Defense Industry

The Department of Defense annually conducts business with some 60,000 prime contractors and hundreds of thousands of other suppliers and subcontractors. Widely publicized investigations and prosecutions of large defense contractors have seriously damaged the reputation of the defense industry. The President's Blue Ribbon Commission on Defense Management concluded, however, that "while fraud constitutes a serious problem, it is not as extensive or costly as many Americans believe. The nation's defense programs lose far more to inefficiency than to dishonesty."

What steps can be taken to restore public confidence in the industry?

Given the size and scope of the defense industry, "no conceivable number of additional federal auditors, inspectors, investigators, and prosecutors can police it fully, much less make it work more effectively." Therefore, the commission strongly recommended the initiation of a program of "corporate self-governance" in the defense industry. More than 45 large defense contractors have made a signed commitment to adopt and implement a rigorous set of principles of business ethics and conduct that acknowledges their corporate responsibilities under procurement laws and to the public. While government audits will remain, the intent is to shift more of the responsibility for the industry's actions to the industry.

Source: *A Quest for Excellence: Final Report*, President's Blue Ribbon Commission on Defense Management, June 1986, pp. 75–79; and Jacques S. Gansler, *Affording Defense* (Cambridge, Mass.: The MIT Press, 1989), p. 207.

Nondefense Procurement

Nondefense procurement is administered by a wide variety of agencies, including cabinet departments (e.g., Health and Human Services, Commerce), commissions (e.g., Federal Trade Commission), the executive branch (e.g., Bureau of Budget), federal agencies (e.g., the Federal Aviation Agency), and federal administrations (e.g., GSA). The Department of Commerce centralizes the procurement of supplies and equipment for its Washington office and all local offices. The Department of the Interior, on the other hand, instructs each area and district office of the Mining Enforcement and Safety Administration to purchase mine-safety equipment and clothing locally.[28]

Like the DLA, the GSA centralizes the procurement of many general-use items (e.g., office furniture, pens, light bulbs) for all civilian government agencies. The Federal Supply Service of the GSA is like the purchasing department of a large diversified corporation because it provides a consolidated purchasing, storing, and distribution network for the federal government. The Federal Supply Service purchases many items commonly used by other government agencies, including office supplies, small tools, paint, paper, furniture, maintenance supplies, and duplicating equipment. The GSA has enormous purchasing power.

---

[28] Gumpert and Timmons, "Penetrating the Government Procurement Maze," p. 18.

INSIDE BUSINESS MARKETING
Federal Government Moves to Buy More Off-the-Shelf Items

A new acronym is in vogue these days among federal procurement personnel. It's COTS, which stands for Commercial Off-the-Shelf, and it means the federal government is buying more products that are regularly available in the private sector. Instead of spending long periods of time developing detailed specifications for every product it buys (it took 17 pages to describe the "specs" for Worcestershire sauce), the government now hopes to procure as many off-the-shelf items as possible.

There appear to be many advantages to the COTS program. Existing commercial products are proven and the items are immediately avail-able (the product development cycle for many standard military items bought by specification has ranged anywhere from one to five years). When COTS items are purchased the manufac-turer does not incur the unnecessary costs of developing distinct, but very similar, military versions. The net result is lower cost to the government. The fact that many COTS products carry a full warranty allows the government to reduce staff involved with inspection, repair, and maintenance. Savings also accrue because the time, effort, and staff devoted to resolving conflicts in cases where specifications are not precisely met are eliminated.

Source: Adapted from: "Success with Commercial Product Procurement," *Contract Management* (August, 1990), p. 24.

Under the Federal Supply Schedule Program, departments within the government may purchase specified items from an approved supplier at an agreed-upon price. This program provides federal agencies with the sources of products such as furniture, appliances, office equipment, laboratory equipment, and the like. Once the supplier has bid and been approved, the schedule may involve an indefinite-quantity contract for a term of one to three years. The schedule permits agencies to place orders directly with suppliers. Currently, there are nearly 200 different schedules under this program.[29]

An important aspect of the GSA's procurement activities is the operation of their Business Service Centers (BSC), through which businesses may obtain advice from trained counselors, information on contract opportunities throughout the federal government, and step-by-step help with contracting procedures.[30] The BSCs are located in 11 major cities across the nation.

Federal Buying

The president may set the procurement process in motion when he signs a congres-sional appropriation bill, or an accountant in the General Accounting Office may initiate the process by requesting a new desktop calculator. It should be understood that the federal government buys almost everything. In fact, it would be difficult to name a product or service that is not listed at least occasionally in the federal government's publication, *Commerce Business Daily* (*CBD*). The *CBD* is published every Monday

---

[29] *Doing Business With the Federal Government,* p. 22.

[30] Ibid., p. 3.

through Saturday by the Department of Commerce. It lists all government procurement proposals, subcontracting leads, contract awards, and sales of surplus property. It is important to note that a proposed procurement action appears in the *CBD* only once. A potential supplier has at least 30 days prior to bid opening in which to respond. By law, all intended procurement actions of $10,000 or more, both civilian and military, are published in CBD. Copies of *CBD* are available at various government field offices as well as local public libraries. Figure 2.3 shows typical listings in the *CBD*.

Once a procurement need is documented and publicly announced, the government will follow one of two general procurement strategies: formal advertising (also know as open bid) or negotiated contract.

Formal Advertising

Formal advertising means the government will solicit bids from appropriate suppliers; usually, the lowest bidder is awarded the contract. This strategy is followed when the product is standardized and the specifications straightforward. The interested supplier must gain a place on a bidder's list (or monitor the CBD on a daily basis—which suggests that a more effective approach is to get on the bidder's list by filing the necessary forms available from the GSA Business Service Centers). Then, each time the government requests bids for a particular product, the supplier receives an invitation to bid. The invitation to bid specifies the item and the quantity to be purchased, provides detailed technical specifications, and stipulates delivery schedules, warranties required, packing requirements, and other purchasing details. The bidding firm bases its bid on its own cost structure and on the anticipation of competitive bid levels.

Procurement personnel review each bid for conformance to specifications. Western Electric was disqualified on a $70 million contract for base PBX systems. Although Western Electric complained that there was no functional need for digital technology in the systems, they were automatically disqualified for not meeting the mandatory bid specifications for a fully digital PBX system.[31] Thus, a critical aspect of marketing strategy for the firm soliciting government business is to develop procedures that ensure all specifications are carefully met. Bid price is obviously another essential strategic dimension in doing business with the government. Contracts are generally awarded to the lowest bidder; however, the government agency may select the next-to-lowest bidder if it can document that the lowest bidder would not responsibly fulfill the contract.

Formal advertising is expensive and time-consuming for all parties, generating a substantial volume of paperwork. However, the process does allow free and open competition. In addition, the government has fairly good assurance that there is no collusion and that it has obtained the lowest possible price.

---

[31] "Western Electric: Air Force Overpays $40 Million on Northern Telecom PBX Pact," *Electronic News,* 27 (July 13, 1981), p. 7.

FIGURE 2.3   **Sample Listings in the *Commerce Business Daily***

Commerce Business Daily

FRIDAY, June 27, 1986
Issue No. PSA-9120

A daily list of U.S. Government procurement invitations, contract awards, subcontracting leads, sales of surplus property and foreign business opportunities

Supplies, Equipment and Material

10 Weapons

Warner Robins ALC Directorate of Contracting and Manufacturing, Robins AFB, GA 31098
10 – **LOCK BOLT HEAD** NSN: 1005001482 324 P/N: 11698279. Dim - approx 1.74'' o/a length x .90'' o/a width, matl - steel carbon spec Q Q-5-698, Func - to lock the track bolts on the gun rotor. 36595 ea appl to: MG1, M61A1 & GAU-4/A. Destn: Robins AFB, GA 31098-5320. Del: 31 May 87 36595 ea. This notice is for Sol FD2060-86-48667 which will be issued approx 23 Aug 86: to: Various sources with an approx closing date of 22 Sep 86. For copy of sol contact: WR-ALC/PMXOA include Mfg Code. For addtl info contact: Callie English/PMXDZ, 912/926-3091. Notes: 3, 44 & 95.
10 – **CHUTE AMMO** NSN: 1005010556 546 P/N: 201F946-3. Dim - approx 2.50'' x 8.00'' x 23.00'' matl - steel & alum, func - provides passageway for RDS moving from access unit to drum. 228 ea appl to: F-16 acft. Destn: Robins AFB, GA 31098-5320. Del: 31 Dec 87 228 ea. This notice is for Sol FO9603-86-R-4299 which will be issued approx 16 Jul 86. To: Nobles Industries Inc, St. Paul, MN 55106 with an approx closing date of 15 Aug 86. For copy of sol contact: WR-ALC/PMXOA include Mfg Code. For addtl info contact: Lenora Pinkett/PMZBA, 912/926-2533 x 2428. Authority: 10 U.S.C. 2304(C)(1), justification: supplies (or services) required are avail from only one responsible source and no other type of supplies or services will satisfy agency reqmts. Notes: 22, 27 & 33. (175)

U.S. Army Armament Munitions & Chemical Command, Attn: AMSMC-PCM-MS, Rock Island, IL 61299,
Tel: 309/782-4664 or 4166
10 – **STOWAGE BRACKET** for ammunition box. Matl is a formed weldment with carc final finish, NSN 1025-00-890-2659, P/N 11619628, end use: M551 Sheridan, Qty 274 ea. FOB Destn. Issue date is o/a 15 Jul 86. DAAA09-86-T-1680. BOD is o/a 15 Aug 86. See Notes 42, 57. To order a copy of this sol, call 309/782-4664 or 4166. For info concerning the Contr Spec and Contr Officer, call Barbara Smart at 309/782-3626 and give PWD No: M1606411M1.
10 – **MOTOR** 1.5 HP DC Motor is source controlled to Skurka Eng Co. P/N G497-CN861, NSN 1005-01-088-4396, P/N 12524473, end use: M242. Qty 76 ea. FOB Destn. Issue date is o/a 15 Jul 86. This is a FY 87 unfunded requirement. DAAA09-86-R 1415, BOD is o/a 14 Aug 86. See Notes 44, 57, 66. To order a copy of this sol, call 309/782-4664 or 4166. For info concerning the Contr Spec and Contr Officer, call Barbara Smart at 309/782-3626 and give PWD No. M1753992M1. (175)

Navy Ships Parts Control Center, PO Box 2020, Mechanicsburg, PA 17055-0788
10 – **BRAKE ASSY** DNG 5517958, except as modified or amplified in RFP, NSN: QH 1015-01-152-0296, (WIMM). Del FOB origin, 37 AY. RFP N00104-86-R-X286. RFP due date 25 Aug 86. 100% opt clause included, 120 days. Offerors are hereby advised that written requests for copies of the Sol and related data package must be accompanied by a letter of intent to return the Tech Data Package upon receipt of contract. The Technical Data Package can only be released to U.S. Manufacturers and Oto Melara, La Spezia, Italy. See Notes 9, 24.
10 – **CIRCUIT CARD ASSY** Dwg 5586091, except as modified or ampl in RFP, NSN: 7H 1020-01-147-7621 (WIMM). Del to Norfolk, VA & Oakland, CA. 46 ea. RFP N000104-86-R-UQ06. RFP due date 11 Aug 86. 100% option clause included. 180 days. See Notes 9, 24. (175)

Naval Sea Systems Command, Code 02511, James Grembi, 202/692-8000, Washington, DC 20362-5101
10 – **ENHANCED BATTLE SHORT MODIFICATION KITS FOR OT-102/SPY-1A TRANSMITTER GROUP IN CG-53.** NAVSEA intends to modify contr N00024-84-C-5124 to provide for the development and installation of modification kits for implementing enhanced Battle Short Design Changes into AN-6901/SPY-1A Amplifier Monitor, AM-6899/SPY-1A radio frequency amplifier PP-7361/SPY-1A high voltage power supply and AM-6900/SPY-1A radio freq amplifier. The contr modification is with Raytheon Co, Equipment Div, Boston Post Rd, Wayland, MA 01778 since this firm is the developer and orig equipment mfr. Sol N00024-86-R-5559/86-5559. (176)

U.S. Army Armament Munitions & Chemical Command, Attn: AMSMC-PCM-MS, Rock Island, IL 61299,
Tel: 309/782-4664 or 4166
10 – **END FITTING** This is a sole source procurement with Standard Armament Inc, 631 Allen Ave, Glendale, CA 91201. End fitting, NSN: 1005-01-215-8175 P/N: 766012-152. End use: Bradley Fighting Vehicle System, Qty: 734 ea. FOB: Dest: DAAA09-86-T-1554, Issue o/a 18 Jul 86 with opening date 18 Aug 86 which is also an approx date. See Note 22 for sol info only. Nancy Moniske 309/782-3136. (175)

Navy Ships Parts Control Center, PO Box 2020, Mechanicsburg, PA 17055-0788
10 – **PISTON ASSY** dwg LD2806641 item 4 as modified or amplified in RFP, NSN 7H 1020-01-201-5849, del to Norfolk, VA & Oakland, CA. 5 ea. RFP N00104-86-R-YE23. RFP due date 11 Aug 86. 100% option clause included. 180 days. See Notes 9, 24 & 42. (175)

Navy Ships Parts Control Center, PO Box 2020, Mechanicsburg, PA 17055-0788
10 – **CAN-LID ASSY** Dwg 2857201, NSN 1H 1010-00-151-3809, del FOB origin. 37 ea. RFQ N00104-86-Q-YE69(7GL). RFQ due 14 Aug 86. See Notes 9, 24, 42.
10 – **COVER** Dwg 5205662, NSN 1H 1045-01-190-9853, del to Norfolk VA 6 ea. RFQ N00104-86-Q-XN33(7JK). RFQ due 14 Aug 86. See Notes 9, 24, 42. (176)

Navy Ships Parts Control Center, PO Box 2020, Mechanicsburg, PA 17055-0788
10 – **REPAIR KIT** Gun Port, Dwg LD624279 except as modified or amplified in IFB, NSN: 1H 1015-01-142-5388 (WIMM), del to var dest, 457 ea. IFB N00104-86-B-0475. BOD 13 Aug 86. 100% opt clause included, 180 days. See Notes 9, 12, 43, 64. (176)

Navy Ships Parts Control Center, PO Box 2020, Mechanicsburg, PA 17055-0788
10 – **TUBE & ADAPTER ASSY,** Dwg LD260465GR14, NSN 1H 1020-00-175-4011, del to Oakland CA. 167 ea. RFQ N00104-86-Q-YE64(7GZ). RFQ due date 11 Aug 86. See Notes 9 & 24. (175)

12 Fire Control Equipment

Warner Robins ALC Directorate of Contracting and Manufacturing, Robins AFB, GA 31098
12 – **ACCELEROMETER** NSN 1270002929411, P/N 113D9430G3. Dim: 1.5'' d x 2'' h, matl: steel alloy, func: measures G forces and provides acft altitude info. 1 ea. appl to ASG-29 sys, F5E/F A/C. Destn: ship to shall be furnished at time of award. Del 30 Sep 86, 1 ea. Item 2: motor gyro, NSN 1270002953528, P/N 701C744G4. Dim: 3'' x 2'' x 2'', matl: steel, wire & magnets, func: used to process the gyro in elevation as required by the lead angle computation. 1 ea, appl to ASG-29 sys, F5E/F A/C. Destn: ship to will be furnished at time of award. Del 30 Sep 86, 1 ea. Item 3: circuit card assy, NSN 127001611710, P/N 292E942G1. Dim: 3'' h x 6 1/2'' l x 1'' t, matl: electronic components, func: provides sensitivity info used in computing lead angles which are required for accurate missile launch and fire control and 4 other items. 4 ea. appl to ASG-29 sys, F5E/F A/C. Destn: ship to shall be furnished at time of award. Del 30 Sep 86, 4 ea. This notice is for Sol FD2060-86-32513 which will be issued approx 16 Jul 86. To: General Electric Co, Binghamton, NY 13902, with an approx closing date of 15 Aug 86. For copy of sol contact Ed McGee, PMZBF, 912/926-2533, ext 2282. Authority 10 USC 2304(C)(1), justification: supplies (or services) required are avail from only one responsible source and no other type of supplies or services will satisfy agency requirements. See Notes 22, 27, 33. (176)

Warner Robins ALC Directorate of Contracting and Manufacturing, Robins AFB, GA 31098
12 – **RETURN HOSE** NSN: 1270001596 162. P/N: 738762 1. Dim - 9.780'' long x 1.634'' wide x 1'' high, matl - metal & rubber, func - allows helium to flow from receiver to compressor. 170 ea appl to: AN/AAD-7, AC130A&E. Destn: Robins AFB, GA 31098-5320. Del: 31 Dec 86 19 ea. This notice is for Sol. FD2060-86-49444 which will be issued approx 23 Aug 86. To Texas Instruments Inc, Dallas, TX 75266 with an approx closing date of 22 Sep 86. For copy of sol contact: WR-ALC/PMXOA include Mfg Code. For addtl info contact: Barbara Grantham/PMXDZ, 912/926-3309. All responsible sources may submit a bid, proposal, or quotation which shall be considered. No tel reqs. Only written reqs received directly from the requestor are acceptable. Notes 27 & 33.
12 – **AMPLIFIER MODULE, EL** NSN 1270009426 170. P/N: 107B7947G1. Dim - approx 1 1/2'' x 3/4'', matl - copper, steel, fiberglass & glass, func - Electronic control amplifier (differential). 142 ea appl to: AN/ASG 22/23/26 sys. Destn: Robins AFB, GA 31098-5320. Del: 30 Jun 87 142 ea. This notice is for Sol. FO9603-86-R-8815 which will be issued approx 23 Aug 86. To: Various sources with an approx closing date of 22 Sep 86. For copy of sol contact: WR-ALC/PMXOA include Mfg Code. For addtl info contact: Callie English/PMXDZ, 912/926-3091. First Article Test required. Notes: 3, 43, 95 & 96. (175)

Reflections of a Shipbuilder

Newport News Shipbuilding, one of the most successful private shipyards in the United States, produces aircraft carriers, tankers, submarines, cruisers, and other military and commercial vessels. Edward J. Campbell, president and chief executive officer, provides these reflections on the government as a customer.

On the plus side:

- The government builds in incentives to reward good performance.

- Government contracts can put a firm at the cutting edge of technology and provide many useful technological spin-offs.

- Government contracts provide solid cash flow; bills are paid regularly if the paperwork is done properly.

- The government is willing to share some of the risks involved in major, long-term shipbuilding contracts.

- The government is becoming more of a partner than an adversary.

On the minus side:

- Compared to the commercial marketplace, buyer–seller relationships are different. Government procurement units are required to get bids—bids they can share with others, even competitors.

- There's a constant "changing of the guard," as key buying influentials are transferred or promoted. Old rules receive new interpretations as these buying influentials change.

- Major government contracts require lengthy review by many committees; years may pass before a decision is made, and the specifications may change throughout this process as the technology changes.

- There are many quality control checkpoints (some of them redundant) throughout the fulfillment of a major government contract.

- Nothing compares to the amount of regulation and paperwork involved in a major government defense contract. Employees of the shipbuilding industry often quip, "We're not finished until the paperwork outweighs the ship."

Source: Edward J. Campbell, president and chief executive officer, Newport News Shipbuilding Company, Lincoln Lecture Series, April 1983, College of Business, Arizona State University.

Negotiated Contract Buying

A negotiated contract is employed to purchase products and services that cannot be differentiated on the basis of price alone (such as complex scientific equipment or R&D projects) or when there are few suppliers. There may be some competition, because the contracting office can conduct negotiations with several suppliers simultaneously.

Obviously, negotiation is a much more flexible procurement procedure; the government buyers may exercise considerable personal judgment. Procurement is based on the more subjective factors of performance and quality as well as on price. The procurement decision for the government is much like that of the large corporation: Which is the best possible product at the lowest price, and will the product be delivered on time? Usually, extensive personal selling by the potential contractor is required to convince the government that the firm can perform. The selling effort should include negotiating favorable terms and reasonable payment dates as well as developing intelligence on future contracts for which the company may want to bid.

Selling to the government is involved, time-consuming, and paper-generating. Government markets are among the most sophisticated and complex environments within which the business marketer operates.

Federal versus Commercial Buying

Table 2.4 compares important characteristics that differentiate the federal acquisition process (in the Department of Defense) from the commercial buying process. Note that much of the initiative for a major system acquisition originates with the buyer in the case of the defense purchase. In addition, there are rigid standards (some defined by law) as to cost, product specifications, completion dates, and technical procedures. As a result, a marketer positioned to sell to the government has a much different marketing strategy focus than does a firm that concentrates on the commercial sector.

The government seller emphasizes (1) understanding the complex rules and standards that must be met; (2) developing an intelligence system to keep informed of each agency's procurement plans; (3) generating a strategy for product development and R&D that facilitates the firm's response to government product needs; (4) developing a communications strategy that focuses on how technology meets agency objectives; and (5) generating a negotiation strategy to secure favorable terms regarding payment, contract completion, and cost overruns due to changes in product specifications.

THE INSTITUTIONAL MARKET: UNIQUE CHARACTERISTICS

The **institutional market** constitutes the third important market component. Institutional buyers make up a sizable market—in 1987, total expenditures on education alone exceeded $241 billion, and national health expenditures totaled over $501 billion.[32] Schools and health-care facilities are important factors in the institutional market, which also includes penal institutions, colleges and universities, libraries, foundations, art galleries, and clinics. On one hand, institutional purchasers are similar to governments in that the purchasing process is often constrained by political considerations and dictated by law. In fact, many institutions are administered by government units— schools, for example. On the other hand, other institutions are privately operated and managed like corporations; they may even have a broader range of purchase requirements than their large corporate counterparts. Like the commercial enterprise, institutions are ever cognizant of the value of efficient purchasing. If a university can save $100,000 through purchasing efficiencies, and its endowment earns 10 percent, the $100,000 savings is equivalent to an endowment gift of $1 million. Because the

---

[32] *Statistical Abstract of the United States*, 1990, pp. 93 and 274.

TABLE 2.4 **Defense Acquisition Process versus Commercial Buying Behavior**

Characteristic	Defense Acquisition Process	Commercial Buying Behavior
Product justification	Established by the agency's mission within overall national defense	Market and economic benefits
Goals and objectives	Match technology to national defense needs at lowest cost; some concern for social goals—compliance, set-asides	Reduce operating cost, improve product quality, etc.
Relationship initiatives	Mostly from the buyer; invited bids	Mostly from the seller
Major product need ideas	Mostly from the buyer	Based on market research and technological innovation
Nature of technical procedures	Complex, regulated by law	Less complex, based on company policy
Complexity of decision-making unit	Multiple agencies; defined roles	Single agency; less defined internal roles
Buyer intrusion on marketers' methods	Considerable	Infrequent
Management procedure for sellers	Endless paperwork	Single contracts and "working agreements"
Level of capital expenditure	Agency mission, technology, congressional appropriation	Investment policy, retained earnings, cash position of buyer
Marketing-mix focus	Communications and technical research and development	Full range of marketing mix elements
Communications thrust	Correct technical capability to meet mission performance	Sales reps convert marketing plan to sales and profits
Pricing methods	Based on customer cost, accounting standards (law)	Based on product life cycle, cash flow, customer financing, competition
Funding and facilities	Often provided by buyer	Nearly always provided by the seller
Economic risk	Largely underwritten by buyer	Underwritten by seller
Relationship	Contractual	Some by contract
Key decision criteria	Conformity to written technical specifications, project completion deadlines, bid price, performance	Full range of quality, price, performance, service criteria

Source: Adapted from Ronald L. Schill, "Buying Process in the U.S. Department of Defense," *Industrial Marketing Management,* 9 (October 1980), p. 295.

institutional market is similar to the other markets, its characteristics will be presented very briefly.

Institutional Buyers: Purchasing Procedures

Diversity is the key element in the institutional market. For example, the institutional marketing manager must first be ready to respond to a school purchasing agent who buys in great quantity for an entire city's school system through a formal bidding procedure, and then be ready to respond to a former pharmacist who has been elevated to purchasing agent for a small rural hospital.

Health-care institutions provide a good example of the diversity of this market. Some small hospitals delegate responsibility for food purchasing to the chief dietitian. Although many of these hospitals have purchasing agents, the agent cannot place an order unless it has been approved by the dietitian. In larger hospitals, decisions may be made by committees composed of a business manager, purchasing agent, dietitian, and cook. In still other cases, hospitals may belong to buying groups consisting of many local hospitals, or meal preparation may be contracted out. In an effort to contain costs, large hospitals have adopted a materials management type of purchasing organization for purchase, storage, movement, and distribution of goods and equipment.[33] Because of these varied purchasing environments, successful institutional marketers usually maintain a separate marketing manager, staff, and sales force in order to tailor marketing efforts to each situation.

For many institutions, once the budget for a department has been established, the department will attempt to spend up to that budget limit. Thus, institutions may buy simply because there are unused funds in the budget. A business marketer should carefully evaluate the budgetary status of potential customers in the institutional segment of the market.

Multiple Buying Influences

The institutional market offers some unique applications for the concept of multiple buying influences (discussed in Chapter 1). Many institutions are staffed with professionals—doctors, professors, researchers, and others. In most cases, depending on size, the institution will employ a purchasing agent and, in large institutions, a sizable purchasing department or materials management department. There is great potential for conflict between those responsible for the purchasing function and the professional staff for whom the purchasing department is buying. The purchasing department is in constant contact with suppliers and can challenge restrictive specifications, can secure information on market availability, and can arrange for product demonstrations from several major suppliers. However, many staff professionals resent losing their authority to buy from whom they wish. Business marketing and sales personnel, in formulating their marketing and personal selling approaches, must understand these conflicts and be able to respond to them. Often, the salesperson must carefully cultivate the professional staff in terms of product benefits and service while developing a delivery timetable, maintenance contract, and price schedule to satisfy the purchasing department.

Group Purchasing

An important factor in institutional purchasing is group purchasing. Hospitals, schools, and universities may join cooperative purchasing associations to obtain quantity discounts. Universities affiliated with the Education and Institutional Purchasing Cooperative enjoy favorable contracts established by the cooperative and can purchase

---

[33] Gary J. Zenz, *Purchasing and the Management of Materials* (New York: John Wiley & Sons, 1987), p. 54.

a wide array of products directly from vendors at the low negotiated prices. The cooperative spends over $75 million on goods annually. Cooperative buying allows institutions to enjoy lower prices, improved quality (through improved testing and vendor selection), reduced administrative cost, standardization, better records, and greater competition.[34]

Hospital group purchasing represents a significant market exceeding $1 billion. Group purchasing has become widely accepted with over 30 percent of public sector hospitals in the United States having membership in some type of affiliated group.[35] Most hospital group purchasing is done at the regional level through hospital associations. However, for-profit hospital chains, which are a growing factor in the health-care field, also engage in a form of group buying. Humana, a chain of over 100 hospitals, buys from its central headquarters for all units in the chain. It is obviously a significant customer for health-care suppliers.

Group purchasing poses special challenges for the business marketer. First, the marketer must be in a position to develop not only strategies for dealing with individual institutions but also unique strategies for the special requirements of cooperative purchasing groups and large hospital chains. The buying centers—individual institution versus cooperative purchasing group—may vary considerably in composition, criteria, and level of expertise. For the purchasing groups, discount pricing will assume special importance. Vendors who sell through purchasing groups must also have distribution systems that effectively deliver products to individual group members. And even though vendors have a contract with a large cooperative association, they must still be prepared to respond individually to each institution that places an order against the contract.

Professional Purchasing on the Rise

Many institutions, particularly health-care facilities, are faced with a severe cash squeeze and have come to recognize the importance of sound management practices in accomplishing their mission (education, health care). As a result, institutions are rapidly adopting purchasing policies and procedures that have proven successful in industry. Business marketers will be increasingly challenged in the institutional market to respond effectively to professional purchasing personnel who are as skilled in their jobs as are those in commercial firms.

Institutional Purchasing Policies

Table 2.5 shows an excerpt from the purchasing policy manual of a large hospital. Note that in many respects the purchasing process is similar to that of a large commercial firm. However, the manual illustrates some important distinctions between institutional and commercial purchasing. The policies regarding cooperative buying, preference to local vendors, and the delegation of purchasing responsibility for food, pharmaceuticals, and a variety of other items are of particular importance. It is just these charac-

---

[34] Michael R. Leenders, Harold E. Fearon, and Wilbur B. England, *Purchasing and Materials Management* (Homewood, IL: Richard D. Irwin, 1989), p. 535.

[35] Zenz, *Purchasing and the Management of Materials,* p. 57.

TABLE 2.5   **Purchasing Policies of a Large Hospital**

A. Basic Purchasing Policies

1. The Administrator has delegated the purchasing function to the Purchasing Department which shall provide service to all other departments. The Administrator may delegate purchasing authority to others.
2. Each department head shall establish the specifications and requirements for supplies and equipment for use in his department. Purchasing will give assistance when requested to do so.
3. Multiple sources of supply are considered for all purchases so as to encourage competition and insure availability of supply.
4. Purchasing through cooperative buying organizations will be pursued whenever an advantage is to be gained by the hospital in cost savings and/or in quality of product.
5. Participation in cost comparison surveys will be done to evaluate the prices we are paying.
6. All items and services not fixed to one source of supply may be subject to bid, negotiation, or contract.
7. All factors being equal, local vendors will be awarded the bid or contract and will always be the preferred source of supply when bids are better than or equal to their competitors.
8. The Product Evaluation Committee will review all requests for change in supplies which have major cost implications, for example, a change from a reusable item to a disposable one, and make recommendations to the Administrator. Every effort will be made to standardize a given item used throughout the hospital.

B. Interdepartmental Relationships

1. The Director of Purchasing has been authorized to initiate, sign, and place all purchase orders for the hospital. Note these exceptions: The Director of Dietary Services purchases all food; the Director of Pharmacy purchases all pharmaceuticals; the Manager of the Hospitality Center purchases all items sold in the Center; the Assistant Administrator, Plant Services, purchases architectural and engineering services, contractors' services, and service agreements for major plant systems; and the Director of Public Relations purchases artwork/printing services.
2. Purchasing will receive and interview all supplier representatives. Other departments requiring information from supplier representatives should make their needs known to Purchasing which will make the necessary arrangements. Purchasing should be kept fully informed of progress by the department in discussions with supplier representatives because of the possibility of involvement in later negotiations.
3. The Director of Purchasing, working with the department head, shall negotiate all purchases or contracts. Purchasing may question quality, quantity, and kind of material requested in order that the best interests of the hospital may be served.
4. In interviews with supplier representatives, employees or staff members outside Purchasing should not commit themselves on preference for any product or on the hospital's source of supply for any product, or give information regarding performance or price. In fairness to all concerned, prices and specific information received from vendors are considered confidential.

Source: Frank J. Roth, Director of Purchasing, Christ Hospital, Cincinnati, Ohio. *Christ Hospital Manual,* Volume 4.

---

teristics that the business marketer must understand in order to carefully develop a sales and communication strategy for this prospective institutional customer.

THE INTERNATIONAL MARKETPLACE FOR INDUSTRIAL GOODS AND SERVICES

A complete picture of the business market must include a horizon that stretches beyond the boundaries of the United States. Probably the most significant business trend over the past ten years has been the development of a truly global economy. Indeed, "the world economy is rapidly becoming irrevocably intertwined. The economic system is more and more like one single interacting organism."[36] Business marketers from machine-tool makers to paper mills are finding that they can no longer limit their marketing activities to the confines of the United States and still assure their long-term profitability. The demand for many industrial products is growing more rapidly in many foreign countries than in the United States. Countries like Germany, Japan, Korea, and Brazil offer large and growing markets for most industrial products. In addition, many U.S. manufacturers are producing components, subassemblies, and even finished products offshore in a desire to reduce labor costs. Thus, the demand for industrial products by many U.S. firms may have its roots in a foreign country.

A significant trend which is having a major impact on industrial marketers is the escalation of **international sourcing**. In 1986, offshore purchases accounted for 11 percent of total purchases by U.S. firms—a percentage that had nearly doubled over 15 years.[37] U.S. firms look to offshore sources for a variety of reasons, including cost, quality, technology, continuity of supply, and competition.[38] Domestic suppliers of industrial parts, components, and materials will be challenged to develop new techniques and strategies to remain competitive with many of their offshore rivals.

United States companies are dramatically expanding their participation in the global market. Data Resources projected that from the mid-80s to the mid-90s growth in American exports would outpace import growth by some 30 percent.[39] An understanding of international markets for industrial products will be a core requirement for the successful business marketing manager of the future. John F. Welch, Jr., chief executive officer at General Electric, notes: "You can't be a world-class competitor with a domestic headset. You've got to think of selling not in 50 states, but in 50 nations. You have to think of sourcing not in one state or one country, but in 50 countries."[40]

What makes the international marketing job different from marketing to domestic industrial customers? A number of factors must be considered by the U.S. marketer when attempting to penetrate international markets, and these factors center on the differences both in the buying process and in the environment in which the transactions take place.

Cultural Differences Affect Purchasing Behavior

Ingrained sociocultural patterns, biases, customs, and attitudes—in short, the cultural underpinnings of a country and its people—have a pervasive impact on how buying decisions are made. These manifestations of culture vary dramatically from country to country. Business marketers must closely examine such cultural differences when

[36] Richard I. Kirkland, Jr., "We're All in This Together," *Fortune,* 115 (February 2, 1987), p. 26.

[37] "More to Imports than Bargains," *Purchasing World,* 30 (March 1986), p. 102.

[38] Eugene L. Magod and John M. Ames, *Total Materials Management* (New York: Van Nostrand Reinhold, 1989), p. 254.

[39] Kirkland, "We're All in This Together," p. 250.

[40] Mark Potts and Peter Behr, *The Leading Edge* (New York: McGraw-Hill Book Company, 1987), p. 21.

formulating strategies for each of their international markets. For example, Japanese culture affects the decision-making process within the typical Japanese company. Decisions are usually made by consensus rather than by upper-management decree.[41] Thus the decision process is very slow and deliberate, and the responsible party is a group rather than an individual. In this type of decision-making climate, patience and low-pressure selling tactics are the keys to success.

In another example, Chinese and Russian buyers differ in their view of the buyer–seller relationship. The Chinese highly value interpersonal relationships; friendship and personal relationships are important for launching a business venture. Trade experts say the Chinese prefer to do business with friends, which often means getting to know potential suppliers in nonwork settings. The Soviets, however, place very little emphasis on personal contacts between their negotiators and their vendor counterparts. Thus, negotiations with Chinese buyers usually include considerable "social time," such as banquets, recreation, sightseeing trips, and tea. By contrast, negotiations with Soviet buyers are typically very formal. Soviets view the negotiating process as a test of potential suppliers: Soviet buyers believe a company that survives this complex process will indeed be the best supplier.[42] Clearly, the business marketer must understand these important cultural impacts on purchase behavior.

Product Use and Application May Vary by Country

Due to the physical characteristics of the people, the state of economic development, geographic considerations, and a host of additional factors, product designs may need to be altered from area to area or from country to country. Some firms gain a competitive advantage by tailoring their products to individual countries. Hyster, a U.S. producer of forklift trucks, carefully adjusts its product offerings to specific countries in which it competes. In Spain, for example, there is a greater need for smaller trucks because of the large food and wine industries; whereas in Germany, with its large automobile industry, the demand is for heavier trucks. Similarly, General Electric Medical Systems designs products specifically for the Japanese market.[43] Their computer-tomography scanners are smaller than similar domestic scanners because Japanese hospitals are smaller than most U.S. facilities and because the product is scaled to the Japanese patient's smaller size.

On the other hand, other companies secure a competitive advantage by standardizing the product design and exploiting similarities across countries. Boeing (aircraft), Canon (copiers), and Caterpillar (heavy equipment) pursue this strategy. Other elements of the marketing program (e.g., marketing communications and service strategies) may be customized to meet the unique needs of buyers in each country.

Remanufacturing—the process in which worn-out products are restored to like-new condition—can also assume a role in many developing markets. This strategy responds to the needs of some potential customers, especially in Third World markets,

---

[41] Kate Bertrand, "Marketing to the Land of the Rising Yen," *Business Marketing,* 71 (October 1986), p. 77.

[42] Misha G. Knight, "The Russian Bear Turns Bullish on Trade," *Business Marketing*, 72 (April 1987), p. 90.

[43] Bertrand, "Marketing to the Land of the Rising Yen," p. 82.

who simply cannot afford new products. Many capital-equipment items sold in South American countries are remanufactured as opposed to new. Remanufactured items are particularly well suited for these markets because they often cost only 40–65 percent of the cost of a new item, and their production is based on unskilled labor as opposed to skilled labor and capital equipment.[44]

Buying Procedures and Policies Are Different

The process of purchasing, including the formal procedures, negotiations, personnel, and bureaucracy, may show marked differences from one country to another. As indicated earlier, decision making is often a group process in many Asian countries. Frequently, these buyers will go to extraordinary lengths to avoid individual action on any decision. Because of the group decision-making process, purchasing decisions are made over a rather long time horizon. The business marketer must be patient and resist the temptation to short-circuit the process.

Different levels of bureaucracy in the purchasing process are encountered in different countries. In the Soviet Union, for example, extensive purchasing negotiations must be carried on with members of various Soviet trading agencies in order to reach agreement on a single contract. Almost 60 foreign trade organizations (FTOs) exist in the Soviet Union, and both an FTO and the end-user ministry are involved in negotiations.[45] For negotiations on major contracts, representatives of other organizations may also participate. Soviet negotiators are deeply sensitive about age, rank, and protocol, typically requiring formal negotiations for literally every purchase; a simple purchase order does not exist. To tap the Soviet market effectively, the business marketer must understand the Soviet negotiating strategy and tactics and must be prepared to respond with an appropriate strategy.

In some purchase contracts negotiated with foreign buyers, the seller will be required to buy a given quantity of some product manufactured in the foreign country or to accept some of its revenue in the form of goods. The seller must then find a market for these items. Such arrangements are referred to as **countertrade**. As an example, Combustion Engineering negotiated a deal with a Brazilian company (government-operated) for $20 million of offshore drilling equipment. In return, Combustion was required to spend $5 million on shoes from Brazil.[46] The ability and willingness to take countertrade is a significant marketing tool that is correlated to success in many foreign markets.

Countertrade is very important in countries with "soft currencies" (currencies that cannot be converted to other currencies). As more firms begin to explore business opportunities in the Soviet Union and other Eastern-Bloc countries, countertrade will play a pivotal role in their success.

---

[44] Diane McConocha and Thomas W. Speh, "Remarketing: Commercialization of Remanufacturing Technology," *Journal of Business and Industrial Marketing,* (January 1991), forthcoming.

[45] This section is based on Misha G. Knight, *How to Do Business with Russians: A Handbook and Guide for Western World Business People* (Westport, CT: Quarum Books, 1987).

[46] "'Creative Deal-Making' Pays Off for Countertrade Unit," *Business Marketing,* 71 (August 1986), p. 24.

FIGURE 2.4   **A Market-Centered Organization**

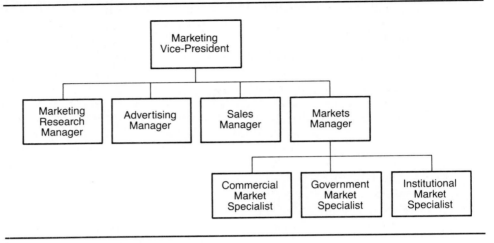

Success in the international business market rests on an understanding of the customer and of the surrounding market forces. While similarities exist in the business marketing process across countries, the marketing strategy must be targeted to the culture, product usage, and buying procedures of the foreign buyers.

DEALING WITH DIVERSITY: A MARKET-CENTERED ORGANIZATION

Because each sector of the business market is unique, many firms have built market specialization into the marketing organization. To illustrate, the industrial products area of the J. M. Smucker Company is organized around market sectors. The institutional, military, and industrial markets are each managed by different individuals, each thoroughly knowledgeable about one particular market. Other companies, such as the Dow Chemical Company, have designed the marketing function to capitalize on their position in the global market. Relying on cross-functional teams located in each geographical area, five product vice presidents manage Dow's global product strategies. Dow's geographical diversity allows the firm to capitalize on local country opportunities. For example, Dow Latin America launched a herbicide for pasture applications in Colombia while Dow Europe was the first to introduce a broad-spectrum herbicide for cereal grains.[47] Mack Hanan refers to such structures as market-centered.[48] He

---

[47] Thomas H. Naylor, *The Corporate Strategy Matrix* (New York: Basic Books, Inc., 1986), pp. 221–223.

[48] Mack Hanan, "Reorganize Your Company Around Its Markets," *Harvard Business Review,* 52 (November–December 1974), pp. 63–74.

contends that the most effective way to satisfy the needs of distinct customer groups is to build the firm's divisions around major customer markets.

One form of a market-centered organizational scheme is illustrated in Figure 2.4. Observe that a market manager supervises and coordinates the activities of three market specialists. Each market specialist examines the buying processes, the product preferences, and the similarities and differences between customers in one sector of the business market. Such an analysis allows the market specialist to further categorize customers within a particular sector into meaningful market segments and to design specialized marketing programs for each segment. A market-centered organization provides the business marketer with a structure for dealing effectively with diversity in the industrial market.

SUMMARY

A large market awaits the business marketing manager. The market can be divided into three major components: commercial enterprises, governments (federal, state, and local), and institutions. Recently, business marketers have seen their market horizons broadened to a global level. The marketer requires an understanding of the unique characteristics and the structure of the purchasing function in each sector.

Commercial enterprises include manufacturers, construction companies, service firms, transportation companies, selected professional groups, and resellers. Of these, manufacturers account for the largest dollar volume of purchases. Furthermore, although the majority of manufacturing firms are small, buying power is concentrated in the hands of relatively few large manufacturing establishments, which are also concentrated geographically. Commercial enterprises such as service establishments and transportation or utility companies are more widely dispersed. Often, the purchasing process is administered by a purchasing manager or purchasing agent. In larger firms, the purchasing function has become quite specialized, placing heavy demands on the industrial salesperson who must match the expertise of potential buyers. In smaller organizations, one person may be responsible for all buying activities. The materials management concept, along with the just-in-time system, which is gaining importance as an approach for reducing inventories and material acquisition costs, requires the careful coordination of a vendor's total marketing and distribution operations.

Many marketers find dealing with the government sector of the industrial market frustrating. However, government is the largest consumer in the United States. The diligent marketer who acquires an understanding of the procurement laws and of the varying contracts employed by the government can find a lucrative market. Federal buying follows two general procurement strategies: formal advertising or negotiated contract. The formal advertising approach, frequently followed for standardized products, involves the solicitation of bids from appropriate suppliers. Negotiated contracts are employed for unique requirements and are typified by discussion and bargaining throughout all phases of the contract.

International buyers represent a large and growing market for most industrial products and services; however, culture, product use, and buying procedures may be radically different from country to country. Each of these elements has a far-reaching and significant impact on the purchasing process.

Diversity is the characteristic that typifies the institutional market. Institutional buyers are somewhere between commercial enterprise and government buyers in terms of their characteristics, orientations, and purchasing processes. Cooperative purchasing—a unique aspect of this segment—necessitates a special strategic response by potential suppliers. Many business marketers have found that a market-centered organization provides the specialization required to meet the needs of each sector of the market.

Discussion Questions

1. Research suggests that an increasing number of buying organizations have adopted the materials management concept. Describe this concept and outline the managerial implications that it raises for the business marketer.

2. Compare and contrast the two general procurement strategies employed by the federal government: (1) formal advertising and (2) negotiated contract.

3. Institutional buyers fall somewhere between commercial enterprises and government buyers in terms of their characteristics, orientation, and purchasing process. Explain.

4. Evaluate the wisdom of this personal selling strategy: the approach that is appropriate for large purchasing departments is equally effective in small purchasing departments.

5. Explain how the decision-making process that a university might employ in selecting a new computer would differ from that of a commercial enterprise. Who would be the key participants in the process in each setting?

6. Fearing red tape and mounds of paperwork, Tom Bronson, president of B&E Electric, has always avoided the government market. A recent discussion with a colleague, however, has rekindled Tom's interest in this business market sector. What steps should B&E Electric take to learn more about this market?

7. Describe the key characteristics that differentiate the federal acquisition process (Department of Defense) from the commercial buying process.

8. Discuss the key factors that a U.S. marketing manager would have to address when developing a strategy to compete in South America and Asia.

9. Why have some industrial firms moved away from product-centered organizations and toward market-centered organizations?

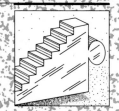

PART II

The Organizational Buying Process

CHAPTER 3

Dimensions of Organizational Buying

An understanding of the organizational buying process is fundamental to the development of sound business marketing strategy. After reading this chapter, you will understand:

1. the importance of examining business marketing management as an exchange process between buyers and sellers.

2. the decision process that organizational buyers apply as they confront differing buying situations and the resulting strategy implications for the business marketer.

3. the pattern that buyer–seller relationships follow over time.

4. the rational and emotional factors that influence organizational members when choosing among the offerings of competing business marketers.

5. the formal evaluation systems and analytical approaches that organizational buyers employ when measuring value and evaluating supplier performance.

AN industrial salesperson might begin the day with a lengthy sales call on a manufacturing facility in the morning, then call on a large hospital and a city government account in the afternoon. The day is characterized by negotiation, bargaining, problem solving, information sharing, and other exchange processes. Knowledge of organizational buying behavior can help the salesperson isolate common elements in the purchasing systems of many organizations. Likewise, examining the nature of exchange relationships between industrial buyers and sellers can provide valuable insights into business marketing management. "Building and maintaining lasting customer ties . . . involves doing a number of things right, consistently, over time."[1] The new era of business marketing is built upon effective relationship management.

The buying procedures of organizations, although more formal, resemble the buying procedures of final consumers. The purchasing agent may automatically order an item just as a shopper routinely selects a preferred brand from the retailer's shelf. Little time, effort, or deliberation goes into the decision. Other decisions, however, involve an elaborate search for information and a careful consideration of alternatives. In such cases, many members of the organization provide input. The household might be considered a group decision-making unit that operates in a similar fashion when major family purchases (e.g., a new car or television) are being considered.

To be effective, the marketer must understand the decision-making process of industrial customers, the key participants in this process, and the criteria they use in making decisions. What process do organizational customers follow in selecting needed products and services? How do they evaluate competing offerings? Clearly, an understanding of the nature of exchange relationships in the business market, coupled with a knowledge of the mechanics of the purchasing system, provides the marketer with a firm base for building responsive business marketing strategy.

EXPLORING BUYER–SELLER INTERACTIONS

Industrial selling, at its most basic level, can be viewed as an exchange process in which two individuals or firms trade items of value. An exchange perspective of business marketing points up not only what the selling organization gains from a transaction, but also what the buying organization secures in return (Figure 3.1). Exchange relationships between the organizational selling center and the organizational buying center are crucial.

The members of the selling organization who are involved in initiating and maintaining exchange relationships with industrial customers constitute the **organizational selling center**.[2] The needs of a particular selling situation, especially the information requirements, significantly influence the composition of the selling center. Its primary objectives are the acquisition and processing of pertinent marketing-related information and the execution of selling strategies. The **organizational buying center** includes those individuals who participate in the purchasing decision and who share the goals and risks arising from that decision. The needs of a particular buying situation dictate the composition of the buying center. To illustrate, a complex buying situation that organizational buyers are encountering for the first time may include several participants representing different functional areas.

---

[1] Barbara Bund Jackson, "Build Customer Relationships that Last," *Harvard Business Review*, 63 (November–December 1985), p. 128. See also F. Robert Dwyer, Paul H. Schurr, and Sejo Oh, "Developing Buyer–Seller Relationships," *Journal of Marketing*, 51 (April 1987), pp. 11–27.

[2] Michael D. Hutt, Wesley J. Johnston, and John R. Ronchetto, Jr., "Selling Centers and Buying Centers: Formulating Strategic Exchange Patterns," *Journal of Personal Selling & Sales Management*, 5 (May 1985), pp. 33–40. For a discussion of the buying center concept, see Frederick E. Webster, Jr., and Yoram Wind, *Organizational Buying Behavior* (Englewood Cliffs, N.J.: Prentice-Hall, 1972), p. 6.

FIGURE 3.1   **Diagnosing Exchange Processes in Business Marketing**

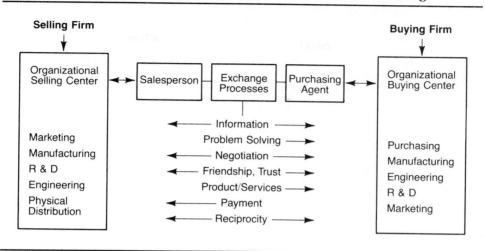

Assuming visible roles in the exchange process are the salesperson (selling-center representative) and the purchasing agent (buying-center representative). The salesperson and the buyer each begin the interaction with particular plans, goals, and intentions. The salesperson exchanges information and assistance in solving a purchasing problem for the reward of a sale given by the buyer or by members of the buying center.

In addition to external negotiations with members of the buying center, the industrial salesperson, acting on behalf of the potential customer, is often involved in internal negotiations with other members of the selling center, such as manufacturing or R&D, to ensure a successful exchange relationship with a particular customer. Internal negotiations also occur within the buying center because various members represent the interests of their functional areas in the selection of suppliers. Complex flows of influence characterize buyer–seller interactions in the business market. To ensure maximum customer satisfaction and the desired market response, business marketers must effectively manage the complex web of influences that intersect in buyer–seller relationships.[3]

Relationship Management

Relationship management, rather than selling, characterizes the role that the business marketer assumes in the exchange process. On one front, the marketer is responsible for coordinating the marketing- or sales-related activities of the firm, while drawing

---

[3] Thomas V. Bonoma and Wesley J. Johnston, "The Social Psychology of Industrial Buying and Selling," *Industrial Marketing Management,* 7 (July 1978), pp. 213–224; see also Nigel C. G. Campbell, John L. Graham, Alain Jolibert, and Hans Gunther Meissner, "Marketing Negotiations in France, Germany, the United Kingdom, and the United States," *Journal of Marketing,* 52 (April 1988), pp. 49–62.

upon the collective strength of the organization. Since the selling organization's competitive advantage is linked directly to the strength of the bonds between functional units that are responsible for the production, service, and support of the company's offering, such coordinative activities are fundamental to the business marketer's strategic role.[4] On another front, the industrial marketer must assume an active role in the procurement decision-making process by defining the customer's need and by demonstrating the value of the marketer's offering.

This exchange perspective also provides a way to trace contemporary changes in buyer–seller relationships in the business market. Changes in the buying environment trigger corresponding adjustments in the selling environment. Consider the strategic approach to purchasing that NCR follows. Through close, long-term partnerships with suppliers, NCR's goal is "co-destiny" status—suppliers who are "so thoroughly integrated into NCR's product development and production processes that they become, in effect, extensions" of those internal activities. James Currier, vice-president of purchasing, asserts that such close relationships will ensure "higher quality at lower costs" as well as provide NCR with "access to leading-edge technology."[5]

As manufacturers face rapidly changing technology, shorter product life cycles, and stiff foreign competition, purchasing becomes even more strategic. In response, purchasing managers are reducing their supplier lists and treating the remaining vendors as strategic partners, sharing information more freely and drawing on supplier expertise in developing new products to meet the quality, cost, and delivery standards that their customers demand.[6] (See Figure 3.2.) Such strategic changes are taking place not only in large corporations such as Motorola, Westinghouse, Caterpillar, and Alcoa, but also in a host of smaller organizations across the business market. In Table 3.1, such key trends in purchasing are linked to adjustments being made by business marketers. These changes highlight the dynamic and challenging nature of exchange relationships in the business market and signal a new era for business marketers.

THE ORGANIZATIONAL BUYING PROCESS

To enhance their effectiveness as a party in the exchange process, industrial salespersons must understand how organizational buyers choose between the competing offerings of industrial marketers. Organizational buying behavior can best be understood from the perspective of the decision process, for organizational buying is viewed as a process rather than as an isolated act or event. Tracing the history of a procurement decision in an organization uncovers critical decision points and evolving information

---

[4] Robert E. Spekman and Wesley J. Johnston, "Relationship Management: Managing the Selling and the Buying Interface," *Journal of Business Research*, 14 (December 1986), pp. 519–531; see also Spekman, "Strategic Supplier Selection: Understanding Long-Term Buyer Relationships," *Business Horizons*, 31 (July–August 1988), pp. 75–81.

[5] Ernest Raia, "NCR: 1989 Medal of Professional Excellence," *Purchasing*, 103 (September 28, 1989), p. 55.

[6] Kate Bertrand, "Crafting 'Win–Win Situations' in Buyer–Seller Relationships," *Business Marketing*, 71 (June 1986), pp. 42–50.

FIGURE 3.2   **An Ad Illustrating the Importance of Close Supplier Relationships**

Source: Courtesy, Ford Motor Company.

requirements. Richard Cardozo contends that "organizational buying consists of several stages, each of which yields a decision."[7] Likewise, the composition of the decision-making unit can vary from one stage to the next as organizational members enter and leave the procurement process.

Table 3.2 highlights the eight-stage model describing the sequence of activities in the organizational buying process.[8] Recognition of a problem or of a potential opportunity triggers the purchasing process. For example, the firm's equipment becomes

---

[7] Richard N. Cardozo, "Modelling Organizational Buying as a Sequence of Decisions," *Industrial Marketing Management,* 12 (February 1983), p. 75.

[8] The discussion in this section is based on Patrick J. Robinson, Charles W. Faris, and Yoram Wind, *Industrial Buying and Creative Marketing* (Boston: Allyn and Bacon, Inc., 1967), pp. 12–18.

TABLE 3.1   **Changing Directions of Buyer–Seller Relationships**

Trend in Purchasing Procurement	Required Adaptation by Business Marketer
Increased status and authority of purchasing managers in the organization	Expand authority of industrial salesperson and utilize more sophisticated selling approaches
Consolidation of purchasing, transportation, traffic, inventory control, and other departments into a materials management department	More carefully synchronize selling and distribution activities (for example, order processing, inventory control, transportation) to meet customer requirements
Centralization of procurement at the headquarters level to consolidate purchasing power for geographically separated manufacturing facilities	Develop a separate sales force tailored to the special needs and selling requirements of these large national accounts
Stronger demands for consistent quality from suppliers and increased adoption of JIT production concepts	Provide a uniform and certified level of quality that eliminates the need for an incoming inspection by customer. Improve logistical performance to meet the precise production schedule of customers
Reduction in the number of suppliers used and treatment of remaining vendors as allies or strategic partners	Adopt a relationship-management rather than a pure selling orientation. Respond to the customer's changing requirements and nurture the development of close ties between multiple layers of the buying and selling organizations

TABLE 3.2   **The Buygrid Framework for Industrial Buying Situations**

	Buying Situations		
Buying Stages	**New Task**	**Modified Rebuy**	**Straight Rebuy**
1. Anticipation or recognition of a problem (need) and a general solution			
2. Determination of characteristics and quantity of needed item			
3. Description of characteristics and quantity of needed item			
4. Search for and qualification of potential sources			
5. Acquisition and analysis of proposals			
6. Evaluation of proposals and selection of supplier(s)			
7. Selection of an order routine			
8. Performance feedback and evaluation			

Note: The most complex buying situations occur in the upper left portion of the buygrid framework and involve the largest number of decision makers and buying influences.

Source: From the Marketing Science Institute Series, *Industrial Buying and Creative Marketing,* by Patrick J. Robinson, Charles W. Faris, and Yoram Wind, Copyright © 1967 by Allyn and Bacon, Inc., Boston. Reprinted with permission.

outmoded or a salesperson initiates consideration of a product by demonstrating opportunities for improving the organization's performance. During the procurement process, many small or incremental decisions are made that ultimately translate into the final selection of a supplier. To illustrate, a quality control engineer might unknowingly establish specifications for a new production system that only supplier A can meet. This type of decision early in the buying process will dramatically influence the favorable evaluation and ultimate selection of supplier A.

Some research suggests that the flow of stages in the eight-stage model of the procurement process may not progress sequentially and may vary with the complexity of the purchasing situation. However, the model provides important insights into the organizational buying process. Certain stages may be completed concurrently; the process may be reoriented at any point by a redefinition of the basic problem; or the process may be discontinued by a change in the external environment or in upper-management thinking. The organizational buying process is shaped by a host of internal and external forces such as changes in economic or competitive conditions or a basic shift in organizational priorities.

Richard Cardozo demonstrates that business marketers can diagnose problems by examining the sequence of decisions.[9] A product manager for technically complex materials noticed that existing customers were consistently repurchasing the product but that the firm had a low success rate in securing business from the hundreds of prospective buyers who requested quotations and information. Further analysis revealed that the sales force was winning new accounts only where the prospective buyer had not formally established specifications. As a result, inquiries from prospective buyers were screened to identify organizations that were at the initial stages of the procurement process. In turn, the sales force was directed to concentrate on this segment of buyers, and new business increased significantly.

BUYING SITUATIONS ANALYZED

The same product may elicit markedly different purchasing patterns in different organizations with various levels of experience and information. Therefore attention must be concentrated on buying situations rather than on products. Three types of buying situations have been delineated: (1) new task, (2) modified rebuy, and (3) straight rebuy.[10] As illustrated in Table 3.2, each type of buying situation must be related to the eight-stage buying process.

---

[9] Cardozo, "Modelling Organizational Buying as a Sequence of Decisions," pp. 75–81.

[10] Robinson, Faris, and Wind, *Industrial Buying and Creative Marketing*, Chapter 1; see also Erin Anderson, Wujin Chu, and Barton Weitz, "Industrial Purchasing: An Empirical Exploration of the Buyclass Framework," *Journal of Marketing*, 51 (July 1987), pp. 71–86; and Morry Ghingold, "Testing the 'Buygrid' Buying Process Model," *Journal of Purchasing and Materials Management*, 22 (Winter 1986), pp. 30–36.

New Task

In the **new-task** buying situation, the problem or need is perceived by organizational decision makers as totally different from previous experiences; therefore, a significant amount of information is required for decision makers to explore alternative ways of solving the problem and to search for alternative suppliers.

When confronting a new-task buying situation, organizational buyers operate in a stage of decision making referred to as **extensive problem solving**.[11] The buying influentials and decision makers lack well-defined criteria for comparing alternative products and suppliers, but they also lack strong predispositions toward a particular solution.

The business marketer confronting a new-task buying situation can gain a differential advantage by participating actively in the initial stages of the procurement process. The marketer should gather information on the problems facing the buying organization, isolate specific requirements, and offer proposals to meet the requirements. Ideas that lead to new products often originate not with the marketer but with the customer.[12]

Marketers who are presently supplying other items to the organization ("in" suppliers) have an edge over other firms; they can see problems unfolding and are familiar with the "personality" and behavior patterns of the organization. The successful business marketer carefully monitors the changing needs of organizations and is prepared to respond to the needs of new-task buyers.

Straight Rebuy

When there is a continuing or recurring requirement, buyers have substantial experience in dealing with the need, and they require little or no new information. Evaluation of new alternative solutions is unnecessary and unlikely to yield appreciable improvements. Thus, a **straight rebuy** approach is appropriate.

Routinized response behavior is the decision process organizational buyers employ in the straight rebuy. Organizational buyers have well-developed choice criteria to apply to the purchase decision. The criteria have been refined over time as the buyers have developed predispositions toward the offerings of one or a few carefully screened suppliers.

The purchasing department handles straight rebuy situations by routinely selecting a supplier from a list (formal or informal) of acceptable vendors and then placing an order. The marketing task appropriate in this situation depends on whether the marketer is an "in" supplier (on the list) or an "out" supplier (not among the chosen few). An "in" supplier must reinforce the buyer–seller relationship, meet the buying organization's expectations, and be alert and responsive to the changing needs of the organization.

---

[11] The levels of decision making discussed in this section are drawn from John A. Howard and Jagdish N. Sheth, *The Theory of Buyer Behavior* (New York: John Wiley and Sons, Inc., 1969), Chapter 2.

[12] Eric von Hippel, "Get New Products from Customers," *Harvard Business Review*, 60 (March–April 1982), pp. 117–122; see also von Hippel, "Successful Industrial Products from Customer Ideas," *Journal of Marketing*, 42 (January 1978), pp. 39–49.

The "out" supplier faces a number of obstacles and must convince the organization that significant benefits can be derived from breaking the routine. This can be difficult because organizational buyers perceive risk in shifting from the known to the unknown; the organizational spotlight shines directly on them if an untested supplier falters. Testing, evaluations, and approvals may be viewed by buyers as costly, time consuming, and unnecessary.

The marketing effort of the "out" supplier rests on an understanding of the basic buying needs of the organization: information gathering is essential. The marketer must convince organizational buyers that their purchasing requirements have changed or that the requirements should be interpreted differently. The objective is to persuade decision makers to reexamine alternative solutions and revise the preferred list to include the new supplier.

Modified Rebuy

In the **modified rebuy** situation, organizational decision makers feel that significant benefits may be derived from a reevaluation of alternatives. The buyers have experience in satisfying the continuing or recurring requirement, but they believe it worthwhile to seek additional information, and perhaps to consider alternative solutions.

Several factors may trigger such a reassessment. Internal forces include the search for quality improvements or cost reductions. A marketer offering cost, quality, or service improvements can be an external precipitating force. The modified rebuy situation is most likely to occur when the firm is displeased with the performance of present suppliers (e.g., poor delivery service).

Limited problem solving best describes the decision-making process for the modified rebuy. Decision makers have well-defined criteria, but are uncertain about which suppliers can best fit their needs.

In a modified rebuy, the direction of the marketing effort depends on whether the marketer is an "in" or an "out" supplier. An "in" supplier should make every effort to understand and satisfy the procurement need and to move decision makers into a straight rebuy. The buying organization perceives potential payoffs from a reexamination of alternatives. The "in" supplier should ask why, and act immediately to remedy any customer problems. The marketer may be out of touch with the buying organization's requirements.

The goal of the "out" supplier should be to hold the organization in modified rebuy status long enough for the buyer to evaluate an alternative offering. Knowing the factors that led decision makers to reexamine alternatives could be pivotal. A particularly effective strategy for an "out" supplier is to offer performance guarantees as part of the proposal.[13] To illustrate, the following guarantee prompted International Circuit Technology, a manufacturer of printed circuit boards, to change to a new supplier for plating chemicals: "Your plating costs will be no more than X cents per square foot or

---

[13] Christopher P. Puto, Wesley E. Patton, III, and Ronald H. King, "Risk Handling Strategies in Industrial Vendor Selection Decisions, *Journal of Marketing*, 49 (Winter 1985), pp. 89–98.

we will make up the difference."[14] Given the nature of the production process, plating costs can be easily monitored by comparing the square footage of circuit boards moving down the plating line with the cost of plating chemicals for the period. Pleased with the performance, International Circuit Technology now routinely reorders from this new supplier.

Each buying situation requires a unique business marketing response. Strategies appropriate for each of the three buying situations are summarized in Table 3.3.

Buying Influentials and the Purchasing Task

Buying decisions typically involve not one but several members of the organization, whether the decisions are made by commercial enterprises, institutions, or governmental organizations. Thus, the relevant unit of analysis for the industrial marketer is the group decision-making unit or the buying center. The **buying center** includes all those individuals and groups that participate in the purchasing decision and that share the goals and the risks arising from the decision.[15] The composition of the buying center and the relative importance of its individual members change rapidly as a firm moves from phase to phase in the decision process.[16]

Locating Buying Influentials

Buyers have differing levels of experience and follow various problem-solving approaches as they move along the learning curve from extended to routine problem solving. To illustrate, the decision to purchase a lathe may be a new-task buying situation in one organization and a modified or straight rebuy in another.

Erin Anderson and her colleagues queried a large sample of sales managers concerning the patterns of organizational buying behavior that their salespeople confront on a daily basis. Sales forces that frequently encounter new-task buying situations generally observe that " . . . the buying center is large, slow to decide, uncertain about its needs and the appropriateness of the possible solutions, more concerned about finding a good solution than getting a low price or assured supply, more willing to entertain proposals from 'out' suppliers and less willing to favor 'in' suppliers, more influenced by technical personnel, [and] less influenced by purchasing agents."[17]

By contrast, sales forces facing more routine purchase situations (i.e., straight and modified rebuys) frequently observe buying centers that are "small, quick to decide, confident in their appraisals of the problem and possible solutions, concerned about

---

[14] Somerby Dowst, "CEO Report: Wanted: Suppliers Adept at Turning Corners," *Purchasing*, 101 (January 29, 1987), pp. 71–72.

[15] Webster and Wind, *Organizational Buying Behavior*, p. 6; see also Robert E. Spekman and Kjell Gronhaug, "Conceptual and Methodological Issues in Buying Center Research," *European Journal of Marketing*, 20, 7 (1986), pp. 50–63.

[16] Gary L. Lilien and M. Anthony Wong, "An Exploratory Investigation of the Structure of the Buying Center in the Metalworking Industry," *Journal of Marketing Research*, 21 (February 1984), pp. 1–11.

[17] Anderson, Chu, and Weitz, "Industrial Purchasing," pp. 71–86.

TABLE 3.3   **Responding to Different Buying Situations:
A Profile of Required Marketing Strategies**

Buying Situations	Supplier Status	
	"In" Supplier	**"Out" Supplier**
New Task	Monitor changes in emerging purchasing needs of the organization.	
	Isolate specific needs.	Isolate specific needs.
	If possible, participate actively in early phases of the buying process by supplying information and technical advice.	If possible, participate actively in early phases of the buying process by supplying information and technical advice.
Straight Rebuy	Reinforce the buyer–seller relationship by meeting the organization's expectations.	Convince the organization that the potential benefits of reexamining requirements and suppliers exceed the costs of doing so.
	Be alert and responsive to changing needs of customer.	Attempt to gain a position on the organization's preferred list of suppliers, even as a second or third choice.
Modified Rebuy	Act immediately to remedy problems with the customer.	Define and respond to the organization's problem with the existing supplier.
	Reexamine and respond to customer needs.	Encourage the organization to sample alternative offerings; offer performance guarantees.

Source: From the Marketing Science Institute Series, *Industrial Buying and Creative Marketing,* by Patrick J. Robinson, Charles W. Faris, and Yoram Wind, (Boston: Allyn and Bacon, Inc., 1967), pp. 183–210.

price and supply, satisfied with 'in' suppliers, and more influenced by purchasing agents."[18]

Strategy Implications

Although past research provides some useful guidelines, great care must be exercised in forecasting the likely composition of the buying center for a particular purchasing situation.[19] The business marketer should attempt to identify purchasing patterns that apply to the firm.[20] To illustrate, the classes of industrial goods introduced in Chapter 1 (e.g., foundation goods versus facilitating goods) involve varying degrees of technical complexity and financial risk for the buying organization.

[18] Ibid., p. 82.

[19] Donald W. Jackson, Jr., Janet E. Keith, and Richard K. Burdick, "Purchasing Agents' Perceptions of Industrial Buying Center Influence," *Journal of Marketing,* 48 (Fall 1984), pp. 75–83; see also Joseph A. Bellizzi and Phillip McVey, "How Valid Is the Buy-Grid Model?" *Industrial Marketing Management,* 12 (February 1983), pp. 57–62.

[20] Roland T. Moriarty and Morton Galper, *Organizational Buying Behavior: A State-of-the-Art Review and Conceptualization* (Cambridge, Mass.: Marketing Science Institute, 1978).

The business marketer must therefore look at the procurement problem or need as the buying organization does. How far has the organization progressed with the specific purchasing problem? How does the organization define the task at hand? How important is the purchase to the organization? The answers will direct and form the business marketer's response and also provide insight into the composition of the decision-making unit. Again, each type of buying situation could represent a different market segment that requires a specialized marketing strategy. Xerox, for example, deploys some sales teams that concentrate on servicing and penetrating existing customers, and others that specialize in obtaining new customers. Attention now turns to the pattern that buyer–seller relationships follow over time.

Relationship Patterns[21]

The trend toward close relationships, or even strategic partnerships, between manufacturers and their suppliers is accelerating in many sectors of the business market. Barbara Bund Jackson suggests that business marketers should assess "the time horizon within which a customer makes a commitment to a vendor and also the actual pattern the relationship follows over time."[22] Figure 3.3 highlights the typical characteristics of customers at the end points of the account behavior spectrum: lost-for-good and always-a-share customers.

Lost-for-Good Customers
The **lost-for-good customer** makes a series of purchases over time, faces high costs in switching to a new supplier, and views the commitment to a particular supplier as relatively permanent. Once won, this type of account is likely to remain loyal to a particular supplier for a long time. If lost, however, it is often "lost for good." This behavior fits some purchasers of computers, office automation systems, communications equipment, and heavy construction equipment. For example, Ford recently decided that it needed a single supplier of office systems to improve communication in its North American operations. Business marketers attempting to secure the Ford account recognize that if they are unsuccessful, years may pass before Ford will consider a totally new system. For the winning bidder, a long, prosperous relationship can be nurtured. Once won, this type of buyer is an asset; while once lost, it is lost for good. Switching costs are especially important to lost-for-good customers.

Switching Costs
In considering possible changes from one selling firm to another, organizational buyers consider two **switching costs**: investments and risk of exposure. First, organizational buyers invest in their relationships with suppliers in many ways: "They invest *money*; they invest in *people*, as in training employees to run new equipment; they invest in

---

[21] This section is based on Barbara Bund Jackson, "Build Customer Relationships that Last," *Harvard Business Review*, 63 (November–December 1985), pp. 120–128; and Jackson, *Winning and Keeping Industrial Customers* (Lexington, Mass.: Lexington Books, 1985).

[22] Jackson, *Winning and Keeping Industrial Customers*, p. 10.

FIGURE 3.3 **Time, Account Behavior, and Marketing Approach**

Long Time Horizon ◄————————► **Short Time Horizon**

Typified by lost-for-good customers	Typified by always-a-share customers
High switching costs	Lower switching costs
Substantial investment actions, especially in procedures and lasting assets	Smaller investment actions
High perceived exposure	Lower perceived exposure
Focus on a technology or on a vendor	Focus on a product or on a person
High importance: strategic, operational, and personal	Lower importance
Relationship Marketing	**Transaction Marketing**

Source: Barbara Bund Jackson, *Winning and Keeping Industrial Customers* (Lexington, Mass.: Lexington Books, 1985), p. 168. Reprinted by permission of the publisher. Copyright D.C. Heath and Company.

lasting assets, such as equipment itself; and they invest in changing basic business *procedures* like inventory handling."[23] Because of these past investments, buyers may be hesitant to incur the disruptions and switching costs that result when new suppliers are selected.

Risk of exposure provides a second major category of switching costs. Attention centers on the risks to organizational buyers of making the wrong choice. Customers perceive more risk exposure when they purchase products important to their operations, when they buy from less-established suppliers, and when they buy technically complex products.

Relationship marketing, targeted on strong and lasting commitments, is especially appropriate for lost-for-good accounts. Business marketers can sensibly invest resources in order to secure commitments and to aid customers with long-range planning. Given the long time horizon and the considerable stakes involved, customers are concerned both with marketers' long-term capabilities and with their immediate performance. Because the customers perceive significant risk, they demand competence and commitment from the selling organization and are easily frightened by even a hint of supplier inadequacy.

Always-a-Share Customers

The **always-a-share customer** (see Figure 3.3) purchases repeatedly from some product category, displays less loyalty or commitment to a particular supplier, and can easily switch part or all of the purchases from one vendor to another. Because of low switching costs, these customers may share their patronage over time with multiple vendors and adopt a short time horizon in their commitments with suppliers. This behavior fits some buyers of commodity chemicals, computer terminals, and shipping

---

[23]Jackson, "Building Customer Relationships that Last," p. 125.

services. A business marketer who offers an immediate, attractive combination of product, price, technical support, and other benefits has a chance of winning business from always-a-share customers. Thus, **transaction marketing**—marketing that emphasizes the individual sale—is most appropriate for the always-a-share buyer.

Intermediate Customers

The behavior of many customers in the business market corresponds to an intermediate point on the account behavior spectrum, somewhere between the lost-for-good model and the always-a-share model. The particular position that a customer occupies depends on a host of factors: the characteristics of the product category, the customer's pattern of product usage, and the actions taken by both the supplier and the customer. For example, purchasers of a commodity such as carbon steel generally fit the always-a-share model. However, a steel user who adopts a just-in-time production system requires close cooperation and scheduling with suppliers. Thus, the customer's usage pattern and the supplier's investment in adapting to the buyer's special requirements can create behavior that corresponds more to the lost-for-good model.

Changing Customers' Commitments

Changes along the account behavior spectrum can be induced by the business marketer. To move a customer closer to the lost-for-good end of the spectrum, there are several ways marketers can raise a buyer's switching costs. First, marketers can raise switching costs by creating buying systems that provide improved efficiency and service for the customer. For example, Baxter's hospital supplies unit provides a system through which customers can order via a computer terminal and receive immediate order confirmation on their own customized forms. Similarly, some industrial distributors provide computer-to-computer links with local customers. These systems provide increased convenience and efficiency for customers, create stronger ties between the buyer and the seller, and move the customer closer to the lost-for-good end of the spectrum.

Second, business marketers can raise customer switching costs by offering system benefits—additional benefits that customers may obtain by relying on a single supplier for most or all of their purchases. To illustrate, a chemical company provides auto body shops with access to a computer program that assists them in matching a car's current color when making touch-ups and repairs. Because the program uses only the supplier's set of pigments, customers are tied to a single source.

On the other hand, to penetrate a competitor's established account, the business marketer may want to move a potential customer closer to the always-a-share end of the spectrum. The appropriate strategy would be to "give the buyers painless ways to mix and match."[24] Many suppliers of computer peripherals and softwares, for example, design and offer products that are IBM compatible. This allows customers to experiment with new vendors and to buy individual items that fit into an existing IBM system.

---

[24] Ibid., p. 127.

To this point, the discussion has centered on three areas that provide a foundation for understanding organizational buying behavior: (1) the buyer–seller exchange process; (2) the multistage procurement process along with the classification of buying situations; and (3) the account behavior spectrum. A fourth factor is the buying motives of organizational buyers.

BUYING MOTIVATIONS OF ORGANIZATIONAL BUYERS

The fate of the business marketer is determined by an organization's evaluation of potential suppliers. Suppliers screened out during the evaluation process may find it difficult to again get the buying firm's attention. The industrial marketer must understand how organizational buyers evaluate potential suppliers.

Organizational members are influenced by both rational and emotional factors when choosing among competing offerings. Rational motives are usually economic, such as price, quality, and service; emotional motives are concerned with such human factors as job security or organizational status. The business marketer has to define the buying motives of the organizational members who will ultimately pass judgment on a product. This is particularly difficult because generalizations about the importance of selected buying motives cannot be made across all types of industrial buying decisions. Members of the buying center often use differing criteria when evaluating suppliers.[25] For example, the purchasing agent may value maximum price economy, but engineers are primarily concerned with product quality. Also, the importance of the criteria varies with the product.[26]

The challenge for the marketer is to view the purchasing decision from the buying organization's perspective, to ascertain the roles of various members of the buying center, and to determine what motivates each member.

Rational Motives

Because commercial enterprises have profit objectives and because governmental units and not-for-profit organizations have budgetary constraints, rational or economic buying motives are significant.

---

[25] For example, see Jagdish N. Sheth, "A Model of Industrial Buyer Behavior," *Journal of Marketing*, 37 (October 1973), pp. 50–56; see also J. Patrick Kelly and James W. Coaker, "Can We Generalize about Choice Criteria for Industrial Purchasing Decisions?" in Kenneth L. Bernhardt, ed., *Marketing: 1776–1976 and Beyond* (Chicago: American Marketing Association, 1976), pp. 330–333.

[26] Donald R. Lehmann and John O'Shaughnessy, "Difference in Attribute Importance for Different Industrial Products," *Journal of Marketing*, 40 (April 1976), pp. 36–42; see also Lehmann and O'Shaughnessy, "Decision Criteria Used in Buying Different Categories of Products," *Journal of Purchasing and Materials Management*, 18 (Spring 1982), pp. 9–14.

Price

The professional buyer evaluates a quoted price from many perspectives. A buyer considering a new piece of capital equipment analyzes potential savings (return) in manpower, energy, and material and relates these factors to the price (investment). Thus, a return on investment (ROI) calculation would be used to compare the offerings of competing equipment firms. In the case of a component part, the buyer might consider price in relation to ease of installation. A higher-priced component that is easier and less costly to install has an edge over a less expensive model that poses cumbersome installation problems. Marketers often overestimate the importance of offering the lowest price. Frequently, the low bidder fails other tests.

Quality

The relentless threat of competition, both foreign and domestic, has elevated the importance of quality for corporate strategists and for purchasing executives alike. George Graham, director of quality at Texas Instruments, captures the theme in procurement for the 1990s: "Quality improvement is a never-ending challenge because its boundaries are being pushed back constantly by customers and suppliers. Suppliers will only understand this if 'quality' is the sole message coming from all levels of your company."[27]

Organizational buyers do not want to pay for more quality than they need; at the same time, they are unwilling to compromise specifications for a reduced price. Uniformity or consistency of product quality is often the crucial factor. Such consistency can: (1) guarantee uniformity of the end product, (2) reduce the need for costly inspections of each incoming shipment, and (3) ensure that the purchased material will not cause delays in the production process. Poor consistency in the quality of materials and components creates costly problems for the buying organization, especially for those who have adopted or are moving toward just-in-time production systems.[28] The goal is to move incoming materials directly to the production line. The just-in-time concept hinges on building in quality rather than on screening out poor quality. Organizational buyers seek business marketers who can provide them with materials and components that are supplier-certified: no incoming quality inspection required.

Motorola, for example, now requires all its suppliers to apply for the Malcolm Baldrige National Quality Award or to provide a time schedule as to when they will apply. George M. C. Fisher, president and CEO at Motorola, notes: "This creates one more demanding review process our suppliers must go through . . . in order to improve quality and efficiency."[29]

---

[27] Tom Stundza, "Good Quality Systems Are Those that Work!" *Purchasing*, 104 (January 18, 1990), p. 160.

[28] For example, see Charles R. O'Neal and Kate Bertrand, *Developing a Winning JIT Marketing Strategy: The Industrial Marketer's Guide* (Englewood Cliffs, NJ: Prentice-Hall, Inc., 1991).

[29] Bernard Avishai and William Taylor, "Customers Drive a Technology-Driven Company: An Interview with George Fisher," *Harvard Business Review*, 67 (November–December 1989), p. 113.

FIGURE 3.4 **How Important Are Various Aspects of Supplier Performance?**

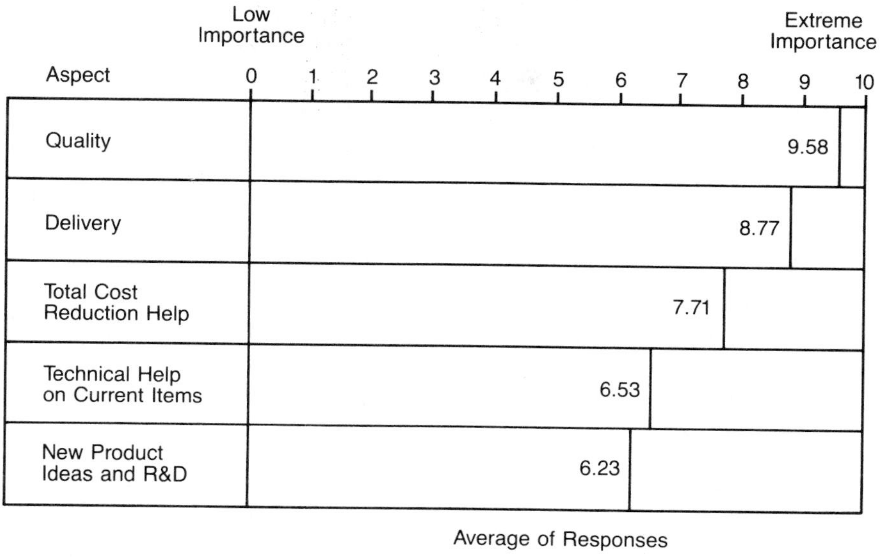

Aspect	Value
Quality	9.58
Delivery	8.77
Total Cost Reduction Help	7.71
Technical Help on Current Items	6.53
New Product Ideas and R&D	6.23

Scale from 0 (Low Importance) to 10 (Extreme Importance). Average of Responses.

Source: Somerby Dowst, "CEO Report: Wanted: Suppliers Adept at Turning Corners," *Purchasing*, 101 (January 29, 1987), p. 73.

Service

All sectors of the business market (commercial enterprises, government units, and institutions) require a broad range of services, including technical assistance, information, delivery, repair capability, spare parts availability, and even financing. Service can be an important means of differentiation for the marketer. A marketer offering sound technical advice, reliable and speedy delivery, and an available supply of replacement parts may have an edge over competing suppliers; the buying organization must make a larger investment in inventory if the supplier's delivery is slow or unpredictable.

The importance of physical distribution to organizational buyers is vividly illustrated in Figure 3.4. This survey of more than 1,000 purchasing managers reveals that delivery (physical distribution) performance ranks second only to product quality in influencing industrial purchase decisions. Observe also the prominent role that other service dimensions assume in the purchase decision. Purchasing managers are eager to locate suppliers who will work closely with them to reduce costs, solve technical problems, and generate new product ideas.

Continuity of Supply

Continuity of supply can be a critical concern of the purchasing manager. Any interruption in the flow of key materials or components can bring the production process to an abrupt halt, resulting in costly delays and lost sales. To guard against contingencies like an unanticipated strike in a supplier's plant, professional buyers are reluctant to rely on a single source of supply; they often choose to spread their business among two or more suppliers whenever possible. As logical as this approach appears, evidence suggests that if a buyer and seller work together in a cooperative single-source relationship, benefits may accrue to both parties in the form of reduced costs for the supplier, lower prices for the buyer, and improved quality for both.[30] How?

The close buyer–seller relationship facilitates a more open exchange of information. Providing the supplier with more accurate production forecasts and more stable purchase requirements may result in lower costs for order processing, transportation, and material handling. In turn, the parties can collaborate to design quality control systems and resolve quality problems promptly. The buyer may also benefit through lower prices, reduced administrative costs, and expanded technical assistance. Although some purchasing managers are uncomfortable with single sourcing—fearing a loss of bargaining power—an expanding segment of the business market is reducing the number of vendors used and relying on single sources.[31] To illustrate, many of the component parts for the Honda Accord, the Macintosh computer, and the forthcoming Boeing 777 aircraft are sole-sourced.

The astute business marketer is alert to potential candidates for a single-source relationship and aware of the special challenges that such relationships present. Organizational buyers who are making strong, long-term commitments " . . . are concerned both with marketers' long-run capabilities and also with their immediate performance. Because the customers feel exposure, they especially demand vendor competence and commitment. They are likely to be frightened by even minor signs of supplier inadequacy."[32]

Reciprocity

Because buyers and sellers often have close relationships in the business market, reciprocal trade possibilities emerge: "If you buy from me, I'll buy from you." The motivation for buying from each other is the key to whether an arrangement involves **reciprocity**, a situation in which the purchase decision is influenced by the *buyer–seller arrangement* rather than by economic or performance factors.

Reciprocal trade relations can be based on friendly or on highly coercive pressure: "If you don't buy X percent more from me, I'll reduce my purchases from you by Y percent!" Reciprocity is legal as long as the arrangement is not enforced through coercive power by one or more parties and as long as the reciprocal agreement does not substantially lessen competition. One authority contends that anticompetitive and coercive reciprocity have been successfully checked by the government in recent years but that friendship reciprocity continues to be a force in the business market.[33]

---

[30] Mark Treleven, "Single Sourcing: A Management Tool for the Quality Supplier," *Journal of Purchasing and Materials Management*, 23 (Spring 1987), pp. 19–24.

[31] Dowst, "CEO Report: Wanted: Suppliers Adept at Turning Corners," p. 60.

[32] Barbara Bund Jackson, "Build Customer Relationships that Last," p. 128.

[33] F. Robert Finney, "Reciprocity: Gone but Not Forgotten," *Journal of Marketing*, 43 (January 1978), pp. 54–59; see also Reed Moyer, "Reciprocity: Retrospect and Prospect," *Journal of Marketing*, 34 (October 1970), pp. 47–54.

A new twist in buyer–seller relationships, reverse reciprocity, is also becoming more prevalent in the business market.[34] Operative during periods of resource shortages, **reverse reciprocity** involves buyers agreeing to sell one set of scarce resources to sellers in return for sellers agreeing to sell a different set of scarce resources to buyers. More simply: "If you'll sell to me, I'll sell to you."

Emotional Motives

A marketer concentrating exclusively on rational motives has an incomplete picture of the organizational buyer. Individuals, not organizations, make buying decisions.

Status and Rewards

Emotional motives include the desire for status within the organization, for promotion, for salary increases, and for increased job security. The industrial salesperson must understand the reward system of the organization and the projects or problems that have priority in the organization. Many firms periodically launch procurement projects geared to achieving significant cost savings during a 12-month period. In this environment, purchasing managers are particularly receptive to proposals from new or existing suppliers.

Perceived Risk

H. Lazo makes the provocative observation that "fear is one of the major influences in industrial buying. Fear of displeasing the boss. Fear of making a wrong decision . . . fear of losing status. Fear, indeed, in extreme cases, of losing one's job."[35] The marketer must ask how each buyer perceives and handles risk.[36] What happens if the product does not perform satisfactorily (functional risk), or if others in the organization view the decision negatively (psychological risk)? The perceived risk concept has two components: (1) *uncertainty* concerning the outcome of a decision and (2) the magnitude of the *consequences* associated with making the wrong choice.

The buyer will often reduce the level of risk by relying on familiar suppliers or by favoring suppliers with the best reputation. Alternatively, an organizational buyer might reduce uncertainty by visiting the supplier's plant, or might reduce the chances of unfavorable consequences by consulting top management before making the decision.

---

[34] Gregory D. Upah and Monroe M. Bird, "Changes in Industrial Buying: Implications for Industrial Marketers," *Industrial Marketing Management*, 9 (May 1980), pp. 117–121.

[35] H. Lazo, "Emotional Aspects of Industrial Buying," in R. R. Hancock, ed., *Proceedings of the American Marketing Association* (Chicago: American Marketing Association, 1960), p. 265.

[36] For example, see Timothy W. Sweeney, H. Lee Mathews, and David T. Wilson, "An Analysis of Industrial Buyers' Risk Reducing Behavior: Some Personality Correlates," *American Marketing Association Proceedings* (Chicago: American Marketing Association, 1973), pp. 217–221.

Friendship

Emotional motives often influence buying decisions in subtle ways. A purchasing manager may be known to select suppliers on the basis of competitive bids, but may work diligently with a friend "to get him competitive" on price level and product specifications.[37]

Emotional motives cannot be overlooked. An understanding of all the buying motives—both rational and nonrational—of the members of the buying center is vital to designing responsive marketing strategy.

HOW ORGANIZATIONAL BUYERS EVALUATE POTENTIAL SUPPLIERS

The rational and emotional buying motives of individual organizational buyers are ultimately reflected in the formal evaluation of suppliers. The buyer's knowledge of the suppliers, coupled with the organization's perception of the value and importance of the purchase, determines the problem-solving approach.

Measuring Value

The accurate measurement of value is crucial to the purchasing function. The principles and tools of value analysis aid the professional buyer in approaching this task. **Value analysis** is a method of weighing the comparative values of materials, components, and manufacturing processes from the standpoint of their purpose, relative merit, and cost in order to uncover ways of improving products, lowering costs, or both. Figure 3.5 provides some examples of how value analysis is used to evaluate the function and design of component parts to result in lower product cost. Note that rather straightforward design and manufacturing alternatives can produce spectacular cost savings. Value is achieved when the proper function is secured for the proper cost. Because functions can be accomplished in a number of different ways, the most cost-efficient way of fully accomplishing a function establishes its value. The value-in-use concept reflects this philosophy.

Value-in-Use[38]

Value-in-use (VIU) is defined as a product's economic value to the user relative to a specific alternative in a particular application. Thus, VIU centers on a specific usage situation and constitutes the price that would equalize the overall costs and benefits of using one product rather than another. Consider this example:

---

[37] Thomas V. Bonoma and Gerald Zaltman, eds., *Organizational Buying Behavior* (Chicago: American Marketing Association, 1978), pp. 3–4.

[38] Material in this section provided by Gary L. Lilien, Research Director, Institute for the Study of Business Markets, The Pennsylvania State University. See also, Valerie Kijewski and Eunsang Yoon, "Market-Based Pricing: Beyond Price-Performance Curves," *Industrial Marketing Management*, 19 (February 1990), pp. 11–19.

FIGURE 3.5   **How Value Analysis Slashes Costs**

Weights mounted on a rotor ring were curved to match the ring curve. Did it need this feature? No. Using a straight piece, the cost dropped from 40¢ to 4¢.	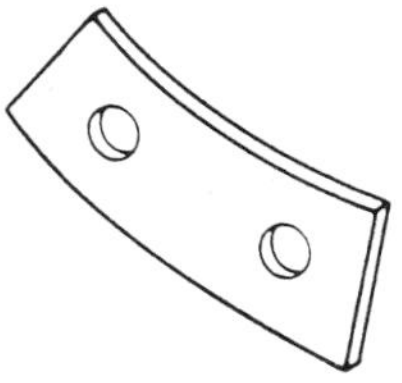 40¢	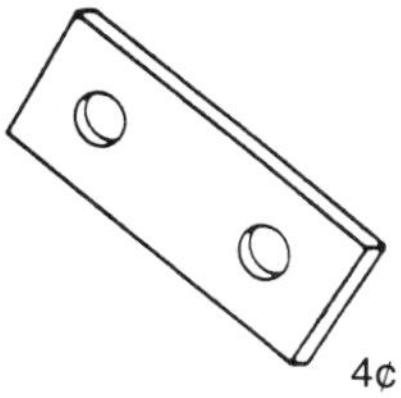 4¢
Field coil supports were machined from stock, but the original design blended nicely into a casting operation. The change resulted in lowering the cost from $1.72 to 36¢ each.	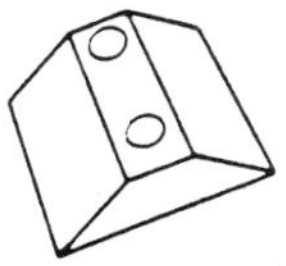 $1.72	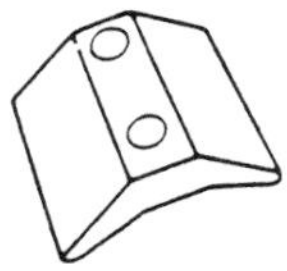 36¢
This insulating washer was made from laminated phenolic resin and fiber. Machined from individual pieces of material, it cost $1.23. A supplier with specialty equipment now fly-cuts the parts, nesting them on full sheets, at 24¢ each.	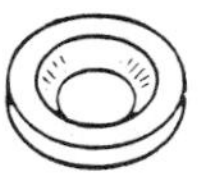 $1.23	 24¢
Standard nipple and elbow required special machining to fit a totally enclosed motor. Casting a special street "L" with a lug eliminated machining and a special assembly jig. The cost dropped from 63¢ to 38¢.	 63¢	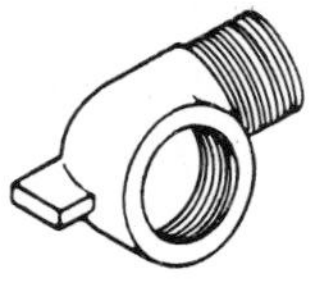 38¢
An insulator costing $4.56 was originally porcelain, leaded extra heavy. Now molded from polyester and glass, it is lighter and virtually indestructible. New cost: $3.25.	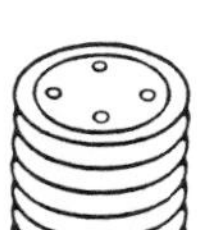 $4.56	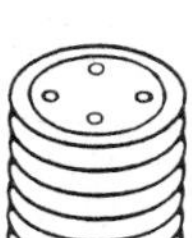 $3.25

Source: Lamar Lee, Jr., and Donald W. Dobler, *Purchasing and Materials Management: Text and Cases* (New York: McGraw-Hill Book Company, 1977), p. 265. Reprinted by permission of McGraw-Hill Book Company.

A chemical plant uses 200 O-rings to seal valves carrying corrosive materials. These O-rings cost $5 each and must be changed during regular maintenance every two months. A purchasing agent located a supplier of a new product which performs the same function while offering twice the corrosive resisting power and twice the useful life (4 months versus 2 months). The value-in-use of the new product might be:

(1) Annual cost of existing product:

$$200 \text{ (Rings)} \times \$5 \text{ per ring} \times 6 \text{ changes per year} = \$6,000$$

(2) Value-in-use of new product:

$$200 \text{ (Rings)} \times 3 \text{ changes per year} \times \text{VIU} = \$6,000$$
$$\text{VIU} = \$10$$

The purchasing agent could pay $10 per unit and receive the same benefits as the existing alternative. Often, other benefits and costs must be considered in VIU calculations.

Suppose that the cost of a plant shutdown is $5,000 and the new product allows a longer period between shutdowns—4 months versus 2 months. When these costs are considered, the value-in-use of the new alternative increases dramatically:

(3) Annual cost of existing product when shutdown cost is considered:

$$\underset{\textit{Equipment Cost}}{(200 \times 6 \times \$5)} + \underset{\textit{Shutdown Cost}}{(\$5,000 \times 6 \text{ plant shutdowns})} = \$36,000$$

(4) Value-in-use of new product when shutdown cost is considered:

$$\underset{\textit{Equipment Cost}}{(200 \times 3 \times \text{VIU})} + \underset{\textit{Shutdown Cost}}{(\$5,000 \times 3 \text{ plant shutdowns})} = \$36,000$$
$$\text{VIU} = \$35$$

Value Analysis: The Marketer's Role

Prudent business marketers are eager to understand customer needs better, to provide the exact level of product design and performance required, and to demonstrate the value-in-use of their products. Such strategy is especially timely given the striking majority of purchasing managers who actively encourage supplier participation in value analysis.[39]

Value analysis projects are usually sponsored or coordinated by the purchasing department, but they often include other departments. The team for a particular project might consist of a purchasing specialist, a design engineer, a production engineer, and representatives from marketing and accounting. Westinghouse Electric used such an approach to reduce the costs of some materials and commodities by over 40 percent.[40]

---

[39] Somerby Dowst and Ernest Raia, "Teaming Up for the '90s," *Purchasing*, 104 (February 1990), pp. 54–59.

[40] Dale C. Weisenstein, "Westinghouse Teams Up for Quality and Productivity," *Purchasing World*, 27 (May 1983), p. 48.

TABLE 3.4 **Supplier Capability: Key Attributes Evaluated by Buyers**

Attribute	Measure
Technical/production capability	Adequacy of equipment, production control, quality control, cost control
Managerial capability	The ability of the supplier to plan, organize, and control operations
Financial condition	The financial stability of the supplier—profit record, cash flow, equity, working capital, credit rating
Service capacity	The supplier's ability to comply with promised product specifications, delivery dates, and technical assistance

For other projects, a purchasing manager might work with a supplier's technical salesperson. Clearly, the industrial salesperson can play an active role by supplying technical assistance, relevant data, and valuable recommendations. In fact, the salesperson of the business marketer is often pivotal in stimulating the purchasing organization to conduct a value analysis study, convincing purchasing or other organizational members that the potential benefits from a particular study exceed its costs.

Evaluating Supplier Capability

A buying organization facing an important purchasing decision must carefully analyze the total capability of suppliers. Observe in Table 3.4 that this assessment covers technical, managerial, financial, and service capabilities. Each provides a measure of ability to comply with promises made to the buying organization.

After the list of potential suppliers has been screened and narrowed, the buying organization generally conducts an on-site inspection of vendor facilities by representatives from purchasing, engineering, and, on occasion, production and finance. The trained observer can quickly appraise the production capability of a supplier: Is the equipment up-to-date? Are scheduling and production control properly organized to allow promised delivery dates to be met? Does the supplier have the talent, resources, and expertise to offer added value in the future?

Buyers also evaluate the financial condition of potential suppliers. A solid financial position usually points to a well-managed operation. Financial stability is critical to continuity of supply and uniformity of product quality. A buyer consults such sources as *Dun and Bradstreet* (D&B) reports, *Moody's Industrials,* or corporate annual reports when assessing the financial condition of a supplier.

The exact meaning of the term *service* varies with the nature of the product and the requirements of the buying organization. **Service** may encompass reliable delivery, technical assistance, innovative suggestions, credit arrangements, rapid support for special needs, and advance notice of impending price changes or shortages of supply. The marketer with strong service capabilities will be in a favorable position.

THE GLOBAL MARKETPLACE
World-Class Suppliers

Several years ago, Intel found that its Japanese competitors were getting near-perfect quality, delivery, and service from its suppliers. Here's the puzzle: Intel was getting a lower level of performance from the same set of suppliers! Thomas Hogue, vice president of administration and materials at Intel, found that performance levels could be improved by developing a closer working relationship with suppliers:

> When a Japanese company places an order, its suppliers can take that order to the bank—there are no changes, cancellations, or other surprises. So, Intel tried it and met with success. Orders are never canceled, and commitment and predict-

ability are the rules when dealing with suppliers.

Intel discovered that such commitments strengthened supplier relationships and boosted quality, service, and efficiency. To further strengthen its suppliers, Intel trains them on the latest quality management procedures, updates them on the latest developments in their products, and ensures that they have the technology available to manufacture new products to support Intel's future needs. Hogue concludes, "What we have been trying to do is to maintain ourselves as a world-class supplier of components and systems and to do that we have to be certain to only use world-class suppliers."

Source: J. William Semich and Somerby Dowst, "How to Push Your Everyday Supplier into World Class Status," *Purchasing*, 103 (August 17, 1989), pp. 74–78.

Evaluating Supplier Performance

Once a contract is awarded to a supplier, the evaluation process takes a different form. Actual performance must be evaluated. Buyers rate supplier performance to assess the quality of past decisions and to make future vendor selections—and as a negotiating tool to gain leverage in buyer–seller relationships. The specific method and the scope of the rating system vary by industry and firm. Three rating systems are briefly described below.[41]

Categorical Plan

Under the categorical plan, supplier performance is evaluated by several departments that maintain informal records on each major vendor, perhaps including purchasing, engineering, quality control, receiving, and inspection. For every major supplier, each individual develops a list of significant performance factors. At a regularly scheduled meeting (usually monthly), each major supplier is tested against each set of criteria and given an overall group evaluation. Suppliers are then categorized as preferred, neutral, or unsatisfactory. Ease of administration is the chief advantage of this highly subjective method.

---

[41] For example, see Ed Timmerman, "An Approach to Vendor Performance Evaluation," *Journal of Purchasing and Materials Management*, 22 (Winter 1986), pp. 2–8.

The Weighted-Point Plan

The buying organization weights each performance factor according to its relative importance. Quality might be given a weight of 40, service 30, and price 30. This system alerts the business marketer to the nature and importance of the evaluative criteria used by a particular organization. The marketer's total offering can then be adjusted to fit the organization's needs more precisely.

Observe in Figure 3.6 how Chrysler Corporation "grades" suppliers of electronic components. Under this program, suppliers can be awarded up to 100 total points, including up to 40 points for quality, 25 points for pricing, 25 points for delivery, and 10 points for technical assistance. Note that a number of dimensions are evaluated for each performance factor. For example, the quality rating is determined by the following:

- The supplier's defect rate
- Conformance to a statistical quality audit (SQA) of the supplier's manufacturing plant in which purchasing and engineering inspect manufacturing processes and controls
- The performance of samples provided by the supplier
- The responsiveness of the supplier to quality problems

Working with other departments, such as engineering and production control, purchasing calculates a performance score for each supplier. Those scoring 91 points or above make the preferred supplier list. It is important to note that only 300 of Chrysler's 1,000 electronics suppliers achieve this distinction, and they receive over 80 percent of the firm's $350 million annual budget for electronic components. Suppliers scoring 83 to 90 points continue to be used, but to a lesser degree than preferred suppliers. Those scoring 70 to 83 points are placed in a marginal category and risk being eliminated from the supplier roster unless they work with Chrysler to improve. Suppliers scoring less than 70 points are usually dropped automatically.

The weighted-point plan is more objective and flexible than the categorical method. The buying organization can adjust the weights of various performance factors to meet particular needs. Likewise, the method forces the organizational buyer to define the key attributes of a supplier.

Cost-Ratio Plan

The cost-ratio method draws upon standard cost analysis. Under this plan, the buying organization evaluates quality, delivery, and service, assigning a minus (–) weight for favorable performance on a factor and a plus (+) weight for unfavorable performance. (That's right—a minus for good performance, a plus for bad performance. You will soon see why.) The weights for each performance factor are derived from standard cost calculations. For the delivery rating, the standard cost base might include the expense of factory downtime and rescheduling caused by a delinquent shipment as well as telephone follow-ups and associated costs. A penalty rating of +0.02 might be assigned for a shipment received one week late and a stronger penalty of +0.05 might

FIGURE 3.6   **How Chrysler Grades Suppliers**

Supplier Rating Chart:

Supplier Name: _____
Shipping Location: _____

Commodity: _____
Annual Sales Dollars: _____

	5 Excellent	4 Good	3 Satisfactory	2 Fair	1 Poor	0 N/A
Quality 40%						
Supplier defect rates						
SQA program conformance						
Sample approval performance						
Responsiveness to quality problems						
Overall rating						
Delivery 25%						
Avoidance of late or overshipments						
Ability to expand production capacity						
Engineering sample delivery performance						
Response to fluctuating supply demands						
Overall delivery rating						
Price 25%						
Price competitiveness						
Absorption of economic price increases						
Submission of cost savings plans						
Payment terms						
Overall price rating						
Technology 10%						
State-of-the-art component technology						
Sharing research development capability						
Capable and willing to provide circuit design services						
Responsiveness to engineering problems						
Overall technology rating						

Buyer: _____   Date: _____
Comments: _____

Source: Courtesy, Chrysler Corporation.

be assigned for a shipment delayed three weeks. Similar weights, based on standard costs, are made for quality and service and then combined into one final composite rating for each supplier. This composite rating is used to calculate an "adjusted price" for each major supplier. As an example, supplier X will be evaluated using this approach.

ILLUSTRATION: The Cost-Ratio Method
Assume that supplier X bids $80 and has a quality cost ratio of +1 percent, a delivery cost ratio of +5 percent, and a service cost ratio of –1 percent. The three cost ratios sum to +5 percent. Thus, the adjusted price for supplier X is $80 + (.05 × 80) = $84. The organizational buyer would select the vendor offering the most economical total

package rather than the supplier with the lowest bid price. Poor delivery performance clearly damaged the position of supplier X. A competing supplier offering solid delivery performance and competitive quality and service would be selected even at a slightly higher bid price.

A computerized cost-accounting system is needed to provide the cost estimates that form the core of the cost-ratio plan. While the method has generated widespread interest, many firms find the weighted-point plan simpler and more flexible. The quality of each method—categorical, weighted-point, and cost-ratio—depends on the accuracy and appropriateness of the underlying assumptions of the evaluator.

Vendor Analysis: Implications for the Marketer

Business marketers must be sensitive to the evaluation criteria of organizational buyers and to how these criteria are weighted. Many criteria may be factored into a buyer's ultimate decision: quality, service, price, company image, capability. Buyers' perceptions are also critical. When products are perceived as highly standardized, price assumes more importance. On the other hand, if products are perceived as unique, other criteria may dominate. The price of a product cannot be separated from the attached bundle of services and other intangible values.

Economic criteria assume significant importance in many industrial buying decisions,[42] especially the anticipated costs associated with buying, storing, and using the product. By contrast, product performance criteria evaluate the extent to which the product is likely to maximize performance. Economic criteria are important in the purchase of standard products of simple construction with standard applications. Performance criteria are more important in the evaluation of complex products or novel applications. By defining the type of vendor evaluation system used by existing or potential customers, the business marketer is better equipped to satisfy their needs profitably.

The marketer who secures a new account must be prepared to pass frequent performance tests. As purchasing departments increase their use of computers, purchasing becomes more centralized, the number of suppliers declines, and the performance of suppliers is subjected to increased quantitative scrutiny.[43]

SUMMARY

Valuable insights into business marketing management can be secured by examining buyer–seller relationships as an exchange process. Relationships, rather than single transactions, provide the central focus. Knowledge of the process that organizational

---

[42]Lehmann and O'Shaughnessy, "Decision Criteria Used in Buying Different Categories of Products," pp. 9–14.

[43]David T. Wilson and H. Lee Mathews, "Impact of Management Information Systems upon Purchasing Decision-Making," pp. 48–56, reported in Thomas V. Bonoma, Gerald Zaltman, and Wesley J. Johnston, *Industrial Buying Behavior* (Cambridge, Mass.: Marketing Science Institute, 1977), p. 114.

buyers follow in making purchasing decisions is fundamental to responsive marketing strategy. As a buying organization moves from the problem recognition phase, in which a procurement need is defined, to later phases, in which suppliers are screened and ultimately chosen, the marketer can play an active role. In fact, the astute marketer often triggers initial awareness of the problem and aids the organization in effectively solving that problem. Incremental decisions made throughout the buying process narrow the field of acceptable suppliers and dramatically influence the ultimate outcome.

The nature of the buying process depends on the organization's level of experience with similar procurement problems. It is thus crucial to know how the organization defines the buying situation: new task, modified rebuy, or straight rebuy. Each buying situation requires a unique problem-solving approach, involves unique buying influentials, and demands a unique marketing response. Valuable insights can also be secured by examining the time horizon within which a customer makes a commitment to a supplier. Switching costs, the level of perceived risk, and the importance of the purchase provide benchmarks for defining the likely pattern a relationship will follow.

Organizational buyers apply a wide range of rational and emotional buying motives to the purchasing decision process. After the decision is made, the buying organization monitors vendor performance, often through the use of a formal rating system. Such systems key on supplier attributes that are important to the buying organization, such as quality, service, delivery, and price. Specific vendor rating systems range from the easily administered categorical plan to the complex cost-ratio method. Many firms have devised their own weighted-point plans. Vendor rating systems define the requirements that the business marketer must meet. Computer technology has markedly improved the ability of organizations to evaluate supplier performance.

Discussion Questions

1. Jim Currier, vice president of purchasing at NCR, notes: "Our chances of bringing innovative solutions to the marketplace will depend on our suppliers; one simply can't afford to 'own' all the requisite technology needed to satisfy customer expectations." What criteria would be important to NCR in evaluating potential suppliers? In building a relationship, who would likely assume a role on the selling side (selling center) and on the buying side (buying center)?

2. "Changes in the organizational buying environment trigger corresponding adjustments in the selling environment." Evaluate this statement, noting recent trends in purchasing.

3. IBM was recently awarded a $200 million contract by Ford to supply new office automation systems. Digital Equipment Corporation and Wang Laboratories, Inc. lost out on the contract, but a Ford official noted, "we're not locked in—we'll go elsewhere if IBM products don't measure up." In your view, what emotional and rational buying motives might have entered into this decision? After losing the first

round, what strategies might Digital Equipment Corporation and Wang Laboratories employ when pursuing the Ford account in the future?

4. What strategic advantage does the marketer gain by reaching the buying organization at the early rather than the late stages of the purchase decision process?

5. Jim Jackson, an industrial salesperson for Pittsburgh Machine Tool, will call on two accounts this afternoon. The first call will be on a buying organization that Jim has been servicing for the past three years. The second call, however, poses more of a challenge. This buying organization has been dealing with a prime competitor of Pittsburgh Machine Tool for five years. Jim, who has a good rapport with the purchasing and engineering departments, feels that the time may be right to penetrate this account. Recently, Jim learned that the purchasing manager was extremely unhappy with the poor delivery service provided by the firm's existing supplier. Define the buying situations confronting Jim, and outline the appropriate strategy that he should follow in each case.

6. Compare and contrast the weighted-point plan and the cost-ratio plan as used by organizational buyers in evaluating alternative suppliers.

7. Organizational buying decisions can be classified as new task, modified rebuy, or straight rebuy. Each elicits a different problem-solving approach and involves different buying influentials. Explain.

8. Describe how the business marketer can profit by understanding the vendor rating system that a particular buying organization employs.

9. Assume that your career path takes you into purchasing rather than marketing. You are assigned the responsibility for purchasing an important component for your firm's final consumer product—personal computers. Describe the criteria that you would apply in evaluating the offerings of various business marketers.

10. Mike Weber, the purchasing agent for Smith Manufacturing, views the purchase of widgets as a routine buying decision. What factors might lead him to alter this position? More important, what factors will determine whether a particular supplier, such as Albany Widget, will be considered by Mike?

CHAPTER 4

Organizational Buying Behavior

The organizational buyer is influenced by a wide array of forces inside and outside the organization. Knowledge of these forces provides the marketer with a foundation on which to build responsive business marketing strategies. After reading this chapter, you will understand:

1. the individual, group, organizational, and environmental variables that influence organizational buying decisions.

2. a model of organizational buying behavior that integrates these important influences.

3. how a knowledge of organizational buying characteristics allows the marketer to make more informed decisions about product design, pricing, and promotion.

GUS Maikish, an IBM account executive, is responsible for a single account—a major New York City bank. Understanding organizational buying behavior is fundamental to Gus's job. "There are many people involved in a major acquisition, and each one has a specific stake in the outcome," he notes. "One will be concerned with reliability, another with processing speed, someone else with obsolescence."[1] A large computer purchase by the bank may involve from 10 to 25 managers who influence the decision. Several such projects are often under way at the bank at the same time. To ensure that the IBM proposal is the centerpiece of the decision-making process, Gus develops detailed records for each project, noting the names of key buying

---

[1] Martin Everett, "This Is the Ultimate in Selling," *Sales & Marketing Management,* 41 (August 1989), p. 32.

influentials, their departments, and the criteria that each deems most important to the decision. These records are constantly updated as the decision process unfolds and they determine the direction of IBM's selling strategy at the bank.

Understanding the dynamics of organizational buying behavior is crucial for identifying profitable segments of the organizational market, for locating buying influences within these segments, and for reaching these organizational buyers efficiently and effectively with an offering that responds to their needs. Each decision the business marketer makes is based on a probable response of organizational buyers. A marketer who is sensitive to the forces that shape organizational buying decisions is best equipped to make sound decisions about product, price, distribution, and promotional strategy.

Chapter 3 provided a framework for analyzing buyer–seller exchange relationships, an eight-stage model of the buying process, and a discussion of the salient characteristics of different purchasing situations. This chapter builds on that foundation and examines the myriad forces that influence organizational buying behavior (Figure 4.1), including environmental forces (e.g., health of the economy); organizational forces (e.g., size of buying organization); group forces (e.g., composition and roles of members); and individual forces (e.g., personal preferences).[2] Each of these forces has a sphere of influence that includes organizational buying decisions.

ENVIRONMENTAL FORCES

Organizational buyers do not make decisions in isolation: they are influenced by a broad range of forces in the external environment. A projected change in business conditions, a technological development, or a new piece of legislation can drastically alter organizational buying plans. Collectively, such environmental influences define the boundaries within which industrial buyers and sellers interact.

Types of Environmental Forces

Six types of environmental forces influence organizational buying behavior: economic, political, legal, cultural, physical, and technological.

Economic Influences

The general condition of the economy is reflected in economic growth, employment, price stability, income, and the availability of resources, money, and credit. Because of the derived nature of industrial demand, the marketer must also be sensitive to the strength of demand in the ultimate consumer market. The demand for many industrial products fluctuates more widely than the general economy.

---

[2] Frederick E. Webster, Jr., and Yoram Wind, *Organizational Buying Behavior* (Englewood Cliffs, N.J.: Prentice-Hall, Inc., 1972), pp. 28–37; see also Stephen T. Parkinson and Michael J. Baker, *Organizational Buying Behavior* (London: The MacMillan Press, Ltd., 1986).

FIGURE 4.1   **Forces Influencing Organizational Buying Behavior**

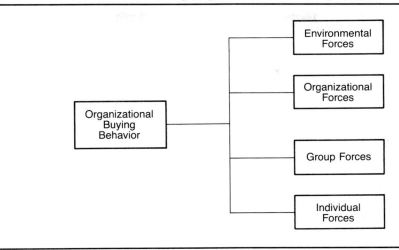

The economic environment influences an organization's ability and, to a degree, its willingness to buy. However, shifts in general economic conditions do not affect all sectors of the market evenly. For example, a rise in interest rates may damage the housing industry (e.g., lumber, cement, insulation) but may have minimal effects on industries such as paper, hospital supplies, office products, and soft drinks. Marketers that serve broad sectors of the organizational market must be particularly sensitive to the differential impact of selective economic shifts on buying behavior. Compared to for-profit organizations, for instance, not-for-profit organizations are more likely to justify a purchase simply because funds were allocated for a particular item in their budget.[3] The rationale is that if the funds are not spent this fiscal year, the budget will be cut next year.

Similarly, when sources of supply are sought worldwide, foreign exchange rates influence organizational buying behavior. For example, a California-based manufacturer spent $500 million on equipment from suppliers in 20 countries and in 14 different currencies.[4] The value of the U.S. dollar against the other currencies (the exchange rate) had a direct impact on these decisions. Fluctuations in the exchange rate also spawn shifts in purchasing behavior. As the value of the dollar declines, particularly against the Japanese yen, some purchasing managers tend to switch back to U.S. sources for particular components.

---

[3] Thomas V. Bonoma and Gerald Zaltman, "Introduction," in Bonoma and Zaltman, eds., *Organizational Buying Behavior* (Chicago: American Marketing Association, 1978), p. 23; see also Kjell Gronhaug, "Exploring Environmental Influences in Organizational Buying, *Journal of Marketing Research,* 13 (August 1976), pp. 225–230.

[4] Somerby Dowst, "Countries, Currencies, and Come-Backers," *Purchasing,* 101 (June 25, 1987), pp. 56–57.

Political and Legal Influences

The political environment includes tariffs and trade agreements with other countries, government funding of selected programs (discussed in Chapter 2), and government attitudes toward business and social service activities. For example, Deere & Company spends more than $250 million on parts and materials from foreign suppliers.[5] Among the factors considered in such international sourcing decisions are the political and economic stability of the country. The legal environment includes forces at the federal, state, and local levels that specify the boundaries of the buyer–seller relationship.[6]

The impact of governmental influences is illustrated in the debate that surrounds the proposal that automobiles must average 40 miles per gallon by the year 2000. To achieve this goal, virtually every part of the automobile will have to be redesigned. This in turn will increase demand for machine tools, aluminum, lightweight steel, plastic, and related materials.

Culture

Culture can be thought of as methods of coping with the environment that are shared by people as members of society and that are passed on from one generation to another. "Culture as reflected in values, mores, customs, habits, norms, traditions and so on will influence the structure and functioning of the organization and the way members of the organization feel and act toward one another and various aspects of the environment."[7]

Physical Influences

The physical environment includes such factors as climate and geographical location of the organization. The availability of labor, selected raw materials, and transportation services often determine the initial selection of a location by an organization. In turn, nearby suppliers often have an advantage in the vendor selection process, particularly when procurement requirements necessitate a close buyer–seller relationship (e.g., just-in-time production system).[8]

Technological Influences

Rapidly changing technology can restructure an industry and dramatically alter organizational buying plans. The technological environment defines the availability of goods and services to the buying organization and, in turn, the quality of goods and services that the organization can provide to its consumers.

---

[5] Shirley Cayer, "Low-Key but Savvy: How Deere & Company Buys," *Purchasing,* 103 (October 12, 1989), pp. 49–55.

[6] For an expanded treatment, see Reed Moyer and Michael D. Hutt, *Macro Marketing* (New York: John Wiley and Sons, Inc., 1978), Chapter 9.

[7] Webster and Wind, *Organizational Buying Behavior,* pp. 45–46.

[8] Charles O'Neal and Kate Bertrand, *Developing a Winning J.I.T. Marketing Strategy: The Industrial Marketer's Guide* (Englewood Cliffs, NJ: Prentice-Hall, Inc., 1991).

THE GLOBAL MARKETPLACE
Negotiating with the Japanese

International business negotiations can break down through failures in cross-cultural communications, even when both parties have much to gain from an agreement. Cultural understanding begins with a sensitivity to cultural differences and a willingness to learn more about the precise meaning of *agreement* in the host culture. Negotiating with Japanese executives is a lengthy exercise, not only because of cultural gaps, but also because the Japanese will not take a position until they have achieved an internal consensus among a great many organization members. However, because of this internal consensus, the Japanese organization can move very quickly once an agreement is reached.

Patience, a virtue in Japan, can also be used as a valuable negotiating tool, especially with impatient Americans. Misreading the situation, U.S. executives often make ill-considered concessions just to keep negotiations moving forward. Ultimately, the Japanese prefer broad agreement rather than a detailed contract. "Like the Greeks, the Japanese do not view the signing of a contract as the end of negotiations. Japanese firms want long-term, exclusive business relations based on *Kan,* a word that can be translated as 'emotional attunement.'"

Source: Franklin R. Root, *Entry Strategies for International Markets* (Lexington Books, 1987), pp. 252–255; see also John L. Graham, "The Influence of Culture on the Process of Business Negotiations: An Exploratory Study," *Journal of Business Studies,* 16 (Spring 1985), pp. 81–96.

The rate of technological change in an industry influences the composition of the decision-making unit in the buying organization.[9] As the pace of technological change increases, the importance of the purchasing manager in the buying process declines. Technical and engineering personnel tend to be more important to the organizational buying process in which the rate of technological change is great.

In the face of rapidly changing technology, buying organizations often use technological procedures to help them forecast the periods in which major changes in technology might occur. The marketer must also actively monitor signs of technological change and be prepared to adapt marketing strategy to deal with new technological environments. Because the most recent wave of technological change is as dramatic as any in history, the implications for organizational decision making are profound and involve changing definitions of industries, new sources of competition, changing product life cycles, and the increased globalization of markets.[10]

---

[9] Bonoma and Zaltman, "Introduction," p. 22.

[10] Noel Capon and Rashi Glazer, "Marketing and Technology: A Strategic Coalignment," *Journal of Marketing,* 51 (July 1987), pp. 1–14.

Environmental Uncertainty

Robert Spekman and Louis Stern suggest that as the information needs of buying groups grow in response to higher environmental uncertainty (e.g., changes in company leadership, or in economic conditions), more people participate in making buying decisions. Spekman and Stern's research indicates further that the influence of the purchasing agent increases with the level of environmental uncertainty. Why? As a firm's external environment becomes more unstable, the information processing function of the purchasing agent "becomes central to a firm's ability to effectively gather, analyze, and act on relevant environmental information,"[11] and purchasing agents thus become more influential.[12] This research highlights the importance of monitoring key environmental trends and tracing their impact on the organizational buying process.

Environmental Influences: Boundaries of the Organizational Buying Process

Collectively, these environmental influences define the general business conditions, the political and legal setting, the availability of products and services, and the values and norms that constrain buying actions. In addition, the environment provides to the organization a stream of information, including marketing communications.[13]

ORGANIZATIONAL FORCES

Understanding the buying organization requires understanding the larger system of interdependent elements. The interaction between purchasing managers and personnel in other departments in the firm can be viewed as an open social action system.[14] The action system consists of a repetitive cycle of purchasing, transforming, and distributing inputs into outputs. Thus, the parts of the organization are joined by the cyclic flow of authority, of work, of information, and of decision processes. Organizational buying processes reflect a history of interaction patterns and a corresponding set of formal and informal relationships that have been nurtured and developed.[15]

Since organizations have unique "personalities," the industrial salesperson must be sensitive to the climate or culture of an organization and also to where the purchasing function is positioned in the executive hierarchy. Both the organizational climate and the status of purchasing vary from firm to firm.

---

[11] Robert E. Spekman and Louis W. Stern, "Environmental Uncertainty and Buying Group Structure: An Empirical Investigation," *Journal of Marketing*, 43 (Spring 1979), p. 56.

[12] Robert E. Spekman, "Information and Influence: An Exploratory Investigation of the Boundary Role Person's Basis of Power," *Academy of Management Journal*, 22 (March 1979), pp. 104–117.

[13] Webster and Wind, *Organizational Buying Behavior*, p. 41.

[14] Robert W. Ruekert and Orville C. Walker, Jr., "Marketing's Interaction with Other Functional Units: A Conceptual Framework and Empirical Evidence," *Journal of Marketing*, 51 (January 1987), pp. 1–19.

[15] John R. Ronchetto, Jr., Michael D. Hutt, and Peter H. Reingen, "Embedded Influence Patterns in Organizational Buying Systems," *Journal of Marketing*, 53 (October 1989), pp. 51–62.

TABLE 4.1   **Selected Dimensions of Organizational Climate**

Dimension	Description
Achievement motivation	The degree to which the organization attempts to excel
Rules orientation	The degree to which rules are revered and followed
Readiness to innovate	The degree to which the organization encourages innovative activity
Industriousness	The degree to which hard work is expected of organizational members

Source: Adapted with modifications from Derek S. Pugh, "The Aston Program Perspective," in Andrew H. Van de Ven and William F. Joyce, eds., *Perspectives on Organization Design and Behavior* (New York: John Wiley and Sons, 1981), p. 155.

Organizational Climate

"In some organizations one may sense spontaneity, happiness, creativity—a place on the go. In other organizations the climate may crackle with tension. Organizational climate can provide one immediate indication of the health or sickness of an organization."[16] Two competitive organizations of comparable size may present markedly different organizational climates. One may encourage innovation and freely allow deviations from rules, the other may be rule oriented and tradition bound.

By understanding the climate of a potential buying organization (Table 4.1), the industrial salesperson can tailor a selling strategy to fit the particular personality of the organization.[17]

Organizational Positioning of Purchasing

An organization that centralizes procurement decisions will approach purchasing differently than will a company where purchasing decisions are made at individual user locations. When purchasing is centralized, a separate organizational unit is given authority for purchases at a regional, divisional, or headquarters level. For example, Mead Corporation's centralized purchasing function serves as a central point for the purchase of common materials used by Mead plants across the United States. Boeing, AT&T, 3M, and Xerox are among other corporations that emphasize centralized procurement.[18] At Xerox, for example, centralized commodity managers buy for all plants worldwide. A marketer who is sensitive to organizational influences can more

---

[16] Kenyon B. DeGreene, *The Adaptive Organization: Anticipation and Management of Crisis* (New York: John Wiley and Sons, 1982), p. 31. See also William J. Qualls and Christopher Puto, "Organizational Climate and Decision Framing: An Integrated Approach to Analyzing Industrial Buying Decisions," *Journal of Marketing Research,* 26 (May 1989), pp. 179–92.

[17] Thomas S. Robertson and Yoram Wind, "Organizational Psychographics and Innovativeness," *Journal of Consumer Research,* 7 (June 1980), pp. 24–31.

[18] For example, see Margaret Nelson, "3M Centralizes Its Office Buy," *Purchasing,* 99 (June 27, 1985), pp. 58–61.

accurately map the decision-making process, isolate buying influentials, identify salient buying criteria, and target marketing strategy for both types of organization.

Centralization versus Decentralization

Centralized and decentralized procurement differ substantially.[19] Centralization leads to specialization. Purchasing specialists for selected items develop comprehensive knowledge of supply and demand conditions, vendor options, supplier cost factors, and other information relevant to the supply environment. This knowledge, and the significant volume of business that specialists control, enhances their buying strength and supplier options.

The priority given to selected buying criteria is also influenced by centralization or decentralization. By identifying the buyer's organizational domain, the marketer can generally identify the purchasing manager's objectives. Centralized purchasing units place more weight on long-term supply availability and the development of a healthy supplier complex. Decentralized buyers may be more concerned with short-term cost efficiency and profit considerations. Organizational buying behavior is greatly influenced by the monitoring system that measures the performance of the unit.

Personal selling skills and the brand preferences of users influence purchasing decisions more at user locations than at centralized buying locations. At user locations, "engineers and other technical personnel, in particular, are prone to be specific in their preferences, while nonspecialized, nontechnical buyers have neither the technical expertise nor the status to challenge them,"[20] as can purchasing specialists at central locations. Differing priorities between central buyers and local users often lead to conflict in the buying organization. In stimulating demand at the user level, the marketer should assess the potential for conflict and attempt to develop a strategy that can resolve any differences between the two organizational units.

The organization of the marketer's selling strategy should parallel the organization of the purchasing function of key accounts. To avoid disjointed selling activities and internal conflict in the sales organization, many business marketers have developed national account management programs to establish a close working relationship "which cuts across multiple levels, functions, and operating units in both the buying and selling organizations."[21] Thus, the trend toward the centralization of the procurement function on the buying side has been matched by the development of national account management programs on the selling side.

---

[19] Joseph A. Bellizzi and Joseph J. Belonax, "Centralized and Decentralized Buying Influences," *Industrial Marketing Management,* 11 (April 1982), pp. 111–115; Arch G. Woodside and David M. Samuel, "Observation of Centralized Corporate Procurement," *Industrial Marketing Management,* 10 (July 1981), pp. 191–205; and E. Raymond Corey, *The Organizational Context of Industrial Buying Behavior* (Cambridge, Mass.: Marketing Science Institute, 1978), pp. 6–12.

[20] Corey, *The Organizational Context,* p. 13.

[21] Benson P. Shapiro and Rowland T. Moriarty, *National Account Management: Emerging Insights* (Cambridge, Mass.: Marketing Science Institute, 1982), p. 8; see also Michael D. Hutt, Wesley J. Johnston, and John R. Ronchetto, Jr., "Selling Centers and Buying Centers: Formulating Strategic Exchange Patterns," *Journal of Personal Selling and Sales Management,* 5 (May 1985), pp. 33–40.

TABLE 4.2   **Factors Contributing to the Centralization of Procurement**

Factor	Description
Commonality of requirements	Two or more procuring units within the organization have common requirements (e.g., sugar and packaging material at General Foods).
Cost-saving potential	Opportunity to strengthen bargaining position, secure lower prices through the aggregation of a firm's total requirements, and achieve economies in inventory control.
Structure of supply industry	Opportunity to consolidate purchasing power and secure favorable terms and service when a few large sellers dominate the supply industry.
Involvement of engineering in purchasing	If engineering involvement is high, purchasing group and the engineering group must be in close organizational and physical proximity.

Source: Adapted from E. Raymond Corey, *The Organizational Context of Industrial Buying Behavior* (Cambridge, Mass.: Marketing Science Institute, 1978), pp. 99–12.

Centralization of Procurement: Contributing Factors

Why is there a trend toward centralizing purchasing? Factors that strongly contribute to this trend are highlighted in Table 4.2.

An organization with multiple plant locations can often achieve cost savings by pooling requirements. Before the procurement function was centralized at General Motors, 106 buying locations spent more than $10 million annually on nearly 24 million pairs of work gloves, buying over 200 styles from 90 sources. The cost savings generated from pooling the requirements for this item alone are substantial.

The nature of the supply environment also can determine whether purchasing is centralized. If the supply environment is dominated by a few large sellers, centralized buying may be particularly useful in securing favorable terms and proper service. If the supply industry consists of many small firms, each covering limited geographical areas, decentralized purchasing may achieve better support.

Finally, note in Table 4.2 that the location of purchasing in the organization often hinges on the location of key buying influences. If engineering plays an active role in the purchasing process, the purchasing function must be in close organizational and physical proximity.

Marketing Implications

Two organizations, with seemingly identical purchasing requirements, may have entirely different philosophies about the "proper" location of the purchasing function, and they may use different operating procedures and markedly different criteria to evaluate suppliers. The marketer who recognizes such differences is best equipped to satisfy their needs.

GROUP FORCES

Purchasing managers rarely make a buying decision independent of the influence of others in the organization.[22] The organizational buying process typically involves a complex set of smaller decisions made or influenced by several individuals. Thus, multiple buying influences and group forces are critical in organizational buying decisions (see Chapter 3). The degree of involvement of group members in the procurement process varies from routine rebuys, in which the purchasing agent simply takes into account the preferences of others, to complex new-task buying situations, in which a group plays an active role throughout the decision process.

The industrial salesperson must address three questions.

- Which organizational members take part in the buying process?
- What is each member's relative influence in the decision?
- What criteria are important to each member in evaluating prospective suppliers?

The salesperson who can correctly answer these questions is ideally prepared to meet the needs of a buying organization and has a high probability of becoming the chosen supplier.

Buying Center

The concept of the buying center (see Chapter 3) provides rich insights into the role of group forces in organizational buying behavior.[23] The buying center, which includes all the organizational members involved in the purchase decision, is an "informal, cross-departmental decision unit in which the primary objective is the acquisition, impartation, and processing of relevant purchasing-related information."[24] The size of the buying center varies, but an average buying center will include more than four persons per purchase; the number of people involved in all stages of one purchase may be as many as 20.[25]

---

[22] Robert J. Thomas, "Correlates of Interpersonal Purchase Influence in Organizations," *Journal of Consumer Research,* 9 (September 1982), pp. 171–182; see also Yoram Wind, "Preference of Relevant Others and Individual Choice Models," *Journal of Consumer Research,* 3 (August 1976), pp. 50–57.

[23] For a comprehensive review of buying center research, see Robert E. Spekman and Kjell Gronhaug, "Conceptual and Methodological Issues in Buying Center Research," *European Journal of Marketing,* 20, 7 (1986), pp. 50–63; Morry Ghingold and David T. Wilson, "Buying Center Structure: An Extended Framework for Research," in Robert E. Spekman and David T. Wilson, eds., *A Strategic Approach to Business Marketing* (Chicago: American Marketing Association, 1985), pp. 180–193; Wesley J. Johnston and Robert E. Spekman, "Industrial Buying Behavior: A Need for an Integrative Approach," *Journal of Business Research,* 10 (June 1982), pp. 135–146; Johnston and Thomas V. Bonoma, "The Buying Center: Structure and Interaction Patterns," *Journal of Marketing,* 45 (Summer 1981), pp. 143–156; Johnston, "Industrial Buying Behavior: A State of the Art Review," in Ben M. Enis and Kenneth J. Roering, eds., *Review of Marketing 1981* (Chicago: American Marketing Association, 1981), pp. 75–87; Yoram Wind, "The Organizational Buying Center: A Research Agenda," in Gerald Zaltman and Thomas V. Bonoma, eds., *Organizational Buying Behavior* (Chicago: American Marketing Association, 1978), pp. 67–76.

[24] Spekman and Stern, "Environmental Uncertainty and Buying Group Structure," p. 56.

[25] For example, see Kate Bertrand, "Survey Finds Many 'Critical' Buying Criteria," *Business Marketing,* 72 (April 1986), pp. 30–31.

TABLE 4.3 **The Involvement of Buying Center Participants at Different Stages of the Procurement Process**

Buying Center	Stages of Procurement Process for a Medical Equipment Purchase			
	Identification of Need	Establishment of Objectives	Identification and Evaluation of Buying Alternatives	Selection of Suppliers
Physicians	High	High	High	High
Nursing	Low	High	High	Low
Administration	Moderate	Moderate	Moderate	High
Engineering	Low	Moderate	Moderate	Low
Purchasing	Low	Low	Low	Moderate

Source: Adapted by permission of the publisher from "An Empirical Study of Hospital Buying," by Gene R. Laczniak, *Industrial Marketing Management*, 8 (January 1979), p. 61. Copyright © 1979 by Elsevier Science Publishing Co., Inc.

The composition of the buying center may change from one purchasing situation to another and is not prescribed by the organizational chart. A buying group evolves during the purchasing process in response to the information requirements of the specific purchase situation. Because organizational buying is a *process* rather than an isolated act, different individuals are important to the process at different times.[26] A design engineer may exert significant influence early in the purchasing process when product specifications are being established; others may assume a more dominant role in later phases. A salesperson must define the buying situation and the information requirements from the organization's perspective in order to anticipate the size and composition of the buying center. Again, the composition of the buying center evolves during the purchasing process, varies from firm to firm, and varies from one purchasing situation to another.

Composition

An important first step in defining the buying center is to define the buying situation and to determine whether the firm is in the early or later stages of the procurement decision-making process. The buying center for a new-task buying situation in the not-for-profit market is presented in Table 4.3. The product, intensive-care monitoring systems, is a complex and costly purchase. Buying center members are drawn from five functional areas, each participating to varying degrees in the decision process. A marketer who concentrated exclusively on the purchasing function would be overlooking key buying influentials.

Because the purchasing function is an easily identifiable element in buying centers in all sectors of the business market, it often provides a convenient starting point for

[26] Gary L. Lilien and M. Anthony Wong, "Exploratory Investigation of the Structure of the Buying Center in the Metalworking Industry," *Journal of Marketing Research*, 21 (February 1984), pp. 1–11.

the industrial salesperson who is attempting to piece together the membership of the buying center. Company policy may dictate that the industrial salesperson must first touch base with the purchasing department before meeting with others. Purchasing managers frown on attempts to bypass purchasing in order to initiate contact at other points in the organization. The purchasing manager plays an important gatekeeping role, controlling the flow of information and the access of salespersons to other members of the buying center. Yet, although purchasing managers can readily identify the individuals included in the buying center, they are often inaccurate in estimating the relative impact of each member on the purchasing decision.[27]

Tracing Communication Flows

Wesley Johnston provides a graphic description of the probable buying center for capital equipment.[28] In Figure 4.2, engineering, purchasing, and manufacturing interact with each other and are central to the buying process for capital equipment. Purchasing and, to a lesser extent, engineering communicate directly with potential industrial suppliers. Accounting and finance, sales and marketing, and receiving play minor supporting roles.

The salesperson should give special attention to a department, such as manufacturing, that is central to the flow of communications within the buying center. Because of their greater access to information and resources, well-connected individuals or departments gain influence.[29] Manufacturing is the only functional area to interact heavily with top management within the buying center, yet few industrial salespersons made direct sales calls on top management or on manufacturing. From the industrial salesperson's perspective, "not going high enough in the buying organization to influence the decision could see many hours of marketing effort overruled."[30]

In approaching a particular buying organization, the industrial salesperson should attempt the following:

1. Define the functional areas that will be involved in a particular buying decision, identifying the organizational member(s) who will represent each area.

2. Examine the patterns of communication within the buying center.

3. Forecast the possible role of top management in the buying process.

---

[27] For a discussion of methodological issues that relate to buying center research, see Alvin J. Silk and Manohar U. Kalwani, "Measuring Influence in Organizational Purchase Decisions," *Journal of Marketing Research*, 19 (May 1982), pp. 165–181; Rowland T. Moriarty and John E. G. Bateson, "Exploring Complex Decision Making Units: A New Approach," *Journal of Marketing Research*, 19 (May 1982), pp. 182–191; Johnston and Spekman, "Industrial Buying Behavior: A Need for an Integrative Approach," pp. 135–146; and Lynn W. Phillips, "Assessing Measurement Error in Key Informant Reports: A Methodological Note on Organizational Analysis in Marketing," *Journal of Marketing Research*, 18 (November 1981), pp. 395–415.

[28] Wesley J. Johnston, *Patterns in Industrial Buying Behavior* (New York: Praeger Publishers, 1981); see also Michael D. Hutt and Peter H. Reingen, "Social Network Analysis: Emergent versus Prescribed Patterns in Organizational Buying Behavior," in Melanie Wallendorf and Paul Anderson, eds., *Advances in Consumer Research*, 14 (Ann Arbor, MI: Association for Consumer Research, 1986), pp. 259–263.

[29] Ronchetto, Hutt, and Reingen, "Embedded Influence Patterns in Organizational Buying Systems," pp. 51–62.

[30] Johnston and Bonoma,"The Buying Center," p. 154.

FIGURE 4.2   **The Probable Buying Center for Capital-Equipment Purchases**

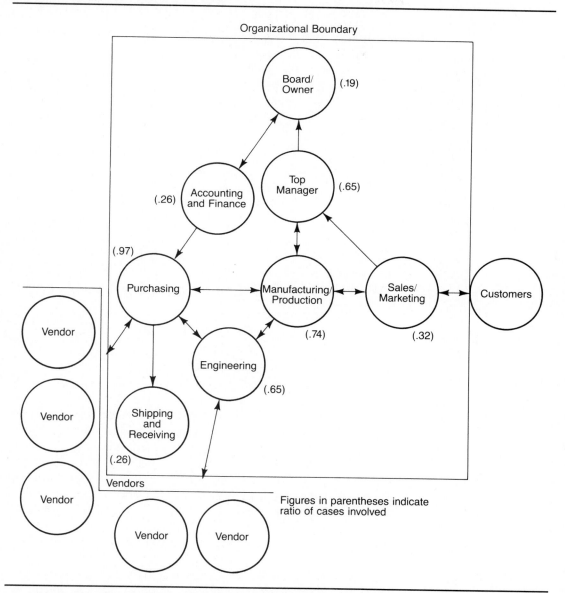

Source: Wesley J. Johnston, *Patterns in Industrial Buying Behavior* (New York: Praeger Publishers, a division of Greenwood Press, Inc., 1981), p. 132. Copyright © 1981 by Praeger Publishers. Reprinted with permission.

Predicting Composition

A marketer can also predict the composition of the buying center by projecting the impact of the industrial product on various functional areas in the buying organization.[31] If the procurement decision will affect the marketability of a firm's product (e.g., product design, price), the marketing department will be active in the decision process. Engineering will be influential in decisions about new capital equipment, materials, and components; setting specifications; defining product performance requirements; and qualifying potential vendors. Manufacturing executives will be included in the buying center for procurement decisions that affect the production mechanism (e.g., the acquisition of materials or parts used in production). When procurement decisions involve a substantial economic commitment or impinge on strategic or policy matters, top management will have considerable influence.

Influencing Composition

The marketer can sometimes influence the composition of the buying center. To illustrate, the desirable attributes of a new material-handling system can best be understood and appreciated by a warehouse supervisor. By directing marketing communications (advertising and personal selling) to receptive users of the product, the marketer can draw them into the buying center and stimulate their active involvement in the procurement process.

The Buying Committee

In some organizations, representatives from several departments make up a committee charged with making a particular purchasing decision. At United Technologies Corporation, for example, 15 separate purchasing councils have been assembled to direct purchasing policy for particular types of requirements such as electronics, bearings, and forgings.[32] The buying committee thus constitutes a more formalized buying center. Universities, hospitals, and industrial firms may assemble a temporary buying committee to choose a computer system; food retailers may use permanent buying committees meeting regularly for multiple decisions such as which new food products should be given shelf space.[33] The philosophy underlying the committee concept is that (1) various viewpoints and a wider range of experience are applied to the decision-making process, (2) decisions are made more scientifically, and (3) the level of pressure in the buyer–seller relationship is lowered.

The industrial salesperson may not be given the opportunity to make a presentation before the full committee, but only to individual committee members. Here the salesperson must provide the accessible committee members with product-related information that may be pertinent to the interests of the inaccessible members.

---

[31] Corey, *The Organizational Context of Industrial Buying Behavior,* pp. 28–36.

[32] "Advice and Consent: United Technologies," *Purchasing,* 100 (November 6, 1986), p. 107.

[33] Michael D. Hutt, "The Retail Buying Committee: A Look at Cohesiveness and Leadership," *Journal of Retailing,* 55 (Winter 1979), pp. 87–97.

INSIDE BUSINESS MARKETING
Stealing a Satisfied Customer

How can a salesperson convince customers to make a change—even when they are perfectly happy with their current supplier? Seasoned experts offer these guidelines.

First, center on those customers who are most likely to benefit substantially from your firm's special capabilities, products, and services. Second, develop a keen understanding of the target company, its industry, and how your product/service package compares to the offerings of competitors. Third, open a dialogue with key decision makers at the target company and listen carefully while probing for their real concerns and problems.

Consider the experience of Bill Meyer, vice president of sales at Chemineer Corporation.

The firm makes fluid agitation and mixing equipment for pharmaceutical, chemical, and paper plants. During a visit to a major chemical company, he perceived that the key decision makers were uneasy about how the required mixing equipment could be installed for a new chemical process. They were particularly concerned about the noise and vibrations that the unusually large mixing tanks might create. The established supplier appeared to be unaware of their concerns. Since Chemineer had already designed and installed a large mixer for a comparable application, Bill responded to their needs and took a $1 million contract out from under a complacent supplier.

Source: Edward Doherty, "How to Steal a Satisfied Customer," *Sales and Marketing Management* (March 1990), p. 41.

Questions and problems that may arise when the committee convenes should be anticipated and addressed.

By working through a liaison to the buying committee, the salesperson attempts to create an advocate for the industrial firm's offering. Ideally, the targeted advocate should possess the required technical expertise and the ability to articulate clearly and convincingly the arguments favoring the vendor.[34] The marketer also should note that the most influential member of the buying group cannot necessarily be determined by comparing the organizational rank of committee members. Past product-related experience, technical expertise, personality traits, and other personal and organizational factors determine the structure of the decision-making unit and the relative influence of individual participants.

Buying Center Influence

Members of the buying center assume different roles throughout the procurement process (Table 4.4); they may be users, influencers, buyers, deciders, and gatekeepers.[35] One person could assume all roles in a purchase situation or each individual could assume a different buying role. To illustrate, as users, personnel from marketing,

---

[34] Robert E. Krapfel, Jr., "An Advocacy Behavior Model of Organizational Buyers' Vendor Choice," *Journal of Marketing,* 49 (Fall 1985), pp. 51–59.

[35] Webster and Wind, *Organizational Buying Behavior,* p. 77.

TABLE 4.4   **Buying Center Roles Defined**

Role	Description
Users	As the role name implies, users are the personnel who will be using the product in question. Users may have anywhere from inconsequential to an extremely important influence on the purchase decision. In some cases, the users initiate the purchase action by requesting the product. They may even develop the product specifications.
Gatekeepers	Gatekeepers control information to be reviewed by other members of the buying center. The control of information may be accomplished by disseminating printed information such as advertisements or by controlling which salesperson will speak to which individuals in the buying center. To illustrate, the purchasing agent might perform this screening role by opening the gate to the buying center for some sales personnel and closing it to others.
Influencers	Influencers affect the purchasing decision by supplying information for the evaluation of alternatives or by setting buying specifications. Typically, technical personnel, such as engineers, quality control personnel, and R&D personnel are significant influences on the purchase decision. Sometimes, individuals outside the buying organization can assume this role (e.g., an engineering consultant or an architect who writes very tight building specifications).
Deciders	Deciders are the individuals who actually make the buying decision, whether or not they have the formal authority to do so. The identity of the decider is the most difficult role to determine: buyers may have formal authority to buy, but the president of the firm may actually make the decision. A decider could be a design engineer who develops a set of specifications that only one vendor can meet.
Buyers	The buyer has formal authority for selecting a supplier and for implementing all procedures connected with securing the product. The power of the buyer is often usurped by more powerful members of the organization. The buyer's role is often assumed by the purchasing agent, who executes the clerical functions associated with a purchase order.

Source: Adapted from Frederick E. Webster, Jr., and Yoram Wind, *Organizational Buying Behavior* (Englewood Cliffs, N.J.: Prentice-Hall, 1972), pp. 77–80.

accounting, purchasing, and production may all have a stake in which new computer is selected. Thus, the buying center can be a very complex organizational phenomenon.

Identifying Patterns of Influence

Key influencers are frequently located outside the purchasing department. Research suggests that the buying center for highly technical products includes the purchasing agent, scientists, engineers, and other managers—with the scientists having the greatest level of influence in the buying group.[36]

A study of the purchasing process for component parts found that only half of product or vendor selection decisions are made by the purchasing department.[37] Functional areas such as design and development engineering, research, and production engineering dominate project initiation and the specification of requirements.

---

[36] James R. McMillan, "Role Differentiation in Industrial Buying Decisions," in *Proceedings of the American Marketing Association* (Chicago: American Marketing Association, 1973), pp. 207–211; see also James R. Cooley, Donald W. Jackson, Jr., and Lonnie L. Ostrom, "Analyzing the Relative Power of Participants in Industrial Buying Decisions," in *Proceedings of the American Marketing Association* (Chicago: American Marketing Association, 1977), pp. 243–246.

[37] Scientific American, Inc., *How Industry Buys/1970* (New York: Scientific American, Inc., 1969), pp. 1–5.

Similar influence patterns emerge in the acquisition of materials and capital equipment. Here researchers found that the typical capital equipment purchase involved an average of four departments, three levels of the management hierarchy (e.g., manager, regional manager, vice president), and seven different individuals.[38] It is interesting to note that a comparative study of organizational buying behavior found striking similarities across four countries (United States, United Kingdom, Australia, and Canada) with regard to the involvement of various departments in the procurement process.[39]

Based on their buying center research, Donald W. Jackson, Jr., and his colleagues provide these strategy recommendations: "Marketing efforts will depend upon which individuals of the buying center are more influential for a given decision. Since engineering and manufacturing are more influential in product selection decisions, they may have to be sold on product characteristics. On the other hand, since purchasing is most influential in supplier selection decisions, they may have to be sold on company characteristics."[40]

Understanding the Power Culture[41]

A key to identifying buying influentials rests on understanding the types of power that organization members either have or appear to have. Unfortunately, one cannot identify powerful buying center members merely by examining a company's organizational chart. Five major power bases are identified in Table 4.5. Note that organization members can derive power from the rewards they can provide for compliance (reward power), or from the penalties they can impose for noncompliance (coercive power). Power can likewise accrue as a result of expertise, personal charm, or status in the organization. Compared to other bases, research suggests that expert power may be the most dominant in shaping preference patterns within the buying center.[42]

By assessing the power culture of a buying organization, the salesperson can more readily identify buying center members, predict the role (e.g., influencer or decider) of each member in the buying process, and estimate the level of each member's influence on the final buying decision. Sensitivity to which power base is likely to be most influential to a particular buying center member can also help the salesperson to develop a personal selling strategy; a manufacturing executive, for example, may rely on personal expertise when new automated production equipment is being considered, thereby requiring a more technical sales presentation.

---

[38] Johnston and Bonoma, "The Buying Center," pp. 143–156; see also Lilien and Wong, "An Exploratory Investigation of the Structure of the Buying Center," pp. 1–11.

[39] Peter Banting, David Ford, Andrew Gross, and George Holmes, "Similarities in Industrial Procurement across Four Countries," *Industrial Marketing Management,* 14 (May 1985), pp. 133–144.

[40] Donald W. Jackson, Jr., Janet E. Keith, and Richard K. Burdick, "Purchasing Agents' Perceptions of Industrial Buying Center Influence: A Situational Approach," *Journal of Marketing,* 48 (Fall 1984), pp. 75–83.

[41] This section is largely based on Thomas V. Bonoma, "Major Sales: Who *Really* Does the Buying?" *Harvard Business Review,* 60 (May–June 1982), pp. 111–119.

[42] Robert J. Thomas, "Bases of Power in Organizational Buying Decisions," *Industrial Marketing Management,* 13 (October 1984), pp. 209–216; see also Ajay Kohli, "Determinants of Influence in Organizational Buying: A Contingency Approach," *Journal of Marketing,* 53 (July 1989), pp. 50–64.

TABLE 4.5   **Bases of Power**

Type of Power	Description
Reward	Ability to provide monetary, social, political, or psychological rewards to others for compliance
Coercive	Ability to provide monetary or other punishments for noncompliance
Attraction	Ability to elicit compliance from others because they like you
Expert	Ability to elicit compliance from others because of technical expertise, either actual or reputed
Status	Compliance-gaining ability derived from a legitimate position of power in a company

Source: John R. P. French and Bertram Raven, "The Bases of Social Power," in Dorwin Cartwright, ed., *Studies in Social Power* (Ann Arbor, MI: University of Michigan Pres, 1959), pp. 150–167, cited in Thomas V. Bonoma, "Major Sales: Who *Really* Does the Buying?" *Harvard Business Review,* 60 (May–June 1982), pp. 111–119.

The Influence of Purchasing

Purchasing assumes a position of power in the buying center when procurement decisions are "in a steady-state condition, that is, when the design of the purchased product is established and vendors have been qualified."[43] Likewise, purchasing is dominant in repetitive buying situations by virtue of technical expertise, knowledge of the dynamics of the supplying industry, and close working relationships with individual suppliers. Recall from Chapter 3 that purchasing managers also assume a central role in evaluating the capabilities and performance of suppliers.

Factors that contribute to purchasing's strength include (1) its level of technical competence and credibility, (2) its base of relevant information, (3) its base of top management support, and (4) its organizational status as an authority in selected procurement areas.[44] Purchasing agents appear to be motivated by a strong desire to enhance their status and position within the organization.[45] The marketer cannot make sweeping generalizations concerning the typical level of power that purchasing possesses in the buying center, but must concentrate on the relative importance of purchasing in the particular buying situation and organizational context.

INDIVIDUAL FORCES

Individuals, not organizations, make buying decisions. Each member of the buying center has a unique personality, a particular set of learned experiences, a specified organizational function, and a perception of how best to achieve both personal and

---

[43] E. Raymond Corey, *The Organizational Context of Industrial Buying Behavior,* p. 34; see also Gloria P. Thomas and John F. Grashof, "Impact of Internal and External Environmental Stability on the Existence of Determinant Buying Rules," *Journal of Business Research,* 10 (June 1982), pp. 159–168.

[44] Corey, ibid., pp. 34–35.

[45] George Strauss, "Tactics of Lateral Relationship," *Administrative Science Quarterly,* 7 (September 1962), pp. 161–186.

ETHICAL BUSINESS MARKETING
Gift Giving and Gift Taking in the Business Market

What policies do industrial firms set on accepting gifts from suppliers?

Practicing purchasing managers, representing 344 manufacturers, were asked about their firms' policies on buyers accepting gifts from suppliers. The results clearly indicate that most manufacturing firms with over 200 employees have made a formal attempt to address the vexing problem of gift giving. Approximately 75 percent of these firms have either said "no gifts" or have set a definite dollar limit on gifts. Most of the remaining firms that reported they have no policy on gifts were small manufac-

turers with fewer than 200 employees. Interestingly, the research also found that 35 percent of the firms have one set of rules on "gift taking" for purchasing personnel, and allow different gift-taking and gift-giving rules to exist for executives in other departments (such as sales or engineering).

Some companies allow gift giving but not gift taking. This raises a challenging question: Should a business marketing firm have one set of rules on gift taking for its buyers and a different set of rules on gift giving to its customers? What do you think?

Source: Monroe M. Bird, "Gift-Giving and Gift-Taking in Industrial Companies," *Industrial Marketing Management*, 18 (May 1989), pp. 91–94.

organizational goals. To understand the organizational buyer, the marketer should be aware of individual perceptions of the buying situation.

Differing Evaluative Criteria

Evaluative criteria are specifications that organizational buyers use to compare alternative industrial products and services; however, these may conflict. Industrial product users generally value prompt delivery and efficient servicing; engineering values product quality, standardization, and pretesting; and purchasing assigns the most importance to maximum price advantage and economy in shipping and forwarding.[46]

Product perceptions and evaluative criteria differ among organizational decision makers as a result of differences in educational backgrounds, source and type of information exposure, interpretation and retention of relevant information (perceptual distortion), and level of satisfaction with past purchases.[47] Engineers have a different educational background from plant managers or purchasing agents; they are exposed to different journals, attend different conferences, and possess different professional goals and values. A sales presentation that is effective with purchasing may be entirely off the mark with engineering.

---

[46]Jagdish N. Sheth, "A Model of Industrial Buyer Behavior," p. 51.

[47]Ibid., pp. 52–54.

Understanding the Reward and Measurement Systems[48]

What factors motivate individual decision makers during the organizational buying process? According to Paul Anderson and Terry Chambers, they are motivated largely by the following:

1. *Intrinsic rewards.* Rewards are attained on a personal basis (e.g., feelings of accomplishment or self-worth).

2. *Extrinsic rewards.* Rewards are distributed by the organization (e.g., salary increases or promotions).

In an experimental setting, the research demonstrated that purchasing managers preferred and chose those vendors that would allow them to attain maximum extrinsic rewards. Thus, the attributes individuals emphasize in evaluating alternative industrial suppliers are likely to reflect the reward and measurement systems of their primary work group. Also, individual expectations about the offerings of alternative suppliers will differ. Purchasing managers have been rewarded for one set of behaviors, such as reducing the cost of materials, whereas engineers have been rewarded for another, such as improving the quality of products. This difference will lead to conflicting advocacy positions within the buying group. How is this conflict resolved?

Recent research suggests that the more the informal and formal reward systems emphasize the local performance of departments, rather than their combined performance in meeting organizational goals, the more likely there is to be interdepartmental conflict in the buying process.[49] In such situations, the salesperson can develop strategies to manage conflict in the decision-making process. For example, the salesperson could create situations where the parties in conflict might be encouraged to confront the conflict and move toward problem solving. A product demonstration, where both departments are invited to participate, could be part of such a strategy.

Responsive Marketing Strategy

A marketer who is sensitive to differences in the product perceptions and evaluative criteria of individual buying center members is well equipped to prepare responsive marketing strategy. To illustrate, a research study examined the industrial adoption of solar air-conditioning systems and identified the criteria of importance to key decision makers (Table 4.6):[50] marketing communications directed at production engineers should center on operating costs and energy savings; heating and air-conditioning (HVAC) consultants should be addressed concerning noise level and initial cost of the system. Knowledge of the criteria that key buying center participants employ is of

---

[48] Paul F. Anderson and Terry M. Chambers, "A Reward/Measurement Model of Organizational Buying Behavior," *Journal of Marketing,* 49 (Spring 1985), pp. 7–23; see also Chambers, Anderson, and B. J. Dunlap, "Preferences, Intentions, and Behavior of Organizational Buyers under Different Reward Conditions," *Journal of Business Research,* 14 (December 1986), pp. 533–547.

[49] Donald W. Barclay, "Interdepartmental Conflict in Organizational Buying: The Impact of Organizational Context," *Journal of Marketing Research,* 28 (May 1991), forthcoming.

[50] Jean-Marie Choffray and Gary L. Lilien, "Assessing Response to Industrial Marketing Strategy," *Journal of Marketing,* 42 (April 1978), pp. 20–31.

TABLE 4.6   **Issues of Importance in the Formation of Individual Preferences**

Decision Makers	Key Importance	Less Importance
Production engineers	Operating cost Energy savings Reliability Complexity	First cost Field-proven
Corporate engineers	First cost Field-proven Reliability Complexity	Energy savings Up-to-date
Plant managers	Operating cost Use of unproductive areas Up-to-date Power failure protection	First cost Complexity
Top managers	Up-to-date Energy savings Operating cost	Noise level in plant Reliability
HVAC consultants	Noise level in plant First cost Reliability	Up-to-date Energy savings Operating cost

Source: Jean-Marie Choffray and Gary L. Lilien, "Assessing Response to Industrial Marketing Strategy," *Journal of Marketing,* 42 (April 1978), p. 30. Reprinted from the *Journal of Marketing,* published by the American Marketing Association.

significant operational value to the marketer when designing new products and when developing and targeting advertising and personal selling presentations.

Information Processing

Volumes of information flow into every organization through direct mail advertising, journal advertising, trade news, word of mouth, and personal sales presentations. What an individual organizational buyer chooses to pay attention to, comprehend, and retain has an important bearing on procurement decisions.

Selective Processes

Information processing is generally encompassed in the broader term **cognition**, which refers to "all the processes by which the sensory input is transformed, reduced, elaborated, stored, recovered, and used."[51] Important to an individual's cognitive structure are the processes of selective exposure, attention, perception, and retention.

1. *Selective exposure.* Individuals tend to accept communication messages that are consistent with their existing attitudes and beliefs. For this reason, a purchasing agent chooses to talk to some salespersons and not to others.

---

[51] U. Neisser, *Cognitive Psychology* (New York: Appleton, 1966), p. 4.

2. *Selective attention.* Individuals filter or screen incoming stimuli in order to admit only certain ones to cognition. Thus, an organizational buyer will be more likely to notice a trade advertisement if it is consistent with his or her needs and values.

3. *Selective perception.* Individuals tend to interpret stimuli in terms of their existing attitudes and beliefs. This explains why organizational buyers may modify or distort a salesperson's message in order to make it more consistent with their predispositions toward the company.

4. *Selective retention.* Individuals tend to store in memory only information pertinent to their own needs and dispositions. An organizational buyer may retain information concerning a particular brand because it matches his or her criteria.

Each of these selective processes influences the way an individual decision maker will respond to marketing stimuli. Because the procurement process often spans several months and because the marketer's contact with the buying organization is infrequent, marketing communications must be carefully designed and targeted.[52] Poorly conceived messages will be "tuned out" or immediately forgotten by key decision makers.

Memory

Some memory theorists hypothesize that individuals possess three types of memory storage systems:[53] a set of sensory stores (SS), a short-term memory store (STS), and a long-term memory store (LTS). According to this theory, information passes from the sense organs to a sensory store, where the information is lost in a fraction of a second unless attention is devoted to the stimulus. If, however, the information is processed, it moves into the STS, which has limited capacity. Here, information can be kept active by further processing. Active information in the STS can be retrieved quickly, and information in the LTS can be called upon as needed to interpret information. Thus, the STS is the center of current processing activity. Finally, part of this information, if properly processed, is transferred to the LTS, which is hypothesized to have unlimited capacity.

What information is likely to be stored? Information that is deemed important to achieving goals or that can be easily stored is likely to be assigned the highest priority.[54] The individual's expectation about how the information will be used also determines what is to be stored and how.

---

[52] Rowland T. Moriarty, Jr. and Robert E. Spekman, "An Empirical Investigation of the Information Sources Used During the Industrial Buying Process," *Journal of Marketing Research,* 21 (May 1984), pp. 137–147.

[53] R. C. Atkinson and Richard M. Shiffrin, "Human Memory: A Proposed System and Its Control Processes," in K. W. Spence and J. T. Spence, eds., *The Psychology of Learning and Motivation: Advances in Research and Theory, Vol 2* (New York: Academic Press, 1968), pp. 89–195, discussed in James R. Bettmen, "Memory Factors in Consumer Choice: A Review," *Journal of Marketing,* 43 (Spring 1979), pp. 37–53.

[54] Richard M. Shiffrin and R. C. Atkinson, "Storage and Retrieval Processes in Long-Term Memory," *Psychological Review,* 76 (1979), pp. 179–93, discussed in James Bettman, ibid.

External Memory

The organizational buyer does have an external memory, which can hold vast amounts of information. Catalogs, technical reports, and on-line computer systems are potential parts of this external memory. A purchasing agent may need to keep only a vendor's name in memory because extensive product-related information can be retrieved from external memory as the need arises. The marketer must therefore provide relevant information in a form that can be assimilated into the buying organization's external memory. Pamphlets and technical reports provided by the industrial salesperson are often retrieved from storage weeks later at critical stages in the procurement process.

Risk-Reduction Strategies

Individuals are motivated by a strong desire to reduce the level of risk in purchase decisions. The perceived risk concept (introduced in Chapter 3) includes two components: (1) uncertainty about the outcome of a decision, and (2) the magnitude of consequences associated with making the wrong choice.

In confronting "risky" purchase decisions, how do organizational buyers behave? Organizational buyers appear to use four risk-reduction strategies:[55]

1. External uncertainty reduction (e.g., visit supplier's plant)

2. Internal uncertainty reduction (e.g., consult with other buyers)

3. External consequences reduction (e.g., multiple sourcing)

4. Internal consequences reduction (e.g., consult with company's top management)

Organizational buyers can also reduce the level of risk by relying on familiar suppliers.[56] Because source loyalty provides the organizational buyer with a convenient method of reducing risk, it constitutes a significant barrier to the entry of an "out" supplier. This makes straight rebuy situations hard for the new supplier to break. When an organizational buyer selects a particular supplier and is rewarded for the decision, the probability of selecting the same supplier again increases.

The reputation of the supplier also influences the perceived level of risk. Theodore Levitt reports that well-known companies, recognized as credible sources, tend to be favored by decision makers facing high-risk decisions.[57] The importance of source credibility appears to increase as the level of perceived risk increases. A first-time purchaser of a computer may feel comfortable in dealing with a large, well-known manufacturer such as IBM.

---

[55] Timothy W. Sweeney, H. Lee Mathews, and David T. Wilson, "An Analysis of Industrial Buyers' Risk Reducing Behavior: Some Personality Correlates," *American Marketing Association Proceedings* (Chicago: American Marketing Association, 1973), pp. 217–221.

[56] For example, see Christopher P. Puto, Wesley E. Patton, III, and Ronald H. King, "Risk Handling Strategies in Industrial Vendor Selection Decisions," *Journal of Marketing,* 49 (Winter 1985), pp. 89–95.

[57] Theodore Levitt, *Industrial Purchasing Behavior: A Study of Communication Effects* (Boston: Division of Research, Graduate School of Business Administration, Harvard University, 1965).

Anticipating Perceived Risk Level

Industrial marketers should carefully consider the level of risk that their product will elicit for a particular buying organization and for specific decision makers. When introducing new products, entering new markets, or approaching new customers, the marketing strategist should evaluate the impact of alternative strategies on perceived risk.

Individual versus Group Decision Making

What factors determine whether a specific buying situation will be a group or an individual decision? Jagdish Sheth theorizes that the following influence the structure of the decision-making unit.[58]

Product-Specific Factors:

1. *Perceived risk.* The higher the level of perceived risk, the greater the likelihood that the decision will be made by a group.

2. *Type of purchase.* New-task buying situations are more likely to involve group decision making (e.g., a first-time purchase of a computer).

3. *Time pressure.* With minimal time constraints, group decision making becomes more feasible.

Company-Specific Factors:

1. *Size.* Large companies tend to use group decision making.

2. *Degree of centralization.* The more decentralized an organization, the more likely decisions will be made by a group.

Sheth notes that these factors are supported by research conducted in the organizational behavior area but that they need empirical verification in the industrial buying context.

THE ORGANIZATIONAL BUYING PROCESS: MAJOR ELEMENTS

The behavior of organizational buyers is influenced by environmental, organizational, group, and individual factors. Each of these spheres of influence has been discussed in an organizational buying context, with particular attention to how the industrial marketer should interpret these forces and, more important, factor them directly into marketing strategy planning. A model of the organizational buying process is presented

---

[58] Sheth, "A Model of Industrial Buyer Behavior," p. 54; see also W.E. Patton, III, Christopher P. Puto, and Ronald H. King, "Which Buying Decisions Are Made by Individuals and Not by Groups?" *Industrial Marketing Management,* 15 (May 1986), pp. 129–138.

in Figure 4.3, which serves to reinforce and integrate the key areas discussed so far in the chapter.[59]

This framework focuses on the relationship between an organization's buying center and the three major stages in the individual purchase decision process:

1. The screening of alternatives which do not meet organizational requirements

2. The formation of decision participants' preferences

3. The formation of organizational preferences

Observe that individual members of the buying center use various evaluative criteria and are exposed to various sources of information, which influence the industrial brands that are included in the buyer's **evoked set of alternatives**—the alternative brands that a buyer calls to mind when a need arises and that represent only a few of the many brands available.[60]

Environmental constraints and organizational requirements influence the procurement process by limiting the number of product alternatives that satisfy organizational needs. For example, capital equipment alternatives that exceed a particular cost (initial or operating) may be eliminated from further consideration. The remaining brands become the **feasible set of alternatives** for the organization, from which individual preferences are defined. The **interaction structure** of the members of the buying center, who have differing criteria and responsibilities, leads to the formation of organizational preferences and ultimately to organizational choice.[61]

An understanding of the organizational buying process allows the marketer to play an active rather than a passive role in stimulating market response. The marketer who identifies organizational screening requirements and the salient evaluative criteria of individual buying-center members can make more informed product design, pricing, and promotional decisions.

---

[59] Choffray and Lilien, "Assessing the Response to Industrial Marketing Strategy," pp. 20–31. Other models of organizational buying behavior include Webster and Wind, *Organizational Buying Behavior,* pp. 28–37; Sheth, "A Model of Industrial Buyer Behavior," pp. 50–56; Anderson and Chambers, "A Reward/Measurement Model of Organizational Buying Behavior," pp. 7–23; Parkinson and Baker, *Organizational Buying Behavior;* Thomas V. Bonoma, Gerald Zaltman, and Wesley J. Johnston, *Industrial Buying Behavior* (Cambridge, Mass.: Marketing Science Institute, 1977), Chapter 2; Rowland T. Moriarty and Morton Galper, *Organizational Buying Behavior: A State-of-the-Art Review and Conceptualization* (Cambridge, Mass.: Marketing Science Institute, 1978); Gene R. Laczniak and Patrick E. Murphy, "Fine Tuning Organizational Buying Models," in Charles W. Lamb and Patrick M. Dunne, Jr., eds., *Theoretical Developments in Marketing* (Chicago: American Marketing Association, 1980), pp. 77–80; Manoj K. Agarwal, Philip C. Burger, and David A. Reid, "A New Model of Organizational Buying Behavior," unpublished working paper (Binghamton: State University of New York, School of Management, 1982); and N. C. G. Campbell, "An Interaction Approach to Organizational Buying Behavior," *Journal of Business Research,* 13 (February 1985), pp. 35–48.

[60] John A. Howard and Jagdish N. Sheth, *The Theory of Buyer Behavior* (New York: John Wiley and Sons, 1969), p. 26; see also Ronald P. LeBlanc, "Environmental Impact on Purchase Decision Structure," *Journal of Purchasing and Materials Management,* 17 (Spring 1981), pp. 30–36; and Lowell E. Crow, Richard W. Olshavsky, and John O. Summers, "Industrial Buyers' Choice Strategies: A Protocol Analysis," *Journal of Marketing Research,* 17 (February 1980), pp. 34–44.

[61] W. C. Buss, "A Comparison of the Predictive Performance of Group–Preference Models," *Proceedings of the American Marketing Association No. 47* (Chicago: American Marketing Association 1981), pp. 174–177.

FIGURE 4.3   **Major Elements of Organizational Buying Behavior**

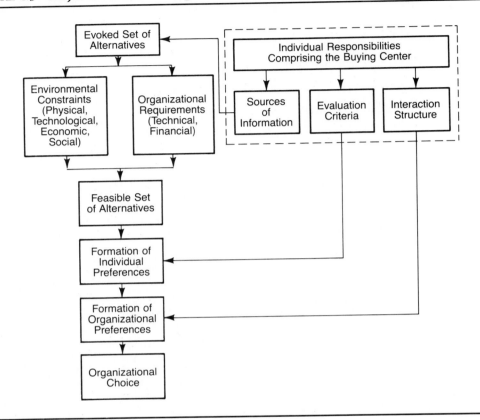

Source: Jean-Marie Choffray and Gary L. Lilien, "Assessing Response to Industrial Marketing Strategy," *Journal of Marketing*, 42 (April 1978), p. 22. Reprinted by permission of the American Marketing Association.

ORGANIZATIONAL BUYING BEHAVIOR: MARKETING STRATEGY IMPLICATIONS

In probing the complex behavioral process of organizational buying, the marketer must systematically gather relevant market information by asking the right questions. Illustrative questions are presented in Table 4.7, which draws together the material of Part II, The Organizational Buying Process. The business marketer can understand an individual decision maker only after examining the broader forces that form the decision-making process and after defining the context of the buying situation, which includes environmental, organizational, product-specific, group, and individual forces. Such analysis will allow the marketer to focus marketing strategy on profitable segments of the organizational market. As we will see in Chapter 6, key dimensions of organizational buying behavior (highlighted in Table 4.7) play a significant role in business market segmentation strategies.

TABLE 4.7 **Organizational Buying Behavior: Forming the Foundation of Marketing Strategy**

Level	Illustrative Questions
Environmental	How will present economic projections for the industry and the economy affect the purchasing plans of this organization?
Organizational	What are the unique *company attributes* (e.g., size, orientation) and *procurement attributes* (e.g., structure and organization position of purchasing) that will influence buyer behavior?
Product-specific	How far has the firm progressed in the *buying process* (early or late phase)?
	What type of *buying situation* does this purchase represent for the organization (new task, straight rebuy)?
	To what degree will organizational buyers perceive *risk* in purchasing this product?
Group	Will the decision be made by an individual or a group?
	Who are the members of the buying center?
	What is each member's relative influence in the decision?
	What is the power base (e.g., status or expert power) of each member of the buying center?
Individual	What criteria are important to each member of the buying center in evaluating prospective suppliers?
	How do potential suppliers rate according to these criteria?

SUMMARY

Upon approaching an organization, the marketer confronts a buyer who is constrained by several forces having strong spheres of influence, which can be classified as environmental, organizational, group, and individual.

First, environmental forces define the boundaries within which buyers and sellers interact. Second, each organization develops a personality that makes it unique. The marketer must understand how organizational buyers approach decisions, set priorities, gather information, resolve conflicts, and establish and revise organizational goals. Both the location of the procurement function in the organizational hierarchy and the type of buying technology available to the purchasing staff directly influence marketing strategy requirements. Third, the relevant unit of analysis for the marketing strategist is the buying center. The composition of this group evolves during the buying process, varies from firm to firm, and changes from one purchasing situation to another. Fourth, the marketer must ultimately concentrate attention on individual members of the buying center. Each has a particular set of experiences and a unique personal and organizational frame of reference to bring to bear on the buying decision. The marketer who is sensitive to individual differences is best equipped to develop responsive marketing communications that will be remembered by the organizational buyer.

Unraveling the complex forces that encircle the organizational buying process is indeed difficult. The goal of this chapter has been to provide a framework that allows the marketing manager to begin this task by asking the right questions. The answers will provide the basis for effective and efficient business marketing strategy.

Discussion Questions

1. Harley-Davidson, the U.S. motorcycle producer, recently purchased some sophisticated manufacturing equipment to enhance its position in a very competitive market. First, what environmental forces might have been important in spawning this capital investment? Second, which functional units were likely to have been represented in the buying center?

2. How does the rate of technological change in an industry influence the composition of the decision-making unit in the buying organization?

3. Fuel economy, exhaust emission, and safety standards are creating changes in the purchasing requirements of automobile manufacturers. In what way will such changes influence the demand for aluminum, steel, rubber, and related materials?

4. Since the composition of the buying center is often made up of individuals who perform differing organizational functions (e.g., production versus purchasing) and who value different product and supplier attributes, how are decisions ever made? What steps can the salesperson take to manage conflict in the decision-making process?

5. An organization that centralizes procurement decisions at regional, division, or headquarters level will approach purchasing differently than will a company that is decentralized with purchasing decisions made at individual user locations. Explain.

6. Explain how the composition of the buying center evolves during the purchasing process and how it varies from one firm to another, as well as from one purchasing situation to another.

7. The Kraus Toy Company recently decided to develop a new electronic game. Can an electrical parts supplier predict the likely composition of the buying center at Kraus Toy? What steps could an industrial salesperson take to influence the composition of the buying center?

8. Why does the influence of the purchasing manager appear to increase as the level of environmental uncertainty rises?

9. Carol Brooks, purchasing manager for Apex Manufacturing Co., read *The Wall Street Journal* this morning and carefully read, clipped, and saved a full-page ad by the Allen-Bradley Company. Ralph Thornton, the production manager at Apex, read several articles from the same paper but could not recall seeing this particular ad or, for that matter, any ads. How could this occur?

10. What factors determine whether a particular buying situation will be a group or an individual decision?

11. The business marketer who identifies organizational screening requirements and the salient evaluative criteria of individual buying center members can make more informed product design and advertising decisions. Explain.

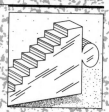

PART III

Assessing Market Opportunities

CHAPTER 5

Business Marketing Intelligence

The cornerstone of creative and effective marketing strategies is good information. Information about the customers, the competitors, and the environment, gathered continuously and organized to support decision making, allows the business marketing manager to base decisions on the realities of the marketplace rather than on hunch and intuition. The result is improved marketing performance. The system for capturing the necessary information for business marketing decision making is the marketing intelligence system. After reading this chapter, you will understand:

1. the components of, and requirements for, an effective marketing intelligence system.

2. the need to develop the information base as a decision support system to ensure maximum managerial relevance.

3. how to use key secondary sources of information for business market planning.

4. the nature and function of marketing research in the business marketing environment.

MARKETING intelligence is a systematic process for generating the information needed to manage business marketing strategy effectively. Marketing strategy decisions will be based on information about market potential, customer requirements, industry and market trends, present and future competitive behavior, expected sales, market-segment size and requirements, and sales and profit performance for customers, products, and territories. Marketing intelligence activities are thus focused on developing the research methodologies, data sources, and processing capabilities necessary to evoke this information in a form that supports marketing strategy development.

This chapter explores the strategic role of information in business marketing management. First, the key components of a marketing intelligence system are delineated. Particular attention is devoted to the decision support system, which is the core of the marketing intelligence function in the industrial firm. Next, the secondary sources of information available to the business marketer are described and evaluated. Third, the role and the unique characteristics of marketing research in the business market environment are analyzed.

THE ROLE OF INFORMATION:　A CASE ILLUSTRATION

The value of marketing intelligence in the marketing decision process is illustrated by the case of an industrial firm trying to compete in a very uncertain market situation.

In the mid-1980s, Beckman Instruments, a wholly owned subsidiary of SmithKline Beckman, faced a major challenge in the hospital market.[1] Beckman produces medical diagnostic products and analytical instruments for use in all types of medical settings. Changes in the Social Security amendments spelled out a new system by which hospitals were to be reimbursed for operating expenses and capital goods purchases. The amendments gave no assurance that medical facilities would be reimbursed for capital goods expenditures, and a three- to four-year period would elapse before the industry would be certain about how reimbursements would be handled. The effect was to slow hospitals' purchases of supply items and to dramatically reduce their capital investments.

Beckman Instruments' dilemma required that several basic questions be answered:

- How long will the situation last?
- How severe will it be?
- How can business from current customers be optimized?
- Who are other potential prospects, outside current customer lists?
- What products are most likely to sell in this environment?
- Who will buy new systems?

To answer these questions and to forge a strategy to respond to the challenge, Beckman Instruments turned to its marketing intelligence system. First, the company reviewed its own customer information system, its list of equipment installations, reports on equipment aging (how long the equipment had been in place), and reports of monthly supplies usage. These elements of data are part of the marketing intelligence system designed to gather data and provide information to management on a periodic basis.

---

[1] This example is based upon Gerald E. Gallwas, "Sales Research and EDP Close the Data Gap," *Marketing Communications* (February 1988), pp. 24–27.

INSIDE BUSINESS MARKETING
Who Needs Market Research?

"About five years ago we hired an MBA from a prestigious eastern university. We manufacture heavy industrial machinery and felt we needed someone 'to do a little market research.' So we gave this MBA the title of market research director—although we weren't sure exactly what he should do. He developed mountains of data and information—but it never seemed to be very useful. Actually, we didn't know what to do with the data or how to use it. After about five months we fired him.

"Reflecting back on our experience, I can now appreciate the value of that data. We recently adopted a formal marketing planning process, and much of that information would be extremely useful today. I wish now that we had the benefit of a five-year-old data base—we are just beginning to develop similar data to enable us to implement our formal planning process."

Source: From a discussion with the director of marketing of an industrial machinery firm.

Once the firm's internal data bases were scanned, a secondary data base (information supplied by an outside source) was reviewed to determine product installations for most hospitals in the United States. Another secondary data source, the American Hospital Association, provided information on historical hospital occupancy data. The secondary data, in conjunction with the firm's internal data, made it possible to compare known Beckman equipment installations with those of its competitors on a demographic basis. The company then used all this information to develop a model of the business and to track likely results through the three- to four-year transition period. High-potential prospects for new equipment were identified, and direct mail, telemarketing, and sales call tactics were formulated from this data.

The combined data sources, both internal and external, along with the business models are important components of Beckman's marketing intelligence system. The information provided by the system enabled the company to track sales of its own products, analyze instances where competitors' equipment was installed, and make projections on how the business scenario would play out over the transition period. The result was that the company was well positioned to create effective marketing strategy and tactics that allowed for the uncertain hospital environment and targeted those areas and hospitals with the highest sales potential.

As this example suggests, marketing intelligence is a multifaceted function that is the primary driving force behind many decisions made by business marketing managers. Valuable marketing information must be created systematically—data from a variety of sources must be transformed into information that will support executive decision making. As Irwin Gross points out, "We are entering the age of information. Suddenly, new means for collecting and disseminating information are bringing costs down and easing availability. Business marketers must make a commitment to information as a necessary part of doing business. Market research and intelligence can no longer be treated as a sporadic and optional activity."[2] The prudent business marketing manager develops an intelligence system that provides the information necessary for making effective decisions.

BUSINESS MARKETING INTELLIGENCE DEFINED

Business marketing intelligence refers to the broad spectrum of information required to make decisions and to manage business marketing strategy effectively. The manager for the marketing intelligence system is responsible for designing and implementing systems and procedures to gather, record, analyze, and interpret all forms of pertinent marketing information. A comprehensive business marketing intelligence system might include:

1. *Formal marketing research studies.* Marketing research may be conducted to determine buyer intentions, analyze primary demand, evaluate competitive behavior and performance, monitor the economic and industry environment, evaluate customer satisfaction, measure market share, analyze advertising effectiveness, determine price elasticity, evaluate distributor performance and satisfaction, or determine buying center composition and behavior.

2. *Market potential and sales forecasting.* The intelligence system must assemble data to determine market potentials and sales forecasts as well as appropriate methodologies.

3. *Financial and accounting performance analysis.* The intelligence system must coordinate the marketing needs with financial and accounting functions. The system should generate periodic reports on revenues, costs, and profits by customer, distributor, product, and territory. These results are compared with objectives set forth in the marketing plan.

4. *New product research.* In many business markets, especially in high-technology industries, success hinges on effective allocation of R&D expenditures. The intelligence function develops procedures for generating new product ideas; monitoring customers, middlemen, and competitors for new product ideas; testing the concepts of new products; test marketing; and evaluating the performance of new products.

5. *Secondary data files.* The sources of published information are diverse and include departments of federal and state governments, local governments, universities, institutes, trade associations, consulting firms, and private research organizations. The marketing intelligence function is responsible for determining which secondary data is relevant and then collecting, analyzing, and disseminating it regularly to the appropriate decision makers.

---

[2] Irwin Gross, "Why All of Industry Needs Research," *Business Marketing,* 72 (April 1987), p. 114.

Marketing intelligence is clearly a broad and complex function whose effectiveness will dramatically affect the quality of industrial marketing decisions. Key components of the business marketing intelligence system are sketched in Figure 5.1.

Components of a Decision Support System

The heart of the marketing intelligence function is what John D. C. Little refers to as a **decision support system** (DSS)—a coordinated collection of data, systems, tools, and techniques with the necessary software and computer hardware through which an organization gathers and interprets relevant information from the business and the environment and turns it into information that can be acted upon.[3] The components of a DSS include:

1. *Data base.* The intelligence function develops and coordinates the flow of information from the multitude of external and internal sources. The primary task is to capture the data so that it can be used with the other components of the DSS to make decisions. A critical objective is to centralize all data in proper form and in sufficient detail so that it is accessible for decision making.

2. *Decision models.* A model may be nothing more sophisticated than a rule of thumb, for example, "for each 1 percent decline in territorial market share, trade promotion advertising should be increased by 5 percent." Or models may be complicated computer-driven mathematical equations. In any case, models are quantitative or qualitative conceptualizations of how a system operates. The model expresses perceptions as to what data and variables are important and how the variables are related.

3. *Statistics and manipulation.* This aspect of the DSS produces meaningful information by relating the data to the models. The typical operation involves segregating numbers into groups, aggregating them, taking ratios, ranking them, plotting, making tables, and so forth. General managerial models (e.g., pro forma profit and loss statements, budgeting statements and forecasting statements) and more complex models (e.g., marketing mix planning, product portfolio analysis, and new product tracking) are aspects of data analysis performed in the statistical manipulation process.

4. *Display.* The display function is the interface between the business marketing manager and the DSS. Much of the communication is achieved through interactive computing. The widespread use of CRTs, PCs, and microcomputer linkups to mainframe computers enhances the manager's ability to interact with the DSS system. It is vital that information be able to flow back and forth between computer and decision maker because business decisions often require that the manager

---

[3]John D. C. Little, Lakshmi Mohan, and Antoine Hatoun, "Using Decision Support Systems," *Industrial Marketing*, 67 (March 1982), p. 50. (This section is based on portions of this article.)

FIGURE 5.1   **A Business Marketing Intelligence System**

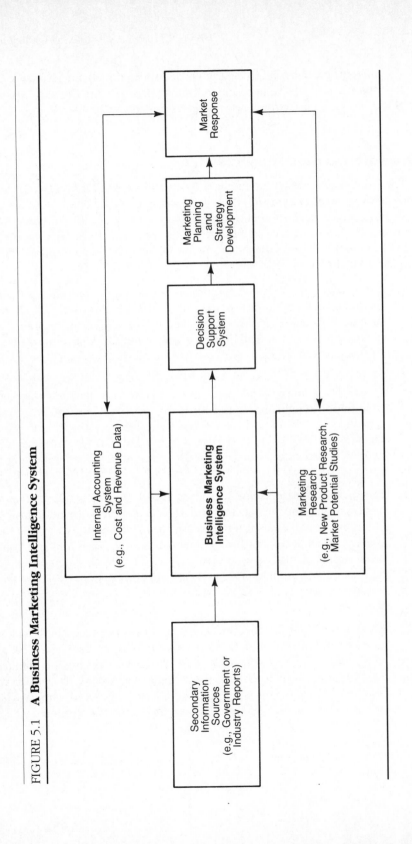

backtrack and experiment with different scenarios before choosing one course of action.[4]

As John Little points out, business marketing is a fertile area for a DSS because the markets are complex and typically heterogeneous, the impact of technological change is significant, and the pricing and sales force decisions are critical.[5] An effective DSS is especially relevant in the industrial sphere; many industrial firms find they have an overload of reports and data and a significant lack of effective information.

Required Decision Support System Attributes

To be effective, the DSS must incorporate four important attributes: managerial capability, analysis, flexibility, and usability. First, the system should be able to provide managers with reports tailored to specific needs and market situations. Systems that impose a common format on all users and that emphasize standardized rather than customized reports fail to meet the marketing manager's needs. Second, the system must be analytical rather than simply generating reports. In addition to capturing historical information, the DSS should allow the evaluation of scenarios (e.g., "what would happen if . . . ."). The DSS should allow the manager to forecast the response of the market to alternative marketing strategies under a range of competitive and business environment scenarios. Third, the system must possess the flexibility and speed to adapt quickly to changes in information requirements. Last, usability implies that the system is "user-friendly"; that is, it is easy to incorporate it into the daily operation of business. The primary need here is to incorporate the personal computer into the use of the DSS.[6] When this linkage of PC and mainframe DSS is achieved, the power of a large data base can be coupled to the flexibility of the PC, and the net result is more effective application of the DSS.

At Conrail, the large northeastern railroad, the need for more precise, flexible, and timely reports is a direct result of the deregulation of the railroad industry.[7] Its DSS uses a combination of batch processing and interactive computers. Conrail's information requirements—the wide range of data associated with each railroad-car load (weight, shipper, destination date, etc.)—dictate the use of batch processing in order to generate the enormous data files. The DSS provides the flexibility to generate data needed by sales reps in the competitive, deregulated environment. Often, information is needed to provide the manager with a stronger and more relevant foundation for making a decision *today*.

In the future, widespread use of expert systems (expert systems are one element of a broad range of computer decision-making systems called artificial intelligence) will vastly expand the capability and influence of the DSS in business marketing.[8]

---

[4] John F. Towey, "Information Please," *Management Accounting* (February 1989), p. 53.

[5] Little, "Using Decision Support Systems," p. 52.

[6] Gallwas, "Sales Research and EDP Close the Data Gap," p. 25.

[7] Ellis Booker, "Computers Help You Win the Game," *Computer Decisions* (September 15, 1984), p. 20.

[8] Towey, "Information Please," p. 53.

The Anatomy of a Decision Support System

For Abbott Laboratories Hospital Products Division (HPD), a decision support system is a necessity for managing the marketing of over 2,000 products sold to thousands of hospitals nationwide. The DSS at Abbott is applied to sales forecasting, pricing analysis, promotional tracking, and new product analysis.

Prior to DSS, many analyses were done by hand or through cumbersome mainframe programs. Now, however, product sales and price data can be easily analyzed for profitability, and a profitability report can be issued in less than an hour. Previously, such reports were manually compiled, and the process took two days.

A particularly effective application of DSS is in the product-mix area. The system can show HPD salespeople when they should attempt to push customers from one product line to another line that is more profitable yet accomplishes the same purpose. In this form of analysis, the "what-if" statistical ability of the DSS comes into play. HPD uses DSS to calculate the projected impact, based on historical data, of a proposed drop in price designed to boost its share in the more profitable line. The system calculates the potential profitability of such a decision.

DSS is also applied to measuring the impact on sales of HPD's product promotion programs. The system tracks actual sales versus planned sales and provides a variance report to indicate whether promotions are on or below target.

In short, HPD's traditional demands for precise marketing information and tight financial control, coupled with its complex product line and vast market, mean that the company can maximize the benefits that a sophisticated DSS offers.

Source: Adapted from Daniel C. Brown, "Anatomy of a Decision Support System," *Business Marketing,* 70 (June 1985), pp. 80–86.

Expert systems and artificial intelligence are powerful tools that go beyond merely providing information; they develop analyses that are able to independently deduce and conclude. In effect, an expert system is a computer program that mimics the behavior of an expert—especially in the realm of problem solving. An expert system can solve difficult problems while offering some rudimentary learning capabilities. The impact is to stimulate the decision maker's thought process as well as to improve the decision-making process itself. The adoption of expert systems and artificial intelligence technology into the DSS framework will enable business marketing managers to "leverage existing expertise to improve the timeliness and performance of many routine but critical business decisions."[9]

Manipulating Data

A DSS is the core of the intelligence function in the industrial firm. The working DSS permits data aggregation at any level desired. For example, sales data can be stored by customer, product, and territory so that management can easily manipulate the data at

[9] Dorothy Leonard-Barton and John J. Sviokla, "Putting Expert Systems to Work," *Harvard Business Review,* 66 (March–April 1988), p. 98.

any level of aggregation. Total sales, sales by top customers, sales by territory, sales by large territories, or sales by product to specified customers in selected territories can all be evaluated. In this way, the intelligence system is totally responsive to the level of analysis required for a specific business marketing decision. A focal point for any market intelligence system is the broad spectrum of secondary information available.

SECONDARY INFORMATION SOURCES

Whether developed through painstaking market research studies or gleaned from existing publications, information exists to support business decisions. Secondary information gathered and published by government agencies, trade associations, trade publications, and independent research firms provides a valuable and often inexpensive start to building knowledge of the market. Of the many external sources of business information, secondary data is the principal source of information about a company's competitive and external environment.[10] Sources of secondary data abound; the real issue is to understand where to look for useful data in the face of so many possibilities.[11] The Standard Industrial Classification (SIC) System is a vital source, because the vast majority of secondary information is reported on the basis of SIC codes.

The Standard Industrial Classification System

In order to develop meaningful data on U.S. businesses, the federal government has segmented all business activity into fairly homogeneous categories. Each category is assigned a code—its Standard Industrial Classification code. The SIC system facilitates the collection, tabulation, and analysis of a wide variety of economic data. The *Standard Industrial Classification Manual,* published by the Office of Management and Budget and distributed through the U.S. Government Printing Office, describes the SIC fully.

The purpose of the SIC system is to identify groups of business firms that produce the same type of product. Every plant and business establishment in the United States is assigned a code that reflects the primary product produced at that location. The SIC coding system works in the following way:

First, the nation's economic activity is divided into ten *basic industries,* each of which is given a two-digit classification code. For example, codes 01–09 represent agriculture, 19–39 manufacturing, 70–89 services, and so on. Next, *major groups* are developed within each basic industry. Each major group has a specific two-digit code. Thus, manufacturing has 20 two-digit codes, each representing a major group such as SIC 34, which is fabricated metal products.

---

[10] James R. Fries, "Library Support for Industrial Marketing Research," *Industrial Marketing Management,* 11 (February 1982), p. 48.

[11] William E. Cox, Jr., *Industrial Marketing Research* (New York: John Wiley and Sons, 1979), p. 30.

Major groups are then further subdivided into three-digit *industry groups*. There are more than 150 industry groups, including SIC 342, which represents hand tools and hardware. The next level of detail, four-digit codes, are specific industries. The SIC contains over 450 specific industries, of which SIC 3423, hand and edge tools, is an example.

The SIC system extends to additional levels of detail in some cases. *Product classes* are defined by five-digit codes; the SIC contains 1,300 of these. Finally, *products* are assigned seven-digit codes; this subdivision contains 10,000 segments.

Figure 5.2 illustrates the basic elements of the SIC system, with hand tools as a specific example. As Figure 5.2 indicates, the more digits, the finer the classification. The most useful level of aggregation is the four-digit code; there is little data published for five- and seven-digit codes. The *Census of Manufactures* does assemble some data at the five- and seven-digit levels, but the census is only published every five years.

The SIC System: Design and Limitations

To use SIC data effectively, the business marketing manager must understand how the codes are developed and what their major limitations are. First, SIC codes are based on the product produced or on the operation performed, with the final product as the major determining factor of classification. Second, codes are given to an establishment, which refers to a single physical location such as a plant, factory, store, mine, farm, bank, office, or mill. Thus, a company may have many SIC codes, each applied to separate plants in the corporate system. Cincinnati Milacron, a billion-dollar producer of industrial manufacturing systems, operates plants in the Cincinnati area that have the following diverse SIC codes:

2869	Industrial organic chemicals
2992	Lubricating oils and grease
3291	Abrasive products
3541	Screw machine products
3559	Special industry machinery
3622	Industrial controls
3679	Electronic components

The classification assigned to an individual establishment will depend on the primary product produced there. If two or more products are made, the primary product is determined by the one with the largest value added (the product with the highest level of incremental value added at the plant).[12] However, sales or shipments are often used because of the difficulty in determining value added for individual products. All statistics for a particular plant will reflect activity associated with the primary and all secondary products. For example, if an electronics plant in Chicago manufactures $2.6 million of transformers (SIC 3612) and $5.9 million of electronic resistors (SIC 3676), an SIC code of 3676 would be assigned, and all data related to employment, investment, and value added would be assigned to SIC 3676 because it is the primary product.

---

[12] *Standard Industrial Classification Manual,* 1972, p. 646.

FIGURE 5.2   **The Standard Industrial Classification**

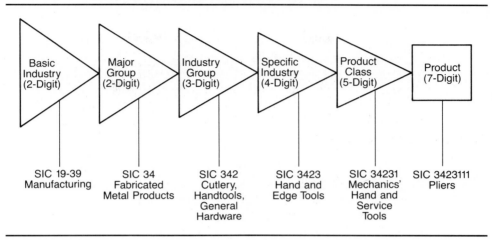

| Basic Industry (2-Digit) | Major Group (2-Digit) | Industry Group (3-Digit) | Specific Industry (4-Digit) | Product Class (5-Digit) | Product (7-Digit) |

| SIC 19-39 Manufacturing | SIC 34 Fabricated Metal Products | SIC 342 Cutlery, Handtools, General Hardware | SIC 3423 Hand and Edge Tools | SIC 34231 Mechanics' Hand and Service Tools | SIC 3423111 Pliers |

A significant problem associated with the SIC is how an entire enterprise will be classified in terms of its four-digit code. Generally, a firm is assigned a four-digit code on the basis of the product group that accounts for the greatest value of all the firm's four-digit product shipments.[13] (This assignment procedure varies from source to source.) The obvious difficulty is that the classification assigned to a firm may not effectively reflect its operations, and therefore the quantitative figures assigned to its industry code (four-digit SIC) are not totally reflective of activity in that industry. In this case, the analyst must be careful to determine whether the data is being presented at the "establishment" (plant) level or at the "enterprise" (firm) level.

Finally, many companies have production facilities that manufacture items to be incorporated into the final product of their parent companies. In this situation, the data for the captive plant is assigned to the SIC of the parent plant's final product. The problem is that the output of the parent plant will thus be overstated, and the data for the industry to which the captive plant belongs will be understated.

Overcoming SIC Problems

In response to some of the difficulties associated with gathering data by establishments and assigning SIC by primary product, the *Census of Manufactures* has developed two corrective ratios. The **primary product specialization ratio** indicates the percentage of total shipments of a given four-digit industry accounted for by its primary product. For example, SIC 3011 (tires and inner tubes) has a specialization ratio of 97 percent, whereas SIC 2812 (alkalis and chlorine) has a ratio of 65 percent. Many firms in SIC 2812 apparently produce secondary products that make up a sizable portion of their total output. The specialization ratio indicates just how much of the production activity in an industry (four-digit SIC) is associated with its primary product. The higher the

---

[13] Richard N. Clarke, "SICs as Delineators of Economic Markets," *Journal of Business,* 62 (January 1989), p. 21.

ratio, the more homogeneous the industry; as a rough rule of thumb, when ratios exceed 90 percent, data for the industry are very reliable.[14]

The **coverage ratio** compares the shipments of a primary product by one four-digit industry to the total shipments of that product by all four-digit industries. For example, SIC 3452 (nuts, bolts, and washers) has a coverage ratio of 90 percent; SIC 2873 (nitrogenous fertilizers) has a ratio of 69 percent. Thus, 31 percent of nitrogenous fertilizer is made by establishments in other SIC groups. Obviously, if a manager is gathering data on a particular four-digit SIC industry with a low coverage ratio, it will be necessary to investigate carefully industries other than the SIC under scrutiny. As with the specialization ratio, a 90 percent coverage ratio indicates that the data is reliable.

The business marketing manager must use caution when using data that is based on the SIC, and should refer to the specialization and coverage ratios in order to assess the reliability of the information to be analyzed. Using SIC data at the firm level is particularly hazardous, as a recent empirical study by Richard Clarke indicated that the SIC is weak at identifying groups of firms that display similar characteristic variables.[15] Clarke suggests that the SIC is more effective at dividing firms into "coarse" industrial groups than at positioning them into finer four-digit segments. Sometimes the manager will need to develop original data through market surveys in order to circumvent the problems associated with the classification system.

However, the limitations of the SIC are in no way an indictment of the system. The process of classifying economic activity in an economy as vast and diverse as that in the United States is a tremendous undertaking. The SIC is an invaluable tool with which business marketers can collect and analyze data about their markets from a variety of sources, knowing that the data are developed from a common base.

Using the SIC

Industrial firms are segmented by the products they produce and by the production processes they employ. If the coverage and specialization ratios are high, each SIC group should be relatively homogeneous in terms of raw materials required, components used, manufacturing processes employed, and problems faced. As a result, the SIC is often an excellent basis on which to segment markets. If the manager understands the needs and requirements of a few firms within an SIC category, requirements can be projected for all firms within that category. For example, most firms manufacturing truck trailers (SIC 3715) will need to purchase components such as wheels, tires, sheet steel, grease, oil, plastic parts, and electric parts. Their requirements will be similar, and potential suppliers can evaluate the total market through a detailed analysis of a few SIC 3715 companies. Suppose a supplier of steel wheels determines through a sales analysis of present customers that SIC 3715 firms spend eight cents per dollar of their final shipments on wheels. A market estimate of total wheel sales to SIC 3715 firms could be developed by referring to an estimate of total shipments: a *Sales and Marketing Management* estimate for 1989 reveals that SIC 3715

---

[14] Francis E. Hummel, *Market and Sales Potentials* (New York: The Ronald Press Company, 1961), p. 77.

[15] Clarke, "SICs as Delineators of Economic Markets," p. 18.

shipped $2,718 million in trailers, which suggests a potential wheel sales volume of $2,718 million × $0.08 = $217.4 million.[16]

Identifying New Customers

The SIC is useful for identifying new customers. The marketing manager can study a four-digit industry to evaluate whether the firms in it could use the marketer's product or service. Although this analysis provides only rough estimates, it is helpful in eliminating industries that are not potential product users. SIC groups that show promise of possible use can be singled out for evaluation in depth.

Segmentation

Since each SIC is relatively homogeneous in terms of problems and processes, segmentation on the basis of SIC is often effective. An understanding of the SIC system is particularly relevant for gathering market information because so many government agencies, trade associations, and private research firms collect data on the basis of SIC codes. As suggested earlier, SIC data is not without fault and caution must be exercised in both the interpretation and the use of the information.

Published Sources of Business Marketing Data

Marketing decisions are only as good as the data used to generate them. The breadth of data available to the business marketing manager provides both an opportunity and a challenge. The opportunity arises from the wealth of available industrial market data. Government at all levels, trade associations, trade publications, and private research companies publish a great deal of economic data on a national, state, and county basis. Most of this data is collected by SIC code, allowing for an analysis industry by industry and, sometimes, product by product. The challenge is to develop familiarity with secondary data sources, to understand the nature of the data in these sources, and to comprehend how the data can enhance business marketing. Table 5.1 provides a compact summary of prime data sources available for defining target segments in the organizational market, estimating market potential, forecasting sales, evaluating competitors, and providing an understanding of market needs.

Federal Government Data Sources

Some of the more important federal government sources are described in Table 5.1. Federal data is industry oriented; the basic unit of analysis is a particular four-digit SIC category. For this reason, federal data sources are often the cornerstone for the determination of market and sales potentials by industry.

The most comprehensive set of federal data is the *Census of Manufactures.* Every five years the Bureau of Census conducts a nationwide census of manufacturing establishments, surveying number of employees, value added, cost of materials, shipments, capital expenditures, and so forth. The data is summarized for four-digit

---

[16]"Data Supplement: U.S. Totals for 4-Digit SIC Industries," *Sales and Marketing Management,* 142 (June 1990), p. 144.

TABLE 5.1   **A Selection of Data Sources for Use in Business Market Analysis**

Source	Title of Publication	Type of Data	Application	Frequency of Publication	Comments
Federal government	*Census of Manufactures* (U.S. Dept. of Commerce)	General data by 4-, 5-, 7-digit SIC on value added, employees, number of establishments, shipments, and materials consumed. Data shown by region, state, employment size, etc.	Provides comprehensive data to determine potential by area and for specific industries.	Every 5 years	Broadest array of industrial data; based on a census, may be dated.
	Annual Survey of Manufactures (U.S. Dept. of Commerce)	Based on a sample of firms, yields current 4-digit SIC data similar to the *Census.*	Similar to the *Census.*	Annually	Less comprehensive and detailed than the *Census;* up to date.
	County Business Patterns (U.S. Dept. of Commerce)	Statistics on number of establishments and employment by 4-digit SIC for all counties in the U.S.	Used to estimate market potential by region; evaluate industry concentration by region.	Annually	Provides effective estimates of potential if number of employees is correlated to industry demand.
	Standard Industrial Classification Manual (U.S. Bureau of the Budget)	Complete description of the SIC system. Describes all 4-digit industries.	Used to evaluate possible industrial users based on products they produce.	Every 5 years	Lists each 4-digit SIC category and its primary products.
	U.S. Industrial Outlook (U.S. Dept. of Commerce)	Overall view of over 200 4-digit SIC industries with past and future growth rates in shipments and employment.	Project future market concentration and potential.	Annually	Reasonably current data; provides useful look at growth prospects in selected industries.
	Current Industrial Reports (U.S. Dept. of Commerce)	Series of over 100 reports covering 5,000 products; usually based on 3-digit SIC, but may use 7-digit codes. Shipment and production data provided.	Provides in-depth analysis of potential by specific industry.	Monthly to annually	Very timely data; published 4–8 weeks after data is collected.
	A Guide to Federal Data Sources on Manufacturing (U.S. Dept. of Commerce)	Describes nature and sources of all federal government data related to manufacturing.	A quick guide to locate appropriate government data.	Annually	Valuable source document for understanding government statistics.
State, local government	State and Local Industrial Directories	Type of data varies, but usually provides individual company data such as SIC code, sales, number of employees, products, and address.	Useful for defining specific potential customers by state and region.	Usually annual	Provides data on firms of all sizes. Particularly useful when markets are concentrated in a few states.
Trade associations	For example: National Machine Tool Builders Association, Glass Container Manufacturers Institute, Iron and Steel Institute, Rubber Manufacturers Association	Sales history of the industry; industrial, financial, and operating data.	Provides an evaluation of past and present growth potentials by industry.	Usually annual	May provide useful industry data not contained in other sources, e.g., average age of equipment.

Source	Title of Publication	Type of Data	Application	Frequency of Publication	Comments
Trade publications	For example: *S&MM* "Special Data Supplement: U.S. Totals for 4-digit SIC Industries"	Number plants and shipments by SIC code by country; country percentage of total U.S. shipments by SIC category.	Provides a ballpark estimate of market potential by state and country.	Updated annually	Very timely source for quickly assessing potential by country and state.
	Iron Age: "Basic Marketing Data on Metal Working"	Census of metalworking industry. Data on plants and employees on a regional basis	Quick estimate of potential for the metalworking industry.	Annual	Useful for easy estimation of potential for a particular industry.
Private industrial directories and research (fee) companies	For example: *Predicasts* (Predicasts, Cleveland, Oh.)	Growth forecasts and market outlook for various industries by SIC.	Can be used to extrapolate potential estimates for the long run.	Quarterly	Up-to-date information on growth trends by 7-digit SIC.
	Dun's Market Identifiers (Dun & Bradstreet, N.Y.)	Data on 3.5 million corporations relative to company SIC, address, locations, sales, and employees.	Provides an evaluation of potential sales by individual company.	Continuous file	Timely information on specific firms can be obtained quickly.
	Standard & Poor's Industry Surveys' Basic Analysis (Standard & Poor's Corp. N.Y.)	Data on major industries and companies.	In-depth data on specific companies.	Weekly	Timely, general data on major industries.
International data sources	For example: *The Yearbook of Industrial Statistics* (United Nations Statistical Office)	Vol. 1: Basic country data and indicators showing global and regional trends in industrial activity.	Trends in worldwide industrial activity.	Annually	Largest compilation of international industrial data. Data covers a ten-year period for each volume.
		Vol. 2: Statistics for 500 industrial commodities and 200 countries.	Industry activity by area; market potential estimation.	Annually	
	The Yearbook of International Trade Statistics (U.N. Statistical Office)	Quantity and value of exports and imports of various commodities over the past several years.	Market potential for various products by country.	Annually	Valuable for assessing trends in product and country imports and exports.
	Ulrich's International Periodicals Directory (R.R. Bowker Co., New York)	Covers 61,000 periodicals throughout the world.	Used to develop data base on international business activity.	Biannually	Information arranged by subject matter and includes titles of publications of international organizations.
	Japan Company Handbook (Toyo Keizai Shinposha, Ltd, Tokyo	Covers 1,003 Japanese corporations.	Evaluation of competition strength and market performance.	Biannually	Provides sales breakdowns, financial statistics, characteristics, and outlooks for over 1,000 Japanese corporations.

SIC categories, geographic regions, and states. Thus, detailed economic statistics can be determined for every SIC category by state and region. Product shipments for five- and seven-digit SIC categories are also presented, allowing the marketing manager to focus on very specific industries within regions and states.

As Table 5.1 suggests, the *Census of Manufactures* makes it possible to investigate, by geographic region, the size and scope of industries that are potential customers. The primary difficulty is the timeliness of the data—the *Census* is published only every five years. In addition, it takes one to three years from data collection to publication.

The problem of the timeliness of the *Census* is partially circumvented by the *Annual Survey of Manufactures.* The *Annual Survey* is a probability sample of 70,000 manufacturers drawn from the *Census of Manufactures* and supplemented by Social Security Administration lists of new establishments. All establishments with over 250 employees in the preceding *Census* are included in the sample. The *Annual Survey* provides essentially the same data as the *Census,* but in less detail and to only the four-digit SIC code level. Survey data is usually published one to two years after collection.

County Business Patterns is an annual publication that provides employment statistics for all manufacturing establishments county by county. Statistics on taxable payrolls, number of employees, and number of reporting units are reported by four-digit SIC group. *County Business Patterns* is especially valuable when demand for a company's product is highly correlated with the size of potential establishments as indicated by the number of employees. In such cases, market potential can be calculated on a county, regional, state, or territorial basis in those industries deemed to be potential markets. A serious limitation of *County Business Patterns* is the nondisclosure rule, which prevents the Census Bureau from publishing data that could identify a specific firm.[17] In such cases, the data for a particular county are not reported, which leads to underestimates of industrial activity there.

There are, of course, many additional federal data sources (see Table 5.1). Sources are more fully described in *A Guide to Federal Data Sources on Manufacturing,* published by the Department of Commerce.

Other Data Sources

The federal government primarily collects statistics on industry; however, states, local governments, and private industrial directories provide data on individual firms. State and local governments publish annual directories of businesses within their jurisdictions. The directories generally include company name, address, SIC code, products produced, sales volume, and number of employees. The directories enable the marketing manager to evaluate market potential firm by firm for well-defined geographic areas. For example, by combining information from industrial directories with sales data from internal sources, a business marketer can create a customer and prospect

---

[17] U.S. Department of Commerce, "A Guide to Federal Data Sources on Manufacturing" (September 1977), p. 45.

INSIDE BUSINESS MARKETING
So You Want to Sell to the Auto Industry?

Predicasts, a leading information and research firm, was asked by a business writer to run a research study for a fictitious chair and sofa manufacturer who wished to enter the auto OEM market as a seat supplier. The purpose of the exercise was to illustrate the type of information that Predicasts can provide. The response from Predicasts was fast and efficient. The customer, had it purchased Predicasts' online service, could have had a complete report almost instantly for $50, a full search for $375.

The information was substantial. Data gathered from hard copy publications, *Predicasts Forecasts* and *Basebook,* indicated market size for a variety of SIC industries dealing with the auto industry, included a time series of sales volume back to 1965 as well as the annual growth rate of the particular market and the source of the data. Further, the *Basebook* reveals that two-door sedans had an annual growth rate of 7.5 percent versus –0.1 percent for four-doors; small auto production grew at 20.9 percent annually compared to minus 1.2 percent for large autos. Bucket seats look good, whereas the prediction for the big roomy back seats was pretty gloomy.

Forecasts reveals that the use of molded urethane seating was expected to drop 0.5 percent in the next ten years. On the bright side, sales of foreign-made cars were expected to increase by as much as 12.3 percent in the next three years. Perhaps the export market would offer the best opportunity.

A computer search of 2,500 publications produced ten feet of printout on the automotive seating market. The news is good and bad. Lear Siegler Automotive had already been chosen to produce a sizable portion of the seats in Ford and GM cars. Hoover Universal had secured a prominent position in the small car program for every major auto manufacturer—up to 40 percent of the domestic market. On the positive side, foreign markets were growing rapidly. The use of plastic seats was expanding in an effort to reduce weight. The sources also showed the leading foreign manufacturers of seating as well as listing major seating contracts signed by various auto manufacturers.

Perhaps the automotive seating market did not look so good after all.

Source: Adapted from Philip Maher, "A Market Researcher's Basic Data Guide," *Industrial Marketing,* 67 (March 1982), p. 80.

profile for each SIC segment. This information would serve as a road map to guide selling and promotion efforts.

Private industrial directories and research companies, such as Dun & Bradstreet or Standard & Poor's, maintain up-to-date files on industrial firms. *Dun's Market Identifiers* provides current information on sales volume, products, employees, and location for more than 3.5 million firms. It provides the manager with quick information on an individual company.

Trade associations often provide industry statistics that are not found in government sources (e.g., average age of capital equipment in the industry). Trade publications also report industry-oriented data. *Iron Age* conducts an annual census of the metalworking industry, which includes data on plants and employees. On a broader scale, *Sales and Marketing Management* publishes an annual "Special Data Supplement," which provides a quick reference to shipments by SIC groups. The publication also makes shipment data on a county basis available to its readers on request. Research firms and business press publishers often publish research studies that focus on purchasing and reading habits in various industries. These studies are often valuable in helping business marketers select appropriate magazines for their advertising messages. One such study, "Purchase Influence in American Business," conducted by a professional market research firm, surveyed more than 5,000 top-level managers to assess their influence on the purchase of over 32 categories of products and services as well as to determine the business publications they read.[18] The results help guide managers in selecting which publication will be most effective for specific types of product advertising.

International Data Sources

The United Nations is the primary source for international industrial data. The Statistical Office of the United Nations in New York publishes a vast array of statistics and reports. The two-volume *Yearbook of Industrial Statistics* reports annually on country and regional trends in business activity as well as statistics on more than 500 industrial products. Import and export data for a variety of commodities is reported by the *Yearbook of International Trade Statistics.* Private research companies are also active. Dun & Bradstreet publishes *Principal International Business,* which provides information on almost 50,000 large companies in 133 countries, arranged both geographically and by SIC number. The rapid ascent of Japan in world markets has spawned a variety of statistical publications on Japan alone. *Japan Company Handbook* supplies sales, financial data, and company outlook for over 1,000 Japanese firms. As business marketing becomes global, the marketing manager must be able to adapt the marketing intelligence system to capture secondary data worldwide.

Developing a Data Base from Secondary Sources

In creating a data bank of secondary data for decision making, business marketers are increasingly turning to on-line computer data base searching. The business marketer pays a fee to an information service and through a personal computer and some communications software, gains access to the desired data base. The periodical and publication base is scanned and the required information is downloaded from the data base to the user's personal computer. On-line data base searching dramatically reduces the time-consuming and costly process of a library search or of gathering the raw data firsthand.

A wide variety of on-line data base services exist, ranging from "supermarket" services such as DIALOG, Nexis, and Orbit, which store hundreds of different data bases from a wide array of independent sources, to specialized vendors such as INVESTEXT, which offers the complete text of financial analyses on publicly held firms. Selection of the appropriate data base is made difficult by the fact that more than 5,000 computer data bases are currently available.[19]

---

[18] Sue Kapp, "Studies Help Direct Ad Dollars," *Business Marketing,* 74 (June, 1989), p. 34.

[19] "Everything You Always Wanted to Know—By PC," *Business Week* (October 1, 1990), p. 176.

INSIDE BUSINESS MARKETING
The Growing Array of Computerized Data Bases

Computerized data bases can be broad based or highly specialized, as the following sample suggests:

Dun's Electronic Yellow Pages: Names, address-es, and phone numbers of eight million companies throughout the United States.

INVESTEXT: Full text of analysts' reports on public corporations.

Coffeeline: 20,000 abstracts and other literature about coffee—from how to grow the plants to coffee's medicinal benefits.

Nexis: A data base supermarket which stores hundreds of data bases from independent sources.

Horse: Pedigrees, breeding records, race records, and earnings of thoroughbreds in North America since 1922.

Human Resources Information Network: Articles from over 100 sources dealing with benefit issues, labor relations, and affirmative action.

ABI/Inform: Scans hundreds of business publications for data on industries, companies, products, and general business topics.

Source: Adapted from "Everything You Always Wanted to Know—By PC," *Business Week*, October 1, 1990, pp. 176, 177.

The information provided by the data bases can be reported in three different formats. These include a simple listing of the articles in bibliographic form, a summary of each article, and the complete text of each article. Most data bases make all these options available. Through these data bases, business marketing managers can customize analyses for specific problems. The types of reports include bibliographies on almost any business topic; time series data on production, consumption, imports, and exports of products and services; financial data on specific companies; or performance trends for industries.[20] Data base searching offers two important advantages for generating secondary information: (1) expediency—extensive library search time is totally eliminated; and (2) custom-designed analyses—all available data bases can be scanned at the same time, or the search can be limited to specific topics, industries, companies, or countries.

Selecting the appropriate data base and vendor is an important and sometimes difficult task. The user must first consider a number of factors including the type of information needed, the format of the information, how current the information must be, and the depth and breadth of the desired data. Choosing the wrong data base can easily lead the user to a dead end and waste company resources. To learn more about on-line data bases, the manager may consult a variety of references. For example, either *The Directory of On-line Data Bases* or *Data Base Directory* provides useful guidance in the selection and use of different data bases.

The development of a secondary data base is one aspect of the marketing intelligence function. An equally important, and often more difficult, aspect is the market research function, the gathering of primary information.

---

[20]Fries, "Library Support for Industrial Marketing Research," p. 49.

BUSINESS MARKETING RESEARCH

Business marketing research is a broad area, defined as "the systematic gathering, recording, and analyzing of information and opportunities relating to the marketing of industrial goods and services."[21] It typically includes sales and market potential analysis, sales forecasting, market surveys, experiments, and observational studies. Formalized marketing research often provides the data used in planning and control. Business marketing research usually undertakes primary data studies—surveys, observation, or experiments—when conclusive research is needed or secondary data is too limited for the decision at hand.

The terms *marketing research* and *marketing intelligence* are frequently confused by students and managers alike. Marketing research is more narrow in scope; it is but one component of the industrial marketing intelligence system. Marketing research is generally undertaken for unique projects with specific objectives. Marketing intelligence is an on-going function designed to provide continuous information for decision making. One aspect is the design and implementation of marketing research projects to create an information base for making individual decisions. What are the distinguishing characteristics of business marketing research?

Marketing research involves certain basic elements that apply generally. In any context, the research study must be planned, a data-gathering instrument designed, and a sampling plan designed. The data must then be gathered, processed, analyzed, and reported. However, because of the environment of the business market and the nature of organizational buying, business marketing research differs from consumer-goods research. Some of the more relevant differences are as follows:

1. *Greater reliance on exploratory studies, secondary data, and expert judgment data in industrial research.* Because of demand concentration, market information tends to be concentrated among a few knowledgeable people, who may be surveyed when time and cost constrain large sample designs. The wealth of government and trade association data by SIC categories provides a valuable secondary data base for many business marketing decisions.

2. *Business marketing research places more emphasis on surveys as opposed to experimental and observational primary data methods.* Experimental and observational studies are not as effective in business as in consumer-goods markets.

3. *Personal interviewing is stressed in business marketing research.* Usually, specific respondents can be identified in the business market (although they are sometimes difficult to reach), and the target population is smaller and more concentrated. Thus, specific individuals in the buying center can be singled out for in-depth interviews.

---

[21] Cox, *Industrial Marketing Research,* p. 3.

4. *Business marketing research is concerned with the determination of market size and potential, as opposed to the consumer research concern for psychological market segmentation.*[22]

5. *Business marketing researchers typically work with smaller samples (because of the smaller universe and concentration of buyers).*[23] Small samples offer the ability to use in-depth interviewing, but sometimes preclude making generalizations from the research findings.

6. *Surveys in business marketing frequently encounter different problems than do surveys in consumer research; as a consequence, the survey process is often quite different.* Table 5.2 compares the survey research processes in industrial and in consumer research. Note the difficulties associated with respondent accessibility and cooperation on the industrial side. These are important, given the prevalence of personal interviewing.

Finally, business marketing research places increasing emphasis on systematic studies of the organizational buying process. Significant advances have been made over the past ten years, but refined marketing research approaches will be required to enable the business marketer to comprehend more fully the buying center in target organizations.

Some experts observe that business marketers are increasingly employing many of the sophisticated research tools utilized by consumer-goods firms. Focus groups, psychological probing techniques, conjoint or trade-off analysis, and quantitative modeling are some of the tools finding application in business marketing settings.[24] This increasing use of sophisticated consumer-research tools is explained by heightened levels of competition and the resulting need to improve understanding of business customer needs and attitudes.

The Tasks of Business Marketing Research

Ronald Paul reports on the usage of various kinds of marketing research by business marketers.[25] Paul indicates that industrial companies use research heavily in the areas of forecasting, business trends, potential, competitive studies, market share, market characteristics, sales analysis and sales quota determination. (Many of these topics will be discussed later in the text.) Clearly, an effective marketing research department is a valuable asset in developing and controlling the business marketing program.

---

[22] The first four items are based on William E. Cox, Jr., and Luis V. Dominguiz, "The Key Issues and Procedures of Industrial Marketing Research," *Industrial Marketing Management,* 8 (January 1979), pp. 81–93.

[23] Rohit Deshpande and Gerald Zaltman, "A Comparison of Factors Affecting the Use of Marketing Information in Consumer and Industrial Firms," *Journal of Marketing Research,* 24 (February 1987), p. 114.

[24] Tom Eisenhart, "Advanced Research Finds a New Market," *Business Marketing,* 74 (March 1989), p. 51.

[25] Ronald Paul, "Research Alternatives for Industrial Marketers," in Edwin E. Bobrow and Mark D. Bobrow, eds., *Marketing Handbook,* Vol. 1 (Homewood, IL: Dow-Jones Irwin, 1985), p. 209.

TABLE 5.2   **Consumer versus Business Marketing Research: What Are the Differences?**

	Consumer	Business
Universe/ Population	Large. Dependent on category under investigation but usually unlimited. Millions of consumers and households.	Small. Fairly limited in total population and even more so if within a defined industry or SIC category.
Respondent Accessibility	Fairly easy. Can interview at home, on the telephone, or using mail techniques.	Difficult. Usually only during working hours at plant, office, or on the road. Respondent is usually preoccupied with other priorities.
Respondent Cooperation	Over the years has become more and more difficult, yet millions of consumers have never been interviewed.	A major concern. Due to the small population, the industrial respondent is being over-researched. The purchaser and decision makers in an industrial firm are the buyers of a variety of products and services from office supplies to heavy equipment.
Sample Size	Can usually be drawn as large as required for statistical confidence since the population is in the hundreds of millions.	Usually much smaller than consumer sample, yet the statistical confidence is equal due to the relationship of the sample to the total population.
Respondent Definitions	Usually fairly simple. Those aware of a category or brand, users of a category or brand, demographic criteria, etc. The ultimate purchaser is also a user for most consumer products and services.	Somewhat more difficult. The user and the purchasing decision maker in most cases are not the same. Factory workers who use heavy equipment, secretaries who use typewriters, and so forth, are the users and, no doubt, best able to evaluate these products and services. However, they tend not to be the ultimate purchasers and, in many cases, do not have any influence on the decision-making process.
Interviewers	Can usually be easily trained. They are also consumers and tend to be somewhat familiar with the area under investigation for most categories.	Difficult to find good executive interviewers. At least a working knowledge of the product class or subject being surveyed is essential. Preferably more than just a working knowledge.
Study Costs	Key indicators of cost are sample size and incidence. Lower incidence usage categories (for example, users of soft moist dog food, powdered breakfast beverages, etc.) or demographic or behavioral screening criteria (attend a movie at least once a month, over 65 years of age, and do not have direct deposit of social security payments, etc.) can up costs considerably.	Relative to consumer research, the critical element resulting in significantly higher per-interview costs are: the lower incidence levels, the difficulties in locating the "right" respondent (that is, the purchase decision maker), and securing cooperation (time and concentration of effort) for the interview itself.

Source: Martin Katz, "Use Same Theory, Skills for Consumer, Industrial Marketing Research," *The Marketing News* (January 12, 1979), p. 16. Reprinted by permission of the American Marketing Association.

Research Methods

Although business marketers rely heavily on secondary data, primary data is often collected to gain firsthand knowledge of customer attitudes, motivations, and buying intentions. For all types of marketing research, the basic methods for gathering primary data are the following:

1. *Surveys.* Interviewers question people who are believed to possess the information desired.

2. *Observation.* People and behavior are viewed and the information is recorded without asking questions.

3. *Experimentation.* Researchers set up a controlled situation in which the outcome of some test is evaluated and in which one or more factors are varied to measure cause-and-effect relationships.

Surveys are the most common research method in business marketing research,[26] because they can provide the type of information business marketers seek.

Applications of Survey Research

Survey techniques are effective for gathering primary data of the following types:[27]

- Awareness and knowledge
- Attitudes and opinions
- Intentions
- Motivations
- Demographic characteristics
- Behavior

As this list suggests, the purpose of the survey is to understand the buying behavior of present and potential industrial customers in order to formulate appropriate marketing strategy. The survey method may be the only way to gather specific data concerning attitudes, motivations and behavior—this material is usually not available in secondary sources. Survey data can also be pivotal in evaluating performance and adjusting market strategies. Let us consider the various methods of applying survey research.

Survey Methods in Business Marketing

Three methods of contact with respondents prevail in business marketing: (1) personal interview, (2) telephone, and (3) mail.

Personal Interviews

Because business marketing research often uses relatively small samples and because much of the information involves in-depth questioning and probing, personal interviewing is the dominant survey approach. Generally, the greater the complexity of the information sought, the more effective personal interviewing is. When technical data, graphs, and illustrations are required, personal interviews are the only choice.

---

[26] Cox, *Industrial Marketing Research,* p. 81.

[27] Ibid., p. 242.

Personal interviewing usually produces high response rates because the interviewer can locate and secure the attention of the correct respondent. In addition, more information can generally be elicited through personal interviews. But personal interviewing is the most expensive and time-consuming form of survey research, and the expense may limit its application.

A research technique that is being increasingly applied to business marketing research problems is the **focus group interview**.[28] A focus group is a group of 6–12 people interviewed in an informal group setting. Open-ended questions are used to stimulate group interaction, and a moderator will lead the discussion much the same as a therapist does in group therapy. Sessions may last up to three hours and they are often videotaped so that different managers can evaluate the sessions.

Business marketing focus groups can be effective in uncovering issues, defining the range of opinions on the issue, testing ad concepts, exploring product needs, and evaluating service perceptions. Standard Register, a business form manufacturer, for example, used a series of focus groups made up of business form buyers to determine buyers' key priorities. Prior to the focus groups the firm believed they "were great service people"; the focus groups indicated that while service was the buyers' number-one priority, Standard Register "had little in terms of service that made them stand out from the crowd."[29] The company quickly created a new customer service management position and initiated a strategy for enhancing responsiveness to customers. Generally, focus groups allow researchers to probe issues in greater depth than they could in structured questionnaires. The information can be gathered and analyzed quickly at relatively low levels of expense. The process is also flexible: the questioning can change direction instantly, and new areas can be explored. Importantly, the data from the focus group session is highly subjective and most experts suggest it should be substantiated through additional quantitative studies.

Telephone Surveys

Telephone interviewing is useful in business marketing research, particularly for evaluating advertising recall, assessing corporate image, and measuring company and brand awareness. If prior contact has been made with respondents who share a vocabulary of technical terms, telephone surveys are a cost-effective way to obtain primary information. For telephone surveys to be effective, the researcher must be able to reach the correct respondent. Telephone interviews are clearly the fastest method for gathering information. Their major drawbacks are (1) the limitations on the amount and kind of information that can be gathered and (2) the inability to detect and control interviewer bias. Telephone interviewers often have difficulty gaining access to the respondent, as secretaries are adept at screening calls. Nevertheless, some firms find telephone surveys effective when advice or opinion is required to make a particular decision rapidly. In this case, a broad listing of firms can be maintained from which a sample can be quickly drawn.

---

[28] Eisenhart, "Advanced Research Finds a New Market," p. 51.

[29] Sue Kapp, "Customer Service is Ex-Fighter Jock's Latest Mission," *Business Marketing,* 75 (August 1990), p. 19.

Mail Surveys

Mail surveys are restricted in terms of the amount and the complexity of information that can be gathered. The quality and quantity of data resulting from a mail survey depend on the respondent's interest in the topic and on the degree of difficulty of the questions. The most severe problem associated with industrial mail surveys is non-response, particularly from large firms. The nonresponse problem has two facets: (1) the original respondent simply fails to return the survey, or (2) the survey is returned by someone other than the original respondent. The latter is often difficult to detect, but does reduce the validity of the survey. Generally, response rates to industrial mail surveys tend to be lower than for consumer surveys. This is a continuing problem and one that business marketing researchers must address.

Mail surveys take more time to construct and administer than telephone surveys, but they are not as demanding as personal interviews. Because of the impersonal nature of the contact and the complexity of the subject matter, the wording and structure of the questionnaire are extremely critical. To secure meaningful response rates, follow-up mailings are frequently required. As one might expect, mail surveys are generally the least expensive survey method.

Table 5.3 uses six criteria to compare the three survey techniques. The inherent trade-offs among the three survey methods must be evaluated in light of the type of information sought, the time and research funds available, and the levels of reliability required. Only then can the appropriate method be selected.

Organizing for Research

The research function can be centralized, decentralized, or contracted out to specialized business marketing research companies. For maximum impact, research findings must be effectively integrated into the decision-making process. The organizational placement of the research function will have a definite effect on whether this goal is accomplished. Deciding how to organize the marketing research function requires consideration of several delicate organizational issues. Generally, marketing research should be free from the influence of those whom its work affects, should have a location that is conducive to maximum operational efficiency, and should have the wholehearted support of the executive to whom it reports.[30]

Two-Tier Research Staff

Large industrial firms often have both a centralized corporate marketing research unit and smaller-scale divisional marketing research units. The central research unit usually has a full-time staff whose major functions are to gather broad-gauged data on the economy and the industry and to conduct studies for product line alternatives, new product opportunities, and acquisitions. The centralized research staff may significantly contribute to the development of marketing plans and strategy. In general, centralized

---

[30] *Marketing, Business and Commercial Research in Industry,* Studies in Business Policy, No. 27 (New York: National Industrial Conference Board, 1955), p. 7, as reported in H. Robert Dodge, *Industrial Marketing* (New York: McGraw-Hill Book Company, 1970), p. 117.

TABLE 5.3   **A Comparison of Business Marketing Survey Methods**

	Criteria					
Approach	**Cost**	**Time**	**Information Quality**	**Information Quantity**	**Nonresponse Problem**	**Interviewer Bias**
Personal Interview	Highest cost per respondent	Most time-consuming	Can elicit in-depth, complex information	Extensive	Few problems, as a result of face-to-face contact	Hard to detect and control
Telephone	Second highest cost	Least time-consuming	Complex information if prior contact established	Limited	Difficult to ensure that contact is made with correct respondent	Hard to detect and control
Mail	Least cost	Moderate	Moderately complex information	Moderate; depends on respondent interest and effort required	Difficult to control who responds and how many will respond	Can be controlled by rigorous pretesting

Source: Adapted from William F. Cox, Jr., *Industrial Marketing Research* (New York: John Wiley and Sons, 1979), pp. 246–51.

research activities affect more than one group or division—preparing economic forecasts, planning support, and researching management science and information systems.[31] Divisional research activities usually affect performance areas such as product sales rates, advertising effectiveness, and market share studies.

Management Support

Regardless of how the business marketing research function is organized, the research unit requires the support of top management. The central research department should report to a high-level executive or even to the president to ensure that (1) marketing research information will be used properly in the decision-making process, and (2) the marketing research function will be given a fair hearing during the corporate budgeting process. The contribution of marketing research can be realized to its fullest extent when top management recognizes its role in the development and control of business marketing strategy.

Utilizing "Outside" Research Specialists

Many types of business marketing research require specialized skills. Studies on organizational buying behavior, company image evaluations, or strategic adjustments required by environmental conditions may dictate outside assistance. The range of alternatives is wide—from free advice provided by advertising agencies to expensive special-purpose studies conducted by management consultants or market research

---

[31] William P. Hall, "Marketing Research for Industrial Products," *Industrial Marketing Management,* 4 (1975), p. 211.

ETHICAL BUSINESS MARKETING
Competitive Information Collection:
Principles for Consultants

A manufacturer's statement about the ethical principles of competitive intelligence gathering:

> There are boundaries to legal and ethical information collection conduct beyond which the efforts of the Company or its consultants must not go. The Company's policy is firm that we must not be involved in "industrial espionage" or theft of trade secrets.

The following specific examples are provided.

1. Information appearing in the press or otherwise generally available may be assembled and distributed, as may legal documents open to public inspection such as patent applications, recorded deeds, SIC reports, and the like. Copies of competitive publications such as annual reports, and public relations releases may be secured and utilized.

2. Photographs of competitive plants may be taken from public highways or sidewalks, but activities which hold competitors or others to unforeseeable standards of self-protection should be avoided. Thus, aerial photography is not to be used since it does not look like the kind of public exposure which a competitor would normally expect to have to defend against.

3. In the course of obtaining information, the consultant should not expressly or impliedly represent that its status is merely that of the general public. For example, the consultant should not participate in public plant tours or visit the vicinity of competitive plants for the purpose of overhearing the conversations of the plant employees.

4. If the consultant receives information which he believes might be confidential or proprietary or in conflict with other obligations he must not provide the information to the Company or otherwise utilize it on behalf of the Company until the Company has had an opportunity to evaluate the manner in which the information was obtained and the propriety of its receiving the data.

Source: A *Fortune* 500 company's policy on competitive information collection.

specialists. Some consulting and marketing organizations specialize in the business marketing field.[32] The purpose and scope of the needed research and the funds available determine which form of outside assistance is most appropriate.

An important mode of industrial research is the multiclient study. A market research firm might propose to study the market for specialty steel products. The research firm circulates a written proposal to firms that might benefit from such a study. If enough firms are willing to participate, the cost of the research is shared by them. A company such as Du Pont receives hundreds of such proposals every year.

---

[32] For example, see Hall, ibid., p. 211.

Business marketing research provides the data necessary to evaluate performance and to plan future marketing strategies. The business marketing research process uses techniques and tools different from those employed in the consumer-goods market. However, sound research methods are equally necessary. The organization of the marketing research function will depend on the size, nature, and role of research in the industrial firm. However, for research to be effective, top management must understand that research plays a vital role in business marketing management.

Using Research in the Business Marketing Process

Market Potential and Sales Forecasting

The marketing intelligence function is responsible for maintaining the data base used to estimate market potential and to forecast sales, as well as for developing the appropriate methodologies and models for generating these estimates. Because of the importance of these estimation procedures, they will be discussed in Chapter 7.

New Product Research

Much of the research activity associated with new products is undertaken through formal market research studies. An important component of this type of research is the formulation of systematic procedures to gather new product ideas from customers, middlemen, sales personnel, competitors, and management. Without formal systems, many new product concepts will go unrecognized, and significant opportunities for sales growth will be lost. Many of the issues associated with new product research will be treated in Chapter 11, Managing Innovation and New Industrial Product Development.

Marketing Control

The success of marketing strategy partially depends on the ability of the marketing manager to understand the requirements of target customers and to develop a marketing mix that will meet those requirements effectively. Equally important is the system whereby the manager evaluates actual against planned performance and objectives, the **marketing control system**. Although the control process is vital in evaluating past performance, it is even more important to the future. Information generated by the marketing control system is an essential element in revising existing marketing strategies, formulating new strategies, and allocating funds to specific programs. The requirements of an effective control system are strict—data must be continuously gathered on the appropriate performance measures. Central to the business marketing intelligence system are (1) systems and procedures for generating the required performance information and (2) readily accessible information banks for continuously evaluating performance. Because the marketing control aspects of the intelligence system are substantial and important, marketing control will be examined in detail in Chapter 18.

Competitor Intelligence

Current approaches to developing business and marketing strategy focus to a significant extent on creating a **competitive strategy**—a strategy based on an analysis

---

INSIDE BUSINESS MARKETING

Market Research Information: It's More than Just Information—It's Motivation

Industrial distributors—wholesalers of industrial products ranging from pipes to PCs—need to know where potential sales volume can be found so they can direct their efforts to capturing the business. Business marketing research can provide the information and in the process, add something extra: incentive for the sales force.

One source of research data on potential for distributors is DMP (Distributor Market Potentials), developed by Industrial Market Information, Inc. A DMP report shows total dollar sales potential for a given product line by county in the distributor's market area. More detailed reports then list the names and addresses of potential buyers along with the sales potential for specific product lines.

The value of the research data is not so much related to its use in planning the distributor's strategy as it is in motivating sales people to exert their best efforts. Typically, sales people will be highly motivated when they realize that a potential payoff exists with a particular prospect. Sales managers report that sales people "attack" accounts more confidently when research data suggest that large potential business exists.

Source: Adapted from Robert C. Clifton, "Market Research Comes of Age," *Industrial Distribution* (December, 1988), p. 64.

---

of the firm's industry, a prediction of the industry's future evolution, an understanding of competitors, and an analysis of the firm's position relative to those competitors.[33] Thus, a core application of marketing research techniques in the business-to-business environment is the collection of accurate and reliable information about competitors. These types of competitive analyses are finding increasing application. A Conference Board study found that 67 percent of surveyed companies planned to increase their competitive intelligence activities, while almost none indicated they would cut back.[34]

Competitive intelligence is a structured approach, and a resulting data set, that develops detailed information about competitors' characteristics, activities, costs, and strategies. The aim of the competitive intelligence system is to create a data base on competitors that will facilitate the company's development of its marketing strategy. The competitive data base makes it possible to quickly identify threats and opportunities, respond rapidly to changes in competitors' strategies, and improve the overall effectiveness of the planning process. The Conference Board study cited earlier indicated that pricing, strategy, and sales data, in that order, are the most useful types of competitive information.[35]

All of the survey research methods can be utilized in developing competitive intelligence, and creative approaches will often be required. In one instance, a researcher trying to discover whether a competitor would open a plant in a particular

---

[33] Kathleen Behof, "The Right Way to Snoop on the Competition," *Sales and Marketing Management,* 139 (May 1986), p. 48.

[34] "Marketers Turn to Competitive Intelligence," *Business Marketing,* 73 (December 1988), p. 23.

[35] Ibid., p. 24.

city visited every country club in the city to inquire about new membership applications. The researcher discovered that the competitor's executives had applied and thereby confirmed the new plant location.[36] Secondary information sources are also used in competitive information gathering, particularly of federal, state, and local government data. Secondary sources, however, have distinct limitations in competitive intelligence because of timeliness and lack of focus on specific issues and current concerns. Primary research—interviews, focus groups, surveys, trade show intelligence, and field observations—will be required, and in most cases, it will be the major ingredient in building a competitor data base.

Sources of competitive intelligence abound—the sales force, annual reports, industry directories, customers, suppliers, on-line data bases. However, effective competitive intelligence depends not only on the information, but on how the information is used. To be effective, a competitive intelligence system must consider the following:

1. *Specific objectives.* To avoid wasted efforts and an overwhelming quantity of data, the manager must carefully determine the exact information to be gathered.

2. *How the data will be used.* Data requirements to plan an ad campaign will be much different from those to develop a manufacturing strategy.

3. *Data gathering approach.* It is important to evaluate the best way to administer the competitive intelligence program. Data can be collected in a number of ways: as part of every marketing manager's job; by the sales force; by a trained competitive intelligence staff; by the marketing research department; or by an outside research firm. If the program is to be permanent or is to become part of strategic planning, then some type of internal process will be required.

4. *Integration into strategic planning.* A system will be required to ensure that the competitive intelligence is provided to managers on a periodic basis for use in the planning process. Monthly computer reports, a competitive intelligence newsletter, or regular competitive intelligence meetings are different approaches for making sure the information is used on an ongoing basis.

The Cost of Primary Research

The substantial cost of collecting primary data must be balanced against its probable value to management. Managers must always take risks because of incomplete information; they cannot afford the luxury of sophisticated research every time a decision must be made. The cost of primary research can be more easily justified as the financial risk of a decision increases. If the level of risk is low, the cost of gathering more information may be greater than the financial loss associated with a poor decision. Primary research should be used when the manager believes that the risk can be greatly reduced at a reasonable cost.

---

[36] Michael E. Porter, *Competitive Strategy* (New York: The Free Press, 1980), p. xiv.

THE GLOBAL MARKETPLACE
Global Competitive Intelligence Gathering Accelerates

The success of Xerox Corporation in recapturing its share of the global copier market shows the tremendous potential of global competitive intelligence. Xerox's global competitive intelligence program helped it determine competitors' manufacturing and distribution costs and to recognize that their copiers were priced 40 percent higher than competitive models and quality levels were subpar. Based on this information, Xerox set about cutting manufacturing costs, improving quality, and enhancing distribution capabilities. The net result? Xerox market share has returned to, and slightly exceeded, prior levels.

Although the use of global competitive intelligence is not widespread among U.S. companies, a number of factors suggest a rapid acceleration in its application. These primary factors stand out:

1. *Europe 1992.* The reduction in trade barriers will enhance the availability of information on EC competitors. More financial information will probably become publicly available.

2. *English as the international business language.* With the acceptance of English as the common language, all aspects of data gathering become easier.

3. *Technology.* Fax machines, electronic mail, and networked computers facilitate the information-gathering process. Data can be sent and received at locally convenient times. The proliferation of on-line data bases on a global basis makes competitive data more readily accessible.

Some multinational firms have instituted sizable global computer networks for competitive intelligence gathering. Digital Equipment, for example, collects and distributes data on global competitors. Its system contains information on competitors' products, strategies, and policies, as well as general market analyses. Data from the system is used for strategic decision making and planning; sales representatives use it to formulate sales tactics.

Source: Adapted from Kate Bertrand, "The Global Spyglass," *Business Marketing,* 75 (September, 1990), pp. 52–56.

SUMMARY

A key aspect of marketing strategy formulation is the development of an information base that facilitates decision making, monitors the environment, and simplifies performance evaluation; the marketing intelligence system accomplishes these objectives. The marketing intelligence system is composed of models, information-gathering procedures, and analysis and marketing research techniques to provide a continuous information flow. This function includes marketing research studies, sales forecasting, market potential estimation, control systems, and secondary data files.

The intelligence system is designed to provide management with a decision support system—data, models, manipulation, and displays that make information accessible for the decision-making process. Gathering and evaluating secondary data is another important dimension of marketing intelligence. The amount of secondary data available to the business marketing manager is staggering; many business marketers are turning to on-line computer searches of secondary data as a means to gather, disseminate, and use such data more effectively.

Marketing research refers to the techniques and procedures for gathering primary data for decision making. Business marketing research is unique as a result of the nature of the business market and of the organizational buying process. Much primary research in the industrial setting is by surveys—personal, mail, or telephone. Gathering the necessary data to control marketing activities also falls within the domain of the intelligence system.

Finally, sales forecasting and market potential estimates require significant data and extensive knowledge of market segments. Specific techniques for segmenting the business market constitute the theme of the next chapter.

Discussion Questions

1. Describe the key components of a business marketing intelligence system and the role that each component assumes in managing the marketing function in an industrial firm.

2. Some experts contend that business marketing is an especially fertile area for the application of a decision support system. First, describe the features of the business market that lend themselves to a DSS. Next, describe the attributes that a DSS should possess to aid the marketing manager.

3. The Tarlton Varnish Company would like to identify furniture manufacturers in Michigan that may be potential users of their product line. What sources of information could they consult in evaluating the potential demand for their products in Michigan? What sources could be used to identify potential customers by name and address?

4. To overcome some of the problems that arise in using SIC data for market planning, two ratios are particularly valuable: the primary product specialization ratio and the coverage ratio. Describe how a business marketer can improve the quality of segmentation decisions by applying these ratios.

5. What information can the business marketer draw from (1) *Census of Manufactures,* (2) *Annual Survey of Manufactures,* and (3) *County Business Patterns?* How is the SIC system used in each?

6. The Alberg Machine Tool Company would like to evaluate the relative attractiveness of selected international markets. Suggest some international data sources that the firm might consult.

7. Compare and contrast marketing research in the business market and in the consumer-goods sector.

8. Houston Electronics recently introduced a new component that appears to have significant potential among manufacturers of personal computers. The firm would like to use a business marketing research study to identify the composition of the buying centers for this product. Develop a research design.

9. Formulate a business marketing research problem that would lend itself to a telephone survey.

10. The marketing research function can be centralized at the corporate level or decentralized at the divisional level. Likewise, the marketing research function can be found in research and development or may be fully integrated into the marketing department. What factors must be considered in positioning the marketing research function in the corporate structure of the industrial firm?

CHAPTER 6

Segmenting the Business Market

The industrial seller faces a market made up of many different types of organizational customers with varying needs. Only when this aggregate market is broken down into meaningful categories can the business marketing strategist readily and profitably respond to unique needs. After reading this chapter, you will understand:

1. the benefits of and requirements for segmenting the business market.
2. the potential bases for segmenting the business market.
3. a procedure for evaluating and selecting market segments.
4. the role of market segmentation in the development of business marketing strategy.

"HIGH-growth companies succeed by identifying and meeting the needs of certain kinds of customers, not all customers, for special kinds of products and services, not all products or all services. Business academics call this market segmentation. Entrepreneurs call it common sense."[1] The business market consists of three broad sectors—commercial enterprises, institutions, and government. Whether marketers elect to operate in one or in all of these sectors, they will encounter diversity in organizations, purchasing structures, and decision-making styles. Each sector has many segments; each segment may have unique needs and require a unique marketing strategy. The business marketer who recognizes the needs of the various segments of the market is best equipped to isolate market opportunities and to respond with an effective marketing program.

---

[1] Donald K. Clifford, Jr., and Richard E. Cavanagh, *The Winning Performance: How America's High-Growth Companies Succeed* (New York: Bantam Books, 1985), p. 53.

The value of market segmentation can be illustrated by briefly examining the computer market. Here IBM is the market leader, drawing more than one quarter of the entire industry's revenue.[2] General Electric, RCA, and Xerox failed in their attempts to compete head-on with IBM in the high end of the market. However, by targeting marketing strategies on particular segments or user needs, others have prospered. Consider the target that Compaq Computer addresses in the personal computer market. "We don't spend a lot of time worrying about the home market or the educational market or some of the other industrial markets. We focus our resources on developing new products to meet the needs of the business PC user."[3] Similarly, rather than attempting a broad assault on the entire market, Steven Jobs at NeXt developed a new generation of personal computers and focused its introduction on the college and university marketplace. Numerous companies offer specialized products to serve other niches: Cray Research (supercomputers), Sun Microsystems and Hewlett-Packard (engineering workstations), Digital Equipment Corporation (minicomputers), NCR (retail-automation products), and Apple Computer (education products).

The goal of this chapter is to demonstrate how the manager can select and evaluate segments of the business market. First, the benefits of and the requirements for successful market segmentation are delineated. Second, specific bases upon which the business market can be segmented are explored and evaluated. This section demonstrates the application of key buyer behavior concepts (examined in Chapter 4) and secondary information sources (Chapter 5) to market segmentation decisions. Third, a framework is provided for evaluating and selecting market segments. Procedures for assessing the costs and benefits of entering alternative market segments and for implementing a segmentation strategy are emphasized.

ORGANIZATIONAL MARKET SEGMENTATION: REQUIREMENTS AND BENEFITS

A **market segment** is "a group of present or potential customers with some common characteristic which is relevant in explaining (and predicting) their response to a supplier's marketing stimuli."[4] Since virtually every market that is made up of more than one potential buying organization could conceivably be divided or segmented, the industrial marketer must understand the requirements for successful segmentation.

---

[2] Brenton R. Schlender, "Who's Ahead in the Computer Wars," *Fortune* (February 12, 1990), p. 59.

[3] Gary Reiner, "Lessons From the World's Best Product Developers," *The Wall Street Journal* (August 6, 1990), p. A-12.

[4] Yoram Wind and Richard N. Cardozo, "Industrial Market Segmentation," *Industrial Marketing Management,* 3 (March 1974), p. 155; see also Peter R. Dickson and James L. Ginter, "Market Segmentation, Product Differentiation, and Marketing Strategy," *Journal of Marketing,* 51 (April 1987), pp. 1–10.

Requirements

A business marketer has four criteria for evaluating the desirability of potential market segments:[5]

1. *Measurability*. Marketers evaluate the degree to which information on the particular buyer characteristic exists or can be obtained.

2. *Accessibility*. Marketers evaluate the degree to which the firm can effectively focus its marketing efforts on chosen segments.

3. *Substantiality*. Marketers evaluate the degree to which the segments are large or profitable enough to be worth considering for separate marketing cultivation.

4. *Compatibility*. Marketers evaluate the degree to which the firm's marketing and business strengths match the present and expected competitive and technological state of the market.

Thus, the art of market segmentation involves identifying groups of consumers that are sufficiently large, and sufficiently unique, to justify a separate marketing strategy. The competitive environment of the market segment is a factor that must be analyzed.

Evaluating the Competitive Environment

In selecting a market segment, the business marketer is also choosing a competitive environment. **Benchmarking** provides a valuable tool for assessing how a firm stands in a particular competitive environment. *Competitive* benchmarking is the process of comparing a firm's products, services, and practices with those of its best competitors. To illustrate, managers at all levels of IBM are asked which competitor is best in the world at what they do—whether R&D, quality assurance, distribution, or software.[6] Attention then turns to the underlying reason for that success and the changes that IBM should make to equal it. At Xerox, senior managers credit competitive benchmarking with producing a shock that, in turn, created the energy the company needed to overhaul its copier business in the 1980s. The analysis revealed to Xerox that, in comparison to competitors, its product quality was poorer, its product design cycles were longer, and its technology was older.[7]

The object company used in benchmarking need not be a direct competitor. *Functional* benchmarking involves a function-against-function comparison using firms drawn from diverse industries. Any excellent company that has the same type of operation, customer group, or information flow can be used. For example, in addition to examining direct competitors, Xerox benchmarked L. L. Bean for distribution

---

[5] The first three of these four were advanced by Philip Kotler, *Marketing Management* (Englewood Cliffs, N.J.: Prentice-Hall, Inc., 1976), p. 143.

[6] George S. Day, *Market Driven Strategy: Processes for Creating Value* (New York: The Free Press, 1990), pp. 156–157.

[7] T. Michael Nevens, Gregory L. Summe, and Bro Uttal, "Commercializing Technology: What the Best Companies Do," *Harvard Business Review,* 68 (May–June 1990), pp. 154–163.

procedures, Procter & Gamble for marketing, Deere & Company for central computer operations, and Florida Power & Light for its quality process. What did Xerox (a copier company) learn from L. L. Bean (an outdoor specialty company)? That L. L. Bean could sort customer orders three times faster in the warehouse than Xerox and that the source of that efficiency was a well-refined computerized order sorting process! Valuable insights were likewise gathered from the other firms and measurable goals were established for each function. Thus, the key to the benchmarking process is not only to record the superior performance level for a particular function but, most importantly, to learn how the reference company achieves its superior level of performance.[8]

Evaluating the Technological Environment

The business marketing strategist must also carefully assess the technological environment in which the firm elects to compete. Consider the technological environment in the computer industry. Manufacturers of mainframe computers upgrade their product lines every four years, personal computer manufacturers replace their models approximately every two years, and manufacturers of engineering workstations advance their technology even more frequently. For example, Sun Microsystems attempts to double the performance of its high-end workstations every eighteen months![9]

Three features of the technological environment are especially relevant: (1) **product technology** (the set of ideas embodied in the product or service); (2) **process technology** (the set of ideas or steps involved in the production of a product or service); and (3) **management technology** (the management procedures associated with selling the product or service and with administering the business).[10] Changes occurring in any of these areas can lead to less market-segment stability, shifts in traditional product-market boundaries, and new sources of competition. To illustrate, technological change is blurring traditional boundaries in the computer, telecommunications, and financial services industries. Michael Porter observes:

> Technology strategy must reinforce the competitive advantage a firm is seeking to achieve and sustain. . . . A firm must know its relative strengths in key technologies, as well as make a realistic assessment of its ability to keep up with technological change. Considerations of pride should not obscure such an assessment or a firm will squander resources in an area in which it has little hope of contributing to its competitive advantage.[11]

---

[8] David T. Kearns, "Leadership through Quality," *Academy of Management Executive,* 4 (May 1990), pp. 86–89; and Robert C. Camp, "Competitive Benchmarking: Xerox's Powerful Quality Tool," in Frank Caropreso, ed., *Making Total Quality Happen* (New York: The Conference Board, 1990), pp. 35–47.

[9] George Stalk, Jr., and Thomas M. Hout, *Competing Against Time: How Time-based Competition Is Re-shaping Global Markets* (New York: Free Press, 1990), p. 102.

[10] Noel Capon and Rashi Glazer, "Marketing and Technology: A Strategic Coalignment," *Journal of Marketing,* 51 (July 1987), pp. 1–14.

[11] Michael E. Porter, "Technology and Competitive Advantage," *Journal of Business Strategy,* 5 (Winter 1985), p. 78; and Porter, *Competitive Advantage: Creating and Sustaining Superior Performance* (New York: Free Press, 1985).

Making a Commitment

Business market segments must be selected with care because of the close working relationship between buyer and seller after the sale.[12] Although producers of consumer goods such as toothpaste can shift from one demographic or life style segment to another relatively quickly, industrial firms may have to realign their entire marketing strategy (e.g., retrain salespersons) and alter the manufacturing process to meet the needs of a new market segment. Posttransaction service commitments to the new segment may continue for months or years. Thus, the decision to enter a particular market segment carries with it significant long-term resource commitments for the industrial firm. Such decisions are not easily reversed.

Benefits

If the requirements for effective segmentation are met, several benefits accrue to the firm. First, the mere attempt to segment the organizational market forces the marketer to become more attuned to the unique needs of customer segments. Although beneficial to firms of any size, market segmentation is crucial to the low market share firm. Often, segments are identified that are being neglected or inadequately served by competitors. "To be successful, a low market share company must compete in the segments where its own strengths will be most highly valued and where its large competitors will be most unlikely to compete."[13]

Second, knowledge of the needs of particular market segments helps the business marketer focus product development efforts, develop profitable pricing strategies, select appropriate channels of distribution, develop and target advertising messages, and train and deploy the sales force. Thus, market segmentation provides the foundation for efficient and effective business marketing strategies.

Third, market segmentation provides the business marketer with guidelines that are of significant value in allocating marketing resources. Industrial firms often serve multiple market segments and must continually monitor the relative attractiveness and performance of these segments. Ultimately, the costs, revenues, and profits accruing to the firm must be evaluated segment by segment. As market or competitive conditions change, corresponding adjustments may be required in the firm's market segmentation strategy. Thus, market segmentation provides a basic unit of analysis for marketing planning and control.

---

[12] B. Charles Ames, "Marketing Planning for Industrial Products," *Harvard Business Review,* 46 (September–October 1968), pp. 100–111.

[13] R. G. Hammermesh, M. J. Anderson, Jr., and J. E. Harris, "Strategies for Low Market Share Businesses," *Harvard Business Review,* 56 (May–June 1978), p. 98.

BASES FOR SEGMENTING BUSINESS MARKETS

While the consumer-goods marketer is interested in securing meaningful profiles of individuals (demographics, life-style, benefits sought), the business marketer profiles organizations (size, end use) and organizational buyers (decision style, criteria). Thus, the business or organizational market can be segmented on several bases,[14] broadly classified into two major categories, macrosegmentation and microsegmentation.

Macrosegmentation centers on the characteristics of the buying organization and the buying situation, thus dividing the market by such organizational characteristics as size, geographic location, SIC category, or organizational structure. In contrast, **microsegmentation** requires a higher degree of market knowledge focusing on the characteristics of decision-making units within each macrosegment—buying decision criteria, perceived importance of the purchase, or attitudes toward vendors. Richard Cardozo and Yoram Wind recommend a two-stage approach to business market segmentation:[15] (1) identify meaningful macrosegments, and then (2) divide the macrosegments into microsegments (Figure 6.1).

In evaluating alternative bases for segmentation, the marketer is attempting to identify good predictors of differences in buyer behavior. Once such differences are recognized, the marketer can approach target segments with appropriate marketing strategy. Secondary sources of information (Chapter 5), coupled with data in company files, can be used to divide the market into macrolevel segments. The concentration of the business market allows some marketers to monitor the purchasing patterns of each customer. For example, a firm that sells industrial products to paper manufacturers is dealing with hundreds of potential buying organizations in the U.S. and Canadian markets; a paper manufacturer selling to ultimate consumers is dealing with millions of potential customers. Such market concentration, coupled with rapidly advancing marketing intelligence systems, makes it easier for the business marketer to monitor the purchasing patterns of individual organizations.[16]

Macrolevel Bases

Selected macrolevel bases of segmentation are presented in Table 6.1. Recall that these are concerned with general characteristics of the buying organization, the nature of the product application, and the characteristics of the buying situation.

---

[14] For a comprehensive review of business market segmentation research, see Richard E. Plank, "A Critical Review of Industrial Market Segmentation," *Industrial Marketing Management,* 14 (May 1985), pp. 79–91; and Robert J. Thomas and Yoram Wind, "Toward Empirical Generalizations on Industrial Market Segmentation," in Robert E. Spekman and David T. Wilson, eds., *Issues in Industrial Marketing: A View to the Future* (Chicago: American Marketing Association, 1982), pp. 1–18.

[15] Wind and Cardozo, "Industrial Market Segmentation," p. 155; see also Richard N. Cardozo, "Analyzing Industrial Markets," in Victor P. Buell, ed., *Handbook of Modern Marketing* (New York: McGraw-Hill Book Company, 1986), pp. 11-1 to 11-11.

[16] Yoram Wind, "Industrial Marketing: Present Status and Future Potential," presentation to the American Marketing Association's Second Annual Faculty Consortium on Industrial Marketing, July 5, 1982.

FIGURE 6.1   **A Hierarchy of Business Market Segmentation**

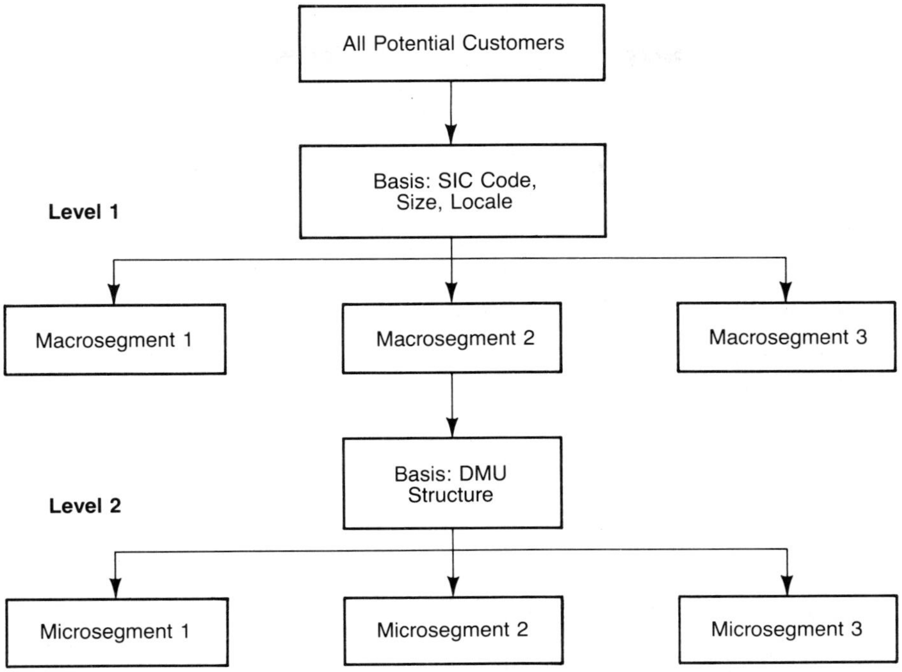

Source: Exhibit 9-11 (page 311) from *Marketing Decision Making: A Model-Building Approach* by Gary L. Lilien and Philip Kotler. Copyright 1983 by Harper & Row Publishers, Inc. Reprinted by permission of the publisher.

Macrolevel Characteristics of Buying Organizations

The marketer may find it useful to partition the market by size of potential buying organizations. Large buying organizations may possess unique requirements and respond to marketing stimuli that are different from those responded to by smaller firms. The influence of presidents, vice presidents, and owners declines with an increase in corporate size; the influence of other participants such as purchasing managers increases.[17] Alternatively, the marketer may recognize regional variations and adopt geographical units as the basis for differentiating marketing strategies.

Usage rate constitutes another macrolevel variable. Buyers are classified on a continuum ranging from nonuser to heavy user. Although this scheme may be more

---

[17] Joseph A. Bellizzi, "Organizational Size and Buying Influences," *Industrial Marketing Management,* 10 (February 1981), pp. 17–21; see also Lowell E. Crow and Jay D. Lindquist, "Impact of Organizational and Buyer Characteristics on the Buying Center," *Industrial Marketing Management,* 14 (February 1985), pp. 49–58; R. Dale Wilson, "Segmentation and Communication in the Industrial Marketplace," *Journal of Business Research,* 14 (December 1986), pp. 487–500; and Jean-Marie Choffray and Gary L. Lilien, "Industrial Market Segmentation by the Structure of the Purchasing Process," *Industrial Marketing Management,* 9 (October 1980), pp. 331–342.

TABLE 6.1   **Selected Macrolevel Bases of Segmentation**

Variables	Illustrative Breakdowns
Characteristics of Buying Organizations	
Size (the scale of operations of the organization)	Small, medium, or large—based on sales or number of employees
Geographical location	New England, Middle Atlantic, South Atlantic, East North Central, etc.
Usage rate	Nonuser, light user, moderate user, heavy user
Structure of procurement	Centralized, decentralized
Product/Service Application	
SIC category	Varies by product or service
End market served	Varies by product or service
Value-in-use	High, low
Characteristics of Purchasing Situation	
Type of buying situation	New task, modified rebuy, straight rebuy
Stage in purchase decision process	Early stages, late stages

appropriate for industrial rather than consumer-goods marketers, limited attention has been given to this segmentation dimension in the business marketing literature.[18] Clearly, a great deal of market knowledge is required to implement this classification effectively, but the potential payoff for distinguishing heavy from light users is high.

The structure of the procurement function constitutes a final macrolevel characteristic of buying organizations. Firms with a centralized purchasing function behave differently than do those with decentralized procurement (see Chapter 4). The structure of the purchasing function influences the degree of buyer specialization, the criteria emphasized, and the composition of the buying center. Centralized buyers place significant weight on long-term supply availability and the development of a healthy supplier complex. Decentralized buyers emphasize short-term cost efficiency.[19] Thus, the position of procurement in the organizational hierarchy provides a base for categorizing organizations and for isolating specific needs and marketing requirements. Many business marketers develop a national accounts sales force to meet the special requirements of large centralized procurement units.

---

[18] Jagdish N. Sheth, "Recent Developments in Organizational Buying Behavior," in Arch Woodside, Jagdish N. Sheth, and Peter D. Bennett, eds., *Consumer and Industrial Buying Behavior* (New York: Elsevier-North Holland, 1977), p. 31.

[19] E. Raymond Corey, *The Organizational Context of Industrial Buyer Behavior* (Cambridge, Mass.: Marketing Science Institute, 1978), pp. 6–12.

FIGURE 6.2   **An Ad Featuring the Benefits of a Technology in One Industry Application—and Its Potential for Others**

Source: Courtesy, Digital Equipment Corporation.

Product/Service Application

Because a specific industrial good is often used in different ways, the marketer can divide the market on the basis of specific end-use applications. Consider Digital Equipment Corporation (see Figure 6.2). The ad for its networking systems features the benefits of the technology in one industry application and its potential for others. The SIC system and related information sources described in the previous chapter are especially valuable when segmenting the market on the basis of end use. To illustrate, the manufacturer of a component such as springs may reach industries incorporating the product into machine tools, bicycles, surgical devices, office equipment, telephones, and missile systems. Observe in Table 6.2 that a similar approach can be employed when segmenting the market for equipment service. By isolating four major classes of service environments, the business marketer is better equipped to differentiate customer requirements and to evaluate emerging opportunities. The required response time, the nature and complexity of equipment in place, and the sophistication of users all vary by service environment.

TABLE 6.2 **Characteristics of Service Market Segments**

Market Segment	Major Features	Service Factors				
		Response and Repair Time	**Technological Complexity of Products**	**Type of Equipment**	**Hardware/ Software Issues**	**Other**
Office environment	Unsophisticated users "White-collar" environment Growing complexity & mix of products supported Low density installed base at each site	8–24 hours	Medium	Electromechanical (e.g., word processing & photocopying equipment)	Generally no	Many service groups present
Manufacturing environment	Sophisticated users High technology orientation High density installed base at each site	1–4 hours	Very high	Electronic (e.g., CAD/CAM equipment)	Generally yes	Generally single vendor service
Distribution environment	Sophisticated users "Blue-collar" environment High density installed base at each site	2–8 hours	High	Electronic, electromechanical & network-related (e.g., order processing, inventory control systems)	Generally yes	Service becoming increasingly important due to technology and regulation changes
Special markets	Unsophisticated users Requires special knowledge of customer Medium density installed base at each site	8–24 hours	Low to medium	Electromechanical (e.g., systems designed for hospitals & hotel/motels)	Yes—very specialized	Typically, specifically oriented suppliers & system integrated

Source: Reprinted by permission of the publisher from Donald F. Blumberg, "Developing Service as a Line of Business," *Management Review,* 76 (February 1987), p. 61 © 1987 American Management Association, New York. All rights reserved.

Some independent third-party maintenance firms have successfully challenged major equipment manufacturers by catering to the total service requirements of selected segments.[20]

---

[20] Diane Lynn Kastiel, "Service and Support," *Business Marketing,* 72 (June 1987), pp. 54–66.

Value-in-Use

Strategic insights are also provided by exploring the value-in-use of various customer applications.[21] Recall our discussion of value analysis in Chapter 3. **Value-in-use** is a product's economic value to the user relative to a specific alternative in a particular application. The economic value of an offering frequently varies by customer application. For example, Cray Research's supercomputers, among the most expensive in the world, are especially well suited to particular applications. NASA found that a Cray-1 costs about one percent of what an IBM 360-50 would cost to perform a standard simulation. For sophisticated users who have unusually complex requirements, the Cray system may be the most economical alternative, providing significant value-in-use. (NASA and the National Center for Atmospheric Research each bought two!)[22]

The segmentation strategy adopted by a manufacturer of precision motors further illuminates the value-in-use concept.[23] The firm found that its customers differed in the motor speed required in their applications and that a new, low-priced machine introduced by a dominant competitor wore out quickly when used in high- and medium-speed applications. The marketer concentrated on this vulnerable segment, demonstrating the superior life cycle cost advantages of the firm's products. A long-term program was also initiated to develop a competitively priced product and service offering for customers in the low-speed segment.

Purchasing Situation

A final macrolevel base for segmenting the organizational market is the purchasing situation. First-time buyers have perceptions and information needs that differ from those of repeat buyers. Therefore, buying organizations are classified as being in the early or late stages of the procurement process, or alternatively, as *new-task, straight rebuy,* or *modified rebuy* organizations (Chapter 3). The position of the firm in the procurement decision process or its location on the buying situation continuum dictates marketing strategy.[24]

These examples illustrate those macrolevel bases of segmentation that business marketers can apply to the organizational market. Other macrolevel bases may more precisely fit a specific situation. A key benefit of segmentation is that it forces the manager to search for bases that explain similarities and differences among buying organizations.

[21] For example, see Horst O. Bender, "Industrial Conversion Framework: A New Tool to Assess Business Markets," in Robert E. Spekman and David T. Wilson, eds., *A Strategic Approach to Business Marketing* (Chicago: American Marketing Association, 1985), pp. 17–29.

[22] Reported in Clifford and Cavanagh, *The Winning Performance,* pp. 176–178.

[23] Robert A. Garda, "How to Carve Niches for Growth in Industrial Markets," *Management Review,* 70 (August 1981), pp. 15–22.

[24] Richard N. Cardozo, "Modelling Organizational Buying as a Sequence of Decisions," *Industrial Marketing Management,* 12 (April 1983), pp. 75–81.

ILLUSTRATION: Macrosegmentation

A producer of capital equipment that is sold to the food processing industry was successful in penetrating small- and medium-sized food manufacturers but had little success with large buying organizations. The firm's marketing strategy centered on providing extensive technical assistance to potential customers planning plant modernization or expansion. Consistent with this strategy, the firm's application engineers often spent days with customers, analyzing technical requirements and proposing design modifications.

While small- and medium-sized organizations, which often have a small engineering staff, responded favorably, large organizations did not. Potential customers with a large engineering staff preferred to handle the technical details in-house. In addition, the plant-level technical staff was often augmented by direct engineering support from the corporate level in large capital projects.

Thus, large customers wanted only manufacturing technology (capital equipment); small- and medium-sized organizations needed technical assistance as well. The business marketer responded by developing a marketing strategy consistent with the needs of each macrosegment.

Microlevel Bases

Having identified macrosegments, the marketer often finds it useful to divide each macrosegment into smaller microsegments on the basis of the similarities and differences between decision-making units.[25] Often, several microsegments—each with unique requirements and unique responses to marketing stimuli—are buried in macrosegments. To isolate them effectively, the marketer must move beyond secondary sources of information by soliciting input from the sales force or conducting a special market segmentation study. Selected microbases of segmentation appear in Table 6.3.

Key Criteria

For some industrial goods, the marketer can divide the market according to which criteria are assigned the most importance in the purchase decision.[26] Criteria include product quality, prompt and reliable delivery, technical support, price, and supply continuity. The marketer also might divide the market based on supplier profiles that appear to be preferred by decision makers (e.g., high quality, prompt delivery, premium price versus standard quality, less-prompt delivery, low price). To illustrate,

---

[25] Wind and Cardozo, "Industrial Market Segmentation," p. 155.

[26] Cardozo, "Segmenting the Industrial Market," in Robert L. King, ed., *Marketing and the New Science of Planning* (Chicago: American Marketing Association, 1968), pp. 433–440; see also Kenneth E. Mast and John M. Hawes, "Perceptual Differences Between Buyers and Engineers," *Journal of Purchasing and Materials Management,* 22 (Spring 1986), pp. 2–6; Donald W. Jackson, Jr., Richard K. Burdick, and Janet E. Keith, "Purchasing Agents' Perceived Importance of Marketing Mix Components in Different Industrial Purchase Situations," *Journal of Business Research,* 13 (August 1985), pp. 361–373; Donald R. Lehmann and John O'Shaughnessy, "Decision Criteria Used in Buying Different Categories of Products," *Journal of Purchasing and Materials Management,* 18 (Spring 1982), pp. 9–14; and Lehmann and O'Shaughnessy, "Differences in Attribute Importance for Different Industrial Products," *Journal of Marketing,* 38 (April 1974), pp. 36–42.

TABLE 6.3   **Selected Microlevel Bases of Segmentation**

Variables	Illustrative Breakdowns
Key criteria	Quality, delivery, supplier reputation
Decision-specific conflict	High . . . low
Purchasing strategies	Optimizer, satisficer
Structure of decision-making unit	Major decision participants, e.g., purchasing manager and plant manager
Importance of purchase	High . . . low
Attitude toward vendors	Favorable . . . unfavorable
Organizational innovativeness	Innovator . . . follower
Personal characteristics	
Demographics	Age, educational background
Decision style	Normative, conservative, mixed mode
Risk	Risk taker, risk avoider
Confidence	High . . . low
Job responsibility	Purchasing, production, engineering

Rowland Moriarty considered this research question: What factors distinguish IBM buyers from non-IBM buyers?[27]

Moriarty found that purchasers of IBM equipment (nonintelligent data terminals) are more concerned about software support and breadth of product line and less concerned about absolute price and price flexibility (i.e., willingness of suppliers to negotiate price). The two microsegments also differed significantly in the importance of the industrial supplier's visibility among top management. "The IBM buyer's emphasis on visibility could also reflect the need of decision participants to minimize their risk in making the decision."[28] (Recall the concept of perceived risk.) Compared to a supplier unknown to top management, IBM is a risk-free choice.

Service responsiveness is assuming an increasingly important role in many industrial buying decisions. Business market customers can be surprisingly sensitive to time and willing to pay a premium price for responsiveness. George Stalk, Jr., and Thomas M. Hout note: "If the customers who are the most sensitive to responsiveness and choice can be locked-up, a time-based competitor secures an almost unassailable and profitable advantage."[29] For example, Atlas Corporation developed a commanding position in the industrial door market by providing customized products in just four weeks, much faster than the industry average of 12 to 15 weeks. Atlas compressed time by building just-in-time factories and, most importantly, by automating its entire order entry, engineering, pricing, and scheduling processes. Nearly all incoming orders can be priced and scheduled while the caller is still on the telephone. The faster information,

---

[27] Rowland T. Moriarty, *Industrial Buying Behavior* (Lexington, Mass.: Lexington Books, 1983); see also Moriarty and David J. Reibstein, "Benefit Segmentation in Industrial Markets," *Journal of Business Research,* 14 (December 1986), pp. 463–486.

[28] Moriarty, *Industrial Buying Behavior,* p. 101.

[29] Stalk and Hout, *Competing Against Time,* p. 102.

decisions, and materials can flow through an organization, the faster the firm can respond to customer orders or adjust to shifts in market demand and competitive conditions. **Fast-cycle companies** manage both the cycle of industrial activities throughout the organization and the cycle time of the entire delivery system—the number of days it takes to develop a new product or to ship a customer's order.

The marketer can benefit by examining the criteria employed by decision-making units in various sectors of the business market—commercial, governmental, and institutional. For example, the institutional market (hospitals, universities, etc.) represents a sector of growing significance in the U.S. economy. Do these noncommercial buyers employ the same criteria as their commercial counterparts? G. E. Kiser and C. P. Rao explore the similarities and differences between industrial purchasing agents and hospital buyers.[30] For standard product-buying situations, reliability (e.g., quality, fairness) and efficiency (e.g., delivery with required follow-up) are of utmost importance to both industrial and hospital buyers. Both buying groups identify cost as important. Hospital buyers, however, assign more importance to service and less to technical capabilities, past experience with suppliers, and direct source. Thus, supplier attributes that are of considerable importance in the commercial segment have little value in the noncommercial segment. This kind of knowledge facilitates the development of differentiated marketing strategies.

Purchasing Strategies

Microsegments can be formed on the basis of the purchasing strategy employed by buying organizations. Two purchasing profiles that have been identified are satisficers and optimizers.[31]

Satisficers approach a given purchasing requirement by contacting familiar suppliers and placing the order with the first to satisfy product and delivery requirements. **Optimizers** consider numerous suppliers, familiar and unfamiliar, solicit bids, and examine all alternative proposals carefully, before selecting a supplier.

These purchasing strategies have numerous implications. A supplier entering the market would have a higher probability of penetrating a decision-making unit made up of optimizers than of penetrating a unit consisting of satisficers who rely on familiar suppliers.

Identifying different purchasing patterns can help the marketer understand differing responses to marketing stimuli. An organizational marketer of deep-frying oil, for example, encounters both satisficers and optimizers. Large universities review and test alternatives carefully, consult with student committees, and analyze the price-per-unit-cooked before selecting a supplier (optimizers). Restaurants and company cafeterias may follow a different pattern. The restaurant manager, consulting with the chef, selects a supplier that provides the required product quality and delivery (satisficer). Remember

---

[30] G. E. Kiser and C. P. Rao, "Important Vendor Factors in Industrial and Hospital Organizations: A Comparison," *Industrial Marketing Management*, 6 (August 1977), pp. 289–296; see also Kjell Gronhaug, "Exploring Environmental Influences in Organizational Buying," *Journal of Marketing Research*, 13 (August 1976), pp. 225–229.

[31] Richard N. Cardozo, "Situational Segmentation of Industrial Markets," *European Journal of Marketing*, 14 (5/6, 1980), pp. 264–276.

that satisficing and optimizing are only two of many purchasing strategies of organizational buyers.

Structure of Decision-Making Unit

The structure of the decision-making unit, or buying center, likewise provides a means of dividing the business market into subsets of customers by isolating the patterns of involvement in the purchasing process of particular decision participants (e.g., engineering versus top management). A comprehensive analysis of the commercial air-conditioning market led to the identification of four microsegments (Table 6.4).[32] Note that the major decision participants in microsegment 3, which represents 32 percent of the potential market, are production engineers and heating ventilating and air-conditioning (HVAC) consultants. These decision participants perceive a high level of risk in purchasing an unreliable system and a low to medium level of satisfaction with their current system. Such an analysis allows the marketer to identify meaningful microsegments and respond with finely tuned marketing communications.

Importance of Purchase

Classifying organizational customers on the basis of the perceived importance of a particular product is especially appropriate when the product is applied in various ways by various customers. Buyer perceptions differ according to the importance of the product to the total mission of the firm. A large commercial enterprise may consider the purchase of an office machine routine; the same purchase for a small manufacturing concern is "an event."

Attitudes toward Vendors

The attitudes of decision-making units toward the vendors in a particular product class provide a means of microsegmentation. An analysis of how various clusters of buyers view alternative sources of supply often uncovers opportunities in the form of vulnerable segments being either neglected or not fully satisfied by competitors.

Organizational Innovativeness

Some organizations are more innovative and willing to purchase new industrial products than others. A study of the adoption of new medical equipment among hospitals found that psychographic variables can improve a marketer's ability to predict the adoption of new products.[33] These include such factors as an organization's level of change resistance or desire to excel. When psychographic variables are combined with organizational demographic variables (e.g., size), accuracy in predicting organizational innovativeness increases.

---

[32] For a complete discussion of the methodology used in the research, see Jean-Marie Choffray and Gary L. Lilien, "A New Approach to Industrial Market Segmentation," *Sloan Management Review,* 19 (Spring 1978), pp. 23–24.

[33] Thomas S. Robertson and Yoram Wind, "Organizational Psychographics and Innovativeness," *Journal of Consumer Research,* 7 (June 1980), pp. 24–31; see also Robertson and Hubert Gatignon, "Competitive Effects on Technology Diffusion," *Journal of Marketing,* 50 (July 1986), pp. 1–12.

TABLE 6.4   **Microsegments for Industrial Air-Conditioning Systems**

Characteristics	Microsegment 1	Microsegment 2	Microsegment 3	Microsegment 4
Major decision participants	Plant managers and HVAC consultants	Production engineers and plant managers	Production engineers and HVAC consultants	Top management and HVAC consultants
Satisfaction with current system	Medium to high	Low	Low to medium	High
Perceived risk of purchasing an uneconomical system	Medium to high	Low	Low to medium	High
Perceived risk of purchasing an unreliable system	Medium to high	Low	High	Low to medium
Percentage of plant area requiring air-conditioning	Medium to large	Small	Large	Medium
Number of separate plants	Medium to large	Small	Large	Small to medium
Company size	Medium	Large	Large	Small
Percentage of potential market	12%	31%	32%	25%

Source: Adapted from Jean-Marie Choffray and Gary L. Lilien, "A New Approach to Industrial Market Segmentation," *Sloan Management Review,* 19 (Spring 1978), pp. 23–24. Reprinted by permission of the publisher. Copyright 1978 by the Sloan Management Review Association. All rights reserved.

Because products will diffuse more rapidly in some segments than in others, microsegmentation on the basis of organizational innovativeness allows the marketer to identify segments that should be targeted first when new products are introduced. The accuracy of new product forecasting is also improved when diffusion patterns are estimated segment by segment.[34]

Personal Characteristics

Some microsegmentation possibilities deal with the personal characteristics of decision makers: demographics (age, education), personality, decision style, risk preference or risk avoidance, confidence, job responsibilities, and related characteristics. Although some interesting studies have shown the viability of segmentation on the basis of individual characteristics, further research is needed to explore its potential as a firm base for microsegmentation.[35]

---

[34] Yoram Wind, Thomas S. Robertson, and Cynthia Fraser, "Industrial Product Diffusion by Market Segment," *Industrial Marketing Management,* 11 (February 1982), pp. 1–8.

[35] For example, see David T. Wilson, "Industrial Buyers' Decision-Making Styles," *Journal of Marketing Research,* 8 (November 1971), p. 433; Wilson, H. Lee Mathews, and Timothy W. Sweeney, "Industrial Buyer Segmentation: A Psychographic Approach," *AMA Proceedings* (Chicago: American Marketing Association, 1971), pp. 327–331; and Timothy W. Sweeney, H. Lee Mathews, and David T. Wilson, "An Analysis of Industrial Buyers' Risk Reducing Behavior: Some Personality Correlates," *AMA Proceedings* (Chicago: American Marketing Association, 1973), pp. 217–221.

ILLUSTRATION: Microsegmentation[36]

Du Pont Company's strategy in the medical X-ray market provides a rich illustration of microsegmentation. The growing importance of buying groups, multihospital chains, and emerging nonhospital health-care delivery systems pointed to the need for a more refined segmentation approach. As a result, Du Pont initiated a formal positioning study among hospital administrators, radiology department administrators, and technical managers in order to identify the firm's relative standing and the specific needs (criteria) for each level of buying influence within each potential segment.

The study indicates that the medical X-ray market can be segmented on the basis of the type of institution and the responsibilities of the decision makers and decision influencers in these institutions:

- Groups selecting a single supplier that must be used by all member hospitals, such as investor-owned hospital chains

- Groups selecting a small set of suppliers from which individual hospitals may select needed products

- Private group practices and the nonhospital segment

In addition to these differences in the way each segment makes decisions, there are also differences in the decision criteria used in each segment. Similar criteria are applied within each segment. These differences and similarities provide the basis for business market strategies tailored to each segment. Du Pont's salespersons, for example, can tailor their presentations to the decision-making dynamics of each segment. In turn, advertising messages can be more precisely targeted.

A MODEL FOR SEGMENTING THE ORGANIZATIONAL MARKET

Macrosegmentation centers on characteristics of buying *organizations* (e.g., size), product application (e.g., end market served), and characteristics of the purchasing situation (e.g., stage in the purchase decision process). Microsegmentation concentrates on characteristics of organizational decision-making *units,* for instance, choice criteria assigned the most importance in the purchase decision.

Identifying Market Segments

The model in Figure 6.3 combines these bases and outlines the steps required for effective segmentation. This approach to organizational market segmentation, developed by Yoram Wind and Richard Cardozo, begins with an analysis of key

---

[36]Gary J. Coles and James D. Culley, "Not All Prospects Are Created Equal," *Business Marketing,* 71 (May 1986), pp. 52–57. For other microsegmentation studies, see Mark J. Bennion, Jr., "Segmentation and Positioning in a Basic Industry," *Industrial Market Management,* 16 (February 1987), pp. 9–18; Arch G. Woodside and Elizabeth J. Wilson, "Combining Macro and Micro Industrial Market Segmentation," in Arch G. Woodside, ed., *Advances in Business Marketing* (Greenwich, CT: JAI Press, Inc., 1986), pp. 241–257; and Peter Doyle and John Saunders, "Market Segmentation and Positioning in Specialized Industrial Markets," *Journal of Marketing,* 49 (Spring 1985), pp. 24–32.

FIGURE 6.3   **An Approach to Segmentation of Business Markets**

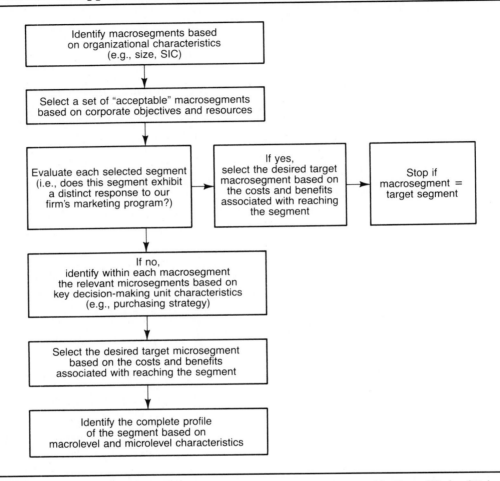

Source: Adapted by permission of the publisher from "Industrial Market Segmentation," by Yoram Wind and Richard Cardozo, *Industrial Marketing Management,* 3 (March 1974), p. 156. Copyright 1974 by Elsevier Science Publishing Co., Inc.

characteristics of the organization and of the buying situation (macro-dimensions)[37] in order to identify, evaluate, and select meaningful macrosegments. Note that the segmentation task is complete at this stage if *each* of the selected macrosegments exhibits a *distinct* response to the firm's marketing stimuli. Since the information needed for macrosegmentation can often be drawn from secondary information sources, the research investment is low.

---

[37] Wind and Cardozo, "Industrial Market Segmentation," pp. 153–166; see also John Morton, "How to Spot the Really Important Prospects," *Business Marketing,* 75 (January 1990), pp. 62–67.

THE GLOBAL MARKETPLACE
Adapting to International Market Segments

Upon entering the international market, many U.S. corporations have stumbled. Foreign companies have had striking success in markets ranging from steel to telecommunications equipment. Yet a growing number of U.S. companies have become remarkably adept overseas, adopting and building on skills foreign competitors were forced to learn years ago. For example, smart international marketers have learned that they must often adapt products to unique conditions.

• Hewlett-Packard reshuffled letters on its computer keyboard to conform to European traditions and adjusted business software to reflect accounting principles overseas.

• Boeing built narrow-bodied 737 planes specifically outfitted to protect against damage on bumpy Third World runways. In addition, Boeing is designing its new 350-seat long distance 777 so that the galley and key cabin features can be reconfigured at an airport with relative ease. Such do-it-yourself features are important to foreign buyers.

• Du Pont produced customized herbicides that attack such specific problems as a weed unique to Brazil and another that damages rice crops in Japan.

Source: Kenneth Labich, "America's International Winners," *Fortune,* 113 (April 14, 1986), pp. 34–46; and Dori Jones Yang and Michael Oneal, "How Boeing Does It," *Business Week* (July 9, 1990), pp. 46–50.

The cost of research increases, however, if microlevel segmentation is required. A marketing research study is often needed to identify characteristics of decision-making units. At this level, chosen macrosegments are divided into microsegments on the basis of similarities and differences between the decision-making units in order to identify small groups of buying organizations that each exhibit a distinct response to the firm's marketing strategy. Observe in Figure 6.3 that the desirability of a particular target segment depends upon the costs and benefits of reaching that segment. The costs are associated with marketing strategy adjustments such as modifying the product, altering personal selling or advertising strategies, or entering new channels of distribution. The benefits include the short- and long-term opportunities that would accrue to the firm for tapping this segment. The marketer must evaluate the potential profitability of alternative segments before investing in separate marketing strategies.

Evaluating Market Segments

To evaluate the relative attractiveness of alternative market segments, the business marketer must assess company, competitive, and market factors. For the global marketer, this analysis extends to the selection of prospective target countries and to an assessment of possible segments within these countries. Franklin Root notes that "the scope of segmentation is greater in large-country markets than in small-country markets; in high-income, technologically sophisticated markets than in low-income, low-technology markets; and for highly differentiated products than for standard or commodity-like products. But segmentation may be profitable in any heterogeneous market . . . ."[38]

Segment Positioning by Country[39]

Figure 6.4 illustrates the importance of evaluating market opportunities and business strengths segment by segment within each target country. This framework includes four components:

- Part A is an assessment of the opportunities and threats offered by alternative market segments in a given country.

- Part B is an analysis of business strengths and weaknesses. Note that this phase involves a situation analysis and marketing audit by country.

- Part C is an evaluation of alternative market segment candidates and of positioning strategies for each segment. S_1P_3 represents the heavy-user segment that is satisfied with a particular product offering and that is motivated to purchase by the product performance.

- Part D is the evaluation of market opportunities in relation to company strengths. Observe that S_1P_3, the heavy user/satisfied segment, provides an attractive market opportunity (high) that matches the company's strength (high). The industrial firm has the manufacturing, R&D, and marketing skills required to satisfy the needs of the market segment. By following this procedure, the most attractive target markets can be identified.

This approach recognizes the interdependence of marketing and other business functions, allows the industrial marketing manager to link company strengths directly to market segment needs, and establishes a foundation for assessing both the risks and expected returns of alternative marketing strategies in an international market context.

International Expansion Strategy

Some experts contend there are two major and opposing multinational expansion strategies: market concentration and market diversification.[40] The focus is the rate of entry into new markets and the allocation of effort among markets. The specific strategy chosen depends on (1) the overall level of marketing effort that the firm is able and willing to invest in the international market and (2) the relative attractiveness of market expansion within the firm's home market. **Market concentration** is typified by

---

[38] Franklin R. Root, *Entry Strategies for International Markets* (Lexington, Mass.: Lexington Books, 1987), p. 176; see also Subhash C. Jain, "Standardization of International Marketing Strategy: Some Research Hypotheses," *Journal of Marketing,* 53 (January 1989), pp. 70–79.

[39] The following discussion is based on Yoram Wind and Thomas S. Robertson, "Marketing Strategy: New Directions for Theory and Research," *Journal of Marketing,* 47 (Spring 1983), pp. 16–22.

[40] Igal Ayal and Jehiel Zif, "Market Expansion Strategies in Multinational Marketing," *Journal of Marketing,* 43 (Spring 1979), pp. 84–93; see also Lindsay N. Meredith and Michael D. Hutt, "Toward an International Perspective of Market Analysis in Industrial Marketing," *Journal of Marketing Education,* 6 (Fall 1984), pp. 15–20.

FIGURE 6.4   **Illustrative Market Opportunities and Business Strength Analysis by Segment Positioning**

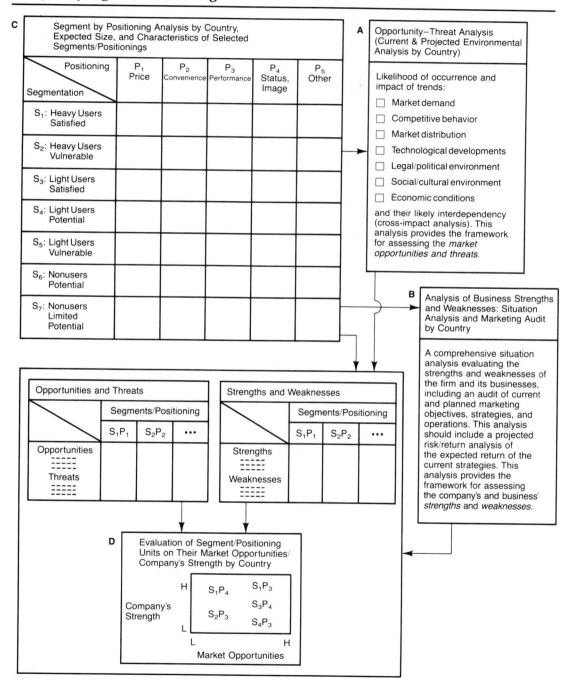

Source: Yoram Wind and Thomas S. Robertson, "Marketing Strategy: New Directions for Theory and Research," *Journal of Marketing,* 47 (Spring 1983), p. 18. Reprinted by permission of the American Marketing Association.

channeling available marketing resources into a small number of markets in an effort to win a significant share of these markets. Once these goals are attained, the firm may expand the scope of its operations to other locations and segments. A concentration strategy may center on a particular country or on particular segments within a country.

By contrast, **market diversification** allocates resources over a large number of markets and segments. For example, attention might center on classifying countries into groups using such variables as economic status, type of industrial structure, or nature of the political system.[41] Further macrosegmentation and microsegmentation may also be required because potential customers may differ in technological sophistication, philosophy and strategy, and emphasis given to price, quality, and service.[42] Among the factors that must be evaluated in choosing a particular market-entry strategy are the growth rate of each market, the need for product and communications adaptation, and the potential economies of scale in distribution. For example, when the growth rate of each international market is high and there is a need for product and communications adaptation, a concentrated strategy is suggested.

IMPLEMENTING A SEGMENTATION STRATEGY

A well-developed segmentation plan will fail without careful attention to how the plan will be implemented.[43] The successful implementation of a segmentation strategy requires attention to certain issues:

- How should the sales force be organized?
- What special technical service requirements will organizations in the new segment have? Who will provide these services?
- Which media outlets can be used to target advertising at the new segment?
- Will adjustments be required in the physical distribution network in order to meet particular inventory requirements?
- What adaptations will be needed to serve selected international market segments?

The astute business marketing strategist must plan, coordinate, and monitor implementation details.

---

[41] For a comprehensive discussion of international market segmentation, see Subhash C. Jain, *International Marketing Management* (2nd ed.; Boston: Kent Publishing Company, 1987), pp. 346–374; and Sudhir H. Kale and D. Sudharshan, "A Strategic Approach to International Segmentation," *International Marketing Review,* 2 (Summer 1987), pp. 60–69.

[42] Susan P. Douglas and Yoram Wind, "The Myth of Globalization," *Columbia Journal of World Business,* 22 (May 1987), pp. 19–29; and Kate Bertrand, "Get Ready for Global Capitalism," *Business Marketing,* 75 (January 1990), pp. 42–54.

[43] For further information on this topic, see Thomas V. Bonoma and Benson P. Shapiro, *Segmenting the Industrial Market* (Lexington, Mass.: Lexington Books, 1983).

SUMMARY

The business market contains a complex mix of customers with diverse needs and objectives. The marketing strategist who analyzes the aggregate market and identifies neglected or inadequately served groups of buyers (segments) is ideally prepared for a market assault. Specific marketing strategy adjustments can be made to fit the unique needs of each target segment. Of course, such differentiated marketing strategies are feasible only if the target segments are measurable, accessible, compatible, and large enough to justify separate attention.

Procedurally, industrial market segmentation involves categorizing actual or potential buying organizations into mutually exclusive clusters (segments) each of which exhibits a relatively homogeneous response to marketing strategy variables. To accomplish this task, the business marketer can draw upon two types of segmentation bases: macrolevel and microlevel. Macrodimensions are the key characteristics of buying organizations and of the purchasing situation. The SIC system, together with other secondary sources of information, is valuable in macrolevel segmentation. Microlevel bases of segmentation center on key characteristics of the decision-making unit and require a higher level of market knowledge.

This chapter outlined a systematic approach for the business marketer to apply when identifying and selecting target segments. Before a final decision is made, the marketer must weigh the costs and benefits of a segmented marketing strategy. The market potential of possible target segments must be calculated, and a careful assessment must be made of company versus competitor strengths. Techniques for measuring market potential (opportunity) provide the theme of the next chapter.

Discussion Questions

1. IBM has been stepping up its campaign to unseat Apple Computer as the leading supplier to primary and secondary schools. Discuss how Apple might use competitive benchmarking strategy as a tool in assessing areas for a counterattack.

2. Two years ago, Jackson Machine Tool selected four SIC categories as key market segments. A unique marketing strategy was then developed for each segment. In retrospect, they wonder whether they are appealing to the right segments of the market. Again this year, sales were up slightly, profits were down rather sharply. They need your help. Outline the approach that you would follow in evaluating the appropriateness of their segmentation.

3. Peter Drucker persuasively argues that traditional accounting systems do not capture the true benefits of automated manufacturing equipment. According to Drucker, such approaches emphasize the costs of *doing* something, (e.g., per-unit production costs), whereas the main benefit of automation lies in eliminating—or at least minimizing—the cost of *not doing something* (e.g., not producing unacceptable quality parts). Explain how a producer of automated equipment might employ a value-in-use segmentation strategy.

4. A recent *Wall Street Journal* article noted that "segment" is the new buzzword for PC retailers such as Computerland and Sears Business Centers. First, suggest possible macro- and microsegments that a PC retailer might wish to consider and describe the process that you would follow in evaluating their relative attractiveness. Second, suggest marketing strategies that the retailer could follow in reaching them.

5. Explain why entry into a particular market segment by an industrial firm often entails a greater commitment than a comparable decision made by a consumer-products company.

6. List some potential macrolevel and microlevel bases of segmentation that a small manufacturer of printed packaging materials might employ.

7. Sara Lee Corporation derives over $1.5 billion of sales each year from the institutional market (e.g., hospitals, schools, restaurants). Explain how a firm such as Sara Lee or General Mills might apply the concept of market segmentation to the institutional market.

8. What personal selling strategy would be most appropriate when dealing with an organizational buyer who is an optimizer? A satisficer?

9. How can the marketing strategist determine whether a particular basis of segmentation (e.g., SIC, company size) is appropriate and meaningful for the firm's product/market situation?

10. Some firms follow a single-stage segmentation approach, using macrodimensions; others use both macrodimensions and microdimensions. As a business marketing manager, what factors would you consider in making a choice between the two methods?

CHAPTER 7

Organizational Demand Analysis

The business marketer confronts the difficult task of predicting the market response of organizational customers. The efficiency and effectiveness of the marketing program rests on the manager's ability to isolate and measure organizational demand patterns and forecast specific levels of sales. Accurate projections of market potential and future sales are among the most significant and challenging dimensions of organizational demand analysis. After reading this chapter, you will understand:

1. the importance of organizational demand analysis to business marketing management.

2. the role of market potential analysis and sales forecasting in the planning and control process.

3. specific techniques that can be effectively applied in measuring market potential and developing a sales forecast.

TO implement business marketing strategy successfully, the business marketing manager must estimate the potential market for the firm's products. Accurate estimates of potential business enable the manager to allocate scarce resources to the customer segments, products, and territories that offer the greatest return. Estimates of market potential also provide the manager with a standard that can be used to assess the firm's performance in the product and market situations targeted. As one management expert suggests, "Without a forecast of total market demand, decisions on investment, marketing support, and other resource allocations will be based on hidden, unconscious assumptions about industrywide requirements, and they'll often be wrong."[1]

---

[1] F. William Barnett, "Four Steps to Forecast Total Market Demand," *Harvard Business Review,* 66 (July–August 1988), p. 28.

Sales forecasting is likewise vital to marketing management. The sales forecast reflects management's estimate of the probable level of company sales, taking into account both potential business and the level and type of marketing effort demanded. Virtually every decision made by the marketer is based on a forecast, formal or informal.

Organizational demand analysis is composed of sales forecasting and market potential analysis, and this chapter explores its role in the planning and control process. First, the market potential estimate and the sales forecast are contrasted as we examine the nature and purpose of each. Once the groundwork is established, several methods of measuring market potential are described, illustrated, and evaluated. The chapter concludes with an examination of the salient dimensions of sales forecasting. Selected sales forecasting techniques are described, illustrated, and evaluated.

ORGANIZATIONAL DEMAND ANALYSIS

The business marketing manager must analyze organizational demand from two perspectives. First, what is the highest possible level of market demand that may accrue to all producers in this industry in a particular time period? The answer constitutes the market potential for a product. It is influenced by the level of industry marketing effort and the assumed conditions in the external environment. Second, what level of sales can the firm reasonably expect to achieve, given a particular level and type of marketing effort and a particular set of environmental conditions? The answer constitutes the firm's sales forecast. Note that the forecast depends on the level of the firm's marketing effort. Thus, the marketing plan must be developed before the sales forecast. This section examines the significance of both components of organizational demand analysis for business marketing management.

The Role of Market Potential in Planning and Control

Market potential is the maximum possible sales of all sellers of a given product in a defined market during a specified time period.[2] If the manager wishes to determine the maximum sales opportunities for a product of an individual company, this is referred to as **sales potential**, which is the maximum share of market potential an individual company might expect for a specific product or product line.[3]

An example will clarify the nature of potentials. Assume that manufacturers of aircraft engines and parts generated shipments of $9 billion this year. What level of market potential would be expected for the industry next year? Based on commercial airline activity, total volume for the industry next year might be projected to increase by 20 percent. Thus, the aircraft-engine industry has a market potential of $10.8 billion ($9 billion × 1.20). Of this, the aircraft-engine division of General Electric in Cincinnati might expect to obtain 14 percent, based on current market share, anticipated marketing

[2] William E. Cox, Jr., and George N. Havens, "Determination of Sales Potentials and Performance for an Industrial Goods Manufacturer," *Journal of Marketing Research,* 14 (November 1977), p. 574.

[3] Francis E. Hummel, *Market and Sales Potentials* (New York: The Ronald Press Company, 1961), p. 8.

INSIDE BUSINESS MARKETING

Market Potential Analysis Helps Guide Bindicator Strategy Adjustments

Marketing managers at Bindicator, a manufacturer of measurement instruments, wanted to refine their marketing strategy in low-performing sales territories. The key issue here was to develop measures that evaluated sales performance fairly.

The solution to the sales measurement problem was the development of relative territory potential. An index of each territory's market potential was created: the index told Bindicator what percentage of U.S. total sales ought to be obtained from each territory. By comparing each territory's percentage of actual total sales to the market potential index, the company was able to spot territories of both weak and strong performance, regardless of market size or industry mix. If the ratio of a territory's actual sales percentage to the market

potential index was above 100, the territory exceeded what would normally be expected; if below 100, the territory was not achieving its potential.

The new measures are utilized to improve market coverage and penetration. For example, two territories with below-average performance were identified, and a change in advertising coverage was made. The advertising campaign targeted the grain industry in the two territories, resulting in a substantial increase in sales leads for both and a healthy increase in their performance measures.

Bindicator's president concluded that "with the sales performance measures, a whole new world of information opens that provides management a broad range of action possibilities previously not available."

Source: Adapted from Karsten Hellebust, "Bindicator Finds a Fair Measure for Sales Territory Performance," *Sales & Marketing Management,* 136 (November 11, 1985), pp. 45–47.

efforts, production capacity, and other factors. General Electric's sales potential is therefore $1.51 billion for next year ($10.8 billion × 0.14).

Potential Represents Opportunity

In most instances, market potentials exceed total market demand and sales potentials exceed actual company sales volume. Market potential is just that—an opportunity to sell. In the example of aircraft engines and parts, market potential may not be converted to demand for a number of reasons: the government may reduce aircraft defense spending, commercial airlines may postpone aircraft orders if passenger airline travel declines, or a strike against major aircraft manufacturers could reduce their production of jet engines. Similarly, sales potentials are ideals based on an assumed set of circumstances: past market performance; a certain level of competitive activity; and a variety of events, both favorable and unfavorable to the firm. Clearly, a change in competitors' actions, a decline in the general economy, or a reduction in the level and effectiveness of marketing may cause actual sales to fall short of sales potential.

Potentials: Planning and Control by Segment

The primary application of market and sales potential information is clearly in the planning and control of marketing strategy by market segment. Recall from Chapter 6 that the term *segments* refers to homogeneous units—customers, products, territories, or channels—for which marketing efforts are tailored. Once sales potentials are determined for each segment, the manager can allocate expenditures on the basis of potential sales volume. There is little benefit in spending huge sums of money on advertising and personal selling in segments where the market opportunity is low. Of course, expenditures would have to be based on both potential and the level of competition. Actual sales in each segment can also be compared with potential sales, taking into account the level of competition, in order to evaluate the effectiveness of the marketing program.

Consider the experience of a Cleveland manufacturer of quick-connective couplings for power transmission systems. For more than 20 years, one of its large distributors had been increasing its sales volume. In fact, this distributor was considered one of the firm's top producers. The firm then analyzed the sales potentials for each of its 31 distributors. The large distributor ranked thirty-first in terms of volume relative to potential, actualizing only 15.4 percent of potential. A later evaluation revealed that the distributor's sales personnel did not know how to sell couplings to its large accounts.

As this discussion demonstrates, market and sales potentials are pivotal in the marketing planning and control process. Therefore, great care must be taken in determining market and sales potential estimates. The business marketing manager must thoroughly understand the various techniques for developing potentials accurately.

The Role of the Sales Forecast

The second component of organizational demand analysis, sales forecasting, likewise poses a significant challenge. The sales forecast answers the question: "What level of sales do we expect next year, given a particular level and type of marketing effort?" Once potentials have been determined, the business marketing manager can allocate resources to the various elements of the marketing mix. Only after the marketing strategy is developed can expected sales be forecast. Many firms are tempted to use the forecast as a tool for deciding the level of marketing expenditures. Clearly, marketing strategy is a determinant of the level of sales and not vice versa. Figure 7.1 illustrates the position of market potential estimates and the sales forecast in the planning process.

The sales forecast represents the firm's best estimate of the sales revenue expected to be generated by a given marketing strategy. The forecast will usually be less than sales potential. The firm may find that it is uneconomical to try to capture all available business. Strong competitors within certain segments may preclude the achievement of total potential sales. Like sales potential data, the sales forecast is an aid in the allocation of resources and in the measurement of performance.

Applying Market Potential and the Sales Forecast

Market potential estimates and sales forecasts complement each other in the marketing planning process. Market potential data are usually vital to sales forecasting: market potential provides direction as to which opportunities the firm should pursue, and the

FIGURE 7.1 **The Relationship of Potential and Forecast: A Planning Framework**

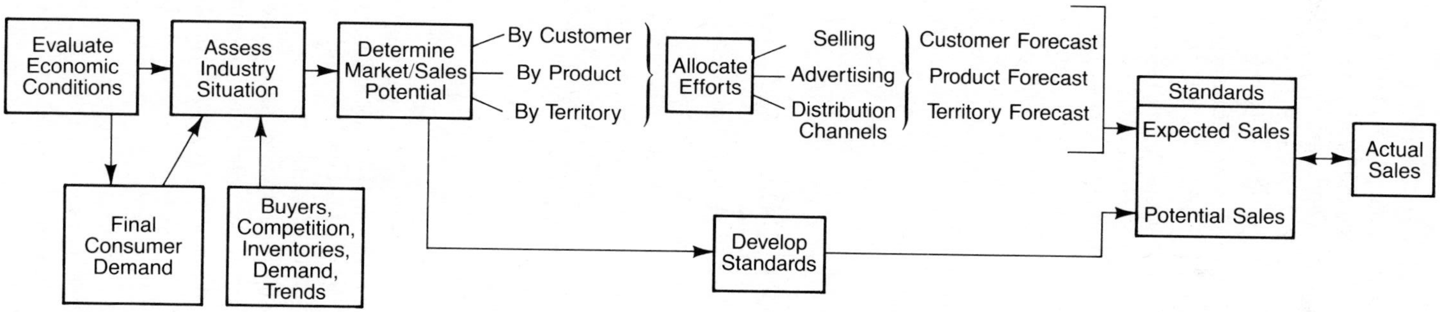

sales forecast is generated once the level of resources to be applied to each opportunity has been decided. Market potential estimates are used to determine where the firm's attention should be focused, the total and relative levels of expenditure to apply to each opportunity, and the benchmarks for evaluating performance. The sales forecast, in contrast, typically provides direction for making short-run, tactical decisions.

Thus, estimates of actual sales over the next year guide management in planning production, estimating purchasing requirements, setting inventory levels, scheduling transportation and the warehouse work force, estimating working capital requirements, and planning short-term expenditures on promotion and advertising. Two- to five-year projections of sales (based on the analysis of market potential) help guide decision making about plant and warehouse facilities and capital requirements and about channel strategy and structure. In summary, market potential provides guidelines for the general direction the firm will take (in terms of markets and product opportunities) and for budget allocations to those opportunities. The sales forecast directs the timing of short-range tactical expenditures and long-term capital spending.

There are specific tools for developing accurate estimates of market potential; the business marketer must understand the purposes of alternative techniques as well as their values and limitations.

DETERMINING MARKET AND SALES POTENTIALS

The secondary data available, whether the product is new or established, the number of potential customers, and the extent of internal company information all play a role in estimating potentials. Estimating market potential requires analysis of variables that relate to, or cause, aggregate demand for the product. It is crucial to find the best measures of the underlying variables so that potential can be measured accurately. This section will examine statistical series methods and survey methods of measuring market and sales potentials.

Statistical Series Methods

Statistical series methods presume a continuing close correlation between the level of product demand and some statistical set (called a statistical series) such as the number of production workers or the value added by manufacturing. Assuming the connection is logical—that is, that there is a sound underlying relationship between the two items—then product demand can be projected indirectly by projecting the statistical series. First, the manager must identify specific industries that either use the firm's product or could use it. Second, a measure of economic activity is determined for each actual and potential consumer industry. The measure of economic activity is assumed to represent the relative sales volume of each industry. For example, the number of production workers is frequently used as the statistical series representing potential demand. Presumably, the larger the work force in an industry, the greater the potential need for a given industrial product, whether it is a component or capital equipment. Other statistical series used include value added, capital-equipment expenditures, materials consumed, total value of shipments, and total employees and payrolls.

The rationale behind using the single series method is that many industrial products have a variety of applications in a multitude of consuming industries. It would be impractical, if not impossible, to estimate directly all the potential applications of the product as well as the total quantities involved. To make the task of estimating market potential manageable, the analyst turns to information that is easily available—a statistical series. The analyst relates one of these series to the demand for the firm's product. Consider aluminum cans. Secondary data reveal that in a given year, the malt beverage industry spent $2.2 billion on aluminum cans and had total shipments of $12 billion. Thus, a relationship between demand for cans and total dollar shipments (the statistical series) can be established. For every dollar of malt beverage sales, 18 cents in aluminum cans will be used. Potential for next year could be estimated either for a given region (by determining estimated malt beverage sales in the region for next year) or for another segment of the malt beverage industry (e.g., by estimating light beer sales for next year). Past relationships between demand for a product and a statistical series provide a reasonably firm basis for evaluating market potential in various market segments and regions.

Single Series Methods

The single series methods calculates market potential on the basis of secondary data reflecting the relative buying power of industrial markets. To employ this procedure, management must have adequate knowledge of the SIC groups that are potential users of a product. Let us consider how this approach may be used to analyze absolute market potential (dollars or units).

Estimates of absolute market potential for the entire United States, various geographic areas, or specific SIC groups can be determined with a statistical series using the following approach:

- Select a statistical series that appears to be related to demand for the product.

- For each target SIC industry, determine the relationship of the series to the demand for the product whose potential is being estimated.

- Forecast the statistical series and its relationship to demand for the desired time frame.

- Determine market potential by relating demand to future values of the statistical series.

Selecting a Statistical Series

To determine market potential using a statistical series, the analyst must first evaluate which statistical series is best related to the demand for the product. The demand for some products may be highly correlated to the number of production workers— uniforms, hand soap, and some office products are good examples. In other cases, value added or the value of shipments is better correlated to demand. For example, due to the high level of automation in the industry, the demand for metal cans by the beverage industry is more closely related to the value of beverage shipments than to the number of industry production workers.

Important criteria in selecting a statistical series are twofold: (1) data on the series must be available and (2) future estimates of the series should be easier to predict than product demand would be. Many of the statistical series reported by the Department of Commerce in the *Census of Manufactures* and *County Business Patterns* can be forecast for one to three years with reasonable accuracy. Private research firms (such as Predicasts and Standard & Poor's), as well as some on-line data services, develop predictions on many of the series for various industries. In addition, *The U.S. Industrial Outlook,* published by the Department of Commerce, makes short- and long-term projections of employment, sales, and capital spending for a vast array of industries. Thus, if an industrial firm determines that consuming industries could use four units of a product per $1,000 of the consuming industry's output, an estimate of market potential for 1995 could be made by consulting a reference source that forecasts 1995 sales of the consuming industry. Market potential would equal 4 units multiplied by the estimated 1995 sales (in thousands of dollars) of the consuming industry.

Determining the Relationship between Demand and Statistical Series

Once the series has been selected, data on the series must be collected and related to demand in order to develop what might be termed a "demand" or a "usage" factor—that is, the quantity of the product demanded per unit of the statistical series.

One approach is to use the *Census of Manufactures* or the more frequently published *Survey of Manufacturers* to develop the data base for the statistical series, and then relate this to prior levels of demand for the product, either by SIC code or by geographic region. Assume we wish to estimate market potential for ball bearings in 1995, and assume SIC 3711 (motor vehicles) and SIC 3715 (truck trailers) are the primary target markets. The statistical series is value of shipments. To determine the usage or demand factor, we relate past ball bearing demand to the value of shipments in SIC 3711 and SIC 3715 (Table 7.1).

Sales of bearings to the target industries would be gleaned from trade sources, whereas the statistical series, value of shipments, could be found in the *Census of Manufactures* or the *Survey of Manufacturers*. Thus, in SIC 3711, 2.2 cents worth of bearings were purchased for each dollar of shipments. An estimate of market potential in 1995 would be developed by multiplying 0.022 by the projected value of shipments to be made by SIC 3711 in 1995.

Suppose a manufacturer of plastic resins wants to analyze market potential in four SIC industries with which the firm has never dealt. There is no published data. A short survey of firms in each SIC group could be implemented to assess resin purchases and some other statistical series such as production workers. The results would be tallied for each SIC group, and a usage factor of resin (pounds) per production worker calculated for each. The result could then be used to forecast market potential in each SIC industry by estimating total production workers in the relevant year and multiplying that by the usage or demand factor. The validity of this approach depends on how well the firms in the sample represent the target industries.

TABLE 7.1 **Usage Factor for Ball Bearings**

Industry	1990 Bearing Sales to the Industry (Millions)	1990 Value of Using Industry Shipments (Millions)	Demand Factor (Bearings per Dollar of Shipments)
SIC 3711	$1,680	$75,271	$.022
SIC 3715	39	2,767	.014

The "Materials Consumed" section of the *Census of Manufactures* shows the quantity and value of materials, containers, and supplies consumed by specific SIC industries (see Table 7.2). A marketer of paper containers could determine from this section that firms in the confectionery industry would use 4.1 cents worth of paper containers for each dollar of shipments by the confectionery industry ($285.1 million in paper containers for $6.98 billion in shipments). Unfortunately, the level of detail for each industry varies. For some industries, specific components and raw materials are not detailed, only total materials consumed. In the case of confectionery products, individual types of paper containers are not indicated. Thus, the manager must use caution in using this type of information.

Estimating a demand or usage factor this way must take into account the limitations of the approach. The analysis is based on averages; an average consumption of a given component per dollar of output or per production worker is computed. The average may or may not hold true for a particular target industry. Product usage may vary considerably from firm to firm, even in the same SIC category. Further, the demand factor is based on historical relationships that may change dramatically; that is, the industry may use more or less of the product as a result of technological change, manufacturing system reconfigurations, or changes in final consumer demand. Nevertheless, carefully derived estimates of the relationship between demand and a statistical series can be powerful tools for measuring market potential.

Forecasting the Statistical Series

Once the relationship of the demand to the series has been documented (the demand or usage factor has been determined), management will estimate future values of the series in one of two ways: by independently forecasting expected values, using their own estimated growth rates; or by relying on forecasts made by government, trade associations, or private research firms. The goal is to project the series forward so that future market potential can be assessed by multiplying the demand factor by the estimated future value of the series.

Future values of the usage factor must also be estimated. The demand or usage factor expresses the relationship between the demand and the series in terms such as "dollar of product per dollar of consuming industry sales" or "pounds of product per production worker." If we are estimating market potential two years into the future, we must ask whether usage of the product per unit of output in the consuming industry will change over that period. Management may want to adjust the demand or usage

TABLE 7.2   **SIC 2064: Candy Products[a]—Materials Consumed**

Materials Consumed	Quantity (Tons)	Dollar Value (Millions)
Sugar	834,600	$393.5
Sugar substitutes (mil lbs.)	25,600	10.0
Cocoa powder	8,100	7.2
Chocolate coatings	143,700	240.9
Unsweetened chocolate	47,200	115.1
Cocoa, pressed cake, and powder	11,300	15.9
Nuts, in shells (mil lbs.)	80,800	61.3
Nutmeats (mil lbs.)	252,600	223.5
Milk	—	165.5
Corn syrup (mil lbs.)	906,800	85.8
High fructose corn syrup (mil lbs.)	80,800	7.7
Crystalline fructose (mil lbs.)	19,300	5.1
Cocoa butter	90,500	201.0
Flavors	—	41.8
Fat and oils (mil lbs.)	81,100	34.1
Paper containers and packaging	—	285.1
Metal cans	—	12.5
Glass	—	17.7
Other materials	—	416.8
Materials, containers, suppliers, NSK	—	257.2

[a]Shipments: $6.98 billion
Cost of Materials: $3.17 billion
Value Added: $3.84 billion

Source: *Census of Manufactures, Industry Series 2061–2068*, U.S. Department of Commerce, Bureau of the Census, 1987, p. 20F-23.

factor to reflect predicted changes in product usage among the targeted industries. An analysis of production processes, technology, competitive actions, and final consumer demand may be required to adjust the usage factor properly. A good example is found in the plastics industry: the move to lighten automobiles in order to enhance gas mileage would indicate a substantial increase in the "pounds of plastic per automobile" usage factor over the next five years. Similarly, in the beverage industry, aluminum cans are increasingly replacing glass containers, but the pounds of aluminum used per dollar of beverage output may also be declining because lighter and lighter aluminum material is being used in the cans.

Determining Market Potential

The final step is the easiest one: the demand or usage factor is multiplied by the forecasted value of the statistical series. Once this stage has been reached, the difficult data and estimation problems have been resolved, and the calculation is routine. Management must be sure that potential is calculated for all relevant market segments. For planning and control purposes, market potential estimates may be required for various customer segments, SIC groups, territories, and distribution channels. A comprehensive example is shown in Table 7.3.

In summary, the effectiveness of the single series method of estimating market potential depends on the following: how well the demand or usage factor represents underlying demand, the quality of the data used, the ability to estimate future values of the series and usage factors, and the extent of distortion caused by using averages and gross estimates. This approach is well suited to industrial products that are in common use. For new products, unique items, and rarely used components, this approach is not appropriate because the data are insufficient. Modifications to the series and considerable management judgment are required to estimate potential. One way to develop better estimates is to use more than one statistical series.

Multiple Statistical Series Method

Because the demand for a product depends on a host of factors, using one variable to estimate demand is frequently insufficient. Business marketers often use sophisticated statistical techniques to measure the combined influence of a number of series on market potential. Those factors most closely associated with industry demand are given the highest weight or relative influence.

For example, a manufacturer of industrial cranes believes that product sales are related to the number of production workers and to customer expenditures on new plant and equipment (P&E). Data for these variables are secured from government sources. Analyzing the data using statistical regression yields an equation that relates crane sales to the number of production workers and to plant and equipment expenditures. The regression equation indicates the nature of the relationship between a dependent variable (industry sales) and the independent variables (expenditures = x_1 and workers = x_2). The resulting equation might look like this:

$$\text{potential crane sales} = 7{,}920 + (0.2363)(\text{P\&E expenditures})$$
$$- (1.024)(\text{production workers})$$

In this case, crane sales increase directly with plant and equipment expenditures, but sales decrease as the size of the work force expands (probably because there is less automation in plants with a large labor force).

Once the crane supplier determines the amount of P&E expenditures and the number of production workers in any given market, total potential can be calculated. If Ohio has 9,000 production workers in user industries, and new P&E expenditures are estimated at $16 million, total potential crane sales in Ohio are:

$$\text{potential} = 7{,}920 + [0.2363\,(\$16 \text{ million})] - [1.024\,(9{,}000)]$$
$$= \$3{,}779{,}504$$

As with the single series method, great care must be taken in selecting the appropriate series. It may be necessary to experiment with several series to see which combination produces the best estimates. Sales potential estimates for prior years can be compared to actual sales in those years to evaluate which combination is most predictive.

TABLE 7.3   Estimating Market Potential with a Statistical Series[a]

Problem: Estimate market potential for metal cans in SIC 2033, 2082, and 2086 for the State of California for 1994.

Product: Metal cans

Market:

    Region: California

    SICs: 2033   Processed fruits and vegetables

           2082   Malt beverages

           2086   Bottled and canned soft drinks

Step 1:   Select Statistical Series: Value of Shipments, 1987

Step 2:   Determine the Relationship of the Demand and the Statistical Series (usage or demand factor)

Consuming Industries	Metal Cans Consumed, 1987[b] (Millions)	Value of Shipments, 1987[b] (Millions)	Usage Factor ($Cans/$Shipments)
2033 Processed fruits and vegetables	$1,079.8	$11,889.5	$.0908
2082 Malt beverages	2,772.3	13,618.6	.2036
2086 Soft drinks	2,560.9	22,006.0	.1164

Source: 1987 *Census of Manufactures, Industry Series 2033, 2082, 2086*, U.S. Department of Commerce, Bureau of the Census, pp. 20C-25, 20H-22, 20C-12, 20H-11.

Step 3:   Forecast the Series for the Desired Time Frame

A. Estimate the value of shipments in California, 1994

SIC	Value of Shipments by California Industries, 1989[b] (Millions)	Projected Annual Growth Rate[c]	Computation	Estimated Value of Shipments by California Industries, 1994 (Millions)
2033	$1,461.6	1.0%	$1,416.6 \times (1.01)^5$	$1,536.0
2082	703.8	.7%	$703.8 \times (1.007)^5$	729.0
2086	582.0	2.0%	$582.0 \times (1.02)^5$	643.0

[a] A similar approach, encompassing four steps—defining the market, dividing the market into segments, forecasting the "demand drivers" in each segment, and conducting sensitivity analyses is presented in F. William Barnett, "Four Steps to Forecast Total Market Demand," *Harvard Business Review*, 66 (July–August 1988), pp. 28–38.

[b] "1989 Business Statistics Report," (New York: Dun's Marketing Services, 1989), pp. 22–34.

[c] *U.S. Industrial Outlook* (Washington, D.C.: U.S. Department of Commerce, International Trade Division, 1990), pp. 34-7, 34-24, 34-39.

Market Surveys

To avoid the problems inherent in historical statistical data, firms can use market surveys to gather primary information on future buyer intentions. Surveys are also used to generate data to be used with the statistical series. The techniques and procedures for conducting industrial market surveys were treated in Chapter 5. For current applications, it is important to note the use of survey results when estimating market and sales potentials, and when determining the demand or usage factor to be used in the single statistical series approach.

B. Adjust usage factor

SIC	Usage Factor	Estimated Usage Change,[d] 1994	Adjusted Usage Factor
2033	$0.0908	(5.0%)	$0.0863
2082	0.2036	0	0.2036
2086	0.1164	2.0%	0.1187

[d]Metal can usage forecasted to decline in foods, remain stable in beer, and increase in the soft drink industry by 1994 (*U.S. Industrial Outlook,* 1990, pp. 11-1, 11-2).

Step 4: Determine Market Potential

SIC	Adjusted Usage Factor	Estimated Value of Shipments by California Industries, 1994 (Millions)	Market Potential for California Industries, 1994 (Millions)
2033	$0.0863	$1,536.0	$132.6
2082	0.2036	729.0	148.4
2086	0.1187	643.0	76.3
			$357.3

The survey method is particularly useful for estimating market potential of new products. Surveys can provide information about whether specific plants are in the market for a new product, about the extent of their needs, and about the likelihood of purchase. Surveys are useful in determining the potential product use by specific SIC groups, the plants in each SIC that have the greatest potential, and the relative importance of each SIC group to total sales. Recall from Chapter 6 that a product's economic value to a user (value-in-use) can vary by market segment. Surveys can be profitably used to determine the value-in-use for various customers or market segments. Surveys have also been utilized to evaluate the purchase potential of individual firms.

A complete enumeration of the market can sometimes be made, and the potential volumes for each prospective customer can be summed to arrive at a total market potential. A complete census of the market is warranted when (1) the markets are very concentrated, (2) there is direct sales contact, (3) orders have a relatively high value, and (4) the unit volume is low.[4] The difficulty is collecting data for all potential users of the product. Typically, the sales force is assigned the task of collecting information. Developing information on existing customers is routine, but it becomes more difficult to solicit information from the user who is not a customer. Sales people often experience difficulties in reaching the individual in a noncustomer firm who has the information they need. They may also be reluctant to allocate a significant amount of time to collecting the data. However, in some industries, buyers are eager to share their

---

[4] William E. Cox, Jr., *Industrial Marketing Research* (New York: John Wiley and Sons, 1979), p. 158.

annual raw material and component requirements with vendors in order to facilitate vendor planning and therefore assure a continuity of supply. The automobile industry, for example, provides steel suppliers with detailed estimates of its requirements for steel.[5]

Uses and Limitations

The survey method is appropriate in estimating the market potential for new products, especially in providing estimates based on objective facts and opinions rather than on executive judgment. In addition, the survey can target specific industries that represent the greatest market potential for new or existing products. Its limitation is the one associated with any survey—the research method used. Nonrepresentative samples and nonresponse bias can distort findings, the wrong person in the respondent companies may fill out the questionnaire, and a small sample size may make sophisticated statistical analysis impossible. A particularly difficult problem is assessing whom to contact. The researcher must invest considerable effort to find the best source of data. It is the responsibility of the marketing manager to resolve the data collection problems and to ensure that the survey design will generate valid results.

Evaluating Market Potential Estimates

Estimating market potential involves considerable art—applying sound judgment to the method and its requirements. An important consideration is the quality of the data used to derive the market potential estimate. Information that is out-of-date or invalid for the situation will not produce viable estimates of demand, regardless of the sophistication and precision of the methodology used.

THE ESSENTIAL DIMENSIONS OF SALES FORECASTING

Selection of a sales forecasting technique depends on many factors, including the period for which the forecast is desired, the purpose of the forecast, the availability of data, the level of technical expertise possessed by the company, the accuracy desired, the nature of the product, and the extent of the product line. Evaluations of each factor suggest the limits within which the firm must work in terms of forecasting methods.

General Approaches to Forecasting

Because all budgets in a company ultimately depend on how many units will be sold, the sales forecast often determines companywide commitments for everything from raw materials and labor to capital equipment and advertising.[6] Various types of forecasts are often required because estimates of future sales are applied to so many

---

[5] Ibid., p. 159.

[6] Geoffrey Lancaster and Robert Lomas, "A Managerial Guide to Forecasting," *International Journal of Physical Distribution and Materials Management,* 16, (1986), p. 6.

activities. A forecast to determine inventory commitments for the next month has to be more precise than one used to set sales quotas, which may differ from expected sales due to their motivational value. A five-year forecast of growth in the machine-tool industry will require a very detailed and sophisticated model incorporating numerous economic variables, whereas a six-month projection of number 28 ball bearing sales may simply require the extrapolation of a trend line. The forecasting process may be administered "top-down" or "bottom-up," or it may be administered as a combination of the two approaches.

Top-Down

In the **top-down** approach, estimates of the general economy and the industry first give managers a picture of the environmental conditions under which they will be operating. These estimates include evaluation of all economic and industry variables that would influence sales of their products. The data base necessary to develop these forecasts might include economic indicators such as GNP, unemployment, capital expenditures, price indexes, industrial production, and housing starts. A model (i.e., a mathematical equation) is created to link the economic indicators to either industry or product sales. For example, Interroyal, a major supplier of commercial and institutional furniture, uses a forecasting model in which current GNP, construction starts 18 months earlier, and current plant and equipment expenditures are linked to expected sales of metal office furniture.

The top-down approach will often include **econometrics**, which refers to large, multivariable, computer-based models of the U.S. economy. Such models attempt to forecast changes in total U.S. economic activity or in specific industries by the use of complex equations that may number over 1,000 for a single model. Econometric models are available from commercial, university, and bank sources. Chase Econometric Associates, for example, provides clients with a monthly report of over 200 economic indicators plus current quarter data and data for the next ten quarters.

A drawback of the top-down approach is the gross level at which the forecasts are made. In some cases, the forecasts are too general to be useful. Some experts believe that the top-down approach limits the value of a forecast in developing strategy and may limit the forecast's overall credibility.[7]

Bottom-Up

Whereas the top-down approach begins with a macrolevel view of the economy and industry and is initiated by upper management, the **bottom-up** method of sales forecasting originates with the sales force and marketing personnel. The logic behind the bottom-up approach is that sales personnel possess a good understanding of the market in terms of customer requirements, inventory situations, and general market trends. Salespeople can also procure economic data from corporate staff so that their

---

[7] Barbara G. Cohen, "A New Approach to Strategic Forecasting," *The Journal of Business Strategy* (September/October 1988), p. 38.

projections will be based not only on historical sales data and customer needs but also on economic and industry data.

The bottom-up approach works well when sales are limited to a well-defined industry. Jet aircraft manufacturers are a good example. A firm supplying gaskets for jets knows that there are long lead times in the production of engines and a limited number of producers. Thus, salespeople know almost exactly what will be built in the next one to three years, and by whom. Specific estimates of the gaskets required can be made, so there is little need for an all-encompassing macroeconomic forecast.

Combination Approach

It is rare that either the top-down or the bottom-up procedure will be used exclusively. The more common approach is to use both, with the marketing executive being responsible for coordinating the estimates. For example, Miracle Adhesives, a marketer of adhesives, sealants, and coatings, develops a sales forecast by polling their territory salespeople in order to estimate sales for the coming year (based on a review of customers and prospects); these forecasts are then reviewed by the divisional sales manager in light of historical sales trends, market trends, economic conditions, and scheduled marketing programs.[8] The final forecast is derived by adjusting the sales force estimates on the basis of the broader economic data.

The Forecasting Time Frame

Sales forecasts may be prepared on a day-to-day basis for inventory control, or an estimate of sales ten years into the future may be needed to plan additional plant and warehouse capacity. The methodologies selected for each of these forecasts would probably differ; each forecasting method is suited for a specific forecasting time frame. In fact, the time horizon for which forecasts are prepared can often serve as a substitute for most of the criteria used to evaluate forecasting techniques. Time horizons reflect such characteristics as the value of accuracy in forecasting, the cost of various methodologies, the timeliness of their results, and the types of data patterns involved in the sales data.[9]

Although the forecast time frame may range from a year to ten or fifteen years, four basic time frames are common.[10]

1. *Immediate term.* Forecasts for this period range from daily to monthly. The purpose is to support operating decisions on such things as delivery scheduling and inventory.

---

[8] Harry R. White, *Sales Forecasting, Timesaving and Profit-Making Strategies that Work* (Glenview, IL: Scott, Foresman and Company, 1984), p. 44.

[9] Spyros Makridakis and Steven Wheelwright, "Forecasting: Issues and Challenges for Marketing Management," *Journal of Marketing,* 41 (October 1977), p. 30.

[10] Adapted from R. A. Lomas and G. A. Lancaster, "Sales Forecasting for the Smaller Organization," *Industrial Marketing Management,* 20 (February 1978), p. 37.

2. *Short-term*. Short-term forecasts range from one to six months. The time frame may overlap with the immediate and intermediate terms. Short-term forecasts are necessary for planning merchandising and promotion, production scheduling, and cash requirements. The seasonal pattern of sales is generally the pattern of interest.

3. *Intermediate term*. This time frame generally ranges from six months to two years. Intermediate-term forecasts are used to set promotional levels, assess sales personnel needs, and set capital requirements. Seasonal, cyclical, and turning points in the sales data are of interest here.

4. *Long-term*. Long-term forecasts extend beyond two years to estimate trends and rates of sales growth for broad product lines. The results are used to make major strategic decisions, including product line changes, capital requirements, distribution channels, and plant expansion.

FORECASTING METHODS

As discussed, the sales forecast may be highly mathematical or informally based on sales force estimates. Two primary approaches to sales forecasting are recognized: (1) qualitative and (2) quantitative, which includes time series and causal analysis. Each category contains a variety of techniques; effective forecasting requires an understanding that "while each technique has strengths and weaknesses, every forecasting situation is limited by constraints like time, funds, competencies, or data. Balancing the advantages and disadvantages of techniques with regard to a situation's limitations and requirements is a formidable but important management task."[11]

Qualitative Techniques

Qualitative techniques, which are also referred to as "management judgment" or "subjective" techniques, rely on informed judgment and rating schemes. The sales force, top-level executives, or distributors may be called upon to use their knowledge of the economy, the market, and the customers to create qualitative estimates of demand. Techniques for qualitative analysis are the executive judgment method, the sales force composite method, and the Delphi method.

The effectiveness of qualitative approaches depends on the close relationships between customers and suppliers that are typical in the industrial market. Qualitative techniques work well for items such as heavy capital equipment or for situations in which the nature of the forecast does not lend itself to mathematical analysis. These techniques are also suitable for new product or new technology forecasts in which historical data are scarce or nonexistent.[12] An important advantage of qualitative approaches is that users of the forecast are brought into the forecasting process. The

---

[11] David M. Georgoff and Robert G. Murdick, "Manager's Guide to Forecasting," *Harvard Business Review*, 64 (January–February 1986), p. 111.

[12] A. Michael Segalo, *The IBM/PC Guide to Sales Forecasting* (Wayne, PA: Banbury Books, 1985), p. 21.

INSIDE BUSINESS MARKETING
Tough Techniques for Improving Forecasting Accuracy

A drawback of all qualitative forecasting techniques is the degree of accuracy of the sales estimates. Metier Management Systems, a marketer of project management systems, has an answer to the accuracy dilemma: ask difficult questions and reward salespeople for forecast accuracy.

Metier holds sales representatives responsible for sales forecasting. Each month sales managers meet with each sales rep to review all the rep's sales prospects. After the meeting, the sales rep develops a forecast based on the estimated sales to each prospect company for the next three months. The preceding prospect review meeting is the catalyst for enhancing sales forecasting accuracy.

For this review, sales managers go through a detailed checklist for all significant prospects. If a sales representative doesn't know the answer to crucial questions, such as who controlled budgets, when a project was to start, whether current equipment was in place, etc., the meeting is stopped and the representative makes the necessary phone calls to get an answer. These meetings are tedious, boring, long, and dreaded by the sales representatives. They are also the basis of *very accurate forecasting*.

This high level of accuracy is the direct result of really knowing each account, not just accepting the sales representative's usually optimistic forecast. If a manager has doubts about a particular account, he can arrange to visit it with the sales representative. This second look at an account usually leads to a clearer picture. Although it is not always possible, visiting an account often contributes to speeding up the sales cycle because it shows an obvious senior management interest on the part of Metier.

To provide further incentives for creating realistic forecasts, each sales manager is evaluated on his forecast accuracy as well as sales volume. In addition, forecast accuracy is considered in the manager's compensation plan. These incentives guide sales managers to work very carefully with their sales reps to fine-tune their sales projections.

Source: Adapted from William E. Gregory, Jr., "Time to Ask Hard-Nosed Questions," *Sales & Marketing Management*, 141 (October 1989), pp. 88–91.

effect is usually an increased understanding of the procedure and a higher level of commitment to the resultant forecast.

Executive Judgment
In a large sample of business firms, the executive judgment method had significantly greater usage than other forecasting procedures.[13] The judgment method is popular because it is easy to apply and to understand. This method combines and averages top executives' estimates of future sales. Typically, executives from a variety of departments, such as sales, marketing, production, finance, and purchasing, are brought together to apply their collective expertise, experience, and opinions to the forecast.

The primary limitation of the approach is that it does not systematically analyze cause-and-effect relationships. Further, because there is no established formula for deriving estimates, new executives may have difficulty making reasonable forecasts.

---

[13] White, *Sales Forecasting*, p. 31.

The resulting forecasts are only as good as the opinions of the executives. The accuracy of the executive judgment approach is also difficult to assess in a way that allows meaningful comparison with alternative techniques.[14]

The executives' "ballpark" estimates for the intermediate and the long-run time frames are often used in conjunction with forecasts developed quantitatively. However, when historical data are limited or unavailable, the executive judgment approach may be the only approach available. Mark Moriarty and Arthur Adams suggest that executive judgment methods produce accurate forecasts when (1) forecasts are made frequently and repetitively, (2) the environment is stable, and (3) the linkage between decision, action, and feedback is short.[15] Business marketers should examine their forecasting situation in light of these factors in order to assess the viability of the executive judgment technique.

Sales Force Composite

The rationale behind the sales force composite approach is that salespeople can effectively estimate future sales volume because they know the customers, the market, and the competition. In addition, participating in the forecasting process gives sales personnel an understanding of how forecasts are derived and a heightened incentive to achieve the desired level of sales. The composite forecast is developed by combining the sales estimates from all salespeople.

Few companies rely solely on sales force estimates, but usually adjust or combine the estimates with forecasts developed either by top management or by quantitative methods. The advantage of the sales force composite method is the ability to draw on sales force knowledge about markets and customers. This advantage is particularly important for the business market in which buyer–seller relationships are close and enduring. The salesperson is often the best source of information about customer purchasing plans and inventory levels. The method can also be executed relatively easily at minimal cost. An added benefit is that the process of creating a forecast forces a sales representative to carefully review these accounts in terms of future sales.[16]

The problems of sales force composites are similar to those associated with the executive judgment approach: they do not involve systematic analysis of cause and effect, and they rely on informed judgment and opinions. Some sales personnel may overestimate sales in order to look good or underestimate them in order to generate a lower quota. All estimates must be carefully reviewed by management.

Salespeople can provide extremely valuable information for forecasting. When good historical data are not available, the salesperson's experience and judgment become the primary input for forecasting. Sales force estimates are relatively accurate for immediate and short-term projections, but they are not very effective for long-range projections.

---

[14] Makridakis and Wheelwright, "Forecasting: Issues and Challenges," p. 31.

[15] Mark M. Moriarty and Arthur J. Adams, "Management Judgment Forecasts, Composite Forecasting Models and Conditional Efficiency," *Journal of Marketing Research,* 21 (August 1984), p. 248.

[16] Stewart A. Washburn, "Don't Let Sales Forecasting Spook You," *Sales and Marketing Management,* 140 (September 1988), p. 118.

Delphi Method

In the Delphi approach to forecasting, the opinions of a panel of experts on future sales are converted into an informed consensus through a highly structured feedback mechanism.[17] As in the executive judgment technique, management officials are used as the panel, but each estimator remains anonymous. On the first round, written opinions about the likelihood of some future event are sought (e.g., sales volume, competitive reaction, or technological breakthroughs). The responses to this first questionnaire are used to produce a second. The objective is to provide feedback to the group so that first-round estimates and information available to some of the experts are made available to the entire group.

After each round of questioning, the analyst who administers the process will assemble, clarify, and consolidate information for dissemination in the succeeding round. Throughout the process, panel members are asked to reevaluate their estimates based on the new information from the group. Opinions are kept anonymous, eliminating both "me too" estimates and the need to defend a position. After continued reevaluation, the goal is to achieve a consensus. The number of experts will vary from six to hundreds, depending on how the process is organized and depending on its purpose. The number of rounds of questionnaires will depend on how rapidly the group reaches consensus.

Delphi Application

The Delphi technique is usually applied to long-range forecasting. The technique is particularly well suited to (1) new product forecasts, (2) estimation of future events for which historical data are limited, or (3) situations that are not suited to quantitative analysis. When the market for a new product is not well defined and the product concept is unique, the Delphi technique can produce some broad-gauged estimates.

The Delphi technique suffers from the same problems as any other qualitative approach, but it may be the only way to develop certain types of estimates. However, there are some shortcomings specific to the approach. Assembling a panel of truly independent experts is extremely difficult. Officials in the same firm or individuals in the same profession tend to read the same literature, have similar training and background, and share the same attitudes on the phenomena under study. Some experts refuse to modify their views in light of feedback, thereby negating the consensus-forming process.

Qualitative forecasting is important in the forecasting process. The techniques can be applied to develop ballpark estimates when the uniqueness of the product, the unavailability of data, and the nature of the situation preclude application of quantitative techniques. The accuracy of qualitative forecasts is difficult to measure due to the lack of standardization. Typically, qualitative estimates will be merged with those developed quantitatively. Table 7.4 summarizes the qualitative approaches.

---

[17] Raymond E. Willis, *A Guide to Forecasting for Planners and Managers* (Englewood Cliffs, NJ: Prentice-Hall, 1987), p. 343.

TABLE 7.4 **Summary of Qualitative Forecasting Techniques**

Technique	Approach	Application
Executive judgment	Combining and averaging top executives' estimates of future sales.	"Ballpark" estimates. New product sales estimates. Intermediate and long-term time frames.
Sales force composite	Combining and averaging individual salespersons' estimates of future sales.	Effective when intimate knowledge of customer plans is important. Useful for short and intermediate terms.
Delphi method	Consensus of opinion on expected future sales volume is obtained by providing each panelist with the projections of all other panelists on preceding "rounds." Panelists modify estimates until a consensus results.	Appropriate for long-term forecasting. Effective for projecting sales of new products or forecasting technological advances.

Quantitative Techniques

Quantitative forecasting, also referred to as "systematic" or "objective" forecasting, offers two primary methodologies: (1) time series and (2) regression or causal. Time series techniques use historical data ordered in time to project the trend and growth rate of sales. The rationale behind time series analysis is that the past pattern of sales will apply to the future. However, to discover the underlying pattern of sales, the analyst must first understand all of the possible patterns that may affect the sales series. Thus, a time series of sales may include trend, seasonal, cyclical, and irregular patterns. Once the effect of each has been isolated, the analyst can then project the expected future of each pattern. Time series methods are well suited to short-range forecasting because the assumption that the future will be like the past is more reasonable over the short run than over the long run.[18]

Regression or causal analysis, on the other hand, uses an opposite approach, identifying factors that have affected sales in the past and fitting them together into a mathematical model.[19] Sales are expressed mathematically as a function of the items that affect it. Recall the earlier discussion of market potential in which a regression equation was used to project potential based on production workers and on new equipment expenditures. A forecast is derived by projecting values for each of the factors in the model, inserting these values into the regression equation, and solving for expected sales. Typically, causal models are more reliable for intermediate-range than for long-range forecasts. The reason is that the magnitude of each factor affecting sales must first be estimated for some future time, which becomes difficult when estimating far into the future.

The remainder of the chapter will consider quantitative forecasting procedures.

---

[18]Spyros Makridakis, "A Survey of Time Series," *International Statistics Review,* 44, No. 1 (1976), p. 63.

[19]Segalo, *Sales Forecasting,* p. 27.

FIGURE 7.2   **Trend, Cycle, and Seasonal Components of Time Series**

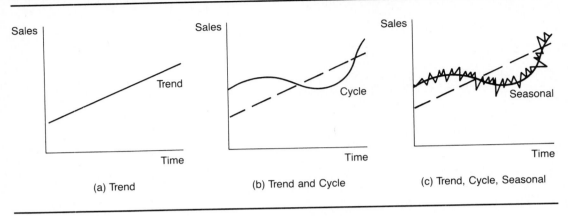

(a) Trend   (b) Trend and Cycle   (c) Trend, Cycle, Seasonal

Time Series Analysis

A **time series** is nothing more than a set of chronologically ordered data points. Company sales reported monthly for the past five years are an example. A time series is composed of measurable patterns, and the objective of the analysis is to identify these patterns so that they may be projected. A time series has four components:

T = Trend
C = Cycle
S = Seasonal
I = Irregular

Figure 7.2 sets out the T, C, and S components.

The **trend** indicates the long-term general direction of the data. The trend may be a straight line of the form $y = a + bx$; or a curve, $y = ab^x$; or $y = bx + cx^2$. A straight-line trend is displayed in Figure 7.2(a). The **cycle** represents the intermediate term with regular upswings and downswings of the data around the trend. For example, the industrial chemical industry in England shows a fairly regular rise and fall in demand over four- or five-year periods. The cycle variations are shown in Figure 7.2(b). The cycle may originate from business cycle movements in the economy as a whole, from business conditions within an industry, from consumer spending fluctuations in finished goods markets, from inventory swings in industry, or from a succession of new product introductions. The cycle is extremely difficult to estimate because reversals need not occur at fixed intervals, and as a result, there may be no regularity to the pattern.

The **seasonal** pattern is depicted in Figure 7.2(c). These patterns represent regular, recurring movements within the year. Data expressed daily, weekly, monthly, and quarterly may show seasonal patterns, which depend on such factors as seasonality of final consumption, end-of-period inventory adjustments, tax dates, business vacations, pipeline inventory adjustments, and scheduling of special promotions.

INSIDE BUSINESS MARKETING
Don't Be Fooled by Historical Sales Trends

The personal computer market virtually exploded overnight—it grew from nothing to a $10 billion market in five years. Such explosive growth trends often coax marketing forecasters into believing that the sales trend can simply be extrapolated into the future. Expectations are high, enthusiasm abounds, and an optimistic forecast is anticipated, if not expected. However, a cautious forecaster cannot be "taken in" by the glorious sales performance of the past but, instead, must objectively appraise the future.

One firm that learned this painful lesson is Computervision, the leader in computer-aided design and manufacturing (CAD/CAM) systems.

In 1984 sales exceeded $500 million and profits were up 35 percent to $48 million. The underlying sales trend indicated that similar increases could be expected for 1985. Unfortunately, the market changed dramatically with both heightened competition and a slackening demand for CAD/CAM systems—factors not considered in the trend extrapolation forecast. When sales slowed, the company anticipated a first-quarter loss of nearly $16 million, and announced the layoff of 950 employees.

As Computervision learned, the fundamental assumptions underlying a forecast must be closely scrutinized. Ill-conceived forecasts can be quite costly.

Source: Adapted from J. Harold Ranck, Jr., "Avoiding the Pitfalls in Sales Forecasting," *Management Accounting,* 68 (September 1986), p. 53.

The **irregular** component in a time series reflects short-term random movements in the data that do not conform to a pattern related to the calendar. Many factors contribute to such random swings in sales patterns (e.g., strikes, competitive actions). Generally, the assumption is that these short-term random effects will average out over a year.

When forecasting future sales volumes, actual sales can be expressed as a combination of all four time series elements:

$$\text{Actual sales} = \text{trend} \times \text{seasonal} \times \text{cycle} \times \text{irregular}$$

To develop a forecast, the analyst must determine each pattern and then extrapolate all four into the future. This requires a significant amount of historical sales information. Once a forecast of each pattern is developed, the sales forecast is assembled by combining the estimates for each pattern.

Regression or Causal Techniques
Causal techniques have as their objective the determination of a relationship between sales and a variable presumed to be related to sales; knowledge of the "causal" variable can be used to determine expected future sales volumes. The method requires a significant amount of historical data to establish a valid relationship. The model mathematically expresses the causal relationship, and the mathematical formula is usually referred to as a regression equation.

A critical aspect of regression analysis is to identify the economic variable(s) to which past sales are related. For forecasting purposes, the *Survey of Current Business*

FIGURE 7.3 **"Freehand" Trend Line of Annual Sales**

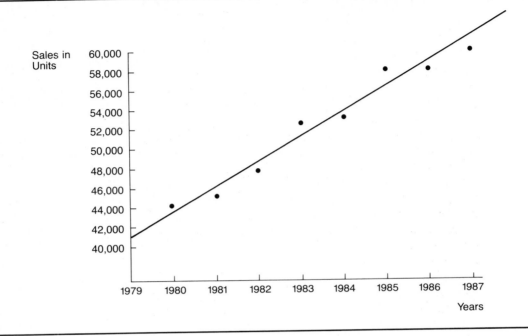

is particularly helpful because it contains monthly, quarterly, and annual figures for hundreds of economic variables. The forecaster can test an array of economic variables from the *Survey* to find the variable(s) with the best relationship to past sales.

As with the statistical series approach, two general rules should be followed in evaluating economic series. First, the economic series (variable) should be logically related to company sales.[20] Forecasters are often tempted to break this rule because they can easily "try out" any number of variables, many of which may not be logically related to company sales. A variable may be found to be highly correlated to past sales, but with no logical connection. Such spurious relationships are not effective for forecasting future sales because they are usually accidental and may not hold true. Second, it should be easier to forecast the economic variable than to project the sales level. The causal approach develops a sales forecast by establishing the relationship of sales to some other economic variable. Knowledge of this relationship is then used to estimate sales by determining future values of the economic variable and the corresponding sales level. If the variable is one for which future projections are either not available or of questionable validity, sales may as well be estimated directly.

---

[20] Frank H. Eby and William J. O'Neill, *The Management of Sales Forecasting* (Lexington, Mass.: Lexington Books, 1977), p. 145.

To create a sales forecast with causal analysis the analyst must first determine the mathematical relationship between sales and the causal variable. This relationship is then expressed in the form of a linear equation: $y = a + bx$, where a and b are the coefficients that express the relationship and x represents the causal variable from which estimates are made. Sales are then forecast by inserting estimated future values of x into the equation.

Use of Regression Techniques

Causal models are the most sophisticated forecasting tools. A study found that only 17 percent of firms regularly use regression techniques for forecasting and that 24 percent have never tried them.[21] Regression models are useful to industrial firms projecting final consumer demand for items of which their products become a part. For example, American Can projects motor oil sales based on a regression model that integrates auto registrations, average miles driven per car, average crankcase size, and average interval between oil changes as causal variables. Finally, an important dimension in forecasting is the ability to predict a turning point in the sales series. To the extent that turning points in causal variables can be foreseen, turns in company sales can be predicted.

Limitations

Although causal methods have measurable levels of accuracy, there are some important caveats and limitations. First, as already discussed, the fact that sales and some causal variables are correlated (associated) does not mean that the independent variable (X) caused sales. The independent variable should be logically related to sales.

Second, because both X and Y have the same trend pattern, one may be, in effect, correlating only trends, whereas the other components (for example, cyclical and seasonal) are not highly correlated.[22] Thus, regression equations whose variables are highly correlated may be unsuitable for short-range projections in which cyclical and seasonal factors are important.

Third, regression methods require considerable historical data if equations are to be valid and reliable, but the data required to establish stable relationships may not be available. Caution must always be used in extrapolating relationships into the future. The equation relates what *has* happened; economic and industry factors may change in the future, making past relationships invalid.

The last, and probably the most crucial, limitation associated with causal methods is the problem of determining future values of independent or causal variables. As we have discussed, before the regression equation can be used to project future sales levels, future values of the independent variables must be determined. Thus, "what is actually done is to shift the burden of forecasting from that of directly predicting some factor of interest (sales) to another one which attempts to estimate several independent

---

[21] Douglas J. Dalrymple, "Sales Forecasting Methods and Accuracy," *Business Horizons,* 18 (December 1975), p. 70.

[22] Paul E. Green and Donald S. Tull, *Research for Marketing Decisions,* 3rd ed. (Englewood Cliffs, NJ: Prentice-Hall, 1975), p. 669.

variables before it can forecast."[23] In the final analysis, the quality of the sales forecast generated by regression models will depend on the forecaster's ability to generate valid and reliable estimates of the independent variables.

Using Several Forecasting Techniques

Recent research on forecasting techniques indicates that improvements in forecasting accuracy can be achieved by combining the results of several forecasting methods.[24] The results of combined forecasts greatly surpass most individual projections, techniques, and analyses by experts.[25] Mark Moriarty and Arthur Adams suggest that managers should use a composite forecasting model that includes both systematic (quantitative) and judgmental (qualitative) factors.[26] In fact, they suggest that a composite forecast be created to provide a standard of comparison in evaluating the results provided by any single forecasting approach. Each forecasting approach relies on varying data to derive sales estimates. By considering a broader range of factors that affect sales, the combined approach provides a more accurate forecast. Rather than searching for the single "best" forecasting technique, business marketers should direct increased attention to the composite forecasting approach.

Role of the Computer in Sales Forecasting

Computers enable the business marketing manager to improve sales forecasting because they can store vast quantities of data, test and compare various forecasting methodologies, and evaluate the reliability of the forecast. The computer is not a technique, but merely a means of making some techniques possible, of making others more effective, and of making the results of some techniques more readily available.[27] The computer is not limited to the quantitative forecasting techniques. It can be useful, for example, in the sales force composite approach by maintaining data files for the sales force and by aggregating the forecasts of individuals.

Managers may use the computer in sales forecasting by developing their own forecasting programs or by purchasing existing software.[28] Most computer hardware manufacturers offer extensive libraries of software applicable to forecasting problems. Independent computer service organizations, including time-sharing firms, have canned programs that will effectively handle most of the popular time series and regression

[23] Makridakis, "A Survey of Time Series," p. 62.

[24] See, for example, Essam Mahmaud, "Accuracy in Forecasting, A Survey," *Journal of Forecasting,* 3 (April–June 1984), p. 139; Spyros Makridakis and Robert L. Winkler, "Averages of Forecasts: Some Empirical Results," *Management Science,* 29 (September 1983), p. 987.

[25] Georgoff and Murdick, "Manager's Guide to Forecasting," p. 119.

[26] Moriarty and Adams, "Management Judgment Forecasts, Composite Forecasting Models and Conditional Efficiency," p. 248.

[27] Gordon J. Bolt, *Market and Sales Forecasting Manual* (Englewood Cliffs, NJ: Prentice-Hall, 1982), p. 270.

[28] Eby and O'Neill, *The Management of Sales Forecasting,* p. 61.

INSIDE BUSINESS MARKETING
The Computer-Assisted Salesperson at Hewlett-Packard

Hewlett-Packard Corporation (HP) has equipped its 2,000 sales representatives with portable personal computers and printers. The goals of the program are to boost sales productivity and to promote a higher level of professionalism by giving the sales force first-hand experience with the solutions that they sell to customers. Because the selling cycles of HP's products (from minicomputers to laboratory instrumentation gear) range from 6 to 18 months, accurate sales forecasts are especially important.

Based on a survey of salesperson needs, a number of software programs have been provided to the sales force, including the Lotus 1-2-3 spreadsheet. Concerning sales forecasting on the new system, William Fritz, an HP salesperson, observes: "I track my product sales and customer payments month-to-month on it and use the graphics to spot trends. . . . The rolling three-month forecast we do at the end of each month is now easier and more accurate because I can plot closing probabilities and likely order dates on a spreadsheet and again have the program do the calculations." A number of databases are being developed to further strengthen the reps' information resources.

Source: Thayer C. Taylor, "Hewlett-Packard Gives Sales Reps a Competitive Edge," *Sales & Marketing Management*, 137 (February 1987), p. 39.

---

techniques. Many general purpose software packages also include sales forecasting procedures.

Although the computer is a powerful tool for forecasting purposes, management must realize that it is only that—a tool. Computer-generated forecasts are only as good as the data and the techniques on which they are grounded. An inappropriate technique does not generate a valid forecast merely because the computer was used to create the forecast. As Gordon Bolt suggests, "Computer forecasts must be 'humanized' by being subjected to human intelligence and judgment."[29] Computers do not replace judgment; in fact they may necessitate higher levels of management judgment in selecting forecasting techniques, imputing correct data, and interpreting computer output.

The widespread application of personal computers to business problems has led to the development of numerous PC-based forecasting programs. Typically, PC-based programs develop forecasts through either expert systems or automatic forecasting.[30] The expert systems method utilizes a set of decision rules appropriate to the particular forecasting situation and helps the user decide on the appropriate approach. Automatic forecasting, on the other hand, typically utilizes a fixed decision sequence to complete the forecast without user intervention. These techniques allow the manager who has limited statistical background to develop effective quantitative sales estimates. Regression techniques and time series analysis are the common forecasting techniques included in the PC-based models.

---

[29] Bolt, *Market and Sales Forecasting Manual*, p. 270.

[30] Marvin Bryan, "Programs Make Forecasting Accessible," *PC Week* (April 24, 1989), p. 100.

Technique Selection

Recognizing that all forecasts are subject to error, management must decide on the degree of error that can be tolerated when seeking a forecasting technique.[31] Ultimately, the technique selected should make the "best" use of available data. The selection of a forecasting technique is based on a variety of criteria; choosing the appropriate approach is a demanding task and requires an understanding of the strengths and weaknesses of the available alternatives. The task is an important one because, by using the best available forecasting approach, more accurate predictions for the future can be made. Business marketers who can better anticipate the future gain an important competitive advantage and enhance the efficiency and effectiveness of their operations.

SUMMARY

Estimating market potential and forecasting sales are the two most significant dimensions of organizational demand analysis. Each is fundamental to marketing planning and control. Knowledge of market potential enables the marketer to isolate market opportunity and efficiently allocate marketing resources to product and customer segments that offer the highest return. Measures of market potential also provide a standard against which the manager can monitor performance. Similarly, the sales forecast—the firm's best estimate of expected sales with a particular marketing plan—forces the manager to ask the right questions and to consider various strategies before allocating resources.

The methods for developing estimates of market potential fall into two categories: (1) statistical series methods and (2) market surveys. The marketer must understand the strengths and weaknesses of each and understand their appropriateness to a particular marketing environment.

Sales forecasts are developed for various periods, ranging from the immediate-term time frame (daily or weekly) to the long-term time frame (two or more years), depending on their purpose.

The forecasting techniques available to the business marketer are (1) qualitative and (2) quantitative. Qualitative techniques rely on informed judgments of future sales and include the executive judgment, the sales force composite, and the Delphi methods. By contrast, quantitative techniques have more complex data requirements and include time series and causal approaches. The time series method uses historical data ordered in time to project the future trend and growth rate of sales. Causal methods, on the other hand, seek to identify factors that have affected sales in the past and to incorporate these factors into a mathematical model. The computer is a valuable tool, facilitating the forecasting process for all methods.

The essence of good forecasting is to combine effectively the forecasts provided by various methods. The process of sales forecasting is challenging and requires a good

---

[31] Lancaster and Lomas, "A Managerial Guide to Forecasting," p. 3.

working knowledge of available alternatives. This chapter has been structured to provide that knowledge.

Discussion Questions

1. Explain how the use of the sales forecast differs from that of an estimate of market potential.
2. What is the underlying logic of statistical series methods used in measuring market potential?
3. What statistical series are provided in the *Census of Manufactures?*
4. Distinguish between single and multiple statistical series methods for estimating market potential.
5. Why are market surveys favored over statistical series methods in measuring the market potential for new industrial products?
6. How could a business marketing manager use SIC information to determine demand potential in the Boston market? Be very specific—this manager is totally unfamiliar with the SIC system.
7. The business marketing manager must develop not one but many forecasts over several time frames. Explain.
8. Compare and contrast the sales force composite and the Delphi methods of developing a sales forecast.
9. Although qualitative forecasting techniques are important in the sales forecasting process in many industrial firms, the marketing manager must understand the limitations of these approaches. Outline these limitations.
10. As alternative methods for sales forecasting, what is the underlying logic of: (1) time series and (2) regression or causal methods?
11. What are the limitations that must be understood before applying and interpreting the sales forecasting results generated by causal methods?
12. What role does a computer have in facilitating the sales forecasting process?
13. What are the features of the business market that support the use of qualitative forecasting approaches? What benefits does the business market analyst gain by combining these qualitative approaches with quantitative forecasting methods?

Exercises

1. The McConocha Company manufactures ink for use in all types of printing operations. The Midwest sales manager is confronted with the need to develop sales quotas for five salespersons located in Pennsylvania, Ohio, Michigan, Indiana, and Illinois. The sales quotas are to be based on the market potential for printing ink in each state; preliminary analysis suggests that SIC 2711 (newspapers), SIC 2721 (periodicals), SIC 2732 (book printing), and SIC 2751 (letterpress commercial printing) are the primary ink-using industries. Historical sales records

suggest that the cost of printing ink constitutes about 0.1 percent of the sales dollar for the using industries. Using the 1987 *Census of Manufactures* or the 1988 *Survey of Business,* determine:

  a.   The total market potential for each SIC industry for the entire five-state area.
  b.   The total market potential for each state.
  c.   The relative market potential for each state.

2. What cautions should the McConocha sales manager be aware of when applying market potential data to the formulation of sales quotas?

3. The Bol Company manufactures electronic controls for sale to book publishing companies. A primary market is New York State, where past sales volumes have not been up to management expectations. Last year the firm had sales of $8.2 million to book publishers in New York State while total U.S. sales to book publishers reached $58.4 million. The following data is gleaned from company and other published sources to evaluate the firm's performance in New York:

Number of Customers in New York State	Total Sales Made by New York State Book Publishers	Total U.S. Sales of All Book Publishers
142	$2.2 Billion	$10 Billion

How well did the company perform last year on the basis of sales volume in New York State? Explain your answer.

4. The Stearns Company requires an estimate of total dollar market potential for the purpose of allocating advertising expenditures to the East Coast market. A small-scale study of a sample of customers in each of the firm's SIC groups provides the following data on "valve purchases per dollar of value added":

SIC	Valve Purchases/Dollar of Value Added	Total Value Added: East Coast
2992	$.11	$21,100
3291	.08	5,600
3541	.07	48,500
3559	.05	28,400
3662	.12	12,500
3679	.10	17,000

Determine the total dollar market potential for the East Coast market.

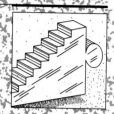

PART IV

Formulating Business Marketing Strategy

CHAPTER 8

Business Marketing Planning: Strategic Perspectives

To this point, the text has examined the techniques available to the business marketing manager for segmenting the business market, forecasting market potential, and forecasting sales. Moreover, you have developed an understanding of organizational buying behavior and of the unique characteristics and strategic role of the business marketing intelligence system. All of this provides a perspective that is of fundamental importance to the business marketing planner.

After reading this chapter, you will understand:

1. the dimensions that characterize market-driven organizations and the importance of this orientation to competitive advantage.

2. the sources of competitive advantage and how they can be converted into superior positions of advantage in the business market.

3. marketing's strategic role in corporate strategy development.

4. the multifunctional nature of business marketing decision making.

5. the essential components of the business marketing planning process.

"CONCERNS about the marketplace are becoming the driving force in business planning and management . . . . Corporate America is growing more marketing-oriented. Strategic market planning is fast turning into the primary means of meeting revenue, profit, market share, and growth goals. In particular, industrial products companies face the strategic marketing challenge most immediately." Whereas some have been slow to respond, "the more forward-looking industrial leaders point to a new marketing direction"[1] These findings, revealed in a recent study by Coopers and Lybrand, capture the growing importance of strategic marketing planning in the business market sector.

To meet the challenges brought on by growing domestic and global competition, industrial firms are increasingly recognizing the vital role that the marketing function assumes in the development and implementation of successful business strategies.[2] Effective business strategies share many common characteristics, but at a minimum, they are responsive to market needs, they exploit the special competencies of the organization, and they employ valid assumptions about environmental trends and competitive behavior. Above all, they must offer a realistic basis for securing and sustaining a competitive advantage. This chapter examines the nature and critical importance of strategy development in the business marketing firm.

First, we examine the characteristics that define market-driven organizations and explore the meaning and strategic value of this orientation. Second, we turn to the sources of competitive advantage and examine the levers a firm can use to convert these sources into superior positions of advantage in the business market. Third, we examine the role that the marketing function assumes in corporate strategy development and we provide a functionally integrated perspective of business marketing planning. This discussion provides a foundation for exploring business marketing strategy on a global scale—the theme of the next chapter.

MARKET-DRIVEN ORGANIZATIONS[3]

Leading-edge organizations stay close to the customer and ahead of competition. Peter Drucker notes that "the single most important thing to remember about any enterprise is that there are no results inside its walls. The result of a business is a satisfied customer . . . . Inside an enterprise there are only cost centers. Results exist only on the outside."[4] A market-driven organization displays a deep and enduring commitment to the principle that the purpose of a business is to attract and satisfy customers at a profit.

George Day suggests that a market-driven organization has a three-level focus that includes:

- "commitment to a set of processes, beliefs, and values that permeate all aspects and activities, that are

---

[1] Dennis Yeskey, "Strategic Marketing: Industrial Companies Face a Critical Challenge," *Management Review,* 75 (April 1986), pp. 20–24.

[2] Orville C. Walker, Jr., and Robert W. Ruekert, "Marketing's Role in the Implementation of Business Strategies: A Critical Review and Strategic Framework," *Journal of Marketing,* 51 (July 1987), pp. 15–33.

[3] The discussion in this section draws on George S. Day, *Market Driven Strategy: Processes for Creating Value* (New York: The Free Press, 1990), Chapter 14; see also Ajay K. Kohli and Bernard J. Jaworski, "Market Orientation: The Construct, Research Propositions, and Managerial Implications," *Journal of Marketing,* 54 (April 1990), pp. 1–18.

[4] Peter F. Drucker, "Management and the World's Work," *Harvard Business Review,* 66 (September–October 1988), pp. 65–76.

- guided by a deep and shared understanding of consumers' needs and behavior, and competitors' capabilities and intentions, for the purpose of

- achieving superior performance by satisfying customers better than the competitors."[5]

In a market-driven organization, this orientation is achieved and sustained by making appropriate moves along four interlocking dimensions: (1) shared beliefs and values, (2) organizational structures and systems, (3) strategy development processes, and (4) supporting programs (see Figure 8.1). Each is highlighted below.

1. *Shared beliefs and values.* All decisions within market-driven organizations begin with the customer and the associated opportunities for advantage. Firms such as Federal Express, IBM, and 3M exhibit these values. Providing superior quality and service on the customer's own terms is a basic value that permeates the entire organization and is continually supported and reinforced by the actions of senior managers. (See Figure 8.2.) In turn, there is attention to service at every level of value creation in the company. Included here are internal activities that encourage production line employees to appreciate that the customer that they must satisfy is the next person on the assembly line.

2. *Organization structure and systems.* Market-driven organizations employ an organization structure that mirrors the segmentation plan of the firm, so that responsibilities for serving each primary market segment are clearly defined. Moreover, the employees closest to the customers are given the power and authority to meet customer needs.

3. *Strategy development.* Rather than relying on rigid systems geared to the preparation of annual budgets, market-driven firms operate with planning systems that are adaptive, participative, and well grounded in appropriate market information. Adaptive planning is facilitated by the astute blending of information from top-down and bottom-up sources, and is directed to helping the organization learn how to cope with a changing environment. Learning takes place in a participative context, largely occurring in multifunctional teams where operating managers debate, resolve strategic issues, and select strategic options.

4. *Supporting programs and actions.* A customer-first orientation is deeply ingrained in a market-driven firm and is particularly apparent in each "moment of truth" for the organization—the point of contact between the customer and the organization.

"When everyone understands the importance of putting the customer first, while staying ahead of the competition, they have a reason for doing their jobs. Then 'quality' becomes an understood dedication rather than an imposed dictum, 'fast response' a meaningful innovation rather than a mechanical metric, 'market share' an earned result rather than a warlike target . . . ."[6]

---

[5] Day, p. 358.

[6] Ibid., p. 375.

FIGURE 8.1   **Dimensions of Market-Driven Management**

Source: George S. Day, *Market Driven Strategy: Processes for Creating Value* (New York: The Free Press, 1990), p. 358.

ASSESSING COMPETITIVE ADVANTAGE[7]

Competitive advantage can be examined from the vantage point of competitors or of customers. A competitor-based assessment targets this question: How do our capabilities and offerings compare with those of competitors? Here the focus is on identifying areas where the firm has relative superiority in skills and resources. In contrast, a customer-oriented assessment involves a detailed analysis of customer benefits by segment to identify those actions a company might take to improve performance.

---

[7] The discussion in this section draws on George S. Day and Robin Wensley, "Assessing Advantage: A Framework for Diagnosing Competitive Superiority," *Journal of Marketing*, 52 (April 1988), pp. 1–20.

FIGURE 8.2 **TRW's Chairman Recognizes Individual Managers and Reinforces Corporate Values**

Source: Courtesy TRW. TRW is the name and mark of TRW Inc.

A competitor-centered perspective leads to a preoccupation with costs and controllable activities that can be compared directly with corresponding activities of close rivals. Customer-focused approaches have the advantage of examining the full range of competitive choices in light of the customers' needs and perceptions of superiority, but lack an obvious connection to activities and variables that are controlled by management.[8]

Observe that a balance of these perspectives is provided in Figure 8.3. Positions of advantage are based on the provision of superior customer value or on the achievement of lower relative costs and the resulting profitability and market share performance. Importantly, positional and performance superiority are derived from relative superiority in the skills and resources that a firm has to deploy. In turn, these skills and resources are an outgrowth of past investments made to enhance a firm's competitive position. To maintain a position of advantage, the firm must erect barriers that make imitation by competitors more difficult. Because these barriers to imitation are continually eroding, the firm must make a continuing stream of investments to sustain or improve the advantage.

---

[8] Ibid., p. 2.

FIGURE 8.3   **The Elements of Competitive Advantage**

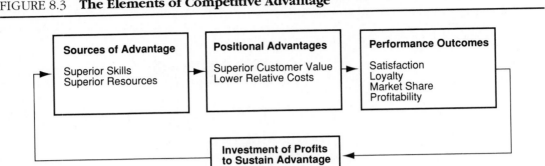

Source: George S. Day and Robin Wensley, "Assessing Advantage: A Framework for Diagnosing Competitive Superiority," *Journal of Marketing,* 52 (April 1988), p. 3. Reprinted with permission of the American Marketing Association.

Sources of Advantage

A business marketing firm gains a competitive advantage through its superior skills and resources. **Superior skills** are the distinctive capabilities of key personnel that set them apart from the personnel of competing firms. Some of the benefits of superior skills emerge from the company's resulting ability to perform individual functions more effectively than other firms. To illustrate, superior engineering may lead to greater reliability in the finished product. Other skills result from the systems and organizational structures that enable a company to adapt faster and more responsively to changing market requirements. For example, Sun Microsystems has developed a strong position in the computer workstation market by introducing new products every 12 months. Carol Bartz, a vice president at Sun, notes:

> We wouldn't hesitate to bring out a new product at a price and performance level that absolutely destroyed an existing line. Why should we wait for the competition to do it? That's a brand new concept in this business, and we're proud you can make money doing it.[9]

Superior resources are more tangible requirements for advantage that enable a firm to exercise its capabilities. Included among superior resources are these:

- Number of salespersons and service representatives by territory, region, and market
- Expenditures on advertising and promotional support
- Distribution coverage (number of industrial distributors who carry the firm's products)
- Scale of manufacturing facilities and the availability of automated assembly lines

[9] "Sun's Sizzling Race to the Top," *Fortune,* 117 (August 17, 1987), p. 89.

- Expenditures on R&D

Often, competitor analysis centers on making direct comparisons and ranking key competitors on each resource dimension.

Positions of Advantage

What we see in the market—from the perspective of customers or competitors—is the positional advantage of a business. Positional advantage can be achieved by providing the lowest delivered cost or by providing superior customer value.

Lowest Delivered Cost Position

An overall cost advantage is obtained by performing most activities at a lower cost than competitors while offering a comparable product. To illustrate, NUCOR has achieved a low-cost position in the steel industry by making extensive use of scrap metal rather than iron ore and by producing all of its steel using the efficient continuous-casting method. To succeed, a cost strategy must offer an acceptable level of value to customers. If the low-cost position is achieved by providing marginal quality or eliminating desired features, the price discount demanded by customers will more than offset the cost advantage.

Value Superiority

"A business is differentiated when some value-adding activities are performed in a way that leads to perceived superiority along dimensions that are valued by customers. For these activities to be profitable, the customer must be willing to pay a premium for the benefits and the premium must exceed the added costs of superior performance."[10] There are many ways for a firm to differentiate products and service.

- Provide superior service or technical assistance through speed, responsiveness to complex orders, or ability to solve special customer problems.
- Provide superior quality that reduces customer costs or improves performance.
- Offer innovative product features that employ new technologies.
- Gain broad distribution coverage.

Converting Skills and Resources into Superior Positions

Michael Porter proposes that the drivers of positional advantage are those particular skills and resources that have the greatest impact on reducing costs or creating value to customers.[11] There are two principal types: cost drivers and drivers of differentiation.

---

[10] Day and Wensley, "Assessing Advantage," pp. 3–4.

[11] Michael E. Porter, *Competitive Advantage: Creating and Sustaining Superior Performance* (New York: The Free Press, 1985).

Drivers of Cost Differences

Cost drivers represent the structural determinants of each activity (e.g., production) that are largely under a company's control. The principal driver is economies of scale. **Economies of scale** reflect increased efficiency due to size. Large plants cost less per unit to build and operate than smaller plants. Scale effects also apply to many other cost elements such as sales, distribution, research and development, and purchasing.

Learning is a second driver of costs and represents efficiency improvements that result from practice and the exercise of skill and ingenuity in repetitive activities. To illustrate, personnel at Intel learned how to improve the performance of a piece of production equipment and thereby reduced the cost of producing an advanced microchip.

A third cost driver is the extent of **linkages** of activities within a firm. The cost of one activity (e.g., inventory) may depend on how another activity is performed (e.g., production). To illustrate, closer coordination between purchasing and production may reduce inventory carrying costs. Other drivers of cost that may be important include the rate of capacity utilization, the degree of vertical integration, and the sharing of activities across several business units (e.g., a common sales force).

Differentiation

Drivers of differentiation represent the possible underlying reasons why one firm outperforms another on attributes important to customers. The principal drivers are

1. **policy choices** concerning what activities to perform and how aggressively to perform them. These include product or service features and performance, level of promotion, and the skills and experience of personnel employed in the activity.

2. **linkages** among key activities, such as coordination between the firm and suppliers to speed product development or between sales and service to improve the effectiveness of order handling.

3. **timing** of entry to provide first-mover advantages in a market.

Other drivers of differentiation include location, synergy from sharing a sales force or other activity with another division of the firm, or learning and scale that permits broader market coverage or more responsive service through a number of locations. When activated by an effective strategy, the drivers of differentiation correspond to the sources of advantage that reside in the superior skills or resources of the firm.

Assessing the Competitive Environment

A business marketer that builds a position of advantage (a differentiation or cost advantage) eventually should be rewarded with a level of market share and/or profit superior to those of key competitors. However, the size of the payoff and its duration will depend on the degree of difficulty that rivals will have in matching or leap-frogging the advantage. The state of competition in business markets ranges from intense, in industries such as steel or metal cans where no company earns spectacular returns on investment, to mild, in industries such as oil field services and equipment where there are opportunities for very high returns. To define the state of competition in a particular environment, the business marketing planner must understand the forces that shape competition in an industry.

Forces Shaping Competition[12]

Michael Porter contends that the state of competition in an industry is determined by the interplay of five basic forces:

1. *The threat of new entrants.* The seriousness of this threat depends on (1) the barriers to entry that are present and (2) the reaction that the newcomer can expect from existing competitors. Barriers to entry include factors such as high capital requirements or economies of scale in the production, distribution, or service enjoyed by existing firms. Thus, the threat of new firms entering a particular industry is weak if barriers to entry are high and if a new entrant can expect sharp retaliation from established competitors.

2. *The threat of substitute products or services.* Substitutes can limit the growth of an industry by placing a ceiling on prices. To illustrate, the profit potential of sugar producers has been limited by the commercialization of high-fructose corn syrup, a sugar substitute.

3. *The bargaining power of suppliers.* By raising prices, powerful suppliers can damage profitability if competitors are unable to recover cost increases by raising their own prices. Also, a powerful supplier can threaten **forward integration** into the industry's business. For example, IBM, a supplier to the computer-controlled machine tool industry, became a competitor in this industry through forward integration.

4. *The bargaining power of buyers.* High-volume buyers can force prices down and demand higher quality or more service. Likewise, large-volume buyers enhance their bargaining power by threatening **backward integration**. General Motors, a large user of computer-controlled machine tools, entered this market through backward integration.

5. *The intensity of rivalry.* The jockeying for position among existing participants relates to the presence of factors such as numerous competitors of roughly equal size and power, a slow rate of industry growth, and a product or service that lacks differentiation.

By examining the interplay of these five forces, the business marketer can gain insight into the present and future profitability of an industry and into the strategic opportunities it offers to the firm. Because foreign competition is a potent force in many industries, the competitive assessment must encompass foreign as well as domestic competitors. A global perspective of competition is required even in firms that choose not to operate in the international market.

---

[12]The discussion in this section is based on Michael E. Porter, "How Competitive Forces Shape Strategy," *Harvard Business Review*, 57 (March–April 1979), pp. 137–145; see also Porter, *Competitive Strategy* (New York: The Free Press, 1980).

FIGURE 8.4 **New Determinants of Competitive Structures in Business Markets**

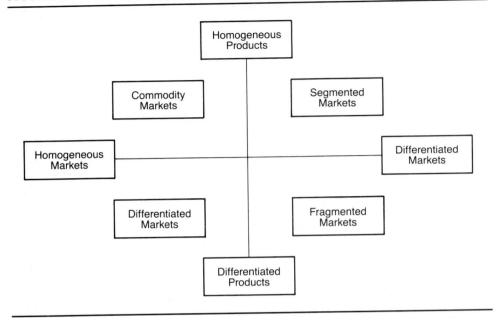

Source: Adapted from Jagdish N. Sheth, "New Determinants of Competitive Structures in Industrial Markets," in Robert E. Spekman and David T. Wilson, eds., *A Strategic Approach to Business Markets* (Chicago: American Marketing Association, 1985), p. 3. Reprinted with permission of the American Marketing Association.

New Determinants of Competitive Structure[13]

Jagdish Sheth argues that different types of competitive structures are emerging in business markets for which the traditional labels such as monopoly, oligopoly, or perfect competition have little relevance. The new determinants of competitive structure are anchored in two dimensions: product differentiation and market differentiation. Observe in Figure 8.4 that four competitive structures are proposed: commodity, differentiated, segmented, and fragmented markets. The strategic relevance of each is explored in Table 8.1. Note that the driving force for a competitive advantage is quite different in each competitive structure: for example, cost efficiency in commodity markets; strong R&D in differentiated markets. Also observe that the fundamental strategic issue varies by competitive market structure. Since superior positions of advantage are being continually challenged, the business marketer must be responsive to changing market needs and alert to fresh initiatives by new and existing competitors.

---

[13] The discussion in this section is based on Jagdish N. Sheth, "New Determinants of Competitive Structures in Industrial Markets," in Robert E. Spekman and David T. Wilson, eds., *A Strategic Approach to Business Marketing* (Chicago: American Marketing Association, 1985), pp. 1–8.

TABLE 8.1   **Major Competitive Structures: Strategic Dimensions**

Competitive Structure	Definition	Driving Force for Competitive Advantage	Fundamental Strategic Issue	Business Market Illustrations
Commodity markets	A handful of suppliers producing highly standardized product offerings and marketing them to customers on a nondifferentiated basis	Economies of scale and cost efficiency in both manufacturing and marketing	Gain market share	Chemical, semiconductors, steel, and copper industries
Differentiated markets	A large number of suppliers providing specialized technologies and products to the market and employing similar marketing programs	Strong R&D and highly differentiated or proprietary products	R&D success and unique manufacturing expertise	Telecommunications and pharmaceutical industries
Segmented markets	A handful of suppliers offering a common but versatile technology to various market segments while employing highly differentiated marketing programs	Application-based segmentation and customization	Market segmentation, market expansion, and a total systems approach	Office automation, computer, and financial services industries
Fragmented markets	A large number of suppliers, each controlling a small market share, providing a unique product offering to a target segment using a highly customized marketing program	Niching or ultraspecialization	Expertise in narrow target segments	Parts suppliers to the automobile and appliance industries

Source: Adapted from Jagdish N. Sheth, "New Determinants of Competitive Structures in Industrial Markets," in Robert E. Spekman and David T. Wilson, eds., *A Strategic Approach to Business Markets* (Chicago: American Marketing Association, 1985), pp. 1–8.

STRATEGIC PLANNING

Many industrial firms have numerous divisions, product lines, products, and brands. Policies established at the corporate level provide the framework for strategy development in each business division to ensure survival and growth of the entire enterprise. In turn, corporate and divisional policies establish the boundaries within which individual product or market managers develop strategy.

The Hierarchy of Strategies

There are three major levels of strategy in most large multiproduct organizations: (1) corporate strategy, (2) business-level strategy, and (3) functional strategy.[14]

Corporate strategy defines the businesses in which a company will compete, preferably in a manner that utilizes resources to convert distinctive competence into competitive advantage. The essential questions at this level are: What businesses are we in? What businesses should we be in? How should we allocate resources across these businesses to achieve our overall organizational goals and objectives? The marketing function assumes a lead role in keeping the firm in step with the changing market environment, for it is "the boundary function between the firm and its customers, distributors, and competitors."[15]

Business-level strategy centers on how a firm will compete in a given industry and will position itself against its competitors. The focus of competition is not between corporations; rather, it is between their individual business units. A **strategic business unit** (SBU) is a single business or collection of businesses that has a distinct mission, a responsible manager, and its own competitors, and that is relatively independent of other business units. Mead Corporation defined 24 SBUs and assigned 24 top executives to the slots by matching expertise with business requirements. The Xerox planning system comprises 34 SBUs. An SBU could be one or more divisions of the industrial firm, a product line within one division, or on occasion, a single product. Strategic business units may share resources such as a sales force with other business units in order to achieve economies of scale. An SBU may serve one or many product-market units.

For each business unit within the corporate portfolio, the essential questions are: How can we compete most effectively for the product market served by the business unit? What distinctive skills can give the business unit a competitive advantage? The marketing function contributes to the planning process at this level by identifying optional long-term competitive positions that will assure customer support and satisfaction, by developing strategies designed to capture these preferred positions, and by serving as a strong advocate for these strategic options with top management and with other functional areas.[16]

Functional strategy centers on how resources allocated to the various functional areas can be used most efficiently and effectively to support the business-level strategy. The primary focus of marketing strategy at this level is to allocate and coordinate marketing resources and activities to achieve the firm's objective within a specific product market. The planning system at 3M can be used to illustrate the hierarchy of strategies in a large multiproduct firm.

---

[14] For a thorough discussion, see Roger A. Kerin, Vijay Mahajan, and P. Rajan Varadarajan, *Strategic Market Planning* (Boston: Allyn and Bacon, 1990).

[15] George S. Day, *Strategic Market Planning: The Pursuit of Competitive Advantage* (St. Paul, MN: West Publishing Co., 1984), p. 3.

[16] Paul F. Anderson, "Marketing, Strategic Planning, and the Theory of the Firm," *Journal of Marketing*, 46 (Spring 1982), pp. 15–26; and Michael D. Hutt, Peter H. Reingen, and John R. Ronchetto, Jr., "Tracing Emergent Processes in Marketing Strategy Formation," *Journal of Marketing*, 52 (January 1988), pp. 4–19.

ILLUSTRATION: 3M's Strategic Planning System[17]

The 3M Corporation defined 20 strategic business centers (comparable to SBUs). Each strategic business center (SBC) is composed of individual operating units—usually divisions or departments responsible for particular products or market segments. Some SBCs cover two or more divisions—for example, Memory Media consists of Data Recording Products and Magnetic A/V Products (see Figure 8.5(a)). Employing a bottom-up approach to strategic planning, SBC plans describe how each 3M business will manage its overall mix of products to secure a competitive advantage consistent with the level of investment and risk that management is willing to accept.

The strategic position of each 3M SBC is typically examined and portrayed on a maturity and competitive position screen. Each SBC uses the approach to examine its portfolio of products and markets. Figure 8.5(b) portrays the strategic condition of a particular 3M business by geographic market. The maturity stages affect the focus of marketing strategy: "In embryonic industries 3M businesses emphasize market- or product-oriented strategies to improve their competitive position. As their industries mature, these businesses will likely emphasize integration, efficiency, and rejuvenation through innovation."[18] In the late stages of maturity, consolidation and divestment will be considered. On the competitive position axis, each 3M business is ranked against its competitors to develop a measure of its relative position. Attention centers on the factors that underlie ultimate success or failure in a particular industry.

In establishing corporate strategies, the complete portfolio of the corporation (see Figure 8.5(c)) is evaluated in terms of competitive position, overall maturity, market attractiveness, future growth prospects, profit and cash generation, and risk. Resources are then allocated to each SBC on the basis of corporate objectives, portfolio balance, and the merits of each SBC strategy.

The 3M strategy approach provides but one example of how a portfolio of businesses or product lines can be examined. Other portfolio models emphasize different performance or descriptive dimensions such as industry growth rate, market share, long-term industry attractiveness, and competitive strength.[19] To gain strategic insights, the business marketer must assemble accurate information, make realistic assumptions, and challenge the underlying premises of each approach. Although formal planning tools assume a role, major strategic decisions emerge incrementally. After tracing the strategy formulation process in ten large corporations, James Quinn observed:

> The most effective strategies of major enterprises tend to emerge step-by-step from an iterative process in which the organization probes the future, experiments, and learns from a series of partial (incremental) commitments rather than through global formulations of total strategies . . . . The process is both logical and incremental. Such logical

---

[17] Michael A. Tita and Robert J. Allio, "3M's Strategy System—Planning in an Innovative Corporation," *Planning Review,* 12 (September 1984), pp. 10–15.

[18] Ibid., p. 13.

[19] For a comprehensive review, see George S. Day, *Analysis of Strategic Market Decisions* (St. Paul: West Publishing Company, 1986).

FIGURE 8.5 **3M's Strategic Planning System**

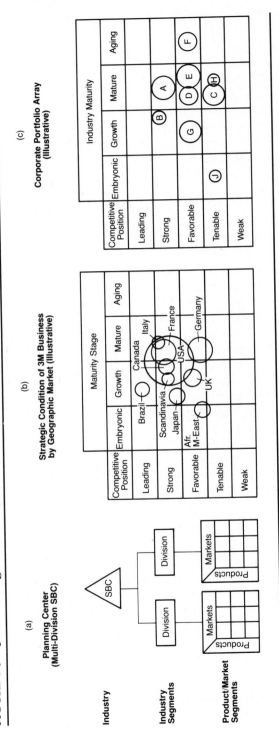

Source: Michael A. Tita and Robert J. Allio, "3M's Strategy System—Planning in an Innovative Corporation," *Planning Review,* 12 (September 1984), pp. 10–15. Reprinted by permission of the Planning Forum.

incrementalism is not "muddling" . . . . Properly managed, it is a conscious, purposeful, proactive, executive practice.[20]

FUNCTIONALLY INTEGRATED MARKETING PLANNING

Business marketing success depends to a large degree on such functional areas in the firm as engineering, research and development, manufacturing, and technical service. Planning in the industrial setting thus requires more functional interdependence and a closer relationship to total corporate strategy than planning in the consumer-goods sector.[21] "Changes in marketing strategy are more likely to involve capital commitments for new equipment, shifts in development activities, or departures from traditional engineering and manufacturing approaches, any one of which would have companywide implications."[22] All business marketing decisions—product, price, promotion, or distribution—are affected, directly or indirectly, by other functional areas. In turn, business decisions in research and development and in manufacturing and procurement, as well as adjustments in the overall corporate strategy, are influenced by marketing considerations.

Business marketing planning must be coordinated and synchronized with corresponding planning efforts in R&D, procurement, finance, production, and other areas (Figure 8.6). For example, the marketing function gives procurement a sales forecast that facilitates material-requirements planning. Procurement both monitors and interprets supply trends that present opportunities or threats to marketing.[23] Business marketing plans must also be consistent with accounting and financial policies, personnel and procurement procedures, and short- and long-term corporate objectives.[24]

This section explores the interrelationships between marketing and three business functions: manufacturing, research and development, and customer service. Each assumes a particularly significant role in the development and execution of business marketing strategy.

Marketing–Manufacturing Interface

Manufacturing capabilities determine the volume, variety, and quality of products that can be marketed and influence the speed with which the industrial marketer can respond to changing market needs or competitive challenges. For efficient production,

[20] James B. Quinn, *Strategies for Change: Logical Incrementalism* (Homewood, IL: Irwin, 1980), p. 58.

[21] Frederick E. Webster, Jr., "Management Science in Industrial Marketing," *Journal of Marketing,* 42 (January 1978), p. 22.

[22] B. Charles Ames, "Trappings vs. Substance in Industrial Marketing," *Harvard Business Review,* 48 (July–August 1976), pp. 95–96.

[23] For example, see John M. Browning, Noel B. Zabriskie, and Alan B. Huellmantel, "Strategic Purchasing Management," *Journal of Purchasing and Materials Management,* 19 (Spring 1983), pp. 19–24.

[24] For a discussion of the marketing–finance interface, see Paul F. Anderson, "The Marketing/Finance Interface," in Neil Beckwith et al., *Educators' Conference Proceedings* (Chicago: American Marketing Association, 1979), pp. 325–329.

FIGURE 8.6 **Business Marketing Planning: A Functionally Integrated Perspective**

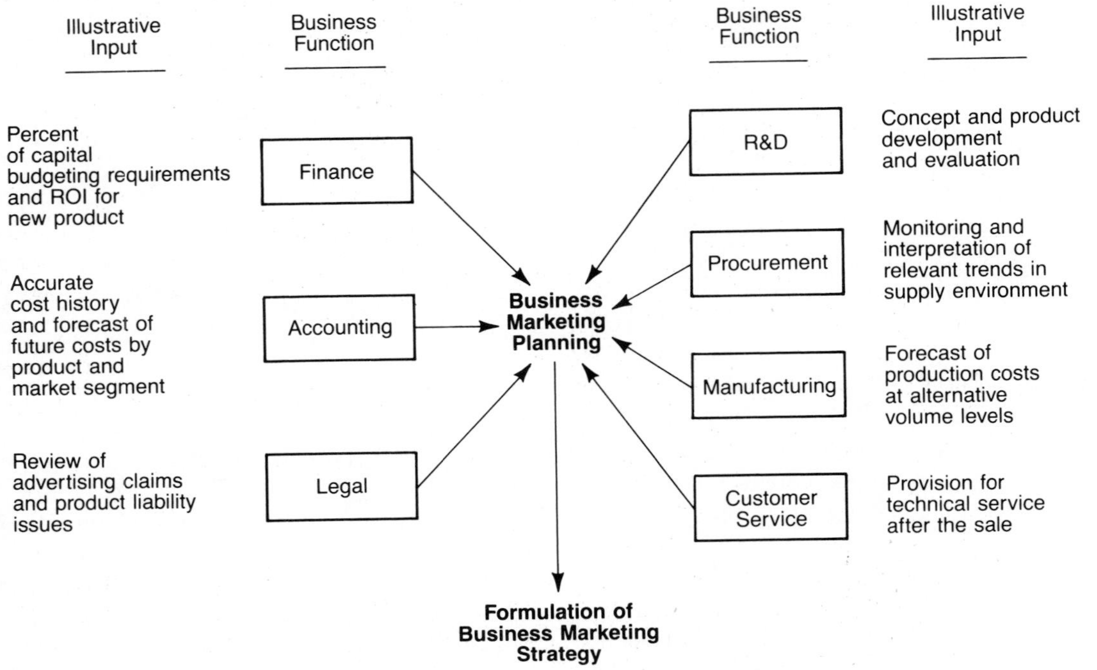

Illustrative Input	Business Function		Business Function	Illustrative Input
Percent of capital budgeting requirements and ROI for new product	Finance	R&D		Concept and product development and evaluation
Accurate cost history and forecast of future costs by product and market segment	Accounting	**Business Marketing Planning**	Procurement	Monitoring and interpretation of relevant trends in supply environment
			Manufacturing	Forecast of production costs at alternative volume levels
Review of advertising claims and product liability issues	Legal		Customer Service	Provision for technical service after the sale

Formulation of Business Marketing Strategy

manufacturing relies heavily on marketing for an accurate sales forecast of the product line.

Manufacturing's Strategic Role

Business marketing firms that require five years to bring new products to market can be quickly overtaken by competitors who can accomplish the same task in three years.[25] To reduce the "cycle time" from conception to production, firms such as Xerox, NCR, Motorola, and IBM have dramatically altered their approach to product development. Traditionally, product development was like a relay race. The marketing department would come up with an idea and hand it off to design. Design engineers would then craft a blueprint and a hand-built prototype. Next, the design would be thrown "over the wall" to manufacturing, where production engineers would struggle to devise a way to bring the blueprint to life. Once everything was set, the purchasing department would call for bids from suppliers for the necessary materials, parts, and equipment. Worst of all, a design glitch would often halt the process until an engineering change could be made. An alternative method tackles all of these tasks concurrently.

---

[25] George Stalk, Jr., and Thomas M. Hout, *Competing Against Time: How Time-Based Competition is Re-shaping Global Markets* (New York: The Free Press, 1990).

Concurrent Engineering[26]

Employing this method, a team—including marketers, design and manufacturing engineers, component suppliers from other companies, production workers, accountants, salespersons, and service representatives—meets to develop a new product and the means to make it. Strict quality goals are established. In turn, competitors' products are carefully researched to find the "best in class" worldwide, with the idea of surpassing these efforts. Using computer-aided design tools, the proposed product can be changed again and again before it is physically constructed.

The group effort ensures that the concerns of each functional area are considered and that the product can be built efficiently when it reaches the factory floor. Rather than passing information from one level of management to another—with management approval required—the cross-functional team mediates their own disputes and makes the decision themselves. By using concurrent engineering at its Atlanta plant where terminals for checkout counters are made, NCR turned out a new product in 22 months—half the normal time. Similarly, AT&T used the approach when it redesigned its main phone-switching computers: the "cycle time" for product development was cut in half and manufacturing defects were reduced by more than 85 percent.

Concurrent engineering touches the entire supply chain and requires a close working relationship between the manufacturer and its supplier network. Approximately 70 percent of Ford's procurement budget goes to suppliers that concurrently engineer component parts. Suppliers must be involved in the new product development process from the start. In addition to tying together the cross-functional team, including key domestic suppliers, new electronic data systems make it possible to use concurrent engineering on a global scale, linking suppliers or corporate functions around the world. For example, in producing its new hard-disk drive, Digital Equipment coordinates design from its Colorado Springs headquarters with final assembly at a plant located in Kaufbeuren, West Germany.

Emerging Manufacturing Technology: Strategic Implications

By altering conventional manufacturing, new technology can alter business marketing strategy. Flexible manufacturing systems, the first step toward computer-integrated manufacturing systems, are a radical departure from the past when economies could be realized only at high levels of production. Because a flexible system can be instantly reprogrammed, goods can be produced economically in small volumes. Flexible manufacturing extends the reflexes, or diversity, of manufacturing to a degree never before available. At its Sommerworth, New Hampshire plant, General Electric uses flexible manufacturing to produce 2,000 different versions of its basic electric meter.[27] Likewise, a Japanese firm employs the approach to offer 11,231,862 variations of a bicycle.[28]

---

[26]This section draws on Otis Port, "A Smarter Way to Manufacture," *Business Week* (April 30, 1990), pp. 110–117; and William J. Cook, "Ringing in Saturn: GM's New Factory Heralds an American Manufacturing Revolution," *U.S. News & World Report* (October 22, 1990).

[27]Gene Bylinsky, "The Race to the Automatic Factory," *Fortune,* 113 (February 21, 1983), p. 54.

[28]Susan Moffat, "Japan's New Personalized Production," *Fortune,* 120 (October 22, 1990), pp. 132–135.

Economies of Scope

The term **economies of scope** describes the capacity of flexible automation to produce a small batch or even a single product as efficiently as a production line that manufactures the same items on a massive scale.[29] Because flexible automation allows the firm to meet the special product requirements of small market segments or large individual customers, lower cost penalties for variety give the business marketer more flexibility in the choice of product and market segmentation strategies.

Flexible manufacturing can also alter buyer–seller relationships in some markets because firms have the option of producing components that they had previously purchased from suppliers. For example, dissatisfied with the quality of a purchased component part, General Motors turned to flexible automation to produce the item itself.

Flexible manufacturing can also alter the nature of competition in selected industrial markets. Efficient production of products in small volumes broadens the scope of markets that competitors can serve. As flexible automation increases, "some companies will find themselves blindsided by competitors they never imagined existed."[30] In monitoring the competitive environment, the business marketer should evaluate the marketing and manufacturing strengths of both existing and potential competitors.

Marketing–R&D Interface

"Ignoring the R&D–marketing interface has resulted in many technology-oriented firms developing products that are the engineer's and scientist's dream and the marketer's nightmare, since they meet no latent or overt consumer needs."[31] The importance of nurturing an effective marketing–R&D interface is reinforced by the sizable investments R&D commands in industrial firms. Motorola and Boeing each spend over $700 million annually, Du Pont and Hewlett-Packard over $1 billion, AT&T over $2.5 billion, and IBM over $5 billion on R&D investments.[32] Many small- and medium-sized firms make a significant investment as a percentage of sales in R&D.

New product development is the focus of the marketing–R&D interface, from idea generation to performance evaluation of the finished product. Successful new product developments depend heavily on marketing research for product features desired by target market segments and for how potential organizational buyers view trade-offs among product attributes.[33] If marketing fails to provide adequate market and competitive information, R&D personnel will be in the precarious position of determining the

---

[29] Harry Thompson and Michael Paris, "The Changing Face of Manufacturing Technology," *The Journal of Business Strategy,* 3 (Summer 1982), pp. 45–52; see also Mariann Jelinek and Joel D. Goldhar, "The Strategic Implications of the Factory of the Future," *Sloan Management Review,* 25 (Summer 1984), pp. 29–37.

[30] Bylinsky, "Automatic Factory," p. 54.

[31] Yoram Wind, "Marketing and the Other Business Functions," in Jagdish N. Sheth, ed., *Research in Marketing,* vol. 3 (Greenwich, CT: JAI Press, 1981), p. 244; see also Noel Capon and Rashi Glazer, "Marketing and Technology: A Strategic Coalignment," *Journal of Marketing,* 51 (July 1987), pp. 1–14.

[32] Emily Smith, "Glimpsing the Future in the Numbers," *Business Week* (June 15, 1990), p. 195.

[33] Yoram Wind, John F. Grashof, and Joel D. Goldhar, "Market Based Guidelines for the Design of Industrial Products," *Journal of Marketing,* 42 (July 1978), pp. 23–27.

direction of new product development without the benefit of market knowledge. A successful relationship between marketing and R&D requires that each understands the strengths, weaknesses, and potential contributions of the other. For instance, a promising new product spawned by R&D may fail because the firm lacks the marketing strengths required to penetrate a particular market segment.

Promoting Cooperation

New product development is successful in an organizational climate that stimulates innovation and encourages interaction between marketing and R&D.[34] What steps can be taken to foster cooperation?

Some firms program regular exchanges of personnel between the two functions, hold frequent information meetings, schedule periodic gripe sessions, and maintain an open invitation for marketers to visit the R&D laboratory. Other industrial firms foster the entrepreneurial spirit in marketing, R&D, and other functional areas by creating mini-enterprises within the larger organization;[35] decentralizing the flow of information, decision-making responsibility, and authority; and providing incentives to reward successful new ventures. A diversified industrial products firm, TRW, has developed a bonus system to stimulate cooperation among its divisions.[36] This firm has also developed an index of its technological capabilities that allows TRW managers working on over 250 independent space and defense contracts to share knowledge.

Marketing–Customer Service Interface

Since organizational buyers evaluate industrial suppliers on many service dimensions, the marketing–customer service interface is also vital to a successful marketing strategy. Two factors assigned particular importance in procurement decisions (see Chapter 3) are (1) the speed and reliability of delivery service and (2) the quality and availability of technical service after the sale. The direct control of these activities often falls outside the marketing function.

Many industrial firms have a separate department that manages physical distribution and still another that provides technical service. Others fully integrate these functions into marketing. Regardless of the organizational location of these functions, effective marketing strategy demands close coordination and open lines of communication among distribution, technical service, and marketing. Organizational buyers enter exchange relationships with business marketers to secure technical assistance, training, and responsive and reliable delivery service, as well as physical products. Carefully designed and coordinated service policies enable business marketers to maximize the value of their total market offerings.

---

[34] Ashok K. Gupta, S. P. Raj, and David Wilemon, "A Model for Studying the R&D–Marketing Interface in the Product Innovation Process," *Journal of Marketing,* 50 (April 1986), pp. 7–17; and Hutt, Reingen, and Ronchetto, "Tracing Emergent Processes."

[35] Thomas J. Peters and Robert H. Waterman, Jr., *In Search of Excellence, Lessons from America's Best-Run Companies* (New York: Harper & Row Publishers, 1982).

[36] "TRW Leads a Revolution in Managing Technology," *Business Week* (November 15, 1982), p. 130.

Functionally Integrated Planning: The Marketing Strategy Center[37]

Rather than operating in isolation from other functional areas, the successful business marketing manager is an integrator—one who understands the capabilities of manufacturing, R&D, and customer service and who exploits their strengths in developing marketing strategies that are responsive to customer needs. **Responsibility charting** is an approach that can be used to classify decision-making roles and to highlight the multifunctional nature of business marketing decision making. The structure of a responsibility chart is provided in Table 8.2. The decision areas (rows) illustrated in the matrix might, for example, relate to a planned product line expansion. The various functional areas that may assume particular roles in this decision process head the columns of the matrix.

The alternative roles that can be assumed by the various managers participating in the decision-making process are defined below:[38]

1. *Responsible* (R). The manager takes the initiative in analyzing the situation, developing alternatives, and assuring consultation with others, and then makes the initial recommendation. Upon approval of decision, the role ends.

2. *Approve* (A). The manager accepts or vetoes a decision before it is implemented, or chooses from alternatives developed by the participants assuming a "responsible" role.

3. *Consult* (C). The manager is consulted or asked for substantive input prior to the approval of the decision but does not possess veto power.

4. *Implement* (M). The manager is accountable for the implementation of the decision, including notification of other relevant participants concerning the decision.

5. *Inform* (I). Although not necessarily consulted before the decision is approved, the manager is informed of the decision once it is made.

Representatives of a particular functional area may, of course, assume more than one role in the decision-making process. The technical service manager may be "consulted" during the new product development process and may also be held accountable for "implementing" service support strategy. Likewise, the marketing manager may be "responsible" for and "approve" many of the decisions related to the product line expansion. For other actions, several decision makers may participate. To illustrate, the business unit manager, after "consulting" R&D, may "approve" (accept or veto) a decision for which the marketing manager is "responsible."

The members of the organization who become involved in the business marketing decision-making process constitute the marketing strategy center. The composition or functional area representation of the strategy center evolves during the marketing

---

[37] Michael D. Hutt and Thomas W. Speh, "The Marketing Strategy Center: Diagnosing the Industrial Marketer's Interdisciplinary Role," *Journal of Marketing,* 48 (Fall 1984), pp. 53–61; see also Robert W. Ruekert and Orville C. Walker, Jr., "Marketing's Interaction with Other Functional Units: A Conceptual Framework and Empirical Evidence," *Journal of Marketing,* 51 (January 1987), pp. 1–19.

[38] Joseph E. McCann and Thomas N. Gilmore, "Diagnosing Organizational Decision Making Through Responsibility Charting," *Sloan Management Review,* 25 (Winter 1983), pp. 3–15.

TABLE 8.2   Interfunctional Involvement in Marketing Decision Making: An Illustrative Responsibility Chart

Organizational Function

Decision Area	Marketing	Manufacturing	R&D	Physical Distribution	Technical Service	Strategic Business Unit Manager	Corporate Level Planner
Product							
Design specifications							
Performance characteristics							
Reliability							
Price							
List price							
Discount structure							
Technical Service Support							
Customer training							
Repair							
Physical Distribution							
Inventory level							
Customer service level							
Sales Force							
Training							
Advertising							
Message development							
Channel							
Selection							

Decision Role Vocabulary: R = Responsible; A = Approve; C = Consult; M = Implement; I = Inform; X = No role in decision.

ETHICAL BUSINESS MARKETING
The Major Ethical Problems Confronting Marketing Managers

Results of an empirical study indicate that marketing managers are confronted with a wide variety of difficult ethical problems. Ethical problems concerning bribery are most frequently cited. However, ethical issues involving fairness, honesty, pricing strategy, product strategy, and personnel decisions are also frequently mentioned. Marketing managers employed by large organizations perceive more ethical problems than those in smaller firms. The primary source of ethical conflict for marketing managers centers on the relationship between corporate interests and the interests of customers. Marketing managers perceive numerous opportunities in their firms and industry to engage in unethical behavior. However, they report that few managers frequently engage in unethical practices.

These findings point to the need to integrate concerns about ethics and social responsibility into the strategic marketing planning process. Here the strategic planner examines the anticipated consequences of marketing programs on all affected publics (e.g., target customers, competitors, managers, employees, stockholders, suppliers). The intent is to develop an ethical profile that isolates how the organization chooses to interact with these publics. This profile acts as a standard for examining the anticipated impact of marketing programs on selected publics and signals the importance of ethical behavior to the organizational climate.

Source: Lawrence B. Chonko and Shelby D. Hunt, "Ethics and Marketing Management: An Empirical Examination," *Journal of Business Research,* 13 (August 1985), pp. 339–359; and R. Eric Reidenbach and Donald P. Robin, *Ethics and Profits: A Convergence of Corporate America's Economic and Social Responsibility* (Englewood Cliffs, NJ: Prentice-Hall, Inc., 1989).

strategy development process, varies from firm to firm, and varies from one strategy situation to another. Likewise, the composition of the marketing strategy center is not strictly prescribed by the organizational chart. The needs of a particular strategy situation, especially the information requirements, significantly influence the composition of the strategy center. Thus, the marketing strategy center shares certain parallels with the buying center (see Chapter 4).

Managing Strategic Interdependencies

A central challenge for the business marketer in the strategy center is to minimize interdepartmental conflict while fostering shared appreciation of the interdependencies with other functional units. Individual strategy center participants are motivated by both personal and organizational goals. Company objectives are interpreted by these individuals in relation to their level in the hierarchy and the department they represent. Various functional units operate under unique reward systems and reflect unique orientations. For example, marketing managers are evaluated on the basis of sales, profits, or market share; production managers on the basis of manufacturing efficiency and cost-effectiveness. In turn, R&D managers may be oriented toward long-term objectives; customer service managers may emphasize more immediate ones. Strategic plans emerge out of a bargaining process among functional areas.

Managing conflict, promoting cooperation, and developing coordinated strategies are all fundamental to the business marketer's interdisciplinary role.

THE BUSINESS MARKETING PLANNING PROCESS

The business marketing planning process is inextricably linked to planning in other functional areas and to overall corporate strategy. It takes place within the larger strategic marketing management process of the corporation. To survive and prosper, the business marketer must properly balance the firm's resources with the objectives and opportunities of the environment. Marketing planning is a continuous process.

A model especially well suited for business marketing is presented in Figure 8.7:[39]

- Section 1 involves an assessment of the current and projected environmental opportunities and threats facing the firm and each of its businesses. An analysis of business strengths and weaknesses is also made.

- Section 2, the heart of the framework, is an evaluation of alternative market-segment candidates and of positioning strategies for each segment. Each is analyzed in terms of market opportunity, the firm's strengths and weaknesses, and the possible common characteristics that may result in positive synergy (e.g., some candidate segments may capitalize on the existing manufacturing or distribution system to a greater degree than others). Figure 8.8 illustrates how a particular segment might look in relation to company strength and requirements for success—good manufacturing fit, poor R&D fit.

- Section 3 is the development of objectives, the evaluation of alternative strategies, and the formulation of the marketing program. Particular attention is also given to designing an implementation and control program for the marketing program.

The approach recognizes the interdependence of marketing and other business functions, allows the business marketing manager to link company strengths directly to market-segment needs, and establishes a foundation for assessing the risks and expected returns of alternative marketing strategies. Furthermore, the approach allows the multinational firm to conduct the analysis by country while exploring common patterns that may provide a competitive advantage on an international scale. "Often, multinational companies err on the side of too little standardization rather than too much, because they let country managers plan, as well as manage, local marketing programs."[40]

---

[39] Yoram Wind and Thomas S. Robertson, "Marketing Strategy: New Directions for Theory and Research," *Journal of Marketing,* 47 (Spring 1983), pp. 12–25.

[40] Franklin R. Root, *Entry Strategies for International Markets* (Lexington, Mass.: Lexington Books, 1987), p. 233.

FIGURE 8.7   **Integrating Marketing and Strategic Planning**

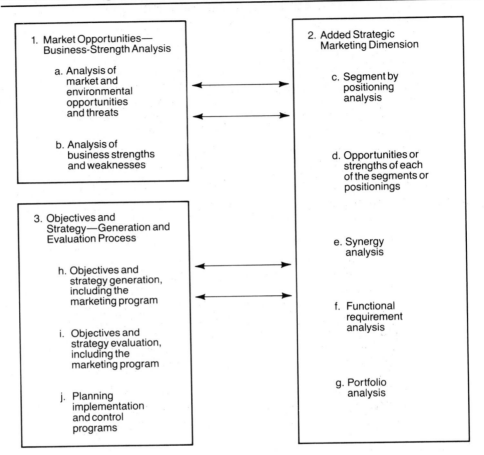

Source: Adpated from Yoram Wind and Thomas S. Robertson, "Marketing Strategy: New Directions for Theory and Research," *Journal of Marketing,* 47 (Spring 1983), p. 16. Reprinted with permission of the American Marketing Association.

The Marketing Plan

Responsive to both corporate and business unit strategy, the marketing plan formally describes all the components of the marketing strategy—markets to be served, products or services to be marketed, price schedules, distribution methods, and so on. A marketing planning guide used by Grumman Corporation is provided in Table 8.3. Note that the planning process format centers on clearly defined markets, a thorough assessment of internal and external problems and opportunities, specific goals, and courses of action. Business marketing intelligence (Chapter 5), market segmentation (Chapter 6), and market potential and sales forecasting (Chapter 7) are fundamental in the planning process.

FIGURE 8.8 **Evaluation of the Functional Requirements for a Particular Candidate Segment**

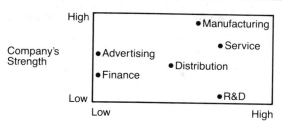

Source: Adapted from Yoram Wind and Thomas S. Robertson, "Marketing Strategy: New Directions for Theory and Research," *Journal of Marketing,* 47 (Spring 1983), p. 17. Reprinted with permission of the American Marketing Association.

Grumman's planning process also emphasizes the central role that the marketing strategy assumes in establishing a course for other functional areas. This is aptly described in the firm's marketing planning guidelines:[41]

> The market strategy is the portion of the business planning process that states *how* the objectives of the business area will be met. The market strategy will govern not only the product-oriented marketing planning in this phase, but also the technical, manufacturing/operations, and financial planning functions. Market strategy is the mainstream guidance from which *all* subsequent planning functions flow. Market strategizing marks the point in the business planning process which is perhaps more pivotal to future profit success than any other phase. For this reason, strategy paths chosen must be entirely realistic with respect to resource capabilities.

Implementing Business Marketing Strategy

Well-conceived strategic plans fail if they are not properly implemented. Strategies may fail because marketing managers are out of touch with the marketplace—they have little direct contact with customers, and they neglect to gather information from the sales force.[42] Other business marketing planning efforts may be irreparable if they are developed without recognizing important internal functional interrelationships. An R&D scientist who works on a product modification, a shop supervisor who sets priorities for the production schedule, a physical distribution manager who expedites the order, a technician who trains customers on product use after the sale—all are part of the implementation of marketing strategy.

---

[41] David S. Hopkins, *The Marketing Plan* (New York: The Conference Board, 1981), p. 123.

[42] Walter Kiechel III, "Three (or Four, or More) Ways to Win," *Fortune,* 111 (October 19, 1981), pp. 181–188.

TABLE 8.3   **Marketing Planning Format: Grumman Corporation**

---

1. **Business/Market Definition**
   a. General statement: categorize customers and users served and their needs.
   b. Quantification of market size: provide forecast of market potential and the rate of growth.
   c. Segmentation analysis: describe customer and user categories and provide an estimate of the size of each segment.
2. **Situation Analysis**
   a. Internal capabilities and current position in each market segment (e.g., market share, sales, profit history)
   b. Analysis of competitors: ranking, market share, strategies, and capabilities of each
   c. Economic conditions and forecast
   d. Regulation: past, pending, and proposed
3. **Problems and Opportunities**
   a. Internal problems and opportunities (e.g., marketing, manufacturing, R&D)
   b. External problems and opportunities (e.g., market segments, competition, regulation)
   c. Planning for the unexpected
4. **Objectives**
   a. Market position (e.g., share, growth rate, image)
   b. Financial (e.g., profit, return on investment, return on assets)
   c. Long-term versus short-term: provide dates
5. **Market Strategy** (This is the mainstream guidance from which *all* subsequent planning functions flow.)
   a. Market segments selected and targeted
   b. Positioning relative to competition
   c. Product strategy
   d. Channel of distribution strategy
   e. Promotion strategy: advertising and personal selling
   f. Pricing strategy
   g. Service strategy
6. **Contingency Plans**

Source: Adapted from David S. Hopkins, *The Marketing Plan* (New York: The Conference Board, 1981), pp. 119–126.

SUMMARY

Guided by a deep understanding of the needs of customers and the capabilities of competitors, market-driven organizations are committed to a set of processes, beliefs, and values that promote the achievement of superior performance by satisfying customers better than competitors. A business marketing firm gains a competitive advantage through its superior skills and resources. Positions of advantage—providing the lowest delivered cost or superior customer value—can be secured by effectively managing and deploying these skills and resources.

Because many industrial firms have numerous divisions, product lines, and brands, there are three major levels of strategy in most large organizations: (1) corporate, (2) business-level, and (3) functional. Business marketing planning must be coordinated and synchronized with corresponding planning efforts in other functional areas. To be successful, the business marketer must be attuned to internal as well as external requirements. Special attention is given to choosing market segments that are well suited to the firm's particular functional strengths (e.g., R&D and manufacturing). A continuous process, marketing planning involves several stages: (1) situation analysis, (2) evaluation of problems and opportunities, (3) formulation of marketing strategy, (4) development of an integrated marketing plan, and (5) measurement and evaluation of results. The result of the planning process is the marketing plan, the formal written description of the marketing strategy. The succeeding chapters will analyze each marketing mix variable.

Discussion Questions

1. Describe the major elements that characterize a market-driven organization and outline the steps a firm might follow in becoming more market driven.

2. The evaluation of new or existing markets requires an analysis of competition. Michael Porter contends that the state of competition in an industry is determined by the interplay of five basic forces. Explain.

3. Select a firm such as Federal Express, Apple Computer, IBM, Boeing, General Electric, or Caterpillar and assess its competitive advantage. Develop a list of particular skills and resources that are especially important to the selected firm's position of advantage. Give particular attention to those skills and resources that competitors would have the most difficulty in matching.

4. Critique this statement: Positions of advantage tend to erode quickly in high-tech markets.

5. One marketing expert argues that traditional labels such as oligopoly and monopolistic competition are being replaced by new determinants of competitive structure that evolve from the concepts of product differentiation and market differentiation. Explain.

6. R&D, manufacturing, customer service, and other functional units assume an important role in the formulation and implementation of marketing strategy. Describe the special interdisciplinary challenges that this presents for the business marketing manager.

7. Describe how flexible manufacturing technology might greatly expand the market segmentation options available to a firm.

8. Compare and contrast the relevance of "economies of scale" and "economies of scope" to the business marketing strategist.

9. John F. Welch, General Electric Company's aggressive chairman and chief executive officer, has stated that he only wants to stay in businesses where G.E. is number 1 or number 2. How will this clear statement of corporate objectives influence marketing objectives and, in turn, marketing strategy?

10. Describe the factors that the business marketing strategist should consider when evaluating the "fit" of a market segment to the firm's distinctive competencies.

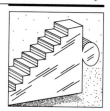

CHAPTER 9

Business Marketing Strategies for Global Markets

Business marketing firms that restrict their attention to the domestic market are overlooking enormous international market opportunities and a challenging field of competitors. After reading this chapter, you will understand:

1. the factors that shape the competitive advantage of a country.

2. the forces that drive the globalization of a particular industry.

3. the spectrum of international market-entry options and the strategic significance of different forms of global market participation.

4. the key strategic marketing issues that emerge as a firm's level of participation in international markets expands.

5. the role that strategic alliances assume in global marketing strategies.

FIRMS that are agile enough to shift from a domestic to an international focus can enjoy significant rewards. Take Marvin Windows, a privately held producer of high-quality windows. Although Warroad, Minnesota, the firm's home base, is about "as far from the oceans as you can get," Marvin Windows is slowly building a position of strength in an unlikely market—the Japanese construction industry. To successfully compete, the firm has significantly improved product quality. Now, only one window in 3,000 arrives in Japan damaged. Ley W. Soltis, an international sales representative with the firm, notes: "If we can take the demands of marketing overseas and apply them to our domestic operations, we'll be more competitive at home."[1] In addition

---

[1] Mike McNamee and Paul Magnusson, "Think Globally, Survive Locally," *Business Week* (November 26, 1990), p. 51.

to extending a firm's base of operations and thereby enhancing sales and profits, participation in global markets can provide an important pathway to a competitive advantage.

Business marketing firms such as General Electric, IBM, Baxter, Dow Chemical, Otis Elevator, Boeing, Caterpillar, Motorola, and others derive a significant portion of their sales and profits from international markets. Likewise, countless small firms with less familiar names enjoy strong ties with international customers. For example, Bauer Aerospace Inc., a Connecticut-based producer of aircraft-engine test equipment, generates 60 percent of its sales from Europe and the Pacific Rim.[2]

The discussion in this chapter is divided into four parts. First, a foundation for understanding global markets is established by examining the forces that shape the competitive advantage of a nation. Second, attention centers on the factors that are reshaping the way that managers think about markets and competitors: the drivers of globalization in an industry. Third, international market-entry options are isolated, described, and then linked to the central strategy questions that must be addressed by firms as their international operations evolve. Fourth, the unprecedented move toward using strategic alliances or partnerships as a component of global strategy is carefully examined.

THE COMPETITIVE ADVANTAGE OF NATIONS[3]

As global competition intensifies, national competitiveness has become a major preoccupation of government and business in every nation. Some see the competitiveness of a country as an outgrowth of plentiful national resources. Others argue that competitiveness is driven by cheap and abundant labor or is a macroeconomic phenomenon shaped by exchange rates, interest rates, or government budgeting policies. But Japan has prospered with limited national resources; Germany has been successful despite high wage rates and labor shortages; Switzerland, despite appreciating currency; Italy, despite high interest rates; and South Korea, despite government budget deficits. Clearly, none of these factors fully explains the competitive position of industries within a particular country.

Michael Porter suggests that to understand national competitiveness, attention should center on specific industries and industry segments and not on the economy as a whole. Supported by a large research team, he conducted a five-year study of ten important trading nations and focused on this question: What are the decisive characteristics of a nation that allow its companies to create and sustain competitive advantage in particular industries? Thus, the study examined those industries in which a nation's companies were internationally successful—that is, possessed a competitive advantage relative to the best worldwide competitors. The findings provide rich insights into the patterns of competition and strategy in the global market.

---

[2] Ibid., p. 50.

[3] This section is based on Michael E. Porter, "The Competitive Advantage of Nations," *Harvard Business Review*, 68 (March–April 1990), pp. 73–93.

Determinants of National Competitive Advantage

Firms achieve competitive advantage through acts of innovation. Such innovation can be reflected in a new product design, a new production process, a new marketing approach, or a new method for training employees. "Much innovation is mundane and incremental, depending more on an accumulation of small insights and advances than on a single, major technological breakthrough. . . . In international markets, innovations that yield competitive advantage anticipate both domestic and foreign needs."[4] Once achieved, a competitive advantage can only be sustained through relentless improvement.

Why are particular companies, based in certain countries, capable of consistent innovation? Michael Porter contends that four broad attributes of a nation, individually and as a system, constitute the playing field that each nation establishes and operates for its industries. (See Figure 9.1.)

Factor Conditions

In technology industries, a nation creates the most important factors of production, such as skilled employees or a scientific base. Moreover, the inventory of factors that a country enjoys at a particular time is less important than the rate and efficiency with which it creates, improves, and deploys them in particular industries. Basic factors of production, such as a pool of labor or a local raw-material source of supply, do not constitute an important advantage in knowledge-intensive industries. In fact, factor disadvantages can force companies to innovate—thereby creating competitive advantage. To illustrate, just-in-time production economizes on the prohibitively expensive space in Japan. Factors that support competitive advantage are those that are highly specialized in relation to an industry's particular needs, such as a pool of venture capital to fund software companies or a scientific institute that specializes in a particular technology.

Demand Conditions

By forcing companies to respond to tough challenges, demand conditions also provide advantages. Japanese companies have pioneered compact, quiet, energy-efficient air-conditioning units to meet the needs of Japanese consumers who must cope with small homes and high energy costs. Across several industries, the tightly constrained space requirements of the Japanese market have forced Japanese companies to innovate, yielding products that are lighter, thinner, shorter, and smaller. Often these are products that are internationally accepted.

Related and Supporting Industries

A third broad determinant of competitive advantage is the presence in the nation of interconnected industries that are all internationally competitive. In addition to providing cost-efficient inputs on a timely basis, home-based suppliers can provide end users with a steady flow of ideas, information, and innovations. Such advantages are an

---

[4] Ibid., p. 74.

FIGURE 9.1 **Determinants of National Competitive Advantage**

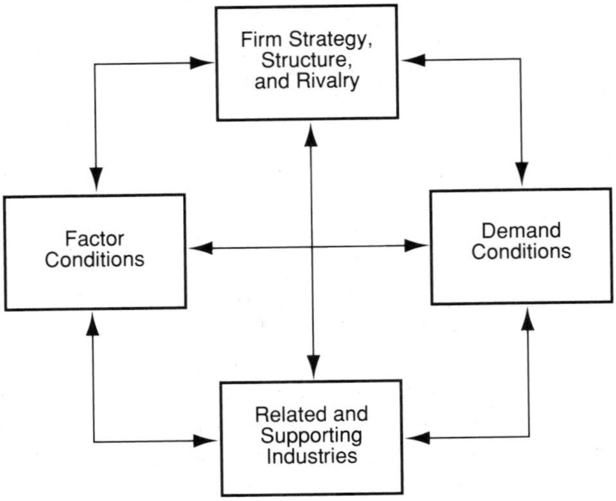

Source: Reprinted by permission of *Harvard Business Review,* from Michael E. Porter, "The Competitive Advantage of Nations," *Harvard Business Review,* 68 (March–April 1990), p. 77. Copyright 1990 by the President and Fellows of Harvard Business School. All rights reserved.

outgrowth of close working relationships that may be easier to form and sustain in a home market. While aided by proximity, the parties must actively manage the relationship for it to prosper. Home-based competitiveness in related industries also provides information flow and technical exchanges that speed the rate of innovation. To illustrate, the success of Swiss firms in the pharmaceutical industry grew out of previous international success in the dye industry.

Firm Strategy, Structure, and Rivalry

"No one managerial system is universally appropriate—notwithstanding the current fascination with Japanese management. Competitiveness in a specific industry results from convergence of the management practices and organizational modes favored in the country and the sources of competitive advantage in the industry."[5] In industries where Italian companies are global market leaders—such as packaging machines, lighting, and woolen fabrics—a company strategy that emphasizes customized products, niche marketing, speed, and flexibility fits both the dynamics of the industry and the nature of the Italian management system. In contrast, German firms, characterized by a highly disciplined management structure, perform well in technical

[5] Ibid., p. 81.

industries—optics, chemicals, machine tools—where complex products require a careful development process and precision manufacturing.

The goals that a country's institutions set for individuals and companies and the prestige it associates with certain industries direct the flow of capital and human resources, thereby affecting the competitive performance and structure of certain industries. Nations tend to be especially competitive in activities from which the country's heroes emerge: banking and pharmaceuticals in Switzerland; agriculture and defense-related industries in Israel.

A final, and extremely powerful, stimulus to the creation and persistence of competitive advantage for a country is the presence of strong local rivals. The United States has secured a leading worldwide position in the computer and software industries, and Japan has a dominant position in machine tools and semiconductors. For each country, vigorous domestic competition goes hand-in-hand with international success. Such rivalry pressures companies to lower costs, to improve quality and service, and to develop new products and processes. Ultimately, vigorous competition in the home market pressures domestic firms to examine global markets and prepares them to succeed in them.

A Self-Reinforcing System

The four determinants of national competitive advantage discussed above and highlighted in Figure 9.1 constitute a self-reinforcing system. For example, domestic rivalry stimulates the formation of unique pools of specialized factors and heightens the expectations of consumers who learn to expect improved products and services. Domestic rivalry also spawns the formation of related and supporting industries. Japan's world-class group of semiconductor producers has been instrumental in spawning world-class Japanese semiconductor-equipment manufacturers. Moreover, countries are rarely home to just one industry that enjoys a national competitive advantage. One competitive industry aids in the development of another.

DRIVERS OF GLOBALIZATION

Several forces are driving companies around the world to globalize by expanding their participation in foreign markets. Trade barriers are falling and nearly every product market—computers, fast food, electronic components, nuts and bolts—includes foreign competitors. Maturity in domestic markets is also driving firms to seek global expansion. For example, U.S. companies, nourished by the large home market, have typically lagged behind their European and Japanese rivals in internationalization. Many of these firms are now finding that strong foreign demand can propel future growth.

Business marketers who wish to pursue international market opportunities must first assess the extent of globalization in their particular industry. Some industries are global in character (e.g., computers and automobiles), others are moving in this direction (e.g., food), while still others remain resolutely national in character (e.g., cement). An industry's potential for globalization is driven by market, economic, environmental, and competitive factors (see Figure 9.2).[6] Market factors determine the customers' receptivity to and acceptance of a global product; economic forces determine whether pursuing a global strategy can provide significant cost advantages; environmental forces address the question of whether the necessary supporting infrastructure is in place; and competitive factors can require firms to match the moves of competing firms in other countries.

Market Factors

Singled out most frequently as a major force driving the globalization of markets is the assertion that customer needs are becoming increasingly homogeneous worldwide.[7] When customers in different countries around the world want essentially the same type of product or service, the opportunity exists to market a global product or brand. While global segments with similar interests and response tendencies may be identified in some product markets, considerable debate surrounds the issue of whether or not this is a universal trend.[8] Some research suggests, however, that compared to consumer goods, industrial and high-technology products (e.g., computers, machine tools) may be more appropriate for global brand strategies.[9]

In the business-to-business market, firms with multinational operations are particularly likely to have common needs and requirements worldwide. Such **global customers** search the world for suppliers, but use the purchased product or service in many countries. The presence of global customers both allows and demands a uniform marketing program—common brand name and corporate image—worldwide. Similarly, some channels of distribution may buy on a global or at least on a regional basis, thereby increasing the viability and importance of standardized marketing programs.

Economic Factors

A single-country market may not be large enough for a firm to realize economies of scale or to warrant the necessary investments in R&D and production equipment. If product standardization is feasible, scale at a given location can be increased by participating in a number of national markets. Similarly, expanded market participation can accelerate the accumulation of learning and experience. Even the largest national markets may be too small to amortize the enormous costs involved in developing a new generation of computers. By developing global or regional products rather than national ones, product development costs can be reduced.

---

[6] The discussion of these factors draws on George S. Yip, "Global Strategy in a World of Nations," *Sloan Management Review,* 31 (Fall 1989), pp. 29–41.

[7] Theodore Levitt, "The Globalization of Markets," *Harvard Business Review,* 61 (May–June 1983), pp. 92–102.

[8] See, for example, Susan A. Douglas and Yoram Wind, "The Myth of Globalization," *Columbia Journal of World Business,* 22 (Winter 1987), pp. 19–29.

[9] Subhash C. Jain, "Standardization of International Marketing Strategy: Some Research Hypotheses," *Journal of Marketing,* 53 (January 1989), pp. 70–79.

FIGURE 9.2   **External Drivers of Industry Potential for Globalization**

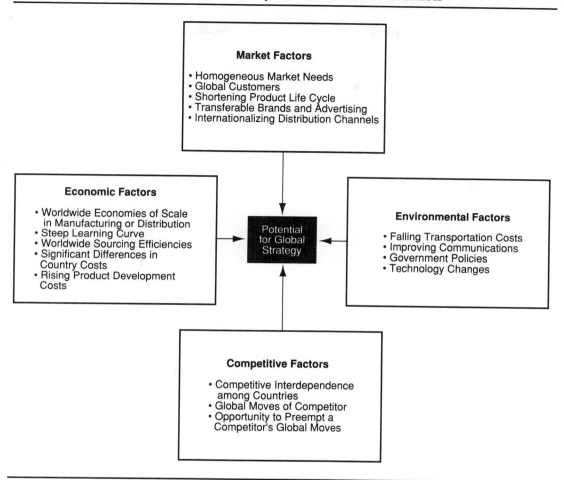

Market Factors

- Homogeneous Market Needs
- Global Customers
- Shortening Product Life Cycle
- Transferable Brands and Advertising
- Internationalizing Distribution Channels

Economic Factors

- Worldwide Economies of Scale in Manufacturing or Distribution
- Steep Learning Curve
- Worldwide Sourcing Efficiencies
- Significant Differences in Country Costs
- Rising Product Development Costs

Potential for Global Strategy

Environmental Factors

- Falling Transportation Costs
- Improving Communications
- Government Policies
- Technology Changes

Competitive Factors

- Competitive Interdependence among Countries
- Global Moves of Competitor
- Opportunity to Preempt a Competitor's Global Moves

Source: George S. Yip, Pierre M. Loewe, and Michael Y. Yoshino, "How to Take Your Company to the Global Market," *Columbia Journal of World Business,* 23 (Winter 1988), p. 40. Reprinted with permission.

Cost advantages can also be secured by seeking suppliers for components and materials on a worldwide basis. Firms such as Xerox, Ford, and Westinghouse have reduced costs by coordinating the purchase of raw materials across their global manufacturing plants. Finally, global firms can exploit differences in the factor costs and skills across countries. To illustrate, hourly labor costs are twice as high in West Germany as in Spain. A firm might increase productivity or reduce costs by concentrating activities in low-cost countries. Of course, the benefits must be weighed against the dangers of training offshore competitors.

Environmental Factors

Host governments affect globalization potential through trade policies, restrictions, and incentives. The liberalization of trade policies can provide a supportive environment for expanded market participation. The harmonization of trade policies in the European Economic Community (EEC) operative at the end of 1992, the U.S.-Canada Free Trade Agreement ratified in 1988, and the formation of a trading zone in the Pacific Rim are all favorable signs.[10] George Day notes that if they function as planned, "the results will be a consolidation into three trading zones that have been called the 'Triad' (Japan, Europe, and the United States). Although there are few impediments to free movements of goods and services within each leg of the triad, there is growing risk that the triad countries may build barriers *between* one another. Global players have little choice but to hedge their bets and build a viable presence within each trading zone for their 'world marketable' products."[11]

Outside the triad, government and trade restrictions can hamper the standardization of marketing programs, for example, through import tariffs and quotas, local content requirements, and constraints on technology transfer. To illustrate, local content requirements, which specify that products contain a certain proportion of component parts manufactured locally, can affect production costs, hamper uniform pricing, and require changes in product design.[12]

Improvements in telecommunications and in logistical systems have markedly increased a firm's capacity to manage operations on a global scale. The spread of FAX systems as well as international computer linkages facilitates highly coordinated global strategies. Likewise, more responsive transportation systems, coupled with computerized inventory systems, reduce the time and cost required to move goods to distant markets.

Competitive Factors

Competitors can raise the globalization potential of their industry by creating competitive interdependence among countries. This is achieved through the sharing of activities. "When activities such as production are shared among countries, a competitor's market share in one country affects its scale and overall cost position in the shared activities. Changes in that scale and cost will affect its competitive position in all countries dependent on the shared activities."[13]

A global orientation can prompt firms to make moves to match or preempt individual competitors. As Ford has become more cost efficient by concentrating production and by sharing activities, Japanese manufacturers are pressured to enter more markets so that increased production volume will cover costs.

---

[10] For an expanded discussion, see for example, Eckart E. Goette, "Europe 1992: Update for Business Planners," *The Journal of Business Strategy,* 11 (March/April 1990), pp. 10–13.

[11] George S. Day, *Market Driven Strategy: Processes for Creating Value* (New York: The Free Press, 1990), p. 262. See also Kenichi Ohmae, *Triad Power* (New York: The Free Press, 1985).

[12] Douglas and Wind, "Myth of Globalization."

[13] Yip, "Global Strategy in a World of Nations," p. 38.

INTERNATIONAL MARKET-ENTRY OPTIONS[14]

A first step in developing effective international marketing strategy centers on understanding the alternative ways that a firm can participate in international markets. The particular mode of entry selected should take into consideration the level of a firm's experience overseas and the stage in the evolution of its international involvement. Figure 9.3 illustrates a spectrum of options for participating in international markets. They range from low-commitment choices, such as exporting, to highly complex levels of participation, such as global strategies. Each is examined below.

Exporting

An industrial firm's first encounter with an overseas market usually involves **exporting** because it involves the least commitment and risk. Goods are produced at one or two home plants and sales are made through distributors or importing agencies in each country. Exporting is a viable entry strategy when the firm lacks the resources to make a significant commitment to the market, wants to minimize political and economic risk, or is unfamiliar with the market requirements and cultural norms of the country.

While preserving flexibility and reducing risk, exporting also limits the future prospects for growth in the country. First, exporting involves giving up direct control of the marketing program, which makes it difficult to coordinate activities, implement strategies, and resolve conflicts with customers and channel members. Customers may sense a lack of commitment on the part of the exporter. "In many international markets customers are loath to form long-run relationships with a company through its agents because they are unsure whether the business will continue to service the market, or will withdraw at the first sign of adversity. This problem has bedeviled U.S. firms in many countries, and only now are they living down a reputation for opportunistically participating in many countries and then withdrawing abruptly to protect short-run profits."[15]

Contracting

A somewhat more involved and complex form of international market entry is **contracting**. Included among contractual entry modes are: (1) licensing, (2) franchising, and (3) management contracts.

Licensing
Under a **licensing** agreement, one firm permits another to use its intellectual property in exchange for royalties or some other form of payment. The property might include trademarks, patents, technology, know-how, or company name. In short, licensing involves exporting intangible assets.

---

[14] The following discussion is based on Franklin R. Root, *Entry Strategy for International Markets* (Lexington, Mass.: D.C. Heath and Company, 1987) and Michael R. Czinkota and Ilka A. Ronkainen, *International Marketing,* 2nd ed. (Hinsdale, IL: The Dryden Press, 1990).

[15] Day, *Market Driven Strategy,* p. 272.

FIGURE 9.3   **Spectrum of Involvement in International Marketing**

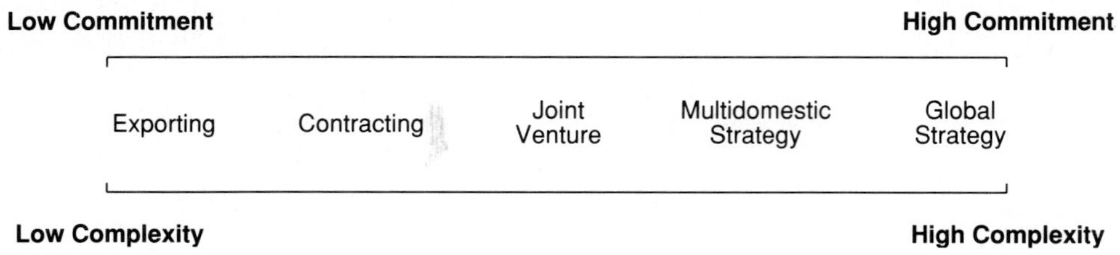

Low Commitment   **High Commitment**

| Exporting | Contracting | Joint
Venture | Multidomestic
Strategy | Global
Strategy |

Low Complexity   **High Complexity**

As an entry strategy, licensing requires neither capital investment nor marketing strength in foreign markets. This provides a means for a firm to test foreign markets without a major commitment of management time or capital. Because the licensee is typically a local company that can serve as a buffer against government action, licensing also reduces the risk of exposure to government action. With increasing host country regulation, licensing may enable the business marketer to enter a foreign market that is closed to either imports or direct foreign investment.

Licensing agreements do pose some limitations. First, some companies are hesitant to enter license agreements because the licensee may become an important competitor in the future. Second, licensing agreements typically include a time limit. Although terms may be extended once after the initial agreement, additional extensions are not readily permitted by a number of foreign governments. Third, a firm has less control over a licensee than over its own exporting or manufacturing abroad.

Franchising

Franchising is a form of licensing in which a parent company (the franchisor) grants another independent entity (the franchisee) the right to do business in a specified manner. This right can include selling the franchisor's product or using its name, production and marketing methods, or general business approach. Franchising has provided an attractive means for U.S. firms, especially service organizations, to penetrate foreign markets at a low cost and to leverage their skills with local knowledge and entrepreneurial spirit. Foreign government intervention represents a major problem for franchise systems in the international arena. For example, government restrictions on franchising and royalties hindered ComputerLand's Manila store from offering a complete range of services, leading to an eventual split between the company and its franchisee.

Despite such problems, franchising provides a viable foreign market entry alternative for business marketing firms—large and small. To illustrate, Automation Papers Company, a New Jersey–based supplier of high-technology paper products, used franchising to gain exclusive representation by a highly motivated sales force in selected foreign markets. The franchisees receive rights to the firm's trademarks, extensive training for local employees, and the benefit of Automation Papers' experience, credit lines, and advertising program.[16]

Other contractual modes of entry have grown in prominence in recent years. **Contract manufacturing** involves sourcing a product from a producer located in a foreign country for sale there or in other countries. Here assistance might be required to ensure that the product meets the desired quality standards. Contract manufacturing is most appropriate when the local market lacks sufficient potential to justify a direct investment, export entry is blocked, and a quality licensee is not available.

Management Contracts

To expand their overseas operations, many firms have turned to management contracts. In a **management contract** the industrial firm assembles a package of skills that will provide an integrated service to the client. When equity participation, either in the form of full ownership or a joint venture, is not feasible or is not permitted by a foreign government, a management contract provides a means for participating in a venture. Management contracts have been employed effectively in the service sector in areas such as computer services, hotel management, and food services. Management contracts can "provide organizational skills not available locally, expertise that is immediately available rather than built up, and management assistance in the form of support services that would be difficult and costly to replicate locally."[17]

One specialized form of a management contract is a **turnkey operation**. This arrangement permits a client to acquire a complete operational system, together with the skills sufficient to allow the unassisted maintenance and operation of the system. Once the package agreement is on line, the system is owned, controlled, and operated by the client. Management contracts provide a means for firms to commercialize their superior skills (know-how) by participating in the international market.

Joint Ventures

In pursuing international-entry options, a corporation confronts a wide variety of ownership choices, ranging from 100 percent ownership to a minority interest. Frequently, full ownership may be a desirable, but not essential, prerequisite for success in the international market arena. Thus a joint venture becomes a feasible option. The **joint venture** involves a joint-ownership arrangement (between, for example, a U.S. firm and one in the host country) to produce and/or market goods in a foreign market. Some joint ventures are structured so that each partner holds an equal share; in others, one partner has a majority stake. The contributions that the partners bring to the joint venture can also vary widely and may include financial resources, technology, sales organizations, know-how, or plant and equipment.

Joint ventures offer a number of advantages. First, joint ventures provide the only path of entry into many foreign markets. In most developing countries and even in

---

[16] Czinkota and Ronkainen, *International Marketing,* pp. 392–396.

[17] Ibid., p. 493.

ETHICAL BUSINESS MARKETING
Bribery and Differing Business Practices

International marketing managers often face a dilemma when home country regulations clash with foreign business practices. To illustrate, The Foreign Corrupt Practices Act makes it a crime for U.S. firms to bribe a foreign official for business purposes. A number of U.S. firms have complained about the law, arguing that it hinders their efforts to compete in the international market against those competitors who operate under no such antibribery laws. Likewise, many managers argue that the United States should not apply its moral principles to other cultures in which bribery and corruption are common. In their view, firms should be free to use the most common methods of competi-tion in the host country. Others counter, how-ever, that if bribes are permitted, a host of un-ethical business practices will follow.

In its Code of Worldwide Business Con-duct, Caterpillar, a global marketer, recognizes that laws in some countries may encourage busi-ness practices that are wasteful or unfavorable. Managers are urged to take a proactive position to alter these practices: "In a world charac-terized by a multiplicity of divergent laws at international, national, state, and local levels, Caterpillar's intentions fall into two parts: (1) to obey the law; and (2) to offer, where ap-propriate, constructive ideas for change in the law."

Source: Michael R. Czinkota and Ilka A. Ronkainen, *International Marketing*, 2nd ed. (Hinsdale, IL: The Dryden Press, 1990), pp. 112–121; and excerpts from Caterpillar Tractor Company's "Code of Worldwide Business Conduct and Operating Principles," in Gene R. Laczniak and Patrick E. Murphy, eds., *Marketing Ethics* (Lexington, Mass: Lexington Books, 1985), pp. 115–116.

some developed countries, the governments require firms to either form or accept joint ventures in order to participate in the local market. Second, joint ventures may open up market opportunities that neither partner to the venture could pursue alone. Here's the logic:

> If you run a pharmaceutical company with a good drug to distribute in Japan but have no sales force to do it, find someone in Japan who also has a good product but no sales force in your country. You get double the profit by putting two strong drugs through your fixed cost sales network, and so does your new ally. Why duplicate such high ex-penses all down the line? . . . Why not join forces to maximize contribution to each other's fixed costs?[18]

Third, joint ventures may provide for better relationships with local organizations (e.g., local authorities) and with customers. By being attuned to the local culture and environment of the host country, the local partner may enable the joint venture to respond to changing market needs and to be more aware of cultural sensitivities.

---

[18]Kenichi Ohmae, "The Global Logic of Strategic Alliances," *Harvard Business Review,* 67 (March–April 1989), p. 147.

Problems can arise in maintaining joint venture relationships. A study suggests that perhaps 70 percent of joint ventures are disbanded or fall short of expectations.[19] The reasons involve problems with the disclosure of sensitive information, disagreements over how profits are to be shared, clashes over management style, and differing perceptions on the course that strategy should follow. The underpinnings of a successful partnership are treated later in the chapter when strategic alliances are examined.

Multidomestic versus Global Strategies

The most complex forms of participation in the global arena are multidomestic and global strategies. Multinational firms have traditionally managed operations outside their home country with **multidomestic strategies** that permit individual subsidiaries to compete independently in different country-markets. The multinational headquarters coordinates marketing policies and financial controls and may centralize R&D and some support activities. Each subsidiary, however, resembles a strategic business unit that is expected to contribute earnings and growth to the organization. The firm can manage its international activities like a portfolio.

In contrast, a **global strategy** seeks competitive advantage with strategic choices that are highly integrated across countries.[20] For example, features of a global strategy might include a standardized core product that requires minimal local adaptation and that is targeted on country-markets chosen on the basis of their contribution to globalization benefits. Major volume and market share advantages might be sought by directing attention to the United States, Europe, and Japan. The value chain concept illuminates the chief differences between a multidomestic and a global strategy.

International Strategy and the Value Chain[21]

To diagnose the sources of competitive advantage, domestic or international, Michael Porter divides the activities performed by a firm into distinct groups. The value chain, displayed in Figure 9.4, provides a framework for categorizing these activities. Primary activities are those involved in the physical creation of the product, the marketing and logistical program, and the service after the sale. Support activities provide the infrastructure and inputs that allow the primary activities to occur. Every activity employs purchased inputs, human resources, and a combination of technologies. Likewise, the firm's infrastructure, including such functions as general management, supports the entire value chain. "A firm may possess two types of competitive advantage: low relative cost or differentiation—its ability to perform the activities in its value chain

---

[19] Based on studies by Coopers and Lybrand and by McKinsey and Company, reported in "Corporate Odd Couples," *Business Week* (July 21, 1986), pp. 100–106.

[20] Yip, "Global Strategy in a World of Nations," pp. 33–35.

[21] Michael E. Porter, "Changing Patterns of International Competition," *California Management Review,* 28 (Winter 1986), pp. 9–40; see also Porter, *Competitive Advantage: Creating and Sustaining Superior Performance* (New York: The Free Press, 1985).

FIGURE 9.4   **The Value Chain: Upstream and Downstream Activities**

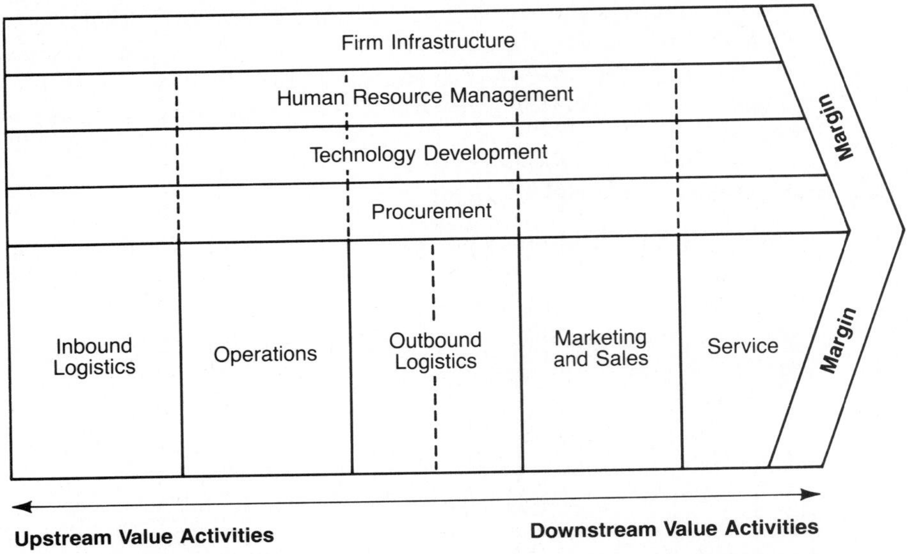

Source: Reprinted from Michael E. Porter, "Changing Patterns of International Competition," *California Management Review,* 28 (Winter 1986), p. 16. Copyright 1986 by the Regents of the University of California; reprinted by permission of the Regents.

either at a lower cost or in a unique way relative to its competitors."[22] A firm that competes in the international market must decide how to spread the activities among countries. Central to this decision is the need to distinguish upstream from downstream activities (see Figure 9.4).

Downstream activities involve those primary activities that are closely tied to where the buyer is located. For example, a business marketer wishing to serve the Japanese market must ensure that a local service network is in place. By contrast, upstream activities (e.g., operations) and support activities (e.g., procurement) are not tied directly to the buyer's location. Caterpillar, for example, uses a few large-scale manufacturing facilities to produce components to meet worldwide demands.

This assessment provides a foundation for valuable strategic insights. Competitive advantage created by downstream activities is largely country-specific: a firm's reputation, brand name, and service network grow out of the firm's activities in a particular country. Competitive advantage in upstream (e.g., manufacturing) and support activities stems more from the entire network of countries in which a firm competes than from its position in any one country.

---

[22] Porter, "Changing Patterns," p. 13.

Source of Advantage: Multidomestic versus Global

When downstream activities (those tied directly to the buyer) are important to competitive advantage, a multidomestic pattern of international competition is common. In **multidomestic industries**, firms pursue separate strategies in each of their foreign markets—competition in each country is essentially independent of competition in other countries (e.g., Alcoa in the aluminum industry, Honeywell in the controls industry).

Global competition is more common in industries in which upstream and support activities (such as technology development and operations) are vital to competitive advantage. A **global industry** is one in which a firm's competitive position in one country is significantly influenced by its position in other countries (e.g., Motorola in the semiconductor industry, Boeing in the commercial aircraft industry).

Coordination and Configuration

Further insights into international strategy can be gained by examining two dimensions of competition in the global market: configuration and coordination. **Configuration** centers on where each activity is performed, including the number of locations. Options range from concentrated (e.g., one production plant serving the world) to dispersed (e.g., a plant in each country—each with a complete value chain).

Coordination refers to how similar activities performed in various countries are coordinated or coupled with each other. If, for example, a firm has three plants—one in the United States, one in England, and one in Japan—how do the activities in these plants relate to each other? There are numerous coordination options because of the many possible levels of coordination and the many ways an activity can be performed. For example, a firm operating three plants could, at one extreme, allow each plant to operate autonomously (unique production processes, unique products). At the other extreme, the three plants could be closely coordinated, utilizing a common information system and producing products with identical features.

Types of International Strategy

Some of the possible variations in international strategy are portrayed in Figure 9.5. Observe that the purest global strategy concentrates as many activities as possible in one country, serves the world market from this home base, and closely coordinates those activities that must be performed near the buyer (e.g., service). Caterpillar, for example, views its battle with the formidable Japanese competitor, Komatsu, in global terms. As well as employing automated manufacturing systems that allow it to fully exploit the economies of scale from its worldwide sales volume, Caterpillar also carefully coordinates activities in its global dealer network. This integrated global strategy gives Caterpillar a competitive advantage in cost and effectiveness.[23]

Figure 9.5 can be used to illustrate other international strategy patterns. Canon, for example, concentrates manufacturing and support activities in Japan but gives local

---

[23] Thomas Hout, Michael E. Porter, and Eileen Rudden, "How Global Companies Win Out," *Harvard Business Review*, 60 (September–October 1982), pp. 98–108; see also Gary Hamel and C. K. Prahalad, "Do You Really Have a Global Strategy?" *Harvard Business Review*, 63 (July–August 1985), pp. 139–148.

FIGURE 9.5   **Types of International Strategy**

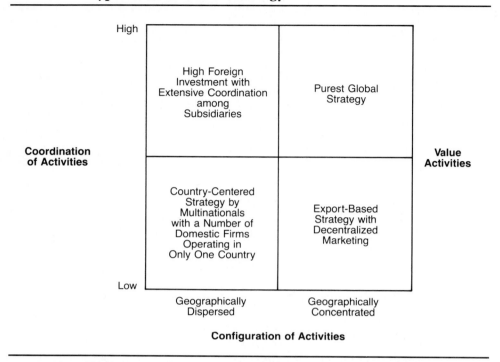

Source: Reprinted from Michael E. Porter, "Changing Patterns of International Competition," *California Management Review,* 28 (Winter 1986), p. 19. Copyright 1986 by the Regents of the University of California; reprinted by permission of the Regents.

marketing subsidiaries significant latitude in each region of the world. Thus, Canon pursues an export-based strategy. In contrast, Xerox concentrates some activities and disperses others. Coordination, however, is extremely high: the Xerox brand, marketing approach, and servicing strategy are standardized worldwide.

Michael Porter notes: "International strategy has often been characterized as a choice between worldwide standardization and local tailoring, or as the tension between the economic imperative (large-scale efficient facilities) and the political imperative (local content, local production). . . . A firm's choice of international strategy involves a search for competitive advantage from configuration/coordination throughout the value chain."[24]

---

[24] Porter, "Changing Patterns," p. 25.

EVOLUTION OF INTERNATIONAL MARKETING STRATEGY[25]

International marketing strategy should be formulated in light of the firm's current position overseas and geared to its vision of growth and future position in worldwide markets. To this point, the chapter has laid a foundation for understanding the forces that shape the competitive advantage of countries and that drive the globalization of markets. In turn, consideration has been given to the array of international market-entry options available to the business marketing firm. For the individual firm, strategy formulation in international markets is an evolutionary process in which the central direction of strategy and the key decisions vary at each successive phase of involvement in international operations.

Figure 9.6 traces the phases in global marketing evolution from the preliminary phase of pre-internationalization through the phases of (1) initial entry, (2) local or national market expansion, and (3) globalization. At each phase a number of triggers may prompt movement into a new phase, thereby stimulating a new strategic direction. Those triggers which prompt a company to reassess its current strategy may be external (e.g., competitive pressures or industry trends) or internal (e.g., management initiative).

Pre-internationalization

A strong domestic orientation may cause a firm to overlook changes that are occurring in target segments and market forces worldwide and to be vulnerable to aggressive foreign competitors. A variety of factors may prompt the domestically oriented firm to reexamine its position, triggering initial entry into international markets. For example, the domestic market may have become saturated or the firm may wish to diversify risk across a range of countries and product markets.

Phase One: Initial International Market Entry

Given the industrial firm's lack of experience and knowledge in international markets, attention centers on identifying the most attractive market opportunities overseas for its existing (i.e., domestic) products and services. The guiding principle is to extend the geographic base of operations to those international markets that provide the closest match to the firm's current offerings and market conditions. By leveraging its domestic competitive position and core competency internationally, the firm seeks to extend economies of scale by establishing a presence in multiple markets. The key decisions in this phase of initial international market entry are: (1) the choice of countries to enter, (2) the timing of entry, and (3) how operations are to be performed in these countries.

---

[25]This section draws on Susan P. Douglas and C. Samuel Craig, "Evolution of Global Marketing Strategy: Scale, Scope, and Synergy," *Columbia Journal of World Business,* 24 (Fall 1989), pp. 47–59.

FIGURE 9.6 **Phases in Global Marketing Evolution**

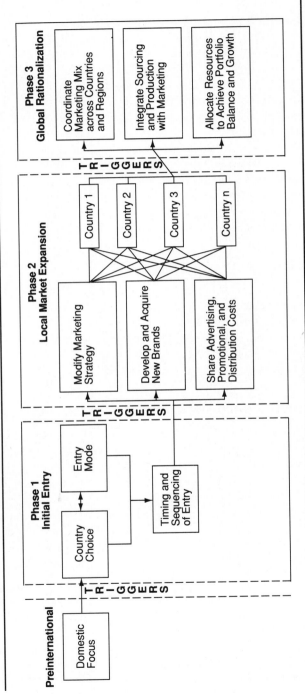

Source: Susan P. Douglas and C. Samuel Craig, "Evolution of Global Marketing Strategy: Scale, Scope, and Synergy," *Columbia Journal of World Business*, 24 (Fall 1989), p. 50. Reprinted with permission.

Choice of Countries

Both risk and opportunities need to be evaluated in choosing which countries to enter. Here the political, financial, and legal risks of entry need to be weighed in relation to the stability and rate of economic growth of a country. Similarly, the size and growth of market potential must be gauged relative to the level of competition and costs of market entry. Difficult trade-offs are common (e.g., high growth potential and high country risks or entry costs). Managers are often prone to choose countries where they have had prior contact or experience. To illustrate, Swedish firms tend to enter neighboring countries such as Denmark, Norway, and Finland first and more distant markets such as Brazil, Argentina, and Australia last.[26]

Timing of Entry

Should the firm enter a number of country-markets simultaneously or, alternatively, should the firm enter one country first to develop a base of experience and then fan out to other countries sequentially? Simultaneous entry might allow the firm to preempt competition by establishing a beachhead in key markets, thereby reducing opportunities for imitation. Multiple market entry may also provide potential scale economies to the firm. Often the determining factor in the decision is the level of resource commitment required to enter a given international market. If, for example, an overseas sales organization must be developed and/or a production facility established, a significant resource commitment is needed.

Mode of Entry

Closely intertwined with the evaluation of market potential and country risk is the decision concerning how to operate in an overseas market. The full range of entry modes, presented earlier in the chapter, may be adopted—ranging from exporting, licensing, and contract manufacturing to joint ventures and wholly owned subsidiaries. In high-risk markets, firms can reduce their equity exposure by adopting low-commitment modes such as licensing, contract manufacturing, or joint ventures with a minority share. Although nonequity modes of entry such as licensing or contract manufacturing involve minimal risk and commitment, they may not provide the desired level of control or financial performance. Joint ventures and wholly owned subsidiaries provide a greater degree of control over operations and greater potential returns.

The choice of a particular entry mode will also depend on the size of the market and its growth potential. Susan P. Douglas and C. Samuel Craig note: "Markets of limited size surrounded by tariff barriers may be supplied most cost effectively via licensing or contract manufacturing. Where there are potential economies of scale, exporting may, however, be preferred. Then, as local market potential builds up . . . a local production and marketing subsidiary may be established."[27]

---

[26] Jan Johanson and Finn Wiedershein-Paul, "The Internationalization of the Firm—Four Swedish Cases," *Journal of Management Studies* (October 1975), pp. 305–322.

[27] Douglas and Craig, "Evolution of Global Marketing Strategy," p. 53.

Once operations are established in a number of foreign markets, the focus often shifts away from foreign opportunity assessment to local market development in each country. This shift might be prompted by the need to respond to local competitors or the desire to more effectively penetrate the local market. Planning and strategy assume a country-by-country focus.

Phase Two: Local Market Expansion

The expansion effort is generally directed by local management in each country rather than from corporate headquarters. The major objective in this phase is to build strategy on the organizational structure developed in each country in order to leverage assets and to more fully utilize core competencies to foster local market growth. Attention centers on capitalizing on R&D and market knowledge, on sharing production and distribution facilities across product lines, and on identifying opportunities for shared marketing expenditures.

Decisions

Economies of scope are provided if the addition of new products or product variants within a country permit a more effective and efficient utilization of an existing operational structure such as the distribution network or the sales force. Thus, priority is given to making product and strategy modifications in each country in order to broaden the local market base and reach new segments. Extensions to the product line and new product research may be explored to more precisely meet local preferences. In developing countries, machine tool manufacturers, for example, may consider streamlining and simplifying their products to reach less sophisticated market segments. The costs of initial entry into a country can be substantial, including the costs of establishing relations with distributors, agents, or local authorities and of gaining familiarity with market conditions and competition. The goal in the local market expansion phase is to capitalize on this resource base by pursuing market development and by realizing economies of scope.

Triggers to a Global Perspective

The country-by-country orientation can yield a patchwork of domestic national businesses. Different marketing strategies are pursued in each country with little or no coordination of operations between countries. The inefficiencies generated by this fragmented system, coupled with external forces that are integrating markets on a global scale, create pressures toward increased coordination across countries. Factors triggering this move include:

- Cost inefficiencies and duplication of effort between the various country operations of the firm
- Opportunities to transfer products, strategies, and experience from one country to another

- Emergence of global customers (e.g., customers such as General Electric that search the world for suppliers and use the purchased product or service in many countries)

- Emergence of global competitors that derive strength from highly coordinated operations worldwide

- Improved linkages between the firm's marketing infrastructure units operating in different countries.

Phase Three: Global Orientation

In the final phase of internationalization, the country-by-country orientation disappears as "markets are viewed as a set of interrelated, interdependent entities which are becoming increasingly integrated and interlinked worldwide."[28] The firm seeks to capitalize on possible synergies and to take maximum advantage of its worldwide operations. Management attention centers on allocating resources and measuring performance on a global scale. The guiding question: What is the optimal allocation of resources across countries, across product-markets, and across target segments to maximize global profits?

Key Decisions

A dual thrust is utilized as a firm adopts a global orientation: (1) improving the efficiency of operations worldwide and (2) formulating a global strategy for expansion and growth.

Efficiency

By coordinating operations across countries and between different functional areas, a firm can reduce worldwide costs in several ways.[29] First, economies of scale can be secured by pooling production, R&D, or other activities for two or more countries. Second, a global firm can reduce costs by moving manufacturing or other activities to low-cost countries. For example, the Mexican side of the U.S.-Mexican border is the site of numerous manufacturing plants established and operated by U.S. companies but employing Mexican labor. Third, a global firm can reduce costs by exploiting flexibility. A company with manufacturing capability in several countries can move production from one location to another to take advantage of the lowest costs at a particular time. Dow Chemical uses this strategy and examines international differences in exchange rates, tax rates, and transportation and labor costs. Production volume for the planning period is then set for each Dow plant. Fourth, efficiency can be enhanced through the coordination across countries of marketing strategies such as brand names, advertising themes, and the standardization of product lines.

---

[28] Ibid., pp. 55–56.

[29] Yip, "Global Strategy in a World of Nations," pp. 33–35.

Strategy Development

A global strategy should define the needs of target segments and determine the geographic configurations of segments. As markets become increasingly international, opportunities for identifying segments that are regional or global in scope, rather than country-specific, are on the increase. In support, one expert notes: "The market for IBM computers or Toshiba laptops is not defined by geographic borders but by the inherent appeal of the product to users, regardless of where they live. And with the proliferation of trade journals, trade shows, and electronic data bases, users have regular access to the same sources of product information."[30]

The global strategy should also include marketing programs tailored to the needs of the regional and global target segments. Often, the organizational structure must be reshaped to successfully implement strategy on a global scale. For example, some companies such as Citibank, that serve multinational corporations, have developed a global account management system whereby an executive is given responsibility for ensuring that the needs of a given client are satisfied worldwide. Importantly, the successful implementation of a global strategy requires the establishment of mechanisms to coordinate and control activities and the flows of information and resources across country boundaries and product-markets.

To recap, strategy formulation in international markets is an evolutionary process in which the key strategic decisions vary at each phase of involvement in international operations. After initial entry and as experience in the international market builds, the firm can often effectively pursue growth opportunities in selected international markets. This forms a foundation for advancing to the next stage and pursuing the more complex challenges of strategy integration and coordination across country-markets.

STRATEGIC ALLIANCES

The traditional management assumption that "good fences make good corporations" has given way to a new philosophy: firms are stretching their formal boundaries by creating strong ties with other firms.[31] **Strategic alliances** or **partnerships** assume a very prominent role in the global strategy of many business marketing firms. Here "there is a formal long-run linkage, funded with direct co-investments by two or more companies, that pools complementary capabilities and resources to achieve generally agreed objectives."[32] Rather than being formed for immediate tactical reasons (as are many joint ventures), strategic alliances are central to the partners' future direction and means of achieving competitive advantages.

---

[30] Ohmae, "Global Logic of Strategic Alliances," p. 144.

[31] Rosabeth Moss Kanter, "Becoming PALS: Pooling, Allying, and Linking Across Companies," *The Academy of Management Executive,* 3 (August 1989), p. 183. See also Robert E. Spekman and Kirti Sawhney, *Toward a Conceptual Understanding of the Antecedents of Strategic Alliances* (Cambridge, Mass.: Marketing Science Institute), Report No. 90–114.

[32] Day, *Market Driven Strategy,* p. 272.

The importance of alliances to global strategy can be illuminated by considering the strategies of IBM and General Electric.

- In Japan alone, IBM has links with Ricoh in distribution and sales of low-end computers, with Nippon Steel in systems integration, with Fuji Bank in financial systems, with NTT in value-added networks, and with others.[33]

- General Electric has over 100 strategic partnerships, and its statement of operating objectives points to more: "To achieve a #1 or #2 global product-market position requires participation in each major market of the world. This requires several different forms of participation: trading technology for market access; trading market access for technology; and trading market access for market access. This 'share to gain' becomes a way of life."[34]

Benefits of Strategic Alliances

Partners to an alliance seek benefits such as (1) access to markets or to technology (as noted above, a motivating force for General Electric); (2) economies of scale that might be gained by combining manufacturing, R&D, or marketing activities; (3) faster entry of new products to markets (e.g., partners with established channels of distribution in different countries swap new products); and (4) sharing of risk.[35] Simply put, there is a tremendous cost—and risk—in a firm's creating its own distribution channels, logistical network, manufacturing plant, and R&D function in every key market in the world. Also, it takes time to develop relationships with channel members and customers and to develop the skills of employees.[36] Alliances provide an option.

Problems of Strategic Alliances

While offering significant benefits, alliances, like joint ventures, often fall short of expectations or dissolve. Why? Among the problems that have been isolated are these:[37]

- Partners are organized quite differently for making marketing and product design decisions, creating *problems in coordination and trust.*

- Partners that combine the best set of skills in one country may be poorly equipped to support each other in other countries, leading to *problems in implementing alliances on a global scale.*

---

[33] Ohmae, "Global Logic of Strategic Alliances," p. 153.

[34] General Electric Company, "Operating Objectives to Meet the Challenges of the 90s" (Fairfield, Conn.: General Electric Company, March 14, 1988), included in Day, *Market Driven Strategy*, p. 273.

[35] See, for example, Ohmae, "Global Logic of Strategic Alliances," and Michael E. Porter and Mark B. Fuller, "Coalitions and Global Strategy," in Michael E. Porter, ed., *Competition in Global Industries* (Boston: Harvard Business School Press, 1986), pp. 315–343.

[36] Ohmae, "Global Logic of Strategic Alliances," p. 146.

[37] Thomas J. Kosnik, "Stumbling Blocks to Global Strategic Alliances," *Systems Integration Age* (October 1988).

- The quick pace of technological change often guarantees that the most attractive partner today may not be the most attractive partner tomorrow, leading to *problems in maintaining alliances over time.*

Managing Strategic Alliances

While significant problems may threaten strategic alliances, a firm that can assemble and manage a portfolio of successful partnerships can secure a competitive advantage in the global market. Indeed, some firms have mastered the art of developing and sustaining successful partnerships. For example, Corning Glass Works is involved in successful partnerships with Dow Chemical, Owens-Illinois, and Eastman Kodak, as well as with partners in France, Great Britain, Australia, West Germany, and China, among others.

Firms that are adept at managing strategic alliances employ an approach that centers on two factors. First, partners are chosen carefully. Observe in Figure 9.7 that potential partners can be evaluated on the basis of their strengths and/or fit across five areas: resources, relationships, reputation, capabilities, and chemistry/culture. This provides a framework for assessing the strengths and weaknesses of a proposed partnership in different country-markets.

Second, firms like Corning are proactive in creating the conditions for mutually beneficial relationships.[38] They employ a flexible approach, letting their alliances evolve in form as conditions change over time; they invest adequate resources and management attention in these relationships; and they integrate the organizations so that the appropriate points of contact and communication are managed. Most importantly, "the partnership is institutionalized—bolstered by a framework of supporting mechanisms, from legal requirements to social ties to shared values, all of which in fact make trust possible."[39]

SUMMARY

Initial insights into the dynamic character of international competition can be secured by addressing this question: Why are certain firms based in certain nations capable of consistent innovations that yield competitive advantage? Research suggests that four broad national attributes, working individually and as a system, determine the competitive advantage of a nation: (1) factor conditions (e.g., skilled labor), (2) demand conditions (e.g., nature of home market demand), (3) related and supporting industries (e.g., excellent supply network), and (4) firm strategy, structure, and rivalry.

In developing international strategy, the business marketer must first assess the globalization potential of the industry. It is driven by market, economic, environmental, and competitive conditions. For example, market forces determine the customers'

---

[38] Kanter, "Becoming PALS," p. 192.

[39] Ibid., p. 192.

FIGURE 9.7 **What Does Each Partner Bring to the Party?**
A Framework for Evaluating Strategic Alliances

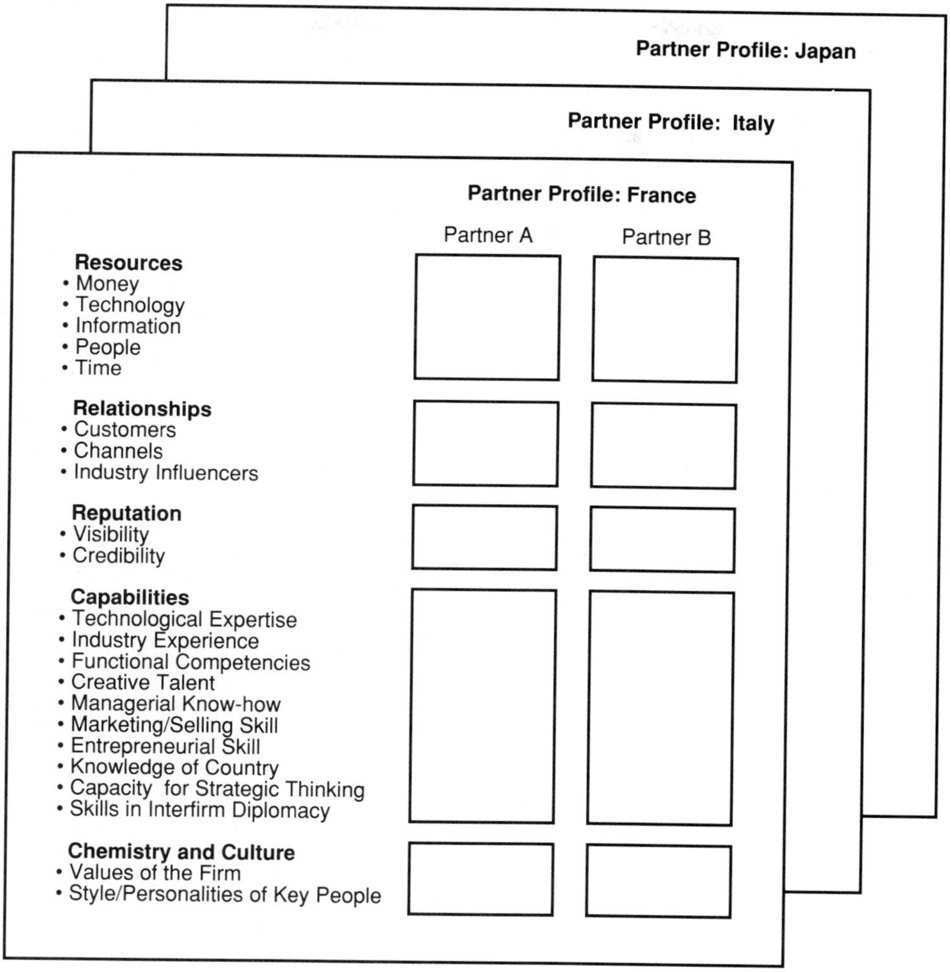

Partner Profile: Japan

Partner Profile: Italy

Partner Profile: France

Partner A   Partner B

Resources
• Money
• Technology
• Information
• People
• Time

Relationships
• Customers
• Channels
• Industry Influencers

Reputation
• Visibility
• Credibility

Capabilities
• Technological Expertise
• Industry Experience
• Functional Competencies
• Creative Talent
• Managerial Know-how
• Marketing/Selling Skill
• Entrepreneurial Skill
• Knowledge of Country
• Capacity for Strategic Thinking
• Skills in Interfirm Diplomacy

Chemistry and Culture
• Values of the Firm
• Style/Personalities of Key People

Source: Rowland T. Moriarty and Thomas J. Kosnik, "High-Tech Marketing: Concepts, Continuity, and Change," *Sloan Management Review,* 31 (Summer 1989), p. 15 by permission of the publisher. Copyright 1989 by the Sloan Management Review Association. All rights reserved.

receptivity to a standardized global product while economic forces dictate whether a global strategy will yield a cost advantage.

Once a business marketing firm decides to sell its products in a particular country, an entry strategy must then be selected. A range of options are available, including exporting, contractual entry modes (e.g., licensing), and joint ventures. A more elaborate form of participation is represented by multinational firms that employ multidomestic strategies. Here a separate strategy might be pursued in each country served. The most advanced level of participation in international markets is provided by firms that employ a global strategy. Such firms seek competitive advantage by pursuing strategies that are highly interdependent across countries.

Strategy in the international arena should be tailored to the firm's degree of experience in overseas markets and its vision of growth and future position in markets worldwide. Strategy formulation in international markets is an evolutionary process, in which a firm's involvement in overseas operations may advance through three phases: (1) initial foreign market entry, (2) local or national market expansion, and (3) globalization. Increasingly, firms are using strategic alliances as a feature of their global strategies.

Discussion Questions

1. Boeing represents one of the premier global competitors based in the United States. The firm's backlog of orders for new planes extends well into the late 1990s. Using the determinants of national competitive advantage as a guide, examine the U.S. aerospace industry.

2. Michael Porter notes: "It is vigorous domestic competition that ultimately pressures domestic companies to look at global markets and it toughens them to succeed in them."[40] Explain.

3. A key premise of the philosophy of global products is that customers' needs are becoming increasingly homogeneous worldwide. Does this trend fit consumer goods more than industrial goods? Does this signal the end of market segmentation strategies?

4. Describe the *competitive* and *economic* factors that are driving the globalization of some industries.

5. A small Michigan-based firm that produces and sells component parts to General Motors, Ford, and Chrysler wishes to extend market coverage to Europe and Japan. What type of market entry strategy would provide the best fit?

6. Global companies must be more than just a bunch of overseas subsidiaries that execute decisions made at headquarters. Using the value chain concept as a guide, compare a global strategy to a multidomestic strategy.

7. Downstream activities in a firm's value chain create competitive advantages that are largely country-specific. Why?

8. The development of effective international marketing strategy should take into consideration the extent of a firm's experience overseas and the stage in the evolution of its international development. Describe the key strategic issues that

---

[40] Porter, "The Competitive Advantage of Nations," p. 83.

must be examined as a firm moves from initial market entry to a more extensive level of involvement in global markets.

9. Discuss the factors that might cause a firm with extensive international operations to shift from a country-by-country orientation to a global perspective.

10. While many business marketers have become quite effective in managing interorganizational relations with channel intermediaries, managing relationships with strategic partners (alliances) poses a different set of challenges. Discuss.

CHAPTER 10

Managing the Product Line for Business Markets

The industrial product constitutes the central force in the marketing mix. The ability of the firm to put together a line of products and services that respond to the needs of customers is the heart of business marketing management. After reading this chapter, you will understand:

1. the concept of the total product.

2. the strategic importance of product quality in business marketing.

3. the various types of industrial product lines.

4. a strategic approach for managing the existing product line.

A business marketer's identity in the marketplace is established through the products and services offered. Without careful product planning and control, marketers are often guilty of introducing products that are inconsistent with market needs, arbitrarily adding items that contribute little to existing product lines, and maintaining weak products that could be profitably eliminated.

Product management is directly linked to market analysis and market selection. As Figure 10.1 illustrates, product policy is a circular process: Products are developed to fit the needs of the market and are modified as those needs change. Drawing upon such tools of demand analysis as organizational market segmentation and market potential forecasting, the marketer evaluates opportunities and selects viable market segments, which in turn determines the direction of product policy. Product policy

FIGURE 10.1   **The Role of Product Policy in Market Analysis**

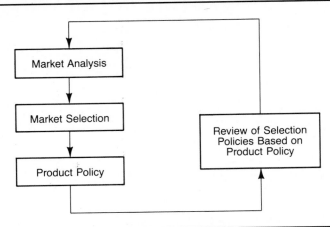

Source: Benson P. Shapiro, *Industrial Product Policy: Managing the Existing Product Line* (Cambridge, Mass.: Marketing Science Institute, 1977), p. 30. Reprinted by permission.

cannot be separated from market selection decisions.[1] In evaluating potential product/market fits, a firm must evaluate market opportunities, determine the number and aggressiveness of competitors, and gauge its own strengths and weaknesses.

Often, a long-term view is critical when managing a product to peak profitability. For example, Du Pont has spent over 20 years nurturing the market for its superstrength Kevlar polymer, which is used in products ranging from commercial fishing boots to tires and bulletproof vests. Irving Shapiro, Du Pont's highly regarded former chairman, notes: "It's taken all that time to build up the end uses and get the quality up to the point where you can start realizing benefits. . . . I don't have any doubts in this world this is a major technological breakthrough that will both have great end uses and will also make money in the late 1980s and 1990s and thereafter. That's the game you're in. You're long past the period when you come up with quick new discoveries that pay off in a year."[2]

This chapter examines the product management function in the business marketing environment. First, we provide a perspective on the definition of an industrial product and explore the rising importance of product quality in business marketing strategy. Second, because industrial goods can assume several forms, we describe the industrial product line options. Third, we discuss how to manage existing product lines. Alternative approaches are described and evaluated.

---

[1] E. Raymond Corey, "Key Options in Market Selection and Product Planning," *Harvard Business Review*, 53 (September–October 1975), pp. 119–128; see also Yoram Wind and Thomas S. Robertson, "Marketing Strategy: New Directions for Theory and Research," *Journal of Marketing*, 47 (Spring 1983), pp. 12–25.

[2] Mark Potts and Peter Behr, *The Leading Edge* (New York: McGraw-Hill Book Company, 1987), p. 195.

THE INDUSTRIAL PRODUCT

What is a product? A business marketer can only respond from the viewpoint of a consumer: A **product** is all of the value satisfactions that a customer derives at both an organizational and a personal level.[3] The purchaser of cold rolled steel is buying physical specifications (thickness, chemical composition), a particular package, technical advice, and delivery reliability.[4] The seller may be able to satisfy more personal needs of the buyer by reducing risk, improving the buyer's organizational status, or merely breaking the monotony of a day with a pleasant discussion about outside interests. Thus, the physical attributes of the product can be augmented in many ways that add extra value to the product. The seller's identity in the market is established not only by the material product or service, but also by the value satisfactions provided to the buyer.

Product Quality

Increasing international competition and rising customer expectations make product quality the strategic issue of the 1990s. All sectors of the business market are affected. To illustrate, a survey of 250 purchasing managers revealed that nearly 75 percent are pressuring suppliers to increase product quality.[5] In turn, the Department of Defense and other governmental units are giving quality an unprecedented level of emphasis in their procurement activities. Although Japanese firms continue to set the pace in the application of sophisticated quality control procedures in manufacturing, significant strides have been made by companies such as Kodak, AT&T, Westinghouse, Ford, Hewlett-Packard, IBM, General Electric, and others. The quest for improved product quality touches the entire supply chain as these and other companies demand improved product quality from their suppliers, large and small. John Young, president and chief executive officer at Hewlett-Packard, notes: "A strategy focused on quality is the best way companies can respond to competition. And surprisingly, an emphasis on quality is one of the most effective ways to control costs."[6]

Internal View of Quality

There are two views of product quality: internal and external.[7] Both can contribute to profitability. The **internal view of quality**, represented on the right side of the

---

[3] Theodore Levitt, *The Marketing Imagination: New Expanded Edition* (New York: The Free Press, 1986), pp. 81–85.

[4] Benson P. Shapiro, *Industrial Product Policy: Managing the Existing Product Line* (Cambridge, Mass.: Marketing Science Institute, 1977), pp. 37–39.

[5] Kate Bertrand, "Marketers Discover What 'Quality' Really Means," *Business Marketing*, 72 (April 1987), p. 61; and "Move Over, Japan; Here Comes U.S. Quality," *Purchasing*, 104 (January 18, 1990), pp. 64–71.

[6] John Young, "The Quality Focus at Hewlett-Packard," *Journal of Business Strategy*, 5 (Winter 1985), p. 6.

[7] Bradley T. Gale and Richard Klavans, "Formulating a Quality Improvement Strategy," *Journal of Business Strategy*, 5 (Winter 1985), pp. 21–32; see also Lynn W. Phillips, Dae R. Chang, and Robert O. Buzzell, "Product Quality, Cost Position and Business Performance: A Test of Some Key Hypotheses," *Journal of Marketing*, 47 (Spring 1983), pp. 26–43.

FIGURE 10.2 **How Quality Drives Profitability and Growth**

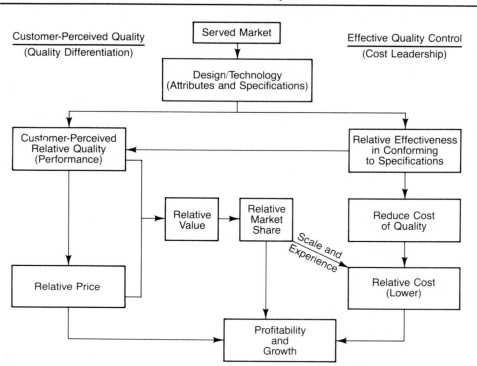

diagram in Figure 10.2, centers on effective quality control and the conformance of the firm's products and services to customer specifications. Customer-perceived quality is enhanced if the business marketer precisely meets the buyer's requirements. By making the product right the first time, effective quality control also reduces manufacturing costs. Many factories invest 20 to 25 percent of their operating budgets in finding and fixing mistakes![8] Cutting the cost of poor quality can lead to dramatic improvements in product profitability.

Consider a defective two-cent resistor entering the manufacturing process at Hewlett-Packard: "If you catch the resistor before it is used and throw it away, you lose two cents. If you don't catch it until it has to be soldered into a computer component, it may cost $100 to repair the part. If you don't catch the component until it is in a computer user's hands, the repair cost will amount to hundreds of dollars and

---

[8] Otis Port, "The Push for Quality," *Business Week* (June 8, 1987), pp. 131–135.

may exceed manufacturing costs."[9] Of course, you may also lose that customer's business in the future.

External View of Quality

"Quality means pleasing consumers, not just protecting them from annoyances."[10] (See Figure 10.3.) The **external view of quality** examines quality from the customer's perspective (see left side of Figure 10.2). Customers choose a particular product over competing offerings because they perceive it as a better "value"—the product's price and performance render it the most desirable alternative. How do product quality improvements contribute to profitability? "By providing the basis for customer acceptance of higher prices, quality improvements boost profits directly. In addition, quality improvements also help profitability indirectly by increasing customer-perceived value. And when value is recognized, the reward is usually a gain in market share—which, in turn, allows lower relative costs."[11] Note in Figure 10.2 that economies of scale and experience (treated later in the chapter) may contribute to lower relative costs.

TRW examined the relationship between product quality and financial performance for 148 product lines. It found that TRW products with the highest quality index enjoyed a much higher return-on-sales (ROS) and return-on-assets-employed (ROAE) than those with a lower quality rating.[12]

Pursuing a Total Quality Strategy

Since organizational buyers evaluate suppliers on the basis of the total offering, three dimensions of quality are important to business marketing strategy: product quality, support quality, and delivery quality. Selected dimensions of each are highlighted in Table 10.1. Observe that the development and implementation of a quality-based strategy requires careful coordination across several functional areas, each of which contributes directly to customer-perceived value.

In developing a sound quality-differentiation strategy the business marketer should (1) identify the relative importance of the various attributes of quality from the customers' perspective and (2) determine how customers rate each attribute of the firm's performance and the performance of major competitors. Importantly, the business marketer must recognize that continuous improvement is the core of the total quality approach. Les Papay, IBM's program director of quality, emphasizes that "total quality creates a culture of uncertainty because customer requirements are constantly

[9] Y. K. Shetty, "Product Quality and Competitive Strategy," *Business Horizons*, 30 (May–June 1987), pp. 49–50.

[10] David A. Garvin, "Competing on the Eight Dimensions of Quality," *Harvard Business Review*, 65 (November–December 1987), p. 103.

[11] Gale and Klavans, "Formulating a Quality Improvement Strategy," p. 23.

[12] John M. Groocock, *The Chain of Quality: Market Dominance Through Product Superiority* (New York: John Wiley & Sons, Inc., 1986), pp. 15–41.

FIGURE 10.3   **A Xerox Ad Defining Quality as Customer Satisfaction**

Source: Courtesy, The Xerox Corporation.

---

changing. Companies have to constantly strive at instilling and maintaining a quality culture to succeed."[13]

Integrated Effort

The development of marketing strategy in general, and product policy in particular, requires a high degree of functional coordination within the enterprise. As suggested above, manufacturing, research and development, engineering, physical distribution, technical service, and marketing together create and deliver the total product with its customer value satisfactions. If perceived benefits such as strong technical support or product quality are not provided, the marketer's reputation may be irreparably damaged.

---

[13] Tom Eisenhart, "'Total Quality' Is the Key to U.S. Competitiveness," *Business Marketing*, 75 (June 1990), p. 32.

TABLE 10.1   **Pursuing a Quality Strategy: A Multifunctional Process**

Main Category	Subcategories	Improvement Responsibility
Product quality	Accurately defining product specifications	Marketing/R&D
	Conformance to product design at time of delivery	Purchasing/manufacturing
	Performance after delivery (e.g., reliability, durability)	R&D
Support quality	Accurately defining customer's needs	Marketing
	After-sales service	Marketing/customer service
Delivery quality	Conformance to promised delivery schedule	Manufacturing/marketing/physical distribution
	Responsiveness to changes in customer's delivery schedule	Manufacturing/marketing/physical distribution

Source: Adapted with modifications from John M. Groocock, *The Chain of Quality: Market Dominance Through Product Superiority* (New York: John Wiley & Sons, 1986), p. 37.

Decisions about modifications or extensions in the product line often cause conflict in the industrial firm. Manufacturing personnel are interested in short product lines with long and smooth production runs. Marketers may prefer to extend rather than cut product lines in the face of competition or changing market requirements.[14] The discussion of organizational buying behavior in Chapter 4 described the kind of interfunctional conflict that often emerges in the buying organization. Such conflict also affects product planning in the selling organization and stems from the same roots: differing backgrounds, perspectives, and departmental objectives.

Organizing the Industrial Product Management Function

Implementing corporate strategy for either business or consumer markets requires a coordinated effort. The need is particularly acute in business marketing. The industrial product management function cannot remain isolated within the organization, but must instead interface with other functional areas. Technical service and research and development groups are part of the product offering. The capability of manufacturing (low cost or high quality) may become a marketing weapon. Cost accounting is important to product management, providing accurate data on the profitability of the product mix. Product managers assume an important coordinating role in the formulation of business marketing strategy.[15]

---

[14] Benson P. Shapiro, "Can Marketing and Manufacturing Coexist?" *Harvard Business Review*, 55 (September–October 1977), pp. 107–114; and Shapiro, "What the Hell is Market Oriented?" *Harvard Business Review*, 66 (November–December 1988), pp. 119–125.

[15] W. Theodore Cummings, Donald W. Jackson, Jr., and Lonnie L. Ostrom, "Differences Between Industrial and Consumer Product Managers," *Industrial Marketing Management*, 13 (August 1984), pp. 171–180; see also Joseph A. Bellizzi, Robert E. Hite, and Jane C. Engle, "Role Ambiguity and Product Management: Comparisons Between Industrial and Consumer Goods Product Managers," in Terrence A. Shimp et al., eds, *1986 AMA Educators' Proceedings* (Chicago: American Marketing Association, 1986), p. 230.

THE GLOBAL MARKETPLACE
Quality: Six Sigma at Motorola

Motorola is a world leader in a range of technology-intensive products such as cellular telephones, pagers, two-way private radio equipment, and automotive and industrial electronics. At a strategy retreat ten years ago, Arthur Sundry, a sales executive at Motorola, ventured the opinion that Motorola was in danger of being buried by the Japanese on quality. His speech, coupled with the rising competitive challenge, put quality at the top of the corporate agenda. To learn more, a team was assembled to travel the world looking for "islands of excellence" among the best manufacturers of cars, watches, cameras, and other technology-intensive products. The Motorola managers spent the most time in Japan, where they found factory managers to be surprisingly receptive.

To meet the quality challenge, Motorola has automated its factories and adopted Japanese-style production techniques, instituted a vast training program covering all 102,000 employees, established a reward system for nearly all employees tied to the quality of what they do, and compelled suppliers to meet rigid quality standards. One supplier notes: "If we can supply Motorola, we can supply God."

Motorola's product quality goal is to achieve **Six Sigma**, the statistical term for 3.4 defects per million. That's 99.9997 percent perfect. Beyond production, all departments at Motorola have their own plans for achieving Six Sigma in what they do. A winner of the Malcolm Baldrige Quality Award, Motorola has become a symbol of how the most effective U.S. firms can hold their own—and even make advances—against formidable Japanese rivals.

Source: Ronald Henkoff, "What Motorola Learns from Japan," *Fortune*, 119 (April 24, 1989), pp. 157–168.

The product management function must link product plans to overall corporate objectives and planning. Firms that overlook this, placing product planning in a vacuum, are often disappointed when the resulting plans clash with corporate goals and capabilities.

The design of the product management function depends upon company and market characteristics. Some industrial firms are organized around products, others around markets.

A business marketing firm offering several products to the same general market might choose the **product manager form of organization**. A **market-centered form of organization** might be more appropriate for a firm that offers the same product to various industry or market segments. With either form, the responsibilities of product management are the same: to plan, coordinate, and control the firm's product mix. Top management must foster the proper environment for product planning.[16]

---

[16] For a comprehensive discussion of organizational design see Victor P. Buell, "Organizing for Industrial Goods Marketing," in Victor P. Buell, ed., *Handbook of Modern Marketing: Second Edition* (New York: McGraw-Hill Book Company, 1986), pp. 51-1 to 51-13; David L. Wilemon, "Product and Market Managers," in Buell, *Handbook of Modern Marketing: Second Edition*, pp. 52-1 to 52-14; Barton Weitz and Erin Anderson, "Organizing the Marketing Function," in Ben M. Enis and Kenneth J. Roering, eds., *Review of Marketing 1981* (Chicago: American Marketing Association, 1981), pp. 134–142; and Stephen Lysonski, "A Boundary Theory Investigation of the Product Manager's Role," *Journal of Marketing*, 49 (Winter 1985), pp. 26–40.

PRODUCT POLICY

Product policy involves the set of all decisions concerning the products and services that the company offers. Three levels of decisions fall into the product policy area: (1) item, a specific version of the product; (2) product line, a group of related items; and (3) product mix, a collection of all items and product lines marketed by the company.

This section is concerned with management of the existing industrial product line. First, various types of industrial product lines are described. Second, decisions about the management of the existing product line are examined. Determining the length of the product line and the strategic position of specific items in the line are emphasized.

Types of Product Lines Defined

Because product lines of industrial firms differ from those of consumer firms, classification is useful. There are four types of industrial product lines:[17]

1. *Proprietary or catalog products.* These items are offered only in certain configurations and produced in anticipation of orders. Product line decisions concern the addition, deletion, or repositioning of products within the line.

2. *Custom-built products.* These items are offered as a set of basic units, with numerous accessories and options. A lathe manufacturer may offer several basic sizes, with a range of options (such as various motor sizes) and accessories for various applications. The marketer offers the organizational buyer a set of building blocks. Product line decisions center on offering the proper mix of options and accessories.

3. *Custom-designed products.* These items are created to meet the needs of one or a small group of customers. Sometimes the product is a unique unit, such as a power plant or a specific machine tool. In addition, some items produced in relatively large quantities, such as an aircraft model, may fall into this category (see Figure 10.4). The product line is described in terms of the company's capability, and the consumer buys that capability. Ultimately, this capability is transformed into a finished good.

4. *Industrial services.* Rather than an actual product, the buyer is purchasing a company's capability in an area such as maintenance, technical service, or management consulting. Special attention is given to services marketing in Chapter 12.

All types of business marketing firms confront product policy decisions, whether they offer physical products, pure services (no physical product), or a product–service combination.[18] Each product situation presents unique problems and opportunities for the business marketer; each draws upon a unique type of capability. Product strategy rests on the intelligent utilization of corporate capability.

---

[17] Shapiro, *Industrial Product Policy,* pp. 17–21.

[18] Albert L. Page and Michael Siemplenski, "Product Systems Marketing," *Industrial Marketing Management,* 12 (April 1983), pp. 89–99.

FIGURE 10.4   **Selected Items in Boeing's Product Line**

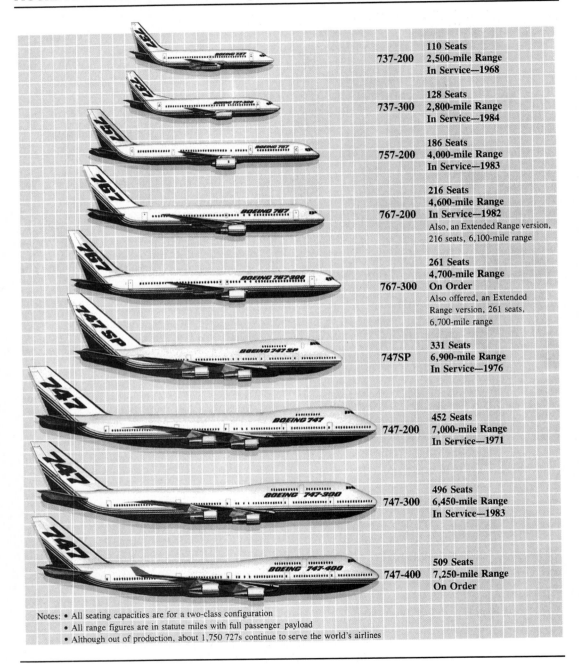

737-200   110 Seats
2,500-mile Range
In Service—1968

737-300   128 Seats
2,800-mile Range
In Service—1984

757-200   186 Seats
4,000-mile Range
In Service—1983

767-200   216 Seats
4,600-mile Range
In Service—1982
Also, an Extended Range version, 216 seats, 6,100-mile range

767-300   261 Seats
4,700-mile Range
On Order
Also offered, an Extended Range version, 261 seats, 6,700-mile range

747SP   331 Seats
6,900-mile Range
In Service—1976

747-200   452 Seats
7,000-mile Range
In Service—1971

747-300   496 Seats
6,450-mile Range
In Service—1983

747-400   509 Seats
7,250-mile Range
On Order

Notes: • All seating capacities are for a two-class configuration
• All range figures are in statute miles with full passenger payload
• Although out of production, about 1,750 727s continue to serve the world's airlines

Source: Courtesy, Boeing Commercial Airplanes.

Product Support: The Service Element

By focusing exclusively on the product, many business marketers overlook the opportunity to use service as a basis for gaining a strong competitive advantage. As emphasized earlier, the business marketer should examine the total product—including the services that augment the offering. Postpurchase service is especially important to buyers in many industrial product categories ranging from computers and machine tools to custom-designed component parts. Responsibility for service support, however, is often diffused throughout various departments such as application engineering, customer relations, or service administration. Significant benefits accrue to the business marketer who designs a product service support strategy that responds to the special needs of organizational buyers.[19]

Defining the Product-Market

An accurate definition of the product-market is fundamental to sound product policy decisions.[20] Careful attention must be given to the alternative ways customer needs can be satisfied. The leading manufacturer of slide rules and drafting equipment was challenged first by producers of hand-held calculators and next by small-computer manufacturers.[21] By excluding products and technology that compete for the same end-user needs, the product strategist can quickly become out of touch with the market. Both customer needs and the ways of satisfying those needs change.

A **product-market** establishes the distinct arena in which the business marketer competes. Four dimensions of a market definition are strategically relevant:

1. *Customer function dimension.* The related benefits are provided to satisfy the needs of organizational buyers.

2. *Technological dimension.* There are alternative ways a particular function can be performed.

3. *Customer segment dimension.* Customer groups have needs that must be served.

4. *Value-added system dimension.* There is a sequence of stages along which competitors serving the market can operate.[22]

Consider the case of a purchasing manager for a stereo manufacturer who is evaluating alternative suppliers of channel display units (a component part). Observe in Figure 10.5 that this need can potentially be satisfied by three different technologies, with perhaps multiple suppliers of each technology. Likewise, some of the suppliers

---

[19] Milind M. Lele and Uday S. Karmarkar, "Good Product Support Is Smart Marketing," *Harvard Business Review*, 61 (November–December 1983), pp. 129–135; see also Lele, "How Service Needs Influence Product Strategy," *Sloan Management Review*, 28 (Fall 1986), pp. 63–70.

[20] For a complete discussion on market definition, see Roger A. Kerin, Vijay Mahajan, and P. Rajan Varadarajan, *Contemporary Perspectives on Strategic Market Planning* (Needham Heights, MA: Allyn & Bacon, 1990).

[21] David W. Cravens, *Strategic Marketing* (Homewood, IL: Richard D. Irwin, Inc., 1987), pp. 159–160.

[22] George S. Day, *Strategic Market Planning: The Pursuit of Competitive Advantage* (St. Paul, Minn.: West Publishing Company, 1984), p. 73.

FIGURE 10.5   **Illustration of a Market Need**

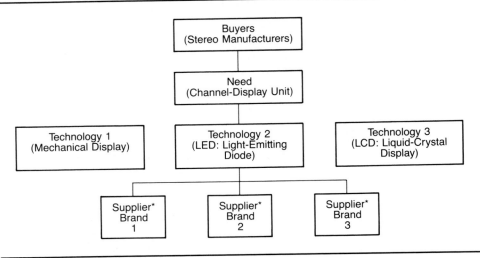

*Suppliers: Electronic Component Manufacturers

Source: Adapted from Gary L. Lilien, "New Product Success in Business/Industrial Markets: Progress, Problems, and a Research Program," Report #2-1985, Institute for the Study of Business Markets, College of Business Administration, Pennsylvania State University, p. 8.

may have the capability to move forward in the value chain and manufacture the complete stereo unit. Competition to satisfy this customer's need exists at the technology level as well as at the supplier or brand level.

By establishing accurate product-market boundaries, the product strategist is better equipped to identify customer needs, the benefits sought by the market segment, and the nature of competition at both the technology and supplier or brand levels. George Day notes: "The strategist seeking to understand a particular market is dealing with a moving target, for change is continuous along each of the key market dimensions of function, technology, customer segmentation, and degree of integration" (value-added system).[23]

Assessing International Product-Market Opportunities

Since an increasing number of sectors of the business market, such as the aerospace, telecommunications, computer, agricultural equipment, and automobile industries, include firms that compete on a worldwide basis, an assessment of the global product-market opportunities is required. Observe in Table 10.2 that the business marketer has several options in developing an international product strategy. The horizontal dimension represents the similarity in or the difference between market needs

[23] Ibid., p. 100.

TABLE 10.2   **Assessment of Global Product-Market Opportunities**

Product Configuration	Market Needs	
	Same	**Different**
Same	Universal or Global Product	Market Segmentation
Different	Product Segmentation (modified product)	Specialty Segmentation (country-tailored product)

Source: Adapted from Jagdish N. Sheth, "Global Markets or Global Competition," *Journal of Consumer Marketing*, 3 (Spring 1986), p. 10.

across countries, while the vertical dimension represents the nature of the product configuration.

A universal or global product assumes that the needs of organizational customers are the same across countries. This assumption may be valid for some classes of industrial products and for some world markets (e.g., Japan, North America, and Western Europe). In fact, some evidence suggests that industrial and high-technology products (e.g., computer hardware, airliners, photographic equipment, machine tools, and heavy equipment) may be most appropriate for global product strategies.[24] Customers with multinational operations are particularly likely to have similar requirements worldwide.[25] For example, where the operations are integrated or coordinated across national boundaries, as in the case of financial institutions, compatibility of operation systems and equipment may be essential. Consequently, such firms may seek business marketers who can supply their global operations.

A **product segmentation** strategy is appropriate when the market needs across countries are the same, but the products must be adapted to fit the local market. Note also from Table 10.2 that a **market segmentation** strategy fits when consumer needs across countries differ, but the product is standardized; other elements of the marketing mix are adapted to reach various target segments. To illustrate, Apple Computer sells a standardized product line worldwide but employs different positioning, promotional, and distribution strategies in each country. Finally, a **specialty segmentation** strategy involves developing tailor-made products for each country. This represents the most extreme form of specialization as market needs vary from country to country.

Susan P. Douglas and Yoram Wind provide this assessment of global product-market strategies:

> A firm's international operations are likely to be characterized by a mix of strategies, including not only global products and brands, but also some regional products and brands and some national products and brands. Similarly, some target segments may be global, others regional and others national. Hybrid strategies of this nature thus enable a

---

[24] Subhash C. Jain, "Standardization of International Marketing Strategy: Some Research Hypotheses," *Journal of Marketing*, 53 (January 1989), pp. 70–74.

[25] Susan P. Douglas and Yoram Wind, "The Myth of Globalization," *Columbia Journal of World Business*, 22 (Winter 1987), pp. 19–30.

company to take advantage of the benefits of standardization, and potential synergies from operating on an international scale, while at the same time not losing those afforded by adaptation to specific country characteristics and consumer preferences.[26]

Product Planning[27]

Once the product-market is defined, attention turns to securing a strong competitive position for the product. **Product positioning** represents the place that a product occupies in a particular market; it is found by measuring organizational buyers' perceptions and preferences for a product in relation to its competitors. Because organizational buyers perceive products as bundles of attributes (e.g., quality, service), the product strategist should examine the attributes that assume a central role in buying decisions.

Determinant Attributes

Particular attention should be given to defining those attributes that are **determinant**—attributes that are both important and differentiating. Figure 10.6 displays the possible types of determinant and nondeterminant attributes. A product manager may find the attributes of his or her brand (see sponsor brand [SB]) in any one of several mutually exclusive categories. In this illustration, only two attributes are determinant; each is considered by organizational buyers to be both important and differentiating. Observe also that another attribute is important but is not differentiating. For example, safety might constitute an attribute that would fit this category in the heavy-duty truck market. Business market customers view safety as being important but may consider the competing products offered by Navistar, Volvo, and Mack Trucks as quite comparable on this dimension. Durability, reliability, and fuel economy might constitute the determinant attributes.

Strategy Matrix

After defining the key attributes and assessing the firm's competitive standing, particular strategy options can be evaluated by the product manager. Figure 10.7 suggests how the attributes portrayed in Figure 10.6 might be changed. Thus, each cell of the strategy matrix provides possible generic strategies that the product manager could pursue to improve the brand's competitive standing. For example, the upper left cell (increase importance and brand differentiation) is a strategy requiring measures to (1) increase the attribute importance to customers, and (2) increase the difference between the competition and the sponsor brand.

Of the attributes displayed in Figure 10.6, D_1 is the attribute most preferred by a product manager—the attribute is important and differentiating, and the sponsor brand is superior to competing brands. Ideally then, the product manager would like to convert attributes wherever possible into the D_1 attribute category. This would require

---

[26] Ibid., p. 28.

[27] This section is based largely on Behram J. Hansotia, Muzzaffar A. Shaikh, and Jagdish N. Sheth, "The Strategic Determinancy Approach to Brand Management," *Business Marketing*, 70 (Fall 1985), pp. 66–69.

FIGURE 10.6   **Determinant and Nondeterminant Attributes**

Attribute

	Determinant		Nondeterminant			
	D₁	**D₂**	**ND₁**	**ND₂**	**ND₃**	**ND₄**
Important	x	x	x			
Not Important				x	x	x
Nondifferentiating (SB=COMP)			x	x		
Differentiating (SB>COMP)	x				x	
(SB<COMP)		x				x

SB: Sponsor Brand   COMP: Competing Brand

Possible Attribute Types

Determinant:
D₁—Attribute is important as well as differentiating, but sponsor brand is superior to competing brand (SB>COMP).
D₂—Attribute is important as well as differentiating, but sponsor brand is inferior to competing brand (SB<COMP).

Nondeterminant:
ND₁—Attribute is important but not differentiating. Statistically, SB and COMP are perceived to be equal (SB=COMP).
ND₂—Attribute is neither important nor differentiating.
ND₃—Attribute is differentiating (SB>COMP), but not important.
ND₄—Attribute is differentiating (SB<COMP), but not important.

Reprinted with permission from Behran J. Hansotia, Muzaffar A. Shaikh, and Jagdish N. Sheth, "The Strategic Determinancy Approach to Brand Management," *Business Marketing*, 70 (February 1985), p. 66. Copyright Crain Communications, Inc.

FIGURE 10.7   **Strategy Matrix**

Brand Difference*

		Increase	Decrease	Maintain
Importance	Increase	ND₂→D₁		ND₃→D₁
	Decrease			D₂→ND₄
	Maintain	ND₁→D₁	D₂→ND₁	ND₄→ND₄ D₁→D₁

*Note: The brand difference may be positive or negative, depending on whether the sponsor brand or the competing brand is perceived as being superior.

Source: Reprinted with permission from Behran J. Hansotia, Muzaffar A. Shaikh, and Jagdish N. Sheth, "The Strategic Determinancy Approach to Brand Management," *Business Marketing,* 70 (February 1985), p. 68. Copyright Crain Communications, Inc.

either increasing brand difference (ND_1) or attribute importance (ND_3). Converting ND_2 into D_1 requires increasing both importance and brand difference.

The least-preferred attribute type for the product manager is D_2—attribute is important and differentiating, but the sponsor brand is inferior to competing brands. Here the product manager attempts to convert it into a nondeterminant attribute.

ILLUSTRATION: Determinancy Analysis

The strategic determinancy approach described above was successfully applied to a capital equipment product at a major corporation. The product that provided the focus of the analysis is sold in three sizes to two market segments: end users and consulting engineers. Through marketing research, fifteen attributes were identified, including such dimensions as reliability, service support, company reputation, and ease of maintenance.

The research found that the firm's brand enjoyed an outstanding rating on product reliability and service support, both attributes generally being determinant for the company against most competitors. To reinforce the importance of both attributes, management decided to offer an enhanced warranty program. Both end users and consulting engineers view warranties as important but not a point of differentiation across competing brands. Management surmised, however, that by establishing a new warranty standard for the industry, the attribute could become determinant, adding to the brand's leverage over competitors. In addition, management felt that the new warranty program might also benefit the brand's reputation on other attributes such as reliability and company reputation.

The study also provided some surprises. Price was not nearly as important to organizational buyers as management had initially believed. This suggested that there were opportunities to increase revenue through product differentiation and service support. Likewise, the research found that the firm's brand dominated all competitors in the large- and medium-sized products, but not in the small-sized products. This particular product had an especially weak competitive position in the consulting engineer segment. Special service support strategies were developed to strengthen the product's standing in this segment. Clearly, determinancy analysis provides a valuable tool for managing products for business markets.

PLANNING INDUSTRIAL PRODUCT STRATEGY

Formulating a strategic marketing plan for an existing product line is the most vital part of a company's marketing planning efforts. Having identified product attributes of importance to organizational buyers, and having compared the firm's product offerings with those of competitors, the planner now considers the current and projected performance of the total product mix. Two tools for planning industrial product line strategy are (1) experience curve analysis and (2) the product evaluation matrix. Each is of value in illuminating the firm's current product-market position as well as establishing clear strategy directions.

FIGURE 10.8   **A Typical Experience Curve (85 Percent)**

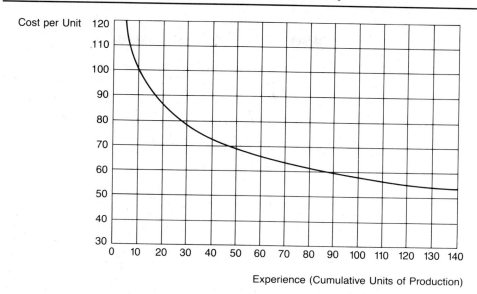

Experience Curve Analysis

The experience curve is based on the discovery that costs (measured in constant dollars) decline by a predictable and constant percentage (usually from 10 to 30 percent) each time accumulated production experience (volume) is doubled.[28] The experience curve effect encompasses a broad range of costs—manufacturing, marketing, distribution, and administrative.

The curve illustrated in Figure 10.8 is an 85 percent experience curve; that is, with every doubling of experience, costs per unit drop to 85 percent of their original level—a 15 percent reduction in costs for every doubling of cumulative production. Various products and industries experience various learning rates (75 percent, 80 percent, 85 percent). The experience curve effect has been supported in studies of numerous industries, including chemical, steel, paper, and electronics. The concept appears to be especially relevant in high-technology markets such as semiconductors and computer memories.[29]

---

[28] William J. Abernathy and Kenneth Wayne, "Limits of the Learning Curve," *Harvard Business Review*, 52 (September–October 1974), pp. 109–119; see also William W. Alberts, "The Experience Curve Doctrine Reconsidered," *Journal of Marketing*, 53 (July 1989), pp. 36–49.

[29] George S. Day, "Analytical Approaches to Strategic Market Planning," in Enis and Roering, eds., *Review of Marketing 1981*, pp. 92–94.

Sources of the Experience Curve Effect

To capitalize on the experience effect, the industrial product manager must understand *why* costs decline with accumulated experience. George Day and David Montgomery isolate three major sources of the experience effect:[30]

1. *Learning by doing.* The efficiency of labor increases because workers of all types become more adept at a job as they repeat it. Similarly, learning includes the discovery, through greater job specialization, of better methods to organize work flows.

2. *Technological improvements.* Economies are derived from new production processes, product standardization, product redesign, or changes in resource mix, such as automation replacing labor.

3. *Economies of scale.* Efficiency increases due to size. "Seldom does an increase in throughput require an equivalent increase in capital investment, size of sales force, or overhead functions."[31] Scale also creates the potential for other cost reductions such as volume discounts and the division of labor.

The experience curve is strategically relevant to the industrial product manager only when these three effects are influential features of the environment.[32] The fact is that as experience is gained, costs do not necessarily decline. Costs that are not carefully managed will inevitably rise. Experience merely gives management the opportunity to seek cost reductions and efficiency improvements. A thorough effort must be made to exploit the benefits of experience. Product standardization, new manufacturing processes, labor efficiency, work specialization—these are a few of the many areas that must be examined to capitalize on the experience curve effect.

Experience curve analysis is also of value when product line modifications are being considered. Often, two or more products in the firm's line share a common resource or involve the same production or distribution activity. Such shared experience is significant because the costs of one item in the product line can be reduced even more because of accumulated experience with other product line items.[33] Clearly, a manager planning to extend the product line must examine whether the item will fit in with the firm's manufacturing and marketing experience.

Experience Curve Analysis and the Product Life Cycle[34]

Experience curve analysis helps the business marketer project costs and prices. The experience curve can be linked to the product life cycle to provide a basis for developing industrial product strategy. The life cycle of a product is often described in

---

[30] George S. Day and David B. Montgomery, "Diagnosing the Experience Curve," *Journal of Marketing*, 47 (Spring 1983), pp. 44–58; see also George S. Day, *Analysis for Strategic Market Decisions* (St. Paul, Minn.: West Publishing Company, 1986), pp. 25–56.

[31] Ibid., Day and Montgomery, p. 47.

[32] Ibid., pp. 44–58.

[33] Derek F. Abell and John S. Hammond, *Strategic Market Planning: Problems and Analytical Approaches* (Englewood Cliffs, N.J.: Prentice-Hall, Inc., 1979), pp. 125–127.

[34] This section is largely based on Day and Montgomery, "Diagnosing the Experience Curve," pp. 50–52. For a related discussion, see Hans B. Thorelli and Stephen C. Burnett, "The Nature of Product Life Cycles for Industrial Goods Businesses," *Journal of Marketing*, 45 (Fall 1981), pp. 97–108.

FIGURE 10.9   **Product Life Cycle Stages and the Industry Price Experience Curve**

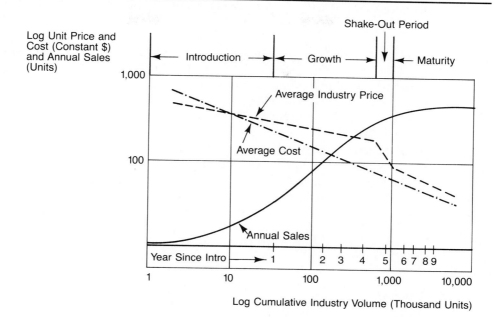

Source: George S. Day and David B. Montgomery, "Diagnosing the Experience Curve," *Journal of Marketing*, 47 (Spring 1983), p. 51. Reprinted by permission of the American Marketing Association.

terms of stages: introduction, growth, maturity, and decline. The product life cycle shows trends in primary demand and patterns of competition.

Selected stages of the product life cycle are joined with an industry price experience curve in Figure 10.9. It shows cumulative experience (not for a single company, but for the industry) across a hypothetical product life cycle. In the introductory stage, the average industry price is below current costs. The demand stimulated by a low price, together with experience-based cost declines, leads to a level of profitability much higher than would be generated by a price policy oriented to covering all costs immediately.[35] Thus, a manager who understands the experience curve can make projections about future profitability that help determine optimal pricing now.

---

[35] Bruce Robinson and Chet Lakhani, "Dynamic Price Models for New Product Planning," *Management Science*, 21 (June 1975), pp. 1113–1122; see also Robert J. Dolan and Abel P. Jeuland, "Experience Curves and Dynamic Demand Models: Implications for Optimal Pricing Strategies," *Journal of Marketing*, 45 (Winter 1981), pp. 52–73; and Louis E. Yelle, "Industrial Life Cycles and Learning Curves: Interaction of Marketing and Production," *Industrial Marketing Management*, 9 (October 1980), pp. 311–318.

Experience curve analysis also provides insights into the relative ease or difficulty with which competitors can enter a product market. If early entrants into a market have significant cost advantages, the experience effect could create substantial entry barriers. In fact, moderate experience slopes seem to create a greater entry barrier than very small or very large slopes.[36] (Consistent with our earlier discussion, a large slope might reflect that costs per unit decline by 40 percent with each doubling of experience, while a small slope reflects a decline of 10 percent.) Small experience effects provide only a minor advantage to the innovator; large experience effects often make it relatively easy for late entrants to catch up with early entrants, perhaps by learning from the innovator's mistakes or by carefully analyzing the design of the innovator's product. When there is a moderately sloped experience curve, however, entry tends to cease after three or four firms enter. Of course, competitive entry patterns are also shaped by the growth rate of the market and by the average margins available to new entrants.

As illustrated in Figure 10.9, a shakeout period can occur between the growth and maturity stages of the product life cycle, triggering a sharp break in the industry price trend. Among the factors that can spawn a shakeout of competitors are (1) a slowing growth rate, (2) a market leader cutting prices to stem erosion of market share, or (3) aggressive late entrants relying on price cuts as the prime force in their marketing strategy. Overall, competitive cost differentials steadily narrow as the market matures.

Strategic Relevance

An astute business marketing manager must understand the strengths and limits of particular strategic planning tools. Experience curve analysis and the product life cycle concept are useful when exploring the underlying dynamics of a market and when evaluating alternative product strategy scenarios. They cannot be used to prescribe simple strategies; they are organizing frameworks.

First, experience curve analysis, as emphasized, is relevant when learning, technology, and economies of scale are important features of the environment. If these are present, the industrial product manager can use experience curve analysis either to capitalize on opportunities for improved efficiency within the firm, or to better understand competitive behavior. Slavish devotion to the experience curve and low-cost strategies can, however, create unintended consequences. One executive noted: "In our hell-bent rush to get costs down, we have given all too short shrift to quality and service. So we wake up, at best, with a great share and a lousy product."[37]

Second, the product life cycle is a versatile framework for organizing hypotheses about strategy alternatives and for "directing management attention toward anticipation

---

[36] Michael A. Spence, "The Learning Curve and Competition," *The Bell Journal of Economics*, 12 (Spring 1981), pp. 49–69.

[37] Quoted in Thomas J. Peters, "Strategy Follows Structure: Developing Distinctive Skills," *California Management Review*, 26 (Spring 1984) and cited by Day, *Analysis for Strategic Market Decisions*, p. 55.

of the consequences of the underlying dynamics of the served market."[38] The concept does not provide generalized universal business marketing strategies.

High and Low Market Share Success

The analysis of experience curves and product life cycles inevitably raises questions about the value of market share to profitability, whether of a firm or of a single product. The rationale for using market share as a performance measure rests on the body of research showing that market share is positively and strongly related to product profitability.[39] Increases in market share are accompanied by a decline in marketing costs as a percentage of sales, a higher profit margin, and higher-quality products that demand a higher price. Recent research, however, indicates that the direct impact of market share on profitability is much smaller than previous studies have suggested.[40] Robert Jacobson and David Aaker argue that other fundamentals can be of equal or greater importance. They suggest that more emphasis be placed on product quality, customer satisfaction, product line appropriateness, and management effectiveness.

A study of successful low market share firms makes it clear that failure to be a market leader need not damage a company's financial position.[41] More than 600 manufacturing companies with a pretax return on investment of at least 20 percent were identified. Most produced frequently purchased components or supplies for the business market. The competitive strategies followed by these successful low market share firms had the following common characteristics:

1. Selectivity—rather than copying the market share leader or trying to serve everyone, these firms concentrated on particular market segments and particular bases of competition, such as product quality and price

2. A reputation for high quality

3. Medium to low relative prices complementing high quality

4. Low total costs, achieved by producing only a narrow line of products for a particular market segment and by spending less than competitors on R&D, advertising, new product introductions, and related activities.

Clearly, the strategy of a firm must be tailored to its distinctive capabilities and the requirements of its competitive environment.

---

[38] George S. Day, "The Product Life Cycle: Analysis and Applications Issues," *Journal of Marketing*, 45 (Fall 1981), p. 65; see also Mary Lambkin and George S. Day, "Evolutionary Processes in Competitive Markets: Beyond the Product Life Cycle," *Journal of Marketing*, 53 (July 1989), pp. 4–20.

[39] Robert D. Buzzell, Bradley T. Gale, and Ralph G. M. Sultan, "Market Share—A Key to Profitability," *Harvard Business Review*, 53 (January–February 1975), pp. 97–106; and Robert D. Buzzell and Frederik D. Wiersema, "Successful Share-Building Strategies," *Harvard Business Review*, 59 (January–February 1981), pp. 135–144.

[40] Robert Jacobson and David A. Aaker, "Is Market Share All That It's Cracked Up to Be?" *Journal of Marketing*, 49 (Fall 1985), pp. 1–12; and Jacobson and Aaker, "The Strategic Role of Product Quality," *Journal of Marketing*, 51 (October 1987), pp. 31–44; see also John E. Prescott, Ajay K. Kohli, and N. Venkatraman, "The Market Share–Profitability Relationship: An Empirical Assessment of Major Assertions and Contradictions," *Strategic Management Journal*, 7 (July–August 1986), pp. 377–394.

[41] Carolyn Y. Woo and Arnold C. Cooper, "The Surprising Case for Low Market Share," *Harvard Business Review*, 60 (November–December 1982), pp. 106–113.

INSIDE BUSINESS MARKETING
High-Growth Market Blues

The conventional wisdom that marketers should invest in growth markets is based upon this line of reasoning: In the early phase of a growth market, share gains are easier and worth more, the experience curve will lead to cost advantages, price pressures will be low, early involvement will provide a technological advantage, and early aggressive entry will deter later entrants. David Aaker and George Day argue that these premises are often shaky. "Numerous firms have entered growth situations only to endure years of painful losses and ultimately an embarrassing, costly, and sometimes fatal exit during a traumatic shakeout phase."

Why do risks often outweigh the rewards of high-growth markets? The authors isolate several factors:

- The number and aggressiveness of competitors is greater than can be supported by the market.

- Adequate distribution may not be available.

- Resources are lacking to maintain a high rate of growth.

- Important success factors change (e.g., from product technology to process or production technology) and the firm cannot adapt.

- Technology changes.

- A competitor enters with a superior product or with a low-cost advantage.

- The market growth fails to materialize.

The effective business marketer must challenge the fundamental strategy premises. "A market is neither inherently attractive nor unattractive because it is experiencing high growth. The real question is whether the firm can exploit the opportunities presented by market growth to gain a competitive advantage."

Source: David A. Aaker and George S. Day, "The Perils of High-Growth Markets," *Strategic Management Journal*, 7 (September–October 1986), pp. 409–421.

In this section we have discussed a strategic planning tool of value to the product strategist operating in the business marketing environment: experience curve analysis. Drawing on recent research, we then moved to an analysis of the significance of market share as a product performance measure. We now consider a procedure for developing a marketing strategy for an industrial product.

Product Evaluation Matrix

Once the strategic position of a product in a particular industry environment has been examined with the help of the experience curve, the manager of an existing line has at hand a second planning aid—a matrix approach developed by Yoram Wind and Henry Claycamp.[42] The matrix is a comprehensive tool integrating three product performance measures: sales, market share, and profitability. As with any other

---

[42] Yoram Wind and Henry J. Claycamp, "Planning Product Line Strategy: A Matrix Approach," *Journal of Marketing*, 40 (January 1976), pp. 2–9; see also Yoram Wind, *Product Policy*, pp. 129–132.

TABLE 10.3 **Levels of Analysis and Specificity of Guidance**

Specificity of Guidance	Nature of Analytical Operation
Lowest	1. Current product position on industry sales, company sales, market share, and profitability.
	2. Projected product position on sales, market share, and profitability, assuming no major changes in the firm's marketing activities, competitive action, and environmental conditions.
	3. Projected product position on sales, market share, and profitability under alternative marketing strategies (conditional forecast), assuming no major changes in competitive action and environmental conditions.
	4. The above plus diagnostic insights into the competitive structure and the effectiveness of the firm's marketing activities.
Highest	5. Projected product position on sales, market share, and profitability under alternative marketing strategies, anticipated competitive action, and alternative environmental conditions (based on computer simulation).

Source: Yoram Wind and Henry J. Claycamp, "Planning Product Line Strategy: A Matrix Approach," *Journal of Marketing*, 40 (January 1976), p. 8. Reprinted by permission of the American Marketing Association.

strategic planning tool, a strong market focus is needed; each product must be examined in relation to the segment it serves.

The approach has five levels providing increasingly specific guidance for product management decisions (Table 10.3). The first step is to profile the product in terms of industry sales, company sales, market share, and profitability. The analysis then proceeds through an evaluation of alternative product strategies under various competitive and external conditions. The approach forces a manager to ask the right questions about the product's current and future position.

Using the Matrix

The matrix approach is implemented using the product evaluation matrix illustrated in Figure 10.10. Company sales are evaluated on the horizontal scale and industry sales on the vertical scale. Each is divided into three categories: growth, stable, or decline. Then profitability is classified as below target, target, or above target, and market share as dominant, average, or marginal. The categories for sales, market share, and profitability are merely illustrative and can be varied as company and industry situations vary. The manager also must define the intervals for each category—for example, for market share: less than 10 percent is marginal; 10 to 24 percent is average; and more than 25 percent is dominant. The appropriate intervals are heavily dependent on the standards for the firm and the industry.[43]

Two products are positioned in the evaluation matrix in Figure 10.10. Product A enjoys a solid performance position, a dominant market share, growing company sales, and profitability at target in a growing industry. Product B, on the other hand, occupies a place in a stable industry with marginal market share and stable company sales, but profits below target. The appropriate marketing strategy for product A would be to

---
[43] Ibid., Wind and Claycamp, p. 4.

FIGURE 10.10 **The Product Evaluation Matrix**

Company Sales		Decline			Stable			Growth		
Industry Sales / Profitability / Market Share		Below Target	Target	Above Target	Below Target	Target	Above Target	Below Target	Target	Above Target
Growth	Dominant								A	
	Average									
	Marginal									
Stable	Dominant									
	Average					B₁				
	Marginal				B					
Decline	Dominant									
	Average									
	Marginal									

Source: Structure provided by Yoram Wind and Henry J. Claycamp, "Planning Product Line Strategy: A Matrix Approach," *Journal of Marketing*, 40 (January 1976), pp. 2–9. Reprinted by permission of the American Marketing Association.

maintain the favorable market position. For product B, however, alternative strategies must be considered. The performance of product B should be considered under a number of various marketing strategy scenarios. The sales, market share, and profitability of product B next year are contingent on the strategy decisions that are made now. Thus, a conditional forecast of product performance should be made for each alternative marketing strategy. The decision support system, the heart of the business marketing intelligence system, facilitates the evaluation of these for each market segment.

In search of the most desirable marketing strategy, the business marketer must also consider potential competitive behavior and projected external conditions. This comprehensive analysis of strategy options and likely external events may lead to a strategy that improves the market position of product B to that shown as product B₁ in Figure 10.10.

Developing a Strategy

Wind and Claycamp identify five strategy options that might be appropriate for a particular product or for an entire line.[44]

1. Maintain the product and its marketing strategy in the present form.

2. Maintain the present form of the product but change its marketing strategy.

---

[44] Ibid., p. 8.

3. Change the product and alter the marketing strategy.

4. Drop the product or the entire product line.[45]

5. Add one or more new items into a line or add new product lines.

The product evaluation matrix allows the product manager to systematically address two basic questions: "Where are we now?" and "Where should we go from here?" The product evaluation matrix provides management with the information required to analyze each product's performance; the combined analyses constitute the firm's current product portfolio. The tool can likewise be applied to assess competitive products, using the same procedure to monitor competitive strategy and performance.

We have concentrated on managing the firm's existing product line using two strategic planning tools of particular value to the business marketing strategist: experience curve analysis and the product evaluation matrix. We also explored the critical importance of product quality to business marketing strategy. Figure 10.11 provides a framework for integrating this discussion.

Observe that the firm's position relative to leading competitors is evaluated in each product or market segment in terms of market share, quality, cost, and technology. Often, the analysis of existing products uncovers market opportunities that could profitably be tapped with new products or technology. Managing the new product development process constitutes the theme of the next chapter.

SUMMARY

The product is usually the most important component of the business marketing mix. Conceptualizing a product must go beyond mere physical description to include all of the benefits and services that provide customer satisfaction. In the face of rising global competition and customer expectations, product quality is emerging as an important strategic issue in business marketing for the 1990s. The formulation of a quality strategy requires a carefully coordinated business marketing strategy—one that recognizes the role that various functional areas assume in providing value to organizational buyers.

Industrial product lines can be broadly classified into (1) proprietary or catalog items, (2) custom-built items, (3) custom-designed items, and (4) industrial services. Industrial product management can best be described as the management of capability. By establishing accurate product-market boundaries on both a domestic and a global scale, the product strategist is better equipped to identify the customer's needs, the benefits sought by market segment, and the nature of the competition. Attention then turns to securing a strong competitive position for the product. A product attribute is determinant if it is both important and differentiating.

In monitoring product performance and in formulating marketing strategy, the industrial marketer can profitably use two planning aids: experience curve analysis

---

[45] For a comprehensive treatment, see George J. Avlonitis, "The Management of the Product Elimination Function: Theoretical and Empirical Analysis," in Arch G. Woodside, ed., *Advances in Business Marketing* (Greenwich, Conn.: JAI Press, Inc., 1986), pp. 1–66.

FIGURE 10.11   **Assess Your Relative Share, Quality, Cost, and Technology Position in Each Cell of the Product Market Matrix**

Products	Your Relative Position*	Market Segments 1. _____	2. _____	3. _____	4. _____
A. _____	Share	_____	_____	_____	_____
	Quality	_____	_____	_____	_____
	Cost	_____	_____	_____	_____
	Technology	_____	_____	_____	_____
B. _____	Share	_____	_____	_____	_____
	Quality	_____	_____	_____	_____
	Cost	_____	_____	_____	_____
	Technology	_____	_____	_____	_____
C. _____	Share	_____	_____	_____	_____
	Quality	_____	_____	_____	_____
	Cost	_____	_____	_____	_____
	Technology	_____	_____	_____	_____
D. _____	Share	_____	_____	_____	_____
	Quality	_____	_____	_____	_____
	Cost	_____	_____	_____	_____
	Technology	_____	_____	_____	_____

*Notes: Relative Share: small, average, large
       Absolute Share: percent
       Quality: inferior, same, superior
       Cost: lower, same, higher
       Technology: behind, same, ahead
         (Product)
         (Process)

Source: Robert D. Buzzell and Bradley T. Gale, *The PIMS Principles: Linking Strategy to Performance* (New York: The Free Press, 1987), p.251. Reprinted with permission of The Free Press, a division of Macmillan, Inc. Copyright © 1987 by The Free Press.

and the product evaluation matrix. Experience curve analysis is relevant when learning, technology, and economies of scale are important features of the environment. In turn, the product evaluation matrix provides management with the information required to analyze each product's performance; the combined analysis constitutes the firm's current product portfolio. Business marketing managers must understand the strengths, weaknesses, and underlying assumptions of various strategic planning tools.

Discussion Questions

1. Bradley Gale, managing director of The Strategic Planning Institute, says: "People systematically knock out income statements and balance sheets, but they often don't monitor the nonfinancial factors that ultimately drive their financial performance. These nonfinancial factors include 'relative customer-perceived quality': how customers view the marketer's offering versus how they perceive competitive offerings." Explain.

2. Critique this statement: "Quality is the exclusive responsibility of the manufacturing sector and of quality-control inspectors."

3. Distinguish between catalog items, custom-built items, custom-designed items, and services. Explain how marketing requirements vary across these classifications.

4. Describe how a product manager might structure a study to identify the determinant attributes for photocopying equipment in the university market.

5. Experience curve analysis and the product life cycle concept are useful tools in exploring the dynamics of a market but cannot be used to derive simple strategy prescriptions. Explain.

6. "Is market share all that it's cracked up to be?" Research suggests that the direct impact of market share on profitability is substantially less than commonly assumed and, in fact, is relatively minor. Discuss the product management implications.

7. Valves play an important role in American industry. They control the flow of liquids and thus serve many users, including chemical-petrochemical complexes, refineries, pipelines, and electric power plants. How much effort should be invested in the development of special valves for the nuclear power market? Given the political, legal, and general uncertainties that surround this potentially large market, what steps should the product planner take?

8. In your position as product manager for the Bronson Machine Tool Company, you must develop a marketing program for existing product X. In determining how much to spend and where to spend it, you are given information on the sales, profitability, and market share of product X for the past five years. You are also provided with a forecast of general economic conditions. Describe how you would develop a strategy for product X.

9. A particular product strategy will stimulate a response from the market, and a corresponding response from competitors. Which specific features of the competitive environment should be evaluated by the industrial product strategist?

10. Some industrial product managers argue that their prime function is to market the "capability" of their firm, rather than physical products. Do you agree or disagree? Explain.

CHAPTER 11

Managing Innovation and New Industrial Product Development

The long-term competitive position of most organizations is tied to their ability to innovate—to provide existing and new customers with a continuing stream of new products and services. Innovation is a high-risk and potentially rewarding process.

After reading this chapter, you will understand:

1. the strategic processes through which product innovations take shape.

2. the role of the technology portfolio in new product planning and the approach that high-performing companies follow in commercializing technology.

3. the process of developing new products.

4. an approach for developing responsive product strategy for business markets.

PRODUCT innovation is important in the history of many prominent firms and in the careers of many legendary managers. Take John (Jack) F. Welch, Jr., chairman of General Electric Company:[1]

> From the very beginning, G.E. veterans say, Welch had a keen appreciation of where the company's strongest competitive edge would come from—its scientists. In his early years, his beat-up Volkswagen was almost a fixture in the parking lot of G.E.'s technology center at Schenectady, New York. . . . Scrimping for every dollar, new employee, and edge he could get, Welch became famous for bootlegging—sneaking money for a new project from another part of the operation. . . . Welch racked up a string of succes-

---

[1] Mark Potts and Peter Behr, *The Leading Edge* (New York: McGraw-Hill Book Company, 1987), pp. 207–208; see also Cynthia Hutton, "The Mind of Jack Welch," *Fortune*, 119 (March 27, 1989), pp. 39–50.

ses, among them the development of Noryl, a tough industrial plastic that moved from the laboratory into the market under Welch, becoming a foundation for a thriving business at G.E. that has grown to more than $1 billion in annual sales. . . . [Today,] Welch cherishes, and champions, lower-level managers at G.E. who share his penchant for innovation and entrepreneurship, and indeed, in many ways, he seems to want to create a company full of Jack Welches, aggressively running their businesses like he's aggressively running the corporation.

The long-term health of industrial companies is tied to their ability to provide existing and new customers with a continuing stream of attractive new products. Many firms derive a significant portion of their sales and profits from products introduced in the recent past. But the risks associated with product innovation are high; there are significant investments involved and the likelihood of failure is high. With shortening product life cycles and accelerating technological change, time is the new battleground in the innovation battle.[2]

This chapter examines product innovation in the business marketing environment. First, we provide a perspective on the management of innovation in the firm. Second, product innovation is positioned within an overall technological strategy for the firm. Attention centers on the characteristics of firms that have recorded superior performance in commercializing technology. Third, key dimensions of the new product development process are examined. The final section of the chapter explores the formulation of strategy for new industrial products.

THE MANAGEMENT OF INNOVATION

Management practices in successful industrial firms reflect the realities of the innovation process itself. "Innovation tends to be individually motivated, opportunistic, customer responsive, tumultuous, nonlinear, and interactive in its development. Managers can plan overall directions and goals, but surprises are likely to abound."[3] Clearly, some new product development efforts are the outgrowth of **deliberate** strategies (intended strategies that become realized), while others result from **emergent** strategies (realized strategies that, at least initially, were never intended).[4] Bearing little resemblance to a rational, analytical process, many strategic decisions involving new products are rather messy, disorderly, and disjointed processes around which competing organizational factions contend. In studying successful innovative companies such as Sony, AT&T, and Hewlett-Packard, James B. Quinn characterized the innovation process as controlled chaos:

---

[2] Ashok K. Gupta and David L. Wilemon, "Accelerating the Development of Technology-Based New Products," *California Management Review*, 32 (Winter 1990), pp. 24–44.

[3] James B. Quinn, "Managing Innovation: Controlled Chaos," *Harvard Business Review*, 63 (May–June 1985), p. 83.

[4] Henry Mintzberg and James A. Walton, "Of Strategies, Deliberate and Emergent," *Strategic Management Journal*, 6 (July–August 1985), pp. 257–272.

Many of the best concepts and solutions come from projects partly hidden or "bootlegged" by the organization. Most successful managers try to build some slacks or buffers into their plans to hedge their bets. . . . They permit chaos and replications in early investigations, but insist on much more formal planning and controls as expensive development and scale-up proceed. But even at these later stages, these managers have learned to maintain flexibility and to avoid the tyranny of paper plans.[5]

Patterns of Strategic Behavior[6]

A planned, deliberate process characterizes the development of some new products while a circuitous and chaotic process typifies others. Why? Research suggests that strategic activity within a large organization falls into two broad categories: induced and autonomous strategic behavior.[7]

Induced Strategic Behavior

Induced strategic behavior is consistent with the firm's traditional concept of strategy and takes place in relationship to its familiar external environment (e.g., its customary markets). By manipulating various administrative mechanisms, top management can influence the perceived interests of managers at the middle and operational levels of the organization and keep strategic behavior in line with the current strategy course. For example, the existing reward and measurement systems may direct the attention of managers to some market opportunities and not to others. Examples of induced strategic behavior might emerge around product development efforts for existing markets.

Autonomous Strategic Behavior

During any period, the bulk of strategic activity in large, complex firms is likely to fit into the induced behavior category. However, large, resource-rich firms are likely to possess a pool of entrepreneurial potential at operational levels, which will express itself in autonomous strategic initiatives. **Autonomous strategic behavior** is conceptually equivalent to entrepreneurial activity and introduces new categories of opportunity into the firm's planning process. Managers at the product-market level conceive of market opportunities that depart from the current strategy course, then engage in product championing activities to mobilize resources and create momentum for further development of the product. Emphasizing political rather than administrative channels, product champions question the firm's current concept of strategy and "provide top management with the opportunity to rationalize, retroactively, successful autonomous

---

[5] Quinn, "Managing Innovation," p. 82.

[6] This section is based on Michael D. Hutt, Peter H. Reingen, and John R. Ronchetto, Jr., "Tracing Emergent Processes in Marketing Strategy Formation," *Journal of Marketing,* 52 (January 1988), pp. 4–19.

[7] Robert A. Burgelman, "A Process Model of Internal Corporate Venturing in the Diversified Major Firm," *Administrative Science Quarterly,* 28 (April 1983), pp. 223–244.

TABLE 11.1   **Induced versus Autonomous Strategic Behavior: Selected Characteristics of the Marketing Strategy Formulation Process**

	Induced	**Autonomous**
Activation of the Strategic Decision Process	An individual manager defines a market need that converges on the organization's concept of strategy.	An individual manager defines a market need that diverges from the organization's concept of strategy.
Nature of the Screening Process	A formal screening of technical and market merit is made using established administrative procedures.	An informal network assesses technical and market merit.
Type of Innovation	Incremental (e.g., new product development for existing markets uses existing organizational resources).	Major (e.g., new product development projects require new combinations of organizational resources).
Nature of Communication	Consistent with organizational work flow.	Departs from organizational work flow in early phase of decision process.
Major Actors	Prescribed by the regular channel of hierarchical decision making.	An informal network emerges based on mobilization efforts of the product champion.
Decision Roles	Roles and responsibilities for participants in the strategy formulation process are well defined.	Roles and responsibilities of participants are poorly defined in the initial phases but become more formalized as the strategy formulation process evolves.
Implications for Strategy Formulation	Strategic alternatives are considered and commitment to a particular strategic course evolves.	Commitment to a particular strategic course emerges in the early phases through the sponsorship efforts of the product champion.

Source: Adapted from Michael D. Hutt, Peter H. Reingen, and John R. Ronchetto, Jr., "Tracing Emergent Processes in Marketing Strategy Formation," *Journal of Marketing*, 52 (January 1988), pp. 4–19.

strategic behavior."[8] Through these political mechanisms, successful autonomous strategic initiatives can become integrated into the firm's concept of strategy.

Product Championing and the Informal Network

Several characteristics that may distinguish induced from autonomous strategic behavior are highlighted in Table 11.1. Observe that autonomous strategic initiatives involve a set of actors and evoke a form of strategic dialogue different from those found in induced initiatives. An individual manager, the product champion, assumes a central role in sensing an opportunity and in mobilizing an informal network to explore the technical feasibility and market potential of the idea. A **product champion** is an organization member who creates, defines, or adopts an idea for an innovation and

---

[8] Robert A. Burgelman, "Corporate Entrepreneurship and Strategic Management: Insights from a Process Study," *Management Science*, 29 (December 1983), p. 1352.

who is willing to assume significant risk (e.g., position or prestige) to make possible the successful implementation of the innovation.[9] Senior managers at 3M Corporation will not commit to a project unless a champion emerges and will not abandon the effort unless the champion "gets tired."[10]

Compared to induced strategic behavior, autonomous initiatives are more likely to involve a communication process that departs from the regular work flow and the hierarchical decision-making channels. The decision roles and responsibilities of managers in this informal network are poorly defined in the early phases of the strategy formulation process but become more formalized as the process evolves. Note in Table 11.1 that autonomous strategic behavior entails a creeping commitment toward a particular strategy course. By contrast, induced strategic initiatives are more likely to involve administrative mechanisms that encourage a more formal and comprehensive assessment of strategic alternatives at various levels in the firm's planning hierarchy.

ILLUSTRATION: Autonomous Strategic Behavior[11]

By tracing the formation of marketing strategy for a set of new technical products, selected dimensions of autonomous strategic behavior can be illuminated. The research discussed here was conducted in a division of a large, diversified, high-technology firm. Twenty-three organization members drawn from four divisions, several functional specialties, and multiple levels in the organization's hierarchy played a role in the new product development process. The communication networks correspond to two critical milestones of the project and are provided in Figure 11.1.

- Milestone 1. An individual manager initiates informal assessment of the market and of the technical feasibility.

- Milestone 2. The organization formally endorses and funds the project.

Project Initiation

The idea that spawned the proposed project originated with a salesperson 19 (Figure 11.1(a)), who had identified a problem that a potential customer was having with a piece of equipment. Because the required product or technology differed significantly from the firm's existing offerings, the salesperson discussed the opportunity with manager 2, who emerged as a product champion. Figure 11.1(a) shows that the product champion basically became the point from which the vast majority of communications radiated. Many of the communications were merely dyadic, involving just the product champion and other organization members. A product manager 8 provided important market information; personnel of other divisions (e.g., managers 12 and 17) provided technical information and some critical equipment (on loan); others provided informal

---

[9] Modesto A. Maidique, "Entrepreneurs, Champions, and Technological Innovations," *Sloan Management Review*, 21 (Spring 1980), pp. 59–76; see also Jane M. Howell, "Champions of Technological Innovation," *Administrative Science Quarterly*, 35 (June 1990), pp. 317–341.

[10] Michael G. Duerr, *The Commercial Development of New Products* (New York: The Conference Board, 1986), p. 32.

[11] Hutt, Reingen, and Ronchetto, "Tracing Emergent Processes in Marketing Strategy Formation," pp. 4–19.

FIGURE 11.1   **Communication Structure**

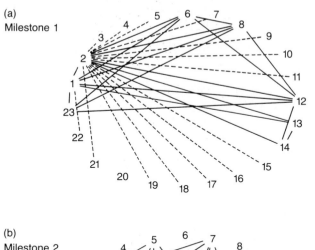

(a)
Milestone 1

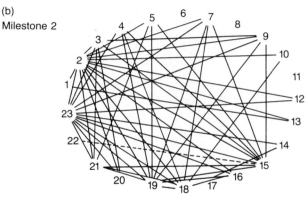

(b)
Milestone 2

——— Dyadic Communication Link within Groups
– – – – Dyadic Communication Link

Source: Adapted from Michael D. Hutt, Peter H. Reingen, and John R. Ronchetto, Jr., "Tracing Emergent Processes in Marketing Strategy Formation," *Journal of Marketing*, 52 (January 1988), p. 11. Published by the American Marketing Association.

support: (R&D director 14, market manager 18, and business unit manager 7, the vice president).

The product champion was instrumental in defining the market opportunity, in exploring the technical feasibility of the project, and in demonstrating this feasibility to customers by using borrowed and adapted equipment. These actions were taken more than one year before the project was funded or formally recognized within the firm's planning hierarchy.

Project Endorsement

Once market interest had been stimulated, the product champion increased the visibility of the project and pursued it more openly within regular corporate channels. As the project moved toward formal corporate approval, other managers assumed prominent roles in the strategy formulation process. A product manager 15 supported the efforts of the product champion and engaged in a web of project-related communications across the division (see Figure 11.1(b)). A market manager 18 and a research engineer 23 were also crucial in keeping top management informed and enthusiastic about the project.

As the momentum for the project increased, the roles and responsibilities of key participants in the process were clarified and the strategy formulation process became more formalized. Note from Figure 11.1(b) how the organization members become tightly interconnected in a web of project-related communications. The autonomous strategic initiative is now a part of the firm's formal planning routine and concept of strategy.

Managing Innovation: Implications

The opposing tendencies toward either stability or change in the new product planning process raise a challenging set of implications for business marketing managers. First, entrepreneurial initiatives cannot be precisely planned, but they can be nurtured and encouraged. Some recommend that the planning and budgeting process should shift away from the primary role of rationing resources toward a role that emphasizes seeking opportunities and taking risks.[12] Others argue that top management ". . . need not encourage entrepreneurship; it need only make sure not to suppress it."[13]

Second, autonomous strategic initiatives could be encouraged by facilitating the exchange of information between the organization's functional areas and business units. For example, distributing an inventory of the R&D projects that are under way throughout the corporation, and indicating the names of the project leaders, would enhance the flow of technical information in both the formal and the informal networks. Nurturing communications among marketing personnel (including field salespersons) and R&D managers would also be profitable. Clearly, the marketing function can assume a pivotal role in the acquisition and dissemination of information crucial to entrepreneurial initiatives.

By gathering critical environmental information concerning threats and opportunities, by serving as an advocate for desired strategic options, and by channeling organizational attention to these options, business marketing managers assume a critical role in the management of innovation within the firm. Crucial to this process in many firms is the development of a technology strategy.

---

[12]James B. Quinn, *Strategies for Change: Logical Incrementalism* (Homewood, IL: Irwin, 1980).

[13]Burgelman, "Corporate Entrepreneurship and Strategic Management: Insights from a Process Study," p. 1361; and Rosabeth Moss Kanter, "Swimming in Newstreams: Mastering Innovation Dilemmas," *California Management Review*, 31 (Summer 1989), pp. 45–69.

THE GLOBAL MARKETPLACE
Innovation and U.S. Competitiveness

After new scientific knowledge yields a radically innovative product such as nylon or the computer chip, there follows a less dramatic and rather grueling process of innovation—a process which is often far more critical to competitive success. Governed by the product life cycle, this cyclic process centers on incremental improvements, not breakthroughs. The firm works to refine the product, customize it for more market segments, make it more reliable, or provide it to the market more cheaply.

A leading technology expert, Ralph E. Gomory, president of the Alfred P. Sloan Foundation, offers this incisive analysis of U.S. competitiveness:

I cannot stress enough that what ground U.S. consumer electronics and automobile producers have already lost *cannot* be attributed to failures of new science or to failures of innovation. We originated those industries and then fell behind in making refinements—behind the Japanese commitment to quality design and careful manufacturing, not behind in science and new ideas. . . . Our weaknesses will not be cured by doing better science. We must reform the way that we approach cyclic product improvement. In the key industries that are problems today, we have been good starters, the Japanese have been good finishers.

Source: Ralph E. Gomory, "From the 'Ladder of Science' to the Product Development Cycle," *Harvard Business Review*, 67 (November–December 1989), pp. 101–102.

THE TECHNOLOGY PORTFOLIO[14]

Eastman Kodak, Lockheed, IBM, and the management teams of other corporations failed to recognize the major technological opportunity that xerographic copying presented. These firms were among the many that turned down the chance to participate with the small and unknown Haloid Company in refining and commercializing this technology. In the end, Haloid pursued it alone and transformed this one technological opportunity into the Xerox Corporation. Among the "tales of high tech," this will remain a classic.

Technological change is "a great equalizer, eroding the competitive advantage of even well-entrenched firms and propelling others to the forefront. Many of today's great firms grew out of technological changes that they were able to exploit."[15] Clearly, the long-run competitive position of most industrial firms depends on their ability to manage, increase, and exploit their technology base.

---

[14] Noel Capon and Rashi Glazer, "Marketing and Technology: A Strategic Coalignment," *Journal of Marketing*, 51 (July 1987), pp. 1–14.

[15] Michael E. Porter, "Technology and Competitive Advantage," *Journal of Business Strategy*, 6 (Winter 1985), p. 60; and Tamara J. Erickson, John F. Magee, Philip A. Roussel, and Komol N. Saad, "Managing Technology as Business Strategy," *Sloan Management Review*, 31 (Spring 1990), pp. 73–83.

The technology portfolio provides a tool that the business marketer can use to evaluate the set of technologies in the firm's asset base, how various technologies complement one another, and how they might be better exploited to gain a competitive advantage. Observe in Figure 11.2 that the entries in the technology portfolio are technologies rather than products. The vertical axis reflects a time dimension and is divided into two intervals reflecting the premarket and postmarket phases of technology exploitation. Each of these phases is further subdivided. The premarket phase is split into the research and the development stages of technology generation, and the postmarket phase is split into the familiar high- and low-growth stages of the product life cycle. Thus, the vertical axis traces the flow of a particular technology through its life cycle, from its conception as a basic research idea through its high growth to its ultimate decline in the low-growth stage of market exploitation.

Competitive Position

The horizontal axis of the technology portfolio captures the relative strength or competitive position of the firm. In the postmarket phase (lower portion of Figure 11.2), attention centers on the relative market share that a particular technology enjoys in the firm's portfolio: high versus low. By contrast, the premarket phase (upper portion) applies to relative technology strength and indicates the extent to which the firm is a leader or follower in the research and/or development of a given technology.

The technology portfolio provides a portrait of how a firm is distributing its resources across its mix of technologies and of where these technologies stand in development, market exploitation, and competitive strength. To ensure both current and future returns, a well-managed set of technologies should be balanced in the matrix in terms of both distribution and size. In particular, heavy concentration of large circles in any part of the portfolio implies that the firm's total flow of resources will be difficult to sustain.

Technology Strategy and Competitive Advantage

Each entry in the technology portfolio may provide the foundation for several products. For example, Honda applies its multivalve cylinder technology to power-generation equipment, cars, motorcycles, and lawn mowers.[16] Because the products derived from a single technology are likely to differ in terms of competitive position and market-segment growth, a single position in the technology portfolio gives rise to multiple entries in the product portfolio (see Figure 11.3). Thus, the single entry in the technology portfolio represents a composite measure (or weighted average) of the associated product portfolio.

---

[16]T. Michael Nevens, Gregory L. Summe, and Bro Uttal, "Commercializing Technology: What the Best Companies Do," *Harvard Business Review*, 60 (May–June 1990), pp. 154–163.

FIGURE 11.2   **The Technology Portfolio**

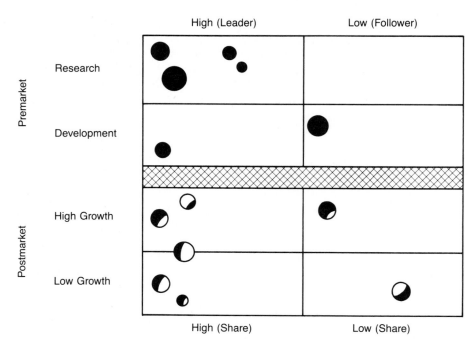

Source: Noel Capon and Rashi Glazer, "Marketing and Technology: A Strategic Coalignment," *Journal of Marketing*, 51 (July 1987), p. 10. Published by the American Marketing Association.

Commercializing Technology: What the Winners Do

In many business markets—such as copiers, facsimile machines, computers, semiconductor production equipment, and pharmaceuticals—industry leadership clearly depends on superior commercialization skills. To isolate the differences between leaders and laggards in commercializing technology, McKinsey & Company examined the process followed by firms in the United States, Japan, and Europe. The study found that high-performing companies such as Hewlett-Packard, which effectively manages the

FIGURE 11.3   **Relationship between Technology and Product Portfolios**

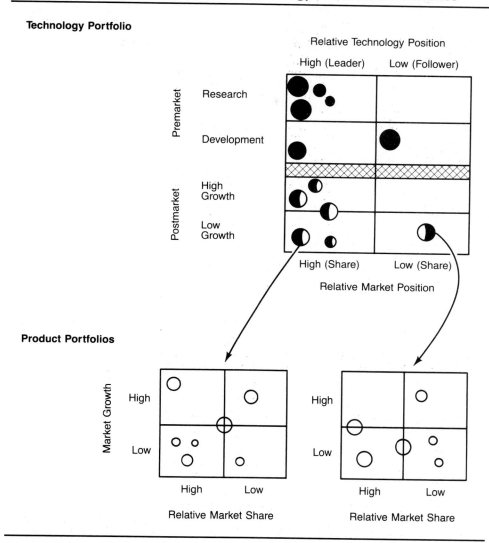

Source: Noel Capon and Rashi Glazer, "Marketing and Technology: A Strategic Coalignment," *Journal of Marketing,* 51 (July 1987), p. 11. Published by the American Marketing Association.

commercialization process, differ from low-performing organizations in four respects. "They get products or processes to the market faster, use their technologies in products across a wider range of markets, introduce more products, and incorporate a greater breadth of technologies in them."[17]

---

[17] Ibid., p. 157.

1. Time to Market

How to speed up the product development cycle is the primary concern of nearly every senior executive of all major industrial corporations. When base technologies are widely available and product life cycles are short, getting to the market quickly can be essential. Fast-cycle companies enjoy many advantages:[18]

- The latest technology can be used closer to the time of introduction.

- Because of the shorter time horizon, customer needs can be forecast more accurately.

- Cost reductions are realized more quickly as new products with more effective designs replace older, less effective designs.

- Customers are willing to pay a premium price for a fresher product or service that more precisely meets their needs.

Xerox, during its widely acclaimed turnaround, cut development cycles from seven years to as little as two years, shaved development costs by as much as two-thirds with a savings of more than $100 million a year, and dramatically improved product quality. Similarly, Hewlett-Packard seized a significant share of the microcomputer printer business by introducing, in quick succession, a broad line of printers based on innovative laser, ink-jet, and software technologies.

2. Range of Markets

High-performing companies recover high development costs by leveraging core technologies across multiple product and geographical markets. For example, Canon exploits its basic investments in the miniaturized motors in its cameras by incorporating these motors in copiers also. Similarly, Hewlett-Packard applies technology from its instrumentation business in six highly differentiated markets, from oscilloscopes to cardiac analyzers. For companies that lack the ability to spread technology costs, joint ventures and technology cross-licensing arrangements are effective solutions.

3. Number of Products

Market fragmentation creates opportunities for organizations that can easily adapt products in order to appeal to market niches. Leading companies serve more market segments than followers. Even in mature industrial markets such as machine tools, there is the opportunity to gain market share by developing models that offer a variety of trade-offs: ease of setup, flexibility, throughput, and price. Successful organizations serve such segments by triggering the commercialization process not just once, but three and four times, and by incorporating incremental changes—not necessarily major breakthroughs—in each new model.

---

[18] George Stalk, Jr., and Thomas M. Hout, *Competing Against Time: How Time-based Competition Is Re-shaping Global Markets* (New York: The Free Press, 1990).

4. Breadth of Technologies

Because products for many markets incorporate an increasing number of technologies, companies must be able to master, or to acquire and integrate, all of these technologies if they are to compete. Consider the copier market. A decade ago, competing in that market meant pursuing innovation in mechanical paper movement, optics, and fusing systems. Competence in these technologies is still needed, but successful competitors today must be at the cutting edge of other technology areas: control hardware and software, organic photoreceptors, and panel displays. Companies that fall behind in any one technology area are at risk of producing an uncompetitive product.

THE NEW PRODUCT DEVELOPMENT PROCESS

To sustain their competitive advantage, leading-edge firms such as Canon, Hewlett-Packard, and Boeing make new product development a top management priority. They get managers and employees from across the organization directly involved to speed actions and decisions. Because new product ventures can represent a significant risk as well as an important opportunity, new product development requires systematic thought. The high expectations ascribed to new products are often not fulfilled. Worse, many new industrial products fail. Although the definitions of failure are somewhat elusive, research suggests that 30 to 40 percent of industrial products fail.[19] While there may be some debate over the number of failures, there is no debate over the fact that a new product rejected by the market constitutes a substantial waste to the firm and to society.

This section examines key components of the new product development process: (1) organization of the new product development effort, (2) sources of new product ideas, (3) new product review and evaluation, and (4) determinants of new product success and failure.

New Product Organizational Arrangements

"Except for the simplest of products and projects—line extensions, product updates and the like—product innovation cannot be a one-department show."[20] The strong need for integrated effort between marketing, production, engineering, and other functional areas in developing business marketing strategy has been emphasized throughout this volume. When product designers pay attention to how the product will be manufactured and take advantage of existing process and support capabilities, and when the design of new processes and new field services is geared to new product

---

[19] See, for example, Robert G. Cooper, "New Product Success in Industrial Firms," *Industrial Marketing Management*, 11 (July 1982), pp. 215–223; and Booz, Allen and Hamilton, *New Product Management for the 1980s* (New York: Booz, Allen and Hamilton, Inc., 1982).

[20] Robert G. Cooper, *Winning at New Products* (Reading, Mass.: Addison-Wesley Publishing Company, 1986), p. 42; and Paul S. Adler, Henry E. Riggs, and Steven C. Wheelwright, "Product Development Know-How: Trading Tactics for Strategy," *Sloan Management Review*, 30 (Fall 1989), pp. 7–17.

plans in the design lab, the firm is likely to capture truly superior performance, quality, and cost advantages.

Although the specific design of the new product function is dependent on many factors such as company size and structure, three elements are worthy of consideration.

1. *New product committee.* A top management committee of representatives from marketing, production, accounting, engineering, and other areas review new product proposals. Although not involved in actual development, the committee must evaluate new product plans. At Eastman Chemicals, this role is performed by the Innovations Committee, chaired by the director of research and development.[21]

2. *New product department.* A department is created in many large firms to generate and evaluate new ideas, to direct and coordinate development, and to implement field testing and precommercialization of the new product. The department head generally has substantial authority and access to top management.

3. *New product venture team.* A group is specifically brought together from various operating departments and charged with the responsibility of bringing a specific product to market or a specific new business into being.[22] To illustrate, Signode Corporation, the leader in plastic and metal stripping systems, found that its plastic sheets had twice the tensile strength of competing products. A venture team was formed to identify new uses and an array of high-performance plastic products was uncovered (e.g., high-strength plastic mesh for holding together paved roads and for preventing dirt slides and beach erosion). The venture team was dissolved once these successful products were established.[23]

Although a number of alternative schemes are used to structure the development process, the need to effectively coordinate the activities of individual functional areas is moving organizations toward the adoption of an integrated, team-based approach. Many industrial firms have learned that it takes more than the accepted basics of high quality, low cost, and differentiation to excel in the fiercely competitive world of commercial new product development: speed and flexibility are also required. Speed, or compressing time-to-market, requires a tighter coupling among functional departments such as marketing, engineering, manufacturing, purchasing, distribution, and services.

Sequential versus Integrated Process[24]

The new emphasis on speed and flexibility calls for a different organizational approach for managing new product development programs. The traditional sequential or "relay-race" approach to product development is similar to a relay race, with one group

---

[21] Duerr, *The Commercial Development of New Products*, p. 33.

[22] John F. Rockart and James F. Short, "IT in the 1990s: Managing Organizational Interdependence," *Sloan Management Review*, 30 (Winter 1989), pp. 7–17.

[23] Duerr, *The Commercial Development of New Products*, p. 44.

[24] Hirotaka Takeuchi and Ikujiro Nohaka, "The New Product Development Game," *Harvard Business Review*, 64 (January–February 1986), pp. 137–146.

of functional specialists passing the baton to the next group. The project moves sequentially from phase to phase: concept development, feasibility testing, development, pilot production, final production, and market launch. As one function waits for another, time is wasted. A bottleneck in one phase can slow or even halt the entire process.

An alternative method, the integrated or "rugby" approach, is being employed by successful time-based competitors. Here the new product development process is characterized by the constant interaction of a hand-picked, interfunctional team whose members work together from start to finish. As in rugby, the ball gets passed within the team—it moves as a unit toward a singular objective. Rather than moving in defined, highly structured stages, the phases overlap considerably with the integrated approach. The shift from a linear to an integrated approach (1) encourages trial and error in the new product development process and (2) stimulates new kinds of learning and thinking within the firm at different levels and functions. "Team members engage in a continual process of trial and error to narrow down the number of alternatives that they must consider. They also acquire broad knowledge and diverse skills, which help them create a versatile team capable of solving an array of problems fast."[25]

Sources of New Product Ideas

The business marketer should be alert to new product ideas and to their sources, both inside and outside the company. Internally, the new product ideas may flow from salespersons who are close to customer needs, from R&D specialists who are close to new technological developments, and from top management who know the company strengths and weaknesses. Externally, ideas may come from channel members, such as distributors or customers, or from an assessment of competitive moves.

Eric von Hippel challenges the traditional view that marketers typically introduce new products to a passive market.[26] His research suggests that the customers in the business market often develop the idea for a new product and even select the supplier to make that product. The customer is responding to the perceived *capability* of the business marketer, rather than to a specific physical product. This points up the need for involving the customers in new product development, and for promoting corporate capability to consumers (idea generators). Consider the strategy of Texas Instruments Incorporated. Figure 11.4 shows an award-winning ad for their digital signal processor. The ad illustrates the benefits of the technology in one industry application and its potential and versatility for others (i.e., "Explore your ideas with us").

Because many industrial product markets for high-technology and, in particular, capital equipment consist of a small number of high-volume buying firms, special attention must be given to the needs of **lead users**, which include a small number of highly influential buying organizations who are consistent early adopters of new

---

[25] Ibid., p. 141.

[26] Eric von Hippel, "Get New Products from Customers," *Harvard Business Review*, 60 (March–April 1982), pp. 117–122; see also von Hippel, *The Sources of Innovation* (New York: Oxford University Press, 1988).

FIGURE 11.4 **An Award-Winning Ad that Suggests the Potential and Versatility of a Technology**

Source: Courtesy, Texas Instruments Incorporated.

technologies.[27] Lead users face needs that will be general in the marketplace, but they confront these needs months or years before the bulk of that marketplace encounters them. In addition, they are positioned to benefit significantly by obtaining a solution that satisfies those needs. For example, Intel is a lead user of production equipment tailored to the delicate task of forming advanced microchips.

Screening New Product Ideas

Before committing resources to the costly process of transforming an idea into a finished industrial product, the firm must scrutinize the idea. Firms that fail to properly assess market needs, the level of demand potential, production requirements, the

---

[27] Eric von Hippel, "Lead Users: A Source of Novel Product Concepts," *Management Science*, 32 (July 1986), pp. 791–805.

INSIDE BUSINESS MARKETING
Seeds for Innovation at G.E.

To speed the transfer of technology from the R&D lab to the market, General Electric encourages its scientists to dream and invent—and then to shop the invention around the various G.E. divisions. While selling their ideas throughout the organization, researchers often uncover promising applications far afield from the original intentions. To illustrate, a medical diagnostic technology used for imaging the human body became a cost-saving device for inspecting jet engines. Sophisticated coating and machining techniques developed for aircraft engines were profitably transferred to G.E.'s power generation business.

To nurture the flow of ideas within the research lab, the director encourages close, informal contacts between researchers of different disciplines. Emphasizing creativity, G.E. regularly treats researchers to art exhibits and classical music concerts in the atrium of the corporate research and development center. Ideas are also exchanged at a regular Friday evening "free beer and pretzel party." Industry analysts contend that this cross-pollination of technology provides an important reason why G.E. dominates in many of its markets. In fact, General Motors and other firms have sent representatives to General Electric's R&D lab to uncover the secret.

Source: Amal Kumar Naj, "G.E.'s Latest Invention: A Way to Move Ideas from Lab to Market," *The Wall Street Journal* (June 14, 1990), pp. A-1, A-9.

nature of the buying process, the aggressiveness of competitors, the extent of technical service requirements, and related factors are doomed to failure.[28] To guard against such omissions, many business marketers have developed elaborate screening procedures for evaluating new products from several perspectives.

Monsanto Corporation uses a new product profile chart (Table 11.2). The major points for analysis include these aspects: (1) financial, (2) marketing and product, (3) production and engineering, and (4) research and development.[29] The chart analyzes the profit, sales, and cash requirements of a venture, as well as the degree to which the potential product fits with the production, the R&D, and the marketing capabilities of the firm. The quality of this review often rests squarely on the firm's knowledge of market needs; each potential application may represent a distinct market segment with special requirements, and it is often necessary to examine each potential application separately.[30] For example, a new control switch might have potential applications in appliances, computers, automobiles, and telephones.

---

[28] Robert G. Cooper and Elko Kleinschmidt, "An Investigation into the New Product Process: Steps, Deficiencies, and Impact," *Journal of Product Innovation Management*, 3 (June 1986), pp. 71–85.

[29] John S. Harris, "New Product Profile Chart," *CHEMTECH* (September 1976), pp. 554–562.

[30] For example, see Pierre Chenu and David L. Wilemon, "A Decision Process for New Product Selection," *Industrial Marketing Management*, 3 (1973), pp. 33–46.

TABLE 11.2   **A New Product Profile Chart**

Financial Aspects	Return on investment (before taxes)
	Estimated annual sales
	New fixed capital payout time
	Time to reach estimated sales volume
Marketing and Product Aspects	Similarity to present product lines
	Effect on present products
	Marketability to present customers
	Number of potential customers
	Suitability of present sales force
	Market stability
	Market trend
	Technical service
Production and Engineering Aspects	Required corporate size
	Raw materials
	Equipment
	Process familiarity
Research and Development Aspects	Research investment payout time
	Development investment payout time
	Research know-how
	Patent status

Source: Reprinted with permission from "New Product Profile Chart," by John S. Harris, *CHEMTECH* (September 1976), p. 559. Copyright 1976 the American Chemical Society.

To implement the new product profile chart, firms may rate each dimension on a scale. For example, the dimension of "marketability to present customers" may be rated as follows:

- -2 entirely different customers
- -1 some present customers
- $+1$ mostly present customers
- $+2$ all present customers

The assignment of numerical values provides a visual indication of the level of desirability of the venture for each criterion. Because the selected criteria are not equally important and because they vary by project, this weighting system does not replace the need for managerial judgment. Management must weigh the relative importance of each criterion to a specific project before evaluating the project on that dimension.

Determinants of New Product Success and Failure

A prime limitation of the new product checklist approach is that neither the screening criteria nor their relative importance is empirically derived. Which factors are most important in determining the success or failure of the new product?

The Determinants of Success

According to Robert Cooper, three factors appear to be crucial to new product success.[31] The **level of product uniqueness and superiority** is the most important. Highly innovative products that improve on competing offerings gain a strong differential advantage. They offer clear benefits, such as reduced customer costs, and are of a higher quality (e.g., more durable) than the products of competitors.

Market knowledge and marketing proficiency are pivotal in new product outcomes. As might be expected, business marketers with a solid understanding of market needs are likely to succeed. Cooper describes the market planning for the successful products he examined: "Market information was very complete: there was a solid understanding of the customers' needs, wants, and preferences; of the customers' buying behavior and price sensitivity; of the size and trends of the market; and of the competitive situation. Finally, the market launch was well planned, well targeted, proficiently executed, and backed by appropriate resources."[32]

Technical and production synergy and proficiency constitute another important new product dimension. When industrial firms can draw upon technical and production resource bases that are compatible, and when they can proficiently pass through the stages of the new product development process (e.g., product development, prototype testing, pilot production, and production start-up), their products succeed.

In addition to the three factors above, an **international orientation** also contributes to the success of product innovation.[33] New products that are designed and developed to meet foreign requirements, and which are targeted at world or nearest-neighbor export markets, outperform domestic products on almost every measure of performance, including success rate, profitability, and domestic and foreign market shares. Underlying this success is a strong international focus in market research, product testing with customers, trial selling, and launch efforts.

Barriers to Success

Cooper uncovered three barriers to success that are likewise worthy of emphasis:

1. A high-priced product, relative to competition, having no economic advantage to the customer

2. A dynamic market that has many new product introductions

3. A competitive market in which customers are already well satisfied.[34]

---

[31] Robert G. Cooper, *Winning at New Products*, pp. 13–33; and Cooper, "The Dimensions of Industrial New Product Success and Failure," *Journal of Marketing*, 43 (Summer 1979), pp. 93–103. See also Gary L. Lilien and Eunsang Yoon, "Determinants of New Industrial Product Performance," Report 4-1986, Institute for the Study of Business Markets, College of Business Administration, The Pennsylvania State University.

[32] Cooper, *Winning at New Products*, p. 29.

[33] Elko J. Kleinschmidt and Robert G. Cooper, "The Performance Impact of an International Orientation on Product Innovation," *European Journal of Marketing*, 22 (9), pp. 56–71.

[34] Cooper, "The Dimensions of Industrial New Product Success and Failure," p. 101.

Overall, this research points up the critical importance of the *product* in business marketing strategy. Likewise, new industrial product success is heavily dependent on strong market orientation blended with strong technical and production capability.

THE NEW INDUSTRIAL PRODUCT ADOPTION PROCESS

The industrial product adoption process has been conceptualized as having two basic stages: (1) the initiation stage and (2) the implementation stage.[35] Each has important substages, briefly described in Table 11.3.

What is the importance of various information sources throughout the adoption process? In general, mass communication, including trade journals, tends to be the most significant information source in triggering awareness of a new industrial product. Salespersons and the proposals they provide dominate the remaining phases.[36] However, other forms of advertising, such as direct mail pieces and catalogs, are also used by decision participants throughout the organizational buying decision process.[37] The organizational buyer's need for information of all types increases as the product moves from initiation to implementation, particularly when a buyer perceives great risk in adoption.

As informal information sources, opinion leaders within the organization are important, especially in the later stages of the process.[38] In contrast to other organization members, opinion leaders tend to have more exposure to trade journals.

In designing promotional support for a new industrial product, the marketer should develop a comprehensive plan that includes several communication vehicles. Technical- and trade-journal advertising stimulates awareness; personal selling identifies the key buying influences and serves as a valued source at all stages during the buying process. Advertising and direct mail can complement and bolster the personal selling effort.

Adoption and Buyer–Seller Relationships

Since many new technologies are customer-initiated, business marketers must be prepared to manage delicate buyer–seller relationships throughout the new product development process. In fact, the firm should "limit the resources and time expended

---

[35] Gerald Zaltman, Robert Duncan, and Jonny Holbek, *Innovations and Organizations* (New York: Wiley-Interscience, 1973), p. 158; see also Urban B. Ozanne and Gilbert A. Churchill, "Adoption Research: Information Sources in the Industrial Purchasing Decision," in Robert L. King, ed., *Marketing and the New Science of Planning* (Chicago: American Marketing Association, 1968), pp. 352–359.

[36] Frederick E. Webster, Jr., "Informal Communication in Industrial Markets," *Journal of Marketing Research*, 7 (May 1970), pp. 186–189; see also Ozanne and Churchill, ibid., pp. 352–359.

[37] Rowland T. Moriarty, Jr., and Robert E. Spekman, "An Empirical Investigation of the Information Sources Used During the Industrial Buying Process," *Journal of Marketing Research*, 21 (May 1984), pp. 137–147.

[38] John A. Martilla, "Word-of-Mouth Communications in the Industrial Adoption Process," *Journal of Marketing Research*, 8 (May 1971), pp. 173–178. For related research, see John A. Czepiel, "Word-of-Mouth Processes in the Diffusion of a Major Technological Innovation," *Journal of Marketing Research*, 11 (May 1974), pp. 172–180.

TABLE 11.3   **Stages of the New Industrial Product**

Stage	Description
I. Initiation Stage	
Knowledge or awareness substage	Organizational decision makers perceive that there is a discrepancy between desired and actual performance.
Formation of attitudes toward the innovation substage	Important attitudinal dimensions include the openness of organizational decision makers to the innovation and their perception of the potential for innovation.
Decision substage	Information concerning the potential innovation is evaluated. If organizational members are highly motivated to innovate, or if their attitudes are highly favorable toward innovation, implementation is likely.
II. Implementation Stage	
Initial implementation substage	The organization makes the first attempt to utilize the specific innovation.
Continued or sustained implementation substage	A successful and relatively trouble-free initial implementation increases the likelihood that the innovation will be further utilized by the organization.

Source: Adapted from Gerald Zaltman, Robert Duncan, and Jonny Holbek, *Innovations and Organizations* (New York: Wiley Interscience, 1973), p. 158.

on developing a new product or technology before expending resources on establishing some form of relationship with potential adopting organizations."[39] Special attention should be given to lead users (discussed earlier). Lead users, "who face tomorrow's needs today, can be instrumental in identifying new product opportunities, testing new product prototypes, and providing opinion leadership for later adopters."[40]

FORMULATING NEW INDUSTRIAL PRODUCT STRATEGY

Market knowledge and marketing proficiency characterize industrial firms that launch successful new products. Before a commitment is made to a particular product design, the industrial product planner must know the key buying criteria or specifications that target market segments use in purchasing such products. Unless the new product has those specifications, it will not be accepted by the market.

---

[39] Roger A. More, "Developer/Adopter Relationships in New Industrial Product Situations," *Journal of Business Research*, 14 (December 1986), p. 515.

[40] Thomas S. Robertson and Hubert Gatignon, "Competitive Effects on Technology Diffusion," *Journal of Marketing*, 50 (July 1986), p. 5; and von Hippel, "Lead Users: A Source of Novel Product Concepts," pp. 791–805.

The Industrial Market Response Model[41]

Jean-Marie Choffray and Gary Lilien provide a model for dealing with new product strategy decisions. Their approach, the industrial market response model, has four components, each directly relating organizational buying behavior to a key product strategy area:

1. *Awareness.* This component relates the level of marketing effort invested in an industrial product to the probability that an individual in an organization will be aware of the product.

2. *Acceptance.* This component relates product "design characteristics to the likelihood that an organization will find the product feasible."[42] Of the organizations surveyed about the purchase of industrial air-conditioning systems, 50 percent require that the cost per ton be less than $988.

3. *Individual evaluation.* These components "relate evaluation of product characteristics to the preferences of each category of decision participants."[43] The criterion of key importance to those evaluating industrial air-conditioning systems varied by job category. Plant managers were most interested in operating costs, top managers in up-to-date technology, and heating and air-conditioning consultants in noise level in the plant.

4. *Group decision.* This component relates group choice to the preference of the members composing the group.

Estimating Market Share and Sales

By using this model as a framework for gathering market information, the industrial marketer can forecast market share and sales for the new product:

$$
\text{Market Share} = \begin{array}{c} \text{Fraction of} \\ \text{potential} \\ \text{buying firms} \\ \text{aware of new} \\ \text{product} \end{array} \times \begin{array}{c} \text{Fraction of firms} \\ \text{for whom the} \\ \text{product} \\ \text{is feasible} \\ \text{(given awareness)} \end{array} \times \begin{array}{c} \text{Fraction of firms} \\ \text{preferring the product} \\ \text{to other alternatives} \\ \text{(given awareness} \\ \text{and feasibility)} \end{array}
$$

$$
\text{Sales} = \begin{array}{c} \text{Market} \\ \text{potential} \\ \text{(opportunity)} \end{array} \times \begin{array}{c} \text{Projected} \\ \text{market} \\ \text{share} \end{array}
$$

---

[41] This section is largely based on Jean-Marie Choffray and Gary L. Lilien, "Assessing Response to Industrial Marketing Strategy," *Journal of Marketing,* 42 (April 1978), pp. 20–31; see also Jerome E. Scott and Stephen K. Keiser, "Forecasting Acceptance of New Industrial Products with Judgment Modeling," *Journal of Marketing,* 48 (Spring 1984), pp. 54–67, and Vijay Mahajan, Eitan Muller, and Frank Bass, "New Product Diffusion Models in Marketing: A Review and Directions for Research," *Journal of Marketing,* 54 (January 1990), pp. 1–26.

[42] Choffray and Lilien, ibid., p. 24.

[43] Ibid., p. 25.

Evaluating Product Design Scenarios

The marketer can also use the industrial market response model to evaluate the impact of alternative product designs on market share and sales. By comparing competitive product designs to the specifications preferred by key market segments, the business marketer can isolate market segments that are inadequately served.[44] Furthermore, customer perceptions of possible product design trade-offs can be examined. Consider the case of a marketer planning a new high-speed packaging system. The marketer must ask how much potential buyers would be willing to pay for incremental improvements in processing speed.

Designing New Product Strategy

The response model can also be used to improve pricing decisions and to develop and target advertising and sales presentations. Advertising messages might emphasize the particular product benefits sought by each member of the buying center. Recall from our discussion in Chapter 4 that messages consistent with the organizational buyer's frame of reference are much more likely to be retained. Clearly, the development of sound industrial marketing strategy rests on knowledge of organizational buying behavior. By linking the two, the industrial market response model makes an important contribution.

Forecasting Performance and Developing a Launch Strategy

Drawing on an international data base of more than 100 industrial product innovations, Eunsang Yoon and Gary L. Lilien explored several features of new product innovation performance.[45] Their model of innovation performance (see Figure 11.5) indicates that R&D and marketing decisions, as well as market characteristics, influence the sales performance of a new product. Observe that two types of new products are the focus of interest: (1) **original new products**, technological breakthroughs that often rely on technologies never before used in the industry, and (2) **reformulated new products**, product line extensions or modifications. Original new products differ from reformulated ones on several counts.

Short-Term Performance

For original new products, first-year market share is higher when (1) the degree of competitiveness in the market is low, (2) the product-class life cycle is in the introductory stage, (3) the market growth rate is low, and (4) the number of competitors is small. Since the success of the original new product depends heavily on uncontrollable market factors, the choice of the specific market opportunity and product is critical.

---

[44] For a comprehensive discussion of the supporting methodology, see Jean-Marie Choffray and Gary L. Lilien, "DESIGNOR: A Decision Support Procedure for Industrial Product Design," *Journal of Business Research*, 10 (June 1982), pp. 185–197.

[45] Eunsang Yoon and Gary L. Lilien, "New Industrial Product Performance: The Effects of Market Characteristics and Strategy," *Journal of Product Innovation Management*, 3 (September 1985), pp. 134–144.

FIGURE 11.5   **A Model of Innovation Performance**

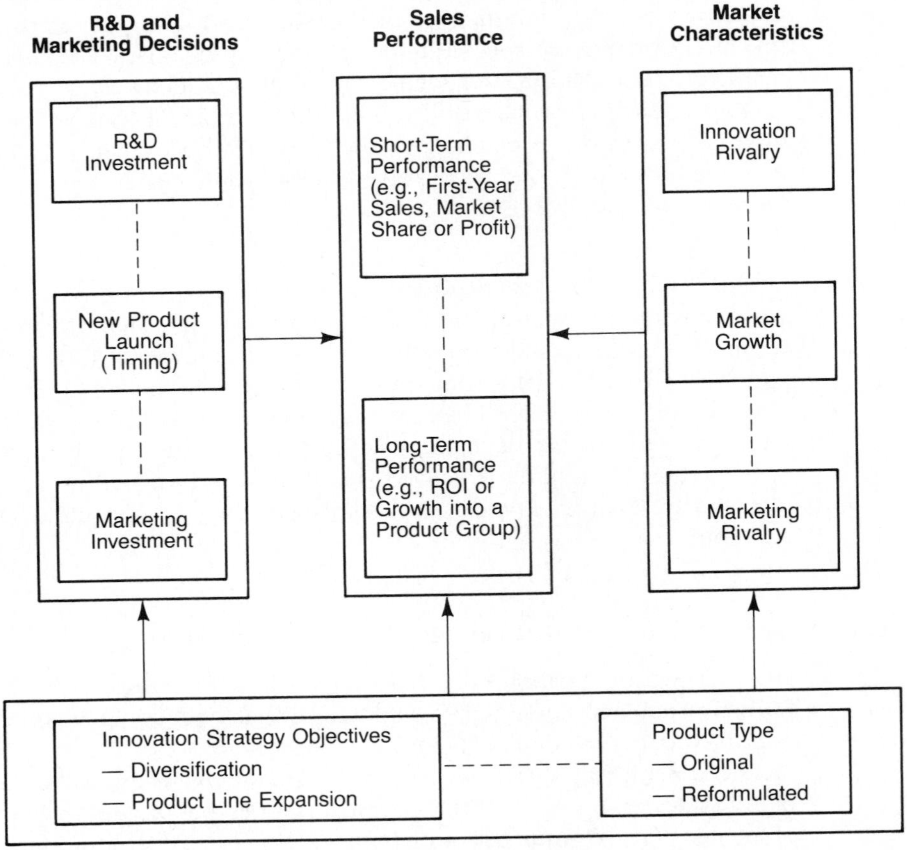

Source: Reprinted by permission of the publisher from Eunsang Yoon and Gary L. Lilien, "New Industrial Product Performance: The Effects of Market Characteristics and Strategy," *Journal of Product Innovation*, 3 (September 1985), p. 136. Copyright 1985 by Elsevier Science Publishing Co., Inc.

A different picture emerges when explaining the initial market share performance of a reformulated product. First-year market share is higher for these products when (1) potential buyers' satisfaction with the service level of existing products is lower, (2) marketing efficiency in advertising and distribution is perceived to be higher, (3) a strategic objective for the reformulated new product is for expansion of the product group, and (4) the number of competitors and the competitiveness level of the market are low. Thus, dimensions related to market potential and competition are critical for explaining short-term performance for original new products, whereas variables related to the level of customer satisfaction with existing products and the strategy–product fit are especially important for reformulated products.

Long-Term Performance

Long-term performance was examined by determining whether or not the product (original or reformulated) developed into a product group. The following factors were found to be important determinants of the long-run success of a new industrial product:

- The degree of expertise in marketing activity of the innovating firm
- The marketing efficiency of the innovating firm
- The stage of the product life cycle at the new product's market launch time.

Launch Time

The initial sales performance of a new product is related to the timing of the product launch. The research uncovered some interesting results: ". . . it pays to launch a reformulated product as early as possible, while success levels were highest for original products where launch was delayed somewhat. This may reflect the greater care taken with new product and market development activities for original new products" (e.g., ironing out technical problems; refining strategy plans).[46]

SUMMARY

Product innovation is a high-risk and potentially rewarding process. Sustained growth is dependent on innovative products that respond to existing or emerging consumer needs. Effective managers of innovation channel and control its main directions, but have learned to maintain flexibility and expect surprises. Marketing managers pursue strategic activity within the firm that falls into two broad categories: induced and autonomous strategic behavior.

New product development efforts for existing businesses or market development projects for the firm's present products are the outgrowth of induced strategic initiatives. In contrast, autonomous strategic efforts take shape outside the firm's current concept of strategy, depart from the current course, and center on new categories of business opportunity; middle managers initiate the project, champion its development, and if successful, see the project integrated into the firm's concept of strategy.

The long-run competitive position of most business marketing firms depends on their ability to manage and increase their technological base. The technology portfolio provides the business marketer with a tool for evaluating the particular mix of technologies in the firm's asset base, analyzing the associated products that issue from each technology, and planning resource allocation for future technology scenarios.

Before committing substantial resources to a new product idea, the proposed venture must be carefully screened. An idea that successfully passes the screening must progress through a well-organized and integrated development process. In turn, marketers must understand that innovative products are carefully evaluated by

---

[46] Ibid., p. 143; see also Gary L. Lilien and Eunsang Yoon, "The Timing of Competitive Market Entry and New Product Performance," Report 3-1987, The Institute for the Study of Business Markets, College of Business Administration, The Pennsylvania State University.

consumers before they are adopted. The industrial market response model is a valuable tool when isolating appropriate product design features and when developing responsive marketing strategies. The initial sales performance of a new product is closely associated with the marketing efficiency of the seller, the market growth rate, the stage in the product life cycle, and the number of competitors in the marketplace.

Discussion Questions

1. Research by James B. Quinn suggests that few major innovations result from highly structured planning systems. What does this imply for the business marketer?

2. Compare and contrast induced and autonomous strategic behavior. Describe the role that the product champion assumes in the new product development process.

3. John Welch, Jr., chairman of General Electric Company, argues that much of the discussion of high-tech versus low-tech companies is misguided. He contends that technology lies at the heart of virtually every organization. Evaluate this position.

4. Illustrate the technology portfolio and discuss its relationship to a firm's product portfolio.

5. Within a given industry, in response to a given competitive environment, why do some firms build a competitive advantage on the basis of technology, while others do not?

6. Measurex Corporation manufactures computer control systems for the continuous-process industries (e.g., the paper industry). The natural tendency for a technology-based company is to slip into a product-driven mode of operation. John Gingerich, executive vice president, contends that the trick is to make the transition from a product-driven to a solutions-driven orientation—providing tangible results for customers. Describe how this orientation could be directly infused into a firm's new product development process.

7. The Los Angeles Motor Works Company has had numerous new products fail in the industrial market. As a marketing consultant, you have been asked to develop a review guide for screening new product ideas. To be useful, this checklist, or guide, should be relatively concise and should highlight priority areas in order of importance. Present your recommendations.

8. Those business marketers who appreciate the unprecedented advantages of getting new products to market sooner and orders to customers faster may well hold the primary tool for achieving competitive prominence in the decade ahead. In the face of this competitive environment, what is the most appropriate way to organize or structure the new product development process?

9. Critique this statement: "Industrial products and consumer products fail for the same basic reasons."

10. Business marketers often face a dilemma when selecting the appropriate time to launch a new product: should we act today and suffer the consequences of a premature introduction (e.g., technical bugs), or should we follow a more deliberate path and risk the loss of a pioneering position to competitors? Advise.

CHAPTER 12

Managing Services for Business Markets

The important and growing market for business services poses special challenges and meaningful opportunities for the marketing manager. This chapter explains the unique aspects of business services and explores the special role they play in the business market environment. After reading this chapter, you will understand:

1. the unique role and distinguishing characteristics of business services.

2. the key purchase criteria, attributes, and choice processes associated with service purchasing.

3. the significant factors that must be considered in formulating a service marketing strategy.

4. the special challenges associated with developing new business services.

5. the role that service plays in support of products and equipment.

6. the nature of, the size of, and the problems associated with international business service marketing.

NCR Corporation, the large, Ohio-based computer manufacturer, earned more than $10 million in revenues from an important account over a recent two-year time span. However, the account *did not* purchase a "product" from NCR until very recently when 50 terminals worth many thousands of dollars were purchased. What the account *did* purchase over the two-year period was a service: NCR performed maintenance service on 7,000 terminals for Online Computer Library Center (OCLC), a nonprofit organization in Dublin, Ohio, that provides data base services to libraries. When OCLC originally contracted with NCR for terminal maintenance, it did not own a single piece of NCR computer equipment. However, the organization was so impressed with the terminal maintenance service that when time came to purchase additional terminals, NCR was the equipment supplier selected.[1]

This example demonstrates the important role that services play in the business marketing environment. Many original equipment manufacturers are now using effective service and support as a core marketing strategy for creating sales growth; moreover, a vast array of "pure service" firms exist to supply businesses and organizations with everything from office cleaning to overnight delivery of correspondence.

Importantly, the marketing of business services has many unique aspects that set it apart from business products marketing. A recent book, *Service Breakthroughs: Changing the Rules of the Game*, succinctly captures the magnitude of the differences:

> Outstanding service organizations are managed differently from their merely 'good' competitors. Missions are stated differently. Managers act differently. Actions are based on totally different assumptions about the way success is achieved. And the results show it, in terms of both conventional measures of performance and the impact these services have on their competitors.[2]

This chapter will examine the nature of business services, the key buying behavior dimensions associated with their purchase, the major strategic elements related to services marketing, and the international environment for business services.

BUSINESS SERVICES: ROLE AND IMPORTANCE

The importance of services marketing is easy to demonstrate: the United States has become a service economy. In fact, fully 74 percent of the employment and 56 percent of the gross national product (GNP) (over $2.2 trillion) in the United States is accounted for by the service sector.[3] In the three years ending in 1988, the services sector added the equivalent of 6.6 million full-time employees, accounting for 92 percent of all new jobs in the period.[4] The dramatic growth in the service sector is occurring in both consumer and business markets.

According to John Case, business services are growing even in regions where manufacturing is in decline. Case suggests that three factors account for the growth of business services:[5]

---

[1] Based on Diane Lynn Kastiel, "Service and Support: High-Tech's New Battleground," *Business Marketing*, 72 (June 1987), p. 55.

[2] James L. Heskett, W. Earl Sasser, Jr., and Christopher W. L. Hart, *Service Breakthroughs: Changing the Rules of the Game* (New York: The Free Press, 1990), p. 1

[3] Jonathan C. Menes and Peter J. Reynolds, "1990 U.S. Industrial Outlook Predicts Continued Growth for Most Industries," *Business America*, 111 (January 29, 1990), p. 5

[4] Ibid., p. 5.

[5] John Case, "The Invisible Powerhouse," *INC.*, 11 (September 1989), p. 25.

1. *Manufacturing growth.* Manufacturing output is still growing despite the decline in the number of manufacturing employees. With this growth, the demand for services like trucking, advertising, and data processing continues its upward trend.

2. *Outsourcing.* Manufacturers of products are buying more services than they used to. The trend is to outsource functions and services that are not the company's core expertise (like the cafeteria, warehousing, and engineering).

3. *Innovations.* New services, never thought about ten years ago, are stimulating increasing services demand. Security systems, waste-management firms, and benefit specialists are examples of service innovations stimulating the rising service demand.

Services in the business-to-business market can be categorized in two distinct groups. The first category is **products supported by services**. In this situation, the wide range of service elements that accompany the physical product are frequently as important as the technical solutions offered by the product itself.[6] (See Chapter 10.) Some examples of product–service linkages include equipment repair and maintenance, consultation services associated with the sale of computers and other technical products, training programs on the use and application of equipment, distribution and delivery service, spare parts, and many others. The business marketing manager must recognize that service activities augment the physical product and can create a differential advantage for the firm in the eyes of organizational buyers. (See Figure 12.1.) Additionally, by developing special expertise in the provision of product-related services, the manufacturer may create the opportunity to market the service as a separate entity. As noted, NCR Corporation is profitably pursuing this strategy and many of Europe's computer companies are currently pursuing strategies that position them as service suppliers rather than equipment manufacturers.[7] These companies see a significant opportunity in supplying specialized services not directly linked to their own equipment.

In the IBM ad in Figure 12.1, for example, note that IBM makes a point of the fact that it services non-IBM equipment. This broad approach allows the companies to provide solutions to almost any corporate problem.

The second category is **pure services**, those that are marketed in their own right without necessarily being associated with a physical product. The list of such business services is vast, including insurance, consulting, banking, maintenance services, transportation, market research, accounting, temporary personnel, security and protection services, and travel booking services. The variety of business services provided and the quantity of services purchased by businesses and organizations appear to be growing rapidly; a recent study of purchasing managers reported that almost 25 percent

---

[6] Lauren K. Wright, "Characterizing Successful New Services: Background and Literature Review," Report #9-1985, Institute for the Study of Business Markets, Pennsylvania State University (April 25, 1985), p. 37.

[7] Sean Milmo, "Computer Companies in Europe Accent Service Market Positions," *Business Marketing*, 74 (January 1989), p. 26.

FIGURE 12.1 **IBM Ad Emphasizing Commitment to Service and Support**

Source: Courtesy, IBM Corporation.

of their purchasing expenditures go for services compared to just 11 percent two years earlier.[8] A number of factors have contributed to the growth of business services:

1. Companies and other organizations increasingly rely on the services of specialists because of the complexity of economic organization and the need to obtain the economies involved in the division and specialization of labor.

2. Technology, particularly in the data collection, manufacturing, and computer information transmission systems, requires the use of outside, specialized services to remain up-to-date. Companies need advice concerning what equipment to buy and continuing advice on how to use it.

3. Organizations can remain flexible and better control their capital commitment by hiring services that provide "use" without "ownership."

4. Time pressures (long lead-time to develop in-house expertise) and lack of available internal resources encourage organizations to use outside services rather than providing services internally.[9]

---

[8] Somerby Dowst, "Service Buying: More of It More Often," *Purchasing*, 102 (June 22, 1987), p. 48.

[9] Based On Donald Cowell, *The Marketing of Services* (London: William Heinemann, 1984), p. 13.

INSIDE BUSINESS MARKETING
The Service War in the Computer Industry

Many manufacturers in the computer industry felt they had won a major battle when they were finally able to establish and effectively operate a service and support function that kept their customers happy and their machines running. Today, it looks as if this is only a small battle in the competitive wars sweeping the computer industry. Companies are now finding they must develop the capability to service their *competitors'* equipment effectively!

Ninety percent of computer networks include products from at least two vendors, and 50 percent include five or more vendors. The trend is toward even more "mixing and matching." As a result, manufacturers must be able to service competitors' equipment or risk losing valuable service contracts—and customer goodwill. Some computer firms, including NCR, Honeywell, Control Data, and Unisys, have officially entered what is referred to as the third-party maintenance sector and now actively market their ability to service a wide variety of manufacturers' products.

Although servicing competitors' equipment creates some problems, such as giving the impression that the manufacturer tacitly approves of another manufacturer's product, its advantages can be significant. First, it gives the manufacturer a reputation for flexibility and enhances its ability to sell equipment. Second, and most important, the market appears to be demanding it. Some computer makers have lost accounts because they could not service equipment other than their own. Even IBM, the market leader, maintains more than 120 non-IBM products that are attached to IBM microcomputers.

What does the future hold? Some industry experts believe that despite the broader service offerings, smart companies will concentrate on becoming experts in a few select areas. To offer a full-service package, manufacturers will probably need to form strategic partnerships with other service providers.

Source: Adapted from Diane L. Kastiel, "Service and Support: High Tech's New Battleground," *Business Marketing*, 72 (June 1987), pp. 54–66.

Current and projected trends in the business environment suggest that these forces will further expand the demand for services in the business market.

Business Service Marketing: Special Challenges

The development of marketing programs for both products and services can be approached from a common perspective, yet the relative importance of various strategic elements and the form of these strategic elements will differ between products and services. The underlying explanation for these strategic differences lies in the distinctions between a product and a service. "Services are intangible; products are tangible. Services are consumed at the time of production, but there is a time lag between the production and consumption of products. Services cannot be stored; products can. Services are highly variable; most products are highly standardized. These differences produce differences in strategic applications that often stand many product marketing principles on their head."[10] Thus, success in the business service marketplace begins with an understanding of the meaning of *service*.

DEFINING BUSINESS SERVICES

Given the diversity of services, special insights can be secured by considering a product–service continuum where the basic underlying variable is *tangibility*. As Donald Cowell suggests, "what is significant about services, where they are objects being marketed, is the relative dominance of intangible attributes in the make-up of the 'service product.' Services are a special kind of product. They may require special understanding and special marketing efforts."[11]

Tangible or Intangible

Figure 12.2 provides a useful tool for understanding the product–service definitional problem. The continuum suggests that there are very few "pure products" or "pure services." For example, industrial grease is a physical object made up of tangible elements (petroleum, chemicals, etc.). However, it does provide a service (lubrication) and delivery service may be an important aspect in marketing the product. Thus, most market offerings comprise a combination of tangible and intangible elements.

Whether an offering is classified as a good or as a service depends on how the organizational buyer views what is being bought—whether the tangible or the intangible elements dominate. On one end of the spectrum, grease and oil are tangible-dominant, and the essence of what is being bought is the physical product. Management seminars, on the other hand, are intangible-dominant because what is being bought—professional development, education, learning—has few, if any, tangible properties. A convention hotel is in the middle of the continuum because the buyer will receive an array of both tangible elements (meals, beverages, notepads, etc.) and intangible benefits (courteous personnel, fast check-ins, meeting room ambience, etc.).

The concept of tangibility is especially useful to the business marketer because many business offerings are composed of product and service combinations. The key management task is to evaluate carefully (from the buyer's standpoint) which elements of the offering dominate. The more the market offering is characterized by intangible elements, the more difficult it is to apply the standard marketing tools that were developed for products. The business marketer must focus on specialized marketing approaches appropriate for services.

The concept also helps the manager to focus clearly on the firm's "total market offering." In addition, it helps the manager recognize that a change in one of the elements of the market offering may completely change the offering in the view of the customer. For example, a business marketer who decides to hold spare parts inventory

---

[10] Henry Assael, *Marketing Management: Strategy and Action* (Boston, Mass.: Kent Publishing Company, 1985), p. 693.

[11] Donald Cowell, *The Marketing of Services*, p. 35.

FIGURE 12.2   **Business Product-Service Classification Based on Tangibility**

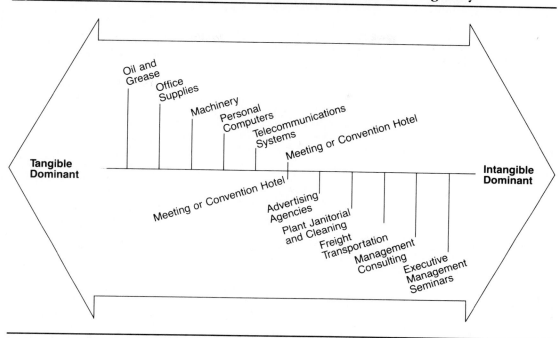

Source: Adapted from G. Lynn Shostack, "Breaking Free from Product Marketing," *Journal of Marketing*, 41 (April 1977), p. 77. Published by the American Marketing Association.

at a central location and use overnight delivery to meet customer requirements must refocus marketing strategy. The offering has moved toward the intangible end of the continuum because of the intangible benefits associated with reduced customer inventory and fast transportation. This new "service," which is less tangible, must be carefully explained and the intangible results of lower inventory costs must be made more concrete to the buyer through an effective promotion program.

In summary, business services are those market offerings that are intangible-dominant. However, few services are totally intangible—they often contain elements with tangible properties. In addition to the tangibility criterion, business services have other important distinguishing characteristics that influence how they are marketed. Table 12.1 provides a summary of the core characteristics that further delineate the nature of business services.

Simultaneous Production and Consumption

Because services are generally *consumed as they are produced*, a critical element in the buyer–seller relationship is the effectiveness of the individual (repair technician, truck driver, consultant) who actually provides the service. From the service firm's

TABLE 12.1   **Unique Service Characteristics**

Characteristic	Example	Marketing Implications
Simultaneous production and consumption	Telephone conference call Management seminar Equipment repair	Direct buyer–seller interaction requires that service be done "right" Requires high-level training for personnel Requires effective screening and recruitment of personnel
Nonstandardized output	Management advice varies with the individual consultant Merchandise damages vary from shipment to shipment	Emphasize strict quality control standards Develop systems that minimize deviation and human error Prepackage the service Look for ways to automate
Perishability: inability to store or stockpile	Unfilled airline seats An idle computer technician Unrented warehouse space	Plan capacity on the basis of peak demand Use pricing and promotion to even out demand peaks and valleys Use overlapping shifts for personnel
Lack of ownership	Use of a railroad car Use of a consultant's know-how Use of a mailing list	Focus promotion on the advantages of nonownership: reduced labor, overhead, and capital Emphasize flexibility

perspective, the entire marketing strategy may rest on how effectively the individual service provider interacts with the customer. The recruiting, hiring, and training of personnel assume special importance in business service firms.

Service Variability

Observe from Table 12.1 that the service offering is *nonstandardized*, meaning that the quality of the service output may vary each time it is provided.[12] Services vary in the amount of equipment and labor that are utilized to provide the service. For example, a significant human element is involved in teaching an executive seminar compared to providing overnight airfreight service. Generally, the more labor involved in a service, the less uniform the output. In these labor-intensive cases, the user may also find it difficult to judge the quality before the service is provided. Because of uniformity problems, business service providers must focus on finely tuned quality-control programs, invest in "systems" to minimize human error, and seek approaches for automating the service.

---

[12] Valarie A. Zeithaml, A. Parasuraman, and Leonard R. Berry, "Problems and Strategies in Services Marketing," *Journal of Marketing*, 49 (Spring 1985), p. 34; see also Zeithaml, Berry, and Parasuraman, "Communication and Control Processes in the Delivery of Service Quality," *Journal of Marketing*, 52 (April 1988), pp. 35–48.

Service Perishability

Generally, services *cannot be stored*; that is, if they are not provided at the time they are available, the lost revenue cannot be recaptured. Tied to this characteristic is the fact that demand for services is often unpredictable and widely fluctuating. The service marketer must carefully evaluate capacity—in a service business, **capacity** is a substitute for inventory. If capacity is set for peak demand, a "service inventory" must exist to supply the highest level of demand. As an example, some airlines that provide air shuttle service between New York, Washington, and Boston offer flights that leave every hour. If, on any flight, the plane is full, another plane is brought to the terminal—even for one passenger. An infinite capacity is set so that no single business traveler will be dissatisfied. Obviously, setting high capacity levels is costly, and the marketer must analyze the cost versus the lost revenue and customer goodwill that might result from maintaining lower capacity.

Nonownership

The final dimension of services shown in Table 12.1 is the fact that the service buyer uses, but *does not own*, the service purchased. Essentially, payment for a service is a payment for the use of, access to, or hire of items. The service marketer must feature the advantages of nonownership in its communications to the marketplace. The key benefits to emphasize are reductions in staff, overhead, and capital associated with a third party providing the service.

Although there may be exceptions to the general prescriptions, these characteristics provide a useful framework for understanding the nature of business services and for isolating special marketing strategy requirements.

BUYING BUSINESS SERVICES

The purchase of business services involves consideration of criteria and factors that are not always associated with the purchase of tangible products. Since business services are intangible and nonstandardized, organizational buyers must grapple with a host of nontraditional purchase criteria such as supplier responsiveness, qualifications and training of supplier personnel, managerial ability, reputation of the supplier, and many others. The effectiveness of a business service firm's marketing strategy will often hinge on a clear understanding of the criteria and the processes used by service customers in evaluating competing service suppliers. A first consideration is the criteria used to guide buying decisions.

Services: Purchase Criteria

The unique aspects of services (e.g., intangibility) focus the buying decision on characteristics that are difficult to define and quantify. When selecting services, buyers tend to rely on surrogate indicators of quality such as surroundings, equipment, service personnel, and price.[13] From a strategic perspective, the issue is why buyers select one service supplier over another. Often, the answer can only be secured through marketing research that addresses such issues as the following:

1. What attributes of a given service are important to a specific segment?
2. Does the importance of each attribute vary among members of the buying center?
3. How are various service providers perceived as performing on these attributes?

Service Attributes

Services have many characteristics that vary from objective, quantifiable measures to highly subjective and perceptual attributes. For example, a business traveler can readily compare airlines on the basis of measurable criteria such as the number of flights, frequent flyer programs, fares, and on-time performance (a service measure that the Department of Transportation has required all airlines to publish since late 1987). Other attributes are more subjective and depend on the traveler's perceptions and interpretation, including quality of the interactions with ticket agents, gate agents, and flight attendants; comfort and amenities in flight; and quality of meals. Business services also embody both people-based and equipment- or facility-based attributes.

The quality of the air travel service, as perceived by the business traveler, depends on a number of people- or equipment-related elements that make up the air service. Some of the tangible **people-based attributes** might include flight attendants, ticket agents, baggage handlers, and pilots. **Equipment-based attributes** include aircraft, seats, meals, and luggage-handling equipment.

Careful consideration must be given to each of the variety of attributes associated with a given service. In the realm of the people/equipment-based dimension, the closer the degree of interaction between the buyer (and the buyer's organization) and the service company, the more likely service personnel and equipment will form an important part of the service product.[14] By looking at the relative importance of people-based and equipment- or facility-based service attributes, management can gain useful insights into which criteria and attributes dominate a particular service package.

Characteristics of the Business Service Package

Table 12.2 shows how some representative business services could be classified on the basis of people/equipment importance. A business service marketer would be well advised to assess carefully how its service package might be classified by potential users. The key perspective is the buyer's perception of the importance of these attributes. Once the manager has a feeling for buyer perceptions, he or she can look for strategic insights from service businesses with similar people/equipment-based emphasis.[15]

---

[13] A. Parasuraman and Valarie A. Zeithaml, "Different Perceptions of Suppliers and Clients of Industrial Services," in Leonard L. Berry, G Lynn Shostack, and Gregory D. Upah, eds., *Emerging Perspectives on Services Marketing* (Chicago: American Marketing Association, 1983), p. 35.

[14] Christopher H. Lovelock, *Services Marketing* (Englewood Cliffs, N.J.: Prentice-Hall, 1984), p. 62.

[15] James A. Rice, Richard S. Slack, and Pamela A. Garside, "Hospitals Can Learn Valuable Marketing Strategies from Hotels," *Hospitals*, 55 (November 16, 1981), p. 22.

TABLE 12.2   **People-Based and Equipment- or Facility-Based Characteristics of a Business Service Package**

Extent to which Equipment- or Facility-Based Attributes Form Part of the Service Package	Extent to which People-Based Attributes Form Part of the Service Package		
	High	**Medium**	**Low**
High	Third-party (public) warehousing Hotel: sales meeting	Airline Automobile rental	Data analysis service Building construction
Medium	Management development seminars Conference party planners	Computer maintenance Audiovisual equipment rental Landscaping and lawn care	Freight transportation Waste disposal service
Low	Corporate banking Management consulting Public accounting Advertising agency	Equipment repair Temporary personnel services	Freight bill payment service Newspaper clipping service Uniform rental

Source: Adapted from Christopher H. Lovelock, *Services Marketing* (Englewood Cliffs, N.J.: Prentice-Hall, 1984), p. 61.

Thus, a public accounting firm might look to a successful advertising agency for prescriptions on marketing strategy. In addition, each cell in the matrix suggests a different emphasis from a marketing standpoint. Services in the high/high cell, hotels for example, must concentrate heavily on both the people and facility dimensions of their offering. Those in the high people/low equipment cell require a different emphasis. Management consulting firms, for example, should consider a host of strategies centered on enhancing the people dimension of their offering—training, recruitment, increasing personal interaction skills, quality control of services, and so on.

The Choice Process

The perceived quality of a business service is a salient factor (along with cost) that focuses on the buyer's comparison of competing service providers. Three important aspects of the choice process should be considered.

1.   *Determinant attributes.* These are the attributes that determine the choice among competing service suppliers. For example, although "cleanliness" is often a top-rated factor among grocery manufacturers when considering the selection of a public warehouse to store their products, most public warehouses in the grocery industry meet USDA cleanliness standards and are generally perceived as equally clean. Thus, cleanliness is usually not an attribute that influences a manufacturer's choice between several major public warehouse companies. The **determinant attributes**, in this case, may be such factors as experience with similar products, management capability, or computer system expertise. These are the attributes in which significant differences between competing suppliers are apparent to potential buyers.

Determinant attributes may be somewhat down the list of service characteristics that are important to buyers. The challenge to the service manager is to identify which attributes are determinant and to use that information to upgrade the company's offering on those attributes and to focus the marketing strategy on them.

2. *Difficulty in evaluating quality.* Because business services are intangible and nonstandardized, buyers tend to have greater difficulty in evaluating services than in evaluating goods. The inability to depend on consistent service performance and quality may lead service buyers to experience more perceived risk.[16] As a result, buyers utilize a variety of prepurchase information sources to reduce risk. Information from current users (word of mouth) is particularly important. In addition, the evaluation process for services tends to be more abstract, more random, and more heavily based on symbology rather than on concrete decision variables.[17] Thus the business service marketer must consider procedures for facilitating the evaluation process. For example, some freight companies provide detailed evaluation models to prospective clients. These models help potential buyers specify the full range of key decision variables and compare competing carriers on the basis of these variables. An important part of services marketing is helping potential buyers make comparisons and thereby reducing the risk associated with the evaluation and selection process.

3. *Perceived quality.* Quality standards are ultimately defined by the business customer. Actual performance by the service provider or the provider's perception of quality are of little relevance compared to the customer's perception of the service. "Good" service results when the service provider meets or exceeds the customer's expectations.[18] (See Figure 12.3.) As a result, many management experts argue that service companies should carefully position themselves so that customers expect a little less than the firm can actually deliver. The strategy: underpromise and overdeliver.

Components of Service Quality

Christian Gronroos suggested that the total quality of a service is a function of three components: **corporate image, technical quality,** and **functional quality**.[19] (Each is described in Table 12.3.) It is difficult to evaluate which aspect of quality is the most

---

[16] Dennis Guseman, "Service Marketing: The Challenge of Stagflation," in James H. Donnelly and William R. George, eds., *Marketing of Services* (Chicago: American Marketing Association, 1981), pp. 200–204.

[17] Valarie A. Zeithaml, "How Consumer Evaluation Processes Differ Between Goods and Services," in Donnelly and George, eds., *Marketing of Services*, pp. 200–204.

[18] William H. Davidow and Bro Uttal, "Service Companies: Focus or Falter," *Harvard Business Review*, 67 (July–August 1989), p. 84.

[19] Christian Gronroos, *Strategic Management and Marketing in the Service Sector* (Cambridge, Mass.: Marketing Science Institute, 1983), p. 25.

FIGURE 12.3 **Federal Express: The First Service Company to Win the Malcolm Baldrige National Quality Award**

Source: Permission granted by Federal Express Corporation.

important from the customer's view. However, all three aspects must be given attention by management. From the marketing manager's perspective, corporate image is the most remote and the most difficult to control, even though it can be important in "excusing" minor deficiencies in the other quality components.

Technical and functional quality are the most readily managed and most easily controlled. It is important to note that these dimensions are very different in nature. Technical quality—*what* the customer receives—is more amenable to measurement and to the application of systems, procedures, and techniques intended to assure its quality. For example, a freight company can employ new trucks, purchase computer programs to route shipments, and use effective driver-training programs in order to improve delivery performance.

Functional quality—*how* the customer is served—is more difficult to measure objectively and may be more difficult to standardize and systematize. For the freight

TABLE 12.3   **The Components of Service Quality**

Component	Description	Examples
Corporate image	The overall image the organization has and its overall attractiveness	United Airlines—friendly Hertz—market leader
Technical quality	Whether the service provides the appropriate technical attributes; *what* the user receives—the material content of the service	A clean building A new marketing strategy from a consultant Goods transported from point A to point B
Functional quality	*How* the service is rendered; this dimension focuses on the way in which the service is provided	Appearance and behavior of a flight attendant Presentation of a consultant's report How rapidly an office machine is repaired

Source: Christian Gronroos, *Strategic Management and Marketing in the Service Sector* (Cambridge, Mass.: Marketing Science Institute, 1983), p. 25.

company, controlling how truck drivers interact with customers is difficult because each driver is performing in a remote location without direct supervision. In addition, the functional quality of the transport service will depend on the customer's perceptions, biases, and prejudices.

Importance of Employees

High-quality service performance will result from a combination of technical and functional effectiveness. A vital question, from the service marketer's standpoint, is which dimension is most important? Research by Christian Gronroos provides some useful insights.[20] His study suggests that the performance of employees who are in contact with the customer may compensate for temporary problems with technical quality. In some cases, performance of these employees may even compensate for a lower level of technical quality. The survey provides strong evidence that functional quality, of which employee performance is a major element, is of utmost importance. Other studies have shown that customers receiving acceptable technical service without adequate functional quality tend to be generally dissatisfied, irrespective of the degree of satisfaction with the technical performance.[21]

Clearly, business service marketers must develop their service packages carefully, with significant attention devoted to the functional aspects, recognizing that functional quality may be the critical ingredient in creating a differential advantage. Business service marketers must not fall into the trap of becoming too technically oriented in regard to service. A common problem experienced by computer users is the difficulty in communicating with computer programmers and technicians who "talk their own language" and seem to patronize the user, who may not be computer literate. Computer

---

[20] Ibid., p. 29.

[21] J. E. Swan and L. J. Comb, "Product Performance and Consumer Satisfaction: A New Concept," *Journal of Marketing*, 40 (April 1976), p. 42.

service companies and software vendors would be well advised to ensure that their representatives and technicians are "user friendly." Recent evidence underscores the impact of treating customers well. Opinion Research Corporation surveyed 400 executives of the nation's largest firms and overwhelmingly they indicated that "how much a firm cares about its customers" is more important than many measurable aspects of their service performance.[22] In a related study, "the personal touch" was considered the most important element of service.

Importance of Quality

An indication of the importance of perceived quality of business services is the fact that those firms having successfully rendered or currently rendering a service are the only firms solicited when a repeat purchase is to be made.[23] Research by A. Parasuraman and Valarie Zeithaml provides further evidence of the need for marketers to evaluate service quality as viewed by the customer.[24] Their results indicate that many suppliers of market research services have a faulty perception of the factors that are important to clients when choosing a market research company. The attributes rated most important by clients—(1) understanding the client's problem and (2) usefulness of research results—were ranked as low as fourth and seventh, respectively, by the research service suppliers. The implications are clear: service firms must strive to adopt a marketing orientation that begins with a careful assessment of customer needs and perceptions.

The quality of service provided to business customers has a major effect on customer "defections"—customers who will not come back. Frederick Reichheld and Earl Sasser point out that customer defections have a powerful impact on the bottom line.[25] They suggest that as a company's relationship with a customer lengthens, profits rise—and generally rise considerably. For example, one service firm found that profit from a fourth-year customer is triple that from a first-year customer.[26] Many additional benefits accrue to service companies that retain their customers: they can charge more, the cost of doing business is reduced, and the long-standing customer provides "free" advertising. The implications are clear—service providers should carefully track customer defections and recognize that continuous improvement in service quality is not a cost, but "an investment in a customer who generates more profit than the margin on a one-time sale."[27]

---

[22] Patricia Sellers, "What Customers Really Want," *Fortune*, 121 (June 4, 1990), p. 58.

[23] Wesley J. Johnston and Thomas V. Bonoma, "Purchase Process for Capital Equipment and Services," *Industrial Marketing Management*, 4 (1981), p. 261.

[24] Parasuraman and Zeithaml, "Differential Perceptions of Suppliers and Clients of Industrial Services," p. 37.

[25] Frederick F. Reichheld and W. Earl Sasser, "Zero Defections: Quality Comes to Services," *Harvard Business Review*, 68 (September–October, 1990), p. 105.

[26] Ibid., p. 106.

[27] Ibid., p. 107.

INSIDE BUSINESS MARKETING
CPAs Develop Marketing Savvy

For years, accounting firms operated under self-imposed restrictions on marketing. In fact, the profession banned any form of marketing, calling it "promiscuous solicitation." Until 1977, marketing by CPA firms was limited to what is termed *country-club marketing*—using public and social visibility to make contacts with potential clients. For CPAs, marketing was polite and gentlemanly until 1977 when a Supreme Court decision overturned professional societies' marketing prohibitions.

A combination of factors—accelerating competition, a loss of differentiation among CPA firms, increased auditor switching by clients, and the new marketing freedom—turned CPAs to marketing in full force. The strategic response by the "Big Eight" CPA firms has been evidenced in the following areas:

- Heavy image-building national promotion campaigns

- Creation of special practice groups—niche marketing—to pursue fast-growing markets

- Expanding the service menu (In 1947 Touche-Ross had two practice areas: accounting and tax service. Today, the firm has 14 service areas and 19 special industry programs.)

- Enhancing technical competence by strengthening training in auditing techniques

- Upgrading the quality of client-interfacing personnel by tightening recruiting standards and increasing entry-level pay

- Improving service consistency by developing uniform methodologies and audit processes (Also, more automation has been introduced to the audit process.)

These many marketing-driven responses to the new accounting environment suggest that marketing has been transformed from a liability to an important asset for many CPA firms.

Source: Adapted from Steven R. Baldwin, "CPAs Learn Marketing ABCs," *Business Marketing*, 72 (October 1987), pp. 42–54.

MARKETING MIX FOR BUSINESS SERVICE FIRMS

To meet the needs of service buyers effectively, an integrated marketing strategy is required. First, target segments must be selected, and then a marketing mix must be tailored to the expectations of each segment. The key elements of the service marketing mix include the development of service packages, pricing, promotion, and distribution. Each requires special consideration by the business marketing manager.

Segmentation

As with any marketing situation, development of the marketing mix will be contingent upon the customer segment to be served. Every facet of the service to be offered, as well as the methods for promoting, pricing, and delivering the service, will hinge upon the needs of a reasonably homogeneous group of customers. The process for segmenting business markets described in Chapter 6 will find application in the services market.

However, William Davidow and Bro Uttal suggest that customer service segments differ from usual market segments in significant ways.[28]

First service segments are often narrower. This situation reflects the fact that many service customers expect services to be customized. Expectations may not be met if the service received is standardized and routine. Secondly, service segmentation focuses on what the business buyers expect as opposed to what they need. The assessment of buyer expectations will play a very large role in selecting a target market and developing the appropriate service package. This assessment is critical because so many studies have shown large differences between the ways that customers define and rank different service activities and the ways suppliers define and rank them.[29]

Finally, segmenting service markets helps the firm to adjust service capacity more effectively. Segmentation will usually reveal that total demand is made up of numerous smaller, yet more predictable, demand patterns. For the demand patterns of a hotel or a convention visitor, business traveler, foreign tourist, or vacationer can all be forecast individually and capacities adjusted for each segment's demand pattern.

Service Packages

The service package can be thought of as the product dimension of service, including decisions involving the essential concept of the service, the range of services provided, and the quality and level of service. In addition, the service package must consider some factors that are unique to services—the personnel who perform the service, the physical evidence that accompanies the service, and the process of providing the service.[30] A useful way to conceptualize the service product is shown in Figure 12.4.

Customer-Benefit Concept

Services are purchased because of the benefits they offer, and a first step in either creating a service or evaluating an existing one is to define the **customer-benefit concept**—that is, evaluate the core benefit that the customer will derive from the service. An understanding of the customer-benefit concept will focus the business marketer's attention on those attributes—functional, effectual, and psychological—that must be not only offered but also tightly monitored from a quality-control standpoint. For example, a sales manager selecting a resort hotel for an annual sales meeting is purchasing a core benefit that could be stated as "a successful meeting." The hotel marketer must then assess the full range of service attributes and components that are necessary to provide a successful meeting. Obviously, a wide variety of service elements will come into play: (1) meeting room size, layout, environment, acoustics; (2) meals; (3) comfortable and quiet sleeping rooms; (4) audiovisual equipment; and (5) staff responsiveness.

---

[28] Davidow and Uttal, "Service Companies: Focus or Falter," p. 79.

[29] Ibid., p. 83.

[30] Cowell, *The Marketing of Services*, p. 73.

FIGURE 12.4 **Conceptualizing the Service Product**

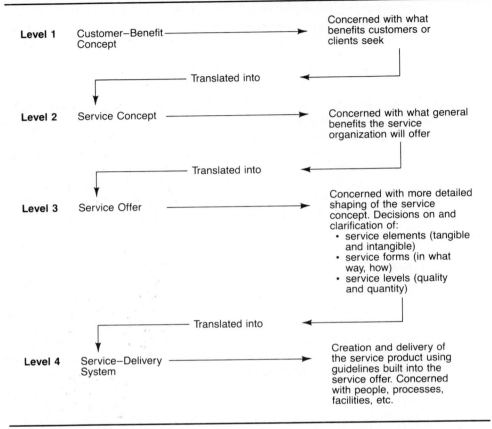

Source: Adapted from Donald Cowell, *The Marketing of Services* (London: William Heinemann, Ltd., 1984), p. 100. Published by Heinemann Professional Publishing, Ltd.

As another example, Dun & Bradstreet does not provide its customers with financial services. Its customer-benefit concept is focused on objective and accurate credit information, security, and even "peace of mind."[31]

Service Concept

Once the customer-benefit concept is understood, the next step is to articulate the **service concept**, which defines the general benefits the service company will provide in terms of the bundle of goods and services sold to the customer. The service concept takes the customer-benefit concept and translates it into the range of benefits the service marketer will *provide*. For a hotel, the service concept might specify the benefits that

---

[31] James L. Heskett, *Managing in the Service Economy* (Boston, Mass.: Harvard Business School Press, 1986), p. 17.

it will develop: flexibility, responsiveness, courteousness in providing flexible meeting rooms; a full range of audiovisual equipment; flexible meal schedules; message services; professional personnel; climate-controlled meeting rooms, and the like.

Service Offer

Intimately linked with service concept is the **service offer,** which spells out in more detail those services to be provided, when they will be provided, how they will be offered, where they will be provided, and to whom. The service elements that make up the total service package, including both tangibles and intangibles, must be determined. The service offer of the hotel includes a multitude of tangible elements (soundproof meeting rooms, overhead projectors, video players, slide projectors, flip charts, refreshments, heating and air-conditioning, meals) and intangible elements (attitude of meeting room set-up personnel, warmth of greetings from desk clerks and bellhops, response to unique requests, meeting room ambience). Generally, management will find it easier to manage the tangible (equipment and physical) elements of the service than to control the intangible elements.

Service Delivery System

The final dimension of the service product is the **service delivery system**—how the service is provided to the customer. The delivery system includes carefully conceived jobs for people; personnel with capabilities and attitudes necessary for successful performance; equipment, facilities, and layouts for effective customer work flow; and carefully developed procedures aimed at a common set of objectives.[32] Thus, the service delivery system should provide a carefully designed blueprint which describes how the service is rendered for the customer.

For physical products, manufacturing and marketing are generally separate and distinct activities; for services, these two activities are often inseparable.[33] The service performance and the delivery system both create the product and deliver it to the customers. This feature of services underscores the important role that people, particularly service providers, play in the marketing process. Technicians, repair personnel, and maintenance engineers are intimately involved in customer contact, and they decidedly influence the customer's perception of service quality. The business service marketer must pay close attention to both people and physical evidence—tangible elements such as uniforms—when designing the service package.

Service Personnel

A first step in creating an effective service package is to ensure that the customer-benefit concept is known, understood, and accepted by all personnel. As Donald Cowell states: "So important are people and their quality to organizations and . . . services that 'internal marketing' is considered to be an important management role to ensure that

[32] Ibid., p. 20.
[33] Cowell, *The Marketing of Services*, p. 110.

INSIDE BUSINESS MARKETING
The Service Encounter

At the heart of every service is the service encounter. Everything flows from it. A service encounter is the event at which a customer comes into contact with a service provider—its people, its communications and other technology, and the services it provides. It is the point in time at which marketing, operations, and human resource management are all brought to bear on the process of creating and delivering a service that meets customers' needs, perceived risks, and expectations. It has been termed by Jan Carlzon, CEO of SAS (Scandinavian Airlines System), the "moment of truth" at which the representatives of a service company must prove to their customers that their company is the best alternative.

Source: James L. Heskett, W. Earl Sasser, Jr., and Christopher W. L. Hart, *Service Breakthroughs: Changing the Rules of the Game*, (New York: The Free Press, 1990), p. 2.

---

all staff are customer conscious."[34] In short, the attitudes, skills, knowledge, and behavior of service personnel have a critical impact on the levels of satisfaction that the user derives from the service. Because service production and consumption are inseparable, a variety of operating personnel have direct contact with the customer and help shape customer perceptions of the service performance.

Two successful service marketers, Marriott Corporation and Delta Airlines, pay particular attention to employee training, involvement, incentives, and in some cases, ownership. Managers are often on a first-name basis with employees, and employees are regularly featured in their ads. Marketing communications directed to employees are as important as those targeted for potential customers. Such internal communications emphasize the company's purpose, its high standards of service, and the role that each employee assumes in creating satisfied customers.[35]

Physical Evidence

The many tangible objects used to create and deliver a service—buildings, computers, equipment, tools, plants, documents—are what Christian Gronroos refers to as the physical/technical resources. "The customer experiences such resources when its personnel come to the service company or when the service employee comes to the customer's location to deliver the service."[36] Physical evidence plays an important role in creating the atmosphere and environment in which a service is bought or performed, and it influences the customer's perception of the service. Physical evidence is the tangible aspect of the service package, which the business service marketer can control to a significant degree.

---

[34] Ibid., p. 110.

[35] This example is based on Heskett, *Managing in the Service Economy*, p. 40.

[36] Christian Gronroos, "An Applied Service Marketing Theory," Working Paper No. 57, Swedish School of Economics and Business Administration, Helsinki, 1980.

The service provider must carefully analyze how physical evidence can be used to create a favorable image of the firm and its service. Xerox's system for providing service and maintenance support for its copying machines is a good illustration of the management of physical evidence. Xerox service representatives wear suits and carry briefcases rather than tool kits. The obvious impact is to create a professional image in the mind of the business machine customer.

When a business attempts to judge a service, particularly before using or buying it, that service will be known by the tangible cues or evidence that surround it.[37] Physical evidence can be used to provide tangible cues in order to strengthen the meaning of the intangible product. Many services cannot be touched, nor can they be defined or grasped mentally. The challenge is to develop tangible representations of the service.

For business service marketers, uniforms, logos, written contracts and guarantees, building appearance, and color schemes are some of the many ways to make their services tangible. An equipment maintenance firm that provides free, written, quarterly inspections helps make its service more tangible. The credit card created by car rental companies is another example of an attempt to make a service more tangible. A key concern for the service marketer is to develop a well-defined strategy for managing physical evidence—to enhance and differentiate service evidence through the creation of tangible clues.

Pricing Business Services

Although product and service pricing policies and strategies share many common threads, the unique characteristics of services create some special pricing problems and opportunities.

Perishability and Managing Demand/Capacity

The demand for services is rarely steady or predictable enough to avoid service perishability. An extremely difficult decision for the business service marketer is to determine the capacity (inventory) of the system—should it meet peak demand, average demand, or somewhere in between? Pricing can be used to manage the timing of demand and align it with capacity levels.

To manage demand, the marketer may offer off-peak pricing schemes and price incentives for service orders that are placed in advance. For example, resort hotels, crowded with pleasure travelers during school vacations and holidays, develop special packages for business groups during the off-season. Similarly, various utilities may offer significant rate reductions for off-peak usage. It may also be possible, depending on demand elasticity and competition, to charge premium rates for services provided at peak demand periods. It is interesting to note, however, that a recent study of

---

[37] G. Lynn Shostack, "Breaking Free from Product Marketing," *Journal of Marketing*, 41 (April 1977), pp. 73–80.

INSIDE BUSINESS MARKETING
People Make the Difference at ServiceMaster

ServiceMaster Company, the Illinois firm that manages support services for hospitals, schools, and industrial companies, has long recognized the importance of people in the success of a service business.

ServiceMaster supervises employees of customers' organizations engaged in housekeeping, food service, and equipment maintenance. Many of these employees are functionally illiterate. The ServiceMaster philosophy, however, is directly focused on these people as well as on their own managers as it states: "Before asking someone to do something, you have to help them be something." The philosophy is operationalized by the provision of educational and motivational programs to help these employees "be something."

For its own employees, ServiceMaster offers an ambitious training program and oppor-
tunities for some responsibilities and advancement. Elaborate training aids and a laboratory for developing new equipment and materials enhance the manager's "be something" feeling. For customers' employees, on the other hand, the "be something" attitude is built through redesigning jobs to enhance productivity and offering educational programs to develop literacy. The attention to the individual results in improved self-respect, self-development, personal satisfaction, and upward mobility for the employees and managers.

Is there a payoff for people development in a service business? There must be. ServiceMaster's return on equity from 1973 to 1985 was the highest of all the larger service or industrial companies in the United States—averaging more than 30 percent after taxes.

Source: Adapted from James L. Heskett, "Lessons in the Service Sector," *Harvard Business Review*, 65 (March–April 1987), pp. 118–126.

---

strategies utilized by service firms showed that many service firms do not reduce prices to increase business during slow periods.[38]

Service Bundling

Many business services include a core service (perhaps several) as well as a variety of peripheral services. How should the services be priced—as an entity, as a service bundle, or individually? **Bundling** is the practice of marketing two or more services in a package for a special price.[39] Bundling makes sense in the business service environment because most service businesses have a high ratio of fixed costs to variable costs and a high degree of cost sharing among their many, related services. Hence the marginal cost of providing additional services to the core service customer is generally low.

A key decision for the service provider is whether to provide pure or mixed bundling.[40] In **pure bundling**, the services are only available in bundled form—they cannot be purchased separately. In **mixed bundling**, the customer can purchase one

---

[38] Zeithaml, Parasuraman, and Berry, "Problems and Strategies in Services Marketing," p. 41.

[39] Joseph P. Guiltinan, "The Price Bundling of Services: A Normative Framework," *Journal of Marketing*, 51 (April 1987), p. 74.

[40] Ibid., p. 75.

or more services individually or purchase the bundle. For example, a public warehouse firm can provide its services—storage, product handling, and clerical activities—in a price-bundled form by charging a single rate (8 cents) for each case received by the warehouse from its manufacturer-client. Or they may market each service separately and provide a rate for each service individually (3 cents per case for storage, 4 cents per case for handling, and 1 cent per case for clerical). Additionally, a multitude of peripheral services can be quoted on an individual basis: physical inventory count, freight company selection and routing, merchandise return and repair, and so on. In this way, the customer can choose the services desired and pay for each separately.

Attracting New Business

Various bundling strategies can be used to expand sales either by **cross-selling**—selling a new service to customers who buy an existing service—or by attracting entirely new customers. In the cross-selling situation for a public warehouse, current customers (utilizing storage services) may be attracted to a new product-labeling service by the offer of a bundled price that results in a discount on the total cost of the two services. Bundling services in order to attract new customers can be efficient when the service attributes can be evaluated before purchase and when the core service is demand elastic.[41] Thus, noncustomized services, where significant competition exists, would seem to be a fertile environment. Bundling insurance coverage with the rental of an automobile may be effective in attracting new business customers for a car rental firm.

In the computer service industry, manufacturers are finding that services formerly sold on an ad hoc basis can be sold more effectively if bundled together. Hewlett-Packard is testing a variety of service bundles with customers in order to determine how customers want to buy the services.[42] Digital Equipment uses service package bundles that are focused on various target markets. Currently, 27 packages exist to serve various market segments. Clearly, the services, how the services are combined, and how the bundle is priced have critical effects on the service firm's success.

Some evidence exists to suggest that business service providers do not recognize the strategic role of pricing. A study by Michael Morris and Donald Fuller found that CPA firms "generally lack a customer orientation in pricing; emphasize formula-based approaches that are cost oriented; are very inflexible in their pricing schemes; do not develop price differentials based on elasticity of different market segments; and rarely attempt to measure customer price sensitivity."[43] The authors suggest that many opportunities are available in the business service sector to improve the pricing of services. Service firms need to adopt pricing strategies that account for the unique aspects of services and define a specific role for the price variable.

---

[41] Ibid., p. 81

[42] Kastiel, "Service and Support: High-Tech's New Battleground," p. 66.

[43] Michael H. Morris and Donald A. Fuller, "Pricing an Industrial Service," *Industrial Marketing Management*, 18 (1989), pp. 139–146.

Services Promotion

The promotional strategies for services follow many of the same prescriptions as do those for products. However, the unique characteristics of business services pose special challenges for the business marketer.

Communication with Employees

Personnel are vital to many people-based service businesses, and they can have a profound effect on the customer's satisfaction with the service. Internal advertising to employees accomplishes the following:

- Promotes an understanding of the firm's mission and customer service benefit
- Influences them on how the service is to be provided
- Motivates them to perform
- Defines management's expectations of them

A current Delta Airlines ad campaign focuses on the theme: "We love to fly and it shows." The copy includes employees and shows situations in which employees take extra steps to assist customers. Even though the ad is ostensibly meant for the customer, it is clearly also aimed at Delta personnel. The ad helps define management's perceptions and expectations of employees.

Word-of-Mouth

Service purchases are frequently considered to be riskier than product purchases because it is more difficult for buyers to evaluate quality and value. As a result, buyers are more apt to be influenced by colleagues, peers, and other professionals who have had experience in purchasing and using the service. Promotion must concentrate on the dominant role of personal influence in the buying process and build on word-of-mouth communication. Donald Cowell suggests that this can be done by:[44]

- Persuading satisfied customers to inform others of their satisfaction
- Developing materials that customers can pass on to noncustomers
- Targeting opinion leaders in ad campaigns
- Encouraging potential customers to talk to existing customers

Service marketers can capitalize on the satisfaction of current customers and word-of-mouth promotion by featuring customers (and their comments) in nonpersonal advertising. The promotional brochures for many management development seminars feature pictures of customers and statements of satisfaction by these prior attendees.

---

[44] Cowell, *The Marketing of Services*, p. 171.

Expectations

Service marketing managers should recognize that many services can be enhanced through efforts to condition buyer expectations about the nature of the service encounter and the results it might produce.[45] As indicated earlier, it is often better to promise less than the firm can deliver in order to establish proper buyer expectations. Advertising, if overly zealous in its claims, can sometimes establish buyer expectations that cannot be met. Some experts believe that Delta airlines created such a situation with its advertising claim, "Delta is ready when you are."[46] Such a slogan is asking for trouble because the buyer is expecting the airline *always* to be ready. Delta dropped the slogan for the much tamer phrase mentioned earlier: "We love to fly, and it shows." Clearly the service marketer does not want to foster performance expectations in its advertising that it has no chance of achieving.

Developing Tangible Clues

As indicated earlier in this chapter, service marketers must concentrate either on featuring the physical evidence elements of their service or on making the intangible elements more tangible. Attempts should be made to translate the image of intangible attributes of a service into something more concrete. In business service marketing, this is typically accomplished by showing pictures of buildings, equipment, and personnel. Federal Express, through a series of highly creative television commercials, helped make their overnight delivery service more tangible by showing situations where shippers did not use their service. The foul-ups that were displayed showed the viewer the results of using a firm other than Federal Express: unhappy superiors, embarrassment, and delayed meetings were tangible results to be avoided.

Operating Personnel as Salespeople

Marketing and operations are generally inseparable in the service business. This means that service personnel also play key selling and marketing roles. The operating personnel must be equipped and ready to deal effectively with the customer; they must also be motivated to do so. At Marriott Corporation, "bellmen are often looked at subconsciously by guests as being 'Mr. Marriott' himself because many times a guest will speak to and deal with the bellman more often during a visit than with any other employees of the hotel." The bellman represents the all-important first and last impression for many guests. . . . They are coached to smile often and do all they can to make the guest feel welcome and special."[47] Many successful business service companies put considerable effort into ensuring that their operating personnel communicate effectively with the customer.

---

[45] Heskett, Sasser, and Hart, *Service Breakthroughs*, p. 7

[46] Patricia Sellers, "How to Handle Customer Gripes," *Fortune*, 118 (October 24, 1988), p. 100.

[47] G. M. Hostage, "Quality Control in the Service Business, *Harvard Business Review*, 53 (July–August 1975), p. 102.

Services Distribution

Distribution decisions in the service industry are focused on how to make the service package available and accessible to the user. Direct sale may be accomplished by the user going to the provider (e.g., a manufacturer using a public warehouse for storing its product) or more generally, by the provider going to the buyer (e.g., typewriter repair). In some instances, service intermediaries can be used.

Service Intermediaries

Financial services, insurance, lodging, warehousing, and transportation are some of the many services sold through intermediaries. For example, in the freight transportation business, selling agents, brokers, and freight forwarders are some of the typical intermediaries used, generally, because they can cost-effectively cover the entire freight service market. In addition, some of these channel members may develop bundles of services from a variety of transportation companies. Thus, a freight forwarder may arrange for a shipment to be moved by three separate modes of transportation—air, rail, and truckline. The forwarder takes care of all arrangements and invoices the customer only once for a single fee.

Franchising

As an alternative channel of distribution, franchising has experienced considerable growth in recent years. Such services as office and factory cleaning, car rental, temporary help, employment agencies, uniform rental, and equipment maintenance are now distributed through franchised dealerships. Franchising works best when the service can be standardized (e.g., office cleaning). Franchising allows the service provider to expand its market coverage rapidly and to minimize capital investment.

The design of the marketing strategy for a business service must be tailored to those unique factors that are associated with an intangible product. In similar fashion, the marketer developing new service packages must also recognize these important elements. The next section will briefly examine the development of new service packages.

DEVELOPING NEW SERVICES

The conventional process for developing new physical products—exploration, screening, business analysis, development, testing, and commercialization—appears to apply equally well to services.[48] (See Chapter 11.) However, the design and introduction of new service offerings has been cited as one of the more difficult challenges for managers in the service sector. As a recent article states:

> New product development is inherently more difficult, messier and less successful in the service sector. If a service company perceives a new need and develops a new service, there is less confidence in the result because the service is not subject to the same rigor

---

[48] Cowell, *The Marketing of Services*, p. 133.

TABLE 12.4   **Steps for Enhancing the New Service Development Process**

Step	Description
1. Establish a culture for entrepreneurship	Facilitate risk taking and new ideas by creating the proper climate: providing R&D funds, doing customer-need research, allowing employees to voice contrary opinions.
2. Create an organization to foster new service development	Assemble a "cast": **Senior Sponsor**, who has authority; **Product Champion**, who provides continuity and enthusiasm; **Integrator**, who brings the functions together and coordinates them; and **Referee**, who establishes rules for the process and then administers them.
3. Test ideas in the marketplace	New ideas must weather the acid test of the marketplace because the service concept is intangible.
4. Monitor results	Establish success measures and evaluate against these. Track customer reaction.
5. Reward risk-takers	Reward those taking good risks, even when they are not consistently successful.

Source: James L. Heskett, *Managing in the Service Economy* (Boston, Mass.: Harvard Business School Press, 1986), pp. 86–90.

and predictable outcomes that new products are subject to in the R&D lab. Most service companies focus on geographic extensions of their service or on minor modifications rather than on truly innovative approaches. Innovation in the service sector is the result of trial and error. . . . Service firms have difficulty in linking innovations and imagination to execution of a new offer.[49]

Although there are important difficulties, the business service firm can take steps to improve the new service development process and resulting marketing success. James Heskett offers five steps that a firm can take to improve the new service development process (see Table 12.4). Consistent with the discussion of product innovation, it is important to create the proper organizational climate (e.g., entrepreneurial culture, championing, taking risks).

Failure of New Services

Pierre Eiglier and Eric Langeard suggest that the lack of success of a new service offering can often be traced to problems that service marketers have in handling four key decisions.[50] They evaluated new service success in a range of service industries and found the four key decision areas to be as follows:

---

[49] "Service Management: The Toughest Game in Town," *Management Practice* (Fall 1984), p. 8.

[50] Pierre Eiglier and Eric Langeard, "A Conceptual Approach of the Service Offering," in H. Larsen and S. Heed, eds., *Proceedings of the E.A.A.R.M., Tenth Annual Workshop* (Copenhagen: E.A.A.R.M., 1981).

1. *The service concept.* To be successful, management must define the consumer benefits the firm intends to supply, the service attributes relating to these benefits, and the ways the service will be produced, sold, and consumed.

2. *The market segment.* The segment dimensions must reflect underlying service needs.

3. *The organization–client interface.* The firm must analyze the participative behavior expected from clients and consider how the interface will be controlled.

4. *The service image.* Decisions must be made on how the total image will be created and sustained through client interaction.

Based on this research, new services are doomed to failure if marketers do not completely understand the customer service concept as it relates to a defined market segment. Once this is carefully articulated, attention must focus on establishing the proper image and client interface.

Support Services

In many respects, services constitute the core business of a large number of business marketers. However, the support service provided by goods-manufacturing firms is an equally important dimension of the business service market. As indicated in Chapter 10, support and service are critical tools for the manufacturer in creating a differential advantage and satisfying customer requirements. Increasingly, service and support are a salient dimension in the selection of a vendor. Furthermore, after-sales service often carries a much higher margin than the sale of the original equipment.

In many industries, market success will depend on the manufacturer's ability to provide any or all of the following services: on-time delivery, inventory reduction, equipment maintenance and repair, education and training in product use, spare parts delivery, software support, on-line communication link-ups, and numerous others. Thus, many goods-producing firms are realistically in the service business because product success is inextricably linked to service performance. Few product marketers can ignore the role of services, and there is an urgent need to develop skill in and understanding of business marketing.

Industrial producers are faced with two scenarios if they fail to provide support and services effectively. First, they could lose a customer, regardless of the quality of their physical product. Second, the service component of the business may be provided by a third party (a service company that services equipment it does not manufacture). This would not only diminish the customer's ties to the manufacturer but also cause the manufacturer to lose the potential profits that could have been garnered from the service element of the business. In the long run, producers may lose the customer entirely.

Services that accompany many products are broadening: an equipment manufacturer can no longer be satisfied with just fixing a machine but must provide technical assistance and solutions to customer problems. If the manufacturer is unable to develop effective service programs, third-party service vendors are waiting to fill the void.

INSIDE BUSINESS MARKETING
The "Service Factory" Advantage

Investors initially balked in 1983 when Bruce D. Smith proposed putting half of his fledgling high-tech company's start-up capital into a customer service organization. Smith's backers protested that the company had yet to launch its product—large switches for private communications networks—and that less expensive approaches to service were available.

Smith wouldn't budge, even if it meant cutting back on research and development. Customers for his switches, he argued, would expect service every bit as good as IBM's. He would provide it because he wasn't just making and selling switches, he was solving customer telecommunications problems.

Smith prevailed on his board and by 1988, Network Equipment Technologies was a $100 million company with one-quarter of its market. Profit ballooned to $15 million, doubling every quarter.

NET's "service factory" is the heart of the company's marketing success. An investment of $12 million and an annual operating budget of $14 million keeps the service factory at the ready for customers.

Large corporations buy NET switches; those customers have their own technical experts who can fix most problems themselves with the help of built-in diagnostic equipment and NET telephone support. But for those 5 percent of service calls requiring an NET engineer's visit, the problem gets fixed in two hours or less. NET's switches keep running more than 99 percent of the time.

NET has created an awesome barrier to competitive entry. Its service prowess allows it to charge a 20 percent price premium, which funds its service infrastructure. "Everything you do, from raising money to the way you design, make, and market the product, has to reflect the philosophy of customer service," Smith insists, calling service "a religious issue that starts at the top."

Source: William H. Davidow, "The Ultimate Marketing Weapon," *Business Marketing,* 74 (October 1989) pp. 56–57.

Third-Party Service Vendors

In the computer equipment industry, equipment manufacturers had 87 percent of the maintenance service market in 1986. However, third-party service firms doubled their volume of business in the following two years and are expected to grow even faster in the future. Similar trends are expected to occur in other high-tech markets such as telecommunications and robotics. It is important to note that many computer firms receive as much as 25 percent of their total revenue from maintenance service.[51]

Thus, much is at stake for computer manufacturers, and the intrusion of third-party service providers will have significant consequences for the firms' profitability. Original equipment manufacturers are beginning to take steps to counteract the inroads being made. Effective strategies for meeting this challenge might include strengthening relationships with current accounts by extending warranties, granting service discounts to new customers, and most of all, improving service quality.

---

[51] Kastiel, "Service and Support: High-Tech's New Battleground," p. 56.

INTERNATIONAL DIMENSIONS OF BUSINESS SERVICES

Many U.S. service businesses realize a considerable portion of their total revenue from sales outside the United States. In 1988, U.S. service companies produced over $70 billion of service exports, an increase of $13 billion over 1987.[52] It is important to note that the United States continues to show a net surplus in service trade: the surplus amounted to $19 billion in 1988.[53] Several years ago, the U.S. Department of Commerce evaluated the extent to which selected service industries generated revenue outside the United States.[54] The results were impressive: the largest (the top 8 to 13) U.S. accounting firms, advertising agencies, and banks realized between 39 and 51 percent of their revenues from non-U.S. sources. Similarly, British, Japanese, and Western European service businesses generate substantial revenue from international trade. Services represent an estimated 25 to 30 percent of total world trade. Although representing significant opportunity, international service markets pose special challenges for the marketing manager.

Key Considerations in Global Services Marketing

The principles of marketing services apply in any context, yet marketing efforts must adjust to the environment in which the firm operates. This section highlights selected factors that business marketers should explore as they contemplate international service offerings.[55]

International Marketing Risks

Some experts suggest that the international expansion of sales of a service package is more risky than expansion of product sales. The increased risk results because products can be introduced gradually to international markets, whereas services, because of their inherent characteristics, must be introduced in totality. This places a heavy burden on service strategy implementation. The service provider must immediately produce on foreign soil, deal directly with customers, and respond to their needs. Immediate on-site procedures, controls, and processes must be established. As a consequence, the business service marketer wishing to reach international markets must give special attention to customer research, service design, and quality control.

Adaptation of Operations to Foreign Markets

Service firms must adjust to the business norms and laws of the host government. Often, service firms are not highly regarded by foreign governments because they provide little capital or technology to the country. Professional service firms—accounting, consulting, and law—have experienced considerable difficulty in adjusting to overseas

---

[52] Sylvia Nasar, "America Still Reigns in Services," *Fortune*, 119, (June 5, 1989), p. 64.

[53] *U.S. Industrial Outlook*, U.S. Department of Commerce, 1990, p. 5.

[54] U.S. Department of Commerce, International Trade Administration, *Current Developments in U.S. International Service Industries* (Washington, D.C., 1980).

[55] Parts of this section are based on Cowell, *The Marketing of Services*, pp. 265–267.

THE GLOBAL MARKETPLACE
Service Exports: Solving Balance of Payment Problems?

In 1989 the United States enjoyed a surplus of $5.1 billion in service trade with Japan. Although not nearly as massive as the $49.7 billion merchandise trade deficit with Japan, the figures suggest that U.S. superiority in services production may be an answer to the chronic balance-of-payment dilemma with the Japanese.

The United States has enjoyed a service trade surplus for almost two decades, and the advantage is growing dramatically. Travel, royalties, and license fees are some of the U.S. exported services that are growing most rapidly. The strength of the U.S. competitive advantage in services lies in superior productivity. American service companies are generally bigger, more automated, and less sheltered from competition than their Japanese counterparts.

In certain service industries the United States enjoys a large productivity advantage: the differential between U.S. and Japanese industries is 156 percent in transportation and communications, 137 percent in business services, and 115 percent in wholesale trade.

The aggressive marketing efforts of many U.S. finance, law, and advertising firms in Japan signal that the service balance should continue to swing in America's favor. In addition, trade barriers have been lowered in such areas as telecommunication services, software, and construction services. Given the skills of many U.S. business marketers in developing and delivering a wide array of services, the huge overall trade deficit with Japan may be on its way out.

Source: Adapted from: N. Chandra Mohan, "Service Exports: Better than You Think," *Fortune*, 121 (June 4, 1990) p. 287.

business practices, client expertise, and lack of client confidence.[56] Careful and extensive research of the business climate is required to address the adaptation problem.

Trade Barriers

Some types of service organizations may be excluded from a particular country by law, by a restrictive licensing system, by tariffs, by takeover, or by nationalization. For example, some countries limit domestic airline routes to domestic companies. Generally, governments all over the world have taken active steps to restrict the growth of multinational services. For example, Australia prohibits foreign banks from opening branches in the country, and Japanese customs officials clear cargo in Tokyo more rapidly for Japanese airlines than for foreign carriers. Clearly, some business service firms may not have the opportunity to expand their international operations. Prior to serious evaluation of potential new markets, careful scrutiny of present and potential governmental regulations is essential.

International markets represent a significant growth opportunity for many business service marketers. Firms seeking to offer their services in overseas markets must

---

[56]R. M. Gaedike, "Selected U.S. Multinational Service Firms in Perspective," *Journal of International Business Studies*, (Spring 1973), p. 61.

carefully evaluate the risks, market setting, and barriers that may restrict their operations and eventual success.

SUMMARY

Business services can be categorized into two segments: pure services, marketed in their own right, and support services, marketed along with goods and equipment. Both segments of the business service market are large, expanding as the world moves toward a service economy. Given the diversity of services, special insights can be secured by classifying business services on a product-service continuum for which the basic underlying factor is tangibility.

Business services are distinguished by their intangibility, linked production and consumption, lack of standardization, perishability, and use as opposed to ownership. Together, these characteristics have profound effects on how services should be marketed. Buyers of business services focus their choice processes on the perceived quality of the service, including people- and equipment-based attributes as well as technical and functional quality. Because of intangibility and lack of uniformity, service buyers have significant difficulty in the comparison and selection of service vendors. Service providers must address this issue in the development of their marketing mix.

The marketing mix for business service centers on the traditional elements—service package, pricing, promotion, and distribution—as well as on service personnel, service delivery system, and physical evidence. A key first step in creating strategies is to define the customer-benefit concept and the related service concept and offer. Pricing concentrates on influencing demand and capacity as well as on the "bundling" of service elements. In the promotion arena, the emphasis is on developing employee communication, enhancing word-of-mouth promotion, providing tangible clues, and developing interpersonal skills of operating personnel. Distribution is accomplished through direct means, through intermediaries, or by franchising.

New service marketing can be made more effective by creating an organizational culture that fosters risk taking and innovation. The failure rate for new services appears to be linked to a poor definition of the customer-benefit concept and the target market.

Support and service are increasing in importance for goods and equipment manufacturers. Third-party vendors have emerged to fill the void created by costly and ineffective service provided by the original equipment manufacturer. Several strategies exist for strengthening the equipment producer's service and support function.

A large and growing international market exists for business service. Transferring services to overseas markets is complex and studded with a variety of challenges. Unique risks, adaptation to foreign settings, and trade barriers are the significant hurdles to be circumvented in the international arena.

Discussion Questions

1. Critique this statement: "The effective business marketer of technical equipment is the one who successfully develops high-quality services to support the product; the less effective firm focuses on technical solutions offered by the product."

2. The Norris Company markets mainframe computers, whereas the Neeb company markets computer maintenance and repair services. Discuss the key characteristics of Neeb's product that distinguish it from Norris' product.

3. Describe a business service that would be classified as "High-High" on the equipment-based and people-based dimensions. Describe a business service that could be classified as "Low-Low" on these dimensions. How would the marketing approach differ between these two services?

4. Explain: "Determinant attributes for the purchase of a business service may be somewhat down the list of service characteristics that are important to buyers."

5. Distinguish between the technical and the functional quality of a business service. Which is most important in terms of customer satisfaction with a service?

6. A new firm has recently been created to provide waste removal for industrial plants. Describe the essential elements to be included in its service product.

7. What is the role of physical evidence in the marketing of a business service?

8. As manager of a luxury resort hotel, what approaches might you utilize to manage business demand for hotel space?

9. Critique this statement: "A key dimension of success in services marketing, as opposed to products marketing, is that operating personnel in the service firm play a critical selling and marketing role."

10. What steps could a manager take to enhance the chances of success for a new business service?

11. Some successful business services become miserable failures when they are marketed in international markets. Discuss some of the factors that might account for their failure in foreign markets.

CHAPTER 13

Managing Business
Marketing Channels

The channel of distribution is the marketing manager's bridge to the market. Designing and managing the business marketing channel is a challenging and ongoing task. The business marketer must ensure that the firm's channel is properly aligned to the needs of important market segments. At the same time, the marketer must also satisfy the needs of channel members, whose support is crucial to the success of business marketing strategy.

After reading this chapter, you will understand:

1. the central components of channel design.

2. the alternative forms of business marketing channels.

3. managerial aids that can be used to evaluate alternative channel structures.

4. the nature and function of industrial distributors and manufacturers' representatives.

5. requirements for managing the existing channel.

6. methods for monitoring channel performance.

A recent book, *Going to Market*, provides an excellent analysis of industrial distribution channels. The book's introduction supplies a rich conception of the industrial channel:

> Channels of distribution, those networks through which industrial products flow from point of manufacture to point of use, are basic to an industrial economy. If farms and factories are the heart of industrial America, distribution networks are its circulatory system. Composed of many thousands of manufacturers' sales branches, wholesalers, agents,

and brokers, industrial distribution systems generate and fulfill demand; they buy and sell, store and transport goods, provide sales financing, often fill the need for after-sale repair and maintenance services, and make markets for used and reconditioned equipment. These distribution networks are loosely organized federations of independent enterprises that are held together by contractual arrangements, information understandings, and mutual expectations.[1]

As suggested in this statement, the marketing channel is the primary means through which the industrial firm finds new prospects for its products, communicates with existing customers, and physically delivers the product. Louis Stern and Frederick Sturdivant indicate the channel's strategic importance: "Of all marketing decisions, the ones regarding distribution are the most far-reaching. A company can easily change its prices or its advertising. It can hire or fire a market research agency, revamp its sales promotion program, even modify its product line. But once a company sets up its distribution channels, it will generally find changing them to be difficult."[2] The selection of the best channel to accomplish objectives is challenging because (1) the alternatives are numerous, (2) marketing goals differ, and (3) the variety of business market segments often requires that separate channels must be employed concurrently.

The channel component of business marketing strategy has two important and related dimensions. First, the channel structure must be designed to accomplish desired marketing objectives. Among the challenges in the design of a distribution channel are specifying channel goals, evaluating constraints on the design, analyzing channel activities, specifying channel alternatives, and selecting channel members. Each requires evaluation.

Second, once the channel structure has been specified, the business marketer must manage the channel to achieve prescribed goals. To administer channel activities effectively, the manager must develop procedures for selecting intermediaries, for motivating them to achieve desired performance, for mediating conflict among channel members, and for evaluating performance.

Channels are pivotal in the overall scheme of business marketing. The purpose of this chapter is to provide a structure for designing and administering the business marketing channel. Chapter 14 will concentrate on the logistics aspects of the channel, which focus on making the product physically available on a timely basis.

THE BUSINESS MARKETING CHANNEL

The link between manufacturers and customers is the channel of distribution. The channel accomplishes all the tasks necessary to effect a sale and to deliver products to the customer. These tasks include making contact with potential buyers, negotiating, contracting, transferring title, communicating, arranging financing, servicing the product,

---

[1] E. Raymond Corey, Frank V. Cespedes, and V. Kasturi Rangan, *Going to Market: Distribution Systems for Industrial Products* (Boston: Harvard University Press, 1989), p. xxvii.

[2] Louis W. Stern and Frederick D. Sturdivant, "Customer-driven Distribution Systems," *Harvard Business Review*, 65 (July–August 1987), p. 34.

and providing local inventory, transportation, and storage. These tasks may be performed entirely by the manufacturer, entirely by intermediaries, or may be shared between them. The customer may even undertake some of these functions; for example, customers granted certain discounts may agree to accept larger inventories and the associated storage costs.

One of the most challenging aspects of business marketing is to allocate the tasks so as to ensure effective performance. The tasks must always be performed as the product moves from the manufacturer to the customer. Figure 13.1 shows the various ways industrial channels can be structured. Some channel structures are **indirect**; that is, some type of intermediary (such as a distributor or dealer) is involved in selling or handling the products. Other channels are **direct**; the manufacturer must accomplish all the marketing functions necessary to create a sale and to deliver products to the customer. The manufacturer's direct sales force and the direct marketing channels are examples.

A basic issue in channel management, then, is how to structure the channel so that the tasks are performed optimally. One alternative is for the manufacturer to do it all.

Direct Distribution

Direct distribution, common in business marketing, is a channel strategy that does not use intermediaries. The manufacturer's own sales force deals directly with the customer, and the manufacturer has full responsibility for performing all the necessary channel tasks. Direct distribution is often required in business marketing because of the nature of the selling situation. The direct sales approach is viable when (1) the customers are large and well defined, (2) the customers insist on direct sales, (3) sales involve extensive negotiations with upper management, and (4) control of the selling job is necessary to ensure proper implementation of the total product package and to guarantee a quick response to market conditions.

A direct sales force may include both generalists and specialists.[3] **Generalists** sell the entire product line to all customers; **specialists** concentrate on certain products, certain customers, or certain industries.

Indirect Distribution

Indirect distribution uses one or more types of intermediaries. Business marketing channels typically include fewer types of intermediaries than do consumer-goods channels. Manufacturers' representatives and industrial distributors account for most of the business handled through indirect industrial channels. Indirect distribution is generally found where (1) markets are fragmented and widely dispersed, (2) low transactions amounts prevail, and (3) buyers typically purchase a number of items, often different brands, in one transaction.[4]

---

[3] Howard Sutton, "Rethinking the Company's Selling and Distribution Channels," The Conference Board, Report #885, 1986, p. 1.

[4] Corey, Cespedes, and Rangan, *Going to Market*, p. 26.

FIGURE 13.1 **Channel Alternatives in the Business Market**

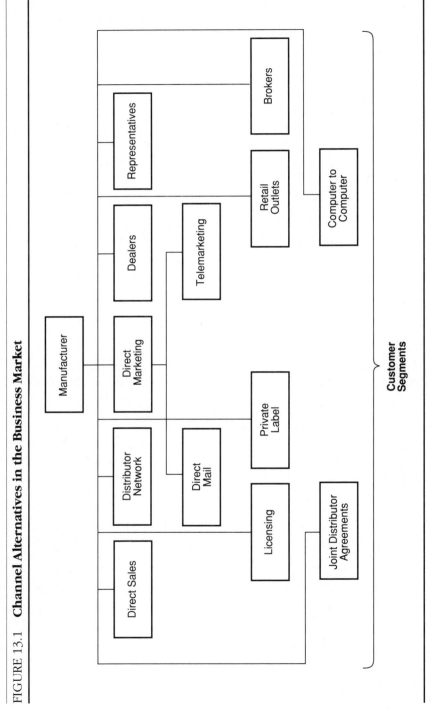

Source: Adapted from David Perry, "How You'll Manage Your 1990's Distribution Portfolio," *Business Marketing*, 74 (June 1989), p. 54.

INSIDE BUSINESS MARKETING
It Takes Five Roads to Reach This Market

One would surmise that overhead projectors and transparency film would be easy to market—they are not sophisticated, they are easy to use, and they don't have a big impact on the buyer's bottom line. The Audio-Visual division at 3M thinks differently. To market 3M projectors effectively, this division has created an elaborate distribution system composed of five distinct marketing channels:

1. *Direct.* Utilizing its own sales force, 3M markets projectors through stores in New York, Chicago, and Los Angeles. These 3M stores (a) provide a performance benchmark against which other dealers are evaluated, (b) provide a testing ground for new products, and (c) allow 3M to maintain contact with end users.

2. *Full-line Dealers.* These dealers are the exclusive distributors of top 3M products. They employ high-level sales forces and receive unlimited support from 3M. The full-line dealers market new products; 25 percent of their product line is new every five years. These dealers focus their effort on large, important customers and sell to high-level decision makers.

3. *Special-line Dealers.* These channel members do not carry the full 3M line. Their efforts are restricted to products that are well along in the product life cycle, and their focus is on bid business—usually schools and institutions that buy on a price basis. In an effort to control expenses, their

efforts are monitored by 3M through telephone as opposed to personal contact. Expenses are further controlled by drop-shipping product directly to end users and avoiding warehousing at the dealer.

4. *Scotch Brand Dealers.* "Commodity" status products are sold through 9,000 of these dealers, who are general-line office supply distributors. These dealers carry many 3M products that support the use of overhead projectors, such as film and supplies. The focus of the Scotch brand dealer is low-volume buyers, too expensive for full-line dealers or the direct sales force to call on. Scotch brand dealers provide broad distribution at low margins and sell projectors that are nearing the end of their product life cycle.

5. *OEM Dealers.* Transparency film is sold to manufacturers of equipment used to make visual slide transparencies (e.g. Hewlett-Packard). The goal is to generate new customers for 3M in the future because the OEM includes the 3M film along with the equipment that is sold to the end user.

The wide array of channels used by 3M reflects the diversity of the industrial marketplace and the importance of channels in establishing a competitive advantage. Each channel is designed on the basis of the buyer's needs, the buyer's purchasing behavior, and the nature of the buying process.

Many Channels Are Often Required

Various combinations of intermediaries and direct selling may be employed in the business marketing channel. In fact, one manufacturer could use several of the avenues shown in Figure 13.1. The wide array of options reflects the many marketing tasks to be performed and the fact that many business marketers are creating unique channel systems to appeal to a wide variety of customer niches.[5] As business markets evolve,

---

[5] David Perry, "How You'll Manage Your 1990's Distribution Portfolio," *Business Marketing*, 74 (June 1989), p. 54.

new channel arrangements have been formed to reach every one of the identifiable segments. For example, direct mail and telemarketing have become important channel systems for many products because they can penetrate the low-sales, low-profit customer segments efficiently and effectively. The insert concerning 3M's "five-road" marketing system illustrates the point. Each of the five 3M channels is utilized to address specific market segments or to perform specific types of marketing tasks.

Use of indirect channels of distribution is common for a wide variety of business products. The quality and performance of the intermediaries have a critical impact on whether the business marketer achieves his or her goals. A channel management strategy begins with an understanding of the various intermediaries that may be utilized in a business marketing channel.

PARTICIPANTS IN THE BUSINESS MARKETING CHANNEL

The types of business marketing intermediaries are distributors, manufacturers' representatives (reps), jobbers, brokers, and commission merchants. Distributors and reps handle the vast preponderance of business-to-business sales made through intermediaries. This section of the chapter will emphasize the role of each intermediary in the business marketing channel and the nature of each operation.

Distributors

Industrial distributors are the most pervasive and important single force in distribution channels. They number close to 12,000 and account for almost $50 billion in sales volume.[6] In one study, 65 percent of the purchasing managers surveyed indicated they purchased between 76 and 100 percent of their maintenance, repair, and operating (MRO) supplies from distributors.[7] In another study, McGraw-Hill found that only 24 percent of all business marketers sell their products directly to end users exclusively; the remaining 76 percent use some type of intermediary, of which industrial distributors are the most prominent.[8] What accounts for the unparalleled position of the distributor in the industrial market? What role do distributors play in the industrial distribution process?

The **Industrial Distributor Profile** presented in Table 13.1 and the insert entitled "Industrial Distributor Operating Characteristics" provide a concise view of the typical industrial distributor. Distributors are generally small, independent businesses serving narrow geographic markets. Sales average almost $2 million, although some top $300 million. Net profits are relatively low as a percentage of sales (4 percent); return on investment averages 11 percent. The typical order is small, and the distributors sell to a multitude of customers in many industries. The typical distributor is able to spread

---

[6] "Profits Up Despite Lagging Sales," *Industrial Distribution*, 77 (July 1987), p. 33.

[7] Somerby Dowst, "MRO Buying Enters a Golden Age," *Purchasing*, 101 (May 7, 1987), p. 47.

[8] "Industry Markets Goods Through Dual Channels, Says McGraw-Hill Study," *Industrial Distribution*, 75 (April 1985), p. 15.

TABLE 13.1   **Profile: Industrial Distributors**

Rubber & Accessories, Inc.

Year Founded: 1972
Headquarters: Lakeland, FL
Branches: Atlanta, GA
Employees: 52
1989 Sales: $12+ million
Warehouse Space: 72,000 sq. ft.
Inventory: $3+ million
Vendors: 300; 25 major
Customers: 4,400
Markets: agriculture, mining, transportation, food, utilities, paper, sugar mills, and construction.
Major lines: conveyor belts, hose and accessories, sheet packing, gaskets, and accessories.

Boyle Machine & Supply Co.

Year Founded: 1935
Headquarters: Peabody, MA
Employees: 19
Warehouse Space: 48,000 sq. ft.
Vendors: 200; 35 major
Customers: 400
Major Lines: hand tools, electric power tools, industrial and hydraulic hose, abrasives, maintenance and safety supplies, fasteners, pt products, and pipe, valves, and fittings.
Markets: light and heavy industry, utilities, municipalities, and all electrical and plumbing contractors.

Source: *Industrial Distribution*, 80 (March 1990 and April 1990), p. 25; p. 30.

its costs over a sizable group of vendors—it stocks goods from between 200 and 300 manufacturers, as shown in the table. Orders are generated by a sales force of outside and inside salespersons. **Outside salespersons** make regular calls on customers and handle normal account servicing and technical assistance. **Inside salespersons** complement these efforts, processing orders and scheduling delivery; their primary duty is to take telephone orders. Most distributors operate from a single location, but some approach the "supermarket" status with as many as 130 branches.

Distributor Responsibilities

An industrial distributor's primary responsibilities are shown in Table 13.2. The products that distributors sell—cutting tools, abrasives, electronic components, ball bearings, handling equipment, pipe, maintenance equipment, and hundreds more— are generally those that buyers need quickly to avoid production disruptions. Thus, the critical elements of the distributor's function are to have these products readily available and to serve as the selling arm of the manufacturer.

   Distributors are full-service middlemen; that is, they take title to the products they sell, and they perform the full range of marketing functions. Some of the more important functions are providing credit, offering wide product assortments, delivering goods, offering technical advice, and meeting emergency requirements. Distributors not only are valuable to their manufacturer-suppliers, but also are generally viewed

TABLE 13.2   **Key Distribution Responsibilities**

Responsibility	Activity
Contact	Reach all customers in a defined territory through an outside sales force that calls on customers or through an inside group that receives telephone orders.
Product availability	Provide a local inventory and include all supporting activities: credit, delivery, order processing, and advice.
Repair	Provide easy access to local repair facilities, which is unavailable from a distant manufacturer.
Assembly and light manufacturing	Purchase material in bulk and shape, form, or assemble to user requirements.

favorably by their customers. Some purchasing agents view the distributor as an extension of their "buying arms" because of the service, technical advice, and product application suggestions provided.

Today, many firms have adopted the just-in-time concept—the buyer demands that the supplies and components it purchases be delivered on a specified day, at a specific time. The effect of this just-in-time trend is to move the distributor into a position of prominence in many channel situations because few manufacturers are organized to make just-in-time deliveries all over the country.[9]

Classification of Distributors

To select the most appropriate distributor for a particular channel, the marketing manager must understand the diversity of distributor operations. Industrial distributors vary according to product lines handled and user markets served. Firms may be ultraspecialized (e.g., selling only to municipal water works), or they may carry a broad line of generalized industrial products. However, three primary distributor classifications are usually recognized.

General-Line Distributors.   **General-line** distributors cater to a broad array of industrial needs. They stock an extensive variety of products and could be likened to the supermarket in consumer-goods markets. Boyle Machine and Supply Company, profiled in Table 13.1, is an example.

Specialists.   **Specialists** focus on one or on a few related lines. Such a distributor may handle only power transmission equipment—belts, pulleys, and bearings. The most common specialty is fasteners, although specialization also occurs in cutting tools, power transmission equipment, pipe, valves, and fittings. Rubber and Accessories, Inc., profiled in Table 13.1, is a specialist in rubber products. There is a trend toward increased specialization as a result of increasing technical complexity of products and the need for higher levels of precision and quality control.

---

[9] Sutton, "Rethinking the Company's Selling and Distribution Channels," p. 3.

INSIDE BUSINESS MARKETING

Industrial Distributor Operating Characteristics

The data below reflect median values for a number of operating variables gleaned from an annual study of industrial distributors.

	Median Values
Annual sales	$1,800,000
Gross profit	27 percent
Net profit	4 percent
ROI	11 percent
Average inventory	$250,000
Inventory turns	5.4
Receivables	$227,000
Sales per employee	$171,000
Number of employees	11.0
Warehouse square feet	7,500
Sales per square foot	$280
Ownership	Independent

Source: John G. F. Bonnanzio, "The Urge to Merge," *Industrial Distribution*, 78 (July 1989), pp. 31–43.

Combination House. A **combination house** operates in two markets: industrial and consumer. Such a distributor might carry electric motors for industrial customers and hardware and automotive parts to be sold through retailers to final consumers.

The selection of a distributor will depend upon the manufacturer's requirements. The general-line distributor offers the advantage of one-stop purchasing to the manufacturer's potential customers. If a high level of service and technical expertise is not required, the general-line distributor is a good choice. The specialist, on the other hand, provides the manufacturer with a high level of technical capability and a well-developed understanding of complex user requirements. Fasteners, for instance, are handled by specialists because of the strict quality-control standards that users impose.

The Distributor as a Valuable Asset

The quality of a firm's distributors is often the difference between a highly successful marketing strategy and an ineffective one. Good distributors are prized by customers, making it all the more necessary to strive continually to engage the best in any given market. Distributors often provide the only economically feasible way of obtaining comprehensive market coverage.

In summary, the industrial distributor is a full-service intermediary who takes title to the products sold; maintains inventories; provides credit, delivery, wide product assortment, and technical assistance; and may even do light assembly and manufacturing. Although the distributor is primarily responsible for contacting and supplying present customers, industrial distributors also solicit new accounts and work to expand the market. Products handled by industrial distributors are generally established products—typically used in manufacturing operations, repair, and maintenance—with a broad and large demand.

Industrial distributors are a powerful force in business marketing channels, and all indications point to an expanded role for them. The manufacturer's representative is an equally viable force in the business marketing channel.

Manufacturers' Representatives

For many business marketers who need a strong selling job with a technically complex product, manufacturers' representatives, or reps, are the only cost-effective answer. **Reps** are salespeople who work independently (or for a rep company), represent several companies in the same geographic area, and sell noncompeting but complementary products. Table 13.3 provides a concise sketch of a typical rep.

The Rep's Responsibilities

A rep neither takes title to nor holds inventory of the products handled. (Some reps do, however, keep a limited inventory of repair and maintenance parts.) The rep's forte is expert product knowledge coupled with a keen understanding of the markets and the customers covered. Reps are usually limited to defined geographical areas; thus, a manufacturer seeking nationwide distribution will usually work with several rep companies.

The Rep-Customer Relationship

Reps are the selling arm for manufacturers—making contact with customers, writing orders, following up on orders, and linking the manufacturer with the industrial end users. Although paid by the manufacturer, the rep is also important to the customers served. Often, the efforts of a rep during a customer emergency (e.g., an equipment failure) means the difference between continuing or stopping production. Most reps are thoroughly experienced in the industries they serve; they can offer technical advice while enhancing the customer's leverage with suppliers in securing parts, repair, and delivery. The rep also provides customers with a continuing flow of information on innovations and trends in equipment, as well as on the industry as a whole.

Commission Basis

Reps are paid a commission on sales; the commission varies by industry and by the nature of the selling job. Table 13.4 provides a sample of average rep commission percentages for various industries in 1986. They range from a low of 4 percent for automotive to 18.1 percent for controls and instrumentation. Percentage commission compensation is attractive to manufacturers because they have few fixed sales costs. Reps are paid only when orders are generated. Because reps are paid on commission, they are motivated to generate high levels of sales—another fact appreciated by the manufacturer.

TABLE 13.3 **Profile of a Manufacturers' Representative**

Company	Alcon Company
Location	Middle Village, N.Y.
End-user market	Bottling and brewery industry
Estimated average commission	10 to 14 percent
Geographic market coverage	New England states, New York, New Jersey, Pennsylvania, Maryland, Delaware, eastern Virginia
Products handled	Bottle filler replacement parts: conveyors, case packers, uncasers, warmers and reusers, empty bottle inspectors, plastic cases, decappers.
Companies represented	P. T. Barkmann & Sons, Hamrich Manufacturing, McQueen Technology, Bacmis Volckening, Kyowa American Corp.

TABLE 13.4 **Manufacturers' Representatives' Commissions**

	Commissions	
Industry	**Average High (Percent)**	**Average Low (Percent)**
Automotive, OEM	6.3	4.0
Chemicals	14.4	9.0
Computers	13.1	6.9
Controls and instrumentation	18.1	9.0
Electronic products	12.2	7.1
Fasteners	7.5	5.2
Office supplies and equipment	13.8	6.0
Paper	15.0	7.3
Steel mills	8.1	4.9

Source: "S&MM's 1987 Survey of Selling Costs," *Sales & Marketing Management* (February 16, 1987), p. 59.

Experience

Reps possess sophisticated product knowledge and typically have extensive experience in the markets they serve. Most reps develop their field experience while working as a salesperson for a manufacturer. They are motivated to become reps by the desire to be independent and to reap the substantial monetary rewards possible on commission.

When Reps Are Used

Large and Small Firms. Small- and medium-sized firms generally have the greatest need for a rep, although many large firms—for example, Dow Chemical and W. R. Grace—use them. The reason is primarily economic: smaller firms cannot justify the expense of maintaining their own sales forces. The rep provides an efficient means to obtaining total market coverage, with costs incurred only as sales are made. The quality of the selling job is often very good as a result of the rep's prior experience and market knowledge.

Limited Market Potential.   The rep also plays a vital role when the manufacturer's market potential is limited. A manufacturer may use a direct sales force in heavily concentrated industrial markets where the demand is sufficient to support the expense and use reps to cover less dense markets. Because the rep carries several lines, expenses can be allocated over a much larger sales volume.

Servicing Distributors.   Reps may also be employed by a firm that markets through distributors. When a manufacturer sells through hundreds of distributors across the United States, reps may sell to and service the distributors.

Reducing Overhead Costs.   Sometimes the commission rate paid to reps exceeds the cost of a direct sales force, yet the supplier continues to use reps. This policy is not as irrational as it appears. Assume, for example, that costs for a direct sales force approximate 8 percent of sales and that a rep's commission rate is 11 percent. The use of reps in this case is often justified because of the hidden costs associated with a sales force. First, the manufacturer does not provide fringe benefits or a fixed salary to reps. Second, the costs of training a rep are usually limited to those required to provide product information. Thus, the use of reps eliminates significant overhead costs.

Other Business Marketing Intermediaries

The importance of distributors and reps far outshadows that of other business marketing intermediaries. Jobbers, brokers, and commission merchants may, however, be vital cogs in the distribution network for certain manufacturers.

Jobbers
Jobbers typically obtain orders from business customers and pass them along to the manufacturers they represent. The distinguishing feature of jobbers is that they take title to the products they sell, but they do not physically handle, stock, or deliver them. The jobber's niche in the industrial marketplace is in marketing products so bulky that additional handling would be prohibitively expensive and only add to the risk of damaging the product. Thus, jobbers deal with products such as coal, iron ore, lumber, and chemicals when bulk shipments in carload quantities do not necessitate any grouping or sorting by the intermediary.

Commission Merchants
Commission merchants deal with bulk commodities—usually raw materials. Typically, they do not have a permanent arrangement with their suppliers, but perform a one-time selling function. An industrial company involved in mining might ship its output to a large central market where buyers inspect the material before purchase. In this case, the commission merchant makes the product available for inspection;

ETHICAL BUSINESS MARKETING
What Does a Manufacturer Owe Its Reps?

The Milton Boiler and Compressor Company, a market leader in its industry, has focused all its marketing attention on markets in the East and Southeast. The company, with a very aggressive and professional sales force, was the clear market share leader in its territories. In 1982, the company's strategic planning task force recommended that the firm expand marketing efforts to the West Coast. The firm carefully evaluated its channel options and made the decision to utilize manufacturers' reps in the new market. Although Milton's sales expertise was widely heralded, it opted for reps because of their vast market knowledge and the fact that the firm had no sales volume at all west of the Mississippi.

George Borne and Associates was selected as the rep firm. Borne was located in Los Angeles, and the firm has sold boiler and compressor equipment in the Southwest and West for almost thirty years. Sales of Milton products were slow at first, but Borne nevertheless worked diligently to establish Milton's line in its territory. Over the first five years of the relationship Borne "invested heavily" in the Milton business: (1) they hired three new salespeople to sell the Milton line, (2) the salespeople were sent to at least four training sessions each year, (3) Borne contracted with a service firm to handle repair and maintenance of Milton equipment, (4) at least $20,000 was invested in sales aides,

promotional material, and catalogs for the Milton line each year, (5) Borne agreed to a lower-than-normal commission for the first three years until sales reached an "acceptable level."

By 1989, sales of Milton original equipment and repair and maintenance parts exceeded $9 million in the western area, and sales appeared to be growing at an annual rate of 12 percent. Although such estimates are difficult, trade publications forecast Milton's western share of market to exceed 13 percent in late 1989. Milton's sales and profit goals were exceeded every year except the first one.

On February 4, 1990, Milton management notified the Borne company that within 90 days Borne would no longer represent Milton in the western territory. Beginning June 1, 1990, Milton would sell product through its own sales force (one individual, it was rumored, was to be hired away from Borne).

Borne management was stunned. They felt cheated and believed they had been used. They felt that Milton had intended all along to sack them as soon as sales volume reached a predetermined level. Most employees believed that Milton management had no ethical standards.

What are the ethical issues underlying this controversial decision by Milton? Does Borne have a right to feel "cheated"? Has Milton breached a faith or violated an ethical standard?

although commission merchants do not take title, they can negotiate prices and execute the sale for the supplier. Commission merchants provide sellers with representation in the marketplace, physical handling of goods, and completion of the transaction.

Brokers

Brokers facilitate transactions between buyers and sellers by providing information on what is demanded and on what is available. Like the commission merchant, the broker operates on a more or less irregular arrangement. A firm desiring to sell used machinery might employ a broker to seek out potential buyers and to complete negotiations leading to eventual sale. The party that engages the broker pays the commission. The broker's role is particularly important when product and market information is nonexistent or inadequate.

Retailers

For some industrial products, **"retail"** stores (sometimes referred to as "Value-Added Resellers") have evolved in response to the need to reach certain market segments in a cost-effective manner. Office supplies, computers, and computer software are examples. In computer software, software retailers are rapidly becoming the preferred source of software for corporate buyers. Software retailers are successful because they can "handle large volumes of product and get it quickly to the customer at a very reasonable price."[10] IBM recently began a pilot program in which IBM-selected resellers will operate IBM-only stores to secure a market at specific college campuses.[11] This retail channel is seen as a way to enhance market share and improve the physical distribution of the product. Delivery, volume, margin, and sales call costs are important factors in the decision to select the retail channel for industrial products.

A clear understanding of the types of channel intermediaries is necessary for effectively designing and managing the business market channel. The next section of the chapter will examine the core dimensions of the channel design process.

CHANNEL DESIGN

Channel design is the dynamic process of developing new channels where none existed and modifying existing channels.[12] The business marketer usually deals with modification of existing channels, although new products and customer segments may require entirely new channels. Regardless of whether the manager is dealing with a new channel or modifying an existing channel, channel design is an active rather than a passive task. Effective distribution channels do not simply evolve; they are developed by management, which takes action on the basis of a well-conceived plan that reflects overall marketing goals.

Channel design is best conceptualized as a series of stages that must be completed so that the business marketing manager can be sure that all important channel dimensions have been evaluated (Figure 13.2). The result of the channel design process is to specify the structure that provides the highest probability of achieving the firm's objectives. Note that the process focuses on channel structure and not on channel participants. **Channel structure** refers to the underlying framework: the number of channel levels, the number and types of intermediaries, and the linkages among channel members. Selection of individual intermediaries is indeed important; it will be examined later in the chapter.

---

[10] Robert F. McCarthy, "Software's Hard-Charging Channel," *Business Marketing*, 74 (October 1989), p. 72.

[11] Albert Pang, "IBM Pairs Colleges, Computer Dealers," *Computer Reseller News*, (September 10, 1990), pp. 1, 32.

[12] Bert Rosenbloom, *Marketing Channels: A Management View* (Hinsdale, Ill.: The Dryden Press, 1978), p. 105.

FIGURE 13.2   **The Channel Design Process**

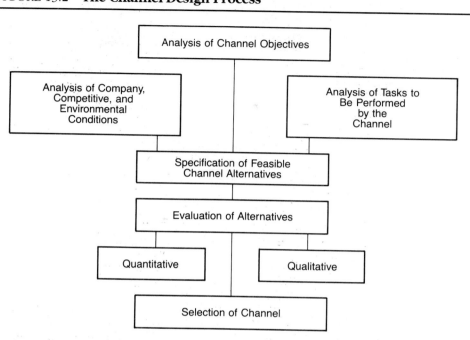

Source: Michael D. Hutt and Thomas W. Speh, "Realigning Industrial Marketing Channels," *Industrial Marketing Management*, 12 (July 1983), p. 171–177.

Stage 1. Channel Objectives

Business firms formulate their marketing strategies to appeal to selected market segments, to earn targeted levels of profits, to maintain or increase sales and market share growth rates, and to achieve all this within specified resource constraints. Each element of the marketing strategy has a specific purpose. Thus, whether the business marketer is designing a totally new channel or redesigning an existing one, the first phase of channel design is to comprehend fully the marketing goals and to formulate corresponding channel objectives.

Structure Based on Profits and Strategy Integration

Profit considerations and asset utilization must be reflected in channel objectives and design. For example, the cost of maintaining a salesperson in the field, including lodging, meals, and auto rental, has increased dramatically over the past decade. *Sales & Marketing Management's* figure for selling cost per call rose 26 percent between 1986 and 1989 for industrial firms.[13] The cost-per-call figure currently approaches $230.

---

[13] "1990 Survey of Selling Costs," *Sales & Marketing Management*, 142 (February 26, 1990), p. 75.

For the manufacturer, these costs are somewhat fixed in the short run. The need to commit working capital to these costs might be eliminated by switching from a direct sales force to manufacturers' reps, whose compensation, as a percentage of sales, is totally variable. Of course, many other factors, such as the quality of the selling job, must also be evaluated. Channel structure must be compatible with all marketing strategy elements.

Channel Objectives Reflect Marketing Goals

Specific distribution objectives are established on the basis of broad marketing objectives. Distribution objectives force the manager to relate channel design decisions to broader marketing goals. A manufacturer of industrial cleaning products might have a distribution objective of providing product availability in every county in the Midwest with over $5 million in market potential. The distribution objective of a supplier of air-conditioning units might be to make contact with industrial plant architects once every month and with industrial contractors once every two months.

Marketing and distribution objectives guide the channel design process and actually limit the range of feasible channel structures. Before the alternative channel structures can be evaluated, the business marketing manager must evaluate other limitations on the choice of channel structures.

Stage 2.   Channel Design Constraints

Frequently, the manager has little flexibility in the selection of channel structures because of trade, competitive, company, and environmental factors. In fact, the decision on channel design may be imposed on the manager. The variety of constraining factors is almost limitless.[14] Figure 13.3 summarizes those factors most relevant to the business marketer.

Stage 3.   Pervasive Channel Tasks

Each channel structure will be evaluated on its ability to perform the required channel activities effectively and efficiently. The concept of a channel as a sequence of activities to be performed, rather than as a set of channel institutions, is essential to channel design. The business marketing manager must creatively structure the tasks necessary to meet customer requirements and company goals rather than merely accepting existing channel structures or traditional distribution patterns.

Manufacturers' reps typically carry no inventory of their suppliers' products. A manufacturer of semiconductors and microcircuits, upon a careful analysis of required channel activities, may decide that although reps can provide the level of sales service

---

[14] For example, see Louis W. Stern and Frederick D. Sturdivant, "Customer-Driven Distribution Systems," *Harvard Business Review*, 65 (July–August 1987), pp. 34–41; Bert Rosenbloom, *Marketing Channels: A Management View* (Hinsdale, Ill.: The Dryden Press, 1978), p. 105; and Louis Stern and Adel I. El-Ansary, *Marketing Channels*, 3rd ed. (Englewood Cliffs, N.J.: Prentice Hall, 1988), pp. 202–223.

FIGURE 13.3   **Factors Limiting Choice of Industrial Channel**

---

1.   **Availability of Good Intermediaries**
     Competitors often "lock up" the better intermediaries.
     Established intermediaries are not always receptive to new products.
2.   **Traditional Channel Patterns**
     Established patterns of distribution are difficult to violate.
     Large customers may demand direct sales.
3.   **Product Characteristics**
     Technical complexity dictates direct distribution.
     Extensive repair requirements may call for local distributors to service the product line.
4.   **Company Financial Resources**
     Capital requirements often preclude direct distribution.
5.   **Competitive Strategies**
     Direct service by competitors may force all firms to sell direct.
6.   **Geographic Dispersion of Customers**
     A widely dispersed market of small customers often requires low-cost representation afforded by
     intermediaries.

---

needed, large accounts need emergency local inventories of a few selected microcircuits. In this case the solution would not be to abandon the rep as a viable channel, but to compensate the rep for carrying a limited inventory of emergency circuits. Analysis of required tasks and a view of the channel as a sequence of activities would lead the firm to a creative solution to the inventory problem.

The backbone of channel design is the analysis of objectives, constraints, and channel activities. Once these are understood, channel alternatives can be evaluated.

Stage 4.   Channel Alternatives

Specification of channel alternatives involves four primary issues:

1.   The number of levels to be included in the channel (i.e., the degree of "directness")
2.   The types of intermediaries to employ
3.   The number of channel intermediaries at each level of the channel
4.   The number of channels to employ

The decisions made for each are predicated upon the objectives, constraints, and activities previously analyzed.

Degree of "Directness"

The issue of directness concerns whether products will be marketed directly to customers or through intermediaries. The critical aspects of this decision were presented earlier in the chapter.

Assessing Product/Market Factors

The number of channel levels depends on a host of company, product, and market variables. The "length" of channels used to market industrial products was studied by

Donald Jackson, Robert Krampf, and Leonard Konopa.[15] Their study of 300 industrial firms suggested that business marketing channel length is influenced by availability of capable intermediaries, market factors, and customer characteristics. Market factors include the number of customers, the geographic concentration of customers, and the industry concentration. Customer characteristics include the significance of the purchase as perceived by the customer and the volume potential of a customer. Channel length increases with greater availability of effective intermediaries and with the number of customers; it decreases when the purchase becomes more significant, when customer potential increases, and when market or industry concentration increases.

There is a greater tendency in business than in consumer-goods marketing to sell directly to the customer. However, direct selling is often not feasible. For products such as tools, abrasives, fasteners, pipes, valves, materials-handling equipment, and wire rope, as much as 97 percent of the annual volume moves through industrial distributors only. These products are typically bought frequently, repetitively (straight rebuy), and in small quantities. Instantaneous availability is fundamental; industrial distributors handle such products efficiently.

Type of Intermediary

A wide array of factors influences the choice of intermediaries, with the tasks they perform being of prime importance. These tasks were carefully detailed for both reps and distributors earlier in the chapter.

A host of product and market conditions also appear to play a role in indicating which type of intermediary will be used. A study by Donald Jackson and Michael d'Amico evaluated the product and market conditions that differed between manufacturer–rep channels and manufacturer–distributor channels.[16] Their findings showed that the manufacturer–rep channel is generally used in the following conditions:

- When the product is not standard but is closer to made-to-order
- When the product tends toward technical complexity
- When the gross margin is not large
- When the market is made up of a relatively few number of customers that are concentrated geographically and concentrated in a few industries
- When these customers order relatively infrequently and allow fairly long lead times

Use of distributors is associated with the opposite conditions. A review of market and product situations should be made when making the rep versus distributor decision.

A second question is whether more than one type of intermediary will be needed to satisfy all target markets. The primary reason for using more than one type of

---

[15] Donald M. Jackson, Robert F. Krampf, and Leonard J. Konopa, "Factors That Influence the Length of Industrial Channels," *Industrial Marketing Management*, 11 (October 1982), pp. 263–268.

[16] Donald M. Jackson and Michael F. d'Amico, "Products and Markets Served by Distributors and Agents," *Industrial Marketing Management*, 18 (February 1989), p. 33.

intermediary for the same product is that different market segments require different channel structures. Some firms use three distinct approaches. Large accounts are called on by the firm's own sales force, distributors handle small repeat orders, and manufacturers' reps develop the market that is made up of medium-sized firms.

Like size of accounts, differences in purchase behavior may also dictate using more than one type of intermediary. If a firm produces a wide line of industrial products, some may require high-caliber selling to a multitude of buying influences within a single buyer's firm. When this occurs, the firm's own sales force would focus on the more complex buying situations, whereas the distributors would sell standardized products from local stocks.

The Number of Intermediaries

How many intermediaries of each type are required to cover a particular market effectively? The answer is sometimes easy—for example, when a firm distributes through reps. Since reps act as the firm's sales force, there would be no point to using more than one rep to call on a specific customer. (Unless, of course, each rep specialized in a unique part of the company's product line.) The business marketer would select the single best rep organization in each of the geographical areas to be covered.

In the case of distribution through industrial distributors, the company may require two, three, or even more carefully selected distributors in a geographic market to ensure adequate market coverage. The policy of carefully choosing channel members in a particular geographical area is referred to as **selective distribution**. The nature of the product and the purchasing process usually dictate a selective policy. Materials-handling equipment, electric motors, power-transmission equipment, and tools typically fall into the category of straight or modified rebuy situations. The time spent in evaluating sources for these products is not great, yet the purchase is not always simple and repetitive. The buyer needs advice about applications, maintenance, and repair, and usually demands rapid product delivery, repair, and service. The manufacturer wants to be represented by a distributor that can satisfy these customer requirements. To ensure that distributors will perform the job required and provide proper emphasis to the manufacturer's line, the number of distributors will be limited to a few in a given market.

Generally, the more standardized the products, the more frequently they are purchased, and the smaller their unit value, the greater the number of distributors in a given market. The abrasives manufacturer who requires up to 1,000 general-line distributors is following an intensive rather than a selective distribution policy. An **intensive distribution** policy is especially appropriate when availability is a requirement. Customers must have a product source in close proximity to their plants.

The Number of Channels

More than one channel will be required when various market segments are served and when the characteristics of the segment dictate a fundamentally unique approach to distribution.

Channels need to change to match the life cycle position of the product. For example, small office copiers were first sold directly through manufacturers' direct sales forces. The Japanese then began marketing copiers through office equipment dealers, and today these machines are available through a variety of channels—direct, dealers, mass merchandisers, and mail order.[17]

Earlier in the chapter, a description of 3M's five channels for audiovisual equipment was presented. In the 3M case, each channel serves a specific target market, and the channel is structured on the basis of buyers' needs, buying behavior, and buying process. For microcomputers, IBM uses a direct sales force to reach the "elite" market—*Fortune* 1,000 companies. A system of more than 2,000 dealers is also employed to reach the 21 percent of the microcomputer market that is made up of small businesses.[18] However, using multiple channels is not without its problems because of the potential competition that exists between the channels. Direct selling activities of manufacturers, sales by nondealer resellers, and compensation splits on joint sales are some of the areas of friction. Managing conflicts of this nature is discussed later in the chapter.

Legal Issues

When a firm maintains more than one channel, some accounts may be double-covered, or various channel members may find themselves competing for business. Business marketers often want to reserve large accounts for their own sales force or restrict certain territories for "selected" distributors. There are complex legal issues associated with such restrictions.

E. Raymond Corey, Frank Cespedes and V. Kasturi Rangan cogently summarize the status of these legal issues:

> The terms and conditions of channel member agreements may require that the reseller do the following:
>
> * Carry the producer's full line
> * Either not stock competing brands or treat them strategically as secondary lines
> * Not solicit business from certain "reserved" accounts, specified classes of trade, and/or beyond the territory in which the reseller is franchised to sell
> * Observe resale price schedules set by the producer
> * Maintain specified inventory levels
> * Meet specified sales quotas
>
> The supplier may secure adherence to these conditions by withholding producer support from nonconforming distributors and by rewarding those which do conform, with resellers resisting such methods of control and sometimes taking legal action against offending suppliers.

---

[17] Milind Lele, "Matching Your Channels to Your Product's Life Cycle," *Business Marketing*, 71 (December 1986), p. 61.

[18] Kate Bertrand, "Changing Channels in the Microcomputer Market," *Business Marketing*, 71 (September 1986), p. 91.

In general, the kinds of terms and conditions outlined above and their enforcement are not illegal per se unless they are construed as being "in restraint of trade or commerce." If franchise conditions serve to build and preserve monopoly power as defined by the Sherman Act, and/or if franchise enforcement is carried out through conspiratorial arrangements, both the conditions and the actions to secure adherence are likely to be judged illegal.[19]

The final task facing the business marketing manager is to select the most effective channel structure from among the feasible alternatives.

Stage 5. Channel Selection

Most channel design decisions are only slight modifications of the channel structure in response to changing markets, expanding geographic coverage, new customer requirements, or new products. Selection of the appropriate modification in channel structure may be fairly straightforward; in fact, the range of choices may be quite limited.

Complex Channel Selection Decisions

The total redesign of an existing channel system or the initiation of a totally new one generally requires a thorough analysis of alternatives. The alternatives are numerous, as are the influencing variables. Although the manager seeks to design the optimal channel for maximum long-run profit, to do so is nearly impossible. Why?

First, the cost and revenue data to support the decision may not be available. So many factors influence the channel decision that it is often impossible to assess their future impact on channel costs and revenues. Second, channels are dynamic, whereas the design decision is made at a single point in time. The optimal channel today may not be optimal in five years, or even one year. Channel design is a process, not a decision. Lastly, the chance of finding all the relevant alternatives is slim.

In spite of such impediments, existing channels must be continually monitored to determine whether a total or a partial change in channel structure is necessary to meet corporate profitability goals. Any change in the channel structure should consider the net impact on channel effectiveness and efficiency.[20] Consequently, the manager must analyze both the direct costs associated with the channel functions to be shifted (selling, storage, service) and those associated with the longer time horizon, as well as the impacts on customer service and sales. Moreover, the manager must consider how potential changes in the channel would fit with the overall marketing strategy.

---

[19] Corey, Cespedes, and Rangan, *Going to Market*, p. 146.

[20] Michael D. Hutt and Thomas W. Speh, "Realigning Industrial Marketing Channels," *Industrial Marketing Management*, 12 (July 1983), pp. 171–177.

Evaluating Alternative Channels

A useful approach to evaluating channel options is provided by Louis Stern and Frederick Sturdivant.[21] The approach, as depicted in Table 13.5, takes into account all the elements of the channel design process as well as important customer requirements. The focus of their approach is to create an "ideal" channel system that fully addresses customer needs; once this system is specified, it is compared to the "feasible" channel system created on the basis of management objectives and constraints. The critical element is to compare both systems on the basis of customer service performance, structure, and costs.

Channel selection is facilitated by looking at "gaps" that may exist between the systems—existing, ideal, and feasible. One of three conclusions could emerge:

1. *All three systems resemble each other.* In this case, the existing system is about as good as it can be. If customer satisfaction is low, the fault is not with the channel design, it is with poor management.

2. *Existing and feasible systems are similar, but differ from the ideal.* Management constraints and objectives may be causing the gap. A careful review is required as specified in Step 6 of Table 13.5.

3. *All three systems are different.* If the feasible system lies between the ideal and existing system, the existing system can be changed without sacrificing management goals. Relaxing management constraints might produce even greater benefits.

An example from IBM illustrates the evaluation process. The ideal channel for marketing the IBM PC to small users was a service-intensive, decentralized network of specialty dealers carrying assorted microcomputer brands as well as other office equipment (for one-stop buying). The existing channel was a direct IBM sales force. The feasible system—prescribed by IBM management in order to control service quality—was composed of IBM retail outlets carrying only IBM products. Comparison shopping in the IBM centers was impossible, and one-stop office equipment buying was prohibited. In 1986, IBM sold its product center network to Nynex. Currently, IBM utilizes over 2,000 independent dealers carrying other brands and products. Clearly, the feasible system (IBM Product Centers) and the existing system (direct) did not match the ideal. When the IBM Product Centers became the existing system, it still differed from the ideal. Eventually, management relaxed its constraints (control), and the ideal system was adopted.

Qualitative Dimensions

The channel decision maker must consider qualitative as well as quantitative factors. Given two channels with nearly similar economic performance, the critical factor may be the degree of *control* that the business marketer can exercise over the channels. A rep as opposed to a distributor channel generally gives the manager more control because the manufacturer maintains title and possession of the goods. The manufacturer

---

[21] Stern and Sturdivant, "Customer-Driven Distribution Systems," pp. 34–41.

TABLE 13.5 **Procedure for Evaluating Channel Alternatives**

Process	Key Analytical Activities
Step 1: Determine customer requirements	Assess desire for sales assistance, locational convenience, one-stop buying, depth of assortment, and the whole range of possible services.
Step 2: Evaluate potential intermediaries	Assess which type of intermediaries are possible, including direct sale.
Step 3: Analyze costs	Involves three dimensions: (1) Is it feasible for the company to satisfy all customer requirements? (2) What types of supplier support are required? (3) What are the costs of the support systems for each type of channel alternative?
Step 4: Specify constraints—create the "bounded" system	Develop management input on key constraints and company long-term objectives. Specify the channel system structure based on these constraints.
Step 5: Compare options	Compare the "ideal system" specified by customers to the "feasible" system specified by constraints and objectives. If an existing channel is being reviewed, compare it to the ideal and feasible system.
Step 6: Review constraints and assumptions	Use experts—consultants, lawyers, accountants—to evaluate assumptions.
Step 7: Evaluate gaps	If gaps exist between the existing, ideal, and feasible systems, analyze the underlying reasons.
Step 8: Implementation	Modify the ideal system according to objectives and constraints.

Source: Adapted from Louis W. Stern and Frederick Sturdivant, "Customer-Driven Distribution Systems," *Harvard Business Review*, 65 (July–August 1987), pp. 34–41.

may be willing to trade off short-run economic benefits in order to gain long-term control over channel activities.

Adaptation by channel members may be important in the long run. Small, undercapitalized distributors may not be able to respond effectively to new competitive thrusts or to problems caused by economic downturns. The viable alternatives, then, will be to sell direct or to use reps and make products available through a system of public warehouses.

Such factors as intermediary image, financial capacity, sales, and merchandising ability must also be analyzed. And once the channel is designed, it must be administered.

CHANNEL ADMINISTRATION

Once a particular industrial channel structure is chosen, channel participants must be selected, and arrangements must be made to ensure that all obligations are assigned. Next, channel members must be motivated to perform the tasks necessary to achieve channel objectives. Third, conflict within the channel must be properly controlled. Last, performance must be controlled and evaluated.

Selection of Intermediaries

Why is the selection of channel members (specific companies, rather than *type*, which is specified in the design process) part of channel management rather than an aspect of channel design? The primary reason is that intermediary selection is an ongoing process; some intermediaries choose to leave the channel, and others are terminated by the supplier. Thus, selection of intermediaries is more or less continuous. Performance of individual channel members must be evaluated continuously. The manufacturer should be prepared to move quickly, replacing poor performers with potentially better ones. Including the selection process in ongoing channel management puts the process in its proper perspective.

Selection Criteria

Because all firms do not have the same channel objectives or activities to be performed, there is no single set of criteria with universal application. Some firms find it impossible to reduce the selection of intermediaries to a rigid procedure, but some means for objectively comparing potential channel members is vital. Ideally, the business marketing manager should examine objective factors concerning the channel situation and sensibly temper these evaluations with personal impressions, opinions, and judgment.

Each business marketer must develop criteria that are relevant to the firm's own product/market situation. Many companies use checklists to compare prospective distributors or reps. The McGraw-Edison Company uses an intensive checklist, and the criteria it considers important are market coverage, product lines, personnel, growth, and financial standing.

Securing Good Intermediaries

The marketer can identify prospective intermediaries through discussions with company salespeople and existing or potential customers, or through trade sources, such as *Industrial Distribution* magazine or the *Verified Directory of Manufacturers' Representatives.* Once the list of potential intermediaries is reduced to a few names, the manufacturer will use the selection criteria to evaluate them.

The formation of the channel is not at all a one-way street. The manufacturer must now induce the intermediaries to become part of the channel system. Some distributors evaluate potential suppliers just as rigorously as the manufacturers rate them and on many of the same dimensions. Manufacturers must often demonstrate the sales and profit potential of their product and be willing to grant the intermediaries some territorial exclusivity.

Motivating Channel Members

Distributors and reps are independent and profit oriented. They are oriented toward their customers and toward whatever means are necessary to satisfy customer needs for industrial products and services. Their perceptions and outlook may vary substantially from those of the manufacturers they represent. As a consequence, marketing strategies can fail because managers at the manufacturers' level do not tailor their programs to the capabilities and orientations of their intermediaries. To manage the business marketing channel effectively, the marketer must understand the intermediaries' perspective and devise methods for motivating these intermediaries to perform in a way that will enhance the manufacturer's long-term success. The manufacturer must continually seek support from intermediaries, and the quality of that support will depend on the motivational techniques employed.

The degree to which an intermediary will comply with manufacturer directives appears to be influenced by the intermediary's dependence on the manufacturer.[22] Manufacturers who wish to enhance their ability to affect the decisions and behavior of their channel members should consider strategies that increase the channel member's dependence on them. Such tactics as increasing commissions, encouraging full-line representation, new product introduction, and increased promotion may be effective at increasing the percentage of sales and profits an intermediary earns from a given manufacturer, and as a consequence, increase its dependence on the manufacturer.[23]

A Partnership

Channel member motivation begins with the understanding that the channel relationship is a *partnership*. Manufacturers and intermediaries are in business together; whatever expertise and assistance the manufacturer can provide to the intermediaries will improve total channel effectiveness. Some business firms recognize the partnership concept by preparing formal contracts to be signed by both parties. Columbus McKinnon Corporation, a large business firm, makes the following agreement with its distributors: "The distributor will maintain an inventory that gives four turns based on last year's sales, will purchase at least $15,000 a year from the supplier, [and] will actively promote the sale of the supplier's products. The supplier (Columbus McKinnon), in turn, extends the latest discount service and freight, contributes a specific amount to joint advertising, works a specified length of time with each distributor salesman, and helps develop annual sales targets."[24]

Both company and distributors agree that a formal contract is the only effective way to operationalize the partnership idea and avoid potential misunderstandings.

One study of channel relationships suggested that manufacturers may be able to increase the level of resources directed to their products by developing a trusting relationship with their reps; by improving communication through recognition programs, product training, and consultation with the reps; and by informing the reps of plans, explicitly detailing objectives, and providing positive feedback.[25] Another study of

---

[22] Janet E. Keith, Donald W. Jackson, and Lawrence A. Crosby, "Effects of Alternative Types of Influence Strategies Under Different Channel Dependence Structures," *Journal of Marketing* 54 (July 1990), p. 37.

[23] Ibid., p. 38.

[24] Duffy Marks, "Post Carborundum: Distributors Evaluate Their Vendor Relations," *Industrial Distribution*, 7 (June 1983), p. 35.

[25] Erin Anderson, Leonard M. Lodish, and Barton A. Weitz, "Resource Allocation Behavior in Conventional Channels," *Journal of Marketing Research*, 24 (February 1987) p. 95. See also Jan B. Heide and George John, "The Role of Dependence Balancing in Safeguarding Transaction-Specific Assets in Conventional Channels," *Journal of Marketing*, 52 (January 1988), pp. 20–35.

INSIDE BUSINESS MARKETING
A Lesson in Effective Manufacturer–Distributor Relationships

The Norton Company is the world's largest manufacturer of abrasive products (sandpaper and grinding wheels). Selling primarily through distributors, Norton has gained market share steadily for over two decades. What factors helped to account for this and for the company's distribution strength? Six major determinants can be cited:

1. The value of the *Norton franchise.* With the broadest product line in the abrasive industry, and long-term reliability as a source of supply, Norton has been able to attract and hold strong distributors.

2. The Norton line as a significant source of *distributor income.* Norton's product line is typically among the three best-selling lines carried by its distributors, accounting on average for about 10 percent of the distributor's sales volume. High distributor margins and a large installed base ensure Norton's distributors of a steady source of revenue and profit.

3. Tactical programs aimed at *motivating* and *monitoring* distributors. The time, money, and attention devoted to nurturing good relationships with its distributors are ul-timately translated into more effective representation of Norton's line by its distributors. Features of Norton's marketing programs—such as a distributor advisory council, incentive programs, and the frequent interactions among individual distributors and Norton's field sales personnel—helped to build these relationships.

4. A clear sense of *selling strategy.* The areas of primary sales coverage for distributors and the direct sales force and the roles of each are clearly understood.

5. *Control* of the franchise. By stipulating that successor distributor managements do not automatically take over the prior owner's franchise, Norton has retained control over the quality as well as the intensity of its representation in local market areas.

6. Ongoing *information* about market segments and distributors' performance. Frequent field visits to distributors by Norton's sales personnel provided Norton with information about the market segments served by distributors.

Source: Adapted from E. Raymond Corey, Frank V. Cespedes, and V. Kasturi Rangan, *Going to Market: Distribution Systems for Industrial Products* (Boston: Harvard University Press, 1989), pp. 134, 135.

distributor–manufacturer working partnerships recommended similar approaches and also suggested that manufacturers and their distributors engage in joint annual planning which focuses on specifying the cooperative efforts each firm requires of its partner to reach its objectives as well as periodic reviews of progress toward objectives.[26] The net result will be trust and satisfaction with the working partnership as the cooperative relationship leads to meeting performance goals.

Strategic partnerships between marketers and distribution intermediaries will become even more important in the future. The Dana Corporation, a manufacturer of industrial and automotive components, provides a meaningful perspective on partnerships:

[26] James C. Anderson and James A. Narus, "A Model of Distribution Firm and Manufacturing Firm Working Partnerships," *Journal of Marketing,* 54 (January 1990), p. 56.

The days are gone when distributors and suppliers in our country can tolerate the inefficiency of an adversarial relationship. The partnership approach is the best way for any industry to achieve the synergy that it takes to be world-class. For our distributors to be truly successful, we feel we must be true marketing partners. A successful distributor is our marketing aim, and we've devoted tremendous time and resources to develop an infrastructure that creates this success.[27]

Clearly, the partnership approach to channel relationships will help eliminate many of the frictions that serve to reduce channelwide efficiency and effectiveness.

Management Aids

Manufacturers often have the size and skill to develop sophisticated management techniques for areas of purchasing, inventory, order processing, and the like, which can be passed on to channel members. Some firms may provide elaborate cost accounting and profitability measurement systems for their distributors in order to assist them in tracking product performance.

Allan Magrath and Kenneth Hardy suggest that a manufacturer should "design a full menu of supports, with sufficient variety to appeal to all its key distributors—small, medium, and large—recognizing that participation in some offerings will vary depending upon the relevance to the particular distributor's size and level of sophistication."[28] The key element is to allow the distributor to choose which programs fit his or her situation.

Dealer Advisory Councils

Distributors or reps may be brought together periodically with the manufacturer's management personnel to review distribution policies, provide advice on marketing strategy, and supply industry intelligence.[29] Intermediaries can voice their opinions on policy matters and are brought directly into the decision-making process for channel operations. Dayco Corporation uses a dealer council to keep abreast of distributors' changing needs.[30] One month after their meeting, council members receive a written report of suggestions they made and of the programs to be implemented as a result. Generally, Dayco enacts 75 percent of distributor proposals. For dealer councils to be effective, the input of channel members must have a meaningful effect on channel policy decisions.

---

[27] Kate Bertrand, "Conference Stresses Partnerships and Customers Relations," *Business Marketing,* 75 (June 1990), p. 34.

[28] Allan J. Magrath and Kenneth G. Hardy, "Gearing Manufacturer Support Programs to Distributors," *Industrial Marketing Management,* 18 (November 1989), p. 244.

[29] Doug Harper, "Councils Launch Sales Ammo," *Industrial Distribution,* 80 (September 1990), pp. 27–30.

[30] James A. Narus and James C. Anderson, "Turn Your Distributors into Partners," *Harvard Business Review,* 64 (March–April 1986), p. 68. See also Gul Butaney and Lawrence H. Wortzel, "Distributor Power Versus Manufacturer Power: The Customer Role," *Journal of Marketing,* 52 (January 1988), pp. 52–63.

Margins and Commission

In the final analysis, the primary motivating device will be compensation. The surest way to lose intermediary support is to use compensation policies that do not meet industry and competitive standards. Reps or distributors who feel cheated on commissions or margins will shift their selling attention to products generating a higher profit. The manufacturer must pay the prevailing compensation rates in the industry and must adjust the rates as conditions change. Inflation in travel, lodging, and entertainment expenses forces many reps and distributors to seek higher commission and margins. Although such increases are painful to the manufacturer, if rates are not adjusted fairly, suppliers can expect a marked reduction in sales effort.

The compensation provided to intermediaries should reflect the marketing tasks performed. If the manufacturer seeks special attention for a new industrial product, most reps will require higher commissions. 3M Corporation has an enlightened attitude regarding compensation of distributors. According to the firm, "We're studying all the distributors' costs—inventory, sales, and so on—and then we're looking at our costs. Maybe we will want to pay the distributor to assume more of the functions we now do. Or maybe we can absorb some activities back here and reduce the distributors' margin. But somebody has to pay for it. We're trying to come up with a classification system so divisions can have different levels of distributor margins, depending on what services the distributor provides."[31]

Market Protection

Most intermediaries want territorial protection from excessive competition with other distributors of the same product. Often, selective distribution will benefit both manufacturer and distributors. The manufacturer receives loyal commitment from the distributor, and the distributor enjoys limited product competition and a relatively large market potential.

Other tools may also be used to motivate business marketing channel members. The success of the motivational program hinges on the overall quality of the firm's channel strategy *and* management's attitude toward channel members. An attitude of assistance, cooperation, and partnership is crucial; this attitude should be reinforced by a well-conceived plan that provides support, training, and communication to the channel participants. Distributors seek working relationships that include reasonable supplier policies in the areas of inventory return, credit, and the number of franchised distributors in a trade area.[32] Better relationships result in distributors who are satisfied and cooperative.

---

[31] Sutton, "Rethinking the Company's Selling and Distribution Channels," p. 6.

[32] James C. Anderson and James A. Narus, "A Model of the Distributor's Perspective of Distributor–Manufacturer Working Relationships," *Journal of Marketing*, 48 (Fall 1984), p. 70.

Conflict: The Need for Interorganizational Management

The very nature of a distribution channel—with each member dependent on another for success—carries the seeds for conflict among the members. Although realizing the need for cooperation, individual members seek to maximize their autonomy and, hence, their profitability. **Channel conflict** occurs when one channel member A perceives another channel member B to be preventing or impeding member A from achieving important goals.[33]

The opportunities for conflict in business marketing channels are limitless—for example, a manufacturer's refusal to increase reps' commissions, a distributor's refusal to maintain required inventory levels, a manufacturer's insistence on a nonexclusive distribution policy. Thus, because channel participants have varying goals, varying perceptions of their roles in the channel, and varying evaluations of their spheres of influence, tensions develop that may cause them to perform in ways that damage channel performance.[34] The business marketer must manage conflict through interorganizational management approaches.[35] Such approaches improve overall channel performance by coordinating relationships among the organizations that make up the channel.

Sources of Conflict

Managers may not recognize a conflict situation until after the fact—when it may be too late to respond to the causes. Clearly, a device is needed for recognizing a potential conflict situation before it occurs. Surveys of distributors and reps at periodic intervals can uncover potential conflict areas by eliciting reps' and distributors' perceptions of how the channel works. Open communication between the company's sales force and channel members is an informal method of assessing potential conflict. Whether using a formal or an informal approach, management must be alert to present or emerging sources of conflict.

Manufacturers Dealing Directly with Large Accounts. Channel intermediaries— both reps and distributors—feel cheated if they are not allowed to reap the economic benefits associated with large accounts. To offset channel conflict of this nature, IBM developed a program called "Customer Fulfillment Option."[36] This program allows

---

[33] Stern and El-Ansary, *Marketing Channels*, pp. 202–223, 283.

[34] Louis W. Stern and James L. Heskett, "Conflict Management in Interorganizational Relations: A Conceptual Framework," in Louis Stern, ed., *Distribution Channels: Behavioral Dimensions* (Boston: Houghton-Mifflin Company, 1969), pp. 293–294.

[35] For example, see Louis W. Stern, Adel I. El-Ansary, and James R. Brown, *Management in Marketing Channels*, (Englewood Cliffs, N.J.: Prentice-Hall, 1989), pp. 369–380; Robert F. Lusch, "Sources of Power: Their Impact on Intrachannel Conflict," *Journal of Marketing Research*, 13 (November 1976), p. 384; Stern and Heskett, "Conflict Management in Interorganizational Relations," p. 293; Larry J. Rosenberg and Louis Stern, "Conflict Measurement in the Distribution Channel," *Journal of Marketing Research*, 8 (November 1971), pp. 437–442; Louis Stern and Ronald H. Gorman, "Conflict in Distribution Channels: An Exploration," in Stern, ed., *Distribution Channels: Behavioral Dimensions*, p. 156; Larry J. Rosenberg, "A New Approach to Distribution Conflict Management," *Business Horizons*, 16 (October 1974), pp. 67–74; and Louis P. Bucklin, "A Theory of Channel Control," *Journal of Marketing*, 37 (January 1973), pp. 39–47.

[36] Bertrand, "Changing Channels in the Microcomputer Market," p. 92.

large corporate buyers to fulfill volume-discount purchasing agreements either through IBM or through authorized dealers. Creative approaches intended to address intermediaries' concerns over large accounts not only increase channel harmony but also allow customers to buy through the most convenient source. To avoid this problem entirely, a manufacturer can establish a policy *never* to sell direct. Steelcase, a huge office equipment manufacturer, has never sold direct to end users in its history.[37] The company has enjoyed unparalleled support from its dealers over the years.

Degree of Effort.   The use of any intermediary by a manufacturer involves a loss of control over the marketing of the product. Business-to-business middlemen are independents, carrying a line of products to satisfy their customers. Their allegiance is to their customers and to those products in their line that are most lucrative. A constant source of friction between the manufacturer and the middleman is the amount of attention devoted to the firm's product. The intermediary often carries products that are easier to sell or that have a higher commission rate or margin than a particular manufacturer's product. The manufacturer can try to enhance the effort given its products by providing sales assistance, training, and promotional support. Interestingly, a recent study provides some evidence that industrial distributors may prefer to *share* responsibility for marketing decisions regarding local markets with their manufacturers.[38] In fact, the distributors felt their performance in the market would be higher if the manufacturer took more responsibility for the channel marketing efforts. Typically, it has been assumed that a distributor would want to increase its power and control over local marketing decisions. However, this research suggests that manufacturer involvement in local marketing strategy would be desired and welcomed.

Compensation.   The commission rates provided to reps or the gross margins offered to distributors are critical conflict areas. Compensation must be fair and must reflect the nature of the tasks performed. To ensure a smooth working channel, intermediaries must be adequately compensated for the portion of the marketing job they are expected to perform.

Intrachannel and Interchannel Competition.   Too many distributors in an area or distributors in competition with reps may result in intense price competition among intermediaries. The general result is to create a group of intermediaries that are unhappy and unsupportive of the manufacturer. A manufacturer may be better off to err on the side of restricted distribution in order to minimize rivalry and to gain maximum support for the product line. If there is intensive territory overlap, the

[37] Kenneth G. Hardy and Allan J. Magrath, *Marketing Channel Management*, (Glenview, IL: Scott, Foresman & Co., 1988), p. 103.

[38] Gul Butaney and Lawrence Wortzel, "Distributor Power Versus Manufacturer Power: The Customer Role," *Journal of Marketing*, 52 (January 1988), p. 61.

manufacturer will need to anticipate the conflict inherent in such a situation.[39] The anticipation should include a plan with specific tactics to manage the level of conflict.

Reducing Conflict

Larry Rosenberg recommends three interorganizational approaches for reducing conflict.

1. *A channelwide committee.* A committee provides a forum for periodically evaluating emerging problems and considering the diverse viewpoints of the channel members.

2. *Joint goal setting.* Although a consensus on goals may not always be possible in any committee or advisory council, the dialogue is beneficial in reducing conflict.

3. *A distribution executive.* An executive position could be established in each major organization in the channel to coordinate internal and external issues that spawn conflict.[40]

The results of conflict management are improved channel performance and enhanced channel solidarity.[41] The reduction of conflict may sometimes be the only means of preserving the channel system.

INTERNATIONAL BUSINESS MARKETING CHANNELS

A variety of channel options are available to a foreign business-to-business marketer. Typically, U.S. business marketers distribute their goods to international markets through three distinct channels (or through some combination of them):[42]

1. *American-based export middlemen.* Domestic export middlemen are utilized by smaller companies that lack experience in foreign sales or by firms that are not deeply involved in international marketing.

2. *Foreign-based middlemen.* Firms that are deeply committed to foreign sales will often use foreign-based middlemen. This decision depends on the availability of good intermediaries, financial requirements, local customs, desired control, and the nature of the product.

3. *Company-managed and company-organized sales force.* This alternative is pursued by firms heavily involved in international sales. For this approach to be effective, the firm must be strong when providing after-sales service, maintaining

---

[39] Allan J. Magrath and Kenneth G. Hardy, "A Strategic Framework for Diagnosing Manufacturer–Reseller Conflict," (Cambridge, MA: Marketing Science Institute, 1988), p. 21.

[40] Larry J. Rosenberg, "A New Approach to Distribution Conflict Management," *Business Horizons,* 17 (October 1974), pp. 67–74.

[41] Stern and El-Ansary, *Marketing Channels,* pp. 290–298.

[42] Phillip R. Cateora, *International Marketing,* Fifth Edition (Homewood, Ill.: Richard D. Irwin, 1983), p. 442.

delivery reliability, supplying spare parts, and providing many other support services.

It is important to recognize that international channels of distribution are not clear-cut, precise, or easily defined entities.[43] A necessary step in developing international channels is to understand the functions of middlemen; international middlemen are referred to by a multitude of misleading titles. The final section of the chapter will briefly examine these middlemen and their roles.

To be effective, global business marketers may have to develop a truly global, integrated channel strategy and be willing to invest considerable resources. James Bolt suggests that successful global competitors are companies that, among other things, "develop an integrated and innovative strategy, aggressively implement it and back it with large investments."[44] In the channels realm, a well-conceived distribution structure, utilizing the best middlemen and backed by the required financial resources, may be a critical element that acts as a barrier to competitors.

Domestic Middlemen

As the name implies, **domestic middlemen** are located in the country of the producer. They are convenient to use, but their critical drawback is the lack of proximity to the foreign marketplace. The quality of representation and the access to market information available through domestic middlemen is limited.

Domestic middlemen can be broadly distinguished by whether they take title to the goods or not. Nontitle, or agent, middlemen include **export management companies** (EMC), **manufacturer's export agents** (MEA), and **brokers**, who are primarily engaged in the selling function, making contact with foreign buyers and negotiating sales. Playing a pivotal role for many small firms, EMCs take over much of the marketing job necessary to reach foreign markets, including responsibility for advertising, credit, and product handling. Agent middlemen are paid on a commission basis.

The other broad groups of domestic middlemen are similar to wholesalers—they take title to the products they sell and perform a broad array of marketing functions. **Export merchants** are wholesalers operating in a foreign market. Middlemen dealing in bulky commodities in foreign markets are referred to as **export jobbers**. **Trading companies** accumulate, transport, and distribute goods from many countries.[45] Recent legislation in the United States has paved the way for the development of American trading companies (ATC).[46] Although early success of the ATCs has been limited, it is expected they will eventually provide effective one-stop export service.

---

[43] Ibid., p. 581.

[44] James F. Bolt, "Global Competitors: Some Criteria for Success," *Business Horizons*, (January–February, 1988), pp. 35, 36.

[45] Cateora, *International Marketing*, p. 590.

[46] Daniel C. Bello and Nicholas C. Williamson, "The American Export Trading Company: Designing a New International Marketing Institution," *Journal of Marketing*, 49 (Fall 1985), p. 60.

Foreign-Based Middlemen

Foreign-based middlemen offer the advantage of close and constant contact with the marketplace and generally provide a more direct channel to the customer. As with domestic middlemen, foreign middlemen are distinguished by whether they take title or not.

Title-holding middlemen include distributors, dealers, and import jobbers. The tasks they perform are similar to those with the same name in domestic settings. In similar fashion, nontitle foreign middlemen include brokers, reps, and factors. Factors are similar to brokers, but are also involved in financing the sale, which is complex and cumbersome in many foreign transactions. Essentially, they eliminate the credit risk for both the buyer and the seller.

Selection of a particular type of foreign-based middleman is dictated by the type of product, margins, and the market conditions.[47] For example, brokers have no inventory and take no risk while importers take title, bear the risk, and guarantee distribution. Consequently, distribution of product through importers will mean a higher landed price for the product because their margins have to be higher to accommodate these risks and additional activities. Whichever type of foreign-based intermediary is used, it may be necessary to creatively structure the initial contract. An importer, for example, may be given a 90-day exclusive contract and agree to buy only 5,000 items. This initial order allows the importer to "test the market." If sales go as expected, large volume commitments can be written into a long-term contract.

Company-Organized Sales Force

The choice between using intermediaries for foreign sales and using a company-organized sales force is complex. The company sales force gives the company control over the international marketing process but also poses serious challenges and risks due to the foreign environment. Erin Anderson and Anne Coughlan suggest that a company-organized sales force is more likely to be used when

1. The product requires a high service level

2. Competing products are differentiated

3. There are fewer legal constraints to direct foreign investment

4. The product is closely related to the firm's core product

5. The country's culture is similar to U.S. culture

6. Competitors utilize a company-organized sales force[48]

Anderson and Coughlan also indicate that the decision-making process in international channels is often nonsystematic and often based on little information. One reason for

---

[47] Jack Nadel, "Distribution, the Key to Success Overseas," *Management Review*, (September 1987), p. 41.

[48] Erin Anderson and Anne T. Coughlan, "International Market Entry and Expansion via Independent or Integrated Channels of Distribution," *Journal of Marketing*, 51 (January 1987), p. 74.

this is that managers operating outside familiar domestic settings have few guidelines to use.

In some foreign markets, business marketers may need a local presence—a plant, a distribution facility, an R&D facility, or a joint venture with a domestic partner in order to participate in the market without substantial penalties (import duties). Many U.S. manufacturers are concerned that the European Community (EC) market may be difficult to penetrate after 1992 because "the single market initiative could lead to a wave of European protectionism."[49] Investment in manufacturing, channel, and physical distribution operations within the EC may prove effective in guarding against these barriers to EC outsiders.

Consequently, channel strategy may enhance a company's ability to compete in the EC through joint ventures or licensing agreements with existing EC channel intermediaries. These partnerships with local firms would be viewed favorably and may allow the firm to avoid any duties imposed on imported, non-EC goods.

The channel decision in the international arena is a difficult one—made complex by the nature of the unfamiliar setting. However, global competition and worldwide marketing are realities of today's business environment, and the business marketing manager must be prepared to accept the challenge of making an informed and well-thought-out choice.

SUMMARY

Channel strategy is an exciting and challenging aspect of business marketing. The challenge comes from the number of alternatives available to the manufacturer in distributing business products. The excitement is there because markets, user needs, and competitors are always changing.

Channel strategy involves two primary management tasks: designing the overall structure and managing the operation of the channel. Channel design includes the evaluation of distribution goals, activities, and potential intermediaries. Channel structure includes the number, types, and levels of intermediaries to be used in the channel. The primary participants in business marketing channels are distributors and reps. Distributors provide the full range of marketing services for their suppliers, although customer contact and product availability are the functions of particular value. Manufacturers' representatives specialize in the selling side of marketing, providing their suppliers with quality representation in the market and with extensive product and market knowledge. The rep is not involved with physical distribution, leaving that burden to the manufacturers.

Channel management is the ongoing task of administering the channel structure in order to achieve distribution objectives. Selection and motivation of intermediaries are two management tasks vital to channel success. The industrial marketing manager may need to apply interorganizational management techniques in order to resolve

---

[49] Kate Bertrand, "Scrambling for 1992," *Business Marketing*, 74 (February 1989), p. 49.

channel conflict. The choice of channels for business marketers competing in overseas markets is both vast and confusing. The manager must choose among domestic and foreign middlemen and a company sales force.

Discussion Questions

1. Explain how a direct channel of distribution may be the lowest-cost alternative for one business marketer and the highest-cost alternative for another competing in the same industry.

2. Describe specific product, market, and competitive conditions that lend themselves to (a) a direct channel of distribution, and (b) an indirect channel of distribution.

3. Compare and contrast the functions performed by industrial distributors and manufacturers' representatives.

4. What product/market factors lend themselves to the use of manufacturers' representatives?

5. Often, the business marketer may have very little latitude in selecting the number of channel *levels*. Explain.

6. Explain how a change in segmentation policy (i.e., entering new markets) may trigger the need for drastic changes in the industrial channel of distribution.

7. Since both industrial marketers and distributors are interested in achieving profit goals, why are manufacturer-distributor relationships characterized by conflict? What steps can the marketer take to reduce the level of conflict and thus improve channel performance?

8. For many years, critics have charged that intermediaries contribute strongly to the rising prices of goods in the American economy. Would business marketers improve the level of efficiency and effectiveness in the channel by reducing as far as possible the number of intermediate links in the channel? Support your position.

CHAPTER 14

Business Marketing Channels: The Logistical Interface

If promised delivery performance is not provided, buyers will search for a new supplier. Organizational buyers assign high importance to responsive physical distribution, or logistical, systems. Therefore, substantial resources are invested to service demand through the logistical system.

After reading this chapter, you will understand:

1. the role of logistical management in business marketing strategy.

2. the importance of achieving the desired interface between logistics and the distribution channel.

3. the importance of cost and service trade-offs in creating effective and efficient logistical systems.

BUSINESS marketers frequently delegate selling and other demand stimulation to intermediaries. Other functions of equal importance, however, must be performed to implement marketing strategies successfully and to satisfy customer needs. Products must be delivered *when* they are required, *where* they are required, and in *usable condition*. Unfortunately, an industrial marketer cannot shift the total burden of these functions to intermediaries. Even if distributors are employed in the channel, manufacturers must be able to deliver products to the distributor efficiently. The business marketer's effectiveness in delivery will dramatically influence the distributor's ability to satisfy delivery requirements of the end user. Direct channels place even greater logistical burdens on the manufacturer. The overall significance of logistics to marketing performance is underscored by the comment made by a corporate president in a recent article:

There are two undeniable truths concerning logistics in the 1990's. The first is that it is a major and increasingly important aspect of the competitive life of most American businesses. The second is that logistics remains one of the few cost elements that can provide a business with significant benefits for the bottom line *without* capital expenditure.[1]

This chapter will describe the role of logistical management in business marketing strategy, both in general and in channel performance.[2] The discussion will be directed by such questions as: How do logistical activities interface with the distribution channel? What are the logistical variables that must be managed to create an effective interface with the channel? What role does logistical service play in the organizational purchase decision? What types of logistical services are sought by buyers? How can these services be designed and implemented most effectively and efficiently? Let us first examine the nature of logistical management.

ELEMENTS OF LOGISTICAL MANAGEMENT

Logistics is an imposing and sometimes mysterious term that originated in the military. In business usage, **logistics** refers to the design and management of all activities (primarily transportation, inventory, and warehousing) necessary to make materials available for manufacturing and to make finished products available to customers as they are needed and in the condition required. Logistics thus embodies two primary product flows: (1) **physical supply**, or those flows that provide raw materials, components, and supplies to the production process and (2) **physical distribution**, or those flows that deliver the completed product to customers and channel intermediaries (Figure 14.1). The flows of physical supply and physical distribution must be coordinated to meet delivery requirements of business customers successfully. The physical supply aspect of logistics requires a business supplier's logistical system to interact with the customer's logistics and manufacturing process. A repair part delivered a few hours late may cost a manufacturer thousands of dollars in lost production time. Although the physical supply dimension of logistics is important, we will concentrate in this chapter on the physical distribution component.

Good business marketing demands efficient, systematic delivery of finished products to intermediaries and industrial users.

---

[1] Michael Goldsmith, "Outsourcing Plays a Role in Corporate Strategies," *Transportation & Distribution, Presidential Issue 1989–1990*, 30 (October 1989), p. 18.

[2] For a comprehensive discussion of all facets of businesses logistics, see James R. Stock and Douglas M. Lambert, *Strategic Logistics Management*, 2nd ed. (Homewood, Ill.: Richard D. Irwin, 1987); James E. Johnson and Donald F. Wood, *Contemporary Physical Distribution and Logistics*, 4th ed. (New York: Macmillan Publishing Company, 1990); and John J. Coyle, Edward J. Bardi, and C. John Langley, Jr., *The Management of Business Logistics*, 4th ed. (St. Paul, MN: West Publishing Company, 1988).

FIGURE 14.1   **The Business-to-Business Logistics System**

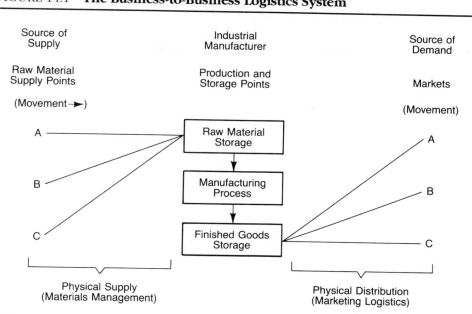

Source: Adapted from John J. Coyle and Edward J. Bardi, *The Management of Business Logistics*, 2d ed. (New York: West Publishing Co., 1984), p. 19.

Timely Logistical Support

Owens-Illinois, a major supplier of glass containers, shows how precisely a supplier must tailor its logistics system to customer needs. Owens-Illinois is a primary supplier to the J. M. Smucker Company, the jam and jelly manufacturer. Because of its vast container requirements, Smucker must carefully manage inventory and delivery of glass containers. To reduce container inventory, Smucker maintains only enough glass containers to run the production line for a few hours. The burden of this policy falls directly on Owens-Illinois. First, Owens-Illinois must schedule the production process at its Toledo plant to provide all the inventories Smucker requires. Then, warehouse systems and reliable motor carriers assure that deliveries match Smucker's inventory policy and avoid production interruptions. Consistent delivery performance to Smucker standards is surely an essential ingredient in this long-term supplier–customer relationship. For Owens-Illinois, logistical service may have created the differential advantage.

In the past, logistics was viewed simply as a cost of doing business, and a function whose only goal was higher productivity.[3] Today, logistics is viewed by many companies as a critical strategic weapon because of its tremendous impact on a customer's

---

[3] Robert Horne, "Charting a Course for Integrated Logistics," *Transportation & Distribution*, 30 (October 1989), p. 46.

INSIDE BUSINESS MARKETING
The Impact of JIT: Quality, Profits, Market Share

Toyota captures 43 percent of the Japanese car market and is the leading foreign car company in the United States. They are also regarded as the master of just-in-time systems, and they have built their entire production process around the just-in-time concept. Under Toyota's system, parts and cars do not get built until orders "move upstream to request them": Japanese dealers use on-line computers to order cars directly from the factory. When a dealer orders a car, it basically reserves a spot on the production line. Rather than the typical wait of several months, customers receive their built-to-order cars in seven to ten days. Savings accrue through the whole process: the factory can balance production and stay in touch with shifting demand; dealers keep very little inventory. Impressively, it is estimated that Toyota needs only 13 man-hours to assemble a car in its best plant, versus 19 to 22 man-hours for Honda and Nissan. Toyota's family cars—Corolla, Camry, and Cressida—all rank tops in their class for assembly quality.

The essence of the JIT system, which took 20 years to perfect, is the network of suppliers whose competence and close ties are the envy of the automaking world. Many experts believe that the close-knit arrangements that Toyota maintains with its suppliers is the principal element in its ability to compress the time it takes to move a new automobile from concept to production (less than four years versus five for U.S. firms and seven for Mercedes-Benz), reduce manufacturing costs, and cut the number of faulty parts to ten parts per million.

Source: Adapted from Alex Taylor, III, "Why Toyota Keeps Getting Better and Better and Better," *Fortune*, 122 (November 1990), pp. 66–79.

operation. For many business marketers, logistics is their *primary* marketing tool for gaining and maintaining competitive superiority. Donald Bowersox reports that after studying more than 1,000 companies "it became clear that some companies stand head and shoulders above their competitors in logistics performance and they use this superiority to gain and keep customer loyalty."[4] These firms typically recognize that logistics performance is an important part of marketing strategy, and they exploit their logistics competencies. Effective logistics competence may even enable a firm to avoid the high cost of extensive promotion or deep price discounts associated with the maturity stage of the product life cycle.[5] In this instance, responsive and reliable logistics service results in a more inelastic demand situation for the product.

Just-in-Time

Many business marketers have realized they have no choice other than to provide almost immediate delivery of their products. The reason is the widespread adoption by U.S. manufacturing firms of the just-in-time inventory principle.[6] Under this

---

[4] Donald J. Bowersox, "The Strategic Benefits of Logistics Alliances," *Harvard Business Review*, 68 (July–August 1990), p. 40.

[5] William R. Darden, Grant M. Davis, and John Ozment, "The Impact of Logistics on the Demand for Mature Industrial Products, *The European Journal of Marketing*, 23 (November 2, 1989), p. 56.

[6] Charles R. O'Neal, "The Buyer-Seller Linkage in a Just-in-Time Environment," *Journal of Purchasing and Materials Management*, 23 (Spring 1987), p. 7

principle, all suppliers must carefully coordinate delivery of parts and supplies with the manufacturer's production schedule—often delivering products just hours before they are to be used. (See Chapter 2.) The objective of a JIT system is to eliminate waste of all kinds from the production process. It requires the delivery of the specified product at the precise time, and in the exact quantity needed. Importantly, the quality must be perfect because there is no opportunity to inspect products in the JIT process. Because JIT attempts to relate purchases to production requirements, the typical order size shrinks, and more frequent deliveries are required. Increased delivery frequency presents a challenge to the business marketing production and logistics system.

A significant effect of JIT purchasing has been the drastic reduction in the number of suppliers utilized by manufacturers.[7] Suppliers who are able to meet customers' JIT requirements will find their share of business growing with the JIT-oriented customer. Meeting the JIT mandate represents a marketing edge, if not an outright survival tactic, for suppliers.[8] The relationship that emerges between JIT suppliers and manufacturers is unique and often requires extensive integration of their operations.[9] As a result, suppliers find that the relationships are longer lasting and are usually formalized with a written contract that may span up to five years. Charles O'Neal summarizes the important JIT impacts on the buyer–seller relationship: "The JIT concept introduces a new philosophy of supplier–customer interorganizational linkage which has significant implications for marketing management. The linkage has many of the attributes of a (positive) marriage relationship, including careful choice of marriage partner, extended time horizon, partner interdependence, intimacy of partners, openness of communications, and provision of support activities to maintain the positive relationship."[10]

Some business marketers effectively capitalize on the JIT concept, gearing their production and logistical systems to match customer needs. Hoover Universal, a manufacturer of steel frames, springs, and seats, delivers seats in specified sizes, colors, and numbers to a Nissan truck plant in Smyrna, Tennessee, within three hours of the time they are bolted into Nissan trucks.[11] As such delivery requirements become industry standards, those business firms with effective and efficient logistical systems already in place will enjoy significant marketing advantages.

Elements of a Logistical System

The controllable variables of a logistical system are set out in Table 14.1. Almost no decision on a particular logistical activity can be made without evaluating its impact on the other areas.

---

[7] A. Ansari, "Strategies for the Implementation of JIT Purchasing," *International Journal of Physical Distribution and Materials Management*, 16, No. 3 (1986), p. 9.

[8] Kate Bertrand, "The Just-in-Time Mandate," *Business Marketing*, 71 (November 1986), p. 45.

[9] Gary L. Frazier, Robert E. Spekman, and Charles R. O'Neal, "Just-in-Time Exchange Relationships in Industrial Markets," *Journal of Marketing*, 52 (October 1988), p. 53.

[10] Charles R. O'Neal, "JIT Procurement and Relationship Marketing," *Industrial Marketing Management*, 18 (February 1989), p. 60.

[11] Bob Woods, "Selling Parts with Service," *Sales and Marketing Management*, 128 (July 4, 1983), p. 31.

TABLE 14.1 **Controllable Elements in a Logistics System**

Elements	Key Aspects
Customer service	The "product" of logistics activities, *customer service* relates to the effectiveness in creating time and place utility. The level of customer service provided by the supplier has a direct impact on total cost, market share, and profitability.
Order processing	Order processing triggers the logistics process and directs activities necessary to deliver products to customers. Speed and accuracy of order processing affect costs and customer service levels.
Logistics communications	Information is exchanged in the distribution process in order to guide the activities of the system. It is the vital link between the firm's logistics system and its customers.
Transportation	The physical movement of products from source of supply through production to customers is the most significant cost area in logistics, and it involves selecting modes and specific carriers as well as routing.
Warehousing	Providing storage space serves as a buffer between production and use. Warehousing may be used to enhance service and to lower transportation costs.
Inventory control	Inventory is used to make products available to customers and to ensure the correct mix of products is at the proper location at the right time.
Packaging	The role of packaging is to provide protection to the product, to maintain product identity throughout the logistics process, and to create effective product density.
Materials handling	Materials handling increases the speed of, and reduces the cost of, picking orders in the warehouse and moving products between storage and the transportation carriers. It is a cost-generating activity that must be controlled.
Production planning	Utilized in conjunction with logistics planning, production planning ensures that products are available for inventory in the correct assortment and quantity.
Plant and warehouse location	Strategic placement of plants and warehouses increases customer service and reduces the cost of transportation.

Source: Adapted from James R. Stock and Douglas M. Lambert, *Strategic Logistics Management*, 2nd ed. (Homewood, IL: Richard D. Irwin, 1987), pp. 14–19.

The system of warehouse facilities, inventory commitments, order-processing methods, and transportation linkages will determine the supplier's ability to provide timely product availability to industrial users. As a result of poor supplier performance, customers may have to bear the extra cost of higher inventories, institute expensive priority-order-expediting systems, develop secondary supply sources, or worst of all, turn to another supplier.

Total-Cost Approach

In the management of logistical activities, two performance variables must be considered: (1) total distribution costs and (2) the level of logistical service provided to customers. The logistical system must be designed and administered to achieve that

---

INSIDE BUSINESS MARKETING
Now That's Logistics!

SCI Systems makes lots of circuit boards for IBM—in fact, it is believed that SCI is IBM's largest subcontractor. To survive and succeed, a company such as SCI must deliver large volumes of high-quality products on time and at prices well below the manufacturing cost of its customers. Sometimes the subcontractor's logistics capabilities are severely tested.

One such test rudely confronted SCI in the wee hours of the morning in 1984. An SCI cargo plane ran out of fuel at 4:00 a.m. and crashed into the Florida Everglades on its way to a "big" customer. Showing its logistics mettle, the com-pany launched a military-like mission to rescue the cargo—circuit boards—from the marshes. Airboats were dispatched to fetch the circuit boards, which were rushed to a motel where SCI technicians tested them for damage.

Back at the Alabama headquarters, sleepy workers opened the plant and rented another airplane. By 10:00 a.m., SCI delivered enough circuit boards from Alabama and the Florida swamp to meet the customer's production schedule for the day.

Now that is truly customer-responsive logistics!

Source: Adapted from Hank Gilman, "SCI, Inc. Flourishes as Main Subcontractor in Electronics Industry," *The Wall Street Journal*, 127 (August 14, 1987), p. 5.

---

combination of cost and service levels that yields maximum profits. First, let us consider the scope and behavior of logistical costs.

Logistical costs vary widely for business marketers, depending on the nature of the product and on the importance of logistical service to the buyer. Logistical costs can consume 16 to 36 percent of each sales dollar at the manufacturing level, and assets required by logistical activities can exceed 40 percent of total assets. Thus logistics can have a significant impact on corporate profitability.[12] It is generally felt that opportunities for productivity gains in production, selling, and promotion have been exploited, and logistics can be considered "the last frontier of cost reduction in American business."[13] How, then, can the marketer manage logistical costs?

The **total-cost** or **trade-off approach** to logistical management offers a guarantee that total logistical costs in the firm and within the channel are minimized. The assumption is that costs associated with individual logistical activities are interactive; that is, a decision about one logistical variable affects all or some of the other variables. Management is thus concerned with the efficiency of the entire system rather than with minimizing the cost of any single logistical activity. The interactions among logistical activities (i.e., transportation, inventory, warehousing) are described as

---

[12] Horne, "Charting a Course for Integrated Logistics," p. 46.

[13] Wendell M. Stewart, "Physical Distribution: Key to Improved Volume and Profits," *Journal of Marketing*, 39 (January 1965), pp. 65–70; see also Thomas W. Speh and Michael D. Hutt, "The Other Half of Marketing: Lost or Found," in Robert S. Franz, Robert M. Hopkins, and Al Toma, eds., *Proceedings: Southern Marketing Association* (University of Southwestern Louisiana: Southern Marketing Association, 1978), pp. 332–35.

cost trade-offs, because a cost increase in one activity is traded for a large cost decrease in another activity, the net result being an overall cost reduction.

Evaluating Cost Patterns

Figure 14.2 shows costs associated with a change in the number of warehouses maintained by an industrial firm. As additional warehouses are added, transportation costs decline as a result of high-volume low-cost shipments entering the warehouses and small-volume high-cost shipments moving only short distances to the customers. Total transportation costs decline with more warehouses because the high-cost small-volume shipments are moved over shorter and shorter distances. Conversely, inventory costs rise as more warehouses are added because more stock is required to maintain the same level of product availability. Combining inventory and transportation costs, the least-cost solution—in which the trade-off of inventory for transportation is optimized—is to maintain ten warehouses. A warehouse decision based either on inventory costs alone or on transportation costs alone would not result in the most cost-effective total system.

Cost trade-offs occur among all logistical activities. Union Carbide makes numerous gases (nitrogen, oxygen, etc.) and delivers them through regional branch operations around the country. In this industry, control of logistics cost is a major competitive advantage. In an attempt to prune total logistics cost, Carbide introduced the "storefront" approach to product distribution: many distribution points become "storefronts," only taking orders and maintaining small inventories of a few products.[14] As a result, most deliveries take place from fewer, centralized plants and distribution points. Important cost trade-offs resulted: storefront branches dramatically lowered inventory and warehousing costs, transportation cost from plants to the branches was eliminated, and double handling of products was reduced. However, overall transportation costs rose because of longer distances from plant to customer and the need for more drivers. In total, overall logistics costs were reduced, service was unaffected, and the firm's competitive position improved.

The widespread application of JIT concepts and the increasing emphasis on total quantity programs suggest that business marketers should carefully consider the "quality costs" generated by their logistics systems.[15] Quality costs, which include costs associated with defective products (higher inventory, additional transport costs for product return), product appraisal (inspection and evaluation expenses), and prevention (training, data analysis, and planning expenses) should be explicitly considered in conjunction with the set of traditional total costs of logistics. The goal is to create a logistics system that delivers a given quality level at the lowest cost.

---

[14] Donald B. Rosenfield, "Storefront Distribution for Industrial Products," *Harvard Business Review*, 67 (July–August 1989), p. 45.

[15] James M. Kenderdine and Paul D. Larson, "Quality and Logistics: A Framework for Strategic Integration," *International Journal of Physical Distribution and Materials Management*, 18 (Number 6, 1988), p. 5.

FIGURE 14.2   **Cost Trade-Offs**

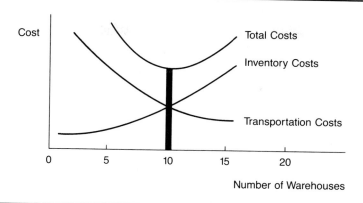

Service/Cost Trade-Offs

If cost is one half of the logistical equation, the other half is service. For many business products, the ability to deliver customer orders rapidly is more important than the logistical costs involved; various levels of service are capable of producing various demand responses.[16] However, each aspect of logistical service has a cost, and that cost must be evaluated in light of the revenue generated. Profitability, as measured by the difference between logistical revenue and cost, is the important control variable.

Channel System Orientation

Part of logistical management is the evaluation of the impact of logistical decisions on the channel members' operations. Manufacturer shifts in inventory policy, transportation modes, and warehouse locations directly affect channel members and end users. Reducing field warehouses from ten to two may require distributors to hold more inventory. Although the manufacturer's warehousing and inventory costs are diminished, distributors' costs will rise, and customer service may be substantially curtailed. The result may dramatically reduce the overall performance of the channel system. Whereas the total-cost framework is a necessary point of departure for the management of industrial logistical strategy, channelwide performance can only be optimized through the systematic evaluation of logistical trade-offs.

---

[16] Ernest B. Uhr, Ernest G. Hauck, and John C. Rogers, "Physical Distribution Service," *Journal of Business Logistics*, 2, No. 2 (1981), pp. 158–69.

BUSINESS-TO-BUSINESS LOGISTICAL SERVICE

A study by *Purchasing Magazine* surveyed more than 1,000 purchasing managers in order to determine the most important aspects of supplier performance. Delivery was rated second only to product quality.[17] In one industry, purchasing agents begin the buying process by calling suppliers with the best delivery service to see whether they are willing to negotiate prices. Similar approaches to vendor selection are evidenced in other industries. This fact, together with the extensive implementation of just-in-time manufacturing systems, makes it clear that logistical service is important to the organizational buyer.

Definition of Customer Service

Logistical service relates to the availability and delivery of products to the customer and can be conceptualized as the series of sales-satisfying activities that begin when the customer places the order and that end with the delivery of the product to customers. Logistical service thus includes whatever aspects of performance are important to the business customer (Table 14.2). These service elements range from delivery time to value-added services, and each of these elements has the potential to affect production processes, final product output, costs, or all three. The importance of logistics service is made clear by the fact that for every hour a Boeing 747 is grounded for lack of a part, it costs $10,000 in interest and depreciation alone. Similarly, a candy manufacturer loses $100 for each minute a candy wrapping machine is idle.[18]

Impacts of Supplier Logistical Service on Business Customers

Supplier logistical service translates into product availability. For a manufacturer to produce or for a distributor to resell, industrial products must be available at the right time, at the right place, and in usable condition. The longer the supplier's delivery time, the less available the product; the more inconsistent the delivery time, the less available the product.

For example, a reduction in the supplier's delivery time permits a buyer to hold less inventory because needs can be met rapidly. The customer reduces the risk of interruption in the production process. Consistent delivery performance allows the buyer to program more effectively, or routinize, the purchasing process, thus lowering buyer costs. A dramatic impact of consistent delivery cycle performance is the opportunity for the buyer to cut the level of buffer or safety stock maintained, thereby cutting the inventory cost. However, for many business products, such as those that are low in unit value and relatively standardized, the overriding concern is not inventory cost, but simply having the products. A malfunctioning 95-cent bearing could shut down a whole production line.

---

[17] Somerby Dowst, "Wanted: Suppliers Adept at Turning Corners," *Purchasing*, 101 (January 29, 1987), p. 73.

[18] Milind M. Lele, "Inventory Management: How to Control Your Critical Marketing Backfield," *Business Marketing*, 71 (May 1986), p. 44.

TABLE 14.2   **Common Elements of Logistics Service**

Elements	Description
Delivery time	The time from the creation of an order to the fulfillment and delivery of that order includes both order-processing time and delivery or transportation time.
Delivery reliability	The most frequently used measure of logistics service, delivery reliability focuses on the capability of having products available to meet customer demand.
Order accuracy	The degree to which items received conform to the specification of the order. The key dimension is the incidence of orders shipped complete and without error.
Information access	The firm's ability to respond to inquiries about order status and product availability.
Damage	A measure of the physical conditions of the product when received by the buyer.
Ease of doing business	A range of factors including the ease with which orders, returns, credits, billing, and adjustments are handled.
Value-added services	Such features as packaging, which facilitates customer handling, or other services such as prepricing and drop shipments.

Source: Reprinted with permission from Jonathon L. S. Byrnes, William C. Copacino, and Peter Metz, "Forge Service into a Weapon with Logistics," *Transportation & Distribution, Presidential Issue,* 28 (September 1987), p. 46.

The Role of Logistical Service in the Buying Decision

Because the impacts of logistical service are so dramatic, it is not surprising that buyers rank logistical service above many other important supplier characteristics.

A recent publication reviewed a multitude of research studies that investigated the importance of logistics service on purchasing decisions. The authors concluded:

> Across multiple products and industries logistics service remains an important element in supplier evaluation, customer perception and satisfaction, and the resulting purchasing decision. It would be tempting to make a definite statement as to the exact importance of logistics service relative to other purchase criteria but it is much more reasonable to state that there is an indication that logistics service stands out as a major factor.[19]

In a number of these studies, logistics service ranked right behind "quality" as a criterion for selecting a vendor.

It is equally important to evaluate logistics service from the standpoint of the cost of poor customer service. Good service can attract and hold customers: ineffective logistics service can harm customer relationships or drive customers away. A study conducted at Ohio State University found that a variety of punitive actions will be taken

---

[19]John T. Mentzer, Roger Gomes, and Robert E. Krapfel, Jr., "Physical Distribution Service: A Fundamental Marketing Concept," *Journal of the Academy of Marketing Science,* 17 (Winter 1989), p. 59.

in response to poor logistics service.[20] For example, chemical companies expect to lose market share in about 50 percent of the situations where their logistics service is unpredictable. In the pharmaceutical and electronics industries, between 16 and 20 percent of the customers would be expected to stop all purchases from the vendor as a result of repeated instances of erratic logistics service. Clearly, the business marketer must develop an effective logistics strategy or risk the loss of substantial business. This key impact of logistics services provides a strong argument for integrating logistics strategy into the overall marketing strategy.

Determining the Level of Service

Obviously, not all products nor all customers require the same level of logistical service. Many business products that are made to order—such as heavy machinery—have relatively low logistical service requirements. Others, such as replacement parts, components, and subassemblies, require extremely demanding logistical performance. Similarly, customers may be more or less responsive to varying levels of logistical service.

Some purchasing agents are far more sensitive to poor service than the majority of purchasing managers. Market segments must be identified on the basis of logistical service sensitivity.[21] For example, buyers of scientific instruments were classified into groups—private firms, government, secondary schools, and so forth. Private firms ranked delivery time more highly than other groups did, and secondary schools ranked ordering convenience more highly than others did. Business marketing managers should attempt to isolate segments and to adjust the logistical service offerings accordingly.

Business purchasers may also vary in terms of their sensitivity to the various elements of logistics service. One study found that consistency of delivery was most important for materials and components; in-stock performance and consistent deliveries were central for supplies; and in-stock performance was most important for small capital items and was perceived to be more important than delivery time.[22] Managers must target their logistics service mix to the requirements of their product type and customer.

Profitability is the major criterion for evaluating the appropriate customer service levels. Information on alternative service levels and their associated sales results must be evaluated in relation to their costs.[23] Figure 14.3 demonstrates the cost/service

---

[20] Bernard J. LaLonde, Martha Cooper, and Thomas G. Noordewier, *Customer Service: A Management Perspective*, (Oak Brook, IL: Council of Logistics Management, 1988), p. 133.

[21] Peter Gilmour, "Customer Service: Differentiating by Market Segment," *International Journal of Physical Distribution and Materials Management*, 12, No. 3 (1982), pp. 37–44.

[22] Donald W. Jackson, Janet E. Keith, and Richard K. Buskick, "Examining the Relative Importance of Physical Distribution Service Elements," *Journal of Business Logistics*, 7 (September 1986), p. 25.

[23] For example, see David P. Herron, "Managing Physical Distribution for Profit," *Harvard Business Review*, 57 (May–June 1979), pp. 121–32; and Harvey N. Shycon and Christopher Sprague, "Put a Price Tag on Your Customer Servicing Levels," *Harvard Business Review*, 53 (July–August 1975), pp. 71–78.

FIGURE 14.3   **Cost/Service Relationship**

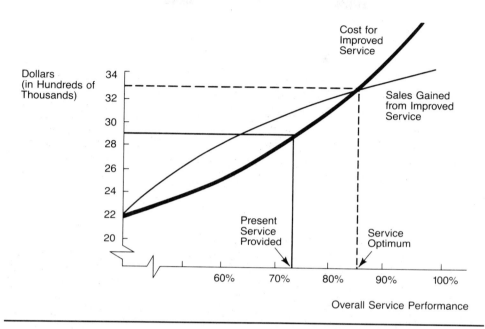

How Much Should You Spend to Improve Service?

Note: How much should a firm spend on customer service in order to gain extra sales? Graph shows how much a typical firm can improve its share of market for each $100,000 spent. Indicated too is the point of diminishing returns at which additional expenditures will exceed the value of increased sales. Though the graph suggests a breakpoint of about 85 percent, a company can determine its own figure only by studying specific conditions in its field. The nature of the product, geographic circumstances, transport characteristics, and other factors all affect the optimum service point.

Source: "Does Your Customer Service Program Stack Up?" *Traffic Management* (September 1982), p. 55.

relationship, showing that profit contribution varies with the service level. In this case, the current service level is 73 percent of orders filled completely. The chart indicates that higher service levels would generate higher levels of profits. The optimal service level is 85 percent because, at service levels below 85 percent, revenue gains exceed the additional costs. At service levels over 85 percent, the marginal costs to produce that level of service exceed the additional revenue that would be gained.

To reiterate, service levels are developed by assessing customer service requirements. The sales and cost effects of various service levels are analyzed to find the service level generating the highest profits. The needs of various customer segments will dictate various logistical system configurations. For example, when logistical service is critical, industrial distributors can provide the vital product availability, whereas customers with less rigorous service demands can be served from factory inventories.

THE INTERFACE OF LOGISTICS IN THE CHANNEL

Logistical activities, whether by manufacturer or intermediary, touch every phase of channel performance and are inherent in the success or failure of most industrial channel systems. The task of the business marketer is, first, to understand the impact of supplier logistical performance on the intermediary's operations, and next, to effect programs that will enhance the intermediary's performance and overall channel coordination.

Logistical Impacts on Industrial Intermediaries

A supplier's logistical system directly affects an intermediary's ability to control cost and service to end users. Delivery time not only influences the customer's inventory requirements but also the operations of channel members. If a supplier provides erratic delivery service to distributors, the distributor is forced to carry higher inventory in order to provide a satisfactory level of product availability to end users.

Inefficient logistics service to the distributors either increases distributor costs (larger inventories) or creates shortages of the supplier's products at the distributor level. Neither result is good. In the first instance, distributor loyalty and marketing efforts will suffer; in the second, end users will eventually change suppliers. 3M Corporation realizes the impact of logistics service on its automotive distributors, and a major reason for opening a new distribution center in Southfield, Michigan, was to support distributors' JIT programs with the auto industry.[24] The new center helps 3M distributors meet JIT requirements for custom orders required by the automobile manufacturers. Observe in Figure 14.4 that Federal-Mogul Corporation, a diversified producer of component parts, emphasizes the benefits that customers can receive from using their responsive distributor network.

Impact on Customer Service

Poor logistical performance is a double-edged sword. It constricts sales possibilities and antagonizes intermediaries. A five percent reduction in customer service can result in a sales decrease of 20 percent.[25] An industrial distributor will not long remain loyal to a manufacturer whose logistical performance reduces service levels to end users. Because inventories typically represent the single largest item among distributor assets, and also the largest distribution expense, distributors are increasingly aware of the impact of supplier logistical service. Also, poor logistics may necessitate use of faster-than-usual freight methods—at premium prices—to get products to customers on time. Because distributors often pass freight charges along to their customers, abnormally high transportation costs can place the manufacturer's product at a price disadvantage in the marketplace.

---

[24] "3M Banks on New Center to Focus Auto Thrust," *Business Marketing*, 70 (February 1985), p. 15.

[25] LaLonde, Cooper, and Noordewier, *Customer Service*, p. 133.

FIGURE 14.4   **Ad Emphasizing Customer Benefits of a Responsive Distribution System**

Source: Courtesy, Federal-Mogul Corporation.

Improving Logistical Performance in the Channel

The business marketer can do much to improve channelwide logistical performance. First, information systems can be developed to provide realistic sales forecasts for individual channel members, and their inventory control systems can be linked to the manufacturer's information system. Second, coordination of logistical activities can be facilitated, perhaps by standardizing packaging, handling, and palletization systems. Third, the manufacturer may perform certain functions (e.g., warehousing) that contribute to improved efficiency for the entire channel. Finally, shipment consolidation is often effective in reducing channelwide transportation costs. Distributors in a particular area might be encouraged to "pool" shipments into a truckload quantity, or to place all of their orders on the same day. In summary, logistics must be integrated channelwide to implement marketing strategy effectively.

BUSINESS-TO-BUSINESS LOGISTICAL MANAGEMENT

The elements of logistics strategy are part of a system, and as such, each affects every other element. The proper focus is the total-cost view. Although the approach taken in this section is to treat the decisions on facilities, transportation, and inventory separately, it must be remembered that they are so intertwined it is impossible to evaluate one without considering the other two.

Logistical Facilities

The strategic development of a warehouse provides the business marketer with the opportunity to increase the level of delivery service to buyers, to reduce transportation costs, or both. Business firms distributing repair, maintenance, and operating supplies often find that the only way to achieve desired levels of delivery service is to locate warehouses in key markets. The warehouse circumvents the need for premium transportation (air freight) and costly order processing by keeping products readily available in local markets.

Servicing Channel Members
The nature of the business-to-business channel affects the warehousing requirements of a supplier. When manufacturers' reps are utilized, the supplier will often require a significant number of strategically located warehouses. On the other hand, a channel system using distributors will offset the need for warehousing. Obviously, local warehousing by the distributor is a real service to the supplier. A few well-located supplier warehouses may be all that is required to service the distributors effectively.

Private or Third-Party
Operating costs, service levels, and investment requirements are essential considerations regarding the type of warehouse to use. The business firm may either own, rent, or lease warehouse space. At a **third-party warehouse**, space may be rented by the

month or leased for a longer time. Short-term arrangements involve **public** warehousing firms, while longer term agreements, including the provision of special services, are provided by **contract** warehousers. The advantage is flexibility—the firm can increase or decrease its use of space in a given market or move into or out of any market quickly. Public warehousing involves no fixed investment; user costs are totally variable. When sales volume is seasonal, erratic, or generally low in a given market, the public warehouse is an economical means of providing excellent product availability. Contract warehousing is effective when the firm requires unique service and special equipment in the warehousing function.

Public or contract warehousing may sometimes supplement or replace distributors in a market. Many public and contract warehouses provide a variety of logistical services for their clients, including packaging, labeling, order processing, and some light assembly. Itel Distribution Services, a public/contract warehouse company based in San Francisco, California, maintains warehouse facilities in a number of major markets. Clients can position inventories in all these markets while dealing with only one firm. Also, Itel can link its computer with the suppliers' computers to facilitate order processing and inventory updating. The Itel warehouse will also repackage products to the end user's order, label, and arrange for local delivery. A business marketer could ship standard products in bulk to the Itel warehouse, gaining transportation economies, and still enjoy excellent customer delivery service. The public or contract warehouse is a feasible alternative to the distributor channel when the sales function can be economically executed either with a direct sales force or with reps.[26]

The alternative to renting or leasing warehouse space is the **private warehouse**, in which the manufacturer makes a capital investment. Although the investment is substantial, private facilities can provide operating cost advantages when they are regularly used at close to capacity. Often more important than the cost and investment aspects is the enhancement of customer service. The private warehouse offers more control over the warehousing operation, permitting efficient levels of operation and delivery service.

Transportation

Transportation is usually the largest single logistical expense, and with the impact of continually rising fuel costs, its importance will probably increase. Typically, the transportation decision involves the evaluation and selection both of a mode of transportation and of the individual carrier(s) that will ensure the best performance at the lowest cost. **Mode** refers to the type of carrier—rail, truck, water, air, or some combination of the four. **Individual carriers** are evaluated on rates and delivery performance.[27] In this section we will consider (1) the role of transportation in industrial

---

[26] Michael D. Hutt and Thomas W. Speh, "Realigning Industrial Marketing Channels," *Industrial Marketing Management,* 12 (July 1983), pp. 171–77.

[27] For example, see Roy J. Sampson, Martin T. Farris, and David L. Schrock, *Domestic Transportation: Practice, Theory and Policy,* (Boston, MA: Houghton Mifflin Company, 1990).

THE GLOBAL MARKETPLACE
"CAT" Gets a Gift from Third-Party Logistics Specialist

In 1983, Caterpillar ceased production of lift trucks in the United States and began manufacturing the trucks in England and Korea. Although savings in manufacturing costs were impressive, the company was left with a substantial logistics problem: how to distribute the lift trucks cost-effectively to the U.S. market.

The answer: produce modular trucks that could be assembled to buyers' specifications after arriving in the states. The key to the strategy, however, was to hire a third-party logistics specialist—a public warehouse firm—to handle the warehousing and assembly work. Such an arrangement allows Caterpillar to con-

centrate on its expertise: the quality and technical aspects of the assembly operation.

Caterpillar "modules" are now shipped to New Orleans where they are received, inspected, and stored in the public warehouse. The warehouse company handles all quality control checks, "checking everything, right down to the thread on nuts and bolts." After receiving and modification operations are completed, the public warehouse ships the completed lift trucks to Caterpillar customers. In all, trucks are now completed and shipped in the same time as when the trucks were manufactured in Ohio while realizing many new economies from offshore manufacturing.

Source: "Profiles of Warehousing Quality," *Distribution*, 85 (December 1986), p. 16.

channels, (2) the criteria for evaluating transportation options, (3) the purpose of expedited logistical systems, and (4) the private carrier alternative.

Transportation and Logistical Service

A business marketer must be able to effectively move finished inventory between facilities, to channel intermediaries, and to customers. The transportation system is the link that binds the logistical network together and ultimately results in timely delivery of products. Efficient warehousing will not enhance customer service levels if transportation is inconsistent or inadequate.

Effective transportation service may be used in combination with warehouse facilities and inventory levels to generate the required customer service level, or it may be used in place of them. Inventory maintained in a variety of market-positioned warehouses can be pulled back to one centralized warehouse if there is rapid transportation service from the central location to business customers. Xerox is one company that uses premium air freight service to offset the need for high inventories and extensive warehouse locations. The decision on transportation modes and particular carriers will depend on the cost trade-offs and service capabilities of each.

Transportation Performance Criteria

Cost of service is the variable cost associated with moving products from origin to destination, including any terminal or accessory charges. The cost of service may range from as little as 0.25 cents per ton-mile via water to as high as 50 cents per ton-mile via air freight. The important aspect of selecting the mode of transportation is not cost per se, but cost relative to the objective to be achieved. Bulk raw materials generally do not require prepaid delivery service, so the cost of anything other than rail or water transportation could not be justified. On the other hand, although air freight may be almost ten times more expensive than motor freight, when a customer needs an emergency shipment of spare parts, the cost is inconsequential. The cost of premium (faster) transportation modes may be justified by the resulting inventory reductions.

Speed of service refers to the elapsed time to move products from one facility (plant or warehouse) to another facility (warehouse or customer plant). Again, speed of service often overrides the cost of service. Rail, a relatively slow mode used for bulk shipments, requires inventory buildups at the supplier's factory and at the destination warehouse. The longer the delivery time, the more inventory customers must maintain to service their needs while the shipment is in transit. The slower modes involve lower variable costs for product movement, yet they result in lower service levels and higher investments in inventory. The faster modes produce just the opposite effect. Not only must a comparison be made between modes in terms of service, but various carriers within a mode must be evaluated on their "door-to-door" delivery time.

Service consistency is usually more important than average delivery time, and all modes of transportation are not equally consistent. Although air provides the lowest average delivery time, generally it has the highest variability in delivery time relative to the average. The wide variations in modal service consistency are particularly critical in business marketing planning. The choice of transportation mode must be made on the basis of cost, average transit time, and consistency if effective customer service is to be achieved.

In summary, because business buyers often place a premium on effective and consistent delivery service, the choice of transportation mode is an important one—one in which the cost of service is often secondary. However, the best decision on transportation carriers will result from a balancing of service, variable costs, and investment requirements. The manager must also consider the transportation requirements of ordinary versus expedited, or rush-order, shipments.

Normal versus Expedited Systems

Logistical systems in business marketing channels are often two-tiered: The routine logistical requirements are satisfied through one system, and the rush-order needs are met through a different system. The normal system is designed to provide low-cost delivery at required service levels. Transportation modes and carriers are selected on the basis of simple efficiency—lowest rates and average delivery performance. A manufacturer of brake shoes may find that rail shipments from factory to distributor or to customer warehouses provide low-cost transportation at a service level that is adequate for most customer orders. However, brake shoes may be rush ordered perhaps 5 percent of the time as a result of increased customer production or abnormally high breakdowns in a truck fleet. The backup system might entail air express shipments from a special warehouse or from any of a number of small package carriers. Such carriers often form the backbone of the second-tier, priority logistical system.

INSIDE BUSINESS MARKETING
Lockheed Transforms Boxcars into Warehouse

How to beat the high cost of warehousing—what firm hasn't wondered about that? Well, if you're lucky enough to have rail tracks on your property, you can do what Lockheed Aeronautical Systems did in its Marietta, Georgia, facility: buy old railroad boxcars and use them as a warehouse on steel wheels.

Lockheed Aeronautical's Georgia Division needed additional warehousing space for its bagged chemicals—and it needed the space quickly. Yet it did not want to lease new warehousing space. The division's traffic manager knew that unused railroad tracks sat adjacent to the existing warehouse and that boxcar capacity in the railroad industry far exceeded demand.

So he visited the railroad serving the plant (CSX), found that it did have excess boxcars it was willing to sell, and bought ten of them at a "very reasonable" price.

The railroad spotted the ten boxcars alongside the warehouse. Platforms were added to give forklifts access to the boxcars from the warehouse dock area. Lockheed strung up lights inside the boxcars for illumination. Then it spraypainted the units to give a clean, uniform appearance. The end result is that Lockheed Aeronautical has handy, long-term storage space in secure boxcars at a fraction of the cost of leasing space.

Source: Frances J. Quinn, "Top 10 Logistics Ideas," *Traffic Management*, 29 (October 1990), p. 36.

Private Carriers

Sometimes the only way for a supplier to achieve the consistent delivery performance required by customers is with its own trucks. Service improvement is the primary justification for a company fleet, because the private fleet may be more expensive than hired transportation. The investment requirements are significant—vehicles, maintenance facilities, and the like—though they can sometimes be reduced by leasing equipment. The decision to operate a private fleet is a complex one.[28] However, the advantages of private ownership and management of transportation service may effectively balance the cost, investment, and service aspects of transportation. Inventory, the third leg of logistical management, is interrelated with the transportation decision.

Inventory Management

Inventory management is the buffer in the logistical system. Inventories are needed in business channels because (1) production and demand are not perfectly matched, (2) operating deficiencies in the logistical system often result in product unavailability (e.g., delayed shipments, inconsistent carrier performance), and (3) industrial customers cannot predict their product needs with certainty (e.g., because a machine may break down or there may be a sudden need to expand production). Inventory may be viewed in the same light as warehouse facilities and transportation: it is an alternative

---

[28] For example, see Johnson and Wood, *Contemporary Physical Distribution and Logistics*, pp. 211–214.

method for providing the level of service required by customers, and the level of inventory is determined on the basis of cost, investment, service required, and anticipated revenue.

Inventory Costs

Inventory costs are subtle and difficult to comprehend because often they are not segregated but found throughout a firm's system of accounts. Inventory costs include four basic cost categories: (1) capital costs, (2) inventory service costs (e.g., cases and insurance), (3) storage space costs, and (4) inventory risk costs (e.g., damage and pilferage).[29]

Together these four cost categories are known as **inventory carrying costs**, typically stated as a percentage of the value of the products held in inventory. (A carrying charge of 20 percent means that the cost of holding one unit in inventory for one year is 20 percent of the value of the product.) Inventory carrying costs usually range from 12 to 35 percent, yet these percentages may be much higher if all relevant inventory-related costs are considered. One company that had historically used a 19 percent carrying charge figure for making inventory decisions was found to have a true carrying charge of 38 percent.[30]

The implications are clear. To make sound inventory decisions, business managers must be able to determine the true cost of holding inventories. Only after the true costs of inventory are known can management evaluate the cost–service and the inventory/transportation trade-offs. Effective inventory policy also demands a product-by-product analysis.

The 80/20 Rule

Most business marketers with extensive product lines are aware that the great bulk of their products do not turn over very rapidly. This is the **80/20 principle**: 80 percent of the sales are generated by 20 percent of the product line.

The major implication of the 80/20 principle is that business marketers must manage their inventory selectively, treating fast- and slow-moving items differently. If a company has half its inventory committed to products that produce only 20 percent of the unit sales volume, significant gains can be made by reducing inventories of the slow sellers to the point at which their turnover rate approximates that of the fast sellers.[31] This rule applies regardless of how the inventory function is handled in the channel. Thus, suppliers can develop more efficient channels and substantially reduce distributor inventory costs by allowing the distributor to cut back inventory on slow-turnover items. Not only will distributor cost performance improve, but enhanced channel goodwill should result.

---

[29] Bernard J. LaLonde and Douglas M. Lambert, "A Methodology for Determining Inventory Carrying Costs: Two Case Studies," in James Robson and John Grabner, eds., *Proceedings of the Fifth Annual Transportation and Logistics Educators Conference* (October 1975), p. 47.

[30] Ibid., p. 39, 47.

[31] James L. Heskett, "Logistics—Essential to Strategy," *Harvard Business Review,* 56 (November–December 1977), p. 89.

Selective Inventory Strategies

The evaluation of selective inventory strategies depends on the cost and service trade-offs involved. First, inventory of slow movers can be reduced at all locations; the result, however, may be a marked reduction in customer service. As with transportation, one workable alternative is to centralize the slow-moving items at a single location, thereby reducing total inventories. The result is a higher sales volume per unit of product at a given location. In turn, inventories of fast-moving items can be expanded, enhancing their service levels.

A selective inventory policy must be applied cautiously. Typically, fast-moving items are standardized items that customers expect to be readily available; slow movers are often nonstandardized, and customers expect to wait to receive them.[32] However, there is no rule that all slow-moving items require low service levels. If a slow-moving item is critical in the production process or is needed to repair a machine, an extremely high level of service is required. Thus, a selective inventory policy mandates that both turnover rates and the criticalness of the product to the customer be evaluated in determining the inventory/transportation system.

The Critical Role: Forecasting and Computers

Estimates of future sales are the primary variable in determining inventory levels throughout the industrial logistics system. Short-term sales forecasts for weekly, monthly, quarterly, or yearly sales are the heart of any inventory planning system because inventories throughout the channel will be based on expected demand. The approaches to forecasting developed in Chapter 7 are relevant to the inventory decision. However, it is often necessary to adapt the broad sales forecasts to logistical purposes. A general forecast used to plan sales and promotional efforts is not usually specific enough for logistical inventory planning. Product-by-product estimates for short intervals are needed so that inventories can be adjusted. These are often not included in the general sales forecast. Finally, forecasting must be integrated within the channel; distributors and suppliers must work from the same sales estimates so that order timing and quantities can be accurately determined for the channel.

Most successful business marketers manage inventory through sophisticated computer programs. The computer is used to track sales histories and product sales as well as to monitor recent stock levels. Decision rules are built into the programs, and these trigger shipments of the product at the right time. Frequently, the computer is linked with portable terminals, and bar-code "wands" are used in the warehouse to record key inventory data. Today, the computer is an indispensable tool for managing inventory to meet service and cost standards.

For example, Kaman Bearing & Supply Corporation, upon finding that more than half of the firm's assets were tied up in inventory, developed a computerized inventory control system.[33] By tracking transaction histories, a complete profile of each of the firm's products was created, and seasonal demand patterns were isolated. Accurate

---

[32] Ibid., p. 29.

[33] Lisa Harrington, "Better Management Means Lower Costs," *Traffic Management*, 21 (November 1982), p. 43.

status reports on inventory levels and improved forecasting capabilities allow Kaman to set product-by-product service levels and to adjust stock levels accordingly. Inventory costs have dropped by more than 25 percent.

The Strategic Role of Logistics

Only recently have business marketers begun to explore the use of logistics as a variable for creating competitive advantage. In contrast to all the other elements of the marketing mix, logistics competency offers the potential to gain a unique differential advantage.[34] Because complex logistics systems require high investments of people, systems, and facilities, it is not likely that logistics system excellence can be easily duplicated. Business marketing managers would be well-advised to carefully evaluate the important strategic role that logistics competence can play in the overall success of their marketing plans. Worldwide sourcing, JIT manufacturing systems, total quality programs, and global competition are key environmental forces that strongly indicate an ever increasing role for logistics in the marketing strategies of business-to-business firms.

SUMMARY

The systems perspective in logistical management cannot be stressed enough—it is the only way that management can be assured that the logistical function will meet prescribed goals. Not only must each logistical variable be analyzed in terms of its impact on every other variable, but the sum of the variables must be evaluated in light of the service level provided to customers. Logistics elements throughout the channel must be integrated to assure smooth product flow.

Logistical service is critical in buyer evaluation of industrial suppliers. Logistical service seems to rank second only to product quality as a desired supplier characteristic. Business marketing managers are faced with a stern challenge to develop cost-effective logistical systems that provide the necessary service levels.

Decisions in the logistical area must be based on cost trade-offs among the logistical variables and on comparisons of the costs and revenues associated with alternative levels of service. The optimal system is one that produces the highest profitability relative to the capital investment required.

The major logistical variables are facilities, transportation, and inventory. Decisions are required on the number of warehouses, whether they are to be owned or rented, the transportation mode and the specific carrier, the level and deployment of inventory, and the selectivity of inventory levels. The systems approach can structure these three variables effectively. The business supplier must monitor the impact of logistics on channel members and on overall channel performance. Finally, the strategic role of

---

[34] Donald J. Bowersox, Patricia Daugherty, Cornelia Dröge, Dale Rogers, and Daniel Wardlow, *Leading Edge Logistics: Competitive Positioning for the 1990's*, (Oak Brook, IL: Council of Logistics Management, 1989), p. 302.

logistics should be carefully evaluated; logistics can provide a strong competitive advantage in many instances.

Discussion Questions

1. Adopting the perspective of an organizational buyer, carefully illustrate how the most economical source of supply might be the firm that offers the highest price but also the fastest and most reliable delivery system.

2. Why is the logistical function often signaled out as "the last frontier of cost reduction in American business"?

3. Describe a situation in which total logistical costs might be reduced by doubling transportation costs.

4. A key goal in logistical management is to find the optimum balance of logistical cost and customer service that yields optimal profits. Explain.

5. Explain how consistent delivery performance gives the organizational buyer the opportunity to cut the level of inventory maintained.

6. Explain how the use of reps versus distributors influences the number of warehouses that the industrial marketer must employ in the logistical system.

7. Why is it often necessary for business marketers to have a two-tiered logistical system: one for routine orders, one for rush orders?

8. Inventory decisions for the business marketer are based on cost–service and inventory/transportation trade-offs. Illustrate the nature of these trade-offs.

9. Excessive premium freight charges and slow inventory turnover are two signs of maldistribution. If these danger signals appear, what steps should the business marketer take?

10. An increasing number of manufacturers are adopting a materials management philosophy (see Chapter 2) and more sophisticated inventory control systems. What are the strategic implications of these developments for business marketers wishing to serve these customers?

CHAPTER 15

Managing the Industrial Pricing Function

The price that a business marketer assigns to a product or service is one of many factors that will be scrutinized by the organizational buyer. Pricing decisions cannot be made in a vacuum; they must be made in concert with other marketing strategy decisions. The diverse nature of the business market presents unique problems and opportunities for the price setter.

After reading this chapter, you will understand:

1. the role of price in the cost/benefit calculations of organizational buyers.

2. the central elements of the industrial pricing process.

3. how effective new product prices are established and the need for periodic adjustment of the prices of existing products.

4. strategic approaches to competitive bidding.

5. the strategic role of lease marketing.

THE business marketing manager must blend the various components of the marketing mix into a total offering that responds to the needs of the market and that provides a return consistent with the firm's objectives. Price must be carefully meshed with the product, distribution, and communication strategies of the firm. "If effective product development, promotion, and distribution sow the seeds of business success, effective pricing is the harvest. While effective pricing can never compensate for poor execution of the first three elements, ineffective pricing can surely prevent these efforts from resulting in financial success. Regrettably, this is a common occurrence."[1]

The interdependence of price and other strategy components must be recognized before the pricing function can be isolated for analysis. Clearly, there is no one best way for establishing the price of a new industrial product or for modifying the price of existing products. The price setter must know the firm's objectives, markets, costs, competition, and customer demand patterns—not easy when time is short, information incomplete, and the competitive and business climate is changing rapidly. Rising expectations for product and service quality, growing competition (foreign and domestic), new technology, changing consumer requirements, and the changing fortunes of different business sectors—these forces call for an active rather than a passive approach to pricing.[2]

This chapter is divided into five parts. First, the special meaning of price is defined in a business marketing context. Second, key determinants of the industrial pricing process are analyzed, and an operational approach to pricing decisions provided. Third, pricing policies for new and existing products will be examined, with emphasis on the need for actively managing a product throughout its life cycle. Fourth, we consider price administration (i.e., types of price adjustments). Last, we turn to two areas of particular importance to the business marketer—competitive bidding and leasing.

THE MEANING OF PRICE IN BUSINESS MARKETS

When members of a buying center select a particular product, they are buying a given level of product quality, technical service, and delivery reliability. Other elements may be of importance—the reputation of the supplier, a feeling of security, friendship, and other personal benefits flowing from the buyer–seller relationship. Observe from Figure 15.1 that the attribute bundles sought by the buying center may fall into three categories: **product-specific** attributes (e.g., product quality), **company-related** attributes (e.g., reputation for technological excellence), and **salesperson-related** attributes (e.g., dependability).[3]

Thus, the total product (as discussed in Chapter 10) is much more than its physical attributes. Likewise, the *cost* of an industrial good includes much more than the seller's *price*. Pricing decisions and product policy decisions are inseparable and must be balanced within the firm's market segmentation plan.[4]

---

[1] Thomas T. Nagle, *The Strategy and Tactics of Pricing: A Guide to Profitable Decision Making* (Englewood Cliffs, N.J.: Prentice-Hall, Inc., 1987), p. 1.

[2] Charles O'Neal and Kate Bertrand, *Developing a Winning J.I.T. Marketing Strategy* (Englewood Cliffs, NJ: Prentice-Hall, Inc., 1991), Chapter 8.

[3] David T. Wilson, "Pricing Industrial Products and Services," Institute for the Study of Business Markets, College of Business Administration, The Pennsylvania State University, Report #9-1986.

[4] Benson P. Shapiro and Barbara B. Jackson, "Industrial Pricing to Meet Customer Needs," *Harvard Business Review*, 56 (November–December 1978), p. 125.

FIGURE 15.1   **Pricing Environment: The Relationship between Buyer, Seller, and Competitor**

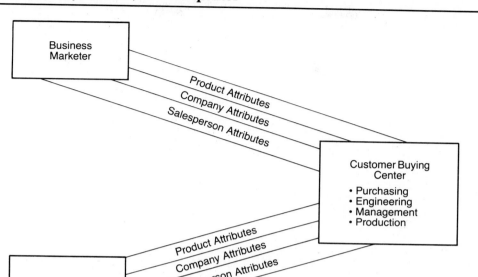

Source: Adapted with modifications from David T. Wilson, "Pricing Industrial Products and Services," Report #9-1986, Institute for the Study of Business Markets, The Pennsylvania State University.

Benefits

Various market segments, each with unique needs, base their evaluation of a product on dimensions of particular value to them. The benefits of a particular product can be functional, operational, financial, or personal.[5] These benefits are of varying degrees of importance to various market segments and to various individuals within the buying center. **Functional benefits** are the design characteristics that might be attractive to technical personnel. **Operational benefits** are durability and reliability, qualities desirable to production managers. **Financial benefits** are favorable terms and opportunities for cost savings, of importance to purchasing managers and controllers. Organizational status, reduced risk, and personal satisfaction are among the **personal benefits** that might accrue to an individual from a particular supplier choice.

[5] Ibid., pp. 119–127.

Costs

A broad perspective is likewise needed in examining the costs a particular alternative may present for the buyer. These costs include not only price, but also transportation, installation, order handling, and inventory carrying costs. Less obvious, but no less important, are the risks of product failure and poor technical and delivery support.[6]

These costs are made especially vivid in buying organizations using formal supplier evaluation programs (see Chapter 3). Systems such as the cost-ratio and the weighted-point methods allow the buyer to measure the total cost of dealing with alternative suppliers.

A buyer may find that the supplier offering the lowest price may be the highest cost alternative in the long run. Clearly, the supplier with the lowest price is not guaranteed an account. This fact was reinforced in a study of purchasers of selected capital items (e.g., liquid transfer and control systems). In an analysis of more than 100 purchase decisions, the low bidder was *not* selected in more than 40 percent of the cases.[7]

THE INDUSTRIAL PRICING PROCESS

There is no easy formula for pricing an industrial product or service. The decision is multidimensional rather than one-dimensional. The interactive variables of demand, cost, competition, profit relationships, and customer usage patterns each assume significance as the marketer formulates the role that price will play in the firm's marketing strategy. Pertinent considerations, illustrated in Figure 15.2, are (1) price objectives, (2) demand determinants, (3) cost determinants, and (4) competition. The additional considerations in the figure, effect on product line and legal implications of a particular pricing decision, are treated later.

Price Objectives

The pricing decision must be based on objectives congruent with marketing and overall corporate objectives. The marketer starts with principal objectives and adds collateral pricing goals: (1) achieving a target return on investment, (2) achieving a market-share goal, or (3) meeting competition. There are many other potential pricing objectives that go beyond profit and market-share goals, taking into account competition, channel relationships, and product line considerations.

---

[6] Ibid.

[7] J. Patrick Kelly and James W. Coaker, "Can We Generalize about Choice Criteria for Industrial Purchasing Decisions?" in Kenneth L. Bernhardt, ed., *Marketing: 1776–1976 and Beyond* (Chicago: American Marketing Association, 1976), pp. 330–333.

FIGURE 15.2   **Key Components of the Industrial Pricing Process**

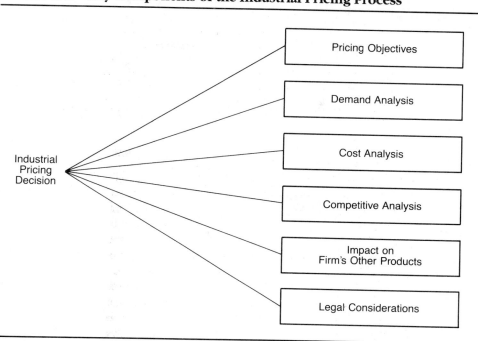

Pricing objectives must be established with care because they have far-reaching effects.[8] Each firm faces unique internal and external environmental forces. Contrasting the strategies of Du Pont and Dow Chemical Company illustrates the importance of a unified corporate direction. Dow's strategy focuses, first, on pricing low-margin commodity goods low to build a dominant market share and, then, on maintaining that dominant share. Du Pont's strategy, on the other hand, emphasizes specialty products that carry a higher margin. Initially, these products are priced at a high level, and prices are reduced as the market expands and competition intensifies. Each firm requires explicit pricing objectives that are consistent with its corporate mission.

Demand Determinants

A strong market perspective is fundamental in pricing. The business market is diverse and complex. A single industrial product can be used in many ways; each market segment may represent a unique application for the product and a separate usage level. The degree of importance of the industrial good in the buyer's end product also varies by market segment. Therefore, potential demand, sensitivity to price, and potential

---

[8] For an expanded treatment of strategic pricing objectives, see Harper W. Boyd, Jr., and Orville C. Walker, Jr., *Marketing Management: A Strategic Approach* (Homewood, IL: Irwin, 1990), pp. 460–467.

profitability can vary markedly across market segments. Once again, a sound market segmentation strategy is pivotal in effective marketing strategy development.

A Customer Focus

A sound industrial pricing perspective involves an analysis of the benefits and costs of the product from the standpoint of the customer.[9] In calculating the benefits of a product, the marketer can examine the physical attributes of a product (hard benefits) and the attached services (soft benefits). Hard benefits may be defined with a price/performance ratio. For example, one performance variable for a piece of earth-moving equipment may be dollars per horsepower or, better yet, yards of earth moved per hour. For computers, the performance variable may be dollars per unit of processing speed or MIPS (million instructions per second): see Figure 15.3. This approach forces the marketer to examine the product from the consumer's perspective and allows for a comparison of the firm's product offering with those of competitors. Soft benefits are more difficult to define precisely, but determining their degree of importance to various market segments should be attempted.

To the organizational customer, cost includes dimensions other than price. The costs of a new packaging machine purchased by a manufacturer begin with the price but also include transportation, installation, repair and maintenance, and energy usage. In calculating the customer costs of such a product, the marketer can apply **life cycle costing** to calculate the total cost of the product over its life span. Life cycle costing includes maintenance, repair, operating costs, and useful product life. Rising labor, energy, and material prices are among factors that have stimulated renewed interest in life cycle costing by government agencies, commercial enterprises, and institutions—and marketing managers.[10]

Although the concept has generally been applied to capital items (e.g., computers, heavy industrial equipment, health facilities), it can also be applied to lighter industrial goods. In using life cycle costing as a marketing tool, the producer of a packaging machine may be able to justify a high initial price if there will be clear savings in energy, material, labor, and maintenance costs over the life of the asset.

Other costs are more difficult to quantify precisely.[11] The buyer of packaging equipment might be concerned about the possibility of a production stoppage due to machine failure. Segments of the market that are sensitive to this risk will be interested in the benefit of reliability, and may be willing to pay a higher price to reduce the risk of system failure.

To recap, the industrial price setter must examine how organizational buyers balance the costs and benefits of alternative offerings. This approach is useful not only in determining an appropriate price but also in facilitating the development of responsive product, advertising, and personal selling strategies.

---

[9] Shapiro and Jackson, "Industrial Pricing to Meet Customer Needs," pp. 123–124.

[10] Robert J. Brown, "A New Marketing Tool: Life Cycle Costing," *Industrial Marketing Management*, 8 (April 1979), pp. 109–113.

[11] Shapiro and Jackson, "Industrial Pricing to Meet Customer Needs," pp. 119–127.

FIGURE 15.3 **An Ad by Sun Microsystems Featuring a Price/Performance Theme**

WHY DID WE INTRODUCE A 12.5 MIPS WORKSTATION FOR $4995?

BECAUSE WE CAN.

SPARCstation™ SLC. By breaking the $5,000 barrier, it turns the economics of computing absolutely upside down. And lets you give your people a system that runs circles around PCs and minicomputers.

Up till now, for this price you'd have to settle for a 386 with one or two little extras. Or a share of a minicomputer. Or maybe an X terminal with an underpowered processor.

But now, you can give everyone a high-performance RISC workstation for the same price. Complete with 12.5 MIPS of processing power. The UNIX® operating system.

8 MB of memory. Even built-in Ethernet*

But more than a hot machine, you can give them all the strategic advantages that come with our SPARC™ technology.

First, our workstations were meant to be networked. So you can have whole groups working on the same project. In perfect synch. And every user has serious processing power. Right at the desktop level. Second, there's the OPEN LOOK™ user interface. Which lets people learn to use UNIX in no time flat. Finally, there's

UNIX itself. With UNIX, your people can create applications that would take a lifetime to develop any other way. In fact, there are over 2,000 SPARCware® applications that are ready to run right now. So you have the added advantage of choosing the world's largest standard for RISC/UNIX software compatibility.

How did we design all this into a $5,000 system? Since 1982, we've built nothing but UNIX workstations. So we've learned a few things. We completely eliminated the processor box.

By building the electronics into the back of the monitor. We gave it a high-resolution monochrome display. And since SPARCstation SLC is designed for workgroups, all the files can be stored in a central server. Or on a local disk, if you'd rather.

For a lot of companies, introducing a machine like this would be next to impossible. But at Sun, it's not exactly our first breakthrough. And this is no announce-it-today, ship-it-next-year product, either. SPARCstation SLC is available in quantity today.

SPARCstation SLC. If you'd like to see how it compares to every other system you could buy, just call 1-800-624-8999 ext. 2066. From anywhere in the U.S. and Canada. And get ready to move your people a quantum leap ahead.

Because now you can.

 sun microsystems

*MIPS = million instructions per second

Source: Courtesy, Sun Microsystems.

Diagnosing Cost/Benefit Trade-Offs[12]

How organizational buyers will evaluate the cost/benefit trade-offs of the total offering determines the appropriateness of a particular industrial pricing strategy. Two competitors with similar products may ask differing prices because their total offerings are perceived as being unique by buyers. In the eyes of the organizational buyer, one firm may provide more value than another.

A core pricing issue is which attributes of the offering contribute most to its perceived value? Several attributes of a total product offering are illustrated in Table 15.1. These attributes, which relate to a particular Du Pont product offering, were identified as those that have value to buyers and that differ among competitors. Two

---

[12]Irwin Gross, "Insights from Pricing Research," in Earl L. Bailey, ed., *Pricing Practices and Strategies* (New York: The Conference Board, 1978), pp. 34–39. See also Valerie Kijewski and Eunsang Yoon, "Market-Based Pricing: Beyond Price-Performance Curves," *Industrial Marketing Management*, 19 (February 1990), pp. 11–19.

TABLE 15.1 **Attributes of a Total Product Offering: Some Trade-Offs**

Attribute	High Level	Low Level
Quality	Impurities less than one part per million	Impurities less than ten parts per million
Delivery	Within one week	Within two weeks
System	Supply total system	Supply chemical only
Innovation	High level of R&D support	Little R&D support
Retraining	Retrain on request	Train on initial purchase
Service	Locally available	Through home office

Source: Irwin Gross, "Insights from Pricing Research," in Earl L. Bailey, ed., *Pricing Practices and Strategies* (New York: The Conference Board, 1978), p. 37. Reprinted by permission of The Conference Board.

levels of performance are provided for each attribute. Since higher costs are incurred in providing higher levels of performance on one or more of the attributes, the strategist should assess the relative importance of the attributes to different market segments and should assess the strength of the firm's offering on each of the important attributes vis-a-vis competitors.

The equation in Figure 15.4 highlights how the relative perceived values of two competing offerings are compared. Irv Gross contends that the relative perceived value of offering A versus offering B "can be thought of as the price differential at which the buyer would be indifferent between the alternatives."[13] As in Figure 15.4, the premium price differential, or perceived relative value, can be broken down into components based on each important attribute: (1) the value of the attribute to the buyer, and (2) the perception of how competing offerings perform on that attribute. By summing all of the component values, we reach the total relative perceived value of an offering. Thus, product offering A may have a total perceived value of $24 per unit, compared to $20 per unit for offering B. The $4 premium might be derived from the value that buyers assign to a high level of product quality and a responsive delivery system, and the perceived advantage of offering A over others on these attributes.

Strategy Implications of the Cost/Benefit Analysis

By isolating the important attributes and the perceptions that enter into the cost/benefit calculations of organizational buyers, the business marketer is better equipped to establish a price and to shape other elements of the marketing strategy. First, if the firm's performance on a highly valued product attribute is truly higher than those offered by competitors, but the market perceives no differences, marketing communications must be devised to bring perceptions into line with reality. Second, marketing communications may also alter the values that organizational buyers assign to a particular attribute. The importance of an attribute such as customer training might

---

[13] Gross, ibid., p. 35.

FIGURE 15.4 **Relative Perceived Value of Two Product Offerings**

$$
\begin{array}{l}
\text{Relative Perceived} \\
\text{Value of} \\
\text{Offering ``A'' vs.} \\
\text{Offering ``B''}
\end{array}
=
\begin{array}{l}
\text{Price Premium for} \\
\text{Indifference}
\end{array}
=
\begin{bmatrix}
\text{First} \\
\text{Attribute} \\
\text{Value}
\end{bmatrix}
\times
\begin{bmatrix}
\text{Perceived} \\
\text{Performance of} \\
\text{Offering ``A'' on} \\
\text{First Attribute}
\end{bmatrix}
-
\begin{array}{l}
\text{Perceived} \\
\text{Performance of} \\
\text{Offering ``B'' on} \\
\text{First Attribute}
\end{array}
+
\begin{bmatrix}
\text{Second} \\
\text{Attribute} \\
\text{Value}
\end{bmatrix}
\times
\begin{bmatrix}
\text{Perceived} \\
\text{Performance of} \\
\text{Offering ``A'' on} \\
\text{Second Attribute}
\end{bmatrix}
-
\begin{array}{l}
\text{Perceived} \\
\text{Performance of} \\
\text{Offering ``B'' on} \\
\text{Second Attribute}
\end{array}
$$

Source: Irwin Gross, "Insights from Pricing Research," in Earl L. Bailey, ed., *Pricing Practices and Strategies* (New York: The Conference Board, 1978), p. 38. Reprinted by permission.

be elevated through marketing communications emphasizing the improved efficiency and safety that training affords the potential buying organization.

Third, the perceived value of the total product offering can be changed by improving the firm's level of performance on attributes that are assigned special importance by organizational buyers. Fourth, knowledge of the cost/benefit perceptions of potential customers presents market segmentation opportunities. For example, good strategy might target those market segments that value the particular product offering attributes that match the distinctive strengths of the firm.

Elasticity Varies by Market Segment

Price elasticity of demand is a measure of the degree to which customers are sensitive to price changes. Specifically, **price elasticity of demand** refers to the rate of percentage change in quantity demanded attributable to the percentage change in price.

Price elasticity of demand is not the same at all prices. An industrial marketer contemplating an alteration in price policy must understand the elasticity of demand. For example, total revenue (price × quantity) will *increase* if price is decreased and demand is price elastic, whereas revenues will *fall* if the price is decreased and demand is price inelastic. Many factors influence the price elasticity of demand—one of them may be buyer perceptions of price/quality relationships. Research suggests that organizational buyers do not associate higher quality with higher price or lower quality with lower price.[14]

Efforts to measure the demand patterns of an individual firm or even of an entire industry are extremely difficult. "No one has yet developed a completely reliable method to measure the price elasticity of demand for a particular brand."[15] Since price is only one of many variables under the control of the marketing manager and only one component of the total product offering, other demand elasticities—promotion, distribution, service—also assume importance. However, recognizing that measurement

---

[14] Phillip D. White and Edward S. Cundiff, "Assessing the Quality of Industrial Products," *Journal of Marketing*, 42 (January 1978), pp. 80–86.

[15] Alfred R. Oxenfeldt, "A Decision-Making Structure for Price Decisions," *Journal of Marketing*, 37 (January 1973), p. 50. See also Steven A. Sinclair and Edward C. Stalling, "How to Identify Differences Between Market Segments with Attribute Analysis," *Industrial Marketing Management*, 19 (February 1990), pp. 31–40.

of price elasticity is difficult should not deter the marketer from attempts to define buyer sensitivity to the price variable across market segments.

Elasticity and End Use

Important insights can be secured by answering this question: How important is the business marketer's product as an input into the total cost of the end product? If the business marketer's product has an insignificant effect on cost, demand is likely inelastic. Consider this example:

> A manufacturer of precision transistors was contemplating an across-the-board price decrease to increase sales. However, an item analysis of the product line revealed that some of its low-volume transistors had exotic applications. A technical customer used the component in an ultrasonic testing apparatus which was sold for $8,000 a unit. This fact prompted the transistor manufacturer to raise the price of the item. Ironically, the firm then experienced a temporary surge of demand for the item as purchasing agents stocked up in anticipation of future price increases.[16]

Of course, the marketer must temper this estimate with an analysis of the costs, availability, and suitability of substitutes. Generally, when the industrial product constitutes an important but low-cost input into the end product, price is less important than quality and delivery reliability.[17]

When the industrial product input assumes a more substantial portion of the final product's total cost, changes in price may have an important effect on the demand for both the final product and the industrial product input. When demand in the final consumer market is price elastic, a reduction in the price of the end item that is caused by a price reduction of an industrial product input generates an increase in demand for the final product and, in turn, for the industrial product.

Because the demand for many industrial products is derived from the demand for the product of which they are a part, a strong end-user focus is needed. The marketer can benefit by examining the trends and changing fortunes of important final consumer markets. Different sectors of the market grow at differing rates, confront differing levels of competition, and face differing short-run and long-run challenges. A downturn in the economy does not fall equally on all sectors. Pricing decisions demand a two-tiered market focus—on organizational customers and on final product customers. "All things being equal, an industrial supplier will have more success in passing on a price increase to customers who are prospering than to customers who are hard pressed."[18]

The value that customers assign to a firm's offering can vary by market segment because the same industrial product may serve differing purposes for various customers. This underscores the important role of market segmentation in the development of profitable pricing strategies.

---

[16] Reed Moyer and Robert J. Boewadt, "The Pricing of Industrial Goods," *Business Horizons*, 14 (June 1971), pp. 27–34; see also George Rostky, "Unveiling Market Segments with Technical Focus Research," *Business Marketing*, 71 (October 1986), pp. 66–69.

[17] Moyer and Boewadt, ibid., p. 28.

[18] Ibid., p. 30.

THE GLOBAL MARKETPLACE
Worldwide Competitive Pricing

A supplier to the automobile industry faces the realities of stiff global competition. Auto manufacturers can no longer pass on cost increases to the marketplace, and their profit margins will not allow them to absorb the increases. The mandate for suppliers is to hold the line on materials and component prices—or in many cases, reduce them—while *increasing* the quality of their product and services.

Statements by senior procurement executives at the big three U.S. auto companies capture the pricing challenge for the business marketer.

- Robert Stone, a vice president on General Motors' material management staff, explains: "As we develop and put a part into the system for the lifetime of one of our products—roughly five years—we have

to . . . find ways to reduce cost. All our ingenuity, technology, innovativeness have to be put toward that principle. This fact frightens a lot of suppliers."

- Davis Platt, vice president of procurement and supply at Chrysler, states: "We'll be supervising suppliers directly and are on an aggressive campaign to reduce our parts and material costs. The emphasis is on cost containment and the shipment of superb quality parts from suppliers."

- Lionel Chicone, vice president of purchasing and supply at Ford, concurs: "What we are trying to do is maximize the opportunity for the supplier to be able to offset cost increases through productivity improvements."

Source: Charles O'Neal and Kate Bertrand, *Developing a Winning J.I.T. Marketing Strategy* (Englewood Cliffs, NJ: Prentice-Hall, Inc., 1991), pp. 126–128.

Methods of Estimating Demand
How can the business marketer measure the price elasticity of demand? Some techniques rely on objective statistical data, others on the intuition and judgment of managers.

Test marketing, as a rule, is considered appropriate only for consumer-goods manufacturers. However, this technique should not be eliminated from the business marketer's repertoire. Industrial products that are sold to a large number of potential users,[19] that have short usage cycles (permitting analysis of repurchase patterns), and that have feasible test market sites lend themselves to test marketing. Whereas most high-priced capital items do not fit this profile, products like industrial paints and maintenance items do.

The **survey approach** examined in Chapter 5 can also be used to measure price elasticity, testing for willingness to buy at various prices or price ranges. On occasion, joint research with a consumer-goods customer could be conducted to survey final consumer demand. Because price is only one variable, the survey instrument must also

---

[19]John Morton and Hugh J. Devine, Jr., "Price Measurements that Hit or Miss," *Business Marketing*, 72 (May 1987), pp. 104–107.

probe for product and service perceptions. It would be useful to ascertain how organizational buyers view price in fundamental cost/benefit trade-offs. This broader perspective is particularly useful in isolating market segments.

When, as often happens, the price setter lacks time and resources, a more informal, subjective approach becomes practical. This technique, drawing upon executive experience, intuition, and judgment, analyzes the relationship of price to other marketing mix variables such as product, promotion, and distribution strategies and a particular competitive setting.[20]

Knowledge of the market is the cornerstone of industrial pricing. A strong market focus, which examines how consumers trade off benefits and costs in their decision making, establishes a base for assigning prices. In this precarious task, the goal is to estimate as precisely as possible the probable demand curve for the firm's product. Knowledge of demand patterns must be augmented by knowledge of costs.

Cost Determinants

Business marketers often pursue a strong internal orientation; they base prices on their own costs, reaching the selling price by calculating unit costs and adding a percentage profit. A strict cost-plus philosophy of pricing overlooks customer perceptions of value, competition, and the interaction of volume and profit.

Costs do, however, establish the lowest pricing point. Since costs fluctuate with volume and vary over time, they must be considered in relation to demand, competition, and pricing objectives. The marketer must know which costs are relevant to the pricing decision and how these costs will fluctuate with volume and over time. Product costs are crucial in projecting the profitability of individual products as well as of the entire product line. Proper classification of costs is essential.

Classifying Costs[21]

The goals of a cost classification system are to (1) properly classify cost data into their fixed and variable components and (2) properly link them to the activity causing them. The manager can then analyze the effects of volume and, more important, identify sources of profit. The following cost concepts are instrumental in the analysis:

1. *Direct traceable or attributable costs.* Costs, fixed or variable, are incurred by and solely for a particular product, customer, or sales territory (e.g., raw materials).

2. *Indirect traceable costs.* Costs, fixed or variable, can be traced to a product, customer, or sales territory (e.g., general plant overhead may be indirectly assigned to a product).

[20] For example, see Bill R. Darden, "An Operational Approach to Product Pricing," *Journal of Marketing*, 32 (April 1969), pp. 29–33.

[21] Kent B. Monroe, *Pricing: Making Profitable Decisions* (New York: McGraw-Hill Book Company, 1979), pp. 52–57; see also Nagle, *The Strategy and Tactics of Pricing*, pp. 14–43.

3. *General costs.* Costs support a number of activities that cannot be objectively assigned to a product on the basis of a direct physical relationship (e.g., the administrative costs of a sales district).

General costs will rarely change because an item is added or deleted from the product line. Marketing, production, and distribution costs must all be classified. When developing a new line or when deleting an item or adding an item to an existing line, the marketer must grasp the cost implications.

- What proportion of the cost of the product is accounted for by purchases of raw materials and components from suppliers?
- How will costs vary at differing levels of production?
- Based on the forecasted level of demand, can economies of scale be expected?
- Does our firm enjoy cost advantages over competitors?
- How does the experience effect impact our cost projections?

Experience Effect

The marketing strategist must also consider the behavior of costs over time. The experience effect is a concept of strategic importance in forecasting costs, and in turn, prices.

Experience curve analysis was introduced in Chapter 10 as a tool to aid product management. The experience curve reflects the theory that costs (measured in constant dollars) decline by a predictable and constant percentage each time accumulated production experience (volume) is doubled. Thus, each time accumulated volume is doubled, the unit costs of many products fall, usually by 20 to 30 percent.[22] The experience curve effect encompasses a broad range of manufacturing, marketing, distribution, and administrative costs.

The three major sources of the experience effect are (1) learning by doing, (2) technological improvements, and (3) economies of scale.[23] Figure 15.5 traces the cost experience for steam turbine generators. The cost per megawatt of output of steam generators followed a 70 percent slope (alternatively, a 30 percent reduction in costs for every doubling in production). The sources of the decline in costs resulted from (1) practice in producing units of each size, which followed an 87 percent slope; (2) scale economies derived from building larger (600-megawatt rather than 200-megawatt) units; and (3) technological improvements in such areas as bearings and high-strength steels, which permitted the design of larger units.[24]

---

[22] William J. Abernathy and Kenneth Wayne, "Limits of the Learning Curve," *Harvard Business Review,* 52 (September–October 1974), pp. 109–119; see also Staff of the Boston Consulting Group, *Perspectives on Experience* (Boston: Boston Consulting Group, Inc., 1972).

[23] George S. Day and David B. Montgomery, "Diagnosing the Experience Curve," *Journal of Marketing,* 47 (Spring 1983), pp. 44–58; see also George S. Day, *Analysis for Strategic Market Decisions* (St. Paul, MN: West Publishing Company, 1986), pp. 25–56.

[24] Ralph Sultan, *Pricing in the Electrical Oligopoly,* Vols. I and II (Cambridge, Mass.: Harvard Graduate School of Business Administration, 1974), cited in Day and Montgomery, "Diagnosing the Experience Curve."

FIGURE 15.5 **Cost Experience for Steam Turbine Generators**

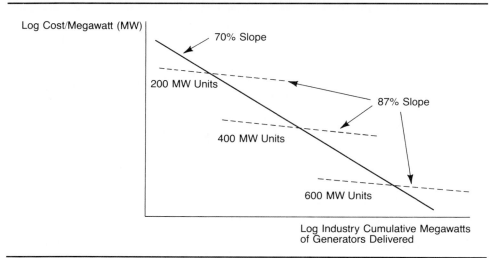

Source: George S. Day and David B. Montgomery, "Diagnosing the Experience Curve," *Journal of Marketing* (Spring 1983), p. 47. Reprinted by permission of the American Marketing Association.

Unfortunately, as experience is gained, costs do not automatically decline. In fact, costs that are not carefully managed will inevitably rise. Experience merely gives management the opportunity to seek cost reductions and efficiency improvements. A thorough effort is needed to exploit the benefits of experience. Product standardization, new production processes, labor efficiency, work specialization—these are only a few of the many areas that must be examined to capitalize on the experience effect.

The experience effect can raise a strategic dilemma for the business marketer. Often, the aggressive pursuit of a cost minimization strategy leads to a reduced ability to make innovative product changes in the face of competition.[25] Clearly, any firm following an efficiency strategy must ensure that its product remains in line with the needs of the market. A product that is efficiently produced and carries a low price can only survive if there are significant market segments that emphasize low price as a choice criterion.

The experience effect can be used to project costs and prices. The concept is also of value when product line modifications are being considered. Often, two or more products in the firm's line share a common resource or involve the same production or distribution activity. With such shared experience, the costs of one item in the product line are reduced even more because of the accumulated experience with the other product-line item. For example, the same production operations may be used to produce high-torque motors for oil exploration and low-torque motors for conveyor

---

[25] Abernathy and Wayne, "Limits of the Learning Curve," pp. 109–119.

belts.[26] The marketer that has carefully classified costs is best equipped to take advantage of shared experience opportunities.

Experience curve analysis is relevant when learning, technology, and economies of scale are important in the environment.[27] The business marketer can use experience curve analysis to project potential cost reduction opportunities.

Break-Even Analysis

Break-even-point analysis, a basic financial tool, inevitably enters the pricing process. Break-even-point analysis allows the decision maker to determine the level of sales required to cover all relevant costs. The break-even point can be calculated as follows:

$$BEQ = \frac{FC}{P - VC}$$

where

BEQ = break-even sales quantity

FC = fixed costs

P = selling price

VC = direct variable costs

Assume that fixed costs are $200,000, that direct variable costs are $15, and that consideration is being given to a selling price of $20. Thus:

$$BEQ = \frac{200,000}{20 - 15} = \frac{200,000}{5} = 40,000 \text{ units}$$

From Figure 15.6, note that break-even analysis assumes that (1) fixed costs remain constant as the volume of production increases and that (2) variable costs increase proportionately with increases in production. Break-even-point calculations are often based heavily on historical cost data when, in fact, projected costs and prices are more critical.

Competition

Competition establishes an upper limit on price. Business marketers seem to regard **competitive level pricing** as the most important pricing strategy.[28] The degree of latitude that the individual industrial firm has in its pricing decision depends heavily on the level of differentiation that the product has in the perceptions of organizational buyers. Price is only one component of the cost/benefit equation of buyers; the marketer can gain a differential advantage over competitors on many dimensions other than physical product characteristics—dimensions such as reputation, technical

[26] Day and Montgomery, "Diagnosing the Experience Curve," p. 54.

[27] Ibid., pp. 56–57.

[28] John G. Udell, *Successful Marketing Strategies* (Madison, WI: Mimir Publishers, Inc., 1972), p. 109.

FIGURE 15.6   **Break-Even Analysis**

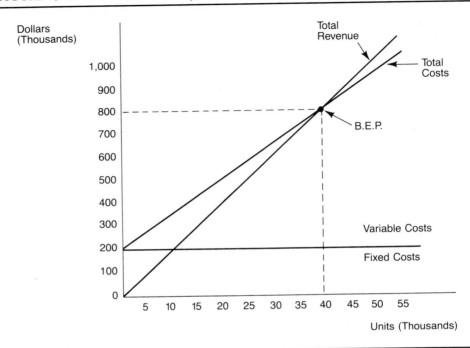

expertise, delivery reliability, and related factors. In addition to assessing the product's degree of differentiation in various market segments, one must ask how competitors will respond to particular pricing decisions.

Gauging Competitive Response

To predict the response of competitors, the marketer can first benefit by examining the cost structure of both direct competitors and producers of potential substitutes. The marketer can draw upon public statements and records (e.g., annual reports) to form rough estimates. The experience effect can also be used to assess the cost structure of competition. Competitors that have ascended the learning curve may have lower costs than those just entering the industry and beginning the climb. An estimate of the cost structure is valuable when gauging how well competitors can respond to price reductions and when projecting the pattern of prices in the future.

Under certain conditions, however, followers into a market may confront lower initial costs than did the pioneer. Why? Some of the reasons are highlighted in Table 15.2. By failing to recognize potential cost advantages of late entrants, the industrial marketer can dramatically overstate cost differences.

The market strategy employed by competing sellers is also important here. Competitors will be more sensitive toward price reductions that threaten market segments

---

TABLE 15.2   **Selected Cost Comparison Issues: Followers versus the Pioneer**

Technology/economies of scale	Followers may benefit by using more current production technology than the pioneer or by building a plant with a larger scale of operations.
Product/market knowledge	Followers may learn from the pioneer's mistakes by analyzing the competitor's product, hiring key personnel, or identifying through market research the problems and unfulfilled expectations of customers and channel members.
Shared experience	Compared to the pioneer, followers may be able to gain advantages on certain cost elements by sharing operations with other parts of the company.
Experience of suppliers	Followers, together with the pioneer, benefit from cost reductions achieved by outside suppliers of components or production equipment.

Source: Adapted from George S. Day and David B. Montgomery, "Diagnosing the Experience Curve," *Journal of Marketing*, 47 (Spring 1983), pp. 48–49.

that they deem important. They learn of price reductions earlier when their market segments overlap. Of course, competitors may choose not to follow a price decrease, especially if their products enjoy a differentiated position.

Industry Structure

When there are few sellers (oligopoly), the actions of one seller produce reactions on the part of its competitors. Examples of oligopolistic industries are computers, aluminum, steel, automobiles, electrical equipment, and glass. In each case, a small number of manufacturers dominate total output. Oligopolies can be either pure or differentiated. In a pure oligopoly, competing firms offer homogeneous products (e.g., steel); a differentiated oligopoly contains producers of differentiated products (e.g., computers). As the extent of product differentiation in an oligopoly increases, the price differences also increase.

The **kinked demand curve** is characteristic of oligopolistic markets. The theory assumes that competing sellers will follow any decrease in price in order to protect their market shares, but that they will refrain from following price increases, in order to capture part of the market share of the price raiser. Thus, the individual firm's demand curve (Figure 15.7) is kinked at the current price-quantity combination. A price decrease results in a relatively small increase in sales. On the other hand, a price increase would lead to a significant reduction in quantity demanded and, thus, total revenue, as customers shift to low-priced competing firms.

There is often a recognized price leader in the business market. **Price leadership** results when one firm essentially serves as the industry spokesman and other sellers in the industry accept its pricing policy. This leadership position can result from technical superiority, size and strength, cost efficiency, power in the channel of distribution, market information, or a combination of these. The industry leader is presumed to bring profitability and stability to an industry by establishing a price that produces satisfactory profits for all sellers.

FIGURE 15.7   **Kinked Demand Curve**

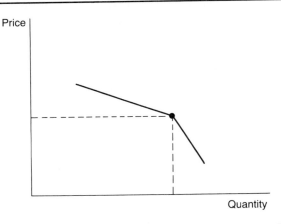

The manager requires a grasp of objectives, demand, cost, competition, and legal factors (discussed later) to approach the multidimensional pricing decision. Price setting is not an act but an ongoing process.

PRICING ACROSS THE PRODUCT LIFE CYCLE

What price should be assigned to a distinctly new industrial product or service? When an item is added to an existing product line, how should it be priced in relation to products already in the line?

Pricing New Products

The strategic decision of pricing new products can be best understood by examining the policies at the boundaries of the continuum—from **skimming** (high initial price) to **penetration** (low initial price). Consider again the pricing strategies of Du Pont and Dow Chemical. Whereas Du Pont assigns an initial high price to new products in order to generate immediate profits or to recover R&D expenditures, Dow Chemical follows a low price strategy with the objective of gaining market share.

In evaluating the merits of skimming compared to penetration, the marketer must again examine price from the buyer's perspective. This approach "recognizes that the upper limit is the price that will produce the minimum acceptable rate of return on the investment of a sufficiently large number of prospects."[29] This is especially important in pricing new products, because the potential profits accruing to buyers of a new

---

[29] Joel Dean, "Pricing Policies for New Products," *Harvard Business Review,* 54 (November–December 1976), p. 151.

ETHICAL BUSINESS MARKETING
On Ethics and Pricing at IBM

John Akers, Chairman of the Board of IBM, argues that business ethics are a key component of our competitiveness as a society. He notes: "No society anywhere will compete very long or successfully with people stabbing each other in the back . . . ; with every squabble ending in litigation; and with government writing reams of regulatory legislation, tying business hand and foot to keep it honest."

Excerpts from IBM's Business Conduct Guidelines reinforce this position and emphasize the importance of fairness in business relationships:

- Everyone you do business with is entitled to fair and even-handed treatment. This is true whether you are buying, selling, or performing in any other capacity for IBM.

- Do not extend to another business enterprise preferential treatment such as unauthorized services or contract terms. IBM, of course, responds to competition in bidding for government and other businesses. However, if the circumstances require modified terms, they must be specifically approved by management.

- IBM extends appropriate terms to each type of customer. For example, distributors, dealers and end users all purchase certain IBM equipment under different terms. But within each category, we strive to treat equally all similarly placed customers, that is, those who are procuring in similar quantities and circumstances.

Source: John F. Akers, "Ethics and Competitiveness: Putting First Things First," *Sloan Management Review*, 30 (Winter 1989), pp. 69–71; and *IBM Business Conduct Guidelines*, Section II (International Business Machines Corporation), pp. 15–19.

machine tool, for example, will vary by market segment, and these market segments may differ in the minimum rate of return that will induce them to invest in the machine tool.

Skimming

A skimming approach, appropriate for a distinctly new product, provides the firm with an opportunity to profitably reach market segments that are not sensitive to the high initial price. As a product ages, as competitors enter the market, and as organizational buyers become accustomed to evaluating and purchasing the product, demand becomes more price elastic. The policy of using skimming at the outset, followed by penetration pricing as the product matures, is referred to by Joel Dean as **time segmentation**.[30] A skimming policy allows the marketer to capture early profits, then reduce the price to reach segments that are more price sensitive. It also allows the innovator to recover high developmental costs more quickly.

Robert Dolan and Abel Jeuland demonstrate that during the innovative firm's monopoly period (1) a skimming policy is optimal if the demand curve is stable over time (no diffusion) and if production costs decline with accumulated volume, and (2)

---

[30] Ibid., p. 152.

a penetration policy is optimal if there is a relatively high repeat purchase rate for nondurable goods or if a durable good's demand is characterized by diffusion.[31]

Penetration

A penetration policy is appropriate when there is (1) high price elasticity of demand, (2) strong threat of imminent competition, and (3) opportunity for a substantial reduction in production costs as volume expands. Drawing upon the experience effect, a firm that can quickly gain substantial market share and experience can gain a strategic advantage over competitors. The viability of this strategy increases with the potential size of the future market. By taking a large share of new sales, experience can be gained when there is a large market growth rate. Of course, the value of additional market share differs markedly between industries and often among products, markets, and competitors within a particular industry.[32] Factors to be assessed in determining the value of additional market share include the investment requirements, potential benefits of experience, expected market trends, likely competitive reaction, and short- and long-term profit implications.

Product Line Considerations

The contemporary industrial firm with a long product line faces the complex problem of achieving balance in pricing the product mix. Firms extend their product lines because the demands for various products are interdependent, because the costs of producing and marketing those items are interdependent, or both.[33] A firm may add to its product line—or even develop a new product line—to fit more precisely the needs of a particular market segment. If both the demand and the costs of individual product-line items are interrelated, production and marketing decisions about one product-line item inevitably influence both the revenues and costs of the others.

Are specific product-line items substitutes or complements? Will a change in the price of one item enhance or retard the usage rate of this or other products in key market segments? Should a new product be priced high at the outset in order to protect other product-line items (e.g., potential substitutes) and in order to give the firm time to revamp other items in the line? Such decisions require a knowledge of demand, costs, competition, and strategic marketing objectives.

Announcements of new product introductions are often accompanied by revisions in the price schedule for other product-line items. Technological advances have been bringing down the prices of computers for years. IBM's introduction of a less expensive, but more sophisticated, central processing unit was paralleled by a reduction in the

---

[31] Robert J. Dolan and Abel P. Jeuland, "Experience Curves and Dynamic Demand Models: Implications for Optimal Pricing Strategies," *Journal of Marketing*, 45 (Winter 1981), pp. 52–62.

[32] Robert Jacobsen and David A. Aaker, "Is Market Share All that It's Cracked Up to Be?" *Journal of Marketing*, 49 (Fall 1985), pp. 11–22; and Yoram Wind and Vijay Mahajan, "Market Share: Concepts, Findings and Directions for Future Research," in Ben M. Enis and Kenneth J. Roering, eds., *Review of Marketing 1981* (Chicago: American Marketing Association, 1981), pp. 31–42.

[33] Monroe, *Pricing*, p. 143; see also Robert J. Dolan, "The Same Make, Many Models Problem: Managing the Product Line," in Robert E. Spekman and David T. Wilson, eds., *A Strategic Approach to Business Marketing* (Chicago: American Marketing Association, 1985), pp. 151–159.

price of older models. Such product line pricing adjustments must be made with care, but are common in the industrial market.

Organizational buyers often screen out product alternatives that fall outside an acceptable price range in order to concentrate on a feasible set of alternatives. Kent Monroe suggests that if all products in a line are priced within the acceptable range, there is a higher probability that a buyer will purchase a product from that line.[34] Thus, success in penetrating a buying organization with one item often means success for other items in the product line.

PRICE ADMINISTRATION

The business marketer deals with various types of customers (e.g., middlemen versus original equipment manufacturers) who buy in varying quantities in various geographical regions. Thus, there is a need to adjust prices to these conditions, and this is the function of price administration.

At the outset, it is important to understand a basic pricing tradition. Industrial sellers often provide a list price and a multiplier. The net price—the price of most importance to the organizational buyer—equals the list price times the multiplier. A product with a list price of $100 and a multiplier of 82 percent has a net price of $82. Why do industrial price setters send their customers on such a circuitous route to the net price? Industrial manufacturers have many items in their product line, and often, many product lines are described in a catalog. Rather than printing a new catalog each time the price of one or more items is adjusted, the firm merely prints a new price schedule and conveys the changes in adjusted multipliers. (For example, the multiplier for the $100 item might be changed to 80 percent, a $2 reduction.) Likewise, the list-price/multiplier system makes it more difficult for competitors to detect price changes as they occur.

Discounts

Price administration requires a discount schedule, which in turn requires decisions about trade, quantity, and cash discounts. Each is defined and illustrated in Table 15.3.

Trade Discounts

Trade discounts, offered to intermediaries or particular classifications of customers, allow the marketer to adjust the price based on the costs and benefits of dealing with various classifications of customers. Trade discounts are offered to distributors because they are performing important services. Trade discounts for original equipment manufacturers could be justified by their high-volume purchasing and low selling requirements. In establishing trade discounts, the marketer must recognize competitive norms and the relative importance of various channel members and customer types to overall marketing objectives.

---

[34] Monroe, *Pricing*, p. 153. For a related discussion, see Joseph P. Guiltinan, "The Price Bundling of Services," *Journal of Marketing*, 51 (April 1987), pp. 74–85.

TABLE 15.3 **Types of Discounts**

Types	Characteristics
Trade discounts	Those offered to various types of customers or middlemen. Often consist of a chain of discounts, subtracted successively from each new net price.
	Example: An item with a $10 list price might be offered to distributors with a discount of 25 + 10 percent:
	$10.00 − .25(10.00) = $7.50 and
	$7.50 − .10(7.50) = $6.75.
Noncumulative quantity discounts	Those granted on the basis of the size (measured in dollars or units) of a single purchase to encourage large orders.

Example:

Size of Order	Percent Off
Less than 20 units	0
20–29 units	2
30 or more units	4

Cumulative quantity discounts	Those granted on the basis of the size (measured in dollars or units) of orders over a specified period of time.

Example:

Annual Customer Purchases	Size of Discount
Less than $1,000	0%
1,000–1,999	3%
2,000–2,999	4%
3,000–3,999	5%

Cash discounts	Those offered for payment of an invoice within a specified period of time.
	Example: 2/10, net 30 (i.e., a 2 percent discount may be taken by the buyer if paid within ten days).

Quantity Discounts

Table 15.3 defines two types of quantity discounts—cumulative and noncumulative. The choice of the type and specific schedule for quantity discounts depends on an assessment of demand, costs, and competition.[35] In determining break points in the discount schedule, a strong customer focus is once again valuable, in terms of inventory carrying costs, order processing costs, transportation costs, and usage rates of various market segments. The marketer can also benefit from examining cost/service trade-offs (see Chapter 14).

Cash Discounts

Cash discounts are offered to encourage prompt payment of invoices, thereby allowing the marketer to maintain a more favorable cash flow. As illustrated in Table 15.3, a 2 percent discount might be offered if the bill is paid within ten days. Often, cash discounts present a delicate problem for marketers. Large buyers pay their bills well

---

[35]James B. Wilcox, Roy D. Howell, Paul Kuzdrell, and Robert Britney, "Price Quantity Discounts: Some Implications for Buyers and Sellers," *Journal of Marketing*, 51 (July 1987), pp. 60–70.

beyond the 10-day period and still deduct the cash discount, especially during periods of high interest rates. The marketer's success in correcting this problem often depends on the power that the industrial firm brings into the buyer–seller relationship. This dilemma is compounded by the fact that the Robinson-Patman Act requires sellers to offer the same terms to all competing buyers, large or small.

Legal Considerations

Since the industrial marketer deals with various classifications of customers and middlemen as well as various types of discounts, an awareness of legal considerations in price administration is vital. The Robinson-Patman Act holds that it is unlawful to "discriminate in price between different purchasers of commodities of like grade and quality . . . where the effect of such discrimination may be substantially to lessen competition or tend to create a monopoly, or to injure, destroy, or prevent competition. . . ." Price differentials are permitted, but they must be based on cost differences or the need to "meet competition."[36] Cost differentials are difficult to justify, and clearly defined policies and procedures are needed in price administration. Such cost justification guidelines are useful not only when making pricing decisions, but also when providing a legal defense against price discrimination charges.

Geographic Pricing

An element in the ultimate price to the buyer is the transportation cost, so geography must play a role in overall price administration. Prices differ according to whether the buyer or the seller assumes transportation costs. The price varies according to the weight and bulk of the product, the nature and location of key market segments, the percentage of the total price represented by transportation costs, the competitive conditions, and industry norms. Transportation is one factor in the buyer's cost/benefit equation, and organizational buyer sensitivity to various types of geographical price arrangements must be taken into account.

The industrial marketer cannot leave price administration to chance. Discounts must be aligned with the firm's pricing policies and related to the requirements of key market segments. Pricing policies are often based on a defensive, or risk-aversive, perspective rather than on a positive one.[37] For example, industrial firms might offer larger quantity discounts in order to partially offset price increases; opportunities for revising discount schedules may emerge as costs change. Tradition-bound firms can easily overlook creative uses of pricing policies.

---

[36] For a comprehensive discussion of the Robinson-Patman Act, see Monroe, *Pricing*, pp. 249–267; see also Steven A. Meyerowitz, "Beware of Price-Discrimination Pitfalls," *Business Marketing*, 71 (June 1986), pp. 136–139.

[37] Joseph P. Guiltinan, "Risk-Aversive Pricing Policies: Problems and Alternatives," *Journal of Marketing*, 40 (January 1976), pp. 10–15.

COMPETITIVE BIDDING

A significant volume of business in the business market is transacted through competitive bidding. Rather than relying on a specific list price, the business marketer must develop a price, or a bid, to meet particular product or service requirements of a customer.

The Buyer's Side of Bidding

Buying by government and other public agencies is done almost exclusively by competitive bidding. Competitive bidding in private industry is less frequent and is usually applied to the purchase of nonstandard materials, complex fabricated products where design and manufacturing methods vary, and products made to the buyer's specifications. The types of item procured through competitive bidding are those for which there is no generally established market level. Competitive bids allow the purchaser to evaluate the appropriateness of the prices.[38] Competitive bidding may be either closed or open.

Closed Bidding

Closed bidding, often used by industrial and governmental buyers, involves a formal invitation to potential suppliers to submit written, sealed bids for a particular business opportunity. All bids are opened and reviewed at the same time, and the contract is generally awarded to the lowest bidder who meets desired specifications. The low bidder is not guaranteed the contract—buyers often make awards to the lowest responsible bidder; the ability of alternative buyers to perform remains part of the bidding process.

Open Bidding

Open bidding is more informal and allows suppliers to make offers (oral and written) up to a certain date. The buyer may deliberate with several suppliers throughout the bidding process. Open bidding may be particularly appropriate when specific requirements are hard to define rigidly or when the products and services of competing suppliers vary substantially.

In selected buying situations, negotiated pricing may be employed. Complex technical requirements or uncertain product specifications may lead buying organizations, first, to evaluate the capabilities of competing industrial firms, and, then, to negotiate the price and the form of the product-service offering. Negotiated pricing is appropriate for procurement decisions in both the commercial and the governmental sectors of the business market (see Chapter 2).

---

[38] Stuart St. P. Slatter, "Strategic Marketing Variables Under Conditions of Competitive Bidding," *Strategic Management Journal*, 11 (May–June 1990), pp. 309–317.

Strategies for Competitive Bidding

Careful planning is fundamental to success in competitive bidding. Planning has three important steps: (1) precise definition of objectives, (2) a screening procedure for evaluating alternative bid opportunities, and (3) a method for assessing the probability of success of a particular bidding strategy.

Objectives

Before preparing a bid for any potential contract, the industrial firm must carefully define its objectives. This helps the firm to decide what types of business to pursue, when to bid, and how much to bid. The objectives may range from profit maximization to company survival. Other objectives might be to keep the plant operating and the labor force intact or to enter a new type of business. The marketer can also benefit by analyzing the objectives of likely bidding rivals.

Screening Bid Opportunities

Because developing bids is costly and time-consuming, contracts to bid on should be chosen with care. Contracts offer differing levels of profitability according to the related technical expertise, past experience, and objectives of the bidding firm. Thus, a screening procedure[39] is required to isolate the contracts that offer the most promise (see Table 15.4).

The use of a screening procedure to evaluate contracts has improved the bidding success of business marketers.[40] The procedure has three steps: First, the firm identifies criteria for evaluating contracts. While the number and nature of the criteria vary by firm and industry, five prebid factors are common:

1. The impact of the contract on plant capacity

2. The degree of experience the firm has had with similar projects

3. Follow-up bid opportunities

4. Expected competition

5. Delivery requirements.

Second, once identified, the prebid factors are assigned weights based on their relative importance to the firm (e.g., a weight of 25 out of the total of 100 is assigned to plant capacity). The third step is to evaluate each factor, giving it a high (10), medium (5), or low (0) value. In Table 15.4, the contract is evaluated favorably on all factors except follow-up bid opportunities. Summing the product of each factor's weight and rating provides a total score. The business marketer can use this procedure to evaluate alternative potential contracts. The firm may wish to establish a minimum acceptable

---

[39] This method is adapted from Stephen Paranka, "Competitive Bidding Strategy," *Business Horizons,* 14 (June 1971), pp. 39–43; see also Stephen Paranka, "Question: To Bid or Not to Bid? Answer: Strategic Prebid Analysis," *Marketing News* (April 4, 1980), p. 16.

[40] For example, see Paul D. Boughton, "The Competitive Bidding Process: Beyond Probability Models," *Industrial Marketing Management,* 16 (May 1987), pp. 87–94.

TABLE 15.4   **Evaluation of a Bid Opportunity**

Prebid Factors	Weight	Rating of			Score
		High 10	**Medium** 5	**Low** 0	
Plant capacity	25	10			250
Degree of experience	20	10			200
Follow-up bid opportunities	15			0	0
Competition	25	10			250
Delivery requirements	15	10			150
Total*	100				850

*Ideal bid score: 1,000
Minimum acceptable score: 750

score before effort will be invested in preparing a bid. Since the bid opportunity evaluated in Table 15.4 yields a score above the cutoff point, a bid would be prepared.

Bidding Strategy

Having isolated a project opportunity, the marketer must now estimate the probabilities of winning the contract at various prices. Assuming that the contract is awarded to the lowest bidder, the chances of the firm winning the contract decline as the bid price increases. How will competitors bid?

In many industries, business marketers confront situations in which the supplier winning the initial contract has the advantage in securing long-term follow-up business. To illustrate, suppliers bidding on contracts to meet 3M's worldwide office equipment needs often provide attractive bids in order to secure an initial relationship with the centralized purchasing unit.[41] Although some immediate profit may be sacrificed, the low bid is seen as an investment that will lead to a continuing stream of profitable follow-up business.

In pursuing this type of bidding strategy, the business marketer must carefully assess the strength of the association between the initial contract and the follow-up business opportunities. For example, the purchase of an office automation system may bond the buyer to a particular seller, thus providing the potential for future business. The costs of switching to another supplier are high because the buyer has made investments in employee training and in new business procedures, as well as in the equipment itself.[42] Such investments create inertia against change. By contrast, for more standardized purchases, such bonding does not occur because the costs of switching to another supplier are quite low for the buyer. In determining the initial bid strategy,

---

[41] Margaret Nelson, "3M Centralizes Its Office Buy," *Purchasing*, 101 (June 25, 1987), pp. 62–65.

[42] Barbara Bund Jackson, "Build Customer Relationships that Last," *Harvard Business Review*, 63 (November–December 1985), pp. 120–128.

the business marketer should examine the strength of the buyer–seller relationship, the probability of securing additional business, and the expected return from that business.

Probabilistic Bidding Models

Business marketers who use probabilistic bidding models seem to be more successful in competitive bidding.[43] Such models aid the firm in exploring its chances of winning a contract at different bid prices and in exploring its level of profit if it does win. Probabilistic bidding models often assume that competitors will behave in the future as they have in the past. Clearly, new competitors may emerge, or existing competitors may alter their bidding strategies. However, probabilistic bidding models give the marketer an objective procedure for evaluating the success probabilities and the potential profits of various bidding scenarios. These formalized bidding approaches do motivate managers to assess carefully the costs, competition, and potential profit opportunities of a particular project. Screening procedures also allow the marketer to isolate those projects that are most consistent with the firm's objectives and capabilities.

THE ROLE OF LEASING IN THE INDUSTRIAL MARKET[44]

Leasing is assuming increased importance in the industrial market. A **lease** is essentially a contract through which the asset owner (lessor) extends the right to use the asset to another party (lessee) in return for periodic payment of rent over a specified period. Approximately 30 percent of all capital goods are leased in the United States, with eight out of ten companies involved in leasing.[45] This section examines the strategic role that leasing can assume in the industrial market.

Financial Leases versus Operating Leases

Leases can be divided into two broad categories: financial (full-payout) and operating leases. **Financial leases** are noncancellable contracts that are usually long term and fully amortized. Lease payments over the contract period equal or exceed the original purchase of the item. A food packaging machine might be purchased outright at a price of $21,000 or leased for five years with lease payments of $5,800 per year. The

---

[43] For a more complete discussion of probabilistic bidding models, see Douglas G. Brooks, "Bidding for the Sake of Follow-On Contracts," *Journal of Marketing*, 42 (January 1978), pp. 35–38; see also Murphy A. Sewall, "A Decision Calculus Model for Contract Bidding," *Journal of Marketing*, 40 (October 1976), pp. 92–98; and Wayne J. Morse, "Probabilistic Bidding Models: A Synthesis," *Business Horizons*, 16 (April 1975), pp. 66–74.

[44] This section is largely based on Paul F. Anderson and William Lazer, "Industrial Lease Marketing," *Journal of Marketing*, 42 (April 1978), pp. 71–79. For additional research in the lease marketing area, see Paul F. Anderson, *Financial Aspects of Industrial Leasing Decisions: Implications for Marketing* (Division of Research, Graduate School of Business Administration, Michigan State University, East Lansing, Mich., 1977).

[45] "Leasing: A New Role," *Business Week* (May 15, 1989), pp. 141–152.

organization leasing the equipment is generally responsible for operating expenses, but the lessor may attach benefits (e.g., maintenance) if competitive pressures dictate. A purchase option is frequently a part of financial leases. This option, which may be exercised at the termination of the contract, is usually the asset's fair market value at the time of exercise.

In contrast, **operating leases** (sometimes called rental agreements) are short-term, cancelable agreements that are not fully amortized. Since the purpose is to provide equipment that is needed only for short periods, a purchase option is usually not included. Operating lease rates are usually higher than financial lease rates because the marketer assumes the operating costs as well as the risks of obsolescence. Financial leasing will receive particular attention.

Lease versus Purchase

As emphasized throughout the chapter, organizational buyers examine the cost/benefit trade-offs of alternative offerings. Thus, buyers contemplating the purchase of capital equipment confront the lease-versus-purchase decision. "A manufacturer's product and service mix is augmented by the additional benefits, largely economic in nature, available to customers through leasing."[46]

How do organizational customers evaluate the benefits and costs of a lease?

Benefits	Costs
Avoidance of cash purchase cost	Cash outflow of lease payments
Avoidance of those operating costs absorbed by lessor	Foregone tax shields resulting from depreciation, interest, and operating expenses
Tax shield provided by lease payments	Sacrifice of asset's salvage value

Essentially, the decision should rest on the present value of the sum of the costs and benefits of the lease: do the cash flow benefits of the lease exceed the cash flow costs?

At the same time, however, buyers may also enter into lease arrangements for reasons not reflected in the lease-versus-purchase cash flow equation.[47] Leasing can preserve credit capacity, minimize equipment disposal problems, allow for the acquisition of equipment when other financing sources are not available, avoid the dilution of ownership or control that accompanies debt or equity financing, and protect against the risks of equipment obsolescence. Thus, the ultimate decision to lease or purchase may depend on a balance between the quantifiable costs of leasing and both the quantifiable and nonquantifiable benefits.

---

[46] Anderson and Lazer, ibid., p. 72.

[47] Paul F. Anderson, "Industrial Equipment Leasing Offers Economic and Competitive Edge," *Marketing News* (April 4, 1980), p. 20; and Paul F. Anderson and Monroe M. Bird, "Marketing to the Industrial Lease Buyer," *Industrial Marketing Management*, 9 (April 1980), pp. 111–116.

Industrial Lease Marketing: Strategic Implications

A firm that markets equipment for either sale or lease must carefully consider the potential customer's needs and concerns. When confronting the lease-versus-purchase decision, many large industrial customers may be using financial techniques that fail to give appropriate weight to the economic benefits of leasing.[48] Paul Anderson and William Lazer contend that a bias against leasing can be overcome by creating a financial specialist position within the lease marketing organization. This specialist would interface with financially-oriented influencers within the buying center and would provide the customer with consulting services and financial, tax, and accounting information.

Xerox Corporation caters to potential lessees through a marketing financial analyst known as a consulting service representative. Customers interested in outright purchase are served by another specialist—the sold equipment representative. Such specialization permits the marketer to respond to the particular needs and objectives of organizational customers. Such services increase the value of the firm's total offering in the minds of organizational buyers and often provide the marketer with a differential advantage over competitors.

Strategic leasing decisions cannot be isolated from product, pricing, and marketing communication decisions. A particularly delicate decision emerges in the development of pricing strategy; a price *and* a lease rate must be established for the same product.

Pricing Strategy

Depending on the firm's objectives, the marketer can establish the lease rate at a level that (1) encourages leasing, (2) encourages outright purchase, or (3) achieves balance between the lease rate and the sales rate. To illustrate, a marketer might offer rates that encourage leasing in order to link buying organizations to the firm's product line or in order to reach market segments that were previously inaccessible. New products that can be tried on a limited or experimental basis diffuse more rapidly than those that cannot.[49] By offering attractive leasing options, the industrial marketer provides potential adopters with the opportunity to experiment with the product on a limited basis.

Alternatively, the business marketer might wish to set relatively high lease rates in order to encourage customers to purchase the capital items outright. Leasing can cause a troublesome cash flow drain for the seller. Thus, marketers might wish to improve their cash flow position by encouraging customers to buy rather than lease. Xerox has provided loans to customers at interest rates two percentage points below the terms available through a bank, thus encouraging outright purchase.[50]

Regardless of the strategy followed, the price setter must have a product line perspective. A change in the price or lease rate of one item may directly or indirectly

---

[48]Paul F. Anderson and John D. Martin, "Lease vs. Purchase Decisions: A Survey of Current Practice," *Financial Management*, 6 (Spring 1977), pp. 41–47.

[49]Everett M. Rogers with F. Floyd Shoemaker, *Communication of Innovations*, 2d ed. (New York: The Free Press, 1971), p. 155.

[50]Jeffrey A. Tannenbaum, "To Prop Sales, Xerox Gives Bargain Loans," *The Wall Street Journal* (January 8, 1981), p. 19.

influence the demand for other items. IBM cut the price of several small computer systems but left the leasing rates unchanged.[51] Such a strategy would encourage customers to purchase the equipment they are currently leasing. Likewise, new customers would be more inclined to purchase rather than lease. To stimulate demand for new items, the firm might prefer to offer attractive lease rates.

The marketer of industrial equipment must understand the benefits and costs of leasing to the customer in order to define the strategic role of leasing in the total industrial marketing program.

SUMMARY

At the outset, the business marketer must assign pricing its role in the firm's overall marketing strategy. Giving a particular industrial product or service an "incorrect" price can trigger a chain of events that undermines the firm's market position, channel relationships, and product and personal selling strategies. Price is but one of the costs that buyers examine in the buying process. Thus, the marketer can profit by adopting a strong end-user focus that gives special attention to the way buyers trade off the costs and benefits of various products.

Price setting is a multidimensional rather than one-dimensional decision. To establish a price, the manager must identify the firm's objectives and analyze the behavior of demand, costs, and competition. Although this task is clouded with uncertainty, the industrial pricing decision must be approached actively rather than passively. Likewise, by isolating demand, cost, or competitive patterns, the manager can gain insights into market behavior and opportunities that have been neglected.

Competitive bidding, a unique feature of the industrial market, calls for a unique strategy. Again, carefully defined objectives are the cornerstone of strategy. These objectives, combined with a meticulous screening procedure, help the firm to identify projects that mesh with company capability. Probabilistic bidding models can be useful when determining the probability of winning and when gauging expected profit outcomes.

Leasing, an area of rising importance in the marketing of industrial equipment, creates numerous strategy options. Successful lease marketing requires a well-integrated marketing program that effectively conveys information on the benefits of leasing to potential customers. The marketer can adjust the relationship between the price and lease rate of a product in order to encourage or discourage leasing and in order to meet changing company or market conditions.

---

[51] "IBM Cuts Quotes for Buying Parts of Small Systems," *The Wall Street Journal* (December 3, 1979), p. 5; and Dennis Kneale, "IBM Maps New Steps to Hold Back PC Clones," *The Wall Street Journal* (July 21. 1986), p. 6.

Discussion Questions

1. Explain why it is often necessary for the business marketer to develop a separate demand curve for various segments of the market. Would one total demand curve be better for making the industrial pricing decision? Explain.

2. NCR introduced its new 3000-series computers that span seven levels of performance. From one processor to 4,000, at prices of $2,500 to $10 million, the line ranges from tiny portables to room-filling multiprocessor machines. First, what factors or criteria would be important to organizational buyers in evaluating the new NCR computers? Second, would these factors vary across market segments? Explain and note the implications for NCR's pricing strategy.

3. The XYZ Manufacturing Corporation has experienced a rather large decline in sales for its component parts. Mary Vantage, vice president of marketing, believes that a 10 percent price cut may get things going again. What factors should Mary consider before reducing the prices of the components?

4. Define the *experience effect* (behavior of costs) and explain why it occurs. Explain how the experience effect relates to strategic pricing decisions.

5. A business marketing manager often has great difficulty in arriving at the optimum price level for a product. First, describe the factors that complicate the pricing decision. Second, outline the approach that you would follow in pricing an industrial product. Be as specific as possible.

6. Leasing is increasingly important in the marketing of capital-equipment items. Describe the factors that the business marketer must consider in determining the relationship of the lease rate to the purchase price (e.g., low lease rate—high purchase price; high lease rate—low purchase price).

7. Explain how a change in the price of one item often contributes to the need for a change in the price of other items in the product line.

8. Evaluate the competitive bidding strategy followed by a West Coast commercial air-conditioning contractor: "To improve my chances of winning contracts, I bid on virtually every contract that comes up in our market area."

CHAPTER 16

Business Marketing Communications: Advertising and Sales Promotion

Advertising supports and supplements personal selling efforts. The share of the marketing budget devoted to advertising is smaller in business than it is in consumer-goods marketing. A well-tailored business-to-business advertising campaign can, however, contribute to the increased efficiency and effectiveness of the overall marketing strategy.

After reading this chapter, you will understand:

1. the specific role of advertising in business marketing strategy.

2. the decisions that must be made when forming a business advertising program.

3. the business media options.

4. the methods for measuring business advertising effectiveness.

COMMUNICATION with existing and potential customers is vital to business marketing success. Experience has taught marketing managers that not even the best products sell themselves: The benefits, problem solutions, and cost efficiencies of those products must be effectively communicated to all of the individuals who influence the purchase decision. As a result of the technical complexity of business products, the relatively small number of potential buyers, and the extensive negotiation process, the primary communication vehicle in business-to-business marketing is the salesperson. However, nonpersonal methods of communication, including advertising, catalogs, and trade shows, have a unique and often crucial role in the communication process. The award-winning ads from AT&T Information Systems and Apple Computer (shown in Figure 16.1) are effective at gaining attention. This type of communication is an important component of the firm's overall communication program.

Consider the difficulty Xerox has encountered selling photocopiers. Over the last several years, Xerox tracked the number of times its salespeople could see corporate decision makers. People selling photocopiers found they could see decision makers in 1 out of 25 calls.[1] Clearly, it is challenging to find who is involved in a purchase decision and, once identified, to be able to make contact with them. However, it is possible that numerous specialists will be involved in the decision, and advertisements can be placed in selected business trade publications to reach these influentials. An important role for business-to-business advertising is to reach those buying influentials inaccessible to the salesperson. Business-to-business advertising and promotion, of course, serve many other functions in the communication strategy as well.

The focus of this chapter is fourfold: (1) to provide a clear understanding of the role of advertising in business marketing strategy; (2) to present a framework for structuring advertising decisions—a framework that integrates the decisions related to objectives, budgets, messages, media, and evaluation; (3) to develop an understanding of each business-to-business advertising decision area; and (4) to evaluate supplementary forms of promotion, including catalogs, trade shows, and trade advertising.

THE ROLE OF ADVERTISING

Integrated Communication Programs

Advertising and sales promotion are rarely employed alone in the business-to-business setting, but are intertwined with the total communications strategy—particularly personal selling. Personal and nonpersonal forms of communication interact to inform key buying influences. The challenge for the business marketer is to create an advertising and sales promotion strategy that effectively blends with personal selling efforts in order to achieve sales and profit objectives. In addition, the advertising and sales promotion tools must be integrated; that is, a comprehensive program of media and sales promotion methods must be coordinated to achieve the desired results.

Nature of Organizational Buying Affects Business Advertising

To understand the role of advertising, we must recognize the forces that shape and influence organizational buying decisions, which are typically joint decisions. The intricacies of the buying center were well documented in Chapter 4. Recall that a

---

[1] Peter Finch, "Xerox Bets All on New Sales Groups," *Business Marketing,* 70 (July 1986), p. 21.

FIGURE 16.1   **Two Award-Winning Business-to-Business Ads**

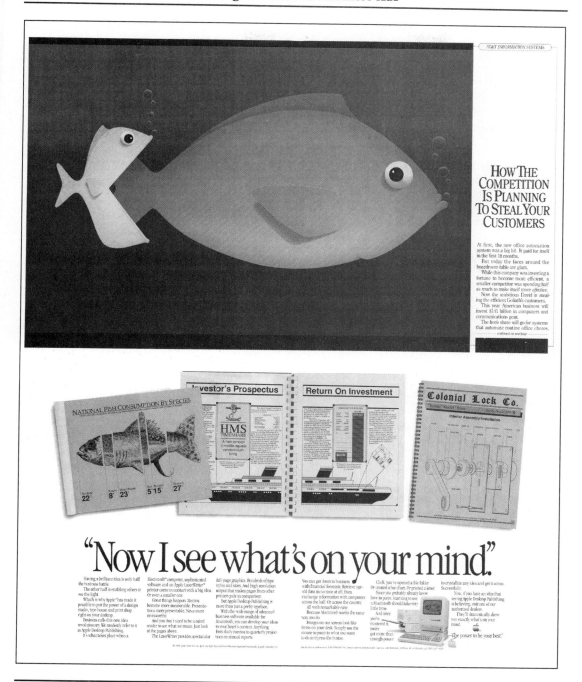

Source: Courtesy, AT&T Business Market Group and Apple Computer. Reprinted by permission of *Nation's Business*, © 1986 U.S. Chamber of Commerce.

business marketer must focus on the full range of individuals involved in the buying center for a particular purchase. The size of the buying center varies, sometimes including as many as 20 people.[2] In most cases, it is not feasible for salespeople to make contact with everyone in the buying center.

The point is clear: Business-to-business advertising fills the void.[3] Carefully targeted advertising extends beyond the salesperson's reach to unidentified buying influentials. Advertising is often the *only* means of communicating the existence of a product to potential buyers. Advertising also increases recognition of the company's name and reputation, enhancing the salesperson's opportunity to create a sale.

Advertising: Enhancing Sales Effectiveness

Effective advertising can make personal selling more productive. John Morrill examined nearly 100,000 interviews on 26 product lines at 30,000 buying locations in order to study the impact of business-to-business advertising on salesperson effectiveness.[4] He concluded that dollar sales per salesperson call were significantly higher when customers had been exposed to advertising. The advertisement by Stanley Vidmar in Figure 16.2 is an effective ad in its own right; notice the focus on user benefits—faster retrieval, less manpower, lower cost. It is important to note that the ad also facilitates the salesperson's job by increasing awareness of the company, its products, and the products' benefits. Buyers who had been exposed to a supplier's advertisement also rated the supplier's sales personnel substantially higher on product knowledge, service,and enthusiasm.[5] A primary role of business-to-business advertising is to enhance the reputation of the supplier.

Business-to-business advertising also contributes to increased sales efficiency. Increased expenditures on advertising lead to greater brand awareness for industrial products, which translates into larger market shares and higher profits.[6] In a recent study, a tightly controlled experimental design was used to measure the impact of business-to-business advertising on sales and profits. For one product in the study, sales, gross margin, and net profit were significantly higher with advertising, compared to the pretest period with no advertising.[7] In fact, gross margins ranged from four to six times higher with advertising, compared to the nonadvertising period.

---

[2] Kate Bertrand, "Survey Finds Many 'Critical' Buying Criteria." *Business Marketing*, 72 (May 1987), p. 55.

[3] A number of studies have documented the ability of advertising to reach industrial buying influentials not accessible to the salesperson. Two of the most frequently cited are *The U.S. Steel/Harnischfeger Study: Industrial Advertising Effectively Reaches Buying Influences at Low Cost* (New York: American Business Press, 1969) and *The Evolution of a Purchase Study* (Bloomfield Hills, Mich.: Bromsom Publishing Company, 1967).

[4] John E. Morrill, "Industrial Advertising Pays Off," *Harvard Business Review*, 48 (March–April 1970), pp. 4–14.

[5] Ibid., p. 6.

[6] "New Proof of Industrial Ad Values," *Marketing and Media Decisions*, (February 1981), p. 64.

[7] "ARF/ABP Release Final Study Findings," *Business Marketing*, 72 (May 1987), p. 55.

FIGURE 16.2   An Example of an Effective Business-to-Business Advertisement

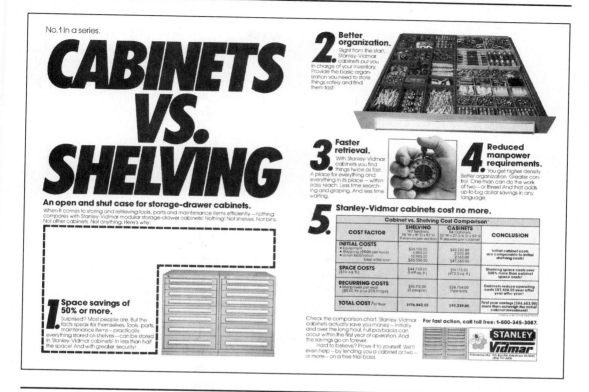

Source: Courtesy, Stanley Vidmar, Inc.

Advertising: Increased Sales Efficiency

The impact of advertising on the overall efficiency of the business marketing program is evidenced in two ways. First, business suppliers frequently need to remind actual and potential buyers of their products or need to make them aware of new products or services. Although these objectives could be partially accomplished through personal selling, the costs of reaching a vast group of buyers would be prohibitive. A properly placed advertisement can reach hundreds of buying influentials for only a few cents each; the average cost of a business sales call is currently approaching $225.[8] The cost of a sales call is determined by the salesperson's wages, travel and entertainment costs, and fringe benefits costs. If these costs total $900 per day and a salesperson can make four calls per day, then each call costs $225.

---

[8] "Survey of Selling Costs," *Sales and Marketing Management*, 142 (February 26, 1990), p. 75.

Second, advertising appears to make all selling activities more effective; therefore, there may be economies of scale associated with business-to-business advertising. Gary Lilien and others reviewed studies assessing the impact of business-to-business advertising expenditures on total marketing costs.[9] The general conclusion was that the larger the advertising budget, the lower the total marketing expenses as a percentage of sales. However, because some studies have shown that economies of scale in advertising do not exist, it is well to avoid assuming that more advertising is necessarily better. Advertising interacts effectively with all communication and selling activities. It can result in higher levels of efficiency for the entire marketing expenditure.

Advertising: Creating Awareness

From a communications standpoint, the buying process can be viewed as taking potential buyers sequentially from unawareness of a product or supplier to awareness, to brand preference, to conviction that a particular purchase will fulfill their requirements, and ultimately, to actual purchase.[10] Business advertising often creates awareness of the supplier and the supplier's products. Sixty-one percent of the design engineers returning an inquiry card from a magazine ad indicated that they were unaware of the company that advertised before seeing the ad.[11] Business advertising may also make some contribution to creating preference for the product—all very cost effectively. In addition, advertising can create a corporate identity or image; ads in a general business publication such as *Business Week*—or even television advertising—may be used to develop desired perceptions in a broad audience.

Buyers of machine tools were surveyed to ascertain the importance of five communication channels in providing information about machine-tool products and services.[12] The channels were (1) salespersons, (2) company catalogs, (3) trade-magazine advertising, (4) trade shows, and (5) direct mail. Trade-magazine advertising was rated the primary source of information for these buyers.

Advertising: Self-Selection

It is often impossible to determine exactly which companies could be potential users of an industrial product. As a result, advertising can prompt unknown prospects to seek product information.[13] If a direct mail or media advertisement can effectively illustrate

---

[9] Gary L. Lilien, Alvin J. Silk, Jean-Marie Choffray, and Murlidhar Rao, "Industrial Advertising Effects and Budgeting Practices," *Journal of Marketing*, 40 (January 1976), pp. 20–21.

[10] Robert J. Lavidge and Gary A. Steiner, "A Model for Predictive Measurement of Advertising Effectiveness," *Journal of Marketing*, 25 (October 1961), pp. 59–61.

[11] Raymond E. Herzog, "How Design Engineering Activity Affects Supplies," *Business Marketing*, 70 (November 1985), p. 143.

[12] Charles H. Patti, "Buyer Information Sources in the Capital Equipment Industry," *Industrial Marketing Management*, 6 (1977), pp. 259–264; see also Alicia Donovan, "Awareness of Trade-Press Advertising," *Journal of Advertising Research*, 19 (April 1979), pp. 33–35.

[13] John L. DeFazio, "An Inquiry-Based MIS," *Business Marketing*, 68 (August 1983), p. 55.

INSIDE BUSINESS MARKETING
Creating a Corporate Image

TRW, Cleveland, began its current corporate campaign 12 years ago, when it became clear that the giant company was largely unknown to the general public.

From the outset, TRW's objectives were clearly stated. In building its reputation, it sought to give each of its audiences certain basic impressions of the company. Specifically, it wanted

- its customers to consider TRW a manufacturer of high-quality products with extra value;

- its employees and prospective employees to think of TRW as a great place to work;

- the financial community to see it as a lean, profitable, growing company that thinks ahead;

- its neighboring residents to feel that it is a good corporate citizen, a worthwhile member of the community; and

- its common stockholders to consider TRW a good investment.

Television spots that are aired during nightly newscasts, election coverage, TV specials, and sports programming are the vehicle used by TRW to heighten awareness of the company and to lay a foundation for creating the firm's image.

Twelve years ago, only 34 percent of the people TRW surveyed knew the company, according to TRW research. In a 1985 survey, approximately 78 percent of the people are familiar with TRW, and two-thirds of them had favorable opinions of the corporation as a whole.

Other research shows that the company is gaining more than reputation. Because of the ads, people perceive TRW as an innovative, well-managed manufacturer of superior high-technology products. Furthermore, people in the cities where ads ran were shown to be twice as likely to invest in TRW as were people in cities where the company did not advertise.

That kind of confidence in a company has ramifications that extend far beyond the price of its stock: it helps sell products.

Source: Adapted from Maureen F. Hartigan and Peter Finch, "The New Emphasis on Strategy in Corporate Advertising," *Business Marketing*, 71 (February 1986), pp. 43–45.

---

important product benefits, potential prospects will **self-select**; that is, they will respond to the advertisement by requesting additional information. In this way, the business marketer can assist the prospect and also collect information about the prospect's product applications, product interests, and potential as a customer.

The Limitations of Business-to-Business Advertising

To develop an effective communications program, the business marketing manager must blend all communication tools into an integrated program, using each tool where it is most effective. Business advertising quite obviously has limitations. Advertising cannot substitute for effective personal selling; it must supplement, support, and complement that effort. In the same way, personal selling is constrained by its costs and should not be used to create awareness or to disseminate information—tasks quite capably performed by advertising.

Generally, advertising alone cannot create product preference; this requires demonstration, explanation, and operational testing. Similarly, conviction and actual purchase can be ensured only by personal selling. Advertising has a supporting role in creating awareness, providing information, and uncovering important leads for salespeople; that is how the marketing manager must use it in order to be effective.

MANAGING BUSINESS-TO-BUSINESS ADVERTISING

The advertising decision model in Figure 16.3 shows the structural elements involved in the management of business-to-business advertising. First, advertising is only one aspect of the entire marketing strategy and must be integrated with other components in order to achieve strategic goals. The advertising decision process begins with the formulation of advertising objectives, which are derived from marketing goals. From this formulation follows a determination of expenditures necessary to achieve those goals. Then, specific communication messages are formulated to achieve the market behavior specified by the objectives. Equally important is the evaluation and selection of the media used to reach the desired audience. The result is an integrated advertising campaign aimed at eliciting a specific attitude or behavior from the target group. The final, and critical, step is to evaluate the effectiveness of the campaign.

Advertising Objectives

Knowing what advertising must accomplish enables the manager to determine an advertising budget more accurately and provides a yardstick against which advertising can be evaluated. In specifying advertising goals, the marketing manager must realize that (1) the advertising mission flows directly from the overall marketing strategy: advertising must fulfill a marketing strategy objective, and the goal set for advertising must reflect the general aim and purpose of the entire strategy; and (2) the objectives of the advertising program must be responsive to the roles for which advertising is suited: creating awareness, providing information, influencing attitudes, and reminding buyers of company and product existence.[14]

Written Objectives

An advertising objective is a time-related, concise statement of the intended outcome of a particular advertising action, phrased in terms of what should happen in the mind of the prospect as a result of reading the advertisement.[15] The objective must speak in unambiguous terms of a specific outcome. The purpose is to establish a single working direction for everyone involved in creating, coordinating, and evaluating the advertising program. Correctly conceived objectives set standards against which the advertising

---

[14] W. H. Grosse, *How Industrial Advertising and Sales Promotion Can Increase Marketing Power* (New York: American Management Association, 1973), p. 41.

[15] Joseph A. Bellizzi and Julie Lehrer, "Developing Better Industrial Advertising," *Industrial Marketing Management*, 12 (February 1983), p. 19.

FIGURE 16.3   **An Advertising Decision Model**

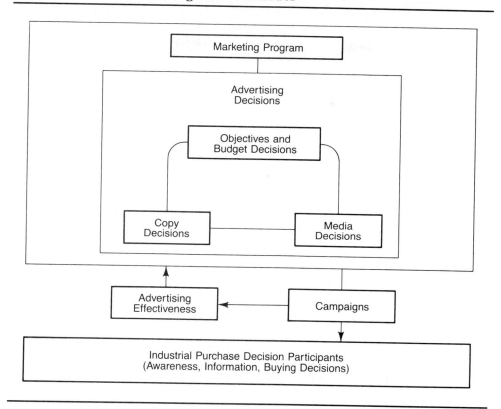

Source: Adapted from David A. Aaker and John G. Myers, *Advertising Management*, 4th ed. (Englewood
Cliffs, N.J.: Prentice-Hall, Inc., 1987), p. 30. Reprinted by permission of Prentice-Hall, Inc.

effort can be evaluated. A specific objective might be: Increase from 15 percent (as
measured in June 1992) to 30 percent (by June 1993) the proportion of design engineers
associating the "lubrication for life" feature with our brand of hydraulic pumps. The
objective directs the manager to create a message related to the major product benefit,
using media that will reach design engineers. The objective also provides a way to
measure accomplishment (awareness among 30 percent of the target audience).

Business advertising objectives frequently bear no direct relationship to specific
dollar sales targets. Although dollar sales results would provide a "hard" measure of
advertising accomplishment, it is often impossible to link advertising directly to sales.
Personal selling, price, product performance, and competitive actions have a more
direct relationship to sales levels, and it is almost impossible to sort out the impact of
advertising. Thus, advertising goals are typically stated in terms of communication
goals such as brand awareness, recognition, and buyer attitudes. These goals can be
measured; it is presumed that achieving them will stimulate sales volume.

Target Audience

A significant task is the specification of target audiences. Because a primary role of advertising is to reach buying influentials inaccessible to the salesperson, the business marketing manager must define the buying influential groups to be reached. Generally, each group of buying influentials is concerned with distinct product and service attributes and criteria, and the advertising must focus on these. Thus, the objectives must specify the intended audience and its relevant decision criteria.

Creative Strategy Statement

A final consideration is the specification of the creative strategy statement. Once objectives and targets are established, the **creative strategy statement** provides guidelines for company and advertising agency personnel on how the product is to be "positioned" in the marketplace. **Product position** relates to how the target market perceives the product.

For example, if the hydraulic pumps cited earlier currently have an unfavorable product position in regard to lubrication, the creative strategy statement might be: Our basic creative strategy is to support a repositioning of the product from that of a reliable pump to a high-performance, reliable self-lubrication pump.

All creative efforts—copy, theme, color, and so forth—as well as media and tactics should be developed to support the creative strategy statement. To plan an effective advertising campaign, one needs objectives upon which to structure media decisions and measure results.

Determining Advertising Expenditures

Typically, business marketers use a blend of intuition, judgment, experience, and only occasionally, more advanced decision-oriented techniques to determine advertising budgets. Some of the techniques most commonly utilized by business marketers are shown in Table 16.1. Among the more common techniques are rules of thumb (e.g., percentage of past years' sales) and objective task.

Rules of Thumb

Often, because advertising is a relatively small part of the total marketing budget for business firms, the value of using sophisticated methods for advertising budgeting is not great. In these cases, managers tend to follow simple **rules of thumb** (e.g., allocate 1 percent of sales to advertising or spend what competition spends). Unfortunately, percentage-of-sales rules are all too pervasive throughout business marketing, even where advertising is an important element.

The fundamental problem with percentage-of-sales rules is that they "implicitly make advertising a consequence rather than a determinant of sales and profits and can easily give rise to dysfunctional policies."[16] Percentage-of-sales rules suggest that the business advertiser reduce advertising when sales volume declines, just when

---

[16] Lilien et al., "Industrial Advertising Effects and Budgeting Practices," p. 22.

TABLE 16.1   Methods Used by Business Marketers to Set Advertising Budgets

Method	Percentage of Respondents Using Each Method[*]
Objective task	74
Affordable	33
Percent of past years' sales	23
Match competitors	21
Percent of anticipated sales	16
Arbitrary	13
Quantitative	3
Per unit of sales	2

[*]Multiple responses.

Source: Vincent Blasko and Charles H. Patti, "The Advertising Budgeting Practices of Industrial Marketers," *Journal of Marketing,* 48 (Fall 1984), p. 106. Reprinted by permission of the American Marketing Association.

increased advertising may be more appropriate. Nevertheless, simple rules of thumb will continue to be applied in budget decisions because they are easy to use, and familiar to management.

Objective-Task Method

The task method for budgeting advertising expenditures is an attempt to relate advertising costs to the objective it is to accomplish. David Nylen capsulizes the dimensions of the task approach: "While acknowledging that the ultimate objective of advertising is profitable sales, the task approach sees a series of intermediate objectives or profit-facilitating tasks assigned to advertising. The budgeting problem under the task approach becomes one of determining how much it will cost to accomplish each of the tasks assigned to advertising."[17] Thus, the task method focuses on the communications effects of advertising, not on the sales effects.

The task method is applied by evaluating the tasks to be performed by advertising, analyzing the costs associated with each task, and summing up the total costs in order to arrive at a final budget. The process can be divided into four steps:

1. Establish specific marketing objectives for the product in terms of such factors as sales volume, market share, profit contribution, and market segments.

2. Assess the communication functions that must be performed in order to realize the marketing objectives and then determine the role of advertising and other elements of the communications mix in performing these functions.

3. Define specific goals for advertising in terms of the measurable communication response required to achieve marketing objectives.

---

[17] David W. Nylen, *Advertising: Planning, Implementation and Control* (Cincinnati: Southwestern Publishing Company, 1975), p. 230.

INSIDE BUSINESS MARKETING
Where Business-to-Business Promotional Dollars Are Spent

Source: David Jacobsen, "Marketers Say They'll Boost Spending," *Business Marketing,* 75, (March 1990), p. 31. Reprinted with permission of *Business Marketing.*

4. Estimate the budget needed to accomplish the advertising goals.[18]

The task method addresses the major problem of the rules-of-thumb methods—funds are applied to accomplish a specific goal so that advertising is a *determinant* of those results, not a consequence. Using the task approach, managers will allocate all the funds necessary to accomplish a specific objective, rather than allocating some arbitrary percentage of sales. The most troubling problem of the method is that management must have some instinct for the proper relationship between expenditure level and communication response. It is difficult to know what will produce a certain level of awareness among business marketing buying influentials. Will 12 two-page

---
[18] Lilien et al., "Industrial Advertising Effects and Budgeting Practices," p. 22.

insertions in *Iron Age* over the next six months create the desired recognition level, or will 24 insertions over one year be necessary?[19]

A recent study in the United Kingdom indicates that the use of the objective-task method is on the rise.[20] The study also found that most business advertisers use several methods to determine the level of advertising expenditures. The researchers concluded that the general trend appears to be "increasing sophistication" in the advertising budgeting process as reflected by greater use of the objective-task method and techniques for tracking advertising effectiveness.[21] Techniques for measuring advertising effectiveness are explored later in the chapter.

Budgeting for advertising must not ignore the political and behavioral aspects of the process. Nigel Piercy's research suggests that attention to budgeting technique is insufficient because organizations operate through structures and processes that are often political in nature.[22] Piercy suggests that what actually determines advertising budgets are the power "interests" in the company and the political behavior of various parties in the budgeting process. An implication of this research is that the manager may be well-served by focusing considerable attention on the budgetary process as a political activity, and not simply as a technique-driven process.

The ADVISOR Project

The lack of specific guidelines for formulating business marketing advertising budgets stimulated two research projects to determine the product and market factors that affect business marketing advertising expenditures. The ADVISOR and ADVISOR 2 projects of Gary Lilien and John Little resulted in a model that specifies the typical size and range of marketing budgets based on a variety of product and market characteristics.[23] The ADVISOR models allow a decision maker to specify product and market characteristics, and then budget and allocation guidelines are provided by the models on the basis of these variables.

Because the budgeting process is so important to advertising effectiveness, managers must not blindly follow rules of thumb. Instead, they should evaluate the tasks required and their associated costs against industry norms. With clear objectives and proper budgetary allocations, the next step is to design effective advertising messages.

---

[19] Some industrial firms have developed quantitative models to relate advertising expenditures to profits or sales. For example, see David A. Aaker and John G. Myers, *Advertising Management*, 3rd ed. (Englewood Cliffs, N.J.: Prentice-Hall, 1987), Chapter 3, pp. 61–80.

[20] James E. Lynch and Graham J. Hooley, "Industrial Advertising Budget Approaches in the U.K.," *Industrial Marketing Management*, 18 (November 1989), p. 266.

[21] Ibid., p. 267.

[22] Nigel Piercy, "Advertising Budgeting: Process and Structure as Explanatory Variables," *Journal of Advertising*, 16, Number 2 (1987), p. 34.

[23] Gary L. Lilien and John D. C. Little, "The ADVISOR Project: A Study of Industrial Marketing Budgets," *Sloan Management Review*, 16 (Spring 1976), pp. 17–31; and Gary L. Lilien, "ADVISOR 2: Modeling the Marketing Mix for Industrial Products," *Management Service*, 25 (February 1979), pp. 191–204.

ETHICAL BUSINESS MARKETING
Deception Saves the Company

Philippe Kahn, in an interview with *Inc.* magazine described with apparent relish how his company, Borland International, got its start by deceiving an ad salesman from *BYTE* magazine.

Inc.: The story goes that Borland was launched by a single ad, without which we wouldn't be sitting here talking about the company. How much of that is apocryphal?

Kahn: It's true: one full-page ad in the November 1983 issue of *BYTE* magazine got the company running. If it had failed, I would have had nowhere else to go.

Inc.: If you were so broke, how did you pay for the ad?

Kahn: Let's put it that we convinced the salesman to give us terms. We wanted to appear only in *BYTE*—not any of the other microcomputer magazines—because *BYTE* is for programmers, and that's who we wanted to reach. But we couldn't afford it. We figured the only way was somehow to convince them to extend us credit terms.

Inc.: And they did?

Kahn: Well, they didn't *offer.* What we did was, before the ad salesman came in—we existed in two small rooms, but I had hired extra people so we would look like a busy, venture-backed company—we prepared a chart with what we pretended was our media plan for the computer magazines. On the chart we had *BYTE* crossed out. When the salesman arrived, we made sure the phones were ringing and the extras were scurrying around. Here was this chart he thought he wasn't supposed to see, so I pushed it out of the way. He said, "Hold on, can we get you in *BYTE?*" I said, "We don't really want to be in your book, it's not the right audience for us." "You've got to try," he pleaded. I said, "Frankly our media plan is done, and we can't afford it." So he offered good terms, if only we'd let him run it just once. We expected we'd sell maybe $20,000 worth of software and at least pay for the ad. We sold $150,000 worth. Looking back now, it's a funny story; then it was a big risk.

Can Borland's action be justified given the stakes involved and the final outcome?

Source: Omar Bhide and Howard H. Stevenson, "Why Be Honest If Honesty Doesn't Pay," *Harvard Business Review,* 68 (September–October 1990), p. 122.

The Advertising Message

Message development is a complex, critical task in industrial advertising. Highlighting a product attribute that is unimportant to a particular buying group is not only a waste of advertising dollars but also a lost opportunity. Both the appeal and the way that appeal is conveyed are vital to successful communication. Thus, creating business-to-business advertising messages involves determining advertising objectives, evaluating the buying criteria of the target audience, and analyzing the most appropriate language, format, and style for presenting the message.

Perception

For an advertising message to be successful, first an individual must be exposed to it and pay attention to it. Then, once the individual has noticed the message, he or she must interpret it as the advertiser intended. Perceptual barriers often prevent the intended message from being perceived by a receiver. A business advertisement must be successful at catching the decision maker's attention. Yet, even though the individual is exposed to an advertisement, there is no guarantee that the message will be processed. In fact, the industrial buyer may read every word of the copy and find a meaning in it opposite to that intended by the advertiser.

The business advertiser must contend with two important elements of perception: attention and interpretation. Buyers tend to screen out messages that are inconsistent with their own attitudes, needs, and beliefs, and they tend to interpret information in the light of those beliefs (see Chapter 4). Thus, unless advertising messages are carefully designed and targeted, they may be disregarded or interpreted improperly. Advertisers must put themselves in the position of the receivers in order to evaluate how the message will appear to them.

Whether or not an ad uses technical wording appears to have some effect on readers' perceptions of both the industrial product and the ad.[24] Technical ads were shown to create less desire in some readers to seek information because such ads suggest "more difficulty in operation." Therefore, it is important to remember that technical readers (engineers, architects, etc.) respond more favorably to the technical ads, and nontechnical readers respond more favorably to nontechnical ads. From a message development viewpoint, the business advertiser must carefully tailor the technical aspects of promotional messages to the appropriate audience.

The Appeal: Benefits

An industrial buyer purchases benefits—a better way to accomplish some task, a less expensive way to produce a final product, a solution to a problem, or a faster delivery time. Advertising messages need to focus on the benefits sought by the target customer and to persuade the reader that the advertiser can deliver the benefit.[25] Messages that have direct appeals or calls to action are viewed to be "stronger" than those with diffuse or indirect appeals to action.

Oftentimes, advertisers tend to concentrate on a physical product, forgetting that the physical product is useless to an industrial buyer unless it solves some problem. Note that the CSX advertisement displayed in Figure 16.4 is clearly focused on the benefits provided to shippers of steel. Product damage is more important than cost, speed of delivery, or reliability in the transportation of many industrial products. CSX has utilized its excellent track record in the area of damage claims to develop this message. It certainly communicates an important shipper benefit in an unambiguous fashion, and product features (5,000 railcars have been refurbished) are only mentioned to reinforce the low-damage-rate benefit.

---

[24]Joseph A. Bellizzi and Jacqueline J. Mohr, "Technical Versus Nontechnical Wording in Industrial Print Advertising," Russell W. Belk et al., eds., *AMA Educators' Proceedings* (Chicago, Ill.: American Marketing Association, 1984), p. 174.

[25]Donald R. Glover, Steven W. Hartley, and Charles H. Patti, "How Advertising Message Strategies Are Set," *Industrial Marketing Management*, 18 (February 1989), p. 22.

FIGURE 16.4   **An Ad Focusing on the Benefits Provided to Users**

Source: Courtesy, CSX Transportation.

Understanding Buyer Motivations

Which product benefits are important to each group of buying influentials? The
business advertiser cannot assume that a standard set of "classical buying motives"
applies in every purchase situation. Business advertisers often do not understand the
buying motives of important market segments.[26]

A methodology for determining the dimensions and benefits perceived by buying
decision participants would be extremely useful to business advertisers. A promising
effort is the business marketing strategy response model of Jean-Marie Choffray and
Gary Lilien,[27] discussed in Chapter 11 in connection with product strategy development.
An application of the model to purchases of industrial cooling systems provided

---

[26] Gordon McAleer, "Do Industrial Advertisers Understand What Influences Their Markets?" *Journal of
Marketing*, 38 (January 1974), pp. 15–23.

[27] Jean-Marie Choffray and Gary L. Lilien, "Assessing Responses to Industrial Marketing Strategy," *Journal of
Marketing*, 42 (April 1978), p. 29.

TABLE 16.2   **Characteristics of Business-to-Business Advertisements that Favorably Affect Each Phase of the Decision-Making Process**

Phase of Decision-Making Process	Ad Elements that Create an Effective Impact
1. Establishing contact	Four-color; color with illustrations; color with product
2. Creating awareness	Product shown by itself; four or more copy blocks; more than 300 words of copy
3. Arousing interest	Product ad; product by itself; use of 800 incoming WATS number, tables, and charts; three to five illustrations
4. Building preference	Product ad; product by itself; four or more copy blocks
5. Keeping customers sold	More than 300 words of copy; product by itself

Source: Bob Donath, "Q: What Makes a Perfect Ad? A: It Depends," *Industrial Marketing*, 67 (August 1982), pp. 89–92.

information useful for developing advertising messages. Product attributes varied in importance for each of the six identified decision participants. Production engineers were concerned with operating cost and energy savings, heating and air-conditioning consultants with noise level in the plant and first cost.

Physical Characteristics of an Advertisement

Once the perception process has been evaluated and the user benefits identified, the business advertiser must decide how the advertisement is to be structured.[28] A wide variety of factors must be considered, including size of the ad, use of color and illustrations, and media placement; readership and recall of business advertisements are strongly related to mechanical and format characteristics (size, color, placement, etc.) of the advertisement.[29]

McGraw-Hill analyzed five years of ad readership scores for nearly 3,600 individual business advertisements in order to evaluate the impact of various elements on the effectiveness of industrial advertisements.[30] Table 16.2 shows which physical characteristics of an advertisement were found to influence effectiveness at various steps of the decision-making process. Note the importance of color in the early phases of establishing contact and the critical importance of copy and product display throughout the later phases. "The copy factor of an advertised proposition contributes perhaps 80 percent of an ad's success or failure."[31] Carborundum, a large abrasives manufacturer, studied how potential buyers responded to various ads used by the company and its

---

[28] For an excellent discussion of how to improve business advertising copy, see Joseph A. Bellizzi and Robert E. Hite, "Improving Industrial Advertising Copy," *Industrial Marketing Management*, 15 (May 1986), pp. 117–122.

[29] Dominique Hanssens and Barton A. Weitz, "The Effectiveness of Industrial Print Advertisements Across Product Categories," *Journal of Marketing Research*, 17 (August 1980), p. 304.

[30] Bob Donath, "Q: What Makes the Perfect Ad? A: It Depends," *Industrial Marketing*, 67 (August 1982), pp. 89–92.

[31] Ibid., p. 90.

competitors. The study concluded that the better the overall quality rating of the ad copy, the more likely it is that readers say they'll take some sort of action.[32] Thus, although certain mechanical aspects help create awareness and interest in the advertisement, its ultimate success will depend on how well the message is targeted to the benefits sought by the buying influential.

In conclusion, to formulate business marketing advertising messages, one must analyze the perceptual process, base the appeal on product benefits, differentiate the buying criteria of the various decision participants, and design the advertisement appropriately.

Business Marketing Advertising Media

Although the message is vital to advertising success, an equally important factor is the medium through which it is presented. Business-to-business media are selected by target audience—the particular purchase decision participants to be reached. Generally, the first decision is whether to use trade publications, direct mail, or both. Selection of particular media also involves budgetary considerations: where are dollars best spent to generate the customer contacts desired?

Business Publications

There are more than 2,700 business publications carrying business-to-business advertising amounting to more than $2 billion. For those specializing in distribution, *Transportation and Distribution*, *Distribution*, *Traffic Management*, and *Modern Materials Handling* are a few of the publications available. *Iron Age* and *Steel* are aimed at individuals in the steel industry. Business publications are either horizontal or vertical. **Horizontal publications** are directed at a specific task, technology, or function whatever the industry. *Advertising Age*, *Purchasing*, and *Handling and Shipping* are horizontal. **Vertical publications**, on the other hand, may be read by everyone from foreman to president within a specific industry. Typical vertical publications are *Glass Industry* or *Manufacturing Confectioner*. Figure 16.5 shows examples of business publications. Note the nature of the readership in terms of circulation and the types of buyers that are targeted.

If a business marketer's product has applications only within a few industries, vertical publications are a logical media choice. When many industries are potential users and well-defined functions are the principal buying influencers, a horizontal publication is effective.

Another important aspect of trade publications is **controlled circulation**, which involves free (as opposed to paid) subscriptions, and which is distributed to selected readers in a position to influence buying decisions. Subscribers must provide their title, function, and buying responsibilities, among other information. Thus, the advertiser can tell whether each publication reaches the desired audience.

---

[32]"Do Buyers Understand Advertising?" *Business Marketing*, 73 (March 1988), p. 102.

FIGURE 16.5 **Examples of Business Publications**

PC World—The Business Magazine of PC Products and Solutions. The largest circulation monthly covering the IBM PC and compatibles market, gives sophisticated business decision makers in-depth, objective solutions to their business problems, and helps them buy personal computers and related products with confidence. *PC World*, 501 Second St., Suite 600, San Francisco, Calif. 94107; 415-546-7722. (RS 205)

P&IM Review with APICS News, the magazine of manufacturing performance, circulated to over 68,000 professionals in production & inventory, purchasing, operations, MIS, marketing, finance and electronic data processing looking to improve operations through manufacturing systems, computer integrated manufacturing, automatic identification systems (bar coding), scale & weighing technologies, and education & consulting. *P&IM Review with APICS News*, 2021 Coolidge St., Hollywood, Fla. 33020; 305-925-5900. (RS 206)

Packaging Digest reaches over 100,000 buying influences across the broad-based packaging function. As the world's leading packaging publication in circulation, advertising, and reader response, *Packaging Digest* presents a unique editorial combination of case history and product news for readers throughout all packaging-intensive markets. *Packaging Digest*, 400 N. Michigan Ave., Chicago, Ill. 60611; 312-222-2000. (RS 207)

Petroleum Engineer International helps petroleum industry engineers and related technical people build profits into oil and gas drilling and producing on land or offshore worldwide. Published monthly, *PEI* emphasizes technical, methods, operating, and engineering advances. *Petroleum Engineer International*, P.O. Box 1589, Dallas, Texas 75221; 214-691-3911. (RS 208)

Pipeline & Gas Journal, a monthly, serves the world-wide energy pipeline and gas distribution business. Feature articles deal with engineering, operating, construction, methods relative to cross-country pipelines that transport crude oil, products, and natural gas, plus facilities that distribute natural gas. *Pipeline & Gas Journal*, P.O. Box 1589, Dallas, Texas 75221; 214-691-3911. (RS 209)

Pipe Line Industry targets the design, engineering, construction, operation, maintenance and management of gas transmission and distribution systems as well as pipe line systems for crude oil, products, water and slurries. It has more advertising, editorial, domestic and international circulation than any magazine in its field. *Pipe Line Industry*, P.O. Box 2608, Houston, Texas 77252; 713-529-4301. (RS 210)

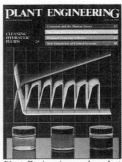

Plant Engineering reaches plant engineers in more plants in the USA than any other publication in its field. Total circulation is now over 128,000 qualified engineers in over 59,000 plants and other industrial operations. *Plant Engineering* provides a broad range of problem-solving editorial which focuses on the application and utilization of technology within the modern plant. *Plant Engineering*, 1301 S. Grove Ave., Barrington, Ill. 60010; 312-361-1840. (RS 211)

Plastics Technology serves manufacturing managers in every plastics processing plant in the U.S. Among *PT* readers, 94% serve one of the four technology buying functions . . . 90% are located in manufacturing facilities. Almost half do not read any other plastics publication. *Plastics Technology*, 633 Third Ave., New York, N.Y. 10017; 212-984-2282. (RS 212)

Source: "The Media Resource File," *Business Marketing*, 73 (September 1987), p. 7. Reprinted by permission, Crain Communications, Inc.

INSIDE BUSINESS MARKETING
The Floppy Disk and Video Cassette Pitch—Companies Find New Ad Media

In the search for creative ways to stimulate sales, some business marketers have discovered new advertising media: floppy disks and video cassettes.

Since many business buyers have microcomputers on their desks, the floppy disk becomes a feasible approach for getting a message across. Some firms mail the disks out with explanatory brochures; others pass them out at trade shows or during sales presentations. Intel promotes its computer hardware and software debugging tools, called incircuit emulators, in its floppy disk ads. The company plans to mail the disks to 15,000 design engineers.

Some business catalog marketers put their entire catalog on diskette. Prospects electronically turn the pages of the diskette catalog with their PCs instead of leafing through one of the many printed catalogs they receive. The diskettes are cheaper to produce than the printed catalog and seem to generate more interest.

The floppies do have their drawbacks: versatility is limited, they can't be read in transit, and the customer must have a microcomputer. However, the disks portray an image of sophistication, and as one Intel spokeswoman stated, "It's not something customers would toss in the garbage."

Video cassettes can have tremendous impact in demonstrating complex products and sophisticated systems. The recipients can view the tape at their leisure, watch it several times, and review elements that interest them. The tapes provide the advertiser with the ability to make its services tangible and also demonstrate credibility by showing highly respected clients with whom they are currently working.

Source: Adapted from Sue Kapp, "The Floppy Disk Pitch: Companies Find New Ad Medium," *Business Marketing*, 72 (June 1987), p. 40; and Tom Eisenhart, "Catalogers Turn to Diskettes for Greater Impact," *Business Marketing*, 75 (April 1990), p. 30.

Obviously, publication choice is predicated on a complete understanding of the range of purchase decision participants and of the industries where the product will be used. Only then can the target audience be matched to the circulation statements of alternative business publications.

Advertising Cost

Circulation is an important criterion in the selection of publications, but circulation must be tempered by cost. First, the total advertising budget must be allocated among the various advertising tools. Most studies indicate that the breakdown of expenditures is approximately as follows:

- Trade publications 40%
- Sales promotion 25%
- Direct mail 25%
- Trade shows 10%

Of course, these allocations vary with company situation and advertising mission. However, the 40 percent allocation to trade publications appears fairly consistent from company to company.

Allocation of the trade publication budget among various journals will depend on their relative effectiveness and efficiency, usually measured in cost per thousand. Thus, the formula is:

$$\text{Cost per thousand} = \frac{\text{Cost per page}}{\text{Circulation in thousands}}.$$

To compare two publications on their actual page rates would be misleading because the publication with the lower circulation will usually be less expensive. The cost-per-thousand calculation should be based on circulation to the *target* audience, not the total audience. Although some publications may appear high on a cost-per-thousand basis, they may in fact be cost-effective, with little wasted circulation.

Frequency and Scheduling

Even the most successful business publication advertisements are seen by only a small percentage of the people who read the magazine; therefore, one-time ads are generally ineffective. Because a number of exposures are required before a message "sinks in," and because the reading audience varies from month to month, a schedule of advertising insertions is required. To build continuity and repetitive value, at least six insertions per year may be required in a monthly publication, and 26 to 52 insertions (with a minimum of 13) in a weekly publication.[33]

Direct Mail Advertising

Direct mail delivers the advertising message first-hand to selected individuals. Possible mailing pieces range from a sales letter introducing a new product to a lengthy brochure or even a product sample. Direct mail can accomplish all of the major advertising functions, but its real contribution is in delivering the message to a precisely defined prospect.

Direct mail is commonly used for corporate image promotion, product and service promotion, sales force support, distribution channel communication, and special marketing problems.[34] In promoting corporate image, as NCR does, direct mail may help to establish a reputation of technological leadership. On the other hand, product advertising by direct mail can be used to put specific product information in the hands of buying influentials. Booklets from Kaiser Aluminum explain aluminum's advantages to industrial buyers and specifiers, whereas messages on how to work with aluminum and a quantity/weight calculator are sent to machine operators and shop foremen.[35]

---

[33] See Stanton G. Cort, David R. Lambert, and Paula L. Garrett, "Effective Business-to-Business Frequency: New Management Perspectives from the Research Literature," *Advertising Research Foundation Literature Review* (October 1983).

[34] Taylor Sims and Herbert E. Brown, "Increasing the Role of Direct Mail Marketing in Industrial Marketing Strategy," *Industrial Marketing Management*, 8 (November 1979), p. 294.

[35] Ibid., p. 295.

Direct Mail: Benefits and Requirements

Direct mail also supports the salespeople—providing leads from returned inquiry cards and paving the way for a first sales call. Direct mail can be used effectively to notify potential customers of the location of local distributors. New products are frequently introduced through a direct mail campaign. In a study by IBM, 60 percent of the executives queried preferred to hear about new office products by mail.[36] In terms of response performance, a typical direct mail package will be equal to something on the order of 10 to 50 print or broadcast exposures.[37] Finally, direct mail applies to a host of special situations such as identifying new customers and markets, meeting competitor claims, and promoting items that are not receiving enough sales support.

From a cost standpoint, direct mail is efficient when compared to other media. Some experts estimated that direct marketing (mail or telephone) returns between $2 and $45 in sales for each dollar spent.[38] The ratios hold true whether direct marketing is used to identify qualified leads or to create immediate sales.

Direct mail is a viable advertising medium when potential buyers can be clearly identified and easily reached through the mail. It can be a wasteful medium if the prospect lists are so general in nature that it is difficult or impossible to find a common denominator among the prospects.

A direct mail advertisement typically gains the full attention of the reader and therefore provides greater impact than a trade publication advertisement. Industrial buyers surveyed by the Business Advertising Research Council claimed to read or at least scan three-quarters of the direct mail promotions sent to them.[39] However, reaching top executives with direct mail may be more difficult. A survey of secretaries of top executives at Fortune 500 companies showed that the average executive receives 175 pieces of unsolicited mail each week, and less than 10 percent of this mail is passed on to the executive.[40] The executives spend only five minutes a day looking at the 17 or so pieces of mail. Clearly, the direct mail piece must have effective copy and headlines to grab the secretary's and the executive's attention.

Timing of direct mail advertising is also flexible; a new price schedule or new service innovation can be communicated to the buyer as needed. Finally, direct mail makes it easy for the buyer to respond—usually a reply postcard is included or the name, address, and phone number of the local salesperson or distributor are provided.

A Planned Response Package

Most direct mail programs seek some type of response. Often, the potential buyer is asked to return a reply card in order to receive additional information such as a sample or a brochure explaining the benefits and applications of a product. Only 1 out of every 40 raw leads developed from a direct mail campaign may be actually worth a

---

[36] Ann Helming, "Direct Mail Leaves Its Indelible Stamp," *Advertising Age*, 53 (June 14, 1983), p. m-12.

[37] Shell R. Alpert, "Testing the 'TOO-Frequent' Assumption," *Business Marketing*, 73 (March 1988), p. 14.

[38] Herbert G. Ahrend, "Direct Marketing Varies for Business-to-Business," *Direct Marketing*, 48 (March 1986), p. 162.

[39] Ann Helming, "Direct Mail Leaves Its Indelible Stamp," p. m-12.

[40] Tom Eisenhart, "Break through Direct Marketing," *Business Marketing*, 75 (August 1990), p. 20.

THE GLOBAL MARKETPLACE
Leveraging a Global Message

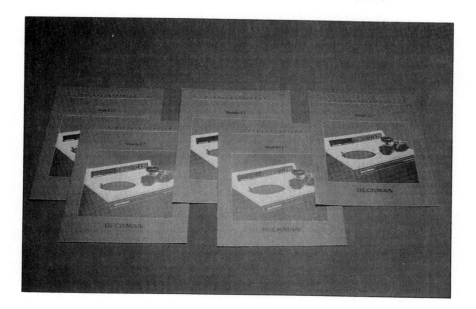

Complex industrial products enjoy a distinct advantage over many standardized industrial items and most consumer goods: these products tend to have "common denominators" in different global markets. The fact that a nuclear reactor meets a certain standard of durability would be as important to an engineer in India as it would to one in Korea. The complexity of the products so limit their application that the applications are generally very similar. In addition, the needs for complex products tend to be the same worldwide—what appeals to a buyer in one country pretty much appeals to most others. The net result is that a single common advertising message can be created for use in *all* markets.

Beckman Instruments follows a global approach to advertising, developing a basic image and message to be communicated to all global markets. The firm feels that this approach provides an "avenue for maximizing advertising results." The firm's director of communication confirms that "we've found a basic message and appearance that's accepted and well received by all countries where we operate. Although it was a challenge to settle on a globally acceptable image and approach, the consistency of purpose and clarity of communications—and, in the end—cost economies we experienced made it well worthwhile." Because purchaser profiles for complex industrial products are similar worldwide, the common advertising message can be communicated over a broader customer base, which results in a high exposure/lower production cost situation. The five brochures for Beckman Instruments' Model L7 Centrifuge, shown above, are an example of "global advertising"—the brochures are identical, except they are written in five different languages.

Source: Adapted from David Perry, "Performance Advertisers Practice What They Preach," *Business Marketing*, 73 (March 1988), pp. 86, 87. Reprinted with permission of *Business Marketing*.

salesperson's attention.[41] As a result, there is often a tendency to adopt a casual approach toward responding to sales leads. However, to realize the potential of direct mail, there must be a formal program to "qualify" each inquiry and respond promptly. Qualification may be accomplished by telephoning the respondent and assessing his or her authority and readiness to purchase. Once the respondent has been qualified, the response program might involve mailing literature to the prospect, referring the prospect to a salesperson, or calling to explain product details. A planned response "package" aims to generate a sale and should include a motivating cover letter, a descriptive brochure, and a reply card that makes it easy to respond.

The Mailing List
The critical ingredient of a direct mail advertising campaign is the list of buying influentials—so the selectivity of direct mail, although its primary advantage, is also its greatest challenge. There are literally hundreds of mailing lists available. Mailing lists for business marketing advertising purposes may be (1) circulation lists provided by trade publications, (2) lists provided by industrial directories, (3) lists provided by mailing-list houses (e.g., firms specifically engaged in renting industrial mailing lists), and (4) self-generated lists of previous customers and prospects. Computers are playing an increasing role in maintaining mailing lists. The computer also allows the advertiser to supplement the list with sales data and SIC codes. A catalog published by Standard Rate and Data Service inventories and describes most of the industrial mailing lists available. These often have names of individual executives. However, if the lists are even slightly out of date, a list by company and functional title should be used.

Telemarketing
Telemarketing not only supplements the personal sales call (see Chapter 17) but can also enhance the effectiveness of direct mail advertising. With the rising cost of a sales call, many business-to-business marketers are turning to telemarketing as a way of reaching buyers cost-effectively. The importance of telemarketing is underscored by the magnitude of expenditures: business-to-business firms spend almost $28 billion on telemarketing annually.[42] Companies in industries as diverse as insurance, agricultural equipment, and computers are using telemarketing to make contact with buyers.

Increasingly, many firms initiate telemarketing by including a toll-free telephone number in their print and direct mail advertisements.[43] Honeywell's Process Control Division's direct mail features a toll-free number.[44] When a prospect responds, the telemarketing operator does preliminary qualifying directly onto a terminal linked to a Honeywell DPS-8 computer. The screen displays questions keyed to a given product,

---

[41] John L. DeFazio, "An Inquiry-Based MIS," p. 54.

[42] George E. Belch and Michael A. Belch, *Introduction to Advertising and Promotion Management*, (Homewood, IL: Richard D. Irwin, 1990), p. 647.

[43] Roy Voorhees and John Coppett, "Telemarketing in Distribution Channels," *Industrial Marketing Management*, 12 (April 1983), p. 105.

[44] Richard G. Webster, "High-Tech Telemarketing Scores for Honeywell Division," *Business Marketing*, 68 (June 1983), p. 102.

and the answers are entered and stored immediately. Once the prospect is qualified, the operator determines whether the response should be mailed information or should receive a sales call. The computerized information is used to create a mailing list. The sales force is notified via electronic mail so that the prospects can be contacted promptly (usually within a day). Telemarketing support for direct mail provides ease of response for the prospect, immediate reply while the idea is fresh, and interactive dialogue to delineate customer needs more fully.[45]

Media Selection: A Recap

In conclusion, selecting business-to-business advertising media is a matching of the media with the target audience. The business advertiser must choose the specific purchase decision participants to which an advertising message will be directed and then match these to the circulations of various journals. The final decision on choice of medium depends on the budget, the cost per thousand of the medium, and the medium's circulation.

Advertising Effectiveness

The business advertiser rarely expects orders to result immediately from advertising. Advertising is designed to create awareness, stimulate loyalty to the company, or create a favorable attitude toward a product. Even though advertising may not directly precipitate a purchase decision, advertising programs must be held accountable. Thus, the business advertiser must be able to measure the results of current advertising in order to improve future advertising and must be able to evaluate the effectiveness of advertising expenditures against expenditures on other elements of marketing strategy.

Measuring Impacts on the Purchase Decision

Measuring advertising effectiveness means assessing advertising's impact on what "intervenes" between the stimulus (advertising) and the resulting behavior (purchase decision).[46] The theory is that advertising can affect awareness, knowledge, and other dimensions that more readily lend themselves to measurement. In essence, the advertiser attempts to gauge advertising's ability to move an individual through the purchase decision process. This approach assumes, correctly or not, that enhancement of any one phase of the decision process or movement from one step to the next increases the ultimate probability of purchase.

A study completed at Rockwell International Corporation suggests that business marketers should also measure the **indirect communication effects** of advertising.[47] This study revealed that advertising affects word-of-mouth communications (indirect effect), and such communications play an important role in buyer decision making.

---

[45] Benson Shapiro and John Wyman, "New Ways to Reach Your Customers," *Harvard Business Review*, 59 (July–August 1981), p. 106.

[46] Aaker and Myers, *Advertising Management*, p. 88.

[47] C. Whan Park, Martin S. Roth, and Philip F. Jacques, "Evaluating the Effects of Advertising and Sales Promotion Campaigns," *Industrial Marketing Management*, 17 (May 1988), p. 130.

INSIDE BUSINESS MARKETING

Business Marketers Find Sports Sponsorship an Effective Advertising Tool

Sports Marketing News estimates that companies spend $6.2 billion annually on sports marketing and sports sponsorship. Although it is not possible to determine how much of that total is spent by industrial firms, the use of sports sponsorship by business-to-business firms appears to be growing rapidly. Industry experts estimate that one large business marketer budgets between $15 and $20 million for its sports sponsorship programs.

What accounts for the increasing popularity of sports sponsorship among business marketers? First, business marketers see a real value in sponsoring sporting events because the events appeal to executives in Fortune 1000 companies—and oftentimes these firms are key target markets for the advertiser. Some companies find that the sporting events provide a good vehicle for increasing contact with customers, while others use the events as sales incentives. Other business marketers enhance the loyalty of dealers and distributors by inviting them to sponsored events. In short, sporting events often have audience demographics that fit the profile of executives who make buying decisions for the company's products, and the events provide a vehicle for entertaining clients and customers.

A number of very large business marketers are engaged in sporting event sponsorship; a sample of these firms and their strategies is profiled below.

MCI Communications spends more than $5 million on sporting events. The company believes the events help cement relationships with business customers. The firm sponsors the Heritage Golf Classic and other events. The firm tracks the increase in business after each sporting event it sponsors. The data suggest that "every event contributes many times the revenue over what it costs."

Konica Business Machines, USA advertises on NFL games shown on ESPN and sponsors numerous events, including the San Jose Golf Classic. The firm brings dealers who are golf enthusiasts to the pro-am tournament preceding the event, which allows executives to interact with dealers on a social basis. In addition, the firm offers a co-op ad program to dealers: dealers can insert local 10-second tags at the end of each of the company's commercials. The firm's sponsorship of cable and network sports programs increased brand awareness from 63 percent to 75 percent over a recent one-year period.

The Automotive Finishes Group of PPG Industries invests almost $9 million a year in auto racing. Most of the funds are used to sponsor the PPG Indy World Series, administered by Championship Auto Racing Teams (CART). Part of the firm's program has included painting every car that has raced at the Indianapolis 500 since 1977. To highlight its role as the leading supplier of automotive paint finishes, the company provides an annual award to the best-looking car at the Indy 500. The company's involvement and sponsorship of auto racing has paid off in closer relationships with automakers.

Source: Adapted from Tom Eisenhart, "Sporting Chances Zap Competitors," *Business Marketing*, 73 (January 1988), pp. 92–97.

Similarly, advertising was shown to indirectly affect buyers on the basis of its impact on overall company reputation and on the sales force's belief that advertising facilitates their selling tasks. It was suggested that advertising effectiveness measurement include a procedure for tracking and measuring the impact of advertising on the indirect communication effects.

TABLE 16.3   **The Five Primary Areas for Advertising Evaluation**

Area	Preevaluation	Postevaluation
Markets	Identifying the market targets at which the advertising is aimed	Measuring extent to which advertising succeeded in reaching its market targets
Motives	Determining what causes people to buy (as a preparatory step toward constructing the advertising message)	Measuring motivating factors after the action (such as a purchase) occurred
Messages	Determining the best ways to construct and communicate messages	Measuring the extent to which the message registered
Media	Determining the best combination of media to reach the market with the messages	Measuring the extent to which various media succeeded in reaching the market with the message
Overall results	Identifying the specific results that advertising is uniquely qualified to perform	Evaluating the extent to which advertising accomplished its objectives as a basis for deciding what to continue, what to change, and how much to spend

Source: Maurice I. Mandell, *Advertising* (Englewood Cliffs, N.J.: Prentice-Hall, Inc., 1974), p. 610. Reprinted by permission of Prentice-Hall, Inc.

In summary, advertising effectiveness will be evaluated against objectives formulated in terms of the elements of the buyer's decision process as well as some of the indirect communication effects. Advertising efforts will also be judged, in the final analysis, on cost per level of achievement (e.g., dollars spent to achieve a certain level of awareness or recognition).

The Measurement Program

A good measurement program entails substantial advanced planning. Table 16.3 shows the basic areas of advertising evaluation. Each has a planning (preevaluation) and an evaluation (postevaluation) aspect. Thus, the manager must determine in advance what is to be measured, how, and in what sequence. The five primary areas for advertising evaluation are (1) markets, (2) motives, (3) messages, (4) media, and (5) results.

The evaluation of business-to-business advertising is demanding and complex, but absolutely essential. Budgetary constraints are generally the limiting factors. Professional research companies are often called on to develop field research studies. When determining the impact of advertising on moving a decision participant from an awareness of the product or company to a readiness to buy, the evaluations will usually measure knowledge, recognition, recall, awareness, preference, and motivation. Measurements of effects on actual sales are unfortunately not often possible.

IBM: Measuring Ad Effectiveness

Observe in Figure 16.6 the approach that IBM, one of the largest business advertisers, uses in assessing its business-to-business advertising. Because a broad array of products are advertised under the IBM brand name, management concentrates on

FIGURE 16.6   **IBM's Campaign Research Measurement Model**

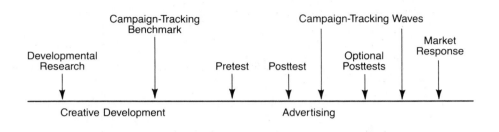

Source: "Features/High-Tech Marketing," *Business Marketing*, 71 (January 1985), p. 108. Reprinted by permission, Crain Communications, Inc. and International Business Machines, Inc.

assessing campaigns in particular business areas rather than on an individual ad's effectiveness.

Creative development constitutes the first stage of the model. Here communication objectives are carefully developed and a concept is designed to convey the proper theme to a particular IBM market segment. For example, in segments where IBM is the preferred product, the ad might be designed to reinforce brand preference to capitalize on the firm's leadership position, and to do so in a warm and upbeat manner. Effectiveness research then involves pretesting and post-introduction tests, tracking studies, impression studies, and focus groups. The IBM approach carefully incorporates evaluations and adjustments before and during the advertising campaign. In turn, periodic tracking surveys monitor how the market's perceptions are changing over time.

SUPPLEMENTARY PROMOTIONAL TOOLS

Media and direct mail advertising constitute the cornerstone of most nonpersonal, business-to-business, promotional programs. Business advertising funds are designated primarily for trade publication and direct mail, but these are reinforced by other promotional activities such as exhibits and trade shows, catalogs, and trade promotion.

Exhibits and Trade Shows

Most industries stage a business show or exhibition annually to display new advances and technological developments in the industry. Some recently published figures indicate that total attendance at 8,000 trade shows approximated 31.5 million, that 91,000 firms displayed their merchandise to potential buyers, and that firms were reported to have spent $7 billion in order to exhibit.[48] Generally, sellers present their

---

[48] Roger A. Kerin and William L. Cron, "Assessing Trade Show Functions and Performance: An Exploratory Study," *Journal of Marketing*, 51 (July 1987), p. 87.

products and services in booths visited by interested industry members. Recently, Digital Equipment created its own show. "The all-Digital show, unique in the industry, let the company show off its . . . products to some 50,000 people, including hundreds of top executives of the world's biggest companies, each personally hosted by a Digital official. Digital is spending more than $20 million on the show, but says resulting revenue may approach $1 billion."[49]

A trade-show exhibit offers a unique opportunity to publicize a significant contribution to technology or to demonstrate new and old products. According to Thomas Bonoma, "For many companies, trade-show expenditures are the major—and for more than a few, the only—form of organized marketing communication activity other than efforts by sales force and distributors."[50] Figure 16.7 shows the lengths some corporations go to when creating a trade-show exhibit. This particular exhibit by Sony was rated as the most memorable in a survey of those attending large shows. Through the trade show,

- An effective selling message can be delivered to a relatively large and interested audience at one time (for example, more than 30,000 people attend the annual Plant Engineering Show).
- New products can be introduced to a mass audience.
- Customers can get hands-on experience with the product in a one-on-one selling situation.
- Potential customers can be identified, providing sales personnel with qualified leads.
- General goodwill can be enhanced.
- Often free publicity is generated for the company.

The cost of reaching a prospect at a trade show is approximately $132, whereas the cost of making an industrial sales call approaches $225.[51]

Trade Shows Are Effective

A study by Exhibit Surveys, Inc., found that an average of 61 percent of the attendees of surveyed trade shows planned to purchase products displayed at the show in the next year.[52] According to the same firm, about 75 percent of the visitors to a sponsor's booth were able to recall the visit and the sponsor eight to ten weeks after the exhibit

---

[49] William M. Bulkeley, "Digital Equipment Gets Bullish Forecasts: Big Trade Show, Competitiveness Are Cited," *The Wall Street Journal* (September 2, 1987) p. 45.

[50] Thomas V. Bonoma, "Get More Out of Your Trade Shows," *Harvard Business Review*, 61 (January–February 1983), p. 76.

[51] "Trade Shows Carry Lower Contact Costs," *Business Marketing*, 74 (March 1989), p. 28.

[52] Richard K. Swandby, Jonathan M. Cox, and Ian K. Sequeira, "Trade Shows Poised for 1990's Growth," *Business Marketing*, 75 (May 1990), p. 48.

FIGURE 16.7   **A Sony Exhibit at the National Association of Broadcasters International Show**

Source: Richard K. Swandby, Robert S. Ciok, and Ian K. Sequeira, "Sony, Halliburton Top Annual Survey," *Business Marketing,* 72 (May 1986), p. 74. Reprinted by permission, Crain Communications, Inc.

closed.[53] Many potential buyers that visit a display booth often have not been visited by the exhibitor's sales force in the preceding year. In fact, 91 percent of the audience attending trade shows in a recent year had not been visited by an exhibitor's sales representative in the previous year.[54] Among business marketing promotion tools for influencing the purchase decision process, trade shows have been ranked third behind peer recommendations and personal selling,[55] and ranked above both print advertising and direct mail. Finally, the Trade Show Bureau reports that the cost of developing and closing a trade-show-generated sales lead is 77 percent less than the cost of closing the average business sale.[56] Although dramatically enhancing sales effectiveness, trade shows can be extremely costly, and must be carefully planned.

[53] John M. Browning and Ronald J. Adams, "Trade Shows: An Effective Promotional Tool for the Small Industrial Business," *Journal of Small Business Management,* 26 (October 1988), p. 33.

[54] Swandby, Cox, and Sequeira, "Trade Shows Poised for 1990's Growth," p. 48.

[55] A. Parasuraman, "The Relative Importance of Industrial Promotion Tools," *Industrial Marketing Management,* 10 (October 1981), pp. 277–81.

[56] "Does Exhibiting Cut Your Selling Costs?" *Business Marketing,* 68 (July 1983), p. 106.

Planning Trade-Show Strategy

To develop an effective trade-show communications strategy, managers must address four questions:

1. What functions should the trade show perform in the total marketing communications program?
2. To whom should the marketing effort at trade shows be directed?
3. What is the appropriate show mix for the company?
4. What should the trade show investment-audit policy be? How should audits be carried out?[57]

Answering these questions helps managers crystallize their thinking about target audiences, about results to be expected, and about how funds should be allocated.

Trade-Show Objectives

Some of the functions of trade shows in generating sales include identifying decision influencers; identifying potential customers; providing product, service, and company information; learning of potential application problems; creating actual sales; and handling current customer problems. In addition to these selling-related functions, the trade show can be a valuable activity for building corporate image, gathering competitive intelligence, and enhancing sales force morale. Specific objectives are needed to guide the development of trade-show strategy and to specify the activities of company personnel while there. Given the importance of establishing clear objectives, it is surprising that the National Trade Show Bureau indicates that only 56 percent of firms that participate in trade shows have specific objectives.[58] However, once specific objectives are formulated, the exhibitor must evaluate alternative trade shows in light of the target market.

Selecting the Shows

The challenge is to decide which trade shows to attend and how much of the promotional budget to expend. Clearly, the firm will want to be represented at those shows frequented by its most important customer segments. A useful service is the *Exposition Audit* provided by Business Publication Audit of Circulation. The audit reports registered attendance at trade shows and a complete profile of each registrant's business, job title, and function. Some firms will use the reports published by Exhibit Surveys, Inc., a company that surveys trade show audiences. Two of the important measures developed by Exhibit Surveys are the **Net Buying Influences** and the **Total Buying Plans**. The first measures the percentage of the show audience that has decision authority for the types of products being exhibited; the second measures the percentage of the audience planning to buy the products being exhibited within the next 12 months. According to Exhibit Surveys, the Net Buying Influence averaged 84

---

[57] Thomas V. Bonoma, "Get More Out of Your Trade Shows," p. 79.

[58] "The Exhibitor: Their Trade Show Practices" (The Trade Show Bureau 1983), Study No. 19.

percent for industrial trade shows in 1989, with a range of 58 to 98 percent.[59] These measures are very useful to the business marketing manager when selecting the most effective shows to attend.

Many firms make a preshow survey of target prospects in order to learn which shows they will attend and what they hope to gain from attending. In this way the exhibitor can prepare its trade show strategy to fit the needs of its potential customers.

Managing the Trade-Show Exhibit

In an effort to generate interest in an exhibit, Nippon Electric runs advertisements in trade publications profiling new projects to be exhibited at the show. Many exhibitors call prospects and customers before the show to make appointments at the show.

Sales personnel must be trained to perform in the trade-show environment. The selling job differs from the typical sales call in that the salesperson may have only five to ten minutes to make a presentation. On a typical sales call, salespersons usually sell themselves first, then the company, and finally the product. At the trade show, the process is reversed.

There must be a system for responding effectively to inquiries generated at the show. Digital Equipment Corporation uses a computer at the show to transmit information to corporate headquarters electronically.[60] Headquarters staff then use word processing to generate a letter and mailing label and to send out the required information. When prospects return to their offices after a show, the material is on their desks.

Finally, a procedure for evaluating a show's effectiveness must be established. Roger Kerin and William Cron indicate that 72 percent of the respondents to a survey on trade shows suggested that a key area for improving their overall trade-show effort was a better means of evaluating performance.[61] A useful step in trade-show evaluation would be to carefully spell out and monitor specific performance measures associated with each trade show objective.

The Trade-Show Budget

How much to budget is hard to decide: "It is strange to find that so little is known about the usefulness of exhibitions, that they are so often an expression of faith rather than fact, with such factors as size of stand and budget determined intuitively by some senior executive."[62] More money is probably wasted at exhibitions than in any other advertising medium. One reason seems to be the apparent need for competitors to outdo each other in creating grand displays.

---

[59] Swandby, Cox, and Sequeira, "Trade Show Poised for 1990's Growth," p. 46.

[60] "DEC Goes On-Line at Showtime," *Sales and Marketing Management*, 128 (February 8, 1982), p. 80.

[61] Robert A. Kerin and William L. Cron, "Assessing Trade Show Functions and Performance: An Exploratory Study," p. 92.

[62] Norman Hart, *Industrial Advertising and Publicity* (New York: John Wiley & Sons, 1978), p. 56.

Basic to the planning process is the estimation of total trade show expenditure and the allocation of funds to various trade show expenses. One way to develop a budget is to "build up" all the expenses to a total budget figure.[63] The primary cost elements include display construction, space rental, set-up and tear-down expenses, and maintenance; these items may make up 80 to 90 percent of the total budget. The overall budget will be affected by such things as the type of show, size of firm, the importance of other promotional tools, and competitive behaviors.

Thomas Bonoma recommends that, if available shows mainly attract *current* customers, a "full-base high-profile" show is most beneficial to companies whose promotion mix is weak for retaining customers but efficient at identifying prospects and selling to them.[64] On the other hand, shows that attract *potential* customers should be exploited by firms whose promotion is effective and efficient in keeping customers, but inefficient in getting them.

Budgeting for trade shows is more art than science. Trade shows are an inherently "sloppy" marketing problem to which sophisticated techniques or models will probably never be applied.[65] Nevertheless, business marketing managers must carefully evaluate each trade show and its associated expenses in terms of the likely sales and corporate image impacts. As with all other promotional vehicles, the planning and budgeting for trade shows must focus on specific objectives. Once these objectives have been determined, the rational approach will then identify the tasks that must be accomplished and the levels of expenditure required.

Catalogs

Because it is not possible for distributors to inventory all items, many manufacturers provide loose-leaf catalogs from which the distributor can order. In addition, many suppliers of products mail extensive catalogs describing their products and potential applications to likely industrial buyers. Catalogs are an efficient way for office- and computer-supply companies, for example, to generate the relatively small dollar sales typical of their business.[66] Catalogs can be a powerful promotional device; if properly distributed, they will be on the shelves of every important potential buyer in the industry.

Catalogs are a form of direct marketing. They generally contain enough information for the reader to make a purchase. In effect, a good catalog is like having a salesperson in the buyer's office at all times. In addition, the catalog will supplement personal selling by providing information between sales calls. Some business marketers

[63] Browning and Adams, "Trade Shows: An Effective Promotional Tool for the Small Industrial Firm," p. 35.

[64] Thomas V. Bonoma, "Get More Out of Your Trade Shows," p. 79.

[65] Ibid., p. 83.

[66] Benson Shapiro and John Wyman, "New Ways to Reach Your Customers," p. 107.

find that catalogs may in fact substitute for a salesperson or a rep in peripheral market areas.

If the supplier distributes the catalog, appropriate mailing lists must be developed, and catalog mailing lists must be continually updated. Important potential buyers may be missed if efforts are not made to add new companies to the list. A business marketer can delegate the catalog distribution function to a firm specializing in such activities. Distributing companies such as Sweets may collect catalogs from a number of firms, bind them together, and distribute them. Users find that the compendium of catalogs reduces search time, and the advertiser is assured of greater life and greater use of its section of the catalog file.

Trade Advertising

Trade advertising refers to a supplier's promotional efforts that are directed at intermediaries. The focus is on communicating product benefits, but trade promotion stresses the profits associated with carrying the manufacturer's line. In addition, promotional pieces are made available to distributors and reps so that they can associate their name with the manufacturer in a local advertising campaign. Suppliers often supply dealer aids such as displays or sales kits to intermediaries in order to enhance their effectiveness. The quality of promotion support provided to distributors can be important when solidifying an effective channel relationship. Note the Hewlett-Packard advertisement in Figure 16.8, directed at dealers, which explains Hewlett-Packard's major television campaign and how it should generate sales for dealers. In addition, it tells dealers they can join a co-op TV campaign that is focused on their individual store.

SUMMARY

Because of the nature of the business-to-business buying process, personal selling is the primary technique for creating sales; advertising supports and supplements personal selling. Yet advertising does perform some tasks that personal selling simply cannot perform. Advertising is able to reach buying influentials that sales personnel cannot.

Advertising supports personal selling by making the company and product known to potential buyers. The result is greater overall selling success. Effective advertising makes the entire marketing strategy more efficient, often lowering total marketing and selling costs. Finally, advertising can provide information and company or product awareness more efficiently than personal selling.

Managing the advertising program begins with the determination of advertising objectives, which must be written and which must be directed to a specific audience. Once objectives are specified, funds must be allocated to advertising efforts. Rules of thumb, though common, are not the ideal methods for specifying advertising budgets. The task method, used with business guidelines established by the ADVISOR studies, is more effective.

FIGURE 16.8   **A Hewlett-Packard Advertisement Directed at Dealers**

Soon we'll be putting spots before your eyes.

The best kind of spots.

This fall, Hewlett-Packard LaserJet printers will be more visible than ever. Because we're adding television to our popular dalmatian print campaign.

The hard-to-miss TV spots, featuring the LaserJet line, do a great job of communicating HP's famous quality and leadership in laser printing. They're sure to generate a lot of interest. Traffic. And sales.

The commercials will be backed by an aggressive television schedule. But that's just the start. Authorized HP dealers will have the opportunity to capitalize on this national exposure with HP's co-op TV ads based on the same concept. You'll be provided with two 30-second commercials that can easily be tailored for your store. Of course, we'll still be running LaserJet dalmatian ads in newspapers and magazines.

You'll be getting more information in your September HP

In Touch Update mailing. If you want all the details, talk to your local Hewlett-Packard sales or marketing communications representative.

Watch for our exciting new spots. And get ready for a busy fall. HP is out to put LaserJets in front of everyone.

© 1990 Hewlett-Packard Company. PE12035

Source: Courtesy of Hewlett-Packard Company.

Advertising messages are created with the understanding that the potential buyer's perceptual process will influence receptivity to the message. The most effective appeal is one that projects product benefits sought by the targeted buying influential.

Advertising media are selected on the basis of their circulation; that is, how well their audience matches the desired audience of buying influentials. Direct mail places advertisements in the hands of precisely defined audiences. Finally, advertising effectiveness must be evaluated against the communication objectives established for the advertising campaign. Readership, recognition, awareness, attitudes, and intention to buy are typical measures of business-to-business advertising performance.

A variety of supplementary promotional tools is available. Trade shows are an effective way to reach large audiences with a single presentation, but funds must be allocated carefully. Catalogs may also lead to direct sales if effectively designed and distributed. Trade advertising emphasizes profitability to intermediaries and provides devices for enhancing their effectiveness.

Discussion Questions

1. Although the bulk of the promotional budget of the business marketing firm is allocated to personal selling, advertising can play an important role in business marketing strategy. Explain.

2. The Hamilton Compressor Company increased advertising expenditures 15 percent in the Chicago market last year, and sales increased 4 percent. Upon seeing the results, Mr. White, the president, turns to you and asks, "Was that increase in advertising worth it?" Outline your reply. (Feel free to include questions that you would ask Mr. White.)

3. Breck Machine Tool would like you to develop a series of ads for a new industrial product. Upon request, Breck's marketing research department will provide you with any data that they have concerning the new product and the market. Outline the approach that you would follow in selecting media and developing messages for the campaign. Specify the types of data that you would draw on to improve the quality of your decisions.

4. Outline how you would evaluate the effectiveness and efficiency of a business firm's advertising function. They would like you to center on budgeting practices and performance results.

5. Explain how a message presented in an industrial advertisement may be favorably evaluated by the production manager, unfavorably evaluated by the purchasing manager, and fail even to trigger the attention of the quality control engineer.

6. Given the rapid rise in the cost of making industrial sales calls, should the industrial marketer attempt to substitute direct mail advertising for personal selling whenever possible? Support your position.

7. What is the role of trade advertising in the industrial marketer's promotional program?

8. It is argued that business advertising is not expected to precipitate sales directly. If business advertising does not persuade organizational buyers to buy brand A versus brand B, what does it do, and how can we measure its impact against expenditures on other marketing strategy elements?

CHAPTER 17

Business Marketing Communications: Managing the Personal Selling Function

Business marketing communications consist of advertising, sales promotion, and personal selling. As explored in the last chapter, advertising and related sales promotion tools supplement and reinforce personal selling. Personal selling is the most important demand-stimulating force in the business marketer's promotional mix. Through the sales force, the marketer links the firm's total product and service offering to the needs of organizational customers.

After reading this chapter, you will understand:

1. the role of personal selling in business marketing strategy.

2. the importance of viewing business marketing management as a buyer–seller interaction process.

3. the nature of the industrial sales management function.

4. the selected managerial tools that can be applied to major sales force decision areas.

GEORGE M. C. Fisher, president and CEO of Motorola, Inc., aptly describes the strategic role that the salesperson assumes in the business market:

Members of our sales force are surrogates for customers. They should be able to reach back into Motorola and pull out technologists and other people that they need to solve

489

problems and anticipate customer needs. We want to put the salesperson at the top of the organization. The rest of us then serve the salesperson. If we could get that mentality ingrained throughout Motorola . . . , I think we could move a long way toward where we need to be.[1]

Personal selling is dominant in business markets because the number of potential customers is relatively small, compared to consumer markets, and the dollar purchases are large. The importance of personal selling in the marketing mix depends on such factors as the nature and composition of the market, the nature of the product line, and the company's objectives and financial capabilities. Business marketers have many potential links to the market. Some may rely on manufacturers' representatives and distributors, others rely exclusively on a direct sales force. Similarly, each firm must determine the relative importance of the various components of the promotional mix—advertising versus sales promotion versus personal selling.

Across all industries, the cost of an industrial sales call averages $225.[2] Computer firms report much higher costs ($453 per sales call) while chemical producers experience much lower ones ($155 per sales call).[3] Of course, these figures vary, depending upon a host of company, product, and market conditions. They do point up, however, that significant resources are invested in personal selling in the business market. To maximize effectiveness and efficiency, the personal selling function must be carefully managed and integrated into the firm's marketing mix.

This chapter first considers how relevant aspects of organizational buying behavior (Chapters 3 and 4) are related to the personal selling process. The chapter then turns to sales force management and the need for defining personal selling objectives, structuring the sales organization, allocating the sales force, and evaluating and controlling sales force operations.

FOUNDATIONS OF PERSONAL SELLING: AN ORGANIZATIONAL CUSTOMER FOCUS

Personal selling is the means through which business marketing strategy is executed. Once the marketer defines target market segments on the basis of organizational characteristics (macrolevel) or the characteristics of decision-making units (microlevel), the sales force is deployed to meet the needs of these segments. The salesperson augments the total product offering and serves as a representative for both seller and buyer. The image, reputation, and need-satisfying ability of the seller firm is

---

[1] Bernard Avishai and William Taylor, "Customers Drive a Technology-Driven Company: An Interview with George Fisher," *Harvard Business Review*, 67 (November–December 1989), pp. 107–114.

[2] William A. O'Connell and William Keenan, Jr., "The Shape of Things to Come," *Sales & Marketing Management* (January 1990), p. 37.

[3] "Surprise! Some Sales Costs Decline," *Sales & Marketing Management* (November 1986), p. 24. For a comprehensive discussion of all aspects of personal selling, see Donald W. Jackson, Jr., William H. Cunningham, and Isabella C. M. Cunningham, *Selling: The Personal Force in Marketing* (New York: John Wiley & Sons, Inc., 1988).

conveyed, to an important degree, by the sales force. By helping procurement decision makers to define requirements and match the firm's product or service to requirements, the salesperson is offering not just a physical product but also ideas, recommendations, technical assistance, experience, confidence, and friendship. A large toy manufacturer, for example, evaluates suppliers on the basis of product quality, delivery reliability, price, *and* the value of ideas and suggestions provided by the sales personnel. This buying organization, in fact, openly solicits ideas, and evaluates suppliers formally on the number and quality of these recommendations.

As a representative for the buyer, the salesperson often articulates the specific needs of a customer to R&D or production personnel in the industrial firm. Product specifications, delivery, and technical service are often negotiated through the salesperson. The salesperson serves as an uncertainty absorption point, reducing conflict in the buyer–seller relationship. John Knopp, a regional sales manager at Hewlett-Packard, identifies this trait in high-performing salespersons: "They know how to get special things done for the customer inside or outside the system. When something has to be done outside of normal policies and practices, they find a way to get it done smoothly."[4]

Organizational Buying Behavior

Successful personal selling relies heavily on a recognition of the unique requirements of each organizational customer. Industrial products may have numerous applications; organizational buyers have varying levels of experience and information in purchasing certain products. A sensitivity to how buying organizations vary, coupled with a knowledge of organizational buying behavior, is the foundation for successful personal selling.

A salesperson can benefit by examining a potential buyer organization from several perspectives. First, how would the organization view this specific buying situation—new-task, modified rebuy, or straight rebuy? As emphasized in Chapter 3, each buying situation calls for a unique personal selling strategy—the exact form depending on whether the marketer is an "in" or an "out" supplier. Second, what are the environmental, organizational, group, and individual influences on the organizational buying process? (See Figure 17.1.)

Among the considerations that will form the personal selling task are the following:[5]

1. *Environmental factor identification.* How do business conditions (e.g., growth, inflation) or political and legal trends (e.g., governmental regulation) affect the industry within which this firm operates?

[4] Thayer C. Taylor, "Anatomy of a Star Salesperson," *Sales & Marketing Management* (May 1986), pp. 49–51.

[5] Richard E. Plank and William A. Dempsey, "A Framework for Personal Selling to Organizations," *Industrial Marketing Management,* 9 (April 1980), pp. 143–149; see also Barton A. Weitz, Harish Sujan, and Mita Sujan, "Knowledge, Motivation, and Adaptive Behavior: A Framework for Improving Selling Effectiveness," *Journal of Marketing,* 50 (October 1986), pp. 174–191; and David M. Szymanski, "Determinants of Selling Effectiveness: The Importance of Declarative Knowledge to the Personal Selling Concept," *Journal of Marketing,* 52 (January 1988), pp. 64–77.

FIGURE 17.1   **Identifying Key Features of the Organizational Buying Environment**

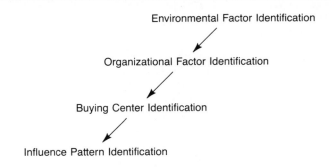

2. *Organizational factor identification.* Is procurement in this buying organization centralized or decentralized? To what extent does the procurement department use the computer in buying and in selecting and evaluating suppliers?

3. *Buying center identification.* Which organization members are included in the buying center?

4. *Influence pattern identification.* Which buying center members exert the most power in the buying decision? What are the selection criteria of each?

Knowledge of the special competitive challenges that the buying firm faces, how the proposed product/service offering will be applied, how it will influence the cost structure and performance of various departments—these are the insights that allow the marketer to focus personal selling strategy sharply. Empathy with the buyer is the core of a mutually beneficial buyer–seller relationship.

Relationship Marketing

The trend toward close relationships, or even strategic partnerships, between manufacturers and their suppliers is accelerating in many sectors of the business market. Several forces, highlighted throughout this volume, support the movement toward closer buyer–seller relationships and away from distant, or even adversarial, relations: rising global competition, the quest for improved quality, rapidly changing technology, and the increased adoption of a just-in-time operations philosophy.[6] Assuming a key role in the relationship marketing program of the firm (see Chapter 3) is the industrial salesperson.

---

[6] See, for example, Charles O'Neal and Kate Bertrand, *Developing a Winning J.I.T. Marketing Strategy* (Englewood Cliffs, NJ: Prentice-Hall, Inc., 1991).

Relationship Quality

By occupying a position close to the customer, the industrial salesperson is often best suited to perform the role of "relationship manager." For many complex purchase decisions, industrial buyers face considerable uncertainty. From the customer's perspective, relationship quality is achieved through the salesperson's ability to reduce this uncertainty. **Relationship quality** is composed of at least two dimensions: (1) trust in the salesperson and (2) satisfaction with the salesperson.[7] Confronting the uncertainty often present in complex industrial exchange settings, relationship quality contributes to a lasting bond by offering assurance that the salesperson will continue to meet the customer's expectations (satisfaction), and not knowingly distort information or otherwise damage the customer's interests (trust). (See Figure 17.2.) "The continuity of interaction that relationship quality provides then creates ongoing opportunities for the seller to identify the customer's unmet needs and propose new business."[8]

MANAGING THE SALES FORCE

Effective management of the industrial sales force is fundamental to the firm's success. Sales management is the planning, organizing, directing, and controlling of personal selling efforts.[9] Figure 17.3 positions sales management activities within the context of the marketing strategy and the environment.

Sales force decisions are tempered by overall marketing objectives and must be integrated with the other elements of the marketing mix. Forecasts of the expected sales response guide the firm in determining the total selling effort required (sales force size) and in organizing and allocating the sales force (perhaps to sales territories). The techniques for estimating market potential and for forecasting sales (discussed in Part III—Assessing Market Opportunities) are particularly valuable in sales planning. Sales management also involves the ongoing activities of selecting, training, deploying, supervising, and motivating sales personnel. Finally, sales operations must be monitored to identify problem areas and to assess the efficiency, effectiveness, and profitability of personal selling units.

This section will consider (1) the role of personal selling in the marketing program, (2) methods for organizing the sales force, (3) the requirements for successful sales

---

[7] Lawrence A. Crosby, Kenneth R. Evans, and Deborah Cowles, "Relationship Quality in Services Selling: An Interpersonal Influence Perspective," *Journal of Marketing*, 54 (July 1990), pp. 68–81. See also Jon M. Hawes, Kenneth E. Mast, and John E. Swan, "Trust Earning Perceptions of Sellers and Buyers," *Journal of Personal Selling & Sales Management*, 9 (September 1989), pp. 1–8.

[8] Crosby, Evans, and Cowles, ibid., p. 76; for a discussion of specific strategies, see James C. Anderson and James A. Narus, "Partnering as a Focused Market Strategy," Working Paper, J. L. Kellogg Graduate School of Management, Northwestern University.

[9] A comprehensive treatment of all aspects of sales management is beyond the scope of this volume. For more extensive discussion, see Gilbert A. Churchill, Jr., Neil M. Ford, and Orville C. Walker, Jr., *Sales Force Management*, 2d ed. (Homewood, IL: Richard D. Irwin, Inc., 1985).

FIGURE 17.2   **A Relationship Marketing Theme in the Business-to-Business Market**

Source: Courtesy, Kodak Copy Products, Eastman Kodak Company.

force administration, and (4) models that can be employed in deploying the industrial sales force.

Defining the Role of Personal Selling in the Business Marketing Program

The specific role of personal selling in the marketing program varies by company and product/market conditions. The following scenarios show two different personal selling roles.

Kim Kelly, a sales representative for Honeywell, Inc., had been competing with the sales personnel of four other firms for a large computer account. He made numerous sales calls to different individuals in the buying organization over a three-year period. In fact, for the last three months as the firm neared a decision, he had worked nearly full time

FIGURE 17.3 **A View of Sales Management Activities within the Context of Marketing Strategy and Environment**

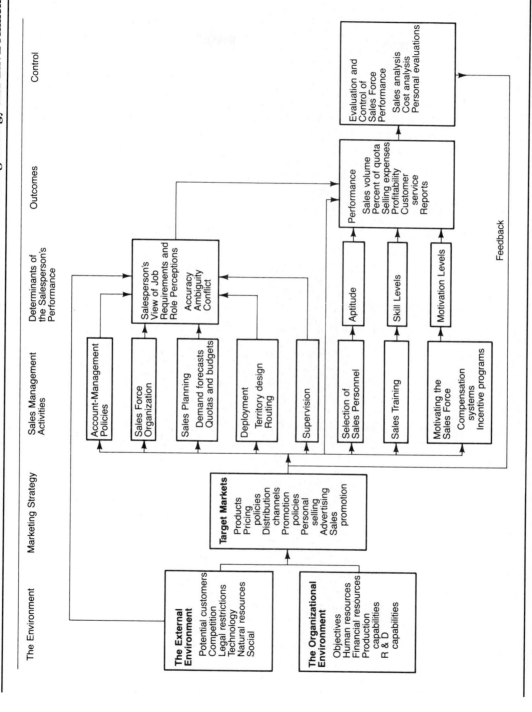

Source: Gilbert A. Churchill, Jr., Neil M. Ford, and Orville C. Walker, Jr., *Sales Force Management*, 2d ed. (Homewood, IL: Richard D. Irwin, 1985), p. 20. Reprinted by permission.

on this account. His diligence and follow-up culminated in an $8 million order on which Kim received an $80,000 commission.[10]

Although supported by advertising, sales promotion, and technical personnel, personal selling is the dominant demand-stimulating force in the communications mix. Kim Kelly's strategy is often referred to as a **push strategy**.

> Adam Hunter is the sales representative for a major manufacturer of industrial accessory equipment. He travels several states calling on industrial distributors who are authorized dealers for his company's product line. These distributors sell the equipment to industrial users. Adam begins his day by stopping at a nearby distributor to solicit an order to replenish inventory levels. Adam checks the distributor's inventory, prepares an order, discusses it with the buyer, and gets it approved and signed. The order is placed in the outgoing mail.
>
> After a 20-minute drive, Adam arrives at another distributor. He is informed that a shipment came in freight collect and should have been freight prepaid. Adam calls his traffic department and authorizes a credit memo for the amount of the shipping charges. With the problem resolved, Adam leaves.
>
> On the third distributor call, Adam learns that a recent bid was lost to a competitor. He gathers all the available information on the missed sale, writes a brief report, and mails it to his sales manager.[11]

Adam's activities go beyond demand stimulation to channel assistance, market intelligence, and strengthening buyer–seller relationships. Adam Hunter's more passive role in personal selling is referred to as a **pull strategy**.

The push strategy is more common in business marketing. Sales personnel may work primarily to stimulate demand while also providing a range of other customer services. Such services are often crucial to the buyer–seller relationship.

Emerging Industrial Selling Styles
Industrial selling is becoming increasingly professional, and selling styles reflect this increased professionalism:[12]

1. *Consultative selling.* The salesperson assumes the role of a consultant helping to improve the profitability of the client. The consultative salesperson, by becoming an expert on the client's business operations, providing analytical expertise, and solving problems, attempts to offer a level of value beyond that offered by competitors.

---

[10] "To Computer Salesmen, The 'Big-Ticket' Deal Is the One to Look For," *The Wall Street Journal* (January 22, 1974), pp. 1, 35.

[11] Noel B. Zabriskie and John Browning, "Measuring Industrial Salespeople's Short-Term Productivity," *Industrial Marketing Management*, 8 (April 1979), pp. 168–169. For a comprehensive discussion of push and pull strategies, see Gary L. Frazier and John O. Summers, "Push and Pull Strategies in Industrial Markets: A Normative Framework," in Gary L. Frazier and Jagdish Sheth, eds., *Contemporary Views on Marketing Practice* (Lexington, Mass.: Lexington Books, 1987).

[12] Thomas R. Wotruba, "The Changing Character of Industrial Selling," *European Journal of Marketing*, 14 (1980), pp. 293–302.

THE GLOBAL MARKETPLACE
International Sales Negotiations

A negotiation style that works for a marketing manager in Chicago may be way off the mark in dealing with potential customers in Brazil or Japan. International salespersons have to adjust their approaches to establishing rapport, information exchange, persuasion, and concession making if they are to be effective in dealing with their clients and partners.

- *Traditions and customs.* Status relations and business procedures should be carefully examined with the assistance of local representatives. In highly structured societies, such as Korea, great respect is paid to age and position.

- *Patience.* Americans often start relatively close to what they consider a fair price in their negotiations, whereas Chinese managers may begin with unreasonable demands. In many countries, such as the Soviet Union and the People's Republic of China, negotiations may take three times as long as they do in Western Europe. Displaying impatience in countries such as Brazil or Thailand may prolong, rather than hasten, negotiations.

- *Persistence.* In some markets, negotiations are seen as a means of forming long-term relationships, not as an event with winners and losers. Insisting on an outcome may be viewed as a threat by negotiating partners abroad.

- *The meaning of agreements.* In many markets, legal contracts are not required. In fact, reference to legal counsel may signal that the relationship is in trouble.

Source: Michael R. Czinkota and Ilkka A. Ronkainen, *International Marketing*, 2nd ed. (Hinsdale, IL: The Dryden Press, 1990), pp. 324–326; and John L. Graham and Roy A. Herberger, Jr., "Negotiations Abroad—Don't Shoot from the Hip," *Harvard Business Review*, 61 (July–August 1983), pp. 160–168.

2. *Negotiative selling.* The negotiation style is designed to maximize the benefits of a transaction for both the buyer and the seller. The goal is to form a salesperson–customer partnership with common objectives, mutually beneficial strategies, and a common defense against others outside the partnership.

3. *Systems selling.* The systems style has evolved to meet the rising sophistication and increased materials management concerns of organizational buyers. The salesperson for a business forms supplier might begin by defining a prospect's record and information needs and then prescribe a package of machines and forms, offer a recommended layout of facilities, establish a training program for employees, and finally design operating procedures and maintenance arrangements.[13]

4. *Team selling.* The industrial seller assembles a team of personnel with functional expertise that matches the specialized knowledge of key buying influentials within the customer firm. The mode of operation adopted by the selling team varies by

[13] Ibid.; see also W. J. Hannaford, "Systems Selling: Problems and Benefits for Buyers and Sellers," *Industrial Marketing Management*, 5 (1976), pp. 139–145.

selling situation. On occasion, the entire sales team will take part in the presentation to the buying center, whereas in other cases, the sales team is contacted at various points in the selling process when the salesperson requires technical expertise.[14]

Telemarketing.

The rising sophistication of telecommunications equipment and services has transformed telephone selling into telemarketing. Over 60 percent of industrial firms now use the telephone for selling, for lead generation, or for both.[15] The distinction between telephone selling and telemarketing centers on the use of trained personnel and meticulous quality control procedures. Only 30 percent of the firms sampled met these requirements.

Since the average cost of an industrial sales call exceeds $200, telephone sales calls at $10 to $20 each provide an economical substitute for personal visits to small accounts. To illustrate, the customers for 3M's Medical-Surgical Division are the more than 6,000 hospitals in the United States.[16] These hospitals are divided into three groups—A, B, and C—based on potential sales volume. Nearly half of the hospitals fall into the low-volume (C) group. 3M developed a successful telephone sales program to serve this customer group. The program has significantly reduced selling costs and improved sales penetration, and it allows field salespersons to concentrate on the high-volume A and B hospitals.

Telemarketing can also be used to supplement personal sales calls: "Often the cost of the required call frequency is greater than the sales volume justifies and, in these cases, telephone calls can supplement personal visits. The visits might be made two to four times per year and the telephone calls eight to ten times per year for a total frequency of one per month—but at a cost substantially lower than twelve visits."[17]

Although many industrial firms have used inside salespeople for years to handle routine transactions, creative applications of telemarketing are an emerging trend.

Organizing the Personal Selling Effort

How should the sales force be organized? The appropriate form depends on many factors, including the nature and length of the product line, the role of intermediaries in the marketing program, the diversity of the market segments served, the nature of the buying behavior in each market segment, and the structure of competitive selling.

---

[14] Frank V. Cespedes, Stephen X. Doyle, and Robert J. Freedman, "Teamwork for Today's Selling," *Harvard Business Review*, 67 (March–April 1989), pp. 44–48.

[15] Murray Roman and Bob Donath, "Exclusive First-Ever Survey: What's Really Happening in Business/Industrial Telemarketing?" *Business Marketing*, 68 (April 1983), pp. 83–90; see also William C. Moncrief, Shannon H. Shipp, Charles W. Lamb, Jr., and David W. Cravens, "Examining the Roles of Telemarketing in Selling Strategy," *Journal of Personal Selling & Sales Management*, 9 (Fall 1989), pp. 1–12.

[16] Howard Sutton, *Rethinking the Company's Selling and Distribution Channels* (New York: The Conference Board, 1986), pp. 23–25.

[17] Benson P. Shapiro and John Wyman, "New Ways to Reach Your Customers," *Harvard Business Review*, 59 (July–August 1981), p. 106.

The size and financial strength of the manufacturer often dictate, to an important degree, the feasibility of particular organizational forms. The business marketer can organize the sales force by geography, product, or market. Large industrial enterprises that market diverse product lines may employ all three at various points throughout the organizational structure.

Geographical Organization

The most common form of sales organization in business marketing is geographical. Each salesperson sells all of the firm's products in a defined geographical area. By reducing travel distance and time between customers, this method usually minimizes costs. Likewise, sales personnel know exactly which customers and prospects fall within their area of responsibility.

The major disadvantage of the geographical sales organization is that each salesperson must be able to perform all of the selling tasks for all of the firm's products and for all customers in a particular territory. If the products have diverse applications, this can be very difficult. A second disadvantage is that the salesperson has substantial flexibility in choosing which products and customers to emphasize. Sales personnel may emphasize those products and end-use applications with which they are most familiar. Of course, this problem can be remedied through training and through capable first-line supervision. Because the salesperson is crucial in implementing the firm's segmentation strategy, careful coordination and control are required to align personal selling effort with marketing objectives.

Product Organization

A product-oriented sales organization is one in which salespersons specialize in relatively narrow components of the total product line. This is especially appropriate when the product line is large, diverse, or technically complex and when a salesperson needs a high degree of application knowledge in order to meet customer needs. Furthermore, various products often elicit various patterns of buying behavior. The salesperson concentrating on a particular product becomes more adept at identifying and communicating with members of buying centers.

A prime benefit of this approach is that it allows the sales force to develop a level of product knowledge that enhances the value of the firm's total offering to customers. The product-oriented sales organization may also facilitate the identification of new market segments.

One drawback is the cost of developing and deploying a specialized sales force. A product must have the potential for generating a level of sales and profit that justifies individual selling attention. Thus, a "critical mass" of demand is required to offset the costs. In turn, several salespersons may be required to meet the diverse product requirements of a single customer. To reduce selling costs and improve productivity, Xerox has launched an ambitious program to convert product specialists into general line specialists.[18] The program is designed, ultimately, to make all 4,000 Xerox salespersons

---

[18] "Xerox's Makeover," *Sales & Marketing Management* (June 1987), p. 68.

knowledgeable about all the firm's products and account strategies. Often, as customers learn to use technology, they outgrow the need for product specialists and prefer working with a single salesperson for all products.

Market-Centered Organization

The business marketer may prefer to organize personal selling effort by customer type. IBM, for example, is realigning its 28,000 salespersons along these lines. Sales offices have been repositioned from a geographical to an industry orientation with IBM salespersons centering on specific vertical markets such as banking or retailing.[19]

By learning the specific requirements of a particular industry or customer type, the salesperson is better prepared to identify and respond to buying influentials. Also, key market segments become more accessible, thus providing the opportunity for differentiated personal selling strategies. The market segments must, of course, be sufficiently large to warrant specialized treatment.

Organizing to Serve National Accounts

To serve large and important customers, an increasing number of business marketers are establishing a national accounts program. The activities of several functional areas in the selling firm, such as design engineering, manufacturing, and logistics, can be carefully integrated to meet special customer needs.

National account management programs have been established by such corporations as Olin Corporation, AT&T, Dow Chemical, Union Carbide, Digital Equipment, and Westinghouse. Why? The concentration of the business market, the trend toward centralized procurement, the rising importance of materials management and the ensuing need for close buyer–seller coordination of inventory and logistical support, the increasing complexity of industrial products—these are among the forces that encourage the development of national account management programs.[20]

National Account Management[21]

As illustrated in Figure 17.4, a distinction can be made between major accounts and national accounts. A **major account** represents a significant amount of potential business. Major accounts are often served through multilevel selling with participation by salespersons, sales and marketing managers, and general managers from the selling organization. **National accounts** are both large and complex, requiring an even more elaborate selling process.

---

[19] "IBM's Travails Test Its Sales Force," *Sales & Marketing Management* (June 1987), p. 60.

[20] Benson P. Shapiro and Rowland T. Moriarty, *National Account Management: Emerging Insights*, Report No. 82-100 (Cambridge, Mass.: Marketing Science Institute, 1982).

[21] Ibid., this section is largely based on Shapiro and Moriarty.

FIGURE 17.4   **Traditional Sales, Major Accounts, and National Accounts**

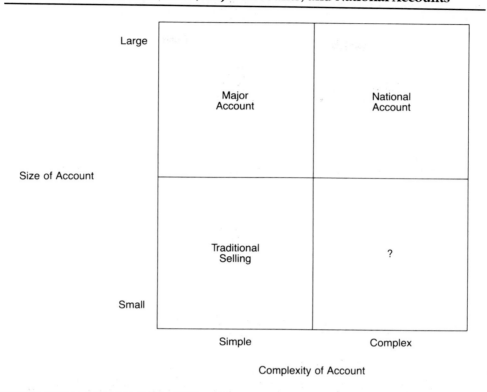

Source: Benson P. Shapiro and Rowland T. Moriarty, *National Account Management: Emerging Insights* (Cambridge, Mass.: Marketing Science Institute, 1982), p. 6. Used with permission.

For example, Pitney Bowes' U.S. Business System Division, a producer of mailing, shipping, and copying products, serves more than one million business market customers.[22] The sales force has the following configuration:

- 50 national account managers serve its 400 largest customers.
- 100 major account managers reach the 1,500 multilocation customers who have centralized procurement.
- 3,500 area sales representatives cover all of its other existing and potential customers (approximately one million).

The complexity that requires a national accounts response can involve the following three customer dimensions:

---

[22] Sutton, *Rethinking the Company's Selling and Distribution Channels*, pp. 10–11.

- Geographical dispersion of customer buying points
- Functional dispersion of customer buying influences—the involvement of two or more functional units in the purchasing process (e.g., procurement, engineering, manufacturing, etc.)
- Operating unit dispersion of customer purchasing activities (e.g., several divisions within a company that operate with some degree of autonomy)

National account management provides a mechanism for responding to these three dimensions of customer complexity. For example, rather than reaching the geographically dispersed plants of the Mead Corporation through geographically dispersed sales offices, a national account management program might be devised to deal with Mead centrally. Such special attention would not be warranted for complex accounts that represent only limited potential business (thus the question mark in Figure 17.4).

Characteristics of National Account Programs

National account management programs vary depending on the company and the industry environment, but they do have some features in common:[23]

1. National accounts are large, relative to other accounts served by the company, sometimes generating more than $50 million in sales revenue each.
2. The national account manager's responsibility often spans multiple divisions in the selling company.
3. The national account manager's team frequently includes support and operations personnel.
4. The selling activities of the national account manager span several functional areas in the buying company and may involve highly conceptual, financially oriented, systems sales.

How national account programs are structured and organized can vary by firm. For example, in some industrial firms the national account manager has line authority over a large, dispersed sales and support team, whereas in others, these managers simply coordinate sales and support personnel. There can be a wide range in the number and size of accounts for which the manager is responsible. Although the organizational structure can vary by company, the common objective of national account management programs is "to provide incremental profits from large or potentially large complex accounts by being the preferred or sole supplier. To accomplish this goal, a supplier seeks to establish, over an extended period of time, an 'institutional' relationship, which cuts across multiple levels, functions, and operating units in both the buying and selling organization."[24]

---

[23] Shapiro and Wyman, "New Ways to Reach Your Customers," pp. 103–110.

[24] Shapiro and Moriarty, *National Account Management*, p. 8.

National Account Success

Research suggests that successful national account units enjoy senior management support; have well-defined objectives, assignments, and implementation procedures; and are staffed by experienced individuals who have a solid grasp of the resources and capabilities of the entire company.[25] Successful national account programs also adopt a strong relationship marketing perspective and consistently demonstrate their ability to meet the customer's immediate and future needs. "Customers making long-term commitments care about longer-term issues: a vendor's general technological capabilities and direction, its financial ability to survive, the staying power of a particular technology, and so on."[26] Xerox ties the compensation plan for its 250 national account managers directly to customer satisfaction. National accounts are regularly queried concerning service, product quality, the salesperson's professionalism and attentiveness, and Xerox's administrative support.[27]

Sales Administration

Successful administration of the sales force involves recruiting and selecting salespersons and training, motivating, supervising, evaluating, and controlling the sales force. The industrial firm should foster an organizational climate that encourages the development of a successful sales force.

Recruitment and Selection of Salespersons

Today more emphasis is being placed on the recruiting process and on reducing salesperson turnover because "today's salesperson must have many talents: knowledge of business, current affairs, and organizational politics; social graces to mingle with company presidents and workers on the shop floor; patience, persistence, and so forth."[28]

The recruiting process presents numerous trade-offs for the business marketer. Should experienced salespersons be sought or should inexperienced individuals be hired and trained by the company? The answer is situation-specific; it varies with the size of the firm, the nature of the selling task, the firm's training capability, and its market experience. Smaller firms often reduce training costs by hiring experienced and more expensive salespersons. In contrast, large organizations with a more complete training function can hire less experienced personnel and support them with a carefully developed training program.

---

[25] Linda Cardillo Platzer, *Managing National Accounts* (New York: The Conference Board, 1984), pp. 13–19.

[26] Barbara Bund Jackson, *Winning and Keeping Industrial Customers* (Lexington, Mass.: Lexington Books, 1985), p. 105.

[27] "Xerox's Makeover," p. 68.

[28] Ben M. Enis and Lawrence B. Chonko, "A Review of Personal Selling: Implications for Managers and Researchers," in Gerald Zaltman and Thomas V. Bonoma, eds., *Review of Marketing 1978* (Chicago: American Marketing Association, 1978), p. 291.

A second trade-off is the quantity-versus-quality question.[29] Often, sales managers screen as many recruits as possible when selecting new salespersons. However, this can overload the selection process, thus hampering the firm's ability to identify quality candidates. Recruiting, like selling, is an exchange process between two parties. A poorly organized recruiting effort that lacks closure leaves candidates with a negative impression. A well-organized recruiting effort ensures that candidates fitting the position requirements are given the proper level of attention in the screening process. Thus, procedures must be established to ensure that inappropriate candidates are screened out early, so that the pool of candidates is reduced to a manageable size.[30]

Responsibility for recruiting and selecting salespersons may lie with the first-line supervisor, who often receives assistance from an immediate superior, or with the personnel department or with other executives at the headquarters level. The latter group tends to be more involved when the sales force is viewed as the training ground for marketing or general managers.

Training

To prepare new industrial salespersons adequately, the training program must be carefully designed. Periodic training is required to sharpen the skills of experienced salespersons, especially when the firm's environment is changing rapidly. Changes in business marketing strategy (e.g., new products, new market segments) require corresponding changes in personal selling styles. The salesperson needs a wealth of knowledge about the company, the product line, customer segments, competition, organizational buying behavior, and effective communication skills. All these must be part of industrial sales training programs.

Effective training builds confidence and motivation in the salesperson, thereby increasing the probability of successful performance. In turn, training helps the business marketer by keeping personal selling in line with marketing program objectives. A successful training effort can reduce the costs of recruiting; many industrial firms have found that salesperson turnover declines as training improves. Clearly, a salesperson who is inadequately prepared to meet the demands of selling can quickly become discouraged, frustrated, and envious of friends who chose other career options. Much of this anxiety—which is especially prevalent in the early stages of many careers—can be removed by effective training and capable first-line supervision.[31]

---

[29] Benson P. Shapiro, *Sales Management: Formulation and Implementation* (New York: McGraw-Hill Book Company, Inc., 1977), p. 457.

[30] Wesley J. Johnston and Martha C. Cooper, "Industrial Sales Force Selection: Current Knowledge and Needed Research," *Journal of Personal Selling and Sales Management*, 1 (Spring/Summer 1981), pp. 49–55.

[31] For a discussion of salesperson turnover, see George H. Lucas, Jr., A. Parasuraman, Robert A. Davis, and Ben M. Enis, "An Empirical Study of Salesforce Turnover," *Journal of Marketing*, 51 (July 1987), pp. 34–59; and Charles A. Futrell and A. Parasuraman, "The Relationship of Satisfaction and Performance to Salesforce Turnover," *Journal of Marketing*, 48 (Fall 1984), pp. 33–40.

FIGURE 17.5   **Determinants of a Salesperson's Performance**

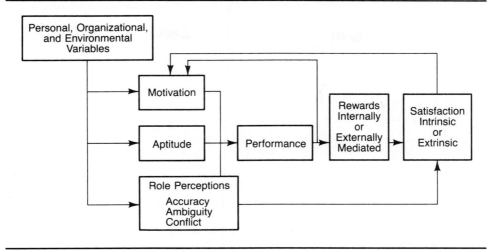

Source: Orville C. Walker, Jr., Gilbert A. Churchill, Jr., and Neil M. Ford, "Motivation and Performance in Industrial Selling: Present Knowledge and Needed Research," *Journal of Marketing Research*, 14 (May 1977), p. 158. Reprinted by permission of the American Marketing Association.

Supervision and Motivation

The sales force must be directed in a way that is consistent with the company's policies and marketing objectives. Critical supervisory tasks are continued training, counseling, assistance (e.g., time planning), and activities that help sales personnel plan and execute their work. Supervision also sets sales performance standards, fulfills company policy, and integrates the sales force with higher organizational levels.

Motivation can be viewed as the amount of effort the salesperson "desires to expend on each of the activities or tasks associated with his(her) job, such as calling on potential new accounts, planning sales presentations, and filling out reports."[32] The model presented in Figure 17.5 hypothesizes that a salesperson's job performance is a function of three factors: (1) level of motivation, (2) aptitude or ability, and (3) perceptions about how his or her role should be performed. Each is influenced by personal variables (e.g., personality), organizational variables (e.g., training programs), and environmental variables (e.g., economic conditions). Sales managers can influence some of the personal and organizational variables through selection, training, and supervision.

Motivation to perform is thought to be related strongly to (1) the individual's perceptions of the types and amounts of rewards that will accrue from various degrees

---

[32] Orville C. Walker, Jr., Gilbert A. Churchill, Jr., and Neil M. Ford, "Motivation and Performance in Industrial Selling: Present Knowledge and Needed Research," *Journal of Marketing Research*, 14 (May 1977), pp. 156–168.

of job performance and (2) the value the salesperson places on these rewards. For a given level of performance, two types of rewards might be offered:

1. *Internally mediated rewards.* The salesperson attains rewards on a personal basis, such as feelings of accomplishment or self-worth.

2. *Externally mediated rewards.* Rewards are controlled and offered by managers or customers, such as financial incentives, pay, or recognition.

The rewards strongly influence salesperson satisfaction with the job and the work environment, which is also influenced by the individual's role perceptions. Job satisfaction is theorized to decline if the salesperson's perception of the role is (1) *inaccurate* in terms of the expectations of superiors, (2) characterized by *conflicting* demands among role partners (company and customer) that the salesperson cannot possibly resolve, or (3) surrounded by *uncertainty* due to a lack of information about the expectations and evaluation criteria of superiors and customers.[33]

Organizational Climate and Job Satisfaction[34]

Gilbert Churchill, Jr., Neil Ford, and Orville Walker, Jr., who contributed the model presented in Figure 17.5, also provide empirical support for some propositions that flow from the model. In examining job satisfaction in a cross section of industrial salespersons, the authors found that role ambiguity and role conflict have a detrimental influence on job satisfaction. Salespersons are likely to experience anxiety and dissatisfaction when they are uncertain about the expectations of role partners or when they feel that role partners (e.g., customers, superiors) are making demands that are incompatible and impossible to satisfy.

An effective approach for reducing role ambiguity among new salespeople is a program of training and socialization that offers sufficient information about role expectations and minimizes potential confusion concerning performance requirements. A socialization program that provides newly hired salespersons with a realistic picture of their job will strengthen their organizational commitment.[35]

Job Satisfaction: Managerial Implications

Salespersons tend to have a higher level of job satisfaction when (1) they perceive that their first-line supervisor closely directs and monitors their activities, (2) management provides them with the assistance and support needed to meet unusual and nonroutine

---

[33] Ibid.

[34] This section is based on Gilbert A. Churchill, Jr., Neil M. Ford, and Orville C. Walker, Jr., "Organizational Climate and Job Satisfaction in the Salesforce," *Journal of Marketing Research*, 13 (November 1976), pp. 323–332. For related discussions, see R. Kenneth Teas and James C. McElroy, "Causal Attributions and Expectancy Estimates: A Framework for Understanding the Dynamics of Salesforce Motivation," *Journal of Marketing*, 50 (January 1986), pp. 75–86; William L. Cron, Alan J. Dubinsky, and Ronald E. Michaels, "The Influence of Career Stages on Components of Salesperson Motivation," *Journal of Marketing*, 52 (January 1988), pp. 78–92; and Jeffrey K. Sager, Charles M. Futrell, and Rajan Varadarajan, "Exploring Salesperson Turnover: A Causal Model," *Journal of Business Research*, 18 (June 1989), pp. 303–326.

[35] Mark W. Johnston, A. Parasuraman, Charles M. Futrell, and William C. Black, "A Longitudinal Assessment of the Impact of Selected Organizational Influences on Salespeople's Organizational Commitment During Early Employment," *Journal of Marketing Research*, 27 (August 1990), pp. 333–343.

problems, and (3) they perceive themselves to have an active part in determining company policies and standards that affect them. Job satisfaction also appears to be related more to the substance of the contact between sales managers and salespersons than to the frequency of contact. Also, salespersons appear to be able to accept direction from a number of departments in the organization without a significant negative impact on job satisfaction; unity of command does not appear to be a prerequisite for high morale.

Performance and individual differences in achievement motivation, self-esteem, and verbal intelligence may also affect job satisfaction. Richard Bagozzi notes: "Salespeople tend to be more satisfied as they perform better, but the relationship is particularly sensitive to the level of motivation and positive self-image of the person. Although management may have no direct control over the performance achieved by salespeople, they can influence the level of motivation and self-esteem through effective incentive and sensitive supervisor–employee programs and thereby indirectly affect both performance and job satisfaction."[36] Although some of the areas that influence job satisfaction and performance are beyond the control of sales managers, this line of research points up the importance of responsive training, supportive supervision, and clearly defined company policies that are congruent with the needs of the sales force.

Evaluation and Control

An ongoing sales management responsibility is the monitoring and control of the industrial sales force at all levels—national, regional, and district—in order to determine whether objectives are being attained and to identify problems, recommend corrective action, and keep the sales organization in tune with changing competitive and market conditions.

The standards by which salespersons are evaluated are the means for comparing the performance of various salespersons or sales units (e.g., districts), as well as for gauging the overall productivity of the sales organization. Managerial experience and judgment are important in developing appropriate standards.

Performance standards are usually related to sales, profit contribution, or activity (e.g., number of new accounts developed, number of prospects contacted). Often, quotas are used for evaluation and motivation. As discussed in Part III, quotas are often derived from the sales forecast and from estimates of market potential. These quotas can be expressed in terms of dollar sales volume, product line sales, new accounts developed, new account sales volume, sales volume by customer type, and number of prospecting calls.[37] The standards must relate to overall marketing objectives, and they must take into account differences in sales territories, for which the number and

---

[36] Richard P. Bagozzi, "Performance and Satisfaction in an Industrial Sales Force: A Causal Modeling Approach," in Bagozzi, ed., *Sales Management: New Developments from Behavioral and Decision Model Research* (Cambridge, Mass.: Marketing Science Institute, 1979), pp. 70–91; see also Bagozzi, "Performance and Satisfaction in an Industrial Sales Force: An Examination of Their Antecedents and Simultaneity," *Journal of Marketing*, 44 (Spring 1980), pp. 65–77.

[37] For a more comprehensive discussion of sales quotas, see Shapiro, *Sales Management*, p. 308.

aggressiveness of competitors, the level of market potential, and the workload can vary markedly.

There is a positive relationship between goal clarity and task performance.[38] Thus, the nature and importance of goals should be clearly defined for salespersons, and feedback on the extent to which they are achieving these goals should be continuous. First-line supervisors are vital in providing salespersons with performance standings against preestablished goals. Supervisors also can help sales personnel take corrective action early.

Toward a Profit Focus

Both large and small business marketing firms appear to be oriented toward sales volume in the evaluation and control of the sales force. "In the quotas they set, the job dimensions they evaluate during performance appraisal, and the bases they use to establish incentive pay (e.g., commission, bonus), the focus is extensively on sales volume generated by sales personnel, rather than on profit contribution or activities/tasks performed."[39] Given the dominant role of personal selling costs in the business marketing budget, there is clearly a need for a stronger profit focus in the sales management function.

The Computer's Role[40]

The microcomputer can help sales managers evaluate the performance of each sales representative, improve time management skills, and teach salespersons to operate their territories as profit centers.

Table 17.1 provides a comparative income statement for a sales district using a spreadsheet program. Each salesperson can be evaluated on several financial criteria, starting with his or her product contribution. Product contribution varies by account because some accounts purchase only low-margin products whereas others purchase a mix of products that generate a higher profit margin. The costs incurred in serving accounts are captured in the comparative income statement. Some accounts require a disproportionate share of costs for freight, inventory, technical service, promotion, or interest on accounts receivable. The performance of each salesperson, as well as the

[38] Charles M. Futrell, John E. Swan, and John T. Todd, "Job Performance Related to Management Control Systems for Pharmaceutical Salesmen," *Journal of Marketing Research*, 13 (February 1976), pp. 25–33; see also Alan J. Dubinsky, Roy D. Howell, Thomas N. Ingram, and Danny N. Bellenger, "Salesforce Socialization," *Journal of Marketing*, 50 (October 1986), pp. 192–207; and Erin Anderson and Richard L. Oliver, "Perspectives on Behavior-Based Versus Outcome-Based Sales Force Control Systems," *Journal of Marketing*, 51 (October 1987), pp. 76–88.

[39] Alan J. Dubinsky and Thomas E. Barry, "A Survey of Sales Management Practices," *Industrial Marketing Management*, 11 (April 1982), pp. 133–141. See also Donald W. Jackson, Jr., Lonnie L. Ostrom, and Kenneth R. Evans, "Measures Used to Evaluate Industrial Marketing Activities," *Industrial Marketing Management*, 11 (October 1982), pp. 269–274.

[40] This section is largely based on G. David Hughes, "Computerized Sales Management," *Harvard Business Review*, 61 (March–April 1983), pp. 102–112. For a related discussion, see Alan J. Dubinsky, "Customer Portfolio Analysis," in Arch G. Woodside, ed., *Advances in Business Marketing*, Vol. I (Greenwich, Conn.: JAI Press, Inc., 1986), pp. 113–139.

TABLE 17.1   **District Comparative Income Statement**

	E. Martin		J. Taylor		W. Jones		District Totals	
	$000	Percent	$000	Percent	$000	Percent	$000	Percent
Sales	2200	100	2500	100	2000	100	6700	100
Account Product Contribution	479	21.77	613	24.52	457	22.85	1549	23.12
Account Costs								
Freight	63	2.86	65	2.60	60	3.00	188	2.81
Inventory	44	2.00	30	1.20	39	1.95	113	1.69
Accounts Receivable	64	2.91	75	3.00	59	2.95	198	2.96
Technical Services	18	0.82	18	0.72	17	0.85	53	0.79
Advertising and Promotion	21	0.95	35	1.40	18	0.90	74	1.10
Total Customer Costs	210	9.55	223	8.92	193	9.65	626	9.34
Personal Selling Costs								
Compensation	31.50	1.43	33.00	1.32	29.90	1.50	94.40	1.41
Transportation	6.00	0.27	5.00	0.20	7.00	0.35	18.00	0.27
Lodging & Meals	3.50	0.16	3.50	0.14	4.00	0.20	11.00	0.16
Telephone	1.35	0.06	1.70	0.07	1.20	0.06	4.25	0.06
Entertainment	3.00	0.14	1.00	0.04	2.50	0.13	6.50	0.10
Samples & Literature	2.00	0.09	2.00	0.08	1.50	0.08	5.50	0.08
Miscellaneous	0.50	0.02	0.50	0.02	0.30	0.02	1.30	0.02
Total Personal Selling Costs	47.85	2.18	46.70	1.87	46.40	2.32	140.95	2.10
Net Territory Contribution ($000)	221.15	10.05	343.30	13.73	217.60	10.88	782.05	11.67
Return on Assets Managed:								
Territory Assets ($000)	800		890		775		2465	
Asset Turnover (Sales/Assets)	2.75		2.81		2.58		2.72	
Add: Interest Inventory		2.00		1.20		1.95		1.69
Interest A/R		2.91		3.00		2.95		2.96
Total Contribution Percent		14.96		17.93		15.78		16.31
Return on Assets Managed (% Contribution × Turnover)		41.14		50.37		40.72		44.34

Source: Reprinted by permission of the *Harvard Business Review.* An exhibit from "Computerized Sales Management," by G. David Hughes, 61 (March/April 1983), p. 109. Copyright © 1983 by the President and Fellows of Harvard College; all rights reserved.

district, can then be evaluated on financial terms including net contribution and return on assets managed. Observe the excellent performance of sales representative J. Taylor.

This illustration deals with the district level, but comparable data could be generated to sharpen selling strategies by account, by territory, or by region. Guidelines for structuring the control system for each level in the sales organization can be coordinated by general sales managers. Overall, the computer can help improve sales force

ETHICAL BUSINESS MARKETING
Ethics in Selling

Scenario 1 In an attempt to negotiate the best price, sales rep Bill Smith tries to communicate to purchasing agents that plant capacity is at a very high level because of the popularity of his product. Bill does this even when plant capacity is low.

Scenario 2 Occasionally customers of Bill Smith ask which of his products he recommends for their company. Regardless of real customer need, Bill recommends one of the more expensive items in his product line.

Scenario 3 An industrial sales representative, Mary Johnson needs to make a yearly quota of $500,000. During the last month of the year, Mary is $10,000 below quota. Toward the end of the month, Mary is still about $5,000 below

quota when she receives an order for $3,000. To make quota, Mary doubles the order without telling the customer. Mary turns in a $6,000 order and makes quota. Mary decides to tell the customer that the order processing department made the mistake. She figures there is a good chance the customer will accept the double order rather than go to the inconvenience of sending the goods back.

As links between their organizations and the customers, salespersons encounter situations that may lead to ethical conflicts. Consider the personal, organizational, and societal stakes that underlie each of these vignettes.

Source: Joseph A. Bellizzi and Robert E. Hite, "Supervising Unethical Salesforce Behavior," *Journal of Marketing*, 53 (April 1989), pp. 36–47.

---

productivity, control expenses, and refine goals and strategies. Computer technology can also be pivotal in solving complex deployment problems for the sales manager. The next section deals with this question: To maximize profitability, how should the sales force be deployed across customers and territories?

MODELS FOR INDUSTRIAL SALES FORCE MANAGEMENT

To this point, our discussion has been concerned with (1) recruiting and selection, (2) training, (3) motivation and supervision, and (4) evaluation and control. Poor decisions in one area can create a backlash in other areas. One critical sales management task remains—deploying the sales force. The objective is to form the most profitable sales territories, deploy salespersons to serve potential customers in those territories, and effectively allocate sales force time among those customers.

Deployment Analysis: A Strategic Approach

The size of the sales force establishes the level of selling effort that can be employed by the business marketer. The selling effort is then organized by designating sales districts and sales territories. Allocation decisions determine how the selling effort is to

TABLE 17.2   **Deployment Decisions Facing Sales Organizations**

Type of Decision	Specific Deployment Decisions
Set total level of selling effort	Determine sales force size
Organize selling effort	Design sales districts
	Design sales territories
Allocate selling effort	Allocate effort to trading areas
	Allocate sales calls to accounts
	Allocate sales calls to prospects
	Allocate sales call time to products
	Determine length of sales call

Source: Reprinted by permission of the publisher from "Steps to Selling Effort Deployment," by Raymond LaForge and David W. Cravens, *Industrial Marketing Management*, 11 (July 1982), p. 184. Copyright © 1982 by Elsevier Science Publishing Co., Inc.

be assigned to customers, prospects, and products. All these are illustrated in Table 17.2.

Proper deployment requires a multistaged approach to find the most effective and efficient means of assigning sales resources (e.g., sales calls, number of salespersons, percentage of salesperson's time) across all of the **planning and control units** (PCUs) served by the firm (e.g., prospects, customers, territories, districts, products).[41] Thus, effective deployment means understanding the factors that influence sales in a particular PCU, such as a territory.

Territory Sales Response

What influences the level of sales that a salesperson might achieve in a particular territory? Eight classes of variables are outlined in Table 17.3. This list shows the complexity of estimating sales response functions. Such estimates are needed, however, to make meaningful sales allocations.

Three territory traits are worthy of particular attention in sales response studies: potential, concentration, and dispersion.[42] Potential (as discussed in Chapter 7) is a measure of the total business opportunity for all sellers in a particular market. Concentration is the degree to which potential is confined to a few larger accounts in that territory. If potential is concentrated, the salesperson can cover with a few calls a large proportion of the potential. Finally, if the territory is geographically dispersed, sales will probably be lower due to time wasted in travel. Past research often centered on **territory workload**—the number of accounts. However, Ryans and Weinberg report that workload is of questionable value in estimating sales response: "From a

---

[41] David W. Cravens and Raymond W. LaForge, "Sales Force Deployment," in Woodside, ibid., *Advances in Business Marketing*, pp. 67–112; and LaForge and Cravens, "Steps in Selling Effort Deployment," *Industrial Marketing Management*, 11 (July 1982), pp. 183–194.

[42] Adrian B. Ryans and Charles B. Weinberg, "Territory Sales Response," *Journal of Marketing Research*, 16 (November 1979), pp. 453–465; see also Ryans and Weinberg, "Territory Sales Response Models: Stability over Time," *Journal of Marketing Research*, 24 (May 1987), pp. 229–233.

TABLE 17.3   **Selected Determinants of Territory Sales Response**

1. Environmental factors (e.g., health of economy)
2. Competition (e.g., number of competitive salespersons)
3. Company marketing strategy and tactics
4. Sales force organization, policies, and procedures
5. Field sales manager characteristics
6. Salesperson characteristics
7. Territory characteristics (e.g., potential)
8. Individual customer factors

Source: Adrian B. Ryans and Charles B. Weinberg, "Territory Sales Response," *Journal of Marketing Research*, 16 (November 1979), pp. 453–465.

managerial standpoint, the recurrent finding of an association between potential and sales results suggests that sales managers should stress territory potential when making sales force decisions."[43]

Sales Resource Opportunity Grid
Deployment analysis matches sales resources to market opportunities. Planning and control units such as sales territories or districts are part of an overall portfolio with various units offering various levels of opportunity and requiring various levels of sales resources. A sales resource opportunity grid can be used to classify the industrial firm's portfolio of PCUs.[44] In Figure 17.6, each PCU is classified on the basis of PCU opportunity and sales organization strength.

PCU opportunity is the total potential that the PCU represents for all sellers, whereas **sales organization strength** includes the competitive advantages or distinctive competencies that the firm enjoys within the PCU. By positioning all PCUs on the grid, the sales manager can assign sales resources to those PCUs that have the greatest level of opportunity and that also capitalize on the particular strengths of the sales organization.

At various points in deployment decision making, the sales resource opportunity grid is important for screening the size of the sales force, the territory design, and the allocation of sales calls to customer segments. This method can isolate deployment problems or deployment opportunities worthy of sales management attention and further data analysis.

Computer-Assisted Deployment
The increased availability of inexpensive, user-friendly computer technology has important implications for analyzing sales force deployment.[45] To illustrate, Honeywell Information Systems, Inc. designed the sales support system highlighted in Figure 17.7.

---

[43] Ibid., p. 464.

[44] LaForge and Cravens, "Steps in Selling Effort Deployment," pp. 183–194.

[45] See, for example, Rowland T. Moriarty and Gordon S. Swartz, "Automating to Boost Sales and Marketing," *Harvard Business Review*, 67 (January–February 1989), pp. 100–108.

FIGURE 17.6   **Sales Resource Opportunity Grid**

PCU Opportunity (High / Low) vs. Sales Organization Strength (High / Low)

High / High:
Opportunity Analysis — PCU offers good opportunity because it has high potential and because sales organization has strong position
Sales Resource Assignment — High level of sales resources to take advantage of opportunity

High / Low:
Opportunity Analysis — PCU may offer good opportunity if sales organization can strengthen its position
Sales Resource Assignment — Either direct a high level of sales resources to improve position and take advantage of opportunity or shift resources to other PCUs

Low / High:
Opportunity Analysis — PCU offers stable opportunity because sales organization has strong position
Sales Resource Assignment — Moderate level of sales resources to keep current position strength

Low / Low:
Opportunity Analysis — PCU offers little opportunity
Sales Resource Assignment — Minimal level of sales resources; selectively eliminate resource coverage; possible elimination of PCU

Source: Reprinted by permission of the publisher from "Steps in Selling Effort Deployment," by Raymond LaForge and David W. Cravens, *Industrial Marketing Management*, 11 (July 1982), p. 187. Copyright © 1982 by Elsevier Science Publishing Co.

Each of the firm's 500 salespersons can get, on demand, account assignment lists, account histories, reminders of planned activities, and daily alerts to key situations. The customer prospect file includes the names, positions, and roles of key buying influentials by account; a description of the company's products, plants, and sales performance; as well as a complete description of its installed computer equipment. Apart from system features dedicated to the field salesperson, sales and marketing managers use the system for forecasting at all levels in the sales organization, culminating in a consolidated forecast for the entire U.S. sales division.

A Model for Allocating Sales Effort

Several models are available to support the decision maker in allocating sales effort.[46] These models can be used in conjunction with the sales resource opportunity grid. To illustrate the workings of these models, the Purchase Attitudes and Interactive

[46]For example, see Leonard M. Lodish, "CALLPLAN: An Interactive Salesman's Call Planning System," *Management Science*, 18 (December 1971), pp. 25–40; see also, Lodish, "Sales Territory Alignment to Maximize Profit," *Journal of Marketing Research*, 12 (February 1975), pp. 30–36; and James M. Comer, "The Computer, Personal Selling and Sales Management," *Journal of Marketing*, 39 (July 1975), pp. 27–33.

FIGURE 17.7   **Flow Diagram of a Typical Support System**

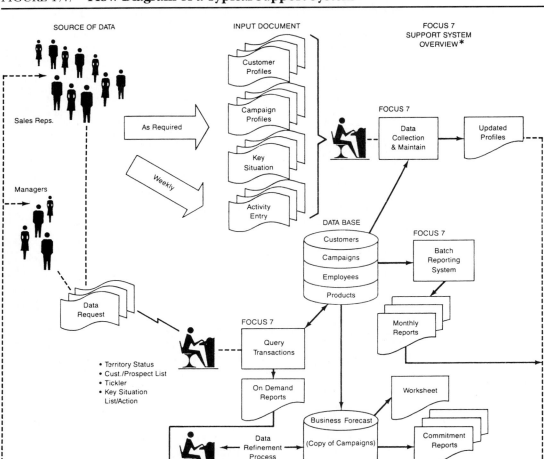

SOURCE OF DATA
INPUT DOCUMENT
FOCUS 7
SUPPORT SYSTEM
OVERVIEW*

* Honeywell Information Systems, Inc.

Source: Louis A. Wallis, *Computers and Sales Support* (New York: The Conference Board, 1986), p. 4. Diagram Courtesy of Honeywell Bull, Inc.

Response to Salesmen (PAIRS) model will be discussed. Developed by A. Parasuraman and Ralph Day, this model draws on the relevant features of earlier models—most notably CALLPLAN—and incorporates some new features.[47] Key components, or building blocks, of this model are discussed in sequence.

---

[47] A. Parasuraman and Ralph L. Day, "A Management-Oriented Model for Allocating Sales Effort," *Journal of Marketing Research*, 14 (February 1977), pp. 22–33. For a comprehensive review and analysis of sales management models, see Gary L. Lilien and Philip Kotler, *Marketing Decision Making: A Model-Building Approach* (New York: Harper & Row, Publishers, 1983), pp. 558–602.

1. Customers in a territory who are similar in their response to selling effort are classified into mutually exclusive and collectively exhaustive groups of approximately equal potential.

2. Salesperson characteristics that management deems useful to the selling job are employed. Selling ability of a salesperson is dependent on characteristics such as education, knowledge of the company's products, and personal traits.

3. The impact of selling effort on a customer in any period depends on the selling ability of sales personnel as well as on the number of sales calls made.

4. The planning horizon is divided into periods of time based on the average length of the purchase cycle or a similar criterion.

5. Variations in the time per sales call for various customers are included.

6. The expected total volume of sales from each type of customer is specified in terms of potential dollar revenue.

7. The model's output consists of an estimate of the sales revenue for each customer or customer group for each period in the planning horizon.

The model draws upon the experience and judgment of sales managers as well as on that of salespersons. Sales managers participate in the development of a salesperson's **effectiveness index** by defining the selling skills viewed as important in dealing with the company's customers. Each salesperson is rated on each characteristic on a scale of 0 (extremely poor) to 10 (excellent). These skills or characteristics are then weighted for each customer category that the firm serves. This approach recognizes that various skills or qualities may be required to reach various market segments or customer types.

Sales personnel also participate in the implementation of the model. They provide three estimates of the potential sales revenues for each customer in each district—a most likely estimate, a pessimistic estimate, and an optimistic estimate. Likewise, sales personnel provide subjective estimates of the sales response at each of four different call levels for each customer, which are used in developing a sales response function for each customer.

An additional significant feature of the PAIRS model is the inclusion of a carryover effect of past sales effort to a current period. To gather the necessary data, sales personnel are asked this question: What share of the customer's business could we obtain next year if *no* sales calls were to be made on the customer after the current period?

This model illustrates the feasibility of examining salesperson–customer interaction in a particular territory. Note that the model does not replace the seasoned judgment of sales managers or the field experience of sales personnel, but instead relies heavily on the experience and judgment of both for key inputs. Such an approach forces all parties involved to ask the right questions and think creatively about the factors that influence territory sales response.

FIGURE 17.8   **The Sales Force as Part of the Corporation's Marketing System**

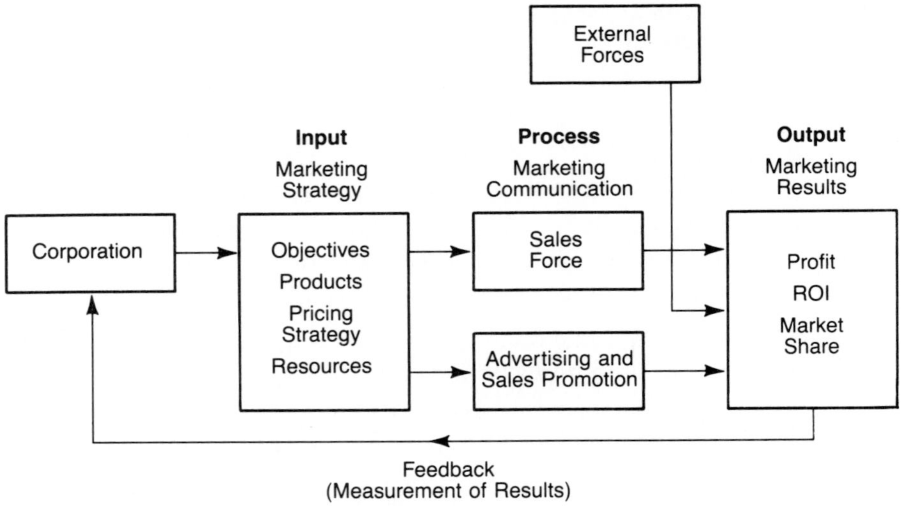

Source: Reprinted by permission of the *Harvard Business Review*. Exhibit from "Manage Your Sales Force as a System," by Porter Henry (March–April 1975). Copyright © 1975 by the President and Fellows of Harvard College, all rights reserved.

SALES MANAGEMENT: A SYSTEMS PERSPECTIVE

To reinforce the strategic role of the sales force in the business marketing communications mix, the chapter closes with a systems view of the marketing function. Note in Figure 17.8 that the inputs of the marketing system include the firm's objectives; product, distribution, and pricing strategies; and the resources to be allocated in order to achieve company objectives in defined market segments. The business marketer communicates the existence of the firm's offerings to organizational market segments (1) through the sales force and (2) through advertising and sales promotion. These have been explored in detail. Both types of marketing communication require evaluation and control for maximum effectiveness and efficiency. Essential to a systems perspective is the measurement of output. The goal of marketing strategy is to achieve specific marketing results—for example, profit, return on investment, and market share.

Reaching Industrial Customers: Evolving Strategies[48]

The rising costs of personal selling, coupled with the desire to improve the efficiency and effectiveness of business marketing strategy, have spawned marketing programs that combine traditional and evolving communication methods. Figure 17.9 integrates

---

[48] This section is largely drawn from Benson P. Shapiro and John Wyman, "New Ways to Reach Your Customers," *Harvard Business Review*, 51 (July–August 1981), pp. 103–110.

FIGURE 17.9   **Comparing Evolving and Traditional Options**

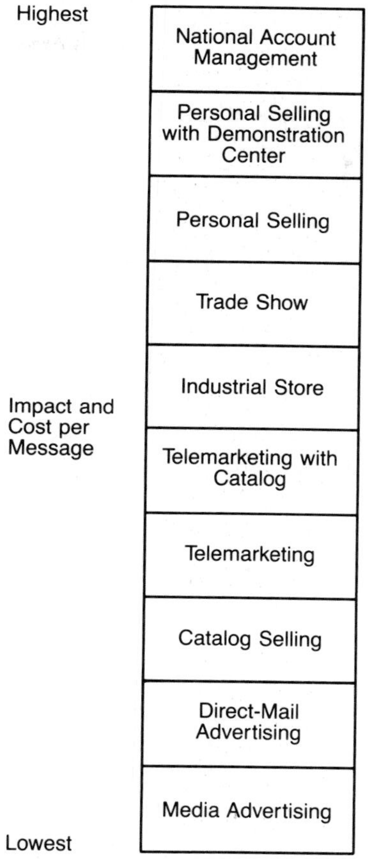

Highest	

Impact and
Cost per
Message

National Account Management
Personal Selling with Demonstration Center
Personal Selling
Trade Show
Industrial Store
Telemarketing with Catalog
Telemarketing
Catalog Selling
Direct-Mail Advertising
Media Advertising

Lowest

the discussion of business marketing communications by illustrating the impact and cost per message of the alternative promotional options available to the marketer.
    The newer communication tools are briefly described here:

1. *National accounts management programs.* A national accounts manager is used to coordinate exchange relationships with the firm's most important customers.

2. *Demonstration centers.* Specially designed showrooms provide customers with the opportunity to examine complex industrial equipment such as data processing equipment, machine tools, electronic test units, and telecommunications equipment.

Such centers provide the opportunity for the seller to provide custom-designed demonstrations that relate directly to the customer's needs.

3. *Industrial stores.* Conventional retailing strategy economically reaches selected segments of the business market. Utilized successfully in the small business computer industry, the store approach is especially appropriate when personal sales in particular customer segments (e.g., small businesses) would be uneconomical and when the product or process lends itself to demonstration.

4. *Telemarketing.* Telephone marketing is used "as a less costly substitute for personal selling, a supplement to personal selling, a higher-impact substitute for direct mail and media advertising, a supplement to direct mail and other media, and a replacement for other slower, less convenient communications techniques."[49]

5. *Catalog selling.* A highly cost-effective approach transmits a significant amount of information to selected prospects and customers in an inexpensive format. Catalog selling is often used in conjunction with a telemarketing system.

Driven by new technology and by the search for increased efficiency and effectiveness, business marketers are formulating integrated marketing communications programs by combining traditional with evolving communication tools. By monitoring the relative impact of these communications options, the business marketing strategist can blend the "old" with the "new" to profitably meet changing customer needs.

SUMMARY

Personal selling is a significant demand-stimulating force in the business market. Given the rapidly escalating cost of industrial sales calls and the massive resources invested in personal selling, the business marketer must carefully manage this function. Recognition of both the needs of organizational customers and the rudiments of organizational buying behavior is fundamental to effective personal selling. Likewise, important insights emerge when the industrial salesperson is viewed as a relationship manager. Attention focuses on defining those market situations that require a relationship-marketing approach rather than a transaction-marketing approach. From the consumer's perspective, relationship quality consists of trust in the salesperson and satisfaction with the salesperson.

The increased professionalism of industrial selling is reflected in the increased prominence of four selling styles: consultative selling, negotiative selling, systems selling, and team selling. Managing the industrial sales force is a multifaceted task. First, the marketer must clearly define the role of personal selling in overall marketing strategy. Second, the sales organization must be appropriately structured—by geography, product, market, or some combination of all three. Regardless of the method used to organize the sales force, an increasing number of industrial firms are also establishing a national account sales force so they can profitably serve large customers

---

[49] Ibid., p. 106.

with complex purchasing requirements. Third, the ongoing process of sales force administration includes recruitment and selection, training, supervision and motivation, and evaluation and control. A particularly challenging sales management task is the deployment of sales effort across products, customer types, and territories. The sales resource opportunity grid is a useful organizing framework for sales deployment decisions. Likewise, the business marketer can benefit by examining management-oriented models that deal with sales allocation problems. By capitalizing on advancing computer technology and user-friendly software, the sales manager is better equipped to plan, organize, and control selling strategies for the business market.

Discussion Questions

1. When planning a sales call on a particular account in the business market, what information would you require concerning the buying center, the purchasing requirements, and the competition?

2. Some business marketers organize their sales force around products; others are market-centered. What factors must be considered in selecting the most appropriate organizational arrangement for the sales force?

3. Christine Lojacono started as a Xerox sales rep several years ago and is now a national accounts manager, directing activities for five national accounts. Compared to the field sales representative, describe how the nature of the job and the nature of the selling task differ for a national accounts manager.

4. A successful sales training program can reduce the costs associated with recruiting. Explain.

5. An emerging body of research suggests that role ambiguity and role conflict have a detrimental impact on the job satisfaction of industrial salespersons. What steps can sales managers take to deal with these problems? What role might a management-by-objectives system play in these efforts?

6. To make effective and efficient sales force allocation decisions, the sales manager must analyze sales territories. Describe how the sales manager can profit by examining (a) the potential, (b) the concentration, and (c) the dispersion of territories.

7. Hewlett-Packard Corporation has outfitted all of its 2,000 sales representatives with portable personal computers and printers. Early results with the new program suggest that sales force productivity has improved—in some cases, rather significantly. Describe some specific dimensions of the salesperson's job that lend themselves to such computer support.

8. What benefits can be derived by examining the business marketing communications mix from a systems perspective?

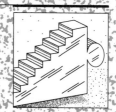

PART V

Evaluating Business Marketing Strategy and Performance

CHAPTER 18

Controlling Business Marketing Strategies

Two business marketing managers facing identical market conditions and possessing equal resources to invest in marketing strategy could generate dramatically different performance results. Why? One manager carefully monitors and controls the performance of marketing strategy; the other does not. The astute marketer evaluates the profitability of alternative segments and examines the effectiveness and efficiency of the components of the marketing mix so that he or she can isolate problems and opportunities and alter the marketing strategy as market or competitive conditions dictate.

After reading this chapter, you will understand:

1. the function and significance of marketing control in business marketing management.

2. the components of the control process.

3. the specific methods for evaluating marketing strategy performance.

4. the importance of execution or implementation to the success of business marketing strategy.

MANAGING a firm's marketing strategy is similar to coaching a football team: the excitement and challenge rests in the formulation of strategy. Shall we focus on running or passing? What weaknesses of the opposition can we exploit? How shall we vary our standard plays? So too, the business marketer applies managerial talent creatively when developing and implementing unique marketing strategies that not only respond to customer needs but also capitalize on competitive weaknesses.

However, formulating effective strategy is only half of coaching, or management. A truly great coach devotes significant energies to evaluating team performance during last week's game in order to set next week's strategy. Did our strategy work? Why? Where did it break down? Similarly, a successful marketing strategy depends on evaluations of marketing performance. The other half of strategy planning is **marketing control**, the system by which a firm checks actual against planned performance, evaluating the profitability of products, customer segments, and territories.

Marketing control systems should focus on two key elements: (1) **activities**—to ensure that marketing activities produce desired results; and (2) **personnel**—to ensure that marketing personnel are behaving in ways that accomplish the desired results.[1] Most control systems are focused on evaluating activities and their results; however, more attention needs to be given to personnel control because of the potential impact on results. In this realm, for example, informal controls (unwritten worker-initiated mechanisms) can significantly influence behavior: sales people may establish norms of low productivity/output which may have more impact on performance than formal management controls (like sales quotas). Thus, the marketing control system should be broad-based enough to account for the more difficult-to-measure control of marketing personnel.

Information generated by the marketing control system is essential for revising current marketing strategies, formulating new strategies, and allocating funds. The requirements for an effective control system are strict—data must be gathered continuously on the appropriate performance measures. Thus, an effective marketing strategy is rooted in a carefully designed and well-applied control system. Such a system must also monitor the quality of strategy implementation. Poor marketing execution may cause the business marketer to doubt even sound strategies because they are masked by implementation problems.[2]

This chapter presents the rudiments of a marketing control system, beginning with a framework incorporating the essential elements of the control process. Next, the types of performance measurement are examined. Finally, attention centers on the particular implementation skills that ultimately shape successful business marketing strategies.

MARKETING STRATEGY: ALLOCATING RESOURCES

The purpose of any marketing strategy is to yield the best possible results to the company. Resources are allocated to marketing in general and to individual strategy elements in particular in order to achieve prescribed objectives. Profit contribution, market share percentage, number of new customers, and level of expenses and sales

---

[1] Bernard J. Jaworski, "Toward A Theory of Marketing Control: Environmental Context Control Types, and Consequences," *Journal of Marketing*, 52 (July 1988), p. 24.

[2] Orville C. Walker, Jr., and Robert W. Ruekert, "Marketing's Role in the Implementation of Business Strategies: A Critical Review and Conceptual Framework," *Journal of Marketing*, 51 (July 1987), pp. 15–33; and Thomas V. Bonoma, *The Marketing Edge: Making Strategies Work* (New York: The Free Press, 1985).

are typical performance criteria; but regardless of the criteria chosen, four interrelated evaluations are required to design a marketing strategy:

1. How much should be spent on marketing in the planning period? (This is the budget for achieving marketing objectives.)

2. How are marketing dollars to be allocated? (e.g., how much is to be spent on advertising? On personal selling?)

3. Within each element of the marketing strategy, how should dollars be allocated to best achieve marketing objectives? (e.g., which advertising media should be selected? How should sales personnel be deployed among customers and prospects?)

4. Which market segments, products, and geographic areas will be most profitable? (Each market segment may require a differing amount of effort as a result of competitive intensity or market potential.)

Guiding Strategy Formulation

The integration of the market strategy formulation and the marketing control system is highlighted by these four decision areas. First, results in the most recent operating period will show how successful past marketing efforts were in obtaining desired objectives. Second, performance below or above what was expected will signal where funds should be reallocated. If the firm expected to reach 20 percent of the OEM market and actually realized only a 12 percent market share, a change in strategy may be required. Performance information provided by the control system might demonstrate that sales personnel in the OEM market were reaching only 45 percent of potential buyers; additional funds could be allocated to expand either the sales force or the advertising budget.

Marketing managers must weigh the interactions among the strategy elements and allocate resources in order to create effective and efficient marketing strategies. In order to develop successful strategies, a system for monitoring past performance is an absolute necessity. In effect, the control system allows management to keep abreast of all facets of performance. This is demonstrated by the control system at Cypress Semiconductor (see Inside Business Marketing box on page 526).

The Marketing Control Process

Marketing control is a process whereby management generates information on marketing performance. Two major forms of control are (1) control over efficient allocation of marketing effort and (2) comparison of planned and actual performance. In the first case, the business marketer may use past profitability data as a standard against which to evaluate future marketing expenditures. The second form of control alerts management to any differences between planned and actual performance and may also reveal reasons for performance discrepancies. In either case, management must have an information system that will provide timely and meaningful data.

INSIDE BUSINESS MARKETING

Cypress Semiconductor: No Excuses Management

The president of Cypress, T. J. Rodgers, explained the essence of Cypress's impressive management control systems in a recent publication:

> At Cypress, our management systems track corporate, departmental, and individual performance so regularly and in such detail that no manager including me, can plausibly claim to be in the dark about critical problems. Our systems give managers the capacity to monitor what's happening at all levels of the organization, to anticipate problems or conflicts, to intervene when appropriate, and to

identify best practices—without creating layers of bureaucracy that bog down decisions and sap morale. The systems are designed to encourage collective thinking and to force each of us to face reality every day.

> Lots of companies espouse a "no surprises" philosophy. At Cypress, "no surprises" is a way of life. We collect information in such detail and share it so widely that the company is virtually transparent. This works against the political infighting and bureaucratic obfuscation that cripple so many organizations.

Source: Adapted from T. J. Rodgers, "No Excuses Management," *Harvard Business Review*, 68 (July–August 1990), pp. 84–86.

Control Is Information

The essence of control is information; in fact, a control system is nothing more than an organized body of information that allows management to evaluate how the firm has done and where future opportunities may lie. Michael Porter and Victor Millar emphasize that information "creates competitive advantage by giving companies new ways to outperform their rivals."[3]

Business marketing strategy requires a vast array of information: sales, expenses, market share, profits, competitive actions, market trends, and environmental data. The components of the business marketing intelligence system were explored in Chapter 5. The internal accounting system (see Figure 18.1) provides sales, expense, and other accounting data fundamental to marketing control. The purpose of the business marketing intelligence system is to obtain information in order to solve specific problems or to evaluate particular market opportunities.

The major sectors of the business market and the important secondary sources of market information were examined in Chapters 2 and 5, and models related to organizational buying, product, pricing, promotion, and distribution were presented in other chapters. The focus of this chapter is on the use of the information when controlling the business marketing process, especially through accounting systems.

---

[3] Michael E. Porter and Victor E. Millar, "How Information Gives You Competitive Advantage," *Harvard Business Review*, 63 (July–August 1985), p. 150.

FIGURE 18.1 **The Business Marketing Intelligence System**

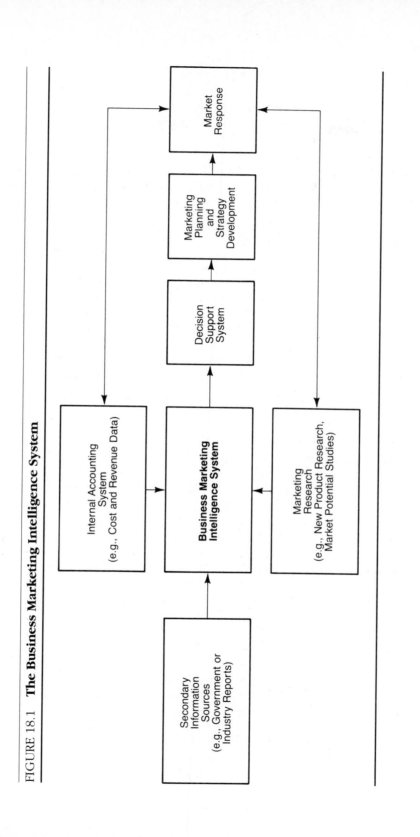

TABLE 18.1 **Levels of Marketing Control**

Type of Control	Primary Responsibility	Purpose of Control	Tools
Strategic control	Top management	To examine whether the company is pursuing its best opportunities with respect to markets, products, and channels	Marketing audit
Annual plan control	Top management, middle management	To examine whether the planned results are being achieved	Sales analysis Market-share analysis Expense-to-sales ratios Other ratios Attitude tracking
Strategic component control	Middle management	To examine how well resources have been utilized in each element of the marketing strategy	Expense ratios Advertising effectiveness measures Market potential Contribution margin analysis
Profitability control	Marketing controller	To examine where the company is making and losing money	Profitability by product territory, market segment, trade channel, order size

Source: Adapted from Philip Kotler, *Marketing Management: Analysis, Planning and Control*, 5th ed. (Englewood Cliffs, N.J.: Prentice-Hall, Inc., 1984), p. 744.

CONTROL AT VARIOUS LEVELS

The control process is universal in that it can be applied to any level of marketing analysis. For example, business marketers must frequently evaluate whether their general strategies are appropriate and effective. However, it is equally important to know whether the individual elements in the marketing strategy are effectively integrated for a given market. Further, management must evaluate resource allocation within a particular element; for example, the effectiveness of direct selling versus the effectiveness of industrial distributors. The control system should work in any of these situations. The four primary levels of marketing control are delineated in Table 18.1.

Strategic Control

Strategic control is based on a comprehensive evaluation of whether the firm is headed in the right direction (see Figure 18.2). Because the business marketing environment is subject to rapid change, existing product/market situations may lose their potential whereas new product/market match-ups provide important opportunities. Philip Kotler suggests that the firm periodically conduct a **marketing audit**, a comprehensive, periodic, and systematic evaluation of the firm's marketing operation that specifically

FIGURE 18.2   **Connecting Information Technology to Strategic Goals: An Illustrative Business Marketing Ad**

Source: Courtesy, Andersen Consulting, Arthur Andersen & Co., S.C.

analyzes the market environment and the firm's internal marketing activities.[4] An analysis of the environment assesses company image, customer characteristics, competitive activities, regulatory constraints, and economic trends. Evaluation of this information suggests areas of potential which the firm may be able to adapt its strategy to target.

An internal evaluation of the marketing system scrutinizes marketing objectives, organization, and implementation. In this way, management may be able to spot situations in which existing products could be adapted to new markets or new products

[4] Philip Kotler, *Marketing Management: Analysis, Planning and Control, 5th ed.* (Englewood Cliffs, N.J.: Prentice-Hall, 1984), p. 764; and Michael P. Mokwa, "The Strategic Marketing Audit: An Adoption/Utilization Perspective," *Journal of Business Strategy,* (Winter 1986), pp. 88–95.

INSIDE BUSINESS MARKETING

Hopping the Lily Pads: A Strategy that Works

The control system indicates that strategy is effective. In the two years since first implementing the "Lily Pad" strategy, sales have grown 45 percent and net income has more than doubled. International sales have grown 64 percent and now account for 63 percent of total sales.

The company is Nordson, a manufacturer of industrial coatings and finishes. The marketing strategy has several components, beginning with organization. To get closer to customers the firm scrapped their old organizational structure based on product lines and divided the company into four geographic divisions: North America, Europe, Japan, and Pacific/South. The new organizational scheme allows Nordson to tailor its sales and marketing efforts to different markets and cultures as well as to compete more effectively with local and regional competitors.

The key ingredient to Nordson's marketing strategy is its approach to market opportunities, and this has been dubbed the "lily pad" strategy.

The essence of the lily pad approach is to slowly evolve the business into new, but closely related, markets or applications. Hence, much like a frog hopping to the closest lily pad, Nordson sticks close to what it knows and takes small steps from its existing areas of strength. The firm focuses on either adapting its existing technology to new markets or developing new technology for its existing markets. As a result, Nordson has gradually evolved from its original business of liquid finishing systems into such areas as powder finishing and electronic coatings. The strategy has allowed the company to control its risk and get the most from existing technology and marketplace knowledge.

The strategic control process at Nordson provides many indications that the company is headed in the right direction. The strategy looks both effective and appropriate to the firm's market situation: sales are projected to increase another 31 percent in the next two years.

Source: Adapted from Sue Kapp, "Chef Extraordinaire," *Business Marketing*, 74 (November 1989), pp. 10–12.

---

could be developed for existing markets. The regular, systematic marketing audit is a valuable technique for evaluating the direction of marketing strategies.[5]

Philip Kotler, et al reviewed their original article on the marketing audit 12 years after it was first published. The authors noted that the audit is sufficiently robust; "that it holds up well today."[6] Table 18.2 summarizes some of the current issues that merit a close review during the marketing audit process.

Strategic Dialogue: Ask Tough Questions!

To offer promise, a strategic option must meet several tests. "Effective business strategies are formed in a crucible of debate and dialogue between and within many levels of management. The challenge is to encourage realism in the dialogue—so critical decisions are not distorted by wishful thinking and myopic analysis—while not suppressing creativity and risk taking."[7] George Day suggests that many strategies fail

---

[5] For example, see Philip Kotler, William T. Gregor, and William Rogers, III, "SMR Classic Reprint: The Marketing Audit Comes of Age," *Sloan Management Review*, 20 (Winter 1989), pp. 49–62; and Mokwa, "The Strategic Marketing Audit," pp. 88–95.

[6] Ibid., pp. 49–62.

[7] George S. Day, "Tough Questions for Developing Strategies," *Journal of Business Strategy*, 7 (Winter 1986), p. 68.

TABLE 18.2 **The Marketing Audit: Current Issues Requiring Analysis**

Current Issues	Focus of the Marketing Audit
Globalization	Those conducting the audit must raise questions about the firm's international opportunities and strategies.
Information Technology	Advanced information technology can provide a substantial competitive advantage. The audit must evaluate the firm's existing technology and opportunities.
Communication/Promotion Technology	"New" media and communications technologies are developing rapidly. The audit must examine the actual or potential use of direct mail, telemarketing, sports marketing, video recorders, video discs, and fax machines.
Analytical Tools	The personal computer and readily available spreadsheet programs make possible the easy evaluation of product line, customer, and distributor profitability. Access to on-line data bases is inexpensive and easy. These technologies need to be fully integrated into the market audit process.
Changing Environments	The changing environment will prompt the need for careful reviews of evolving situations. Deregulation of the communications, financial services, and transportation industries has stimulated a marketing audit in order to determine how to compete in the new environment.
Implementation	Effective implementation of strategy remains a critical issue. To enhance the chances of success, operating managers must be involved in the audit process so that "ownership" of the audit process and its results is achieved among those who will implement the strategic changes.

Source: Adapted from Philip Kotler, William T. Gregor, and William H. Rodgers, III, "SMR Classic Reprint: The Marketing Audit Comes of Age," *Sloan Management Review* 20 (Winter 1989), pp. 49–62.

because the right questions are not asked at the right time during the strategy formulation process. He offers several insightful questions to guide the analysis of strategy options; see Table 18.3. These tough questions are fundamental to the strategic control process.

Competitive Analysis[8]

A thorough assessment of the firm's positioning relative to its competitors is fundamental to strategic control. An assessment of an industrial firm's profitability relative to competition includes demand as well as supply factors (Figure 18.3). Consider two alternative paths to a position of competitive strength.

ILLUSTRATION: Supply and Demand Factors

Firm A follows a strategy geared toward building volume and reducing production and distribution costs. The strategy exploits the experience effect (see Chapter 10) and scale economies, thereby achieving cost advantages over competitors. This strategy centers on *supply* factors.

---

[8] This section is largely based on George Day, "Gaining Insights through Strategy Analysis," *Journal of Business Strategy,* 4 (Summer 1983), pp. 51–58.

TABLE 18.3 **Reviewing Strategic Options: Seven Tough Questions**

---

1. **Suitability: Is there a sustainable advantage?**
   (e.g., assess each strategy option in light of the capabilities of the business and the likely responses of key competitors)
2. **Validity: Are the assumptions realistic?**
   (e.g., assumptions concerning sales, profits, competition)
3. **Flexibility: Do we have the skills, resources, and commitments?**
   (e.g., adequate sales force, advertising budget, commitment of key personnel)
4. **Consistency: Does the strategy hang together?**
   (e.g., Is it internally consistent across the functional areas in the firm?)
5. **Vulnerability: What are the risks and contingencies?**
   (e.g., If important assumptions are wrong, what are the risks inherent in each strategy alternative?)
6. **Adaptability: Can we retain our flexibility?**
   (e.g., If a major contingency occurs, could the strategy be reversed in the future?)
7. **Financial Desirability: How much economic value is created?**
   (e.g., the attractiveness of expected performance relative to the probable risk of each option)

Source: George S. Day, "Tough Questions for Developing Strategies," *Journal of Business Strategy*, 7 (Winter 1986), pp. 60–68.

In contrast, firm B follows a strategy that centers on *demand* factors. By providing a high-quality product and by augmenting the offering with technical services, the firm commands a premium price in certain market segments. The segments served by firm B exhibit low demand elasticity.

Firm A's strategy is to gain a competitive cost advantage (supply factors), whereas firm B's strategy is to secure a perceived quality advantage (demand factors). Often, however, there is not a clear choice, and the strategic perspective must consider relative competitive position from both the supply and the demand sides.

George Day contends that "the relative importance of supply versus demand factors can differ dramatically, depending on perceived differences among products and the ability of competitors to match any cost advantages or provide equivalent customer values."[9] Thus, the marketing control system must consider multiple measures of market share. From a supply perspective, the market definition should encompass all related products that influence the size of the production experience base and the ability to achieve economies of scale; the market for the product is broadly defined. A demand perspective, in contrast, has a narrower customer-oriented market definition, and it asks: What is the firm's relative share of the profitable segments of the market? Consistent with Figure 18.3, multiple market share measures that isolate key features of the demand and supply environment enrich strategic control.

George Day and Robin Wensley further suggest that to effectively evaluate its competitive advantage, a firm must make competitor-centered assessments as well as customer-focused assessments.[10] Individually, each type of assessment only provides

---

[9] Ibid., p. 54.

[10] George S. Day and Robin Wensely, "Assessing Advantage: A Framework for Diagnosing Competitive Superiority," *Journal of Marketing,* 52 (April 1988), p. 9.

FIGURE 18.3   **Sources of Profitability**

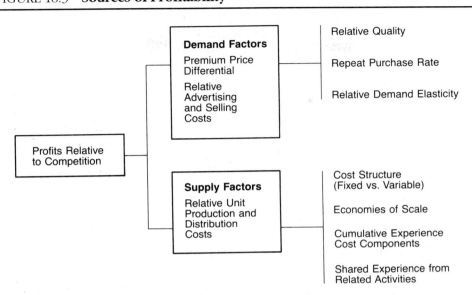

a partial picture of the competitive advantage situation. A comprehensive diagnosis can be gained only with a combination of methods. Table 18.4 provides a list of the types of measures used in each type of assessment, and indicates that each assessment focuses on different variables.

Annual Plan Control

In annual plan control, the objectives specified in the plan become the performance standards against which actual results are compared. Sales volume, profits, and market share are the typical performance standards for business marketers. **Sales analysis** is an attempt to determine why actual sales varied from planned sales. Expected sales may not be realized because of price reductions, inadequate volume, or both. A sales analysis separates the effects of these variables so that corrective action can be taken.

Market share analysis is an assessment of how the firm is doing relative to competition. A machine-tool manufacturer may experience a 10-percent sales gain that, on the surface, appears favorable. However, if total machine-tool industry sales are up 25 percent, an analysis of market share would show that the firm has not fared well relative to competitors.

Finally, **expense-to-sales ratios** are analyses of the efficiency of marketing operations. In this regard, management is concerned with overspending or underspending.

TABLE 18.4   **Methods of Assessing Competitive Advantage**

Competitor-Centered	**Customer-Focused**

A. Assessing Sources (Distinctive Competencies)
1. Management judgments of strengths and weaknesses
2. Comparison of resource commitments and capabilities
3. Marketing skills audit

B. Indicators of Positional Advantage

4. Competitive cost and activity comparisons	5. Customer comparisons of attributes of firm versus competitors
a. Value chain comparisons of relative costs	a. Choice models
b. Cross-section experience curves	b. Conjoint analysis
	c. Market maps

C. Identifying Key Success Factors
6. Comparison of winning versus losing competitors
7. Identifying high leverage phenomena
   a. Management estimates of market share elasticities
   b. Drivers of activities in the value chain

D. Measures of Performance

10a. Market share	8. Customer satisfaction surveys
11. Relative profitability (return on sales and return on assets)	9. Loyalty (customer franchise)
	10b. Relative share of end-user segments

Source: George S. Day and Robin Wensley, "Assessing Advantage: A Framework for Diagnosing Competitive Superiority," Journal of Marketing, 52 (April, 1988), p. 9. Reprinted by permission of the American Marketing Association.

Frequently, industry standards or past company ratios are used for standards of comparison. Total marketing expenses and expenses of each strategic marketing element are evaluated in relation to sales. Recall the discussion in Chapter 16 on advertising expenditures, which provided a range of advertising expense-to-sales ratios for industrial firms. These figures provide management with a basis for evaluating the company's performance.

A Framework for Marketing Control

James Hulbert and Norman Toy suggest a comprehensive framework for integrating such measures into a marketing control system.[11] The basic approach is to identify the factors that caused a variance of actual product profitability from planned profitability (Table 18.5). The objective is to isolate the reasons for the differences between planned

---

[11] James M. Hulbert and Norman E. Toy, "A Strategic Framework for Marketing Control," *Journal of Marketing*, 41 (April 1977), pp. 12–19; see also Nigel F. Percy, "The Marketing Budgeting Process: Marketing Management Implications," *Journal of Marketing*, 51 (October 1987), pp. 45–59.

TABLE 18.5   **Operating Results for a Sample Product**

Item	Planned	Actual	Variance
Revenues			
Sales (units)	20,000,000	22,000,000	+2,000,000
Price per unit ($)	0.50	0.4773	−0.0227
Total market (units)	40,000,000	50,000,000	−10,000,000
Share of market	50%	44%	−6%
Revenues ($)	10,000,000	10,500,000	+500,000
Variable costs ($.30 unit) ($)	6,000,000	6,600,000	−600,000
Profit contribution ($)	4,000,000	3,900,000	−100,000

Source: Adapted from James M. Hulbert and Norman E. Toy, "A Strategic Framework for Marketing Control," *Journal of Marketing*, 41 (April 1977), p. 13.

and actual results (the variances displayed in column 3), specifically the profit contribution variance.

In this case, management seeks to understand why actual profit contribution was $100,000 less than planned profits. A detailed analysis of the data shows that although total sales were larger than expected (22 million versus 20 million units), the firm failed to achieve its targeted market share. In addition, the firm was unable to maintain its price policy. Management must review its forecasting, considering that the market size was underestimated by 25 percent (40 million versus 50 million). To the extent that marketing strategy allocations are predicated on estimated market size, the firm may have failed to allocate sufficient effort to this market. The variances point to some real weaknesses in the forecasting process.

Because the firm did not share proportionately with its competitors in the market growth, the entire marketing strategy must be reevaluated. Management apparently underestimated the magnitude of price reductions necessary to expand volume. Clearly, annual plan control provides valuable insights into where the plan faltered and suggests the type of remedial action that should be taken.

Strategic Component Control

Some of the measures used for annual plan control can be applied to evaluating the performance of individual marketing strategy elements (e.g., pricing). A good control system will provide continuing data on which to evaluate the efficiency of resources used for a given element of marketing strategy. Table 18.6 provides a representative sample of the types of data required. Performance measures and standards will vary by company and situation, according to the goals and objectives delineated in the marketing plan.

Recall the extensive discussion in Chapter 7 that dealt with techniques and procedures for calculating market potential. Because potential represents the opportunity to sell, it provides an excellent benchmark against which to measure performance.

TABLE 18.6   **Illustrative Measures for Strategic Component Control**

Product
Sales by market segments
Sales relative to potential
Sales growth rates
Market share
Contribution margin
Percentage of total profits
Return on investment

Distribution
Sales, expenses, and contribution by channel type
Sales and contribution margin by intermediary type and individual intermediaries
Sales relative to market potential by channel, intermediary type, and specific intermediaries
Expense-to-sales ratio by channel, etc.
Order cycle performance by channel, etc.
Logistics cost by logistics activity by channel

Communication
Advertising effectiveness by type of media
Actual audience/target audience ratio
Cost per contact
Number of calls, inquiries, and information requests by type of media
Dollar sales per sales call
Sales per territory relative to potential
Selling expenses to sales ratios
New accounts per time period

Pricing
Price changes relative to sales volume
Discount structure related to sales volume
Bid strategy related to new contracts
Margin structure related to marketing expenses
General price policy related to sales volume
Margins related to channel member performance

Analysis of performance relative to potential can be made for distribution channels, channel members, and products. The results are sometimes combined with profitability control, the last area of a comprehensive control system.

Profitability Control

The essence of profitability control is to describe where the firm is making or losing money in terms of the important segments of its business. A **segment** is the unit of analysis used by management for control purposes; it may be customer segments, product lines, territories, or channel structures. Suppose an industrial firm focuses on three customer segments: machine tools, aircraft parts, and electronics manufacturers. To allocate the marketing budget among the three segments, management must consider the profit contribution associated with each segment and its expected potential. Profitability control, then, provides a methodology for associating marketing costs and revenues to specific segments of the business.

Profitability by Market Segment

Relating sales revenues and marketing costs to market segments improves decision making. More specifically:

> For both strategic and tactical decisions, marketing managers may profit by knowing the impact of the marketing mix upon the target segment at which marketing efforts are aimed. If the programs are to be responsive to environmental change, a monitoring system is needed to locate problems and guide adjustments in marketing decisions. Tracing the profitability of segments permits improved pricing, selling, advertising, channel, and product management decisions. The success of marketing policies and programs may be appraised by a dollar-and-cents measure of profitability by segment.[12]

Profitability control, a prerequisite to strategy planning and implementation, has stringent information requirements. To be effective, the firm needs a marketing-accounting information system.

The accounting system must first be able to associate costs with the various marketing functions and activities and must then attach these "functional" costs to the important segments to be analyzed.[13] Thus, as a particular cost is incurred, the cost is coded according to the function and the segment to which it applies. In the case of warehouse salaries, for example, the distribution function is debited with the expense. If the salaries can be related to the handling of specific products for specific customer segments, the proportion of expense applicable to each product and customer segment is coded. Similarly, each sale to customers is coded by product and by segment. The final result is a data base that allows management to evaluate each segment of the business on the basis of its costs and revenues.

The critical element in the process of determining the appropriate marketing costs associated with a product or customer segment is to trace all costs to the activities (warehousing, advertising, etc.) for which the resources are used and then to the products or segments that consume them.[14] Such an **activity-** or **function-based cost system** replaces systems in which support and overhead costs are allocated on some simplistic basis like percent of sales volume. Rather than assuming that a product that represents 10 percent of total volume should be assigned 10 percent of the support and overhead cost, an activity-based cost system seeks to examine the demands made by products or segments on indirect resources. Once the factors that trigger the use of support activities are determined, the cost of these activities can be traced to specific

---

[12] Leland L. Beik and Stephen L. Buzby, "Profitability Analysis by Market Segments," *Journal of Marketing*, 37 (July 1973), p. 49.

[13] Frank H. Mossman, Paul M. Fischer, and W. J. E. Crissy, "New Approaches for Analyzing Marketing Profitability," *Journal of Marketing*, 38 (April 1974), p. 44.

[14] Robin Coopera nd Robert S. Kaplan, "Measure Costs Right: Make the Right Decisions," *Harvard Business Review*, 66 (September–October 1988), p. 96.

products. For example, a building supply company used six different channels to reach its industrial customers.[15] Using conventional methods, selling, general, and administrative expenses were assigned to each channel on the basis of the company average (each channel was allocated about 16 percent of sales for SG&A expenses). The original equipment manufacturer (OEM) channel, under this process, was determined to be the worst of the six channel systems with 27 percent gross margin and 2 percent operating margin. Application of activity-based systems for developing SG&A costs showed the OEM channel did not use many SG&A activities—the OEMs required no advertising, catalog, or sales promotion expense. As a result, OEMs' actual SG&A expenses were only 9 percent of sales, well below the 16 percent average for the six channels. The operating profit, under the new analysis, turned out to be 9 percent, not 2 percent. Clearly, an activity-based costing system provides more accurate information on which to make important marketing decisions.

Hewlett-Packard has recently changed its accounting system to an activity-based system.[16] The costs of producing a printed circuit board are determined by first evaluating the activities required to produce the board and then costing out each of the activities. For example, each printed circuit board has diodes inserted into it, and the firm analyzed the cost of each insertion. If one insertion costs 6 cents, then the diode insertion activity can be determined by multiplying $.06 times the number of diodes. The remaining costs are built up in the same fashion. This costing process creates more accurate costs because the system measures the factors that truly drive costs.

Creating Cost Modules

Frank Mossman and his colleagues use the term **modular data base** to refer to systems that allow the capture of costs by product or segment.[17] By coding costs and revenues according to function and segment, **cost modules** are created, which allow management to regroup costs and revenues for a particular type of analysis. Cost modules can be regrouped in three ways:

1. Under common responsibilities (i.e., all costs associated with physical distribution), allowing a comparison of estimated and actual costs by function

2. By marketing segments; when these costs are added to manufacturing costs of individual products, the total can be deducted from revenues to produce segment profitability

3. By expense groupings, for typical external reporting purposes[18]

Clearly, cost modules cannot be applied universally. Advertising expenses cannot logically be allocated to specific customers; however, some can be associated with products or territories.

---

[15] Ibid., pp. 100, 101.

[16] Debbie Berlont, Reese Browning, and George Foster, "How Hewlett-Packard Gets Numbers It Can Trust," *Harvard Business Review*, 68 (January–February 1990), pp. 178–183.

[17] Mossman, Fischer, and Crissy, "New Approaches for Analyzing Marketing Profitability," p. 44.

[18] Ibid.

In summary, profitability control requires a marketing-accounting system that codes expenses, as they are incurred, to the relevant functions and marketing segments. The result is a data base composed of cost modules that can be easily manipulated to determine profit performance by marketing segments—customers, products, and territories. How can the cost and revenue data be combined most effectively to provide a measure of profit performance?

Contribution to Profit

The important concept is *contribution to profit* rather than net profit; to arrive at a net profit figure, certain cost elements that either are fixed or are not within the control of the marketing manager must be deducted from revenues. For example, administrative and overhead costs do not vary with the level of marketing effort in the short run, and thus no attempt should be made to allocate them arbitrarily. Certain fixed costs assigned to an unprofitable territory would not be eliminated by an elimination of service to that territory. Net profit figures require too many arbitrary allocations to make them suitable for control and performance evaluation purposes.

A more useful and valid measure of performance is **controllable profit contribution**, that is, revenue associated with a marketing segment (product sales, sales to a particular customer group) minus the costs that can be directly attributed to that segment. Controllable costs are those costs that originate in a particular department (marketing) and over which the manager has some influence.[19] For example, the expenditure of $1,500 for a two-page, six-issue advertisement in *Plastics World* is a controllable cost for the marketing department. The expense could not be assigned to customer segments because there is no meaningful basis for allocating the cost, but it can be assigned to one specific product.

Net Segment Margin

The net result of contribution margin analysis is the **segment margin statement** (Table 18.7). Each measure of segment performance permits a unique type of analysis. The **segment contribution margin** represents the contribution to profits of the segment based on the revenue generated and on the controllable costs; the goal is to maximize revenue with respect to the controllable costs. The **segment controllable margin** includes a subtraction of those costs that are controllable by the manager, but that do not vary directly with the level of sales. For example, if the salespersons who sell to OEM accounts are paid a straight salary, the sales expense does not vary with the level of sales; but if OEM accounts were dropped, the expense would disappear. The controllable margin represents the net impact (positive or negative) of the segment on the firm's operation during the period. If a long-term view is desired, the **net segment margin** is determined by subtracting current costs associated with long-term assets. Net segment margin is not as useful as the other measures for decision-making purposes because it requires some arbitrary cost allocations.

---

[19] Patrick M. Dunne and Harry L. Wolk, "Marketing Cost Analysis: A Modularized Contribution Approach, *Journal of Marketing*, 41 (July 1977), p. 84.

TABLE 18.7   **Segment Margin Statement**

Revenue	$800,000
Less the production and marketing costs directly attributable to the segment	300,000
Segment Contribution Margin	500,000
Less the nonvariable costs incurred specifically for the segment	180,000
Segment Controllable Margin	320,000
Less a charge for the use of assets used by the segment, whose benefits apply over many future periods	80,000
Net Segment Margin	$240,000

Source: Adapted from Frank H. Mossman, Paul M. Fischer, and W. J. E. Crissy, "New Approaches to Analyzing Marketing Profitability," *Journal of Marketing*, 38 (April 1974), p. 46. Reprinted by permission of the American Marketing Association.

However, Charles Ames and James Hlavacek argue that the creation of net profitability statements is an effective method of focusing management attention on large elements of overhead or shared cost. As they state, "when firms allocate these costs to products or segments, they show up as a charge against earnings and managers responsible for profits carefully scrutinize and challenge them. This can be a powerful force toward reducing and getting large chunks of overhead costs under control that would otherwise never be scrutinized by someone with a direct profit responsibility."[20] Thus, although it is difficult and oftentimes impossible to effectively allocate overhead costs to segments, it may be useful as a motivator to get management to try to control overhead expenditures.

The contribution margin statements can be used for budgeting, performance analysis, short-run decision making, pricing, and evaluating alternatives(e.g., whether to keep a territory or to drop it, whether to use a distributor or a direct channel).[21] Because costs are developed first by functional areas and then by segments, the information system can be used to evaluate various marketing functions—for example, personal selling, distribution, and advertising.

In summary, profitability control evaluates the performance of various marketing segments. The key to successful profitability control is the marketing-accounting information system from which the manager develops segmented contribution statements. The segment controllable margin is the primary segmental performance measure; it relates controllable costs to segment revenues.

---

[20] B. Charles Ames and James D. Hlavacek, "Vital Truths About Managing Your Costs," *Harvard Business Review*, 68 (January–February 1990), p. 146.

[21] Dunne and Wolk, "Marketing Cost Analysis: A Modularized Contribution Approach," p. 85.

Marketing Control Systems: Industry Practices

How do business marketing managers evaluate marketing activities? This was the question posed in a study of the control measures used by 146 industrial manufacturers whose sales volumes ranged from $100 million to $500 million, with an average volume of about $150 million.[22]

Sales volume is the most typical measure used to evaluate product performance, followed by contribution of product to profit. Surprisingly, expenses incurred by the product were monitored by only 40 percent of the firms sampled. Sales volume is also the most frequently used measure of customer performance. The net profit from a customer is monitored by relatively few industrial firms.

The same pattern emerged with respect to geographical area performance measures. Again, sales performance was predominant, with only a fraction of the firms monitoring net profit by region. Only one-quarter of the total sample (37 responding firms) used order size performance measures, and most of these used sales volume rather than the net profit by order size. The analysis of order size is useful in developing quantity discounts, alternative forms of shipping, and differentiated sales commission rates.

Improving Efficiency and Effectiveness

The survey of industry marketing control practices suggests that there are significant opportunities for improving business marketing efficiency and effectiveness. The control phase continues to be the weak link in marketing management.[23] Given the rising concern about productivity and the sizable asset commitments of many industrial firms, return-on-assets would appear to be a valuable performance measure, yet it is one used by very few of the industrial firms sampled.

In analyzing profitability by market segment, predominant attention is given to output measures such as sales, and only limited attention is given to inputs or expenses. By linking sales to expenses by product, customer, territory, and order size, the business marketer is better equipped to allocate the marketing budget, establish strategic priorities, and uncover reasons for variations.

IMPLEMENTATION OF BUSINESS MARKETING STRATEGY

Many marketing plans fail because they are poorly implemented. **Marketing implementation** is the process that translates marketing plans into action assignments and ensures that such assignments are executed in a manner that will accomplish a plan's defined objectives.[24] Richard Williams, vice president of market strategy and

---

[22] Donald W. Jackson, Jr., Lonnie L. Ostrom, and Kenneth R. Evans, "Measures Used to Evaluate Industrial Marketing Activities," *Industrial Marketing Management*, 11 (1982), pp. 269–274.

[23] Dana Smith Morgan and Fred W. Morgan, "Marketing Cost Controls: A Survey of Industry Practices," *Industrial Marketing Management*, 9 (July 1980), pp. 217–221.

[24] Philip Kotler, *Marketing Management: Analysis, Planning, and Control*, p. 738.

THE GLOBAL MARKETPLACE
Information Technology and Global Strategy

Many forms of competitive advantage for the global marketer derive less from *where* the firm performs activities (e.g., manufacturing or R&D) than from *how* it performs them on a worldwide scale. Information technology increases a firm's ability to coordinate its activities on a regional, national, or global basis. To illustrate, Boeing employs computer-aided design technology to jointly design component parts on-line with foreign suppliers.

Michael Porter observes that "one of the patent advantages of the global firm is that it can spread activities among locations to reflect different preferred locations for different activities,

something a domestic or country-centered competitor does not do. Thus components can be made in Taiwan, software written in India, and basic R&D performed in the Silicon Valley, for example." Communication and coordination costs have dropped sharply, due to dramatic advances in information systems and telecommunication technology.

"Today's game of global strategy seems increasingly to be a game of coordination—getting more and more dispersed production facilities, R&D laboratories, and marketing activities to truly work together."

Source: Michael E. Porter, "Changing Patterns of International Competition," *California Management Review*, 28 (Winter 1986), pp. 9–40.

development at Unisys, commented during an interview that "great strategies poorly implemented are disasters; we've got to pay attention to high-quality execution."[25] Special implementation challenges emerge for the marketing manager because diverse functional areas participate in both the development and the execution of business marketing strategy.

The Strategy–Implementation Fit

"Marketing strategy and implementation affect each other. While strategy obviously affects actions, execution also affects marketing strategies, especially over time."[26] Although the dividing line between strategy and execution is a bit fuzzy, it is often not difficult to diagnose implementation problems and to distinguish them from strategy deficiencies. Consider the following:

> A firm introduced a new portable microcomputer that incorporated a number of features that the target market valued. The new product appeared to be well positioned in a rapidly growing market, but initial sales results were miserable. Why? The 50-person sales force had little incentive to grapple with a new unfamiliar product and continued to emphasize the older models. Given the significant market potential, management had

---

[25] Kate Bertrand, "Harvesting the Best," *Business Marketing*, 73 (October 1988), p. 41.

[26] Thomas V. Bonoma, "Making Your Marketing Strategy Work," *Harvard Business Review*, 62 (March–April 1984), pp. 69–76.

FIGURE 18.4   **Diagnosis of Marketing Strategy and Implementation**

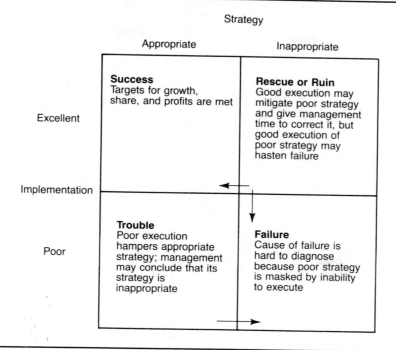

Source: Reprinted by permission of the *Harvard Business Review.* An exhibit from "Making Your Market-ing Strategy Work," by Thomas V. Bonoma (March–April 1984), p. 71. Copyright © 1984 by the President and Fellows of Harvard College, all rights reserved.

decided to set the sales incentive compensation level lower on the new machines than on the older ones. The older models had a selling cycle one-half as long as the new product and required no software knowledge or support.

In this case, poor execution damaged good strategy.[27]

Observe in Figure 18.4 how marketing strategy and implementation affect each other. When both strategy and implementation are appropriate, the firm is likely to be successful in achieving its objectives. Diagnosis becomes more difficult in other cases. For example, the cause of a marketing problem may be hard to detect when the strategy is on the mark but the implementation is poor. The business marketer may never become aware of the soundness of the strategy. Note also that excellent implementa-tion of a poor strategy (upper right cell) may give managers time to see the problem and correct it.

---

[27] Ibid., p. 70.

Implementation Skills

Thomas Bonoma identifies four implementation skills that are particularly important to the marketing manager: (1) interacting, (2) allocating, (3) monitoring, and (4) organizing.[28] Each assumes special significance in the business marketing environment.

Marketing managers are continually *interacting* with others both within and outside the corporation. Inside, a number of peers (e.g., R&D personnel) over whom the marketer has little power often assume a crucial role in strategy development and implementation. Outside, the marketer deals with important customers, channel members, advertising agencies, and the like. The best implementers have good bargaining skills and the ability to understand how others feel.

The implementer must also *allocate* time, assignments, people, dollars, and other resources among the marketing tasks at hand. Astute marketing managers are "tough and fair in putting people and dollars where they will be most effective. The less able ones routinely allocate too many dollars and people to mature programs and too few to richer ones."[29]

Marketing managers with good *monitoring* skills exhibit flexibility and intelligence in dealing with the firm's information and control systems. "Good implementers struggle and wrestle with their markets and businesses until they can simply and powerfully express the 'back of the envelope' ratios necessary to run the business, regardless of formal control system inadequacies."[30]

Finally, the best implementers are effective at *organizing*. Sound execution often hinges on the marketer's ability to work with both the formal and the informal networks within the organization. The manager customizes an informal organization in order to solve problems and to facilitate good execution.

The Marketing Strategy Center: An Implementation Guide[31]

Diverse functional areas participate to differing degrees in the development and implementation of business marketing strategy. Research and development, manufacturing, technical service, physical distribution, and other functional areas play fundamental roles. Ronald McTavish points out that "marketing specialists understand markets, but know a good deal less about the nuts and bolts of the company's operations—its internal terrain. This is the domain of the operating specialist. We need to bring these different specialists together in a 'synergistic pooling' of knowledge and viewpoint to achieve the best fit of the company's skills with the market and the

---

[28] Ibid., p. 70.

[29] Ibid., p. 75.

[30] Ibid., p. 75.

[31] Michael D. Hutt and Thomas W. Speh, "The Marketing Strategy Center: Diagnosing the Industrial Marketer's Interdisciplinary Role," *Journal of Marketing*, 48 (Fall 1984), pp. 53–61; and Michael D. Hutt, Peter H. Reingen, and John R. Ronchetto, Jr., "Tracing Emergent Processes in Marketing Strategy Formation," *Journal of Marketing*, 52 (January 1988), pp. 4–19.

INSIDE BUSINESS MARKETING

Marketing Expert Puts Strategy–Implementation Issues in Perspective

Thomas Bonoma, commenting in the *Marketing News*, offers some candid observations on the importance of effective strategy execution.

Strategic brilliance can't compensate for dim tactical follow-through. Researchers, teachers, and students must grapple with *marketing-as-practiced,* instead of focusing solely on strategic problems that can only define *marketing-as-conceived.*

The last 25 years have witnessed remarkable progress in management's strategic marketing sophistication. Trouble is, strategic brilliance isn't what's lacking in a world where corporations nominated as "key accounts" by their vendors don't know whom to call with a buying problem, and where airline travel, even "up front," is a dice throw of disappointments be-

tween the indigestible food and the surly service.

If strategies often fail to work, it's usually not because the plans aren't clever enough. It's because of the near total academic, consulting, and research emphasis on strategic brilliance versus tactical follow-through as the be-all and end-all of the marketing discipline.

It's not even clear whether firms *can* be strategically differentiated any longer. But, managing the quality with which the strategies are executed and seeking imaginative tactics for putting plans into practice can make all the difference. Unfortunately, most firms are far better at proposing effective action than at disposing it, as are most marketing academics.

Source: Adapted from Thomas V. Bonoma, "Enough About Strategy! Let's Get Some Clever Execution," *Marketing News* (February 13, 1989), p. 10.

company's approach to it."[32] This suggests a challenging and pivotal interdisciplinary role for the marketing manager in the industrial firm.

The marketing strategy center (discussed in Chapter 8) provides a framework for highlighting this interdisciplinary role and for exploring key implementation requirements. Observe that important strategic topics examined throughout this volume are highlighted in Table 18.8. In each case, nonmarketing personnel play active implementation roles. For example, product quality is directly or indirectly affected by several departments: manufacturing, research and development, technical service, and others. In turn, successful product innovation reflects the collective efforts of individuals drawn from several functional areas. Clearly, effective strategy implementation requires well-defined decision roles, responsibilities, timetables, and coordination mechanisms.

On a global market scale, special coordination challenges emerge when selected activities such as R&D are concentrated in one country and other strategy center activities such as manufacturing are dispersed across countries. Xerox, for example, has been successful in maintaining a high level of coordination across such dispersed

---

[32] Ronald McTavish, "Implementing Marketing Strategy," *Industrial Marketing Management*, 26 (Number 5, 1988), p. 10.

TABLE 18.8 Interfunctional Involvement in Marketing Strategy Implementation: An Illustrative Responsibility Chart*

Decision Area	Marketing	Sales	Manufacturing	R&D	Purchasing	Physical Distribution	Technical Service	Strategic Business Unit Manager	Corporate-Level Planner
Product/ service quality									
Technical service support									
Physical distribution service									
National accounts management									
Channel relations									
Sales support									
Product/ service innovation									

*Decision role vocabulary: R = Responsible   M = Implement
A = Approve   I = Inform
C = Consult   X = No role in decision

activities. The Xerox brand, marketing approach, and servicing procedures are standardized worldwide.[33]

The Marketer's Role

To ensure maximum customer satisfaction and the desired market response, the business marketer must assume an active role in the strategy center by negotiating market-sensitive agreements and by developing coordinated strategies with other members. While being influenced by other functional areas to varying degrees in the marketing decision-making process, the marketer can potentially serve as an influencer in key areas such as the design of the logistical system, the selection of manufacturing technology, or the structure of a materials management system. Such negotiation with other functional areas is fundamental to the business marketer's strategic interdisciplinary role. Thus, the successful business marketing manager performs as an integrator by drawing on the collective strengths of the enterprise to satisfy customer needs profitably.

LOOKING BACK

Figure 18.5 synthesizes the central components of business marketing management and highlights the material presented in this volume. Part I introduced the major classes of customers that constitute the business market—commercial enterprises, governmental units, and institutions. The buying behavior of these consumers was considered in Part II, with particular attention to the myriad forces that act upon organizational decision makers and decision influencers. Part III discussed the business marketing intelligence system and the tools for assessing market opportunities; it explored techniques for measuring market potential, identifying market segments, and forecasting sales. Functionally integrated marketing planning provides a framework for dealing with each component of the business marketing mix, as detailed in Part IV.

Once business marketing strategy is formulated, the manager must evaluate the response of target market segments in order to ensure that any discrepancy between planned and actual results is minimized. This chapter, Part V, explored the critical dimensions of the marketing control process, which is the final loop in the model presented in Figure 18.5—planning for and acquiring marketing information. Such information forms the core of the firm's management information system; it is derived internally through the marketing-accounting system and externally through the marketing research function. The evaluation and control process enables the marketer to reassess business market opportunities and to make adjustments as needed in business marketing strategy.

---

[33] Michael E. Porter, "Changing Patterns of International Competition," *California Management Review*, 28 (Winter 1986), pp. 9–40.

FIGURE 18.5 **A Framework for Business Marketing Management**

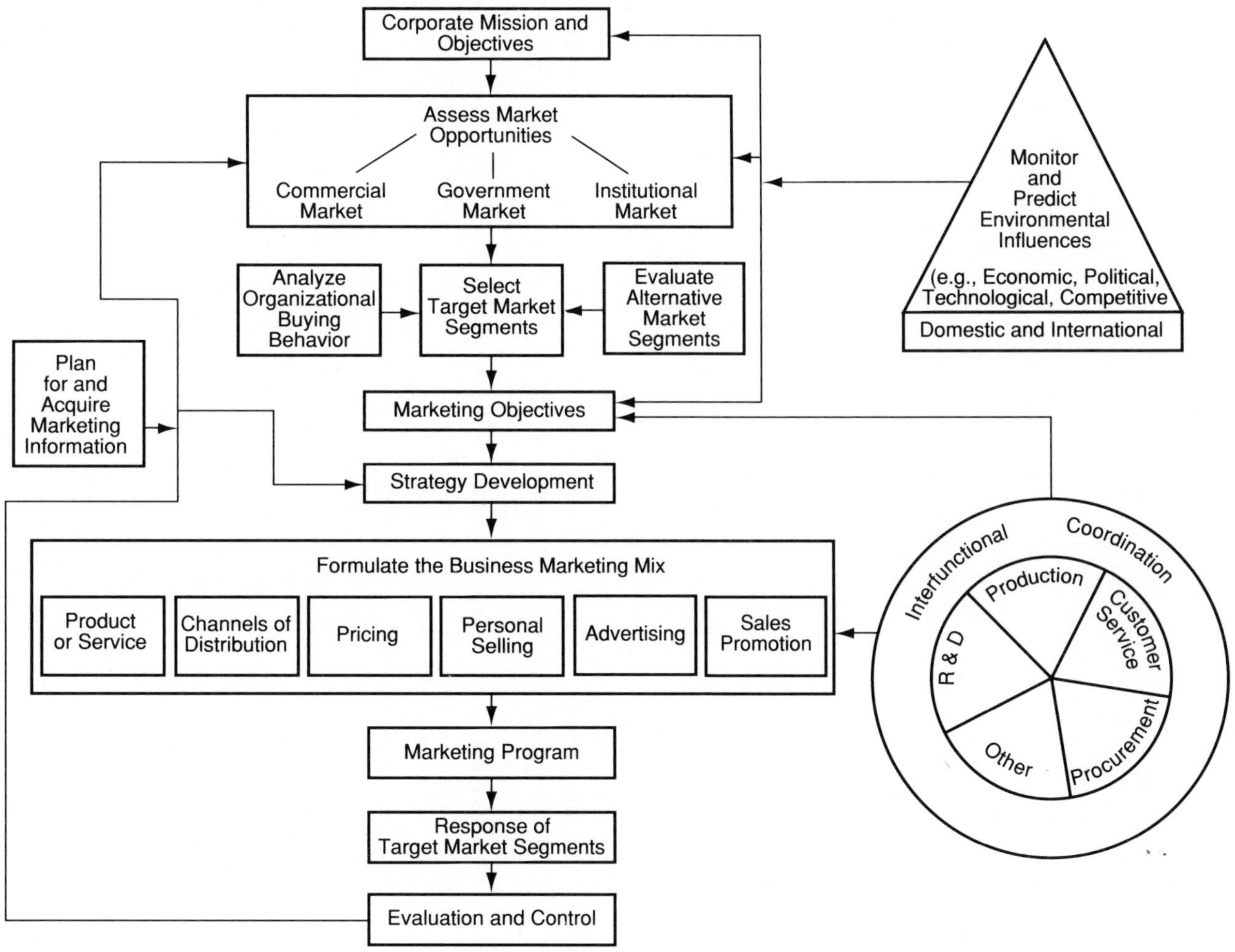

SUMMARY

Central to market strategy is the allocation of resources to each strategy element and the application of marketing efforts to segments. The marketing control system is the process by which the industrial firm generates information to make these decisions. Moreover, the marketing control system is the means by which current performance can be evaluated and steps can be taken to correct deficiencies.

An effective control system has four distinct components. Strategic control, which is operationalized through the marketing audit, provides evaluative information on the present and future course of the firm's basic product/market mission. Annual plan control compares annual to planned results in order to provide input for future planning. Strategic component control focuses on the effectiveness of each element in the marketing strategy. Finally, profitability control seeks to evaluate profitability by segment.

Many business marketing plans fail because they are poorly executed. Marketing implementation is the process that translates marketing plans into action assignments and ensures that such assignments are executed in a timely and effective manner. Four implementation skills are particularly important to the business marketing manager: (1) interacting, (2) allocating, (3) monitoring, and (4) organizing. Nonmarketing personnel play active roles in the implementation of business marketing strategy. This suggests a challenging and pivotal interdisciplinary role for the marketing manager.

Discussion Questions

1. Last December, Lisa Schmitt, vice president of marketing at Bock Machine Tool, identified four market segments that her firm would attempt to penetrate this year. As the year comes to an end, Lisa would like to evaluate the firm's performance in each of these segments. Of course, Lisa turns to you for assistance. First, what information would you seek from the firm's marketing information system in order to perform the analysis? Second, how would you know whether the firm's performance in a particular market segment was good or bad?

2. Susan Breck, president of Breck Chemical Corporation, added three new products to the firm's line two years ago in order to serve the needs of five SIC groups. Each of the products has a separate advertising budget, although they are sold by the same salespersons. Susan requests your assistance in determining what type of information the firm should be gathering in order to monitor and control the performance of these products. Outline your reply.

3. Assume that the information you requested in Question 2 has been gathered for you. How would you determine whether advertising and personal selling funds should be shifted from one product to another?

4. Hamilton Tucker, president of Tucker Manufacturing Company, is concerned about the seat-of-the-pants approach used by managers in allocating the marketing budget. He cites the Midwest and the East as examples. The firm increased its demand-stimulating expenditures (e.g., advertising, personal selling) in the

Midwest by 20 percent, but sales climbed only 6 percent last year. In contrast, demand-stimulating expenditures were cut by 17 percent in the East, and sales dropped by 22 percent. Hamilton would like you to assist the midwestern and eastern regional managers in allocating their funds next year. Carefully outline the approach you would follow.

5. Delineate the central components of the marketing control process. Describe the role of the control system in formal marketing planning.

6. Distinguish between *contribution to profit* and *net profit.*

7. Using the marketing strategy center concept as a guide, describe how a strategy that is entirely appropriate for a particular target market might fail due to poor implementation in the logistics and technical service areas.

8. Describe how the strategy implementation challenges for a marketing manager working at Du Pont (industrial firm) might be different from those for a marketing manager working at Pillsbury (consumer-goods firm).

PART VI

Cases

Case Planning Guide

Page	Case #	Case Title	1	2	3	4	5	6	7	8	9	10	11	12	13	14	15	16	17	18
	1	E. I. du Pont de Nemours & Co., Inc.							x	x		x						x		x
	2	Ideal Brands, Inc.	x	x	x															
	3	Cameron Auto Parts		x	x															
	4	Southwestern Ohio Steel Co. (A)					x	x		x	x		x			x	x			
	5	Trus Joist Corporation (B)			x	x		x		x			x				x			
	6	Caterpillar Tractor Company										x	x		x		x			
	7	The McKenzie Company (A)													x				x	
	8	The McKenzie Company (B)													x					
	9	Beta Pharmaceuticals: Pennsylvania Distribution System													x	x				
	10	S. C. Johnson and Son, Limited (R)	x	x				x							x	x	x		x	
	11	Texas Instruments: Electronic Appliance Controls				x				x		x	x				x			x
	12	Afton Industries															x			
	13	Rogers, Nagel, Langhart (RNL PC), Architects and Planners			x	x		x	x	x	x	x		x	x	x		x	x	x
	14	Microsoft Corporation						x		x	x	x		x			x	x		
	15	Brand Pipe Company				x		x		x		x			x	x	x	x	x	
	16	Lectron Corporation				x	x	x	x	x		x	x		x	x		x	x	x
	17	Multicon, Incorporated (A)							x	x		x	x	x						
	18	Ethical Dilemmas in Business Marketing	x	x	x															

E. I. du Pont de Nemours & Co., Inc.

David T. Blake, marketing director for the Spunbonded Division in the Textile Fibers Department of du Pont, reviewed the 1984 marketing plan as he thought about the 1985 plan, which was due in a few weeks. The overall strategy for Sontara fiber in the surgical gown and drape market and for Tyvek fiber in the construction industry had already been formulated; now he wondered whether the budget proposals on his desk fit the strategies.

Company Background

Du Pont, with 1983 sales of $35.4 billion, ranked seventh in the Fortune 500 list of companies. Comprising 90 major businesses and operating in more than 50 countries, du Pont organized its more than 1,700 products in eight industry segments: biomedical products; coal; petroleum exploration and production; industrial and consumer products; polymers; agricultural and industrial chemicals; petroleum refining, marketing, and transportation; and fibers (see Exhibit 1.1).

The fibers segment (1983 sales: $4.8 billion) marketed the world's most extensive offering of man-made fibers, including fiber products for apparel, carpets, tire and aircraft component reinforcement, road support, packaging, protective clothing, and medical apparel. The company sold the fiber products to textile and other

Source: This case was written by Jonathan Guiliano, MBA 1985, under the supervision of Professor Cornelius A. de Kluyver, as the basis for class discussion rather than to illustrate effective or ineffective handling of an administrative situation. Copyright 1984 by the Darden Graduate Business School Foundation, Charlottesville, Virginia.

EXHIBIT 1.1 **Industry Segments: E. I. du Pont de Nemours & Co., Inc.**

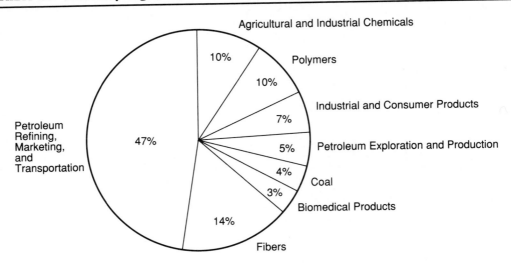

Industry Segment	1983 Sales (billions)	Products
• Petroleum refining, marketing, and transportation	16.8	Gasoline, jet fuel, diesel fuel, heating oil, fuel oil, asphalt, petroleum coke, natural gas liquids
• Fibers	4.8	Man-made fibers
• Agricultural and industrial chemicals	3.5	Fungicides, herbicides, insecticides, pigments, organic chemicals, fluorochemicals, petroleum additives, mineral acids.
• Polymer products	3.4	Plastic resins, elastomers, films
• Industrial and consumer products	2.5	Photographic products, electronic products, analytic instruments, explosives, nonstick coatings, sporting firearms and ammunition
• Petroleum exploration and production	1.9	Crude oil, natural gas
• Coal	1.4	Steam coal, metallurgical coal
• Biomedical products	1.1	Clinical instruments, biomedical instruments, prescription pharmaceuticals, radio pharmaceuticals

manufacturers that processed them into consumer goods. Four groups made up this segment of the business: apparel fibers, carpet fibers, industrial fibers, and spunbonded products.

The Spunbonded Products Division

The Spunbonded Division (1983 sales: $500 million) produced and marketed four products:

EXHIBIT 1.2   **Spunbonded Product Manufacture**

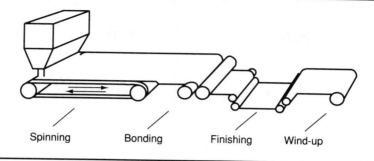

Spinning   Bonding   Finishing   Wind-up

REEMAY®—spunbonded polyester
TYPAR®—spunbonded polypropylene
TYVEK®—spunbonded olefin
SONTARA®—spunlaced fabrics

Manufacturing the first three of these generally involved a continuous process of spinning, bonding, and finishing, as diagrammed in Exhibit 1.2; the process to make Sontara involved fiber entanglement and related steps.

REEMAY®, a polyester, was a lightweight, hygienically safe, heat-resistant fiber that was used as apparel interliner, coverstock (e.g., to cover diapers), and agricultural crop cover. TYPAR® was a strong, stable, low-cost polypropylene used as primary carpet backing, as a geotextile (to provide drainage under roads), and in furniture as a replacement for burlap. TYVEK®, a strong and opaque olefin with a protective barrier, was used for envelopes, disposable apparel, sterile packaging, bookcovers, tags and labels, and "housewrap" (material to provide a barrier against air infiltration). SON-TARA® structures were noted for softness, absorbency, and comfort, and were used in curtains, bedspreads, and surgical gowns and drapes.

The Spunbonded Division was managed by a division director. Reporting to him were a technical director, a manufacturing director, and a marketing director, David T. Blake. Reporting to Mr. Blake were a number of marketing managers responsible for various end-user markets for the division's products; each marketing manager was assisted by several marketing and technical representatives. Throughout the Spunbonded Division, managers used a communications network through personal computers, on which they also ran their own software for analysis and control. The Spunbonded Division was one of the first divisions to use computer networking at du Pont.

Marketing managers submitted annual budget proposals to the marketing director, who reviewed and usually approved them. If Mr. Blake thought a proposal was unreasonable, he asked the marketing manager to modify it and then combined the various proposals into an overall marketing plan for consideration by the division director.

EXHIBIT 1.3   **U.S. Surgical Gown and Drape Market Trends**

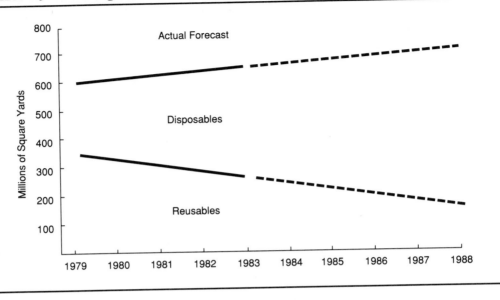

Sontara Spunlaced Products

Sontara, introduced in 1975, was a sheet structure of entangled fibers. It looked and felt like a conventional textile, and was made from 100 percent polyester, or a blend of polyester and rayon, or from a woodpulp/polyester blend. This last was used primarily for disposable surgical gowns and drapes in hospital operating rooms; the gowns were worn by operating personnel and the drapes were used for patient apparel and to cover objects. Sontara accounted for about 17 percent of all division sales in 1983.

The Surgical Gown and Drape Market

The U.S. market for surgical gowns and drapes in 1983 was approximately 637 million square yards, and its annual growth rate was about 2 percent. The market was divided into two parts: reusable fabric, or cotton; and disposable fabrics, such as Sontara. The benefits of cotton such as comfort, absorbency, and in the short term, cost, were increasingly becoming outweighed by the advantages of disposables—principally, convenience and infection-barrier qualities. Market share for disposables was 55 percent in 1983 with a forecast annual growth rate of 8 percent for the next few years (see Exhibit 1.3 for market trends). It was thought unlikely that more than 90 percent of the market would ever switch to disposables. Fabric manufacturers, or fabric suppliers, in the disposables market, made the fabric and sold it to firms that made the gowns and drapes and sold them to hospitals. Unlike du Pont, several companies were both fabric manufacturers and gown and drape makers and suppliers, as shown in

EXHIBIT 1.4   **Relationships among Companies in the U.S. Surgical Gown and Drape Market**   The companies in the first column manufacture fabric that they sell to respective companies in the second column, which in turn make gowns and drapes and sell them directly to hospitals.

Fabrics and Manufacturers	Gown and Drape Makers and Hospital Suppliers
Chicopee (Johnson & Johnson)	Johnson & Johnson
Sontara (du Pont)	American Hospital Supply
Regard (Kimberly-Clark)	
Spunguard (Kimberly-Clark)	Kimberly-Clark
Boundary (Procter & Gamble)	
Signature (Procter & Gamble)	Procter & Gamble
Assure I (Dexter)	
Assure III (Dexter)	AHS and others

Exhibit 1.4. Du Pont sold Sontara to Johnson & Johnson (J&J) and to American Hospital Supply (AHS). J&J also manufactured a fabric, Chicopee, or Fabric 450, which it made into gowns and drapes and sold to hospitals. AHS sold gowns and drapes of both Sontara and Regard, a Kimberly-Clark (K-C) product. Besides Regard, K-C, the first company in the disposables market, also manufactured Spunguard, a fabric which K-C made into gowns and drapes and sold to hospitals. Procter & Gamble (P&G) manufactured two fabrics, Boundary and Signature, also made them into gowns and drapes, and sold them to hospitals.

Among companies selling gowns and drapes to hospitals, AHS held a dominant position, with J&J and P&G a strong second and third. Among disposable materials used for gowns and drapes, Sontara barely trailed the two K-C products combined, as shown in Exhibit 1.5. Du Pont's Tyvek also held a one percent share of all gown and drape fabric sales. Exhibits 1.6 and 1.7 provide additional information on U.S. surgical and drape market.

Competition, which had already eroded gownmaker profit margins, was widely expected to grow more intense. Du Pont's main competitors were K-C, P&G, and J&J's Chicopee Division. K-C (1983 total sales: $3.3 billion), though steadily losing market share, had begun to consolidate its position as a fully integrated supplier to the medical apparel market; it had recently added production capacity and expanded its sales force. K-C's Regard continued to lose share to Sontara at AHS; of course, because K-C also supplied hospitals with gowns and drapes made of its Spunguard, AHS both bought from K-C and competed against it. P&G (1983 sales: $12.5 billion) had entered the market several years ago as a vertically integrated supplier and touched off protracted price competition. To strengthen its position, P&G had reorganized its highly visible medical apparel sales force, a few years previously. Like P&G, J&J (1983 sales: $6.0 billion) recently had invested heavily in research and development. Production costs at Chicopee were now high, but because of J&J's large volume, it was expected that the company would move quickly down the experience curve and costs would drop.

EXHIBIT 1.5

A. Market Shares of Companies Selling Directly to Hospitals

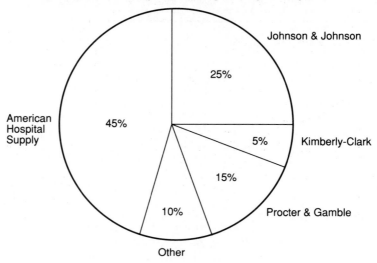

- Johnson & Johnson — 25%
- Kimberly-Clark — 5%
- Procter & Gamble — 15%
- Other — 10%
- American Hospital Supply — 45%

B. Market Shares of Materials Used by Hospitals

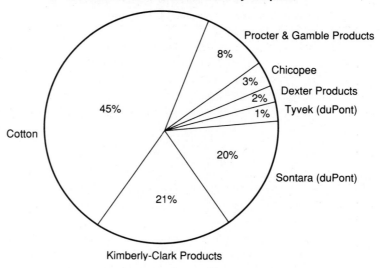

- Procter & Gamble Products — 8%
- Chicopee — 3%
- Dexter Products — 2%
- Tyvek (duPont) — 1%
- Sontara (duPont) — 20%
- Kimberly-Clark Products — 21%
- Cotton — 45%

EXHIBIT 1.6 **U.S. Surgical Gown and Drape Market**

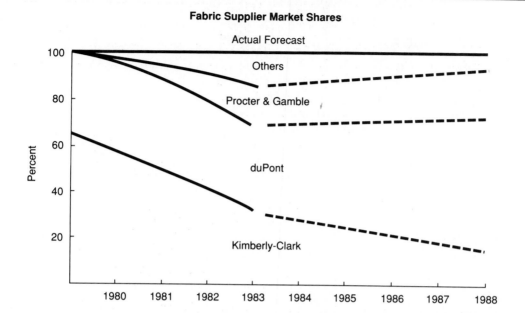

Fabric Supplier Market Shares

EXHIBIT 1.7 **U.S. Surgical Gown and Drape Market**

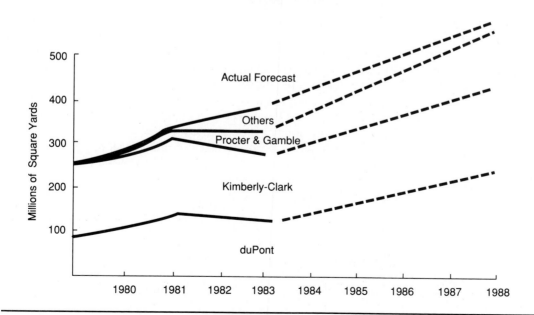

Fabric Supplier Sales

J&J's Chicopee was much softer than Sontara, but was therefore also more difficult to process. J&J often sold gowns and drapes made of Sontara and later substituted Chicopee, which was relatively simple to do because neither J&J nor AHS used the Sontara name on their products.

In addition to these complex company rivalries and relationships, there were still others of possible significance. K-C, for example, also competed against Sontara in the home furnishings, furniture, and bedding market, and against Tyvek in the industrial apparel market. Although a competitor of du Pont, P&G was also a customer; P&G used du Pont's spunbonded fabric Reemay as a coverstock for disposable diapers. And although the Spunbonded Products Division was engaged in sales of Sontara only to hospital suppliers and not in sales of Sontara apparel to hospitals, du Pont did have sales forces that sold other du Pont products directly to hospitals.

Cost, "barrier," and "flexural rigidity" were the three most important qualities used to compare surgical gowns and drapes. "Barrier" referred to how well the fabric protected against infection, and "flexural rigidity" defined the material's comfort and wear. Exhibit 1.8 diagrams the relative positions of the competing fabrics in terms of each of these three qualities; the fabrics most directly comparable and competitive with Sontara were P&G's Boundary and J&J's Chicopee.

Strategy and Tactics for Sontara

The future of Sontara involved several problems. First, because of increasing price competition, R&D was needed to lower unit production costs. Second, end-user brand awareness for Sontara was relatively low, primarily because J&J and AHS never identified the Sontara name. Third, hospitals, under government pressure to reduce costs, were becoming more price sensitive, and purchase decisions were increasingly made by administrators rather than by operating room nurses who used the gowns and drapes and understood Sontara's value. Fourth, every hospital had its own accounting system, so it was difficult to prove the long-term cost-effectiveness of Sontara products. Fifth, because hospitals would rarely admit to incidences of post-operative infection, it was also difficult to demonstrate Sontara's ability to reduce such infections. Sixth, disposables threatened to become commodities as more hospitals switched from cotton to disposable products. Finally, du Pont faced potentially severe capacity limitations, which impeded the company's ability to compete aggressively.

Despite these problems, the market offered opportunities as the preference for disposable fabric increased, as professional groups, such as the Association of Operating Room Nurses (AORN), made statements favoring disposables as more clinical proof of Sontara's efficacy became available, and as new uses for Sontara, such as for scrub suits, developed.

In view of these circumstances, du Pont's two principal strategic objectives for Sontara were (i) to at least maintain market share over the next two years, without further price erosion, until the capacity problems had been resolved, and (ii) to convince garment makers that du Pont could support them in promoting Sontara to end-users and would remain a strong force in the disposable fabric business. At the

EXHIBIT 1.8 **Key Fabric Properties of Surgical Gowns and Drapes**

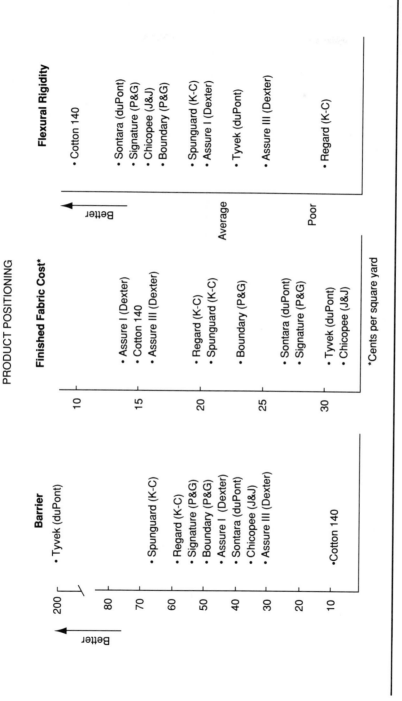

PRODUCT POSITIONING

same time, the company planned to continue R&D to lower production costs as a hedge against further price reductions and to restore profit margins.

To implement this strategy, the 1984 budget for Sontara had consisted of $450,000 for the sales force and $92,000 for advertising and promotion. Advertising and promotion were principally targeted toward operating room nurses, who traditionally decided what garments and drapes to buy. About $50,000 of this amount was spent on repeating the "Scrubby the Surgical Bear" campaign at the next annual AORN conference. Nurses had to listen to a 10-minute presentation about Sontara by a mind reader to receive a small teddy bear dressed in Sontara surgical garb and enclosed in a Tyvek sterile package. Scrubby had become a favorite at the conferences, and many nurses would stop by "Bear Mountain" to hear Scrubby's message:

> Hi!
> I'm Scrubby the Surgical Bear! I'm wearing soft, single-use surgical garments made with SONTARA spunlaced fabric from du Pont. SONTARA keeps me cool and comfortable, and helps prevent infections in my patients.
>
> Notice that my package has a tough lid of TYVEK spunbonded olefin from du Pont. Sterile packing of TYVEK gives me superior protection. It keeps out water and bacteria, resists punctures and tears, peels open cleanly and has proven shelf life.
>
> Take good care of me, just as SONTARA and TYVEK take good care of you and your patients in the O.R.!
>
> Love,
>
> Scrubby

The cost of the bears was $20,000. Brochures depicting Scrubby were $10,000. Du Pont also sent direct mail material (shown in Exhibit 1.9) to AORN nurses at a cost of $7,000, and ran advertisements (shown in Exhibit 1.10) at a cost of $5,000, in the AORN Journal (circulation 50,000) to give away big Scrubbies (Exhibit 1.10). Du Pont estimated that over the past two years, this program had put Sontara in touch with 25 percent of the 55,000 operating room nurses in the U.S.

The sales force allocation for Sontara was an estimate. It assumed that the marketing division assigned the equivalent of four-and-one-half people to the gown and drape market, and that each person represented about $100,000 in total cost. Tentative plans for 1985 called for the same sales force expenditure and an increase of 25 percent for each item in the advertising and promotion budget.

Tyvek

Tyvek spunbonded olefin was a sheet of extremely fine, high-density polyethylene fibers. It was a high-strength, high-barrier, low-weight structure, resistant to tearing, puncturing, shrinking, and rotting. One of the many uses for Tyvek was as "housewrap," an air infiltration barrier for homes, introduced in 1981. U.S. sales for Tyvek housewrap in 1983 were $2.8 million, or 800,000 pounds, while international sales were $0.8 million, or 400,000 pounds. Total Tyvek sales in 1983 were in excess of $100 million.

EXHIBIT 1.9   **The du Pont Bear Lair**   Sample of mailer sent out to 6,000 preregistered O.R. nurses prior to the 1984 A.O.R.N. Congress in Atlanta.

Mailer tied together the "bear theme," also made it easier for nurses to find du Pont booth among the hundreds they could visit, and promoted the annual du Pont Vacation Sweepstakes (which helps pull traffic to the booth).

Make Tracks
for the du Pont Bear Mountain
- Scrubby the Surgical Bear
- The Amazing Zellman, Psychic Perceptionist
- The du Pont 1984 AORN Vacation Sweepstakes

THE
DU PONT
BEAR
LAIR

EXHIBIT 1.10   **Win Your Own "Scrubby the Bear"**

Just answer these easy questions about SONTARA® spunlaced fabric for single-use O.R. gowns and drapes.

You may be one of 75 lucky O.R. nurses who'll win a 3-foot high "Scrubby the Surgical Bear" dressed in cap, mask and gown of SONTARA.* SONTARA is the *soft* gown and drape fabric . . . the one with over 10 years' proven O.R. experience. And made only by du Pont, a leader in health-care product research.

You're always a winner if you ask for SONTARA by name . . . from such leading O.R. gown and drape manufacturers as American Convertors, Surgikos, Kendall, and Mars.

Now . . . answer the questions, and qualify to win a giant "Scrubby" bear. Use either this form or a reasonable facsimile.

	Yes	No
• SONTARA is the most cloth-like, single-use O.R. fabric.	☐	☐
• SONTARA is remarkably strong, light, and comfortable.	☐	☐
• SONTARA is a proven barrier material.	☐	☐
• SONTARA lints less than reinforced paper or cotton.	☐	☐
• SONTARA fabric is available in gowns and drapes from leading manufacturers.	☐	☐

Winners will be selected at random from all entries received before March 1, 1984. You must be an O.R. nurse to win. Send your completed entry form to:

"Scrubby" Contest, du Pont Company, Room X40201, Wilmington, DE 19898

Name _____   Title _____

Hospital _____   Address _____

City, State, Zip _____

*Du Pont registered trademark. Du Pont makes SONTARA® spunlaced fabric, not gowns and drapes.

Tyvek housewrap was stapled to the sheathing of a home under construction before siding was put up. An average house required 16 pounds of Tyvek; the cost of Tyvek to the home builder averaged less than $200, including labor, for a conventional woodframe house. In a National Association of Home Builders study, Tyvek was reported to reduce heating costs by an average of 30 percent and air conditioning expenses by approximately 10 percent. The Tyvek wrap covered cracks and seams, thereby enhancing or protecting the effectiveness of a home's insulation.

The Market for Housewrap

Housewrap sales were directly related to new housing starts. As interest rates declined in 1983, starts for one-family houses soared to 0.9 million, and Tyvek housewrap sales exceeded forecasts by 60 percent. The 1984 forecast for new one-family homes was 1.0 million. It was estimated that Tyvek housewrap sales in the United States would reach 2.3 million pounds in 1984 (see Exhibit 1.11).

Tyvek's only direct competitor as a housewrap was 15-pound felt, or tar paper, which was thick, heavy and difficult to install because it tore easily. Although tar paper's price was about one-third less, Tyvek cost less overall because of labor savings during installation.

Because of the size of the market, and despite numerous patents on Tyvek, du Pont expected competition for housewrap to increase significantly in the near future. Among potential competitors were Boise Cascade (1983 sales: $3.5 billion), Certain-Teed (1983 sales: $1.0 billion), Georgia-Pacific (1983 sales: $6.5 billion), and Kimberly-Clark (1983 sales: $3.3 billion).

Du Pont sold Tyvek to 42 leading building supply distributors with 83 warehouses throughout the United States. These distributors, carefully selected by du Pont, sold to dealers, who in turn sold to home builders. In some areas, the distributor's sales force called directly on home builders.

Builders were the key buying influence for housewrap. Secondary influences included architects, government agencies, city and state building code officials, and energy conservation specialists at public utilities. Home buyers, increasingly energy-conscious, were also becoming more important.

Strategy and Tactics for Tyvek

Du Pont's principal objective for Tyvek was to achieve maximum market penetration in the shortest possible time. The 1985 strategy for Tyvek, therefore, was to continue to gain visibility, to strengthen the distributor network, and to promote the product as effectively as possible.

The 1984 budget for Tyvek housewrap had consisted of $250,000 for sales and as detailed in Exhibit 1.12, $475,000 for advertising and promotion. Ads, such as the one shown in Exhibit 1.13, were placed in trade and professional magazines to reach home builders and architects. Sales aids were developed for distributors, dealers, and home builders; and a direct mail campaign was mounted to buyers of blueprints for house

EXHIBIT 1.11   **Sales of Tyvek Housewrap**

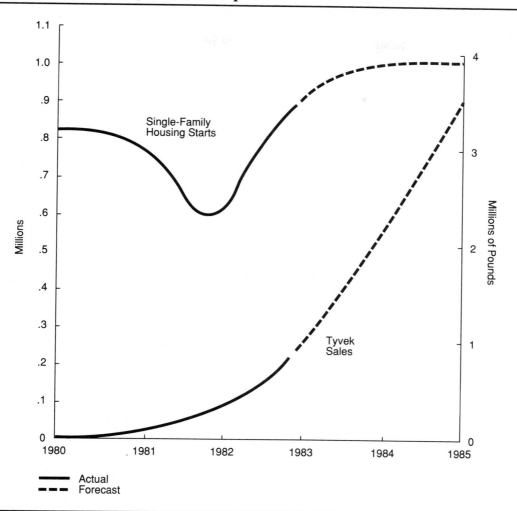

designs from certain companies. (See Exhibit 1.14 for a Tyvek direct mail piece.) In addition, the division had initiated co-op advertising with distributors, and made information about research findings on Tyvek's ability to conserve energy available to various publications through press releases. Finally, the budget covered trade shows, such as du Pont's exhibit at the National Association of Home Builders' annual convention. Tentative budget plans for 1985 kept the sales force expenditure at the current level and increased advertising and promotion by 50 percent, with allocations similar to those of the 1984 plan.

EXHIBIT 1.12   **Tyvek 1984 Advertising and Promotion Budget**

Advertising
BUILDER magazine, 8X	$ 55,000
PROFESSIONAL BUILDER, 8X	53,000
MULTI-HOUSING WORLD, 8X	28,000
PROGRESSIVE ARCHITECTURE, 8X	16,000
Sweet's 1985	8,000
Test publications	5,000
Preparation	12,000
du Pont magazine	1,000
TOTAL	$178,000

Sales Aids
Builder Support:
Model home display	$ 3,000
Homebuyer sell sheet	2,000
'Wise Builder' certificate	4,000
Mailing to HOME PLANNERS and HOME MAGAZINE plan buyers	10,000

Retailer Support:
Literature	50,000
Co-op support	110,000
Co-op merchandising	1,000

Distributor Support:
Distributor sales meeting	9,000
Distributor handbook	2,000
Sweet's brochure	8,000
LaBelle presentation	7,000
Masthead mailings	6,000
NAHB exhibit	20,000
Multi-Housing World exhibit	20,000
Regional shows	12,000
Manufactured-home support	12,000
Inquiry handling	1,000
Postage/freight	1,000
Store room	1,500
List maintenance	500
TOTAL	$280,000

Product Information
Press release production	$ 8,000
Press release distribution	3,000
COST SAVING release	4,000
Photography	2,000
TOTAL	$ 17,000

TOTAL Advertising and Promotion 1984	$475,000

EXHIBIT 1.13   **TYVEK Housewrap**

New test proves TYVEK Housewrap cuts heating costs 29%. And that sells homes.

Give yourself a competitive edge and a faster sale by offering homebuyers the extra value of TYVEK Housewrap.

The NAHB Research Foundation determined that there is a 29% reduction in heating costs in a home wrapped with TYVEK.* Placed over sheathing, TYVEK seals cracks and seams and significantly reduces interior air exchange rate.

It also keeps air out of the wall cavity, preserving insulation R-value and reducing heat loss through walls. And because it passes moisture vapor, it won't cause in-wall condensation.

It costs under $200 to wrap an average-size house. That includes labor. Two workers can put up 1,800 square feet in less than two hours with just a knife and staple gun.

TYVEK helps homes sell faster, and du Pont helps you get the word out with free literature and model display.

Order TYVEK Housewrap—made only by du Pont—from your building supply dealer. And for free test data literature and the name of your nearest distributor, call (302) 999-5088. Or write du Pont Company, Room G-39982, Wilmington, DE 19898.

*Before-and-after test on a conventionally constructed 2-by-4 wood-frame home with R-11 insulation in walls. Your savings may be more or less depending on climate and construction.

TYVEK Housewrap is a du Pont trademark for its air infiltration barrier.

EXHIBIT 1.14   **TYVEK Housewrap**

Energy-saving air infiltration barrier
A simple, inexpensive way to improve energy efficiency and make your homes more appealing.

Cold air infiltration consumes up to 40% of home heat. At the same time, cold air passing through insulation significantly reduces R-value. Housewrap of TYVEK* spunbonded elefin seals cracks and seams in sheathing and at plates and sills. It keeps cold air out of insulation, so insulation delivers its full R-value. And it keeps cold air out of the house and warm air in.

TYVEK reduces heat loss
Tests on an NAHB research home showed a 29% reduction in heating costs after applying TYVEK.† That's the kind of energy-savings home buyers are looking for. And it costs very little to add to your homes.

TYVEK won't cause condensation build-up
It's a durable sheet of high-density polyethylene fibers. It's not a film or paper. It allows moisture vapor to pass through (94 perm), so there's no danger of in-wall condensation. It's lightweight, tear-resistant and will never rot or shrink.

TYVEK is easy to install
Start at one corner and roll over the entire wall, wrapping around corners and over doors and windows. One man rolls, the other follows, applying staples or roofing nails.

When house is wrapped, go back and x-out windows and doors, pulling TYVEK in over window frame.

TYVEK comes in two sizes: 3 ft. wide rolls covering 999 sq. ft. and 9 ft. rolls covering 1755 sq. ft. One 9 ft. roll covers an average-size house and weights only sixteen pounds. Two men can do a typical house in less than two hours, so labor cost is minimal. Find out from your building dealer how little it costs to add this important energy-saving feature to your homes.

The 1984 Budget Review

In considering how the 1985 budget proposals fit his strategies for Sontara and Tyvek, Mr. Blake had several questions. How would each product's push and pull emphasis change in 1985? How did the marketing mix affect push and pull, and how did the elements of the mix interact? What results would the various elements cause at different expenditure levels? He wondered how competitors' marketing strategies affected Sontara. He also thought about buyer behavior: How well would each product do in a use test at the current price? Of the total value that buyers of Sontara and Tyvek received, how much of that value was built into the product and how much was added by marketing? Which mix elements contributed the most value? To find answers to these questions, he talked with the Sontara and Tyvek marketing managers.

John Murray, marketing manager for Sontara in the surgical gown and drape market, described the emphasis behind the 1984 budget as push rather than pull. He estimated that 75 percent of the current effort was push and that the percentage should go unchanged until he had something with which to launch a cost-effective pull campaign. For example, Sontara was under clinical study for the next two or three years, after which he could put the findings in professional journal ads and in direct mail to doctors, nurses, hospital administrators, and others. With this type of campaign, the push/pull percentage could approach 50/50.

Mr. Murray believed that it was misleading to identify specific budget items in the 1984 advertising and promotion budget as mix elements. It was more accurate, he said, to think of the overall budget as one-third advertising activity and two-thirds trade support. He said that the difference between the two was that the intent of advertising was to create a favorable image for the product, and the intent of trade support was to assist indirectly the sales effort of du Pont customers. Because all budget items were part advertising and part trade support, it was more useful to look at the total budget rather than at each item. The $92,000 advertising and promotion expenditure in 1984, he said, was in effect $31,000 for advertising and $61,000 for trade support. He thought that the same proportion was appropriate for the 1985 proposal of $115,000: $40,000 for advertising, and $75,000 for trade support. So, with $450,000 for the sales force, the three general mix elements were sales force, advertising, and trade support.

As he looked at the market, however, Mr. Murray found that these three elements did not fully capture the marketing activity of both du Pont and its competitors. He believed that the sales force actually involved two functions: to maintain the current sales effort, and to do missionary sales. He said that he could make the same distinction concerning trade support, and that he could divide advertising between advertising to intermediate-users (i.e., gown and drape makers) and to end-users (i.e., hospitals). The 1985 proposal, he said, thus involved six mix elements: $450,000 in sales force/maintenance, $0 in sales force/missionary, $75,000 in trade support/maintenance, $0 in trade support/missionary, $10,000 in advertising/intermediate-users, and $30,000 in advertising/end-users.

Mr. Murray believed that the effective level of competitors' marketing spending was $900,000 sales force/maintenance, $100,000 sales force/missionary, $150,000 trade support/maintenance, $75,000 trade support/missionary, $25,000 advertising/intermediate-users, and $100,000 advertising/end-users.

Regarding how the various marketing mix elements interrelated, he said he was inclined to believe that the effectiveness of each element depended on the effectiveness of the others. The effectiveness of additional expenditures, he said, followed a concave curve for sales force/maintenance, trade support/maintenance, and advertising/intermediate-users. For the other three elements, the curve was S-shaped.

The weighted-average price for Sontara was $.26 per square yard, and the variable cost was $.12. Sontara's relatively high price did not discourage purchases, he thought;

for example, he said, in a use test, roughly 30 percent of the respondents said they would buy Sontara on the next occasion.

Mr. Murray described the effect of budget changes on sales in terms of three scenarios: (i) sales expected with the proposed budget, (ii) the effect on sales of raising one mix element to its maximum reasonable expenditure level while holding the others constant at the proposed level, and (iii) the impact of reducing one mix element to zero while holding the others at their proposed spending level.

With the current proposal of $565,000 he estimated that 1985 sales could reach 210 million square yards. This represented 32 percent of the total market or 50 percent of the smaller disposable market. If sales force/maintenance expenditures were to be raised from the proposed level of $450,000 to a maximum reasonable expenditure level of $550,000 while holding other spending to what had been proposed, Mr. Murray thought market share could reach 35 percent of the total market. Similarly, if the other mix elements were increased to their maximum reasonable levels while holding the remaining expenditures at their proposed levels, he thought market share increases would be likely as well although not as dramatically. Specifically, if $200,000 were to be spent on sales force/missionary instead of the proposed $0, he thought market share would increase to 33 percent; if trade support/maintenance would be increased to $100,000, a 33 percent market share would result; if $100,000 would be spent on trade support/missionary, market share would be 33 percent; if advertising to intermediate users were to be increased to $50,000, the net effect would be a 1 percent increase in market share; while an increase in advertising to end-users to $300,000 would also result in a 1 percent share gain.

Reductions in spending were thought to have the opposite effect. Reducing sales force/maintenance expenditures to zero while holding other spending at the proposed level was thought to reduce share to 22 percent of the total market during the next twelve months. Similarly, reductions to zero spending for sales force/missionary expenditures, trade support/maintenance, support/missionary, advertising to intermediaries, and advertising to end-users were thought to reduce expected market share to 32, 27, 32, 31, and 28 percent, respectively.

As a validity check on the above estimates, Mr. Murray described what he thought would happen if all mix elements were to be raised simultaneously to their maximum reasonable expenditure levels, or if all support were to be withdrawn from the product. With maximum effort he thought a 39 percent share could be realized although he was not sure how viable such an aggressive strategy would be for the long run. If all support were to be withdrawn, he estimated that market share would drop to 22 percent in the next twelve months before declining further.

Glenn White, marketing manager for Tyvek housewrap, said his marketing emphasis was mostly push, but increasingly pull. The push/pull percentage was 95/5 in 1984, he believed, and would become 65/35 in 1985, and 50/50 in 1986.

Mr. White categorized his marketing plan in terms of seven mix elements: sales force, advertising/end-users, advertising/intermediate-users, press releases, builder support, retailer support, and distributor support. He believed that interactive effects could occur among the mix elements, though he did not know what they were or how to account for them. For advertising/end-users, he believed that the effectiveness of additional expenditures followed an S-shaped curve, and that for the other elements the curve was concave.

The current price for Tyvek housewrap was $3.60 per pound, and the variable cost was about $1.50. In a use test, Mr. White estimated that between 20 percent and 25 percent would purchase the housewrap on the next occasion.

Mr. White, as Mr. Murray, described the effects of budget changes on Tyvek sales in terms of a number of scenarios: (i) sales expected from the baseline proposal, (ii) the effects of item-by-item budget increases, and (iii) the effects of item-by-item reductions as well as what would happen if all budget elements were increased to their maximum reasonable expenditure levels or if all support for the product would be withdrawn.

Specifically, Mr. White thought the proposed budget of $250,000 for the sales force, $0 for advertising to end-users, $230,000 for advertising to intermediaries, $25,000 for press releases, $35,000 for builder support, $225,000 for retailer support, and $195,000 for distributor support would result in sales of 3.6 million pounds which translates into a 23 percent market share.

Raising the budget on an item-by-item basis was thought to have the following effects: sales force expenditures to $800,000 a 4 percent share increase, advertising to end-users of $1,100,000—a pull campaign—an 8 percent share increase, more advertising to intermediaries (to $460,000) an additional three share points, increased builder support (to $100,000) a 1 percent share gain, additional funds for press coverage (to $30,000) 1 percent share increase, and finally, additional distributor support (to $250,000) a 3 percent share increase. In similar fashion, reduction of the above mix elements to zero was thought to reduce market share for sales force expenditures to 20 percent, for advertising to end-users to 23 percent, for advertising to intermediaries to 20 percent, for press releases to 21 percent, for builder support to 22 percent, for retail support to 17 percent and for distributor support to 19 percent.

In judging the overall effects of budget adjustments, Mr. White thought that if all elements were increased to their maximum reasonable expenditure limits, market share could reach 33 percent. On the other hand, if all support was withdrawn, a likely market share of 13 percent would result.

Conclusion

As he listened to the various arguments and estimates, Mr. Blake wondered about their consistency and what their implications would be for the 1985 budget. Should the Sontara and Tyvek budget proposals be revised? If so, how?

Ideal Brands, Inc.

David Johnson, group research manager at Ideal Brands, looked at the envelope and its contents again. The check for $1,000 was made out to him and the accompanying note said only "Thank you." It was signed by the owner of Creative Research, Inc., a supplier to whom Johnson had just awarded a $220,000 contract. No other explanation was needed. Johnson knew the check was a "gift" in exchange for the contract. But what should he do with this check? This was the first time he had received anything other than a thank you from a supplier.

Background Information

David Johnson received his M.S. in marketing from the University of Minnesota in 1985 with minors in statistics and psychology, and joined Ideal Brands, Inc. as a research analyst in the Consumer Research Department. His first assignments related to research on two of Ideal's smaller entries in the soft drink market.

In 1987, Johnson was promoted to research manager and in 1988 to group research manager. He supervised all research on three brands that accounted for approximately $525 million in annual sales (IB's total sales were $850 million).

The distribution of Johnson's $2 million research budget by type of research was:

Source: This case was prepared by James W. Cagley and Dale A. Lunsford, both at the University of Tulsa, as a basis for class discussion, and is not designed to illustrate effective or ineffective handling of managerial situations.

Advertising creative studies	30%
Problem market studies	30
Product concept testing	20
Test market/market tracking	10
Miscellaneous	10
TOTAL	100%

Seventy-five percent of Johnson's research budget was used for outside suppliers. The decision to use external firms for research was based on such considerations as expertise, experience, credibility with both advertising agency and Ideal management, expedience, a cost–benefit evaluation, and a general "feel" or "comfort level" between project supervisor and supplier.

Introduction of Peter Salinger

The Consumer Research Department reported directly to the Vice President of Marketing. (An abbreviated organization chart for Marketing is presented in Exhibit 2.1 and shows the reporting relationships within the department.) Some uncertainty had been introduced in the spring of 1989 when Peter Salinger was appointed as the new Vice President of Marketing. He was new to the soft drink industry, having spent 15 years with two cereal marketers. He had been extremely successful and was, of course, expected to do similarly well with Ideal Brands.

Johnson, Tom Goodwin, the other Group Research Manager, and the Director of Consumer Research, Ted Allert, had spent a great deal of time bringing Salinger "up to speed" on all research that impacted his decision areas. Johnson was impressed with Salinger—his grasp of the importance of research and his ability to synthesize findings from disparate studies and methodologies.

The Research Process

At Ideal Brands, individual projects were developed by research groups and presented to the marketing group for discussion and "blessing" before research was fielded. In June, Johnson, Allert, and Salinger were discussing preliminary plans for a large-scale study related to the 1991 advertising pool. Salinger asked about recent approaches to evaluating advertising creative. The conversation went:

Johnson: In the two years I've been involved, we have used primarily qualitative techniques, specifically focus groups, to evaluate our creative.

Salinger: Who have you been using for these groups?

Johnson: We have used a firm named Dynamic Research—they have had a lot of experience in the soft drink industry and have brought a lot of insight to our brands.

Allert: We also used them before Dave was put in charge of advertising creative research.

Salinger: It might be time to seek a fresh approach to our research. While at (previous cereal employer), we used a firm named Creative Research, Inc. for most of our

EXHIBIT 2.1 **Abbreviated Marketing Department Organization Chart**

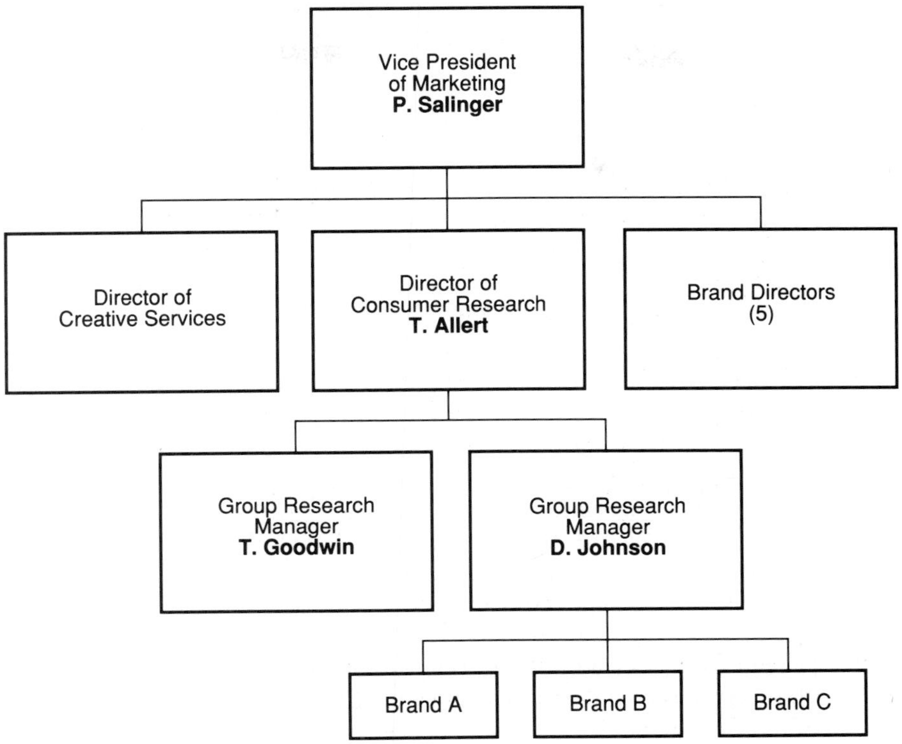

```
                        ┌──────────────────┐
                        │  Vice President  │
                        │   of Marketing   │
                        │   P. Salinger    │
                        └──────────────────┘
           ┌──────────────────┼──────────────────┐
   ┌───────────────┐  ┌──────────────────┐  ┌───────────────┐
   │  Director of  │  │   Director of    │  │ Brand Directors│
   │Creative Services│ │Consumer Research │  │     (5)       │
   │               │  │    T. Allert     │  │               │
   └───────────────┘  └──────────────────┘  └───────────────┘
                 ┌────────────┴────────────┐
        ┌──────────────────┐    ┌──────────────────┐
        │ Group Research   │    │ Group Research   │
        │    Manager       │    │    Manager       │
        │   T. Goodwin     │    │   D. Johnson     │
        └──────────────────┘    └──────────────────┘
                      ┌──────────┼──────────┐
                 ┌─────────┐ ┌─────────┐ ┌─────────┐
                 │ Brand A │ │ Brand B │ │ Brand C │
                 └─────────┘ └─────────┘ └─────────┘
```

qualitative work. I think it would be appropriate if we would talk to them about the 1990 creative study.

The Proposed Research Project

The proposed methodology for the 1990 creative study involved an initial set of 24 focus groups in six cities to be fielded early in 1990. Results would be presented to a combination of agency and Ideal management in May and creative direction for the 1991 pool would be based largely on this study. A follow-up study using rough creative (animatics or storyboards) would be conducted in August of 1990. This follow-up study was slated to include 8 to 10 focus groups and would serve as a final concept check before production began for the budgeted $40 million advertising campaign.

Vendors

In the process of developing the final research proposal, Johnson sought proposals from three research firms—Dynamic, Creative Research, and Quality First Research. A brief description of each follows:

- Dynamic Research had been involved with Ideal Brands' research for five years—being the primary qualitative vendor for the past two years. Allert and Johnson had been pleased with their work although it bothered both of them that it appeared as though Ideal was becoming too dependent on Dynamic. The owner of Dynamic was withdrawing from active, hands-on management and had recently hired two people from competitive research houses to handle most of the moderation and analysis.

- Creative Research, Inc. was a research firm that specialized in qualitative research applied to advertising creative, basic consumer positioning, and concept testing. Its owner and principal had earned a Ph.D. in Social Psychology from the University of Southern California and had an impressive list of former and ongoing clients, including automobile companies, financial institutions, and consumer goods firms.

- Quality First Research was an unknown quantity to Allert and Johnson but had, at one point in time, been the primary supplier for one of Ideal's largest competitors. They had a solid reputation for quality—field, moderation, and analysis—but were known as a relatively high-cost firm.

The Supplier Decision

The final supplier decision fell to Johnson and Allert. Each of the potential suppliers' proposals followed the two-stage plan. Johnson was relatively comfortable with each firm and their primary people and felt that any of the three would do an adequate job.

Prices for the proposals ranged from $200,000 (Dynamic) to $245,000 (Quality First). Remembering Salinger's "suggestion," both Johnson and Allert felt that Creative Research warranted a favored position. Their price of $220,000, plus presentation travel expenses, was not out of line with the budget Johnson envisioned. Creative Research was selected, the final proposal was presented to the marketing group, "blessed," and a contract was signed in November of 1989.

The Dilemma

On December 5, 1989, Johnson received a letter from Creative Research with "Personal" stamped on the envelope. As noted at the beginning of this case, inside was a check for $1,000 made out to Johnson and a note saying "Thank you" signed by the owner of CRI.

Johnson wondered what to do. This was the first time he had received anything more than a thank you note from a supplier.

Cameron Auto Parts

Alex Cameron's first years in business were unusually harsh and turbulent. He graduated from a leading Canadian business school in 1982 when the Canadian economy was in the midst of one of the worst recessions in its history. It was not that Alex had difficulty finding a job, however; in fact, he took over the reins of the family business. His father timed his retirement to coincide with Alex's graduation and left him with the unenviable task of cutting back the work force to match the severe sales declines the company was experiencing.

Cameron Auto Parts was founded in 1965 by Alex's father to seize opportunities created by the signing of the Auto Pact between Canada and the United States. The Auto Pact permitted the Big Three automotive manufacturers to ship cars, trucks, and original equipment (OEM) parts between Canada and the United States tariff free, as long as they maintained auto assembly facilities on both sides of the border. The pact had been very successful with the result a lot of auto parts firms sprang up in Canada to supply the Big Three. Cameron Auto Parts prospered in this environment until by 1980, sales had reached $60 million with profits of $1.75 million. The product focus was largely on small engine parts and auto accessories such as oil and air filters, fan belts, and wiper blades; all sold as original equipment under the Auto Pact.

When Alex took over in 1982, the company's financial position was precarious. Sales in 1981 had dropped to $48 million and for the first six months of 1982 to $18 million. Not only were car sales declining in North America, but also the Japanese were taking an increasing share of the market. As a result, the major North American auto producers were frantically trying to advance their technology and lower their prices at the same time. It was not a good year to be one of their suppliers. In 1981, Cameron Auto Parts lost $2.5 million and had lost the same amount again in the first six months

Source: This case was prepared by Professor Harold Crookell of The University of Western Ontario. Copyright © 1987, The University of Western Ontario.

of 1982. Pressure for modernization and cost reduction had required new investment in equipment and computer-assisted design and manufacturing systems of close to $4 million. As a result, the company had taken up over $10 million of its $12 million line of bank credit at an interest rate of 16 percent.

Alex's first six months in the business were spent in what he later referred to as "operation survival." There was not much he could do about working capital management as both inventory and receivables were kept relatively low anyway via contract arrangements with the Big Three. Marketing costs were negligible. Where costs had to be cut was in production and specifically in people, many of whom had been with the company for over 15 years and were personal friends of Alex's father. Nevertheless, by the end of 1982, the work force had been cut from 720 to 470, the losses had been stemmed, and the company saved from almost certain bankruptcy. Having to be the hatchet man, however, left an indelible impression on Alex. As things began to pick up during 1983 and 1984, he added as few permanent workers as possible relying instead on overtime, part-timers, or subcontracting.

Recovery and Diversification

For Cameron Auto Parts, the year 1982 ended with sales of $38 million and losses of $3.5 million (Exhibit 3.1). Sales began to pick up in 1983, reaching $45 million by year end with a small profit. By mid-1984 it was clear the recovery was well underway as Canada emerged as a major exporter of automotive products to the United States. Alex, however, while welcoming the turnaround, was suspicious of the basis for it. Cameron's own sales hit $27 million in the first six months of 1984 and company profits were over $2 million. The Canadian dollar had dropped as low as 73 cents in terms of U.S. currency, and the Big Three had begun to recognize the advantage of sourcing in Canada as extensively as possible. The short-term future for Cameron seemed distinctly positive, but the continued Japanese threat coupled with growing U.S. protectionism left Alex feeling vulnerable to continued total dependence on the volatile automotive industry. Diversification was on his mind as early as 1982. He had an ambition to take the company public by 1988, and diversification was an important part of that ambition.

Unfortunately, working as an OEM parts supplier to the automotive industry did little to prepare Cameron to become more innovative. The auto industry tended to standardize its parts requirements to the point that Cameron's products were made to precise industry specifications and consequently did not find a ready market outside the industry. Without a major product innovation, it appeared that Cameron's dependence on the Big Three was likely to continue. Furthermore, the company had developed no "in-house" design and engineering strength from which to launch an attempt at new product development. Because product specifications had always come down in detail from the Big Three, Cameron had never needed to design and develop its own products and had never hired any design engineers.

In the midst of "operation survival" in mid-1982, Alex boldly decided to do something about diversification. He personally brought in a team of four design engineers and instructed them to concentrate on developing products related to the existing line but with a wider "nonautomotive" market appeal. Their first year together

EXHIBIT 3.1 **Income Statements[a] for Years Ended December 31, 1982–1984 ($000s)**

	1982	1983	1984
Net sales	$38,150	$45,200	$67,875
Cost of goods sold			
Direct materials	6,750	8,050	12,400
Direct labor	12,900	10,550	12,875
Overhead (including depreciation)	16,450	19,650	27,600
Total	$36,100	$38,250	$52,875
Gross profit	$ 2,050	$ 6,950	$15,000
Expenses			
Selling and administration (including design team)	3,150	3,800	6,200
Other (including interest)	2,400	2,900	3,000
Total	$ 5,500	$ 6,700	$ 9,200
Net profit before tax	(3,500)	250	5,800
Income tax	(500)	—	200
Net profit after tax	$(3,000)	$ 250	$ 5,600

[a]Alex expected sales to reach $85 million in 1985 with profits before tax of $10 million. Flexible couplings were expected to contribute sales of $30 million and profits of $5 million on assets of $12 million.

showed little positive progress, and the question of whether to fund the team for another year (estimated budget $425,000) came to the management group.

Alex: Maybe we just expected too much in the first year. They did come up with the flexible coupling idea, but you didn't seem to encourage them, Andy.

Andy McIntyre: [Production manager] That's right! They had no idea at all how to produce such a thing in our facilities. Just a lot of ideas about how it could be used. When I told them an American outfit was already producing them, the team sort of lost interest.

John Ellis: [Finance] We might as well face the fact that we made a mistake and cut it off before we sink any more money into it. This is hardly the time for unnecessary risks.

Alex: Why don't we shorten the whole process by getting a production license from the U.S. firm? We could start out that way and then build up our own technology over time.

Andy: The team looked into that, but it turned out the Americans already had a subsidiary operating in Canada—not too well from what I can gather—and they are not anxious to license anyone to compete with it.

Alex: Is the product patented?

Andy: Yes, but apparently it doesn't have long to run.

At this point a set of ideas began to form in Alex's mind, and in a matter of months he had lured away a key engineer from the U.S. firm with an $80,000 salary offer and put him in charge of the product development team. By mid-1984 the company had developed its own line of flexible couplings with an advanced design and an efficient production process using the latest in production equipment. In retrospect, Alex commented:

> We were very fortunate in the speed with which we got things done. Even then the project as a whole had cost us close to $1 million in salaries and related costs.

Marketing the New Product

Alex continued,

> We then faced a very difficult set of problems, because of uncertainties in the marketplace. We knew there was a good market for the flexible type coupling because of its wide application across so many different industries, but we didn't know how big the market was or how much of it we could secure. This meant we weren't sure what volume to tool up for, what kind or size of equipment to purchase, or how to go about the marketing job. We were tempted to start small and grow as our share of market grew, but this could be costly too and could allow too much time for competitive response. Our U.S. engineer was very helpful here. He had a lot of confidence in our product and had seen it marketed in the States. At his suggestion we tooled up for a sales estimate of $30 million—which was pretty daring. In addition we hired eight field salespeople to back up the nationwide distributor and soon afterward hired five U.S.-based salespeople to cover major markets there. We found that our key U.S. competitor was pricing rather high and had not cultivated very friendly customer relations. We were able to pay U.S. tariffs and still come in at or slightly below its prices. We were surprised how quickly we were able to secure significant penetration into the U.S. market. It just wasn't being well serviced.

During 1984 the company actually spent a total of $2.5 million on equipment for flexible coupling production. In addition, a fixed commitment of $1.5 million a year in marketing expenditures on flexible couplings arose from the hiring of salespeople. A small amount of trade advertising was included in this sum. The total commitment represented a significant part of the company's resources and threatened serious damage to the company's financial position if the sales failed to materialize. A breakdown of division sales is shown in Exhibit 3.2.

"It was quite a gamble at the time," Alex added. By the end of 1984, it was clear that the gamble was going to pay off."

Cameron's approach to competition in flexible couplings was to stress product quality, service, and speed of delivery, but not price. Certain sizes of couplings were priced slightly below competition but others were not. In the words of one Cameron salesperson,

> Our job is really a technical function. Certainly we help predispose the customer to buy and we'll even take orders, but we put them through our distributors. Flexible couplings can be used in almost all areas of secondary industry, by both large and small firms. This is why we need a large distributor with wide reach in the market. What we do is give

EXHIBIT 3.2   **Sales by Market Sector, 1980–1984 ($ millions)**

	OEM Parts	Flexible Couplings	Total Sales	Profits
1980	$60	Nil	$60	$1.75
1981	48	Nil	48	(2.50)
1982	38	Nil	38	(3.50)
1983	45	Nil	45	0.25
1984	58	10 (six months)	68	5.80

our product the kind of emphasis a distributor can't give. We develop relationships with key buyers in most major industries, and we work with them to keep abreast of new potential uses for our product, or of changes in size requirements or other performance characteristics. Then we feed this kind of information back to our design group. We meet with the design group quite often to find out what new types of couplings are being developed and what the intended uses are, etc. Sometimes they help us solve a customer's problem. Of course, these "solutions" are usually built around the use of one of our products.

Financing Plant Capacity

When Alex first set his diversification plans in motion in 1982 the company's plant in Chatham, Ontario (about 100 km from the Big Three's Detroit head offices), was operating at 50 percent capacity. However, by early 1985 sales of auto parts had recovered almost to 1980 levels, and the flexible coupling line was squeezed for space. Andy McIntyre put the problem this way:

I don't see how we can get sales of more than $85 million out of this plant without going to a permanent two-shift system, which Alex doesn't want to do. With two full shifts we could probably reach sales of $125 million. The problem is that both our product lines are growing very quickly. Auto parts could easily hit $80 million on their own this year, and flexible couplings! Well, who would have thought we'd sell $10 million in the first six months? Our salespeople are looking for $35–40 million during 1985. It's wild! We just have to have more capacity.

There are two problems pressing us to consider putting flexible couplings under a different roof. The first is internal: we are making more and more types and sizes, and sales are growing to such a point that we may be able to produce more efficiently in a separate facility. The second is external: the Big Three like to tour our plant regularly and tell us how to make auto parts cheaper. Having those flexible couplings all over the place seems to upset them, because they have trouble determining how much of our costs belong to Auto Parts. If it were left to me I'd just let them be upset, but Alex feels differently. He's afraid of losing orders. Sometimes I wonder if he's right. Maybe we should lose a few orders to the Big Three and fill up the plant with our own product instead of expanding.

Flexible couplings were produced on a batch basis, and there were considerable savings involved as batches got larger. Thus as sales grew, and inventory requirements made large batches possible, unit production costs decreased, sometimes substantially. McIntyre estimated that unit production costs would decline by some 20 percent as annual sales climbed from $20 million to $100 million, and by a further 10 percent at $250 million. Scale economies beyond sales of $250 million were not expected to be significant.

John Ellis, the company's financial manager, expressed his own reservations about new plant expansion from a cash flow perspective.

> We really don't have the balance sheet (Exhibit 3.3) ready for major plant expansion yet. I think we should grow more slowly and safely for two more years and pay off our debts. If we could hold sales at $75 million for 1985 and $85 million for 1986, we would be able to put ourselves in a much stronger financial position. The problem is that people only look at the profits. They don't realize that every dollar of flexible coupling sales requires an investment in inventory and receivables of about 30 cents. It's not like selling to the Big Three. You have to manufacture to inventory and then wait for payment from a variety of sources.
>
> As it is, Alex wants to invest $10 million in new plant and equipment right away to allow flexible coupling sales to grow as fast as the market will allow. We have the space on our existing site to add a separate plant for flexible couplings. It's the money I worry about.

Foreign Markets

As the company's market position in North America began to improve, Alex began to wonder about foreign markets. The company had always been a major exporter to the United States, but it had never had to market there. The Big Three placed their orders often a year or two in advance, and Cameron just supplied them. As Alex put it,

> It was different with the flexible coupling. We had to find our own way into the market. The U.S. engineer was useful in this regard in that he knew personally a lot of key U.S. customers and was able to help us choose some good U.S. salespeople.
>
> One unexpected benefit of entering the U.S. market was that we started getting orders from Europe and South America, at first from the subsidiaries of our U.S. customers and then from a few other firms as word got around. We got $40,000 in orders during 1984 and the same amount during the first four months of 1985. This was a time when we were frantically busy and hopelessly understaffed in the management area, so all we did was fill the orders on an FOB, Chatham basis. The customers had to pay import duties of 15 percent into most European countries and 20–50 percent into South America on top of the freight and insurance, and still orders came in.

A Licensing Opportunity

In the spring of 1985, Alex made a vacation trip to Scotland and decided while he was there to drop in on one of the company's new foreign customers, McTaggart Supplies Ltd. Cameron Auto Parts had received unsolicited orders from overseas amounting to $40,000 in the first four months of 1985, and over 10 percent of these had come from

EXHIBIT 3.3 **Balance Sheets for Years Ended December 31, 1982–1984 ($000s)**

	1982	1983	1984
Assets			
Cash	$ 615	$ 430	$ 400
Accounts receivable	5,850	6,850	10,400
Inventories	4,995	4,920	7,500
Total current assets	$11,460	$12,200	$18,300
Property, plant, and equipment (net)	10,790	11,800	13,000
Total assets	$22,250	$24,000	$31,300
Liabilities			
Accounts payable	$ 4,850	$ 5,900	$ 9,500
Bank loan	11,500	12,000	10,000
Accrued items (including taxes)	450	400	500
Total current liabilities	$16,800	$18,300	$20,000
Common stock (held by Cameron family)	500	500	500
Retained earnings	4,950	5,200	10,800
Total equity	$ 5,450	$ 5,700	$11,300
Total liabilities and equity	$22,250	$24,000	$31,000

McTaggart. Alex was pleasantly surprised at the reception given to him by Sandy McTaggart, the 60-year-old head of the company.

Sandy: Come in! Talk of the devil. We were just saying what a shame it is you don't make those flexible couplings in this part of the world. There's a very good market for them. Why my people can even sell them to the English.

Alex: Well, we're delighted to supply your needs. I think we've always shipped your orders promptly, and I don't see why we can't continue . . .

Sandy: That's not the point, laddie! That's not the point! Those orders are already sold before we place them. The point is we can't really build the market here on the basis of shipments from Canada. There's a 15 percent tariff coming in, freight and insurance cost us another 10 percent on top of your price, and then there's the matter of currency values. I get my orders in pounds, but I have to pay you in dollars. And on top of all that, I never know how long the goods will take to get here, especially with all the dock strikes we have to put up with. Listen, why don't you license us to produce flexible couplings here?

After a lengthy bargaining session, during which Alex secured the information shown in Exhibit 3.4, he came round to the view that a license agreement with McTaggart might be a good way of achieving swift penetration of the U.K. market via McTaggart's sales force. McTaggart's production skills were not as up to date as Cameron's, but his plant showed evidence of a lot of original ideas to keep manufacturing costs down. Furthermore, the firm seemed committed enough to invest in some

EXHIBIT 3.4 Selected Financial Data on McTaggart Supplies Ltd.

1984 sales: £35 million (down from £44 million in 1982).

Total assets: £11 million, equity £6.5 million.

Net profit after tax: ± £1.5 million.

Control: McTaggart family.

Market coverage: 15 sales in United Kingdom, 2 in Europe, 1 in Australia, 1 in New Zealand, 1 in India.

Average factory wage rate: £3.25 per hour (versus $11.50 in Canada).

Factory: Old and larger than necessary. Some very imaginative manufacturing know-how in evidence.

Reputation: Excellent credit record, business now 130 years old, good market contacts (high-caliber sales force).

Other: Company sales took a beating during 1982–1983 as one of the company's staple products was badly hurt by a U.S. product of superior technology. Company filled out its line by distributing products obtained from other manufacturers. Currently about one-half of company sales are purchased from others. Company has capacity to increase production substantially.

Pricing	Index
Cameron's price to McTaggart (same as distributor price in Canada)	100
Import duty	15
Freight and insurance	10
Total cost to McTaggart	125
Price charged by McTaggart	160
Price charged by Canadian distributor	120

new equipment and to put a major effort into developing the U.K. market. At this point the two executives began to discuss specific terms of the license arrangement.

Alex: Let's talk about price. I think a figure around 3 percent of your sales of flexible couplings would be about right.

Sandy: That's a bit high for an industrial license of this kind. I think 1½ percent is more normal.

Alex: That may be, but we're going to be providing more than just blueprints. We'll have to help you choose equipment and train your operators as well.

Sandy: Aye, so you will. But we'll pay you for that separately. It's going to cost us £500,000 in special equipment as it is, plus, let's say, a $100,000 fee to you to help set things up. Now you have to give us a chance to price competitively in the market, or neither of us will benefit. With a royalty of 1½ percent I reckon we could reach sales of £500,000 in our first year and £1 million in our second.

Alex: The equipment will let you produce up to £4 million of annual output. Surely you can sell more than a million. We're getting unsolicited orders without even trying.

Sandy: With the right kind of incentive, we might do a lot better. Why don't we agree to a royalty of 2½ percent of the first million in sales and 1½ percent after that. Now mind you, we're to become exclusive agents for the U.K. market. We'll supply your present customers from our own plant.

Alex: But just in the United Kingdom! Now 2 percent is as low as I'm prepared to go. You make those figures 3 percent and 2 percent, and you have a deal. But it has to include a free technology flowback clause in the event you make any improvements or adaptations to our manufacturing process.

Sandy: You drive a hard bargain! But it's your product, and we do want it. I'll have our lawyers draw up a contract accordingly.

Alex signed the contract the same week and then headed back to Canada to break the news. He traveled with mixed feelings, however. On the one hand, he felt he had got the better of Sandy McTaggart in the bargaining, while on the other, he felt he had no objective yardstick against which to evaluate the royalty rate he had agreed on. He was also aware that talk was beginning to surface in Canada about a "free trade" agreement with the United States, and he wondered how this might affect the company's strategy. This was pretty much the way he presented the situation to his executive group when he got home.

Alex: . . . so I think it's a good contract, and I have a check here for $100,000 to cover our costs in helping McTaggart get set up.

John: [Finance] We can certainly use the cash right now. And there doesn't seem to be any risk involved. I like the idea, Alex.

Andy: [Production] Well, I don't. And Chuck (head of the Cameron design team) won't either when he hears about it. I think you've sold out the whole U.K. market for a pittance. I thought you wanted to capture foreign markets directly in order to get out from under the threat of U.S. protectionism.

Alex: But Andy, we just don't have the resources to capture foreign markets ourselves. We might as well get what we can through licensing, now that we've patented our process. And anyway, if Canada signs a free trade deal with the United States, we may not have to worry any more about U.S. protectionism.

Andy: Well, maybe. But I don't like it. It's the thin edge of the wedge if you ask me. Our know-how on the production of this product is pretty special, and it's getting better all the time. I hate to hand it over to old McTaggart on a silver platter. I reckon we're going to sell over $20 million in flexible couplings in Canada alone during 1985.

Alex: If this deal works out with McTaggart, we can use the experience to sign a joint venture with someone else to cover the rest of the Common Market countries.

Southwestern Ohio Steel Company (A)

In October, 1988, Dan Wilson, Sales Manager for Southwestern Ohio Steel (SOS), was concerned over the company's deteriorating relations with one of their larger customers, Consolidated Metal Stampings. Wilson had received a telephone call from Consolidated's purchasing manager earlier in the week, which suggested that Consolidated might stop buying from SOS entirely if a proposed price increase went into effect.

Consolidated purchased roughly 30,000 tons of steel each year, twenty percent of which it bought through steel service centers; the remainder was purchased mill-direct. Consolidated contracted with suppliers on an annual basis by guaranteeing to provide a certain tonnage at a specified price to be "released" as needed during the year. The price increase at issue was SOS's bid price for the coming year's contract.

The situation was complicated by the market supply of the grade of steel Consolidated would be buying. A shortage had existed for some time which caused many steel mills to place customers on allocation. The shortage had caused prices to increase from 10 to 20 percent in the past year. Even with the price increases, it was often difficult for users to obtain sufficient supplies. In fact, SOS's primary mill source had established a deadline for placement of orders for the upcoming year. The deadline was today, and Wilson had not heard a definitive answer from Consolidated.

Source: This case was prepared by Dr. David W. Rosenthal of Miami University and is intended to be used as a basis for class discussion rather than to illustrate either effective or ineffective handling of the situation. The names of the firms, individuals, locations, and/or financial information have been disguised to preserve the firm's desire for anonymity.

Presented and accepted by the Referees Midwest Society for Case Research. All rights reserved to the author and the MSCR. Copyrighted © 1989 by David W. Rosenthal.

The price SOS had offered Consolidated was ten percent over last year's prices, yet some ten percent under the prevailing market prices. Wilson believed that the pricing was fair, but wondered what he should do. He could lower the price to Consolidated to the 1987 figure. He could lower the price and ask for concessions on shipping quantities and timing. He could simply place SOS's order for steel but without Consolidated's tonnage figured in. His recommendations had to be made quickly as they would affect the supply of steel from the mills for the coming year.

Company and Industry Background

SOS was founded in 1945 in order to bridge the gap between the large order quantities required by steel mills in Southwestern Ohio and the service requirements of regional businesses. The company had grown consistently and was currently one of the largest steel service centers in the country.

Until 1985 SOS had operated as a family business; but with the retirement of the founder, the management had executed a leveraged buyout of the company. The SOS organization chart is show in Exhibit 4.1.

SOS maintained three locations: Hamilton, Ohio; Middletown, Ohio; Lawrenceburg, Tennessee. Each facility consisted of a processing center and warehousing and shipping facility. In addition to slitting and shearing machinery, and rack storage for steel coil, SOS also owned and operated a fleet of tractor-trailer trucks for the delivery of steel orders. In all, SOS employed some 400 people and shipped 285,000 tons of steel in 1987.

The role of steel service centers in the market had grown considerably over the past decade. Traditionally, steel service centers had taken large shipments of steel in the form of master coils from the mills, and had, in turn, sold smaller quantities to users who did not require sufficiently large amounts to buy direct. The service centers were able to purchase sufficient quantities to receive price discounts from the mills, and were able to command price premiums from the smaller buyers.

While the traditional "bulk breaking" role continued, new functions and services had been developed. One such service was slitting the coiled steel lengthwise to meet the manufacturing needs of the users more closely. The result was to reduce the amount of scrap generated by the users. In some cases, the users who had been doing their own slitting found that the service center could do the task more efficiently and at lower cost than they could internally.

Similarly, "levelling" or "cut to length" were services which were increasingly provided by service centers. Some users found it to their advantage to have the coils unrolled, flattened, and pieces cut to specified rectangular dimensions, then stacked for use.

Quality control, metallurgical assistance in design and material specification, and inventory management had all increased the role of steel service centers in the market. The advent of "just-in-time" (JIT) inventory systems had increased demand from the service centers dramatically. For even some of the largest steel users, the instant inventory required by JIT was not available directly from the mills. As a result, service centers were increasingly used as a source of fast inventory supply.

EXHIBIT 4.1 Organization Chart

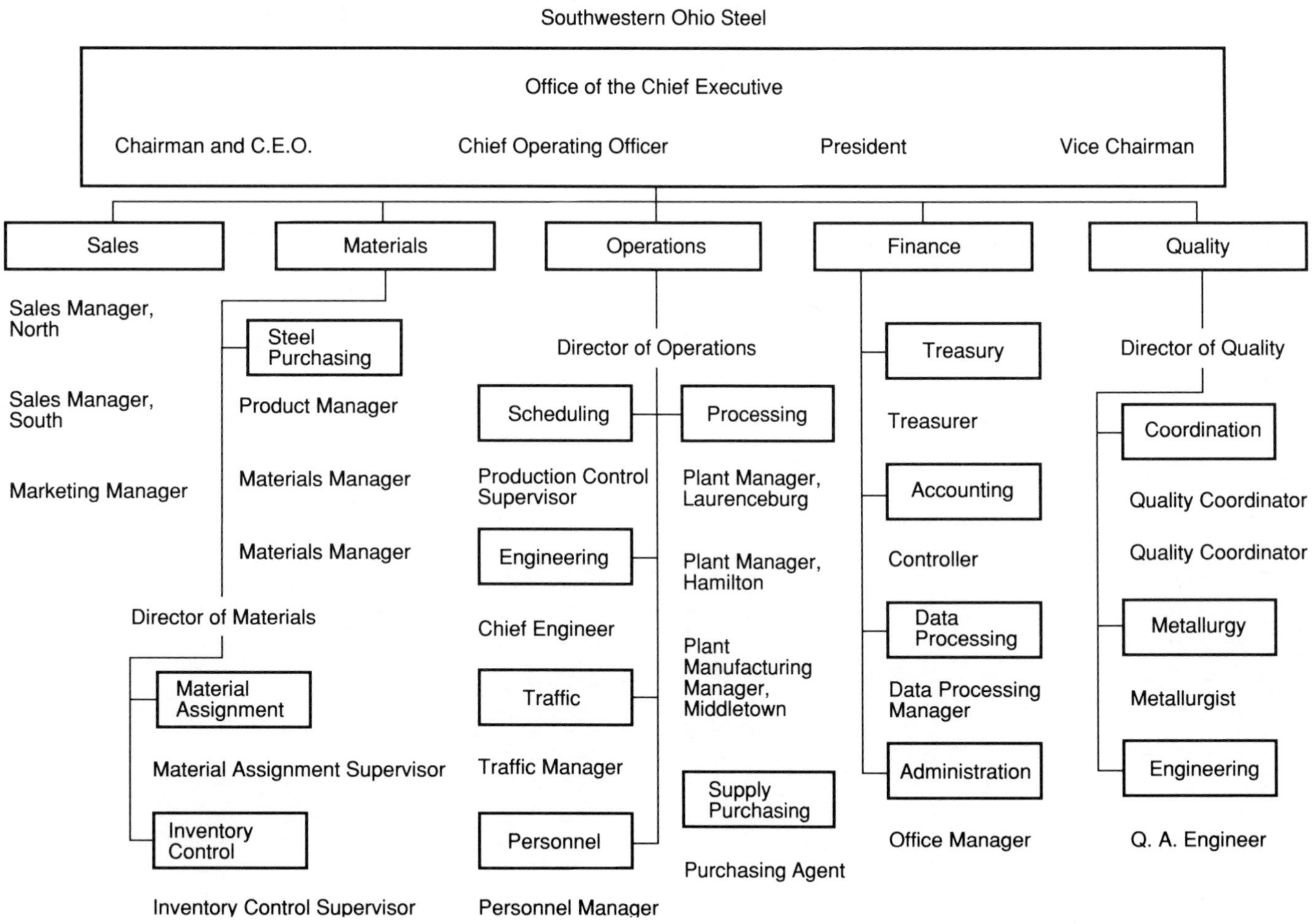

Southwestern Ohio Steel

Office of the Chief Executive

- Chairman and C.E.O.
- Chief Operating Officer
- President
- Vice Chairman

Sales
- Sales Manager, North
- Sales Manager, South
- Marketing Manager

Materials

Director of Materials

- Steel Purchasing — Product Manager
- Materials Manager
- Materials Manager
- Material Assignment — Material Assignment Supervisor
- Inventory Control — Inventory Control Supervisor

Operations

Director of Operations

- Scheduling — Production Control Supervisor
- Processing
- Plant Manager, Laurenceburg
- Plant Manager, Hamilton
- Engineering — Chief Engineer
- Plant Manufacturing Manager, Middletown
- Traffic — Traffic Manager
- Supply Purchasing — Purchasing Agent
- Personnel — Personnel Manager

Finance
- Treasury — Treasurer
- Accounting — Controller
- Data Processing — Data Processing Manager
- Administration — Office Manager

Quality

Director of Quality

- Coordination
  - Quality Coordinator
  - Quality Coordinator
- Metallurgy — Metallurgist
- Engineering — Q. A. Engineer

SOS was considered by steel users to be one of the best quality service centers in the United States. On-time delivery, quality of material provided, and price level were the normal criteria on which service centers were evaluated. SOS was generally perceived to be among the best suppliers on each criterion.

Additionally, in times of short supplies, users of steel were strongly concerned over the ability of a service center to provide continuity of supply over time. A supplier without metal was of no help to users. Thus, the relationship of a service center with a particular steel mill was often an important consideration in placing an ongoing order. If a service center had a strong relationship with a particular mill or mills, they could be expected to have metal available consistently. SOS was widely known to have strong ties to Armco Steel in Middletown, Ohio, thus providing them with an edge over competition in both supply and material quality.

The increasing share of market served by the steel service centers had caused some of the steel mills to begin to take steps to recapture lost sales. Some of the actions included changes in pricing structures, shipping priorities, and outright purchases of service centers by the mills. SOS, however, was the second largest customer of Armco and the two companies had worked closely over the years to maintain a quality relationship and even to build new business jointly.

Nationally the relationship between mills and service centers was changing. Service centers had gained a significant share of market, but the mills were beginning to strike back with pricing structures which were more favorable to end users and less favorable to service centers, generally. (See Exhibit 4.2.) In fact, sales of service centers were flat in 1988.

Recent Company Performance

SOS had been experiencing a period of exceptional growth in sales, both in terms of tons, dollars, and share of market. In 1985 SOS shipped approximately 215,000 tons of steel. In 1987 the level of shipments had risen to nearly 300,000 tons. Projections called for the growth to continue, reaching shipments of nearly 400,000 tons in 1990. (See Exhibit 4.3.)

SOS's solid performance was in large part the result of management's dedication to improved information and control systems. The company boasted an advanced, custom designed, computerized inventory control and materials management system which enabled customer inquiries about availability and status of orders to be answered instantly.

The company had also added new high-speed splitting lines and a tension levelling line that was one of the most advanced in the industry. The investment in new equipment allowed SOS to improve production efficiency and improve the quality of output significantly. Thus, for some items which required straight cuts or square dimensions or exceptional flatness within close tolerances, SOS was the only supplier considered by some buyers. Additionally, Statistical Process Control (SPC) was increasingly being required by steel purchasers. SPC referred to a system of production controls and documentation which showed conformance with specifications on an ongoing basis. The automotive industry was particularly concerned with SPC because

---

EXHIBIT 4.2   **The "Cross Over" Change in Mill Pricing Policies**

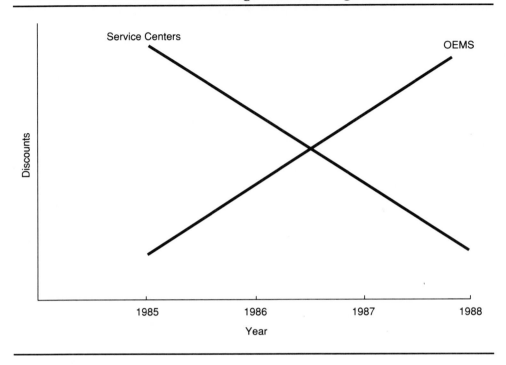

---

of its commitment to JIT, and other industries seemed to be following. SOS was an industry leader in the application of SPC in their production.

SOS's sales mix reflected the changes in demands for various types of products and the company's investments in production facilities. The value-added portions of the business, slit coil and cut-to-length, were increasing in volume. (See Exhibit 4.4.)

Marketing of Sheet and Strip Steel

SOS segmented their market into: (1) "inquiry" or "spot" buyers and (2) "contract" buyers. Inquiry or spot buyers bought material on an as-needed basis in order to meet changing needs. An order could consist of anything from a few thousand pounds to several truck-loads. Inquiry accounts bought on an irregular basis, but were not necessarily small accounts.

Inquiry accounts were often approached by SOS representatives with special offerings. As a result of mill overruns, mill errors in the chemical composition of a quantity of steel in its production, or mill-direct customers canceling orders, SOS was often able to buy steel at less than its normal cost. When such an opportunity occurred, SOS salespeople would contact those buyers who could use that particular type of steel

EXHIBIT 4.3   **Growth of SOS Shipments**

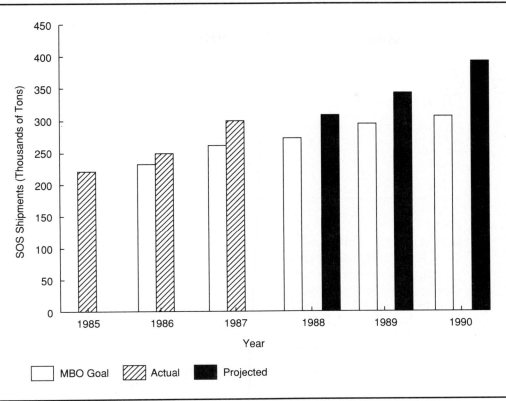

MBO Goal   Actual   Projected

EXHIBIT 4.4   **SOS Sales Mix by Product Type**

	Typical Month			
	1986 Shipments Tons/Month	**Pct. of Shipments**	**1987 Shipments Tons/Month**	**Pct. of Shipments**
Stock	1,472	7.0	1,307	5.4
Slit Coil	13,975	66.9	17,379	72.0
Cut To Length	2,618	12.5	2,799	11.6
High Volume Blanks	1,395	6.7	1,390	6.0
Manual Shearing	1,332	6.4	1,110	4.7
Safe Edge	95	.5	67	.3
	20,887	100.0%	24,052	100.0%

EXHIBIT 4.5   **SOS Geographic Sales Distribution**

Geographic Market	1986 Percent of Sales	1987 Percent of Sales
Tri-State Market (OH, KY, IN)	64.0	64.8
Lawrenceburg Market (TN, AL, MS, GA, LA)	18.6	15.6
Eastern Market (VA, NC, WV, PA, NJ, SC, FL, MD)	7.8	9.9
North/Northwestern Market (IA, MI, IL, NE, WI)	5.3	7.4
Southwest Market (MO, AR)	3.5	2.3
Other	.8	.0
	100.0%	100.0%

and "inquire" about their needs. In many instances SOS could provide usable material to the buyer at significant savings over prevailing market prices.

Contract accounts tended to buy steel on the basis of a year-long agreement for a supplier to provide material at a specified quantity and price over the length of the contract. Specific shipments of steel were "released" against the overall contract on a schedule determined in the contract negotiations. Contract accounts were often large, and the materials were used on a relatively stable basis. SOS management indicated that sales (tonnage) were split roughly 50-50 between contract and inquiry.

SOS also segmented their market according to geography. By its nature, steel engendered high transportation costs. Shipments beyond 150–200 miles were generally infeasible because of the additional costs. SOS customers were typically located within this distance from their warehouse in Hamilton and Middletown, Ohio, and Lawrenceburg, Tennessee. The geographic distribution of SOS sales is shown in Exhibit 4.5.

SOS's top 200 customers accounted for nearly all of the company's tonnage, but no individual customer accounted for more than about 3 percent. Similarly, SOS sold to a diverse mix of customers who used the steel for everything from automobiles to office furniture. No one industry accounted for more than 15–20 percent of SOS's sales. (See Exhibit 4.6.)

SOS maintained a sales staff consisting of both "inside" and "outside" sales personnel. The inside staff consisted of 13 salespeople. They were responsible for customer service, order placement, order facilitating, and scheduling shipping. Much of the inside salesperson's time was spent on the telephone, either answering customers' questions about availability of material or status of shipments, or making price quotes. Inside salespeople were also responsible for making offering calls and entering orders or releases into the system.

It was common for buyers to develop a strong professional attachment to their assigned inside salesperson. The salesperson had access to the records of purchases made, the materials used, the prices charged, and the market availability. At a given point a buyer could have literally hundreds of orders in process. An inside salesperson,

EXHIBIT 4.6   **SOS—Percent of Shipments by Industry**

Industry	1986	1987
Appliance	12.0	15.6
Automotive Direct	3.3	4.0
Automotive Related	11.7	8.0
Construction Related	9.4	7.8
Office Furniture	7.3	7.5
Shelving	6.2	5.6
Heating and Air-Conditioning	5.9	3.9
Tool Boxes	5.7	5.3
Electrical Closures	4.7	6.9
Farm Gates and Products	4.6	6.1
Health Care and Caskets	3.0	3.7
Recreational Equipment	2.8	1.7
Furniture Hardware	2.3	3.9
Small Manufactured PDTs	17.8	17.5
	100.0%	100.0%

by knowing the customer's portfolio, could provide invaluable service in tracking orders and in offering special opportunities as they arose. Buyers often insisted on talking with only "their" inside salesperson because of their knowledge and expertise.

SOS's six outside salespeople were responsible for actually visiting the steel users' production facilities and meeting with the buyers and the production people. The outside salespersons' responsibilities included prospecting for new accounts, evaluating production items and making recommendations for the steel requirements, examining rejected steel, and making adjustments for its dispensation. The outside salespeople worked closely with the inside salespeople to first determine the needs of the users, and then to service those needs accurately on a long-term basis.

SOS had recently initiated an ongoing research project to track trends in buyer needs, perceptions, and behavior. Several trends had become evident from the research. First, JIT inventory, or at least approximations of JIT, were increasingly being followed by steel users. The result of the increased attention being given to inventory levels was that lead times for suppliers such as SOS in providing materials were being shortened considerably. Safety stocks were being lowered as well. Buyers often required steel service centers to provide material with only 24 hours advance notice, although the average lead time was approximately one week.

Because lead times and safety stocks were being cut, quality control issues were becoming more important. Users simply could no longer afford to have a nonconforming shipment because they did not have material available to continue manufacturing while the unsatisfactory material was replaced.

Second, there was a trend for larger, process oriented steel users to reduce the numbers of their suppliers. The necessity of exchanging information on production scheduling, materials and inventory needs made working with more than a very few suppliers unwieldy and inefficient. As a result, large buyers of steel had been looking for means of evaluating suppliers and limiting the number from whom they bought.

Third, the trend of buying from service centers rather than direct from mills continued. The research findings indicated that the buyers simply did not perceive the mills as being able to provide sufficiently fast turnaround on orders to make them compatible with JIT systems.

The Current Situation

SOS had been selling steel to Consolidated Metal Stampings since 1965. Consolidated bought roughly 30,000 tons of steel each year, about 80 percent of which was bought mill-direct. The remaining 20 percent was bought through steel service centers. Over the past few years Consolidated's steel usage had increased at the rate of about 3 percent per year.

Consolidated bought from service centers on a contractual basis, and contracts were let on a yearly basis. Typically, there were some 20 service centers who bid on the Consolidated contracts each year. For the most part, SOS had fared better than most of the other service centers on Consolidated's quotations. The reason for SOS's success was attributed to their proximity to Consolidated's manufacturing facilities, thus enabling SOS to enjoy a slight freight advantage over the competitors. (SOS sales to Consolidated for the past four years are shown in Exhibit 4.7.)

The service center portion of Consolidated's steel purchases was particularly attractive to the service centers, and as a result the competition among suppliers for the contracts was termed by SOS management as "brutal." The Consolidated package offered large tonnage, relatively stable orders, and very simple quality requirements. The steel was to be used for unexposed parts, making the finish/surface requirements unimportant. The order consisted mostly of hot-rolled, pickled, and oiled (HRPO), one of the lowest grades of steel.

At the same time, the Consolidated account was not without its difficulties. Over the past few years the service requirements of the Consolidated account had become increasingly stringent. Items that had been released in truck-load quantities in the past were now being released in 5,000 pound and 10,000 pound increments, thus increasing the number of transactions and shipments, but without increasing the weight. Since service centers sold by weight, the increased costs of shipping were eroding the profitability of the account. In addition, deliveries which had been full truck loads every third day had been changed to less-than-full truck loads delivered daily. The vendors had generally been forced to absorb these additional costs, probably about 1 percent of selling price, because of competitive pressure.

Recent market events had created a shortage of HRPO products at the mill level. Some of the large steel mills had taken furnaces off-line for repair and upgrading. At the same time some of the mills had shifted their product offerings away from the low-priced, low-margin HRPO products. The result had been a tight supply of HRPO in the market, and many mill-direct customers had been placed on an allocation, including SOS.

EXHIBIT 4.7   **SOS Sales to Consolidated Metal Stampings**

	Year			
	1987	**1986**	**1985**	**1984**
Tons	4,200	2,500	2,500	3,000

Because of the shortfall in HRPO, and aggressive pricing on the part of the mills, prices of HRPO on the spot market had risen steadily over the past year. Market prices now averaged $520 per ton, some 10 to 20 percent over last year's prices, but demand had not slackened, and inventories of HRPO were low. Users of this type of steel were able to substitute other materials, but usually of a higher quality and cost per pound. The better grade materials were available in quantity while HRPO was often difficult to locate. SOS's market intelligence indicated that the shortage conditions were not likely to change over the next year.

Consolidated's call for bids had gone out only a few weeks before, but during the past six months SOS salespeople had steadily passed on the message to Consolidated's buyers that the market was tight, and that under the allocations prevalent in the market some price increases were inevitable.

Over the past three years SOS had been holding the price of HRPO stable for Consolidated. In fact, Consolidated had not paid a single increase over that time. The current bid was $450 per ton, exactly 10 percent over last year's price, but SOS market intelligence told them that the bid price was some 10 percent *under* the prevailing market price, and slightly lower than the prices offered by other bidders. Wilson, in agreement with SOS management, believed that the offer had been more than reasonable under the circumstances and was therefore somewhat surprised by the harsh response of the Consolidated management. However, given some changes in the management of Consolidated, they were not totally shocked.

In 1985, Ben Ingalls was appointed President and CEO of Consolidated. Ingalls was a cost cutting expert from the automotive industry, and was well known for his tough dealings with vendors in contract negotiations. Since his coming on board, Consolidated had removed several long-standing vendors of other products solely for price reasons. In the view of SOS management, the 1986 and 1987 steel service center negotiations had deteriorated to a crisis atmosphere, with SOS kept in the dark until the final award was made. It became apparent over this time that Ingalls had been playing a major role in raw-materials purchase decisions.

The Telephone Call

On November 16, 1987, Frank Shields, the purchasing manager for Consolidated, called Dan Wilson to respond to the SOS bid. Wilson had been calling Shields repeatedly during the previous week in order to find out how things stood. Armco had originally given SOS only until November 13 to place their order for the first quarter of

1988, but Wilson had asked them to postpone their deadline for one week, until he could obtain a commitment from Consolidated.

In previous conversations Wilson had learned that SOS's prices had been the lowest of the service centers who had bid, and that he, Shields, was going to recommend that SOS receive the business at the 100 percent level. SOS had actually placed two bids, one offering a specific level of prices for a partial commitment of Consolidated's needs, and a lower level of prices for a contract covering all of Consolidated's service center needs.

Shields opened the conversation, "Dan, I'm sorry about taking so long to get back to you on this, but we've been having lots of discussions on the bids we received. I guess it is no secret that we are under some serious pressure to keep our manufacturing costs down. This tight market really has us over a barrel, so we've been exploring some options."

"That's okay, Frank," Wilson replied, mustering as much warmth to his voice as he could. The buyer for Consolidated had known some two months previously that the deadline was approaching and that SOS would need a solid answer. "What sort of options are you thinking about? Maybe we can help."

"Well, look. We just can't live with this 10 percent increase in material costs over last year. I know that you are doing your best to give us the best price you can, but it just isn't good enough. Somehow we've got to find a way to reduce the unit cost on HRPO. Is there anything that you can do for us?" Shields urged.

"Not really, Frank. Even if we have a commitment from you for 100 percent of Consolidated's service center orders, we still can't go below the price that we quoted you. You know as well as I do how tight the market is. Why, we could sell the same steel that we are offering you for a 10 percent premium over the price we quoted you. We want your business, you know that, but we have to have an answer in to our supplier by Friday," said Wilson.

"I know, and I recommended to the president, Ben Ingalls, that we accept your bid, and at the 100 percent level. We have had good service from SOS over the years, and the price was the best that we could expect to see, given the circumstances. But Ben was adamant that we couldn't absorb a 10 percent increase," said Shields.

"Frank, have him call our president. Maybe if he hears it straight from the horse's mouth instead of through us, then he'll recognize the kind of a deal we are offering. But, we just can't go any lower . . . not without taking all of the profit out of it for us. And at this point we can't even go back to the supplier. They would just laugh at us if we asked for price concessions from them at this late date," Wilson noted as one of his salespeople handed him a telephone memo.

"I'll ask him, but from past experience, I already know the answer. Ben Ingalls just doesn't believe in speaking with vendors, or getting to know them in any way. I do wish we could clear this mess up. God knows that we don't want a slitter in here . . ."

"Okay, but don't wait on this. We've only got until Friday, and our supplier won't allow us another extension," said Wilson.

"We'll get you an answer. As you know, I'm recommending that SOS be awarded 100 percent of the business at the prices you've quoted. Ten percent seems like an awful lot, but in today's crazy steel market, it really isn't that bad. Dan, just don't cut me off! I think that SOS should make sure that I'm covered."

As he ended the conversation, he wondered what Shields had meant about a slitter. It would cost Consolidated $750,000 to $1 million to install a slitting line, and at the same time, their costs would go up as a result of the space requirements of the line, the storage requirements for the steel to be cut, and the inventory that had already been cut. Additional carrying charges and scrappage would probably top off the costs of a new line, making the real cost of material as high as ever . . . *if* they could find the steel in the first place.

Wilson estimated that Consolidated would incur direct slitting costs of about $10 per ton, scrappage costs of $20 per ton, holding costs of $10 per ton, and allocation for space and overhead anywhere from $5 to $15 per ton. Still, at $400 per ton, the price of steel would look attractive if they bought mill-direct, and the mills were certainly doing all that they could to recapture end users' business. Frequently, these additional costs were either not considered or underestimated by users, but Shields had seemed to have a good grasp of the real cost situation.

Wilson's Options

The telephone conversation had occurred on Monday, and as of today, Friday, neither Wilson nor SOS's president, Timothy Harson, had heard further from Consolidated. In the meantime, the mill had called several times asking for SOS's order quantities and configurations.

One option was for Wilson to reduce the prices offered to a 3–3.5 percent maximum increase. The indications were that a price reduction of this magnitude would be required in order to gain Ingall's approval. Wilson felt confident that Consolidated would accept such an offer immediately. SOS could justify such a reduction only by assuming they would "underwrite" the account through this difficult period, then "make up" profits in future years.

From a financial standpoint, Wilson wondered at the extent of the losses to SOS, and in addition, he thought that he ought to consider the profits that were being missed by not selling the same tonnage to other customers at the higher market prices. Generally speaking a good rule of thumb for pricing was that 2,000 tons of steel sold for $1 million. Most service centers achieved a 2–4 percent profit before tax.

Wilson was concerned over the response of other customers if and when they learned of the success of Consolidated in "beating down" SOS's prices. Price protection and stability were valued by steel users, and SOS had gained considerable business over the years by dealing honestly and fairly with their customers in times of price instability.

A smaller price reduction together with concessions on delivery and transportation would provide a better financial package to SOS. By shipping full truckloads, and strict adherence to a delivery schedule Wilson estimated that SOS could save as much as 1 percent of sales to Consolidated.

In the past Consolidated had been unwilling to fulfill its obligations on such contract covenants. Consolidated had sought bids and signed contracts for specific quantities of steel, and then had actually "released" as little as 35–50 percent of that amount. Shipping requirements of full truckloads had been ignored, and schedules had varied widely. Further, Wilson had no assurance that such a plan would be acceptable to Consolidated management either in terms of price or conditions, and he was running out of time to place SOS's order.

Wilson's other option was simply to place the order without Consolidated, and to use the steel to supply other SOS customers who were clamoring for HRPO. Once the commitment was made to these other customers SOS could not supply Consolidated if they turned around and wanted to buy through SOS.

Consolidated had consistently been one of SOS's largest customers, often ranking in the top 25. Wilson was proud of the increases in sales to Consolidated over the past year or two since Consolidated had cut the number of suppliers they used down to only a handful. SOS's quality and service levels were clearly making an impression.

Consolidated had been a regular customer of SOS for over 25 years, and the entire SOS organization felt that some loyalty was appropriate. Market conditions shifted, but long-term customer relationships were difficult to establish and maintain. In the difficult market that currently existed, Wilson felt that cutting Consolidated off could damage relations to the extent that they might never order from SOS again. Driving customers into the arms of the competition was not consistent with SOS's growth plans nor management philosophy. In fact, Tim Harson, the CEO of SOS, had commented to Wilson on the Consolidated situation, "It has been a long-standing SOS policy not to allow a foolish short-term decision to affect a long-term relationship. Let's not start now."

Wilson believed that the pricing had been fair but only under the prevailing market conditions. If the market were to ease, then the prices would come down, and the levels sought by Consolidated would be reasonable after all. The forecasts indicated that it would be a year before supply was plentiful, but the forecasts had been wrong before.

Wilson glared at the papers on his desk and contemplated giving Consolidated one last telephone call. Their supplier couldn't wait any longer, and he had put in too much time on this one issue already.

Trus Joist Corporation (B)

Mr. Mike Kalish, salesman for the Micro=Lam;® Division of Trus Joist Corporation, had just received another moderately sized order for the product Micro=Lam laminated veneer lumber; however, the order held particular interest for him. The unique feature of the order was that the material Micro=Lam was to be used as a truck trailer bedding material. This represented the second largest order ever processed for that function.

Earlier in the fall of 1978, Mr. Kalish had spent some time in contacting prospective customers for truck trailer flooring in the Northwest and Midwest; however, the response from manufacturers had been disappointing. Despite this reception, smaller local builders of truck trailers were interested and placed several small orders for Micro=Lam laminated veneer lumber. The order Mr. Kalish had just received was from one of the midwestern companies he had contacted earlier, thus renewing his belief that the trailer manufacturing industry held great potential for Micro=Lam laminated veneer lumber as a flooring material.

Company Background

The Trus Joist Corporation, headquartered in Boise, Idaho, is a manufacturer of structural wood products with plants located in the Pacific Northwest, Midwest, Southeast, and Southwest. Annual sales, which totaled over $78 million in 1978, were broken down into three major product categories: the Micro=Lam Division, contributing 7 percent of sales (the majority of Micro=Lam sales were internal); the Commerical Divisions, with 82 percent of sales; and the Residential Sales Program, with 11 percent of sales.

Source: This case is produced with the permission of Dr. Stuart U. Rich, Professor of Marketing, and Director Emeritus, Forest Industries Management Center, College of Business Administration, University of Oregon, Eugene, Oregon.

In the late 1950s, Art Troutner and Harold Thomas developed a unique concept in joist design, implemented a manufacturing process for the design, and then founded the Trus Joint Corporation. By 1978, the company employed over 1,000 people, of whom about 180 were sales personnel. The majority of salesmen were assigned to the regional Commercial Division sales offices; four outside salesmen were assigned to the Micro=Lam Division. The functions of selling and manufacturing were performed at each of the five geographically organized Commerical Divisions; therefore, the salesmen concentrated on geographic selling. The Micro=Lam Division was more centralized in nature, conducting all nationwide sales and manufacturing activities from Eugene, Oregon.

In 1971, Trus Joist first introduced and patented Micro=Lam laminated veneer lumber. The product is made of thin $\frac{1}{10}$-inch- or $\frac{1}{8}$-inch-thick veneer sheets of Douglas fir glued together by a waterproof phenol formaldehyde adhesive. Under exact and specified conditions, the glued sheets are heated and pressed together. The Micro=Lam lumber, or billet,[1] is "extruded" from specially made equipment in 80-foot lengths and 24-foot widths. The billets can be cut to any customer-desired length or width within those limiting dimensions. The billets come in several thicknesses ranging from $\frac{3}{4}$ inch to $2\frac{1}{2}$ inches; however, $1\frac{1}{2}$ inches and $1\frac{3}{4}$ inches are the two sizes produced regularly in volume.

Marketing Micro=Lam

When Micro=Lam was first introduced, Trus Joist executives asked an independent research group to perform a study indicating possible industrial applications for the product. The first application for Micro=Lam was to replace the high-quality solid sawn lumber 2-by-4-inch trus chords[2] in its open web joist designs and the solid sawn lumber flanges[3] on its wooden I-beam joist (TJI). Into the fall of 1978, this still represented the majority of Micro=Lam production. The findings of the research report suggested that Micro=Lam could be used as scaffold planking, mobile home trus chords, and housing components. These products accounted for about 25 percent of the Micro=Lam production. Mr. Kalish had also begun to develop new markets for Micro=Lam, including ladder rails and framing material for office partitions.

When marketing Micro=Lam to potential customers, Trus Joist emphasized the superior structural qualities of the product over conventional lumber. Micro=Lam did not possess the undesirable characteristics of warping, checking, and twisting, yet it did show greater bending strength and more structural stability. (One ad claimed, "Testing proves Micro=Lam to be approximately 30 percent stiffer than number 1 dense select structural Douglas fir.") In some applications, Micro=Lam offered distinct price advantages over its competing wood alternatives, and this factor always proved to be

---

[1] Micro=Lam is manufactured in units called billets, and the basic unit is one billet foot. The actual dimensions of a billet foot are 1-by-2-by-1½ inches and one billet is 80 feet-by 24 feet-by 1½ inches.

[2] Trus chords are the top and bottom components in an open web trus incorporating wood chords and tubular steel webs.

[3] Flanges are the top and bottom components in an all-wood I-beam. Refer to Exhibit 5.1.

EXHIBIT 5.1   **End View of an All-Wood I-Beam (TJI)**

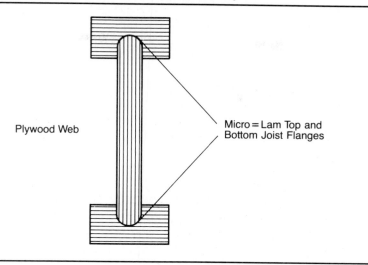

Plywood Web

Micro=Lam Top and
Bottom Joist Flanges

a good selling point. Manufacturers were often concerned about the lead/delivery time involved in ordering Micro=Lam. Trus Joist promised to deliver within one to three weeks of an order, which was often a full two weeks to two months ahead of other wood manufacturers.

The industrial application report had also suggested using Micro=Lam as a decking material for truck trailers. This use became a reality when Sherman Brothers Trucking, a local trucking firm that frequently transported Micro=Lam, made a request for Micro=Lam to redeck some of its worn-out trailers. To increase the durability of the flooring surface, the manufacturing department of Trus Joist replaced the top two veneer sheets of Douglas fir with apitong. Apitong was a Southeast Asian wood known for its strength, durability, and high specific gravity. This foreign hardwood had been used in the United States for several years because of the diminishing supplies of domestic hardwoods. (See Exhibit 5.2.)

The pioneer advertisement for Micro=Lam as a trailer deck material had consisted of one ad in a national trade journal and had depicted the Micro=Lam cut so that the edges were used as the top surface. (See Exhibit 5.3.) The response from this ad had been dismal and had resulted in only one or two orders. The latest advertisement depicting Micro=Lam as it was currently being used (with apitong as the top veneer layers) had better results. This ad, sent to every major truck or trailer manufacturing journal as a news release on a new product, resulted in 30 to 50 inquiries, which turned into 10 to 15 orders. Approximately 15 decks were sold as a result of the promotion.

Everyone at Trus Joist believed that the current price on Micro=Lam was the absolute rock bottom price possible. In fact, most people believed that Micro=Lam was underpriced. The current price of Micro=Lam included a gross margin of 20 percent. The price of 1¼-inch-thick and 1½-inch-thick Micro=Lam was based on the costs of

---

EXHIBIT 5.2 **Mechanical Properties of Wood Used for Trailer Decking**

Common Name of Species	Specific Gravity (Percent Moisture Content)	Modules of Elasticity (Million psi)	Compression Parallel to Grain and Fiber Strength Maximum Crush Strength (psi)
Apitong	0.59	2.35	8.540
Douglas fir	0.48	1.95	7.240
Alaska yellow cedar	0.42	1.59	6.640
White oak	0.68	1.78	7.440
Northern red oak	0.63	1.82	6.760
Micro=Lam	0.55	2.20	8.200

Micro=Lam using Douglas fir as the veneer faces of the lumber.

Source: *Wood Handbook: Wood as an Engineering Material,* USDA Handbook no. 72, rev. ed., 174: U.S. Forest Products Laboratory.

EXHIBIT 5.3 **End View of Remanufactured Micro=Lam**

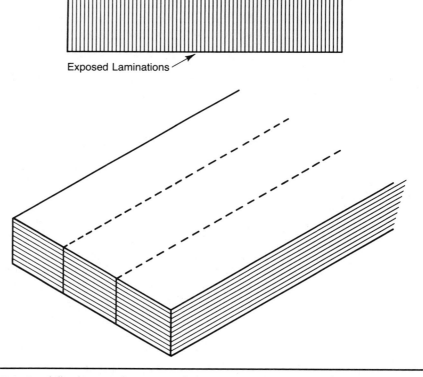

Exposed Laminations

Original Micro=Lam billet depicting the cutting path (- - - - - -) during the remanufacturing process.

EXHIBIT 5.4 **Truck Trailer Shipments and Dollar Value (by Calendar Year)**

	1975	1974	1973	1972	1971
Complete trailers and chassis	67,888	191,262	167,201	141,143	103,784
Value	$613,702,000	$1,198,520,000	$956,708,000	$795,500,000	$585,264,000
Containers	4,183*	10,108*	18,626	18,166	8,734
Value	$18,071,000	$27,343,000	$60,159,000	$51,527,000	$26,514,000
Container chassis	2,936	12,883	12,790	15,498	9,775
Value	$14,898,000	$42,076,000	$33,143,000	$39,028,000	$24,999,000
Total units	75,007	214,253	198,617	174,807	122,293
Value	$646,671,000	$1,267,939,000	$1,050,010,000	$886,055,000	$636,777,000

Truck Trailer Manufacturers Association Data for 1975 preliminary and subject to slight possible change.

*Containers not reported June–October 1974 and January–March 1975.

Source: *Ward's Automotive Yearbook,* 1978, p. 91.

a 1½-inch billet. The total variable costs of 1½-inch material were multiplied by ⅚ to estimate the same costs of 1¼-inch material. There had recently been some discussion over the appropriateness of this ratio. Some of the marketing personnel believed that a more appropriate estimate of the variable costs for the 1¼-inch Micro=Lam would be the ratio of the number of veneers in a 1¼-inch billet to the number of veneers in a 1½-inch billet, or ¹⁴⁄₁₆. At the present time, the costs of veneer represented 55 percent of the selling price. Glue cost was approximately 13 cents per square foot; fixed overhead represented 14 cents per square foot; and other variable costs amounted to approximately 12½ cents per square foot. The total variable costs were divided by 0.80 to cover all selling and administrative expenses and to secure a profit.[4]

In 1977, truck trailer manufacturers ordered and used 46 million square feet for installation in new truck trailer construction. This figure was understated because redecking or replacement of worn-out floors of trailers had not been incorporated, and there was little organized information to determine what this potential could be. As of 1975, 236 truck trailer manufacturers produced $646.7 million in trailers. (See Exhibits 5.4 and 5.5.)

The problem Mr. Kalish saw with this aggregate data was that it was not broken down into the various segments of trailer builders. For example, not all of the 236 manufacturers produced trailers which used wooden floors. Among those not using wooden floors were tankers and logging trailers. Mr. Kalish believed that the real key to selling Micro=Lam in this industry would be to determine the segment of the trailer industry on which he should concentrate his selling efforts. Mr. Kalish also knew that he somehow had to determine trailer manufacturers' requirements for trailer decking. The Eugene-Portland, Oregon, area offered what he thought to be a good cross section of the type of trailer manufacturers that might be interested in Micro=Lam. He had already contacted some of those firms about buying Micro=Lam.

[4] All cost figures have been disguised.

EXHIBIT 5.5 **Truck Trailer Manufacturers**

Allentown Brake & Wheel Service, Inc., Allentown, Pa.
Allied Products Corp., Chicago, Ill.
Aluminum Body Corp., Montebello, Calif.
American Body & Equipment Co., Grand Prairie, Tex.
American Trailers, Inc., Oklahoma City, Okla.
Anthony Co., Streator, Ill.
Atlantic International Corp., Baltimore, Md.
Atlantic International Marketing Corp., Baltimore, Md.
Atlantic Manufacturing Corp., Baltimore, Md.
Atlantic Mobile Corp., Cockeysville, Md.
Atlas Hoist & Body, Inc., Montreal, Que., Can.
Bartlett Trailer Corp., Chicago, Ill.
Bethlehem Fabricators, Inc., Bethlehem, Pa.
Adam Black & Sons, Inc., Jersey City, N.J.
Black Diamond Enterprises, Inc., Bristol, Va.
Herman Born & Sons, Inc., Baltimore, Md.
Budd Co., Troy, Mich.
Centennial Industries Division, Columbus, Ga.
Copco Trailer Division, South Bend, Ind.
Custom Trailers Inc., Springfield, Mo.
Delta Truck Trailer Co., Inc., Camden, Ark.
Distribution International Corp., Ft. Washington, Pa.
Dorsey Corp., Chattanooga, Tenn.
Dorsey Trailers, Inc., Elba, Ala.
Dura Corp., Southfield, Mich.
Durobilt Mfg. Co., El Monte, Calif.
Eight Point Trailer Corp., Los Angeles, Calif.
Essick Mfg. Co., Los Angeles, Calif.
Evans Products, Portland, Ore.
Expediter Systems, Inc., Birmingham, Ala.
Firmers Lumber & Supply Co., Sioux City, Iowa
Ford Motor Co., Dearborn, Mich.
Ford Motor Co. of Canada Ltd., Oakville, Ont., Can.
Fruehauf Corp., Detroit, Mich.
Fruehauf Trailer Co. of Canada Ltd., Dixie, Ont., Can.
General Body Mfg. Co., Inc., Kansas City, Mo.
Gerstenslager Co., Wooster, Ohio
Great Dane Trailers, Inc., Savannah, Ga.
Hawker Siddeley Canada Ltd., Toronto, Ont., Can.
Hendrickson Mfg. Co., Lyons, Ill.
Hercules Mfg. Co., Henderson, Ky.

Source: *Poor's Register.*

Hesse Corp., Kansas City, Mo.
Highway Trailers of Canada Ltd., Cooksville, Ont., Can.
Hobbs Trailers, Fort Worth, Tex.
Hyster Co., Portland, Ore.
Leland Equipment Co., Tulsa, Okla.
Lodestar Corp., Niles, Ohio
McCade-Powers Body Co., St. Louis, Mo.
McQuerry Trailer Co., Fort Worth, Tex.
Meyers Industries, Inc., Tecumseh, Mich.
Mindustrial Corp., Ltd., Toronto, Ont., Can.
Mitsubishi Electric Corp., Chiyoda-ku, Tokyo, 100, Japan
Moline Body Co., Moline, Ill.
Montone Mfg. Co., Hazelton, Pa.
Nabors Trailers, Inc., West Palm Beach, Fla.
Noble Division (Waterloo Plant), Waterloo, Iowa
OMC-Lincoln, Lincoln, Neb.
Ohio Body Mfg. Co., New London, Ohio
Olson Trailer & Body Builders Co., Green Bay, Wis.
Pike Trailer Co., Los Angeles, Calif.
Pointer Truck Trailer Co., Renton, Wash.
Polar Manufacturing Co., Holdingford, Minn.
Pullman, Inc., Chicago, Ill.
Pullman Trailmobile, Chicago, Ill.
Ravens-Metal Products, North Parkersburg, W.Va.
Reliance Trailer Manufacturing, Cotati, Calif.
Remke, Inc., Roseville, Mich.
Rogers Bros. Corp., Albion, Pa.
Shetky Equipment Corp., Portland, Ore.
Southwest Truck Body Company, St. Louis, Mo.
Starcraft Corp., Goshen, Ind.
Sterling Precision Corp., West Palm Beach, Fla.
Thiele, Inc., Windber, Pa.
Timpte, Inc., Denver, Colo.
Timpte Industries, Inc., Denver, Colo.
Trailco, Hummels Wharf, Pa.
Transport Trailers, Cedar Rapids, Iowa
Troyler Corp., Scranton, Pa.
Utility Tool & Body Co., Clintonville, Wis.
Valley Tow-Rite, Lodi, Calif.
Peter Wendel & Sons, Inc., Irvington, N.J.
Whitehead & Kales Co., River Rouge, Mich.
Williamsen Truck Equipment Corp., Salt Lake City, Utah

General Trailer Company

Mr. Jim Walline had been the purchasing agent for General Trailer Company of Springfield, Oregon for the past two and a half years. He stated, "The engineering department makes the decisions on what materials to buy. I place the orders after the requisition has been placed on my desk."

General Trailer Company was a manufacturer of several different types of trailers: low-boys, chip trailers, log trailers, and flatbeds. In 1977, General manufactured five flatbeds and redecked five flatbeds. General did most of its business with the local timber industry; however, it sold three flatbeds in 1977 to local firms in the steel industry.

The flatbeds General Trailer manufactured were 40 feet to 45 feet long and approximately 7 feet wide. Log trailers were approximately 20 feet to 25 feet long.

General Trailer manufactured trailers primarily for the West Coast market, although it had sold a few trailers to users in Alaska. On the West Coast, General's major competitors were Peerless, Fruehauf, and Trailmobile, all large-scale manufacturers of truck trailers. Even though General was comparatively small in size, it did not feel threatened because "we build a top-quality trailer which is not mass-produced," as Mr. Walline put it.

General had been using apitong as a trailer decking material until customers complained of its weight and its expansion/contraction characteristics when exposed to weather. At that time, Mr. Schmidt, the general manager and head of the engineering department, made the decision to switch from apitong to laminated fir.

Laminated fir (consisting of solid sawn lumber strips glued together) was currently being used as the material for decking flatbeds, and Pacific Laminated Company of Vancouver, Washington, supplied all of General's fir decking, so General would only order material when a customer bought a new trailer or needed to have a trailer redecked. Mr. Walline was disappointed with the two- to three-week delivery time, since it often meant that much more time before the customer's trailer was ready.

Laminated fir in 40-foot lengths, 11¾-inch widths, and 1¼-inch thicknesses was used by General. General paid approximately $2 to $3 per square foot for this decking.

Even though Pacific Laminated could provide customer-cut and edged pieces with no additional lead time, General preferred ship-lapped fir in the previously noted dimensions, with the top two layers treated with a waterproof coating.

The different types of trailers General manufactured required different decking materials. Low-boys required material 2¼ inches thick and General used 3-by-12-inch rough-cut fir lumber. Chip trailers required ⅝-inch-thick MDO (medium density overlay) plywood with a slick surface.

Mr. Walline said General had used Micro=Lam on one trailer; however, the customer had not been expecting it and was very displeased with the job.[5] Therefore, the current policy was to use only laminated fir for the local market unless a customer

---

[5] After purchasing Micro=Lam, General Trailer modified the material by ripping the billets into 1½-inch widths and then relaminating these strips back into 12- or 24-inch-wide pieces of lumber. This remanufacturing added substantial costs. Also, the laminations were now directly exposed to the weather. Moisture could more easily seep into cracks or voids, causing swells and buckling. (See Exhibit 5.3.)

specifically ordered a different decking material. Trailers headed for Alaska were decked with laminated oak, supplied by a vendor other than Pacific Laminated.

Mr. Walline said that if he wanted to make a recommendation to change decking materials, he would need to know price advantages, lead times, moisture content, availability, and industry experience with the material.

Sherman Brothers Trucking

"We already use Micro=Lam on our trailers," was the response of Mr. Sherman, president of Mayflower Moving and Storage Company, when asked about the trailer decking material his company used. He went on to say, "In fact, we had hauled several shipments for Trus Joist when we initiated a call to them asking if they could make a decking material for us."

Mayflower Moving and Storage owned 60 trailers (flatbeds) which it used to haul heavy equipment and machinery. It had been in a dilemma for eight years about the types of materials used to replace the original decks. Nothing seemed to be satisfactory. Solid apitong was tough, but it was too heavy and it did not weather very well. Plywood did not provide adequate weight distribution and had too many joints. Often the small wheels of the forklifts would break through the decking, or heavy equipment with steel legs would punch a hole through the decks. Laminated fir was too expensive.

Mayflower Moving and Storage was currently redecking a trailer per week. It usually patched the decks until the whole bed fell apart; then the trailer would sit in the yard waiting for a major overhaul. By this time the trailers needed to have the crossbeams repaired and new bearings as well as a new deck.

Mr. Sherman went on to say, "The shop mechanic just loves Micro=Lam. This is because it used to take the mechanic and one other employee two days to redeck a trailer, and now it just takes the shop mechanic one day to do the same job." Advantages (over plywood and apitong) of the 2-by-40-foot Micro=Lam pieces were ease of installation, excellent weight distribution due to the reduced number of seams, and reduced total weight of the bed.

Mr. Sherman explained that Mayflower Moving and Storage usually purchased four or five decks at a time, and warehoused some of the materials until a trailer needed redecking.

Mr. Sherman thought the original decking on flatbeds was some type of hardwood, probably oak, which could last up to five years; however, a similar decking material had not been found for a reasonable price. The plywood and fir decks used in the past eight to ten years had lasted anywhere from one to two years, and some had worn out in as little as six months. After using Micro=Lam for six months, Mr. Sherman expected the decking to last up to three to five years.

When asked about the type of flooring used in the company's moving vans, Mr. Sherman emphasized the top care that those floors received. "We sand, buff, and wax them just like a household floor; in fact, we take such good care of these floors they will occasionally outlast the trailer." The original floors in moving vans were made out of a laminated oak and had to be kept extremely smooth, allowing freight to slide freely without the possibility of damaging items of freight with legs. The local company purchased all of its moving vans through Mayflower Moving Vans. The only problem with floors in moving vans was that the jointed floors would occasionally buckle because of swelling.

The fact that Micro=Lam protruded ⅛ inch above the metal lip[6] that edged the flatbed trailers posed no problem for Sherman Brothers. "All we had to do was plane the edge at 40 degrees. In fact, the best fit will have the decking protrude a hair above the metal edge," Mr. Sherman said. Just prior to this, Mr. Sherman had recounted an experience that occurred with the first shipment of Micro=Lam. Because the deck was too thick, Mayflower Moving and Storage had about ⅛ inch planed from one side of the decking material. However, the company shaved off the apitong veneer, exposing the fir. Mr. Sherman said that he laughed about it now, but at the time he was not too pleased.

Peerless Trucking Company

"Sure, I've heard of Micro=Lam. They [Trus Joist salesmen] have been in here . . . but we don't need that good a material." This was the response of Mel Rogers, head of Peerless' Purchasing Department, Tualatin, Oregon, when asked about the use of Micro=Lam as a truck decking material. Mr. Rogers, a 30-year veteran of the trailer manufacturing industry, seemed very skeptical of all laminated decking materials.

The primary products manufactured by Peerless (in Tualatin) required bedding materials very different from Micro=Lam. Chip trailers and rail car dumpers required metal beds to facilitate unloading. Low-boys required a heavy decking material (usually 2-by-12-inch or 3-by-12-inch rough planking) because Caterpillar tractors were frequently driven on them. Logging trailers had no beds.

Approximately 60 decks per year were required by Peerless in the manufacture of flatbeds and in redecking jobs. Micro=Lam could have been used in these applications, but fir planking was used exclusively, except for some special overseas jobs. Fir planking was available in full trailer lengths, requiring eight man-hours to install on new equipment. Usually, five or six decks were stocked at a time. The estimated life of a new deck was two to three years.

Fir planking was selected for decking applications on the basis of price and durability. Peerless purchased fir planking for $1,000 per MBF. Tradition supported fir planking in durability, as it was a well-known product.

Decking material thickness was critical, according to Mr. Rogers, because any deviation from the industry standard of 1⅜ inches required extensive retooling.

Any new decking materials for use in original equipment manufacture had to be approved by the Peerless engineering department. Alternative decking materials could have been used locally if specified by the customer.

Mr. Rogers was certainly going to be a hard person to sell on the use of Micro=Lam, Mr. Kalish felt. "Why use Micro=Lam when I can buy fir planking for less?" Rogers had said.

---

[6] Refer to Exhibit 5.6.

EXHIBIT 5.6   **Cross-Sectional End View of Trailer Decking (Tongue and Groove)**

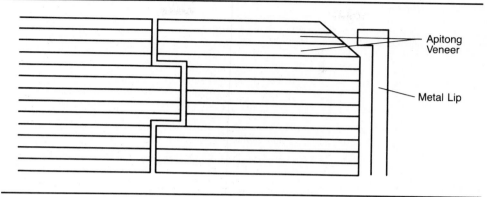

Apitong
Veneer

Metal Lip

Fruehauf Trucking Company

"I'd be very happy if someone would come up with a durable [trailer] deck at a reasonable price," was the response of Wayne Peterson when asked about Fruehauf's experience with decking materials. Mr. Peterson was service manager for Fruehauf's factory branch in Milwaukie, Oregon. Fruehauf Corporation, with its principal manufacturing facilities in Detroit, Michigan, was one of the nation's largest manufacturers of truck trailers.

The manufacturing facilities in Milwaukie produced 40-ton low-beds as well as assembled truck bodies manufactured in Detroit. The low-beds were subjected to heavy use, often with forklifts, which required a decking material of extreme strength and durability. Laminated decking materials then available were therefore excluded from this application.

The decking materials used in the truck bodies were specified by the sales department in Detroit, based on customer input. Generally, apitong or laminated oak was installed at the factory. Any new product to be used in original equipment manufacture had to be approved by Fruehauf's well-developed factory engineering department.

The Milwaukie operation also did about 15 redecking jobs per year. The decking material was specified by the customer on the basis of price and weathering characteristics. The materials used were laminated oak (11½ wide by 40 feet long), apitong (7-by-⅛ inches—random lengths), Alaska yellow cedar (2-by-6-inch T&G), fir planking (2-by-6-inch T&G), and laminated fir (24 feet wide by 40 feet long). Alaska yellow cedar was priced below all other decking materials, followed (in order) by fir planking, laminated fir, laminated oak, and apitong.

Fruehauf's suppliers of decking materials were as follows: laminated fir—Pacific Laminating, Vancouver, Washington; Alaska yellow cedar—Al Disdero Lumber Company, Portland, Oregon; and apitong—Builterials, Portland, Oregon. There were no specific suppliers for the other materials.

EXHIBIT 5.7   **Decking Material Prices, November 1978**

Product	Price	Form
Alaska yellow cedar	$650/MBF	2″ × 6″ T&B 15′ lengths
Apitong	$1.30–$2/lineal foot*	1⅜″ × 7″ random lengths
Fir planking	$1/board foot	2″ × 6″ T&G random lengths
Fir laminated	$2.50/square foot	1¼″ × 11¾″ × 40′
Micro=Lam	$1.30/square foot	1¼″ × 24″ × 40′
	$1.50/square foot	1½″ × 24″ × 40′
Oak laminated	$2.20/square foot	1⅜″ × 1½″ × 40′

*Lineal foot—price per unit length of the product

Source: Al Disdero Lumber Company, Portland, Oregon, Builterials, Portland, Oregon.

A minimum inventory of decking materials was kept on hand to allow for immediate repair needs only. Orders were placed for complete decks as needed.

A redecking job typically required 30 man-hours per 7-by-40-foot trailer, including the removal of the old deck and installation of the new one. Decking materials that were available in full trailer lengths were preferred because they greatly reduced installation time, improved weight distribution, and had fewer joints along which failure could occur.

The use of alternative products, such as composition flooring of wood and aluminum, was not under consideration.

Alaska yellow cedar and fir planking had the best weathering characteristics, while apitong and laminated oak weathered poorly. Oak and apitong did, however, have a hard, nonscratching surface that was desirable in enclosed use. When asked about the weathering characteristics of laminated flooring in general, Mr. Peterson responded, "It's all right for the dry states, but not around here."

Competition

There were a large number of materials with which Micro=Lam competed in the trailer flooring market, ranging from fir plywood to aluminum floors. Trus Joist felt that the greatest obstacles to Micro=Lam's success would be from the old standard products like laminated fir and oak, which had a great deal of industry respect. For years, oak had been the premier flooring material; recently, however, supplies had been short and delivery times long (two months in some cases), and prices were becoming prohibitive. (See Exhibit 5.7.)

Mr. Kalish had found that in the Northwest, Pacific Laminated Company was one of the major flooring suppliers to local manufacturers. Pacific Laminated produced a Douglas fir laminated product that was highly popular; however, like oak, it was relatively high-priced. Despite the price, Pacific Laminated could cut the product to dimensions up to 2 feet wide and 40 feet long. Delivery time was excellent for its customers, even with special milling for shiplapped or tongue and groove edges and manufacturing to user thickness.

Conclusion

Although Mr. Kalish had had limited success marketing Micro=Lam to truck trailer manufacturers, he was concerned with the marketing program for his product. Several trailer manufacturers had raised important questions concerning the price and durability of Micro=Lam compared to alternative decking materials. He knew Micro=Lam had some strong attributes, yet he was hesitant to expand beyond the local market. Mr. Kalish was also wondering about the action he should eventually take in order to determine the additional information he would need to successfully introduce Micro=Lam nationally as a trailer decking material. One thought that crossed his mind was to define the company's marketing strategy for this product. Meanwhile, small orders continued to trickle in.

Caterpillar Tractor Company

Background

Caterpillar Tractor Company is a large industrial manufacturing firm headquartered in Peoria, Illinois. Its familiar "CAT" logo and yellow paint are known throughout the world. Indeed, in its business Caterpillar has an estimated 37 percent of the world market; its closest rival, Japan's Komatsu, has an estimated 15 percent.

A multinational company, Caterpillar has manufacturing and dealer representatives throughout the world. The products which the firm designs, manufactures, and markets can be classified into two basic categories:

1. Earthmoving, construction and materials-handling equipment—track-type tractors, bulldozers, rippers, track- and wheel-type loaders, pipelayers, wheel dozers, compactors, wheel tractor-scrapers, off-highway trucks and tractors, motor graders, hydraulic excavators, log skidders, lift trucks, and related parts and equipment.

2. Engines—for earthmoving and construction machines, on-highway trucks, marine petroleum, agricultural, industrial, and electric power generation systems. Engines, either diesel or natural gas, have power ranges from 85 to 1,600 horsepower, or, in generator set versions, from 55 to 1,200 kilowatts. Turbines range from 25 to 10,600 horsepower, and, in generator set configurations, from 10 to 7,900 kilowatts.

Strategy

Caterpillar's market success is based upon two areas of strategic importance—product and after-sale support. The guiding principles of the CAT product strategy are fourfold. First, advanced technology is incorporated into machines so that users derive optimal

Source: This case was prepared by Dr. George B. Glisan, Illinois State University. Copyright 1984.

productivity and efficiency. To maintain the flow of product applications, the organization commits hundreds of millions of dollars each year to research and development. A second product guideline is quality. Within the last ten years several billion dollars have been spent on plant and equipment to ensure the quality of Caterpillar products. Customers demand quality to avoid costly downtime and to ensure reliability in the hostile operating environments the machines endure.

Another aspect of the product strategy is to offer a full line of products. This implies machines capable of performing on jobsites as small as a residential lot or as large as the Alaskan pipeline and on jobsites as forbidding as the Amazon jungle, the Sahara desert, or the Arctic tundra. The CAT product line offers over 100 different machines with a nearly infinite number of options/modifications. A final principle of the product strategy is to design and build only machines that can be produced on an assembly line, to take advantage of the manufacturing expertise and efficiency of the Caterpillar plants, and to provide significant economies of scale.

The other key area of strategic importance to Caterpillar's market success is after-sale support. The core of this effort is the network of 248 independent industrial distributors that represent the firm in the United States (93) and 140 other countries (155). The typical CAT dealer is a very large organization. The combined capitalization of all dealers, in fact, nearly equals the $3+ billion net worth of Caterpillar.

The dealer organization offers after-sale support in two ways—services and parts supply. All Caterpillar dealers are staffed with highly trained technicians and have well-equipped facilities for servicing customer machines. A typical dealer will offer:

1. Customer Track Service—dealer technicians examine the track of track-type machines to detect signs of unusual wear and potential failure before they shut down the machine.

2. Field Service—dealers, through a fleet of specially equipped trucks, can perform many repairs for customers at the jobsite.

3. Technical Analysis—a field check of major mechanical, electrical, cooling, and hydraulic systems as a means of preventive maintenance.

4. Scheduled Oil Sampling—customers can have samples of the motor oil in their machines subjected to sophisticated chemical analysis to detect signs of internal engine wear.

Caterpillar facilitates the quality of this service by providing training clinics for technicians at the dealership and by conducting schools at the Service Training Center in East Peoria, Illinois.

Servicing ability is moot without the necessary parts. Furthermore, many customers service their own machines, requiring only parts from their CAT dealer. As a result a well-stocked inventory of parts is essential. Caterpillar first analyzes the population of machines within a dealer's sales territory and, based upon this analysis, recommends the appropriate parts to inventory, as well as the quantity. This minimizes the inventory cost to the dealer by eliminating unneeded and slow-moving parts, as well as maximizing service to users. With this suggested inventory configuration, slightly more than 90 percent of all parts requests can be filled from the dealer's inventory.

Caterpillar also facilitates parts supply by providing a way to meet the unfilled parts requests. All U.S. dealers of Caterpillar are linked by computer terminal to a parts distribution system. First, a dealer checks to determine if nearby CAT dealers have the needed parts. If not, a dealer then searches the inventory of the nearest Caterpillar parts depot (there are eleven depots in the United States to back up dealers for emergency parts needs). Routine orders placed by dealers (typically weekly) are supplied by one of four regional distribution departments. Exhibit 6.1 shows how this system is structured. The system assures a customer of receiving a part within 48 hours.

Oil Filters

Part of Caterpillar's after-sale system of support is its line of supply items. These are parts that preserve and maintain the operating efficiency of machines and engines. The engine oil filter plays a critical maintenance role. While Caterpillar does not actually manufacture oil filters, it does design and engineer filters and prescribe to suppliers the performance parameters that filters must meet. All such filters carry the Caterpillar label.

One of Caterpillar's procurement policies is to have multiple suppliers for its oil filters. These suppliers are given the design specifications for the filters and a commitment by Caterpillar to purchase all filters ordered that meet performance standards. Most suppliers produce and market filters for Caterpillar equipment under their own brand as well. These filters, however, enter each supplier's own channel of distribution and are not available at the Caterpillar dealer.

After suppliers manufacture the CAT filters they are shipped to Caterpillar's main parts distribution center at Morton, Illinois. There filters are randomly selected from shipments and sent to the metallurgical laboratory for testing to determine their acceptability. If a shipment is accepted, the filters are packaged in Caterpillar containers and placed in inventory, ready for shipment through the distribution system.

The New Filter

Recently several problems associated with oil filters have surfaced at Caterpillar. One concerns a new filter design. Initial reports showed sales to be far lower than expected. Optimism for the new design was based upon several improvements over the older design that provide extended protection of users' engines. Specific improvements in the new filter design included full rubber grommets and metal end caps to provide better sealing for maximum oil filtration, a helical coil spring to keep the filter firmly in place under all operating conditions, a superior bypass valve that operates under low- as well as high-pressure conditions to prevent oil starvation to the engine, and a larger filtration element.

Parts marketing representatives have investigated the situation to determine the reasons for the sales resistance and have found that dealers' and customers' resistance is due to the price of the new filter. There are nearly a dozen competitive brands of oil filters for Caterpillar diesel engines. The mean unit price of these competitive filters is $2.71, whereas the Caterpillar filter is priced at $3.08. With the distinct design

EXHIBIT 6.1   **Caterpillar Parts Distribution System**

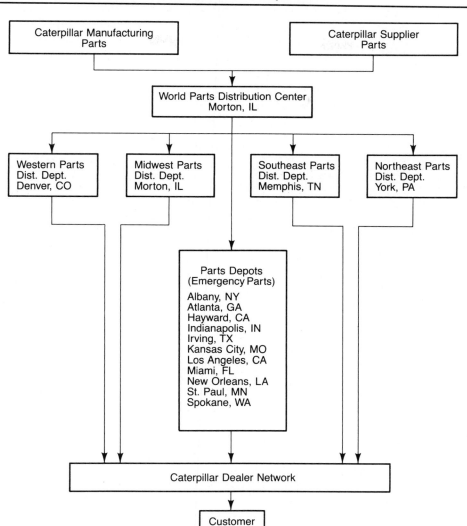

advantages of the new filter, as well as the quality assurance of the CAT name, management felt that the 10 percent price premium was more than justified.

Confirming the reduced sales of filters have been the reports coming from the engine remanufacturing facility at Bettendorf, Iowa. The engines sent to the facility originate from customers who trade their used engine for one that has been remanufactured by Caterpillar. During the inspection of customers' trade-in engines, personnel record the brand of oil filter on the engines. Recent reports show that competitors' oil filters outnumber the Caterpillar brand on the traded engines.

The Dirty Filter

While assessing the situation of the new design filter, management has been notified of the discovery of defective filters during routine testing at the metallurgical laboratory in Morton. Technicians report that one of the tests performed on a sample of filters shows that they are "dirty." This means that during the manufacturing process foreign contaminants were trapped inside the filters. If such a filter were to be used by a customer, these contaminants would enter the engine oil unfiltered. The result would be premature engine damage leading to repairs costing several thousand dollars as well as lost income due to downtime on the jobsite. Additional testing by the lab has revealed that the scope of the problem is much larger than first thought and that several hundred thousand filters may be defective. The lab also reports that the filters in question came from only one supplier. The dilemma is double edged for management. Although the decision to return the rejected oil filters to the supplier in question is obvious, because there are so many filters involved, there will be a filter shortage in the distribution system. Not only will lost sales result, but competitors will have an opportunity to sell to CAT filter buyers at a time when it is difficult to maintain loyalty due to the price differential.

Supplier Difficulties

A final disturbing problem has emerged. The rejected oil filters that were returned to the supplier have started turning up in customer engines. The rejected filters were simply relabeled by the supplier with their own brand and placed into their own distribution system. Additionally, close inspection of the relabeled filters reveals that it is not difficult to detect the CAT logo on the filters, which were simply spray painted. Such an action violates one of the covenants of the supplier agreement, that all rejected filters will be destroyed. An interview with the president of the filter supplier reveals that this action was done against company policy and without his personal knowledge. An immediate dilemma is that customers think they are buying, in effect, an equivalent quality Caterpillar filter. Dealers report that unsuspecting customers using the rejected/relabeled filters have been suffering severe engine damage and are asking that Caterpillar stand behind the engines under warranty repair.

Needless to say, management is confronted with several difficulties. At this point they have not made any final decisions. They would like to attack all their problems with a coordinated strategy.

The McKenzie Company (A)

Martin McKenzie waited impatiently in the service department of the Mercedes dealership. He was anxious to return to his office, for later that afternoon he would have to tell the sales manager of Hosunwa America whether he had chosen to continue to represent either Hosunwa or Elm Grove Capacitor. Elm Grove had introduced a new product line that had brought the two companies into competition.

As owner of an electronics sales representative company, McKenzie could sell only noncompeting products. The conflict of interest that had arisen between two of his largest principals required that McKenzie choose between them. As each had contributed about 20 percent of his firm's 1981 revenues, loss of either was going to have a significant impact on McKenzie's income. Even in a good year, the choice would have been unpleasant, but in the spring of 1982, it was especially onerous. For the last 18 months, McKenzie had felt like the Red Queen in *Alice in Wonderland*—running as fast as he could to stay in the same place.

Background

A tall man whose sandy hair and complexion reflected his Scottish ancestry, McKenzie had come to California from the Midwest to go to college. After receiving an electrical engineering degree from Cal Tech, he had gone to work for a small engineering firm that had a defense subcontract from Honeywell. When the contract ended, McKenzie chose not to return to the laboratory. He moved into one of Honeywell's sales divisions and, within three years, was made a sales manager. Shortly thereafter, his division was reorganized. The resulting policy changes were not to his liking, so when he was

---

The McKenzie Company does not exist. Issues presented herein for a classroom discussion were drawn from the composite experiences of a number of electronics sales representative firms and are typical problems faced within their industry.

Source: © 1982 Dan R. E. Thomas and Christine Hunt Blouke.

offered a job by an electronics sales representative firm in Los Angeles, he gladly accepted.

Smith Associates, founded seven years earlier by Richard Smith, 44, had three other employees: Smith's son-in-law, Andrew Edwards, a bookkeeper, and a sales secretary who also handled customer calls. The firm represented eight small component manufacturers or "principals," including three Japanese lines. Taken on three years before, the Japanese lines had, to Smith's surprise, come to account for approximately 60 percent of the firm's sales. Smith had begun to receive some pressure from several of the manufacturers to increase his sales staff to provide them with better market coverage in the Los Angeles territory, so he offered McKenzie a job.

Smith's selection of McKenzie was a good one, for McKenzie learned the business quickly. Finding himself in a position to substantially increase his previous income through commissions, McKenzie was highly motivated. He was well organized in his sales efforts and did not neglect the American lines. He soon built a good rapport with the sales managers of two of the American principals who had wanted Smith to add staff, and through McKenzie's efforts, sales of those two lines increased significantly.

Within three years McKenzie was generating 40 percent of the firm's revenues. In spite of the "easy sales" of the Japanese components (the Japanese enjoyed a sole-source position in several specialized markets), McKenzie continued to generate 60 percent of his sales from the American lines. In contrast, sales made by Smith and his son-in-law were about 60 percent Japanese components. Sales percentages for the firm are illustrated in Exhibit 7.1

McKenzie began to feel that the firm should be more aggressive. While Smith was content with the status quo, his American principals were again pushing him to enlarge the sales force. Fully realizing his own role in the growth of the firm's revenues, McKenzie approached Smith, asking to be made a partner. Smith's response did not satisfy McKenzie. Smith intimated that he had been considering offering 25 percent of the firm to his son-in-law and 25 percent to McKenzie "in a few more years." Smith's son-in-law, Edwards, was a low-key man with a lackluster sales record; he had assumed most of the office management chores, for which Smith was grateful, but Edwards' sales contribution was below average.

Several months after McKenzie suggested partnership, the sales manager of Elm Grove Capacitor Company, one of Smith Associates' American principals, asked McKenzie to have lunch with him. Elm Grove had acquired a film capacitor manufacturer. The addition of film to Elm Grove's ceramic and tantalum capacitor product line brought the company into direct competition with Smith's largest principal, Misan Electronics. Pleased with McKenzie's past performance, the sales manager offered him Elm Grove's account and encouraged him to start his own firm. After thinking it over for two weeks, McKenzie decided to go ahead.

McKenzie had signed a strict noncompete agreement with Smith Associates that prohibited him from becoming a direct competitor of Smith and from working for any of Smith's principals for one year after leaving Smith's employ. However, McKenzie's lawyer advised him that the courts were unlikely to uphold the agreement because it prohibited him from pursuing his livelihood. McKenzie felt that Smith would be

---

EXHIBIT 7.1   **Smith Associates' Revenue by Salesperson and Manufacturers**

	Total	Japanese Manufacturers	American Manufacturers
McKenzie	40%	16%	24%
Smith and Son-in-Law	60	36	24
Total	100%	52%	48%

---

unlikely to undertake litigation, in part because of Smith's intense dislike of lawyers. In addition, the conflict of interest between the Japanese product and the Elm Grove product would cause Smith to drop the smaller American line which had accounted for less than 16 percent of Smith's revenues in the preceding year.

The McKenzie Company

Eight weeks later, in January 1978, the McKenzie Company was formed. McKenzie hired a part-time secretary and subleased an office from Circuit Specialists, a new business started by two former employees of the engineering firm that had been McKenzie's first employer.

In addition to Elm Grove's line of electrolytic capacitors, McKenzie began to represent the custom-designed hybrid circuits that his landlords were manufacturing.

In March 1978, McKenzie answered three ads in a trade journal and was successful in adding all three lines. He was interviewed and hired by Genesis Gate Array, a small local company that did semi-custom circuit design. Genesis's founders had contacts in the aerospace industry which had generated enough business to get them established. Recent advances in software tools had made it possible for Genesis to serve a broader set of customers. They had concluded that it was time for them to enlarge their market and that hiring a sales representative made more sense than hiring their own direct sales force.

McKenzie also was hired by two New England-based manufacturers, Waltham Resistor, which made resistor networks, and Pronto Circuit Company, which made two-sided and multilayer printed circuit boards.

Hybrid circuit sales generally involved a long lead time for development. Commission on sales could lag behind orders by up to 18 months. Gate Array technology was just emerging in 1978. However, McKenzie's three other product lines—capacitors, resistor networks, and printed circuits—began to produce steady revenues. McKenzie completed his first year in business slightly ahead of the goal he had targeted for himself. His 1978 revenues were $70,000, and his target had been $60,000. Sixty percent of his revenues came from the sale of Elm Grove's capacitors.

In August 1979, McKenzie was approached by Flexico, another small printed circuit board manufacturer that specialized in flexible circuits. McKenzie happily accepted Flexico's line.

EXHIBIT 7.2 **Percentages of Revenue/Principal**

	1979
Elm Grove Capacitor	40.0%
Circuit Specialists	15.0
Genesis Gate Array	14.0
Waltham Resistor	16.0
Pronto Circuit	14.0
Flexico (10/79)	1.0
	100.0%

McKenzie's second year went well. He hired a bookkeeper who also handled customers' telephone orders. His revenues were $115,000 in 1979. His revenues per principal are shown in Exhibit 7.2.

At a lunch to celebrate his second anniversary with Elm Grove's sales manager, McKenzie was introduced to Donald Monroe. Monroe had been the sales manager in Elm Grove's Boston office for three years. When Monroe's wife was offered a job in Los Angeles, the couple decided to relocate. Monroe had decided to find an outside sales job, believing it would offer both greater independence and more money. Following lunch, Elm Grove's sales manager spent an hour with McKenzie. He gave Monroe glowing references and urged McKenzie to hire him "to give us better sales coverage in this territory."

At dinner with Monroe and his wife two days later, McKenzie discovered that they had mutual friends from college and that Monroe also loved sailing. After dinner McKenzie gave the Monroes an office tour then took them to see his sailboat. Over drinks at a bar overlooking the marina, McKenzie offered Monroe a job.

Monroe accompanied McKenzie on sales calls for four weeks, emphasizing the northern end of Los Angeles County, which would be Monroe's territory. The men had lunch or dinner with each of the company's principals, and McKenzie spent time explaining the "politics" of each principal.

McKenzie had anticipated that within about nine months, Monroe would be paying his own way. He was delighted when Monroe was able to write orders for Elm Grove's product line on his first solo sales call. However, McKenzie's expectations proved unrealistic. He had thoroughly underestimated how long it would take a person to learn how to effectively sell multiple lines of electronic components. Since McKenzie's engineering experience had made him familiar with most electronic technologies, he had assumed that Monroe had as diverse a background as he had. However, Monroe's experience was much more specific, derived from working with Elm Grove. He tended to emphasize the products and technologies he knew best and to avoid any appearance of ignorance before McKenzie or a customer.

McKenzie did not speak directly to Monroe about his sales performance. He did, however, grumble about what Monroe was costing him to a few friends who were also in the sales business. Their response surprised McKenzie for they all supported Monroe,

EXHIBIT 7.3   **Monroe's Performance**

1/80–12/80	Cost to McKenzie (Salary, Car Expenses)	Incremental Commission Revenues on Sales*
1st Quarter	$15,000	$ 1,000
2nd Quarter	15,000	2,500
3rd Quarter	15,000	5,500
4th Quarter	15,000	8,500
	$60,000	$17,500

*Commission revenues from Monroe's new accounts.

told McKenzie he had to give a new man at least 12 to 18 months to pay his way, and suggested he spend more time with Monroe. McKenzie, feeling he had to increase his own sales to cover his additional expenses, did not take their advice.

Exhibit 7.3 shows Monroe's performance during his first year with McKenzie.

In June 1980, McKenzie added the line of Alba Electronics, an integrated circuit socket manufacturer. In November 1980, McKenzie's firm was one of three to be interviewed by the new American subsidiary of Hosunwa Electronics of Japan. Hosunwa manufactured aluminum electrolytic capacitors. The line went to McKenzie in part because Hosunwa America's new sales manager was as avid a sailor as were McKenzie and Monroe. Exhibit 7.4 shows McKenzie's revenues per principal for 1980.

1981

Between 1978 and 1980, the price of tantalite ore had risen approximately 270 percent. In keeping with industry trends, the price of Elm Grove's tantalum electrolytic capacitors had been driven up 115% in 1980. Many of McKenzie's customers had begun to switch to cheaper aluminum electrolytic capacitors.

The McKenzie Company's sales of Elm Grove's capacitors were flat in the first two quarters of 1981. Increased supply caused the price of tantalum powder to drop, allowing Elm Grove to reduce its prices. By the third quarter of 1981, prices of tantalum electrolytic capacitors were down 25 percent, but this effort to hold market share only served to hold the company's sales in this segment at 1980 levels.

Elm Grove was also forced to drop prices for its ceramic monolythic capacitors in an effort to maintain sales in the face of significant industry overcapacity. Rising material costs forced Elm Grove's film capacitor prices up 5 percent.

By the end of the third quarter, Elm Grove's sales were 4 percent below 1980 levels, with some sales regions posting 8 percent declines. McKenzie and Monroe had managed to hold sales at 1980 levels within the Los Angeles territory, which was not feeling the effects of the recession quite as sharply as other regions.

Many of McKenzie's accounts began to switch to cheaper aluminum capacitors. The Hosunwa line not only allowed McKenzie to maintain sales that would otherwise have been lost, but opened avenues to new markets. Although aluminum electrolytic

EXHIBIT 7.4   **Percentage of Revenue/Principal**

	1979	1980
Elm Grove Capacitor	40.0%	33.0%
Circuit Specialists	15.0	15.0
Genesis Gate Array	14.0	19.5
Waltham Resistor	16.0	12.0
Pronto Circuit	14.0	14.0
Flexico	1.0	5.5
Alba Electronics (8/80)	—	1.0
Hosunwa America (12/80)	—	—
	100.0%	100.0%

capacitors were manufactured throughout the Far East, the Japanese product was judged to be superior in quality and technology. McKenzie gained market share from other aluminum electrolytic capacitor manufacturers as well as from former tantalum users.

The Hosunwa line experienced rapid sales growth at the expense of their competitors. The company was very price competitive and anxious to gain share quickly. McKenzie's revenues from Hosunwa sales equalled market revenues from Elm Grove sales by the end of the second quarter of 1981. However, the Hosunwa sales manager was working toward a quota determined by Hosunwa of Japan's five-year strategic plan, which did not anticipate the 1980–1981 recession. He was often critical of the McKenzie Company's performance, even though McKenzie's sales were 10 to 30 percent above those of the other Hosunwa representatives' quotas in the western region. He developed the habit of calling the office to suggest that McKenzie or Monroe be sure to see "so-and-so as soon as possible this week," using a tone of voice that quickly raised the listener's anger.

After 18 months with the McKenzie Company, Donald Monroe had hit full stride. He had become comfortable with all the company's lines, and the rising sales volumes for Hosunwa America products were as much his doing as McKenzie's. Although McKenzie was slow to praise Monroe directly, he emphasized the man's abilities to the company's principals.

In June of 1981, McKenzie hired a second salesman, James Hadinata, who was a Los Angeles native. He had spent his senior year in high school as an exchange student in Japan and, after graduating from UCLA, had gone to work for Nippon Electric Company's first U.S. subsidiary. Starting in sales, he had received several promotions during his four years with the firm and was a marketing manager for Nippon's 16 K RAM when Nippon's president's daughter abruptly broke their engagement, and Hadinata elected to leave the company.

McKenzie had known Hadinata casually for two years (their boats were in adjacent moorings), and Monroe and Hadinata had raced against each other in several local regattas. When Monroe mentioned that Hadinata was job hunting, McKenzie reached for the phone, asked Hadinata to join them for dinner, and the following Monday, Hadinata joined the firm.

EXHIBIT 7.5 **Percentage of Revenue/Principal**

	1979	1980	1981
Elm Grove Capacitor	40.0%	33.0%	20.5%
Circuit Specialists	15.0	15.0	16.0
Genesis Gate Array	14.0	19.5	22.0
Waltham Resistor	16.0	12.0	6.0
Pronto Circuit	14.0	14.0	9.0
Flexico	1.0	5.5	4.0
Alba Electronics	—	1.0	2.0
Hosunwa America	—	—	20.5
	100.0%	100.0%	100.0%

The entire passive components/semiconductor industry experienced a sales slump in the first half of 1981. Waltham Resistor, Pronto Circuit, Flexico, and Alba Electronics all had flat sales through the first two quarters. Only Genesis Gate Array and Circuit Specialists were immune to the recession. Their sales doubled from the same period the previous year.

During good times, McKenzie had been diligent in communicating with his principals, sending short notes with competitive information or market forecasts at least bimonthly. Now McKenzie went to greater lengths, calling or writing at least every four weeks to trace the extent of the recession, identify any bright spots, and assure his principals that the drop in orders in no way reflected the amount of service they were receiving.

As the recession deepened in the third quarter of 1981, an anti-Japanese feeling appeared to be growing within the electronic components industry as imports continued to take share from American products. Several of McKenzie's American principals, and in particular Elm Grove, made comments about McKenzie's Japanese line. These ranged from small jokes to unusually hostile remarks about supporting American-made products during hard times. This attitude on the part of the American principals made it even more difficult for McKenzie to keep his temper with Hosunwa's sales manager. Whenever possible he had Hadinata take the calls, which were briefer and less vitriolic when Japanese was spoken.

Ironically Hosunwa's sales continued to increase beyond expectation. The company had a product of superior quality, an American service staff that gave extremely prompt and courteous customer service, plus low prices. By the end of 1981, revenues from McKenzie's sales of Hosunwa's line exceeded revenues of Elm Grove. Exhibit 7.5 shows McKenzie's revenue per principal for 1981.

1982

In December 1981, Circuit Specialists was acquired by the Roundy Corporation, a Boston-based semiconductor manufacturer. Circuit Specialists was Roundy's seventh acquisition in three years. The aggressive, rapid-growth company had developed a diversification plan that hinged on its acquisition of small companies with leading-edge technologies within the semiconductor industry.

As more than 60 percent of Roundy's sales were made in New England, the company maintained a direct sales force in the East. The balance of the company sales were made through electronic sales representative firms. In January 1982, Roundy fired Circuit Specialists' New England representative and added the line to their own sales portfolio. Circuit Specialists' president invited McKenzie to lunch January 5 to tell him of the new arrangements and, "to assure you that Roundy has no intention of extending their direct sales force outside New England." However, as a matter of company policy, McKenzie was given a copy of Roundy's standard contract which would supersede Circuit Specialists' contract with McKenzie Company in 90 days. While commission rates were not affected, the new contract had a 30-day cancellation clause, with commission paid on outstanding orders for only 60 days. In contrast, Circuit Specialists' contract had had a 90-day termination clause with commission to be paid on all outstanding backlog. Given the long development time associated with custom circuit design, only a very small percentage of outstanding commissions would be collected in 60 days.

Roundy's main line of semiconductors was presently under contract with the largest sales representative firm in Los Angeles. McKenzie wondered if Roundy would also wish to consolidate their subsidiaries' lines with one firm. In spite of the personal assurances from his old friend at Circuit Specialists, McKenzie was troubled.

Even more alarming news came from Elm Grove's sales manager on January 10, 1982. Elm Grove had adopted a strategic plan to improve its performance in the capacitor marketplace: In order to try to recapture sales volume lost to aluminum electrolytic capacitors, Elm Grove had decided to add an aluminum capacitor manufactured in Taiwan to their product line. This addition would become effective April 1, and at that time McKenzie would probably have to choose between his two major principals.

Elm Grove had also decided that the company must now move to avoid further erosion of the market share. IC chips had displaced discrete capacitors and resistors in many electronics applications between 1978 and 1981. The decline in market share was offset slightly by technological constraints that limited the amount of capacitance that could be incorporated into an IC chip. To bridge this gap, discrete capacitors could be mounted externally on a printed circuit board supporting the IC. Elm Grove had quietly invested the lion's share of their 1981 R&D money in the development of capacitor chips. Some industry observers had predicted that the chip format could gain 20 percent of the capacitor market by the mid-1980s. Elm Grove's sales manager expected that the company would have their new product ready for market within eight months, by August 1982, although no date for official introduction had been announced.

For McKenzie's customers the choice between Hosunwa's line and the Taiwanese capacitor would be equivalent to choosing between an unknown generic product and a well-advertised major name brand. As McKenzie knew only too well, the Hosunwa line had an enthusiastic clientele who would not be easily persuaded to switch to an unknown product, particularly when cost was equal and the quality of the Taiwanese capacitor was unproven.

McKenzie, Monroe, and Hadinata met to objectively evaluate the two principals. Monroe supported Elm Grove. He argued that the company was mature, reliable, prompt to pay commissions, and its sales manager was a friend. Although not a market leader in the past, its new strategy could signal a more aggressive approach that might generate larger sales if the company's predictions for capacitor chips and its new products proved sound. The contract with Elm Grove had a 90-day cancellation clause, and commission would be paid on all outstanding orders.

Hosunwa was certainly the more dynamic company. It was aggressively pursuing market share. Its R&D expenditures were believed to be high. The company had suffered some growing pains; its policies kept changing with its management as people moved up. The present sales manager was a pain in the neck, but the man's ambition was such that Hadinata predicted that he would seek promotion successfully and move on within the company. There were rumors that the company planned to expand its product line. Twice Hosunwa's sales manager had cut McKenzie's commission rate on large sales. In addition, as the recession had continued, Hosunwa had dropped its maximum commission for sales to a single customer.

McKenzie found it hard to assess the anti-Japanese sentiments so recently surfacing among his American principals and in the electronics industry as a whole. There had been talk in Washington about raising tariffs or imposing quotas on Japanese imports. McKenzie wondered if his possession of one major Japanese line might attract others. Remembering Smith Associates' experience with Japanese products, McKenzie thought of them as "money in the bank," assuming they did not grow so big that they found it more profitable to move away from sales reps and into direct sales.

Conclusion

Back in his office, McKenzie again weighed Elm Grove against Hosunwa. He realized that whatever course he chose, he could expect a substantial drop in revenue in 1982. After nine months with McKenzie, Hadinata was performing beyond any expectation and would show a profit above his costs to the company within three months if he continued at his present pace. McKenzie knew that with the loss of either principal, the McKenzie Company's sales would probably be off at least 20 percent. In the short run, he would be hard pressed to keep Hadinata, yet in the long run, he had no choice if the firm was to grow. And if McKenzie's firm was to grow as he wished, he knew he needed to take a long look at his principals and their futures (see Exhibits 7.6–7.8).

EXHIBIT 7.6 **The McKenzie Company**

Time Line for Personnel and Principals Added

Personnel (Date of Hire)	1978 Jan Mar Jun Oct	1979 Jan Mar Jun Oct	1980 Jan Mar Jun Oct	1981 Jan Mar Jun Oct	1982 Jan Mar Jun Oct
McKenzie					
Secretary					
Bookkeeper	(part time 1978)				
Monroe					
Hadinata					
Principals:					
Elm Grove	60%	40%	33%	20.5%	
Circuit Specialists	4%	15%	15%	16%	
Genesis G. A.	6%	14%	19.5%	22%	
Waltham Resistor	15%	16%	12%	6%	
Pronto P. C.	13%	14%	14%	9%	
Flexico		1%	5.5%	4%	
Alba			1%	2%	
Hosunwa				20.5%	

Monroe now fully productive.

EXHIBIT 7.7   **The McKenzie Company's Income Statement 1978–1981**

Commission Revenue	1978 $70,000	1979 $115,000	1980 $153,900	1981 $263,000
Expenses				
Business meals and entertainment	$ 3,640	$ 5,980	$ 8,003	$ 13,676
Dues and subscriptions	70	115	154	263
Group insurance	1,750	2,875	3,847	6,575
Insurance	378	621	831	1,420
Payroll taxes	3,211	5,155	7,002	11,902
Postage	189	310	416	710
Professional services	2,800	4,600	6,156	10,520
Rent and office expenses	3,570	5,865	7,849	13,413
Salaries and commissions	49,394	79,312	107,730	183,112
Telephone and telegraph	3,241	5,324	7,126	12,177
Travel	1,407	2,312	3,093	5,286
Total operating expenses	$69,650	$112,470	$152,207	$259,055
Net income before tax	350	2,530	1,693	3,945
Taxes	168	1,214	813	1,894
Net income after tax	$ 182	$ 1,316	$ 880	$ 2,051

EXHIBIT 7.8   **The McKenzie Company: Percentage of Revenue per Principal per Year**

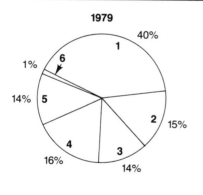

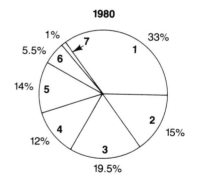

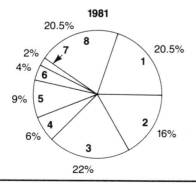

1 Elm Grove Capacitor
2 Circuit Specialists
3 Genesis Gate Array
4 Waltham Resistor
5 Pronto Circuit
6 Flexico
7 Alba Electronics
8 Hosunwa, America

The McKenzie Company (B)

In May 1982, one of the McKenzie Company's former principals, Hosunwa of Japan, reached a cooperative agreement with two other Japanese passive component manufacturers. The three merged to form a new corporation. Hosunwa America was to be enlarged. Its management staff would take responsibility for introducing the other product lines in the United States.

Hosunwa America's sales manager, Bill Tanabe, was given responsibility for all three product lines. He immediately exercised a 30-day termination clause with all Hosunwa's U.S. sales representatives and began to set up a direct sales force. One of his first job offers went to James Hadinata, to whom he offered a sales position in Hosunwa's Western Region. Tanabe implied that he expected a promotion soon and that Hadinata would be in line for his job as sales manager.

Hadinata received Hosunwa's offer on May 28. Unexpected and unsolicited, it nevertheless appeared to be an extraordinary opportunity. Hadinata spent the Memorial Day weekend trying to evaluate the offer from all perspectives. On Tuesday, June 1, he came into the office early to catch McKenzie before he could leave to make sales calls, and he bluntly outlined Hosunwa's offer and its apparent advantages, which included a $4,000 raise and bonus/commission potential that appeared likely to increase his present income by about 30 percent within twelve months.

"It's a great opportunity for me, Mac. The only really negative thing about it is that I'd report directly to Tanabe. But I've managed to work with him from here, even though I don't like him. If his market projections are sound Hosunwa offers real potential for advancement. I told him I'd give him my answer on Friday after I had a chance to think about it and talk to you."

Source: © 1982 Dan R. E. Thomas and Christine Hunt Blouke.

McKenzie suggested Hadinata join him for dinner the following evening, and Hadinata left the office. With effort, McKenzie restrained himself from putting his fist through the wall. He immediately called his lawyer to determine whether he could legally prevent Hadinata from taking the job through the noncompete agreement Hadinata had signed.

McKenzie's lawyer was immediately pessimistic. McKenzie had terminated the Hosunwa contract in April 1982 when a conflict of interest between Elm Grove Capacitor and Hosunwa had arisen. In general, McKenzie's lawyer felt that noncompete contracts were difficult to enforce. Likely costs of litigation, in time and energy as well as in money, could be high.

Once his anger cooled, McKenzie began to consider what other options he had available. Hadinata was a superb salesman and he worked well with McKenzie and Monroe. It would be difficult to attract another large principal with only one salesman besides himself to cover the territory, and even Hadinata who was far from typical had taken 12 months of training to begin to pay his way.

Beta Pharmaceuticals: Pennsylvania Distribution System

Jack Sexton, manager of logistics planning, walked out of his boss's office with a frown on his face. He had just learned that the top management of his company, Beta Pharmaceutical, had been taking a closer look at cost levels in the company's distribution system. In particular, high transportation costs resulting from frequent minimum-size LTL shipments to customers and low-volume resupply shipments to the smaller warehouses were beginning to raise eyebrows. Total warehousing and material-handling costs had also been questioned.

When he got back to his office, Mr. Sexton sat back and thought the problem over. He recalled that the present plant, warehouse, and customer configuration had evolved during a period of high-growth years, without the systematic development of a master distribution plan. Warehouse location and customer service decisions were based mainly on marketing-centered recommendations, competitive pressures, and customer desires. Customer order frequency and shipment size had been largely in the control of the customer. Basically, Beta believed that to achieve and maintain industry leadership, it was necessary to meet customer demand 100 percent of the time. Thus the cost of customer service, inclusive of distribution, had historically been very high.

Several days later Mr. Sexton settled on a course of action. Calling in a logistics consulting firm, HLW and Associates, he asked that a pilot study be conducted to evaluate a portion of the present product logistics system for cost-service effectiveness.

Source: This case was prepared by Harvey Boatman, Paul Liguori, and Gary Wiser under the direction of Professor Alan J. Stenger.

EXHIBIT 9.1   **Project Description**

Project: How should Beta Pharmaceuticals distribute products to customers in the state of Pennsylvania?

Background: Beta currently distributes products to customers from public warehouses in Pittsburgh, Harrisburg, and Philadelphia.

- Cartage carriers are used in the three metropolitan areas.
- Common carriers are used in the balance of the state.
- Customers (hospitals) order both in patterns and randomly.
- Shipments are made within 24 to 48 hours of order receipt.
- Shipment sizes are small, from under 100 pounds to a few thousand pounds.
- The full product line is stocked in Philadelphia and Pittsburgh, but only a partial line is stocked in Harrisburg.
- Distribution costs are a significant element of total costs.

Objective: Determine the best method to distribute products to customers, considering the effects on:

- Distribution costs (freight and handling).
- Levels of customer service.
- Inventory levels.

Scope: The scope of the project should be restricted to the state of Pennsylvania to keep it manageable.

- Inventory policies and methods of replenishing warehouses should be ignored. However, the relationship between aggregate inventory levels and warehouse volume must be recognized.
- Customer order patterns can be assumed to be controllable within certain limits, to be defined. Customer contact will not be allowed.
- The number and location of warehouses should be determined.
- Methods of delivery should be determined, including such alternatives as (1) direct shipment or (2) scheduling of customer orders for pooled delivery, including contact with carriers for rates and feasibility.

The state of Pennsylvania was determined to be a "typical" subsystem within the national distribution network and was designated by Mr. Sexton as the focal point for the study.[1] An outline of the study proposal is shown in Exhibit 9.1.

Background

The Company

Beta Pharmaceuticals is a multidivisional manufacturer and distributor of a diversified line of medical care products. Manufacturing, sales, and distribution facilities are located throughout the world, with major operations existing in Europe, Africa, South America, Australia, Asia, Canada, and the United States. Products include intravenous solutions, artificial organs, disposable medical devices, clinical testing and diagnostic supplies and equipment, blood collecting and storage equipment, prescription drugs, and industrial and medical enzymes.

---

[1] Pennsylvania represents a "mini model" of the total system in that it contains a three-warehouse configuration, two customer service areas, a customer service representative, and a dollar demand pattern consistent with the rest of the national system.

Beta has 12 production or research facilities in the United States, and markets its products through five customer-service or distribution-center regions. The company employs 13,600 persons throughout its worldwide system.

The backbone of Beta's strong marketing position in the hospital supply industry is a well-funded R&D program. New products, as well as improvements to existing products, are constantly being developed and exploited as a key element in market strategy and industry leadership. As a result of this philosophy, Beta increased the 1984 expenditures for research and development by 25.7 percent over 1983 for a total dollar investment of $46.7 million.

The aggressive competitive stance, supported by resourceful research and development, effective quality control, and customer-oriented distribution, has enabled the company to build a 16-year compound growth rate in sales and earnings per share of 20 percent. Its 1984 sales were $855.9 million, which represented a 27.7 percent increase over 1983. Earnings per share for 1984 were $1.95, a 23.4 percent increase over 1983.

The Distribution System

The current distribution system used by Beta within the state of Pennsylvania makes use of three public warehouses: Philadelphia, Pittsburgh, and Harrisburg. From these three warehouses, Beta is able to serve most of its customers in 49 of the 67 counties in Pennsylvania: this service is supplemented by shipments from nearby out-of-state warehouses or by carload shipments direct from a Beta plant. The distribution responsibilities of the three Pennsylvania warehouses include shipments to out-of-state customers as well as to the Pennsylvania customers.

Beta maintains either a company-salaried customer service representative or a warehouse employee at each warehouse to handle orders and customer inquiries. Whenever an order is received, company policy dictates that it be filled and tendered to a carrier within 48 hours. Orders are received either by phone or mail, direct at the warehouse or at company headquarters in Chicago. The 48-hour service goal starts at the point the order is received within the Beta system.

Once the warehouse receives the order, two possibilities exist. If the items are in stock, a bill of lading is cut and the freight is tendered to a common carrier or a cartage carrier. Of those shipments tendered to common carriers, 95 percent are delivered by the second morning. This means a maximum order filling time—including transportation—of four days 95 percent of the time. If the customer is located within the commercial zone of the city and a cartage carrier can be used, total time from order receipt by Beta to delivery to the customer is reduced to two days 95 percent of the time.

When sufficient stock is not available, the warehouse representative will contact the regional distribution center to which the warehouse is assigned. The regional distribution center will review the inventory levels of the surrounding warehouses and assign the order to one of these warehouses. Transportation cost is used as the basis for which warehouse should receive the order. If the item is not available in any of the surrounding warehouses, it will be back-ordered and expedited from a production facility. Since Beta wants to maintain high customer service levels, every attempt is made to maintain inventories high enough to avoid the need of back ordering to Chicago.

The majority of Beta's customers are hospitals. As such, they have limited storage space. They also cannot afford to wait very long after ordering items because their inventory averages approximately one week's demand. Since Beta is the major supplier of medical products in the Pennsylvania area, it falls upon them to provide hospitals with the required service. Traditional performance and marketing pressure have forced Beta into the position of maintaining inventory for its customers. However, very few of the shipments made by Beta are on a life-or-death basis for a patient.

Preliminary Findings and Plans of the Consultants

Beta's present distribution system is structured around basic customer service objectives. Competitive stress and rapid growth contributed to the piecemeal development of the present structure, wherein the customer sets the rules. This resulted in a number of marginal, close-to-the-customer warehouses. Warehouse-to-customer shipments are made without consideration of economic order quantities or potential savings to be recognized by shipping in consolidated lots. Many customers avoid assuming inventory responsibility and cost by ordering frequently, often at random intervals and in varying order quantities. Beta provides 24-hour delivery to all customers within the commercial zone of each warehouse, and 48-hour delivery to other customers. This situation has necessitated the establishment of safety stock of nearly 100 percent at most warehouses.

The piecemeal pattern of development has presented coordination problems at the corporate level. Many problems common to several areas are still handled on an individual basis at the local level. Rarely is the experience and information gained at one point generalized for the benefit of other areas of the system. The nearly exclusive use of public warehouses compounds this situation, particularly when quality control, damage, or liability become the question. The use of public warehouses also complicates the information-gathering process as well as making the control aspects of inventory more difficult to handle.

Even though growth potential remains high for Beta, a plateau has been reached in many areas. For example, the climb to leadership in the medical products industry has been achieved; a reputation for high standards, effective quality control, and an understanding for the specialized problems experienced by hospitals has been established; an impressive record of innovation and responsible research and development has been compiled. In essence, Beta has created a "pull" situation, in the marketing sense, for the products bearing the Beta trademark.

Beta presently has good information potential. Most operations-related facts are collected in the present system, but unfortunately those items not lost due to pure volume are presented in a manner that makes their usefulness limited and suspect. Feedback and information update is slow and complicated under the present system of hand tallies, verbal order placement at each warehouse, and conflicting loyalties (due to the nearly exclusive use of public warehouses). Control at the warehouse level is shaky at best.

The Pennsylvania Subsystem

The following information is available for the Pennsylvania subsystem:

1. *Monthly demand for Pennsylvania customers.* A computer printout for March 1985 gives demand by customers for each of Beta's major product lines. It shows how many bills of lading were cut and the number of cases per product line on each bill. Every order shipped within the state of Pennsylvania is included, with coded identification of which warehouse filled the order. There is a considerable amount of overlap in the territory served by various warehouses. Out-of-state warehouses appear throughout the printout, indicating service to cities also serviced by the Pennsylvania warehouses. The monthly demand information gives no indication of the timing throughout the month for the orders. It is easy to identify how many shipments a customer received but not when they were received. Finally, there is no indication that March 1985 was a typical month in terms of demand level. A quarterly demand schedule was requested but not provided. As a result, the assumption that March 1985 is a typical month had to be made.

2. *Quarterly transportation cost.* This is a summary of the air and truck costs incurred by each of Beta's warehouses on an outbound basis by product line only. It does show total pieces and weight of each product line shipped by air and truck, but it does not break total cost down past a total for air and truck. Since the total cost is a three-month figure for all shipments out of a warehouse, an average cost would not truly reflect the intrastate rate levels.

3. *March payments to carriers.* Beta provided a list of the total billings for transportation charges paid to carriers in March 1985. The charges are broken down by product line pieces and weight. The list is not very useful because it is for bills paid in March, not for shipments made during March. Also, no information was provided concerning the number of shipments each carrier handled or the destination of these shipments.

4. *Warehouse throughput.* Beta was able to provide estimates of the average monthly throughput in terms of total cases for the three Pennsylvania warehouses, as follows:

Philadelphia:	50,000 cases
Pittsburgh:	35,000 cases
Harrisburg:	9,000 cases

    Warehouse capacity in both Philadelphia and Pittsburgh is large enough to handle the entire throughput of Harrisburg should that location be eliminated. Average monthly throughput would be useful in evaluating the methods of warehouse replenishment.

5. *Warehouse cost.* The three Pennsylvania facilities are public warehouses. Under the contract agreements with Philadelphia and Harrisburg, a single charge is assessed for each carton that comes into the warehouse. There is no annual rental fee, no quantity discount, and no penalty for falling below a minimum level. The single rate per carton includes storage, handling, stenciling, and anything else the

warehouse people might have to do to the case. The charge in Philadelphia is 44 cents per case, while the Harrisburg charge is 43 cents per case. Pittsburgh, which does not have the same type of arrangements, pays an average of 46 cents per case. There is no indication of how this figure would vary with different inventory levels. An additional 10 cents per case is assigned by Beta to each case handled through the Pittsburgh warehouse due to the presence of a Beta customer service representative in that city.

6. *Warehouse replenishment policy.* Beta will not retain a warehouse unless it can be replenished at least once a month in carload quantity. The information provided by Beta concerning actual replenishment schedules is very sketchy. Philadelphia and Pittsburgh are replenished on a carload basis once a week. However, no information was available as to how many cars per week were used, whether they get the 40,000-pound or the 60,000-pound carload rate, or whether additional demand would also move at carload rates. If Harrisburg is eliminated, inbound freight costs to Philadelphia and Pittsburgh will change. The Harrisburg replenishment schedule was stated to be once every two to three weeks and once a month.

7. *Average inventory level.* Both Philadelphia and Pittsburgh hold six weeks' demand in inventory, whereas Harrisburg holds eight weeks' demand in inventory. These figures were unfortunately subject to some uncertainty.

8. *Truck rates.* Evaluating configuration changes in the current system requires a comparison of total cost for both the present and proposed systems. Costing out a system requires a close estimate of the transportation costs generated by that system. In light of the restrictions of a linear programming algorithm in terms of homogeneous product and potential system requirement of over 2,000 rates, weighted rate per county was used. Since the three Pennsylvania warehouses service 49 counties in Pennsylvania, 40 weighted rates were obtained. A weighted rate assumes that all freight destined to a specific county is going to the one city where the major customers' demand is located. By selecting the city having the maximum flow of freight, variation from the actual rates is minimized. The weight break to that city is computed in terms of the average weekly tonnage coming into the entire county. This requires that a maximum of four shipments per month be allowed for any county. After one rate for each commodity group was established, the four rates were combined into one weighted rate, based on the percentage of the total weekly tonnage that the product line accounted for.

Propose several ways in which the Pennsylvania distribution system *might* be improved.

S. C. Johnson and Son, Limited (R)

Four months ago, in November 1980, George Styan had been appointed Division Manager of INNOCHEM, at S. C. Johnson and Son, Limited[1] (SCJ), a Canadian subsidiary of S. C. Johnson and Son, Inc. INNOCHEM's sole product line consisted of industrial cleaning chemicals for use by business, institutions, and government. Styan was concerned by the Division's poor market share, particularly in Montreal and Toronto. Together, these two cities represented approximately 35 percent of Canadian demand for industrial cleaning chemicals, but less than 10 percent of INNOCHEM sales. It appeared the SCJ distributors could not match the aggressive discounting practiced by direct selling manufacturers in metropolitan markets.

Recently, Styan had received a rebate proposal from his staff designed to increase the distributor's ability to cut end-user prices by "sharing" part of the total margin with SCJ when competitive conditions demanded discounts of 30 percent or more off the list price to end users. George had to decide if the rebate plan was the best way to penetrate price-sensitive markets. Moreover, he wondered about the plan's ultimate impact on divisional profit performance. George had to either develop an implementation plan for the rebate plan or draft an alternative proposal to unveil at the 1981 Distributors' Annual Spring Convention, three weeks away.

Source: Copyright © 1982, School of Business Administration, The University of Western Ontario. This case was written by Carolyn Vose under the supervision of Professor Roger More. Reprinted with permission.

[1] Popularly known as "Canadian Johnson Wax."

The Canadian Market for Industrial Cleaning Chemicals

In 1980, the Canadian market for industrial cleaning chemicals was approximately $100 million at end-user prices. Growth was stable at an overall rate of approximately 3 percent per year.

"Industrial cleaning chemicals" included all chemical products designed to clean, disinfect, sanitize, or protect industrial, commercial, and institutional buildings and equipment. The label was broadly applied to general purpose cleaners, floor maintenance products (strippers, sealers, finishes, and detergents), carpet cleaners and deodorizers, disinfectants, air fresheners, and a host of specialty chemicals such as insecticides, pesticides, drain cleaners, oven cleaners, and sweeping compounds.

Industrial cleaning chemicals were distinct from equivalent consumer products typically sold through grocery stores. Heavy-duty industrial products were packaged in larger containers in bulk and marketed directly by the cleaning chemical manufacturers or sold through distributors to a variety of end users. Exhibit 10.1 shows market segmentation by primary end-user categories, including janitorial service contractors and the in-house maintenance departments of government, institutions, and companies.

Building Maintenance Contractors

In Canada, maintenance contractors purchased 17 percent of the industrial cleaning chemicals sold during 1980 (end-user price). The segment was growing at approximately 10–15 percent a year, chiefly at the expense of other end-user categories. *Canadian Business* reported, "Contract cleaners have made sweeping inroads into the traditional preserve of in-house janitorial staffs, selling themselves on the strength of cost efficiency."[2] Maintenance contract billings reached an estimated $1 billion in 1980.

Frequently, demand for building maintenance services was highly price sensitive, and since barriers to entry were low (small capitalization, simple technology), competition squeezed contractor gross margins below 6 percent (before tax). Variable cost control was a matter of survival, and only products bringing compensatory labor savings could command a premium price in this segment of the cleaning chemical market.

A handful of contract cleaners did specialize in higher margin services to prestige office complexes, luxury apartments, art museums, and other "quality-conscious" customers. However, even contractors serving this select clientele did not necessarily buy premium cleaning supplies.

In-House Maintenance Departments

Government

In 1980, cleaning chemical sales to various government offices (federal, provincial, and local) approached $2 million. Typically, a government body solicited bids by formally advertising for quotations for given quantities of particular cleaning chemicals.

---

[2] "Contract Cleaners Want to Whisk Away Ring-Around-the-Office" *Canadian Business* (1981), p. 22.

EXHIBIT 10.1   Segmentation of the Canadian Market for Industrial Cleaning Chemicals

(1) By End-User Category

End-User Category	% Total Canadian Market for Industrial Cleaning Chemicals (End-User Value)
Retail Outlets	25%
Contractors	17
Hospitals	15
Industrial and Office	13
Schools, Colleges	8
Hotels, Motels	6
Nursing Homes	5
Recreation	3
Government	3
Fast Food	2
Full Service Restaurants	2
All Others	1
Total	100% = $95 million

(2) By Product Category

Product Category	% Total Canadian Market for Industrial Cleaning Chemicals
Floor Care Products	40%
General Purpose Cleaners	16
Disinfectants	12
Carpet Care Products	8
Odor Control Products	5
Glass Cleaners	4
All Others	15
Total	100% = $95 million

Although bid requests often named specific brands, suppliers were permitted to offer "equivalent substitutes." Separate competitions were held for each item and normally covered 12 months' supply with provision for delivery "as required." Contracts were frequently awarded solely on the basis of price.

Institutions

Like government bodies, most institutions were price sensitive owing to restrictive budgets and limited ability to pass on expenses to users. Educational institutions and hospitals were the largest consumers of cleaning chemicals in this segment. School boards used an open bid system patterned on the government model. Heavy sales time requirements and demands for frequent delivery of small shipments to as many as 100 locations were characteristic.

Colleges and universities tended to be operated somewhat differently. Dan Stalport, purchasing agent responsible for maintenance supplies at The University of Western Ontario, offered the following comments:

> Sales reps come to UWO year 'round. If one of us (in the buying group) talks to a salesman who seems to have something—say, a labor-saving feature—we get a sample and test it . . . Testing can take up to a year. Floor covering, for example, has to be exposed to seasonal changes in weather and traffic.
>
> If we're having problems with a particular item, we'll compare the performance and price of three or four competitors. There are usually plenty of products that do the job. Basically, we want value—acceptable performance at the lowest available price.

Hospitals accounted for 15 percent of cleaning chemical sales. Procurement policies at University Hospital (UH), a medium-sized (450-bed) facility in London, Ontario, were typical. UH distinguished between "critical" and "noncritical" products. Critical cleaning chemicals (i.e., those significantly affecting patient health, such as phenolic germicide), could be bought only on approval of the staff microbiologist who tested the "kill factor." This measure of effectiveness was regularly retested, and any downgrading of product performance could void a supplier's contract. In contrast, noncritical supplies, such as general purpose cleaners, floor finishes, and the like, were the exclusive province of Bob Chandler, purchasing agent attached to the Housekeeping Department. Bob explained that performance of noncritical cleaning chemicals was informally judged and monitored by the housekeeping staff:

> Just last year, for example, the cleaners found the floor polish was streaking badly. We (the Housekeeping Department) tested and compared five or six brands—all in the ballpark price-wise—and chose the best.

Business

The corporate segment was highly diverse, embracing both service and manufacturing industries. Large-volume users tended to be price sensitive—particularly when profits were low. Often, however, cleaning products represented such a small percentage of the total operating budget that the cost of searching for the lowest cost supplier would be expected to exceed any realizable saving. Under such conditions, the typical industrial customer sought efficiencies in the purchasing process itself, for example, by dealing with the supplier offering the broadest mix of janitorial products (chemicals, paper supplies, equipment, etc.). Guy Breton, purchasing agent for Securitech, a Montreal-based security systems manufacturer, commented on the time-economies of "one-stop shopping":

> With cleaning chemicals, it simply isn't worth the trouble to shop around and stage elaborate product performance tests . . . . I buy all our chemicals, brushes, dusters, towelling—the works—from one or two suppliers . . . buying reputable brands from familiar suppliers saves hassles—back-orders are rare and Maintenance seldom complains.

Distribution Channels for Industrial Cleaning Chemicals

The Canadian market for industrial cleaning chemicals was supplied through three main channels, each characterized by a distinctive set of strengths and weaknesses:

1. Distributor sales of national brands
2. Distributor sales of private label products
3. Direct sale by manufacturers

Direct sellers held a 61 percent share of the Canadian market for industrial cleaning chemicals, while the distributors of national brands and private label products held shares of 25 percent and 14 percent, respectively. Relative market shares varied geographically, however. In Montreal and Toronto, for example, the direct marketers' share rose to 70 percent and private labellers' to 18 percent, reducing the national brand share to 12 percent. The pattern shown in Exhibit 10.2 reflected an interplay of two areas of channel differentiation, namely, the discount capability at the end-user level and the cost of serving geographically dispersed customers.

Distributor Sales of National Brand Cleaning Chemicals

National brand manufacturers, such as S. C. Johnson and Son, Airkem, and National Labs, produced a relatively limited range of "high-quality" janitorial products, including many special purpose formulations of narrow market interest. Incomplete product range combined with shortage of manpower and limited warehousing made direct distribution infeasible in most cases. Normally, a national brand company would negotiate with distributors who handled a broad array of complementary products (equipment, tools, and supplies) by different manufacturers. "Bundling" of goods brought the distributors' cost efficiencies in selling, warehousing, and delivery by spreading fixed costs over a large sales volume. Distributors were therefore better able to absorb the costs of after-hour emergency service, frequent routine sales and service calls to many potential buyers, and shipments of small quantities of cleaning chemicals to multiple destinations. As a rule, the greater the geographic dispersion of customers and the smaller the average order, the greater the relative economies of distributor marketing.

Comparatively high gross margins (approximately 50 percent of wholesale price) enabled national brand manufacturers to offer distributors strong marketing support and sales training along with liberal terms of payment and freight plus low minimum order requirements. Distributors readily agreed to handle national brand chemicals, and in metropolitan markets, each brand was sold through several distributors. By the same token, most distributors carried several directly competitive product lines. Styan suspected that some distributor salesmen only used national brands to "lead" with and tended to offer private label whenever a customer proved price sensitive or a competitor handled the same national brand. Using an industry rule of thumb, he estimated that most distributors needed at least 20 percent gross margin on retail sales to cover their salesmen's commission of 10 percent on retail sales plus delivery and inventory expenses.

EXHIBIT 10.2 **Effect of Geography on Market Share of Different Distribution Channels**

Supplier Type	Share Nationwide	Share in Montreal and Toronto
Direct Marketers	61%[1]	70%
Private Label Distributors	14%	18%
National Brands Distributors	25%[2]	12%

[1]
Dustbane	17%
G. H. Wood	13
All Others	31
Total	61%

[2]
SCJ	8%
N/L	4
Airkem	3
All Others	10
Total	25%

Distributor Sales of Private Label Cleaning Chemicals

Direct selling manufacturers were dominating urban markets by aggressively discounting end-user prices—sometimes below the wholesale price national brand manufacturers charged their distributors. To compete against the direct seller, increasing numbers of distributors were adding low-cost private label cleaning chemicals to their product lines. Private labelling also helped differentiate a particular distributor from others carrying the same national brands.

Sizable minimum order requirements restricted the private label strategy to the largest distributors. Private label manufacturers produced to order, formulating to meet low prices specified by distributors. The relatively narrow margins (30–35 percent wholesale price) associated with private label manufacture precluded the extensive marketing and sales support national brand manufacturers characteristically provided to distributors. Private label producers pared their expenses further still by requiring distributors to bear the cost of inventory and accept rigid terms of payment as well as delivery (net 30 days, FOB plant).

In addition to absorbing these selling expenses normally assumed by the manufacturer, distributors paid their salesmen higher commissions on private label sales (15 percent of resale) than on national brands (10 percent of resale). However, the incremental administration and selling expenses associated with private label business were more than offset by the differential savings on private label wholesale goods. By pricing private label chemicals at competitive parity with national brands, the distributor could enjoy approximately a 50 percent gross margin at resale list while preserving considerable resale discount capability.

Private label products were seldom sold outside the metropolitan areas where most were manufactured. First, the high costs of moving bulky, low-value freight diminished the relative cost advantage of private label chemicals. Second, generally speaking, it was only in metro areas that distributors dealt in volumes great enough to satisfy the private labeller's minimum order requirement. Finally, outside the city, distributors were less likely to be in direct local competition with others handling the same national brand, reducing value of the private label as a source of supplier differentiation.

For some very large distributors, backward integration into chemical production was a logical extension of the private labelling strategy. Recently, several distributors had become direct marketers through acquisition of captive manufacturers.

Direct Sale by Manufacturers of Industrial Cleaning Chemicals

Manufacturers dealing directly with the end user increased their gross margins to 60–70 percent of retail list price. Greater margins increased their ability to discount end-user price—a distinct advantage in the price-competitive urban marketplace. Overall, direct marketers averaged a gross margin of 50 percent.

Many manufacturers of industrial cleaning chemicals attempted some direct selling, but relatively few relied on this channel exclusively. Satisfactory adoption of a full-time direct selling strategy required the manufacturer to match distributor's sales and delivery capabilities without sacrificing overall profitability. These conflicting demands had been resolved successfully by two types of company, large scale powder chemical manufacturers and full-time janitorial products manufacturers.

Large Scale Powder Chemical Manufacturers. Economies of large-scale production plus experience in the capital-intensive manufacture of powder chemicals enabled a few established firms, such as Diversey-Wyandotte, to dominate the market for powder warewash and vehicle cleansers. Selling through distributors offered these producers few advantages. Direct selling expense was almost entirely commission (i.e., variable). Moreover, powder concentrates were characterized by comparatively high value-to-bulk ratios, and so could absorb delivery costs even where demand was geographically dispersed. Thus, any marginal benefits from using middlemen were more than offset by the higher margins (and associated discount capability) possible through direct distribution. Among these chemicals firms, competition was not limited to price. The provision of dispensing and metering equipment was important, as was 24-hour servicing.

Full-Line Janitorial Products Manufacturers. These manufacturers offered a complete range of maintenance products including paper supplies, janitorial chemicals, tools, and mechanical equipment. Although high margins greatly enhanced retail price flexibility, overall profitability depended on securing a balance of high- and low-margin business, as well as controlling selling and distribution expenses. This was accomplished in several ways, including:

- focusing on market areas of concentrated demand to minimize costs of warehousing, sales travel, and the like;
- increasing average order size, either by adding product lines which could be sold to existing customers, or by seeking new large-volume customers; and

- tying sales commission to profitability to motivate sales personnel to sell volume, without unnecessary discounting of end-user price.

Direct marketers of maintenance products varied in scale from established nationwide companies to hundreds of regional operators. The two largest direct marketers, G. H. Wood and Dustbane, together supplied almost a third of Canadian demand for industrial cleaning chemicals.

S. C. Johnson and Son, Limited

SCJ was one of 42 foreign subsidiaries owned by the U.S.-based multinational, S. C. Johnson and Son, Inc. It was ranked globally as one of the largest privately held companies. SCJ contributed substantially to worldwide sales and profits and was based in Brantford, Ontario, close to the Canadian urban markets of Hamilton, Kitchener, Toronto, London, and Niagara Falls. About 300 people worked at the head office and plant; another 100 were employed in field sales.

INNOCHEM Division

INNOCHEM (Innovative Chemicals for Professional Use) was a special division established to serve corporate, institutional, and government customers of SCJ. The division manufactured an extensive line of industrial cleaning chemicals, including general purpose cleansers, waxes, polishes, and disinfectants, plus a number of specialty products of limited application, as shown in Exhibit 10.3. In 1980, INNOCHEM sold $4.5 million in industrial cleaning chemicals through distributors and $0.2 million direct to end users. Financial statements for INNOCHEM are shown in Exhibit 10.4.

INNOCHEM Marketing Strategy. Divisional strategy hinged on reliable product performance, product innovation, active promotion, and mixed channel distribution. Steve Remen, market development manager, maintained that "customers know our products are of excellent quality. They know that the products will always perform as expected."

At SCJ, performance requirements were detailed and tolerances precisely defined. The Department of Quality Control routinely inspected and tested raw materials, work in process, packaging, and finished goods. At any phase during the manufacturing cycle, Quality Control was empowered to halt the process and quarantine suspect products or materials. SCJ maintained that nothing left the plant "without approval from Quality Control."

"Keeping the new product shelf well stocked" was central to divisional strategy, as the name INNOCHEM implies. Products launched over the past three years represented 33 percent of divisional gross sales, 40 percent of gross profits, and 100 percent of growth.

INNOCHEM had a sales force of ten that sold and serviced the distributor accounts. These salespeople were paid almost all salary, with some bonus potential up to 10 percent for exceptional sales volume increases. The company had also recently committed one salesperson to work with large direct accounts. The advertising budget

EXHIBIT 10.3   **INNOCHEM Product Line**

—for all floors except unsealed wood and unsealed cork

Stripper:	**Step-Off**—powerful, fast action
Finish:	**Pronto**—fast drying, good gloss, minimum maintenance
Spray-Buff Solution:	**The Shiner Liquid Spray Cleaner** or **The Shiner Aerosol Spray Finish**
Maintainer:	**Forward**—cleans, disinfects, deodorizes, sanitizes

—for all floors except unsealed wood and unsealed cork

Stripper:	**Step-Off**—powerful, fast stripper
Finish:	**Carefree**—tough, beauty, durable minimum maintenance
Maintainer:	**Forward**—cleans, disinfects, deodorizes, sanitizes

—for all floors except unsealed wood and unsealed cork

Stripper:	**Step-Off**—for selective stripping
Sealer:	**Over & Under-Plus**—undercoater-sealer
Finish:	**Scrubbable Step-Ahead**—brilliant, scrubbable
Maintainer:	**Forward**—cleans, disinfects, sanitizes, deodorizes.

—for all floors except unsealed wood and cork

Stripper:	**Step-Off**—powerful, fast stripper
Finish:	**Easy Street**—high solids, high gloss, spray buffs to a "wet look" appearance
Maintainer:	**Forward**—cleans, disinfects, deodorizes **Expose**—phenolic cleaner disinfectant

—for all floors except unsealed wood and unsealed cork

Stripper:	**Step-Off**—for selective stripping
Sealer:	**Over & Under-Plus**—undercoater-sealer
Finishes:	**Traffic Grade**—heavy-duty, floor wax **Waxtral**—extra tough, high solids
Maintainer:	**Forward**—cleans, disinfects, sanitizes, deodorizes

—for all floors except asphalt, mastic and rubber tile. Use sealer and wax finishes on wood, cork, and cured concrete; sealer-finish on terrazzo, marble, clay, and ceramic tile; wax finish only on vinyl, linoleum, and magnesite.

Sealer:	**Johnson Gym Finish**—sealer and top-coater cleans as it waxes
Wax Finishes:	**Traffic Wax Paste**—heavy-duty buffing wax **Beautiflor Traffic Wax**—liquid buffing wax
Maintainers:	**Forward**—cleans, disinfects, sanitizes, deodorizes **Conq-r-Dust**—mop treatment
Stripper:	**Step-Off**—stripper for sealer and finish
Sealer:	**Secure**—fast-bonding, smooth, long-lasting
Finish:	**Traffic Grade**—heavy-duty floor wax
Maintainer:	**Forward,** or **Big Bare**

Sealer-Finish:	**Johnson Gym Finish**—seal and top-coater
Maintainer:	**Conq-r-Dust**—mop treatment
General Cleaning:	**Break-Up**—cleans soap and body scum fast **Forward**—cleans, disinfects, sanitizes, deodorizes **Bon Ami**—instant cleaner, pressurized, or pump, disinfects
Toilet-Urinals:	**Go-Getter**—"Working Foam" cleaner
Glass:	**Bon Ami**—spray-on foam or liquid cleaner
Disinfectant Spray:	**End-Bac II**—controls bacteria, odors
Air Freshener:	**Glade**—dewy-fresh fragrances
Spot Cleaning:	**Johnson's Pledge**—cleans, waxes, polishes **Johnson's Lemon Pledge**—refreshing scent **Bon Ami Stainless Steel Cleaner**—cleans, polishes and protects
All-Purpose Cleaners:	**Forward**—cleans, disinfects, sanitizes, deodorizes **Break-Up**—degreaser for animal and vegetable fats **Big Bare**—heavy-duty industrial cleaner
Carpets:	**Rugbee Powder & Liquid Extraction Cleaner**— **Rugbee Soil Release Concentrate**—for pre-spraying and bonnet buffing **Rugbee Shampoo**—for power shampoo machines **Rugbee Spotter**—spot remover
Furniture:	**Johnson's Pledge**—cleans, waxes, polishes **Johnson's Lemon Pledge**—refreshing scent **Shine-Up Liquid**—general purpose cleaning
Disinfectant Spray:	**End-Bac II**—controls bacteria, odors
Air Freshener:	**Glade**—dewy-fresh fragrances
Glass:	**Bon Ami**—spray-on foam or liquid cleaner
Cleaning:	**Break-Up**—special degreaser designed to remove animal and vegetable fats
Equipment:	**Break-Up Foamer**—special generator designed to dispense Break-Up Cleaner
General Cleaning:	**Forward**—fast-working germicidal cleaner for floors, walls—all washable surfaces **Expose**—phenolic disinfectant cleaner
Sanitizing:	**J80 Sanitizer**—liquid for total environmental control of bacteria. No rinse necessary if used as directed
Disinfectant Spray:	**End-Bac II Spray**—controls bacteria, odors
Flying Insects:	Bolt Liquid Airborne, or Pressurized Airborne, P3610 through E10 dispenser
Crawling Insects:	Bolt Liquid Residual or Pressurized Residual, P3610 through E10 dispenser Bolt Roach Bait
Rodents:	Bolt Rodenticide—for effective control of rats and mice, use with Bolt Bait Box

Johnson Wax is a systems innovator. Frequently, a new product leads to a whole new system of doing things—a Johnson system of "matched" products formulated to work together. This makes the most of your time, your effort and your expense. Call today and see how these Johnson systems can give you maximum results at a minimum cost.

EXHIBIT 10.4   **Profit Statement of the Division**

Profit Statement

	$000
Gross Sales	4,682
Returns	46
Allowances	1
Cash Discounts	18
Net Sales	4,617
Cost of Sales	2,314
Gross Profit	2,303
Advertising	75
Promotions	144
Deals	—
External Marketing Services	2
Sales Freight	292
Other Distribution Expenses	176
Service Fees	184[1]
Total Direct Expenses	873
Sales Force	592
Marketing Administration	147
Provision for Bad Debts	—
Research and Development	30[2]
Financial	68
Information Resource Mgt.	47
Administration Management	56
Total Functional Expenses	940
Total Operating Expenses	1,813
Operating Profit	490

[1]Fees paid to SCJ (Corporate) for corporate services.

[2]A portion of a research chemist's cost to conduct R&D specifically for industrial products.

of $75,000 was primarily allocated to trade magazines and direct-mail advertisements to large segments of end users such as maintenance contractors. Sales promotions, by contrast, were directed mainly at distributors and consisted largely of special pricing and packaging deals to get distributors to more aggressively bid Johnson products in their offers to end users.

Mixed Distribution Strategy. INNOCHEM used a mixed distribution system to broaden market coverage. Eighty-seven percent of divisional sales were handled by a force of 200 distributor salesmen and serviced from 50 distributor warehouses representing 35 distributors. The indirect channel was particularly effective outside Ontario and Quebec. In part, the tendency for SCJ market penetration to increase with distances from Montreal and Toronto reflected Canadian demographics and the general economics of distribution. Outside the two production centers, demand was dispersed and delivery distances long.

Distributor salesmen were virtually all paid a straight commission on sales, and were responsible for selling a wide variety of products in addition to S. C. Johnson's. Several of the distributors had sales levels much higher than INNOCHEM.

For INNOCHEM, the impact of geography was compounded by a significant freight cost advantage: piggybacking industrial cleaning chemicals with SCJ consumer goods. In Toronto, for example, the cost of SCJ to a distributor was 30 percent above private label, while the differential in British Columbia was only 8 percent. On lower value products, the "freight effect" was even more pronounced.

SCJ had neither the salesmen nor the delivery capabilities to reach large-volume end users who demanded heavy selling effort or frequent shipments of small quantities. Furthermore, it was unlikely that SCJ could develop the necessary selling and distribution strength economically, given the narrowness of the division's range of janitorial products (i.e., industrial cleaning chemicals only).

The Rebate Plan

The key strategic problem facing INNOCHEM was how best to challenge the direct marketer (and private label distributor) for large-volume, price-sensitive customers with heavy service requirements, particularly in markets where SCJ had no freight advantage. In this connection George had observed:

> Our gravest weakness is our inability to manage the total margin between the manufactured cost and end-user price in a way that is equitable and sufficiently profitable to support the investment and expenses of both the distributors and ourselves.
>
> Our prime competition across Canada is from direct selling national and regional manufacturers. These companies control both the manufacturing and distribution gross margins. Under our pricing system, the distributors' margin at end-user list on sales is 43 percent. Our margin (the manufacturing margin) is 50 percent on sales. When these margins are combined, as in the case of direct selling manufacturers, the margin becomes 70 percent at list. This long margin provides significant price flexibility in a price-competitive marketplace. We must find a way to profitably attack the direct marketer's 61 percent market share.

The rebate plan Styan was now evaluating had been devised to meet the competition head-on.

"Profitable partnership" between INNOCHEM and the distributor was the underlying philosophy of the plan. Rebates offered a means to "share fairly the margins available between factory cost and consumer price." Whenever competitive conditions required a distributor to discount the resale list price by 30 percent or more, SCJ would give a certain percentage of the wholesale price back to the distributor. SCJ would sacrifice part of its margin to help offset a heavy end-user discount. Rebate percentages would vary with the rate of discount, following a set schedule. Different schedules were to be established for each product type and size. Exhibits 10.5, 10.6 and 10.7 outline

EXHIBIT 10.5 **Distributors' Rebate Pricing Schedule: An Example Using Pronto Floor Wax**

Code 04055	Product Pronto	Description Fast Dry Fin	Size 209 Lit	Pack 1

Eff. Date: 03-31-81
Resale List Price 71 613.750
Distributor Price List 74 349.837
Percent Markup on Cost with Carload and Rebate

Dis-count %[1]	Quote (FST) (incl)[2]	Rebate %[3]	Rebate DLRS[4]	2% Net[5]	2% MU-%[6]	3% Net	3% MU-%	4% Net	4% MU-%	5% Net	5% MU-%
30.0	429.63	8.0	27.99	314.85	36	311.35	38	307.86	40	304.36	41
35.0	398.94	12.0	41.98	300.86	33	297.36	34	293.86	36	290.36	27
40.0	368.25	17.0	59.47	283.37	30	279.87	32	276.37	33	272.87	35
41.0	362.11	17.5	61.22	281.62	29	278.12	30	274.62	32	271.12	34
42.0	355.98	18.0	62.97	279.87	27	276.37	29	272.87	30	269.37	32
43.0	349.84	18.5	64.72	278.12	26	274.62	27	271.12	29	267.63	31
44.0	343.70	19.0	66.47	276.37	24	272.87	26	269.37	28	265.88	29
45.0	337.56	20.0	69.97	272.87	24	269.37	25	265.88	27	262.38	29
46.0	331.43	20.5	71.72	271.12	22	267.63	24	264.13	25	260.63	27
47.0	325.29	21.0	73.47	269.37	21	265.88	22	262.38	24	258.88	26
48.0	319.15	21.5	75.21	267.63	19	264.13	21	260.63	22	257.13	24
49.0	313.01	22.0	76.96	265.88	18	262.38	19	258.88	21	255.38	23
50.0	306.88	23.0	80.46	262.38	17	258.88	19	255.38	20	251.88	22
51.0	300.74	24.0	83.96	258.88	16	255.38	18	251.88	19	248.38	21
52.0	294.60	25.0	87.46	255.38	15	251.88	17	248.38	19	244.89	20
53.0	288.46	26.0	90.96	251.88	15	248.38	16	244.89	18	241.39	19
54.0	282.33	28.0	97.95	244.89	15	241.39	17	237.89	19	234.39	20
55.0	276.19	30.0	104.95	237.89	16	234.39	18	230.89	20	227.39	21

[1]Discount extended to end user on resale list price.

[2]Resale price at given discount level (includes federal sales tax).

[3]Percentage of distributor's price ($613.75) rebated by SCJ.

[4]Actual dollar amount of rebate by SCJ.

[5]Actual net cost to distributor after deduction of rebate and "carload" (quantity) discount.

[6]Effective rate of distributor markup.

the effect of rebates on both the unit gross margins of SCJ and individual distributors for a specific product example.

The rebate plan was designed for new, "incremental" business only, not for existing distributor accounts. Distributors would be required to seek SCJ approval for end-user discounts of over 30 percent of resale list. The maximum allowable end-user discount would rarely exceed 50 percent. To request rebate payments, distributors

---

EXHIBIT 10.6 **Effect of Rebate Plan on Manufacturer and Distributor Margins: The Example of One 209-Liter Pack of Pronto Floor Finish Retailed at 40 Percent below Resale List Price**

I. Under Present Arrangements

Base price to distributor	$349.84
Price to distributor, assuming 2 percent carload discount[1]	342.84
SCJ cost	174.92
∴ SCJ margin	$167.92
Resale list price	613.75
Resale list price minus 40 percent discount	368.25
Distributor price, assuming 2 percent carload discount	342.84
∴ Distributor's margin	$ 25.41

II. Under Rebate Plan

Rebate to distributor giving 40 percent discount off resale price amounted to 17 percent distributor's base price	$ 59.47
SCJ margin (minus rebate)	108.45
Distributor margin (plus rebate)	84.88

III. Competitive Prices

For this example, George estimated that a distributor could buy a private-branded "comparable" product for approximately $244.

---

[1] A form of quantity discount which, in this case, drops the price the distributor pays to SCJ from $349.84 to $342.84.

would send SCJ a copy of the resale invoice along with a written claim. The rebate would then be paid within 60 days.

Proponents of the plan maintained that the resulting resale price flexibility would not only enhance INNOCHEM competitiveness among end users but would also diminish distributor attraction to private label.

As he studied the plan, George questioned whether all the implications were fully understood and wondered what other strategies, if any, might increase urban market penetration. Any plan he devised would have to be sold to distributors as well as to corporate management. George had only three weeks to develop an appropriate action plan.

EXHIBIT 10.7   **Effect of End-User Discount Level on Manufacturer and Distributor Margins under Proposed Rebate Plan**

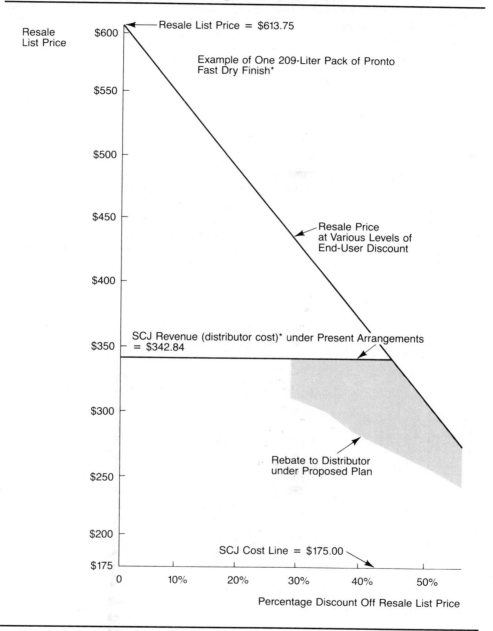

*Assuming 2 percent quantity ("carload") discount off the price to distributor.

Texas Instruments: Electronic Appliance Controls

The telephone was ringing as Charles Ames, Manager of Appliance Controls Engineering, entered his office on the morning of June 21, 1976. The call was from the Director of Engineering for Electronic Cooking Incorporated (ECI), who told Ames that a competitor had underbid Texas Instruments for an order of electronic controls for microwave ovens. Mr. Ames was confident that the competitor's bid price was unrealistically low since Texas Instruments, with its accumulated experience, could meet the bid only by pricing with profit margins significantly less than the TI model for this product line.

While assembling his staff to discuss the ramifications of the competitive bid, Ames realized that a decision of this importance would significantly affect the direction of TI market growth. Accordingly, a meeting time that afternoon was set to bring together Ames, his staff, and their group vice president to formulate a course of action.

The Company

Texas Instruments Incorporated (TI) is a world leader in electronic technology innovation, production, and applications. In 1975, 84 percent of TI's total business was electronics based. TI is a major producer of handheld calculators in terms of dollar volume.

Source: From Roger A. Kerin and Robert A. Peterson, *Strategic Marketing Problems: Cases and Comments.* Third Edition. Copyright © 1984 by Allyn and Bacon, Inc.

Past and Future Performance

TI has experienced almost a threefold increase in net sales in the last decade. Net sales volume in 1975 was approximately $1.4 billion compared with net sales of about $580 million in 1966. TI was ranked 152 in the *Fortune* 500 in 1975. Abbreviated TI 1976 financial statements are shown in Exhibit 11.1

Two years ago, TI announced its goal to grow to $10 billion in net sales by the late 1980s. The guidelines for achieving the $10-billion goal were articulated in the *First Quarter and Stockholders Meeting Report, 1976:*

- We will model TI's business to self-fund growth.

- We intend to rely primarily on internal growth rather than on major acquisitions.

- We will optimize our resources to improve TI's share position.

- We will emphasize expansion of served markets into contiguous new segments, taking advantage of intra-TI shared experience.

- We will rely primarily on opportunities related to electronics, particularly those in which our semi-conductor skills can be decisive.

The operating guidelines for reaching the $10-billion goal were also outlined in the 1976 document:

- We must meet TI's return on assets goals to allow the growth to be self-funded.

- We must meet the operating model parameters to generate adequate OST[1] funds.

- OST funds must be invested in TI's major growth thrusts, that is, products that serve markets with a high growth rate and in which TI can develop a profitable position.

- We must retain and build upon TI philosophies and methods to manage profitable growth. This is why the institutionalism of TI's management culture has been emphasized through mechanisms such as the OST system, People and Asset Effectiveness, and Design-to-Cost.[2]

- TI must continue to increase its basic technological strength, especially in semi-conductors. This includes not only the design and development of key components but also the application of these components to advanced systems and services.

- We must make Success Sharing[3] work because it is the key to increased productivity.

OST Budgetary Procedure

An OST program—Objectives, Strategies, and Tactics—is the action plan for a particular endeavor. An OST program states not only what a particular endeavor expects to achieve but also how it will be achieved and the actions necessary to achieve it,

---

[1] The TI Objectives, Strategies, and Tactics (OST) system is described briefly in the OST budgetary procedure section of this case.

[2] Design-to-Cost is described briefly in the text.

[3] Success Sharing is a term used to designate the total package of TI employees' pension, profit sharing, and stock option purchase plans.

EXHIBIT 11.1   **Abbreviated Texas Instruments' Consolidated Financial Statements for the Year Ended December 31, 1975 (in thousands of dollars)**

Income Statement

Net Sales		$1,367,621
Operating Costs and Expenses		
Cost of goods and services sold	1,004,133	
General, administrative, and marketing	227,515	
Employees' retirement and profit sharing plans	21,185	
Total		1,252,833
Profit from operations		$ 114,788
Other income (net)		11,971
Interest on loans		(10,822)
Income before provision for income taxes		$ 115,937
Provision for income taxes		53,795
Net income		$ 62,142

Balance Sheet

Current Assets	
Cash and short-term investments	$ 266,578
Accounts receivable	245,785
Inventories (net of progress billings)	142,880
Prepaid expenses	7,322
Total	$ 662,565
Property, plant and equipment (net)	253,709
Other assets and deferred charges	25,203
Total assets	$ 941,477
Liabilities and Stockholders' Equity	
Current liabilities	$ 301,843
Deferred liabilities	54,346
Stockholders' equity	585,288
Total liabilities and stockholders' equity	$ 941,477

Source: Annual Report.

including the costs of engineering, marketing, and production. OST funding is derived from a portion of operating profits intended to support a new business strategy and is controlled at the department (profit and loss center) level. Funding for OST programs is competitive in that division managers obtain inputs from each of the department managers and subsequently submit funding requests to a budget committee. OST programs are ranked according to their growth and profitability potential by the budget committee, with funds allocated accordingly.

The annual budgeting procedure is highly refined and well controlled. Flexibility is retained, however, to modify a product or program definition operating within the OST system. Programs are defined in the fourth quarter for the coming calendar year and are reviewed monthly and quarterly. The flexibility of the process is illustrated by Mr. Ames' reflection on the Electronic Controls program:

In 1973, the Oven Temp Sensor Program was funded $50,000 and the Electronic Control Program was allocated $10,000. In 1974, Oven Temp was allocated $60,000, while the Electronic Controls Department was allocated nothing. Then, in December 1974, a group of vice-presidents from a microwave oven manufacturer visited TI. The prospects outlined by these executives allowed for an improved Electronic Control Program to be developed. Funds from another program were immediately diverted to Electronic Controls, which marked the beginning of the program as it now stands.

Mr. Ames noted that this episode was not uncommon, given TI's corporate position that OST funds should be invested in products that serve growth markets and in which TI could develop a profitable position. Existing programs exhibiting poor performance could lose funding. Mr. Ames was very much aware of this fact: "The sequence of events that benefited the Electronic Controls Program could work against it unless the program could be made profitable."

Tactical Action Program: Electronic Controls

Pre-1975

Texas Instruments executives had decided to examine the electronic control market for microwave ovens in late 1972 in order to utilize and expand TI's semiconductor expertise. Microwave oven volume had grown substantially in the late 1960s and early 1970s. According to industry estimates, total industry sales in 1972 were 320,000 units, compared with 20,000 units in 1968. Total industry sales in 1974 were approximately 785,000 units. During this period, ECI held the major share of the market, accounting for about 40 percent of the microwave oven units sold.

Controls for microwave ovens prior to 1975 were produced by electromechanical companies. However, industry sources indicated that these companies were experimenting with electronic controls. Other firms with semiconductor technology were showing signs of interest in producing electronic controls; yet, no firm had openly entered the market. "But TI had the right product at the right time, the capacity to support the potential demand, and the recognized technological expertise from calculators and related products to enter the market," Ames noted.

January–June 1975

On January 27, 1975, Charles Ames was assigned as manager of TI's Electronic Controls Program, then called the Tactical Action Program (TAP). Ames was responsible for both the engineering and marketing functions. He had responsibility for designing the product in addition to developing proposals for microwave oven producers.

Within two weeks of his appointment, Ames made his first presentation to ECI. The proposal was rejected in March. In April, he presented a proposal to AMEX Ovens for electronic controls with a unit sales price of $55.00. AMEX made a verbal commitment in June for 50,000 units.

During this period, Ames' energies were devoted to designing the electronic controls to cost requirements imposed by the cost-conscious appliance industry. The idea of Design-to-Cost (DTC) is central to TI's production and marketing thrust. Briefly, this concept involves designing a product from the start to achieve specific performance, cost, and profit goals. This practice involves the reduction in product cost necessary to perform a function due to a lower material and labor content. The impact of the DTC process for a TI hand-held calculator serves as a typical illustration. In 1974, forty-seven total parts (including 16 electronic parts) were required to build the TI19 model calculator. By 1976, the TI1200 calculator, identical in function, required 23 parts, and only two parts were electronic. Mr. Ames' efforts were focused on similar DTC activities for electronic controls.

The guide used by Ames in charting cost reductions was the learning or experience curve phenomenon. In effect, Ames hoped that he could realize a 20-percent reduction in electronic control assembly labor cost each time his volume doubled for a new design. Similar curves would be developed for each proposal to microwave oven producers and would reflect Ames' ability to economize on material and labor content for each succeeding generation of controls. Mr. Ames realized, however, that a practical limit existed in how much he could reduce overall costs.

July–December 1975

On July 2, Mr. Ames received a call from a Superior Cooking Products (SCP) executive requesting that he prepare a proposal for them. This proposal included a bid price per unit of $45. On August 14, SCP placed the first confirmed order for 50,000 units.

Mr. Ames received a call from ECI on November 28 asking for a proposal. A new proposal was developed to the ECI specifications, and a price of $36 per unit was bid. The difference in prices between the AMEX, SCP, and ECI prices arose from TI manufacturing cost savings due to order size (250,000 per year for ECI) and different control specifications.

During this period, Ames consolidated and generated a variety of data pertaining to the appliance market and the electronic controls market for the purpose of forecasting TI's potential market growth and identifying possible areas of product superiority. These data would serve as inputs for his OST funding requests and for preparation of financial planning and control indices.

Appliance Market and Microwave Ovens. Frequent discussions with marketing executives of appliance manufacturers revealed that technological innovation was the single most distinguishable factor separating competing products. Accordingly, appliance manufacturers were constantly seeking out new product features, provided the costs of product innovation were commensurate with the benefits. One reason for the search for new product designs was the saturation level of appliances in American homes. According to industry estimates, about 70 percent of the 72.7 million electrically-wired homes in the United States had electric ranges in 1975. Approximately six of ten electric ranges sold in 1975 were replacement purchases rather than net new purchases.

Microwave oven unit volume had grown substantially since the early 1970s, in spite of unfavorable publicity regarding the potential for radiation emission. Exhibit 11.2 shows Ames' forecast of microwave oven unit sales and penetration of electronic controls in the total market through 1980, based on discussions with appliance manufacturer executives. Ames believed that these estimates might be optimistic

EXHIBIT 11.2   **Forecast of Microwave and Electric Range Unit Volume and Penetration of Electronic Controls (unit volume in millions)**

	1977	1978	1979	1980
Microwave units	2	2.8	3.5	4
Percentage of microwave units with electronic controls	30%	45%	60%	80%
Electric ranges	2.9	2.87	2.85	2.8
Percentage of electric ranges with electronic controls	0%	3%	5%	10%

because some industry observers were forecasting a 17-percent saturation level among American homes by 1980. The annual rate of increase in the number of homes was about 2.3 percent, and the replacement cycle of microwave ovens had not been determined.

Also of interest to Ames was potential market share of major microwave oven producers. ECI had been a major supplier in the market prior to 1975. However, Home Appliance (HAI), Superior Appliance, and AMEX had made competitive inroads and would continue to do so, according to industry sources. Despite some disagreement among microwave oven producers as to their respective market shares, Exhibit 11.3 shows the market share ranges described by industry observers.

Microwave Oven Controls Competition. Two major suppliers of electromechanical controls existed in late 1975. Relays and Wire (R&W) and the Contact-Switch Company (C-S). Both firms had made progress in designing electromechanical controls at competitive prices. However, Ames believed that inherent limitations in the electromechanical technology would prohibit them from making major cost reductions or offering the innovative control features possible through semiconductor technology in the future. Nevertheless, in 1975, electromechanical technology was able to supply controls at a lower cost than semiconductor technology, and this competitive advantage was forecast to exist until 1979. This would happen "provided semiconductor producers could penetrate the market, the microwave oven growth potential was realized, and so on and so forth," Ames opined. "A lot depends on how long semiconductor firms will stay with it, given very limited profit margins in the short run of maybe four to five years."

January–June 1976

On February 26, 1976, Ames was notified that ECI had accepted his bid price. During the remaining spring months, Ames directed an increasing amount of his time toward DTC efforts for second-generation controls for TI customers and the ensuing production of first-generation controls. Time was also spent preparing OST funding and planning schedules.

EXHIBIT 11.3 **Estimated Market Shares of Microwave Producers, 1975, 1976, 1980**

	1975 (%)	1976 (%)	1980 (%)
Electronic Cooking	25–33	25–30	15
Superior Appliance	16–25	20–25	15
Amex Ovens	10–18	15–25	12–20
Home Appliance	10	10–12	20–25
Other U.S. Producers	5–7	7–8	15–20
Japanese Producers	8–18	8–15	5–8

On April 19, 1976, Ames was asked to bid on a second-generation control for ECI. Given the nature of the bid, including the specifications and quantity (150,000 units), Ames proposed a price of $44 (see the cost schedule in Exhibit 11.4). Shortly thereafter, Ames was advised that the competitive bid level was $42 per unit, which TI met after considerable discussion. Then, on June 21, 1976, Ames was informed that TI had been underbid by a major semiconductor manufacturing company at a price of $37. He assembled his staff to discuss the ramifications of the bid.

Ames had forecast an 80 percent labor learning curve for his bid, as shown in the exhibit. The labor estimate early in the process was about 1.75 hours per unit, but would decrease to about 0.36 hours per unit at the 150,000th unit. The midpoint at 75,000 units was 0.45 hours per unit. Hence, one-half of the unit volume would require more than 0.45 hours per unit to build, and one-half would require less.

The 80 percent labor learning curve corresponded to the doubling of unit volume from 150,000 to 300,000. The flattening of the curve was a fact of life: learning gains would be less dramatic beyond 150,000 units without redesign and major change to the configuration. The labor hours per unit of the 300,000th unit would be 0.325, with the midpoint being approximately 0.34 labor hours per unit at the 225,000th unit produced.

Ames did not forecast reductions in material or yield cost since he did not plan an interim design change that would be fruitful in the short run. Furthermore, labor-cost-per-unit reductions, assuming that he would bid for an additional 150,000 second-generation ECI controls, did not look promising.

Overshadowing the entire situation was the question of whether the competitor was also forecasting prices and costs on an 80 percent labor learning curve. If so, then Ames would have to consider how long his group would stay in the electronic range control business. This factor was critical if volume doubled again for the ECI account.

Ames was also plagued by other considerations. First, the future of cumulative microwave sales volume remained a question. Second, even if Ames received the contract, all 150,000 units might not be shipped since the customer could stop shipment of controls at any time. In other words, as few as 50,000 to 75,000 units could be

EXHIBIT 11.4 **ECI Second-Generation Control Cost Estimate**

The cost estimate developed by Ames is shown below:

$26.50	Yielded material cost
6.50	.45 hours/unit (@ $14.45/hour)*
$33.00	Total material, labor and overhead or "manufactured cost"
11.00	25% gross margin objective
$44.00	Control selling price at 150,000 unit volume

Estimated Labor Learning Curve for the ECI Second Generation Control

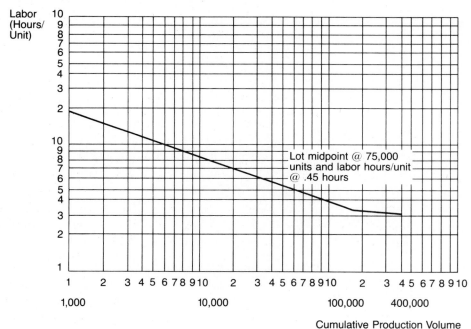

*.45 hours = lot midpoint of the 150,000-unit lot;
   $14.45 = hourly rate including factory overhead.

shipped, and the order could be stopped. Third, TI policy held that every contract must achieve profit from operation objectives consistent with total company operations. Future OST funding for electronic appliance controls would depend, to a significant degree, on his ability to meet these objectives.

Afton Industries

In January 1988, the director of sales and the director of planning and administration of Afton Industries met to prepare a joint recommendation to the president on the pricing of the firm's line of asphalt shingles. Afton Industries had been a price leader over the years; when the firm announced its price on asphalt shingles, competitive manufacturers followed. Afton had announced and implemented a price increase on January 1, 1986, but this time competitors did not follow suit. The firm had since experienced a measurable decline in market share.

Approximately 80 percent of the homes in Afton's region have asphalt shingles. About 90 percent of the homeowners contracting for new roofs use asphalt shingles. Nevertheless, the market for shingles has plateaued in recent years because of depressed conditions in new home construction and a lower incidence of reroofing owing to uncertain economic conditions.

Sales and marketing efforts for asphalt shingles focus on roofing material distributors. Distributors provide a warehousing function for shingle manufacturers and sell shingles to roofing contractors or applicators who install the shingles.

Afton Industries is a major regional manufacturer of asphalt shingles for single-family houses. Company sales in 1987 were $10 million. The company's line of asphalt shingles is highly regarded by roofing material applicators in its region, and virtually all major distributors carry the company's line. None of its competitors have distribution through more than half of the distributors in the region.

The company had enjoyed a leadership position in its region because large, national producers of shingles (for example, GAF Corporation, Georgia-Pacific

Source: This case was prepared by Professor Roger A. Kerin, Edwin L. Cox School of Business, Southern Methodist University, as a basis for class discussion and is not designed to illustrate effective or ineffective handling of an administrative situation. Certain names and data have been disguised. Reprinted with permission from Roger A. Kerin and Robert A. Peterson, *Strategic Marketing Problems: Cases and Comments,* Fifth ed. (Allyn and Bacon, 1990), pp. 538–541.

EXHIBIT 12.1 **Volume and Price Behavior for Asphalt Shingle Squares: 1979–1987**

| Year | Volume of Squares (000s) | | Price per Square | |
	Region	Afton Industries	Competitors	Afton Industries
1979	830	500	$17	$17
1980	977	586	$17	$17
1981	1,085	651	$15	$15
1982	1,205	723	$15	$15
1983	1,339	803	$17	$17
1984	1,488	893	$18	$18
1985	1,600	960	$18	$18
1986	1,500	750	$18	$20
1987	1,250	500	$18	$20

Corporation) did not have manufacturing facilities in the region. Costs of freight due to the weight of asphalt shingles precluded national firms from shipping shingles into the region from their present plant sites.

In January 1986, Afton raised its price per square of asphalt shingles from $18 to $20.[1] Although the company was strong financially, the price increase was prompted in part by a decision by the company's board of directors to embark on an extensive plant modernization and expansion program. The price increase was one of several changes directed by the board to improve the company's working capital position.

Contrary to past behavior, the five competitors of Afton Industries did not increase their prices. Rather, they held their prices at $18 per square. In 1987, Afton recorded the same sales volume level as had been achieved in 1979 (see Exhibit 12.1). Afton's president instructed the director of sales and the director of planning and administration to prepare a recommendation on the company's price policy and competitive posture soon after the end-of-year totals were recorded.

During the course of the initial meeting, the director of sales presented data on projected housing starts and the age of the existing housing stock (to estimate reroofing potential) in the region, to arrive at a volume forecast for asphalt shingle squares. The figure both executives believed realistic was 1.2 million asphalt shingle squares for the region in 1988.

A week later the executives met and discussed their options. After a lengthy discussion, they concluded that two options existed. They could recommend maintaining the price at $20 per square or reducing the price to $18. The option of

---

[1] A *square* is a unit of measurement used in the roofing industry. One square contains approximately 80 individual shingles. A rule of thumb in the industry holds that 25 squares are needed to roof an average single-family dwelling.

recommending a price increase to $22 was dismissed on the grounds that the price differential between Afton Industries and its competitors would be entirely too great. In the sales director's opinion, it was unlikely that competitors would reduce their prices in the near future regardless of whether Afton lowered its price or maintained the $20 price. He noted that competitors were experiencing financial difficulties. However, he believed nothing was impossible and that a 10-percent chance of competitors' lowering their price below $18 existed. The director of planning and administration felt that the probability was conceivably higher but was unable to assign a probability estimate.

During the discussion on competitive response, the director of sales commented that if Afton kept its price at $20, an additional loss of 10 percentage points in market share would result regardless of the actions by competitors. He felt that lowering the price to $18 would lead to a gain of 10 percentage points in market share in 1988 if competitors stayed at the $18 price. If the price were reduced to $18 and competitors retaliated with an additional price cut, however, Afton could expect a loss of 15 percentage points in market share in 1988. These assessments were based on discussions with the company's sales force indicating that a number of large construction contracts were locked into the $20 price and that Afton's quality image would preclude a major downward movement in market share. Also, several sales representatives indicated that many applicators who purchased shingles from competitors at $18 per square were marking up the product in such a manner that the installed price to homeowners and builders was equal to Afton's installed price at typical markup levels. The installed price parity was annoying to competitors because they had no cost advantage at the point-of-sale or in the bidding process for new construction. In addition, it was believed that competitors had higher direct labor and material costs than Afton did. The effect of this cost disadvantage was that competitors' contribution margins were lower than that of Afton Industries.

Later in the same week, the accounting department submitted a cost breakdown on the company's line of asphalt shingles. These data are shown in Exhibit 12.2. In addition, the accounting department, in consultation with market research personnel, prepared a summary of the operating performance of the five competitors, shown in Exhibit 12.3. Afton Industries had planned to maintain selling and administrative expenses at 1987 levels.

EXHIBIT 12.2   **Afton Estimated per-Square Costs of Asphalt Shingles at 500,000-Square Volume**

Direct labor	$8.00
Direct material	5.00
Scrappage	0.50
Product line expense	
Direct expenses[a]	0.50
Indirect expenses[b]	1.50
Selling and general administrative expenses[c]	2.00
Total cost per square	$17.50

[a]Includes supplies, repairs, power, etc. (all variable costs).

[b]Includes depreciation, supervision, etc. (all fixed expenses).

[c]All costs were fixed, but allocated on a per-unit basis for expository purposes.

EXHIBIT 12.3   **Selected Operating Data on Afton's Competitors, 1987**

	Competitors				
	A	**B**	**C**	**D**	**E**
Unit (square) volume	200,000	190,000	150,000	150,000	60,000
Cost of goods sold/unit	$15.00	$15.50	$16.00	$16.00	$16.25
Selling and general administrative expenses	$500,000	$475,000	$425,000	$425,000	$350,000

Rogers, Nagel, Langhart (RNL PC), Architects and Planners

It was August 1984. John B. Rogers, one of the founders and a principal stockholder in RNL, had just completed the University of Colorado's Executive MBA program. Throughout the program John had tried to relate the concepts and principles covered in his courses to the problems of managing a large architectural practice. In particular, he was concerned about the marketing efforts of his firm. As he put it, "Marketing is still a new, and sometimes distasteful, word to most architects. Nevertheless, the firms that survive and prosper in the future are going to be those which learn how to market as effectively as they design. At RNL we are still struggling with what it means to be a marketing organization, but we feel it's a critical question that must be answered if we're going to meet our projections of roughly doubling by 1989, and we're giving it lots of attention."

RNL

In 1984, with sales (design fees) of approximately $3,300,000, RNL was one of the largest local architectural firms in Denver and the Rocky Mountain region. The firm evolved from the individual practices of John B. Rogers, Jerome K. Nagel, and Victor D. Langhart. All started their architectural careers in Denver in the 1950s. The partnership of

Source: This case was prepared by H. Michael Hayes, Professor of Marketing and Strategic Management, Graduate School of Business Administration, University of Colorado at Denver, as the basis for class discussion rather than to illustrate either effective or ineffective handling of an administrative situation. Copyright © 1985 by H. Michael Hayes.

Rogers, Nagel, Langhart was formed from the three individual proprietorships in 1966, and became a professional corporation in 1970.

In 1984 the firm provided professional design services to commercial, corporate, and governmental clients, not only in Denver, but throughout Colorado and, increasingly, throughout the western United States. In addition to basic architectural design services, three subsidiaries had recently been formed:

- Interplan, which provides prearchitectural services, programming, planning, budgeting, scheduling, and cost projections, utilized in corporate budgeting and governmental bond issues.

- Denver Enterprises, formed to hold equity interests in selected projects designed by RNL and to take risk by furnishing design services early in a project and by participating in the capital requirements of a project.

- Space Management Systems (SMS), which provides larger corporations with the necessary services (heavily computer-system supported) to facilitate control of their facilities with respect to space, furnishings, equipment, and the cost of change.

In 1984, the firm had 72 employees. John Rogers served as chairman, and Vic Langhart served as president. Nagel had retired in 1976. (See Exhibit 13.1 for an organization chart.) Development of broad-based management had been a priority since 1975. The firm had seven vice presidents. Two of these vice presidents, Phil Goedert and Rich von Luhrte, served on the Board of Directors, together with Rogers and Langhart.

Growth was financed through retained earnings. In addition, a plan to provide for more employee ownership, principally through profit sharing (ESOP in 1984), was initiated in 1973. Rogers and Langhart held 56 percent of RNL stock, and 66 percent was held by the four board members. The Colorado National Bank Profit Sharing Trust held 12 percent in its name. The remaining 22 percent was controlled by 23 other employees, either personally or through their individual profit-sharing accounts. It was a goal of the firm to eventually vest stock ownership throughout the firm, in the interest of longevity and continuity.

The firm's principal assets were its human resources. Rogers and Langhart, however, had significant ownership in a limited partnership, which owned a 20,000-square-foot building in a prestigious location in downtown Denver. In 1984, RNL occupied 15,000 square feet. Use of the remaining 5,000 square feet could accommodate up to 30 percent growth in personnel. Through utilization of automation and computers, RNL felt it could double its 1984 volume of work without acquiring additional space.

Architectural Services

> Architecture: the profession of designing buildings, open areas, communities, and other artificial constructions and environments, usually with some regard to aesthetic effect. The professional services of an architect often include design or selection of furnishings and decorations, supervision of construction work, and the examination, restoration, or remodeling of existing buildings.
>
> *Random House Dictionary*

EXHIBIT 13.1 **Corporate Organization**

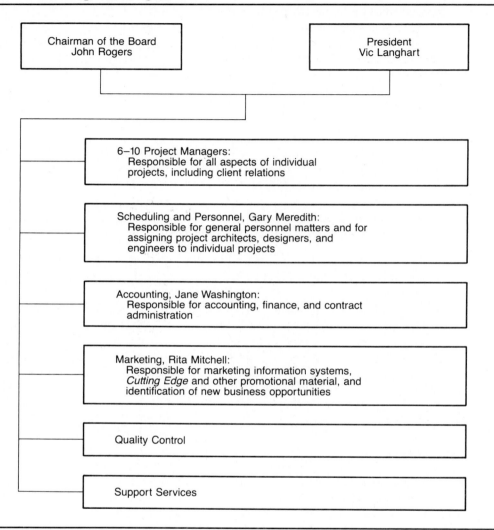

Chairman of the Board	President
John Rogers	Vic Langhart

6–10 Project Managers:
Responsible for all aspects of individual projects, including client relations

Scheduling and Personnel, Gary Meredith:
Responsible for general personnel matters and for assigning project architects, designers, and engineers to individual projects

Accounting, Jane Washington:
Responsible for accounting, finance, and contract administration

Marketing, Rita Mitchell:
Responsible for marketing information systems, *Cutting Edge* and other promotional material, and identification of new business opportunities

Quality Control

Support Services

Note: RNL does not have a formal organization chart, as such. This exhibit was developed by the case writer to portray the general nature of work assignments and reporting relationships in the firm. As a rule, project managers report either to John Rogers or to Vic Langhart. Most administrative staff functions report to Vic Langhart. At the operational level, Interplan and SMS projects are handled like RNL projects.

Demand for architectural services is closely tied to population growth and to the level of construction activity. The population in the Denver metropolitan area grew from 929,000 in 1960 to 1,620,000 in 1980, and it is estimated to grow to 1,958,000 by 1990. Denver's annual population change of 3.4 percent in the decade 1970–1980 ranked tenth for major American cities (Dallas and Phoenix ranked first and second). The projected population growth for the Denver metropolitan area from 1978 to 1983 ranked third in the nation, and Colorado was predicted to be one of the ten fastest-growing states during the 1980s.

Commercial construction permits grew from 340 in 1970, with an estimated value of $70,818,000, to 1,235 in 1980, with an estimated value of $400,294,000. This growth was not steady, however. Year-to-year changes in dollar value of commercial construction varied from 0.2 percent to 91.6 percent, and the number of permits dropped from a high of 2,245 in 1978 to 1,235 in 1980. Similar patterns of growth and variation characterized industrial construction.

Translating construction growth into estimates of demand for architectural services is difficult. One rule of thumb holds that each additional person added to the population base requires 1,000 square feet of homes, schools, churches, offices, hospitals, manufacturing facilities, retail and shopping facilities, and transportation facilities. In the Denver metro area alone, this could mean 338 million square feet. At $50 average per square foot, total construction expenditure over the decade could reach $16.9 billion, involving as much as $845 million in design fees during the 1980s.

The past and projected growth in demand for architectural services was accompanied by a significant growth in the number of architects in Colorado. From 1979 to 1982, the number of state registrations of individual architects grew from 1,400 to 3,381, an increase of 141.5 percent. Over 100 architectural firms competed actively in the Denver market. (Over 500 architects are listed in the Yellow Pages of the Denver metro area phone directory.) In recent years, a number of national firms (e.g., Skidmore, Owens and Merrill) opened offices in Denver. Other major firms came to Colorado to do one job and then returned to their home offices (e.g., Yamasaki for the Colorado National Bank Office Tower, TAC for Mansville World Headquarters). Of the 26 major firms working on 38 selected jobs in Denver in 1983, 16, or 61.5 percent, were Denver based. Of the other ten, which have headquarters offices elsewhere, all but two had offices in Denver.

Major categories of customers for architectural services include:

- Industrial
- Commercial
    Owner
    Developer
- Government
    Federal
    State
    Municipal
- Residential (note: RNL did not compete in this market)

Within these categories, however, not all architectural work is available to independent firms, and not all architectural work on a project is awarded to one architect. A recent Denver survey, for example, indicated that of 49 commercial jobs under construction with a known architect, 11 were handled by an "inside" architect. Of the remaining 38 jobs, 20 included shell and space design, whereas 18 involved space design only. In the 18 space designs, only 50 percent were actually done by architects.

The rapid growth in the construction market in Denver came to an abrupt halt in February 1982. Triggered by the broad realization that the oil boom was over, or had at least slowed significantly, project after project was put on hold. Construction of office space literally came to a halt. Of particular concern to RNL, which had just completed negotiations for a $1 million contract with Exxon, was the Exxon announcement of the closure of its Colorado Oil Shale activities at Parachute, Colorado.

It was against the backdrop of these changes that RNL felt the pressing need to review its marketing activities.

Marketing of Architectural Services

The basis of competing for architectural work has changed dramatically over the past several decades. As John Rogers recalled:

> At the beginning of my practice in 1956, you could establish an office, put a sign on your door, print calling cards, and have a "news" announcement with your picture in the *Daily Journal* that you had established a new practice of architecture. Beyond that, it was appropriate to suggest to friends and acquaintances that I was in business now, and I hoped that they might recommend me to someone they knew. The Code of Ethics of the American Institute of Architects, like many other professions at the time, prohibited any kind of aggressive marketing or sales effort as practiced in recent times.
>
> In fact, after convincing one School Board member (an artist) in Jefferson County that design was important, and then being awarded a commission to design an elementary school, which led to another and another, it was not surprising to read in the *Daily Journal* that the School Board had met the previous evening and had elected me to design a new junior high school, one that I hadn't even known about. I called and said, "Thank you." Marketing expense was zero with the exception of an occasional lunch or courtesy call here and there.
>
> Today, the situation is vastly different. We have to compete for most jobs, against both local firms and, increasingly, large national firms. Clients are becoming more sophisticated regarding the purchase of architectural services [see Exhibit 13.2 for a brief description of buyer behavior]. Promotion, of some kind, and concepts such as segmentation have become a way of life.

During the 1960s, development of an architectural practice was a slow process, characterized by heavy reliance on word of mouth regarding professional experience and expertise. Overt communication about an architect's qualifications was limited to brochures. Personal acquaintances played a significant role in the development of new clients. Personal relations between principals and clients were an important part of continuing and new relations. This method of practice development tended to favor local firms, whose reputation could be checked out on a personal basis, and small firms, whose principals could provide personal management and design of client projects.

As Denver grew, the market changed. The advantage of being a successful, local architect and knowing the local business community diminished. Newcomers to

EXHIBIT 13.2   **Buyer Behavior**

Purchase of architectural services is both complex and varied. Subject to many qualifications, however, there seems to be a number of steps that most buying situations have in common.

Development of a list of potential architects.

Identification of those architects from whom proposals will be solicited for a specific job (usually called the short list).

Invitations to submit proposals.

Evaluation of proposals and screening of final candidates.

Selection of a finalist, based on proposal evaluation, or invitations to finalists to make oral presentations to an evaluation group.

From a marketing standpoint, the focus of interest is the process of getting on the short list and the process by which the final selection is made.

The Short List

Prospective clients find out about architects in a variety of ways. Those who are frequent users of architectural services will generally keep a file of architects, sometimes classified as to type or practice. Additions to the file can come from mailed brochures, personal calls, advertisements, press releases, or in fact, almost any form of communication. When a specific requirement develops, the file is reviewed for apparent fit. With many variations, a short list is developed, and proposals are solicited.

Those who use architects infrequently tend to rely on various business or social networks to develop what is in essence their short list. In either case, a previously used architect is almost always on the short list, provided the past experience was satisfactory.

As the largest single customer for architectural services, agencies of the federal government follow a well-defined series of steps, including advertisement in the *Commerce Business Daily* and mail solicitation of local firms.

The Selection Process

The selection process is significantly influenced by the nature and scope of the work and its importance to the firm. Architect selection on major buildings is usually made at the highest level in the organization: by a principal or the president in a private organization or by various forms of boards in not-for-profit organizations such as churches. In some instances, the principal, president, or board is actively involved in all phases of the process. In others, the management of the process is delegated to others who develop recommendations to the decision makers. On smaller jobs, and those of an ongoing nature (e.g., space management), the decision is usually at lower levels and may involve a plant engineer or facilities manager of some kind.

continued

Denver tended to rely on relationships with architects in other cities. For local architects there was not time to rely on traditional communication networks to establish relationships with these newcomers. The size of projects grew, requiring growth in the size of architectural staffs. Personal attention to every client by principals was no longer possible.

Concomitantly, there was a growing change in the attitude toward the marketing of professional services. New entrants in the fields of medicine and law, as well as architecture, were becoming impatient with the slowness of traditional methods of practice development. A Supreme Court decision significantly reduced the restrictions that state bar associations could impose on lawyers with respect to their pricing and advertising practices. In a similar vein, the American Institute of Architects signed a consent decree with the Justice Department, which prohibited the organization from publishing fee schedules for architectural services.

Perhaps of most significance for architects, however, was the start of the so-called proposal age. Investigations in Maryland and Kansas, among other states, had revealed improper involvement of architects and engineers with state officials. Financial

---

EXHIBIT 13.2   *(continued)*

Regardless of the level at which the selection process is made, there seem to be two well-defined patterns to the process. The first, and predominant one, evaluates the firms on the short list, taking into prime consideration nonprice factors such as reputation, performance on previous jobs, and current workload. Based on this evaluation, one firm is selected, and a final agreement is then negotiated as to the scope of the work, the nature of the working relationship, the project team, and specific details as to price. The second pattern, of limited but growing use, attempts to specify the requirements so completely that a firm price can accompany the proposal. In some instances, the price and the proposal are submitted separately. Evaluation of the proposals includes a dollar differential, and these dollar differentials are applied to the price quotation to determine the low evaluated bidder.

Regardless of the process, there appear to be three main criteria on which firms are evaluated:

1. *The ability of the firm to perform the particular assignment.* For standard work this assessment is relatively easy and relies on the nature of past work, size of the organization, current backlogs, and so forth. For more creative work, the assessment becomes more difficult. Much importance is put on past work, but the proposal starts to take on additional importance. Sketches, drawings, and sometimes, extensive models may be requested with the proposal. In some instances, there may actually be a design competition. Much of this evaluation is, perforce, of a subjective nature.

2. *The comfort level with the project team that will be assigned to do the work.* For any but the most standard work there is recognition that there will be constant interaction between representatives of the client's organization and members of the architectural firm. Almost without exception, therefore, some kind of evaluation is made of the project team, or at least its leaders, in terms of the client's comfort level with the personalities involved.

3. *Finally, the matter of cost.* While direct price competition is not a factor in most transactions, the cost of architectural services is always a concern. This has two components. First, there is concern with the total cost of the project, over which the architect has great control. Second, there is growing concern with the size of the architect's fee, per se.

At least some assessment of the reputation of the architect with respect to controlling project costs is made in determining the short list. Once final selection is made, there is likely to be much discussion and negotiation as to the method of calculating the fee. The traditional method of simply charging a percentage of the construction price seems to be on the wane. Increasingly, clients for architectural services are attempting to establish a fixed fee for a well-defined project. The nature of architectural work, however, is such that changes are a fact of life and that many projects cannot be sufficiently defined in the initial stages to allow precise estimation of the design costs. Some basis for modifying a basic fee must, therefore, be established. Typically this is on some kind of direct-cost basis plus an overhead adder. Direct costs for various classes of staff and overhead rates obviously become matters for negotiation. In the case of the federal government, the right is reserved to audit an architect's books to determine the appropriateness of charges for changes.

---

kickbacks were proven on many state projects. Formal proposals, it was felt, would eliminate or reduce the likelihood of contract awards made on the basis of cronyism or kickbacks. Starting in the government sector, the requirement for proposals spread rapidly to all major clients. In 1984, for example, even a small church could receive as many as 20 detailed proposals on a modestly sized assignment.

Marketing at RNL

In 1984, RNL was engaged in a number of marketing activities. In addition to proposal preparation, major activities included:

- Professional involvement in the business community by principals, which provides contacts with potential clients. This included memberships in a wide variety of organizations such as the Downtown Denver Board, Chamber of Commerce, and Denver Art Museum.

- Participation in, and appearances at, conferences, both professional and business oriented.

- Daily review of *Commerce Business Daily* (a federal publication of all construction projects) along with other news services that indicate developing projects.

- Maintenance of past client contacts. (RNL found this difficult but assigned the activity to its project managers.)

- Development of relationships with potential clients, usually by giving a tour through the office plus lunch.

- VIP gourmet catered lunches for six invited guests, held once a month in the office. These involved a tour of the office and lively conversation, with some attempt at subsequent follow-up.

- Participation in appropriate local, regional, or national exhibits of architectural projects.

- Occasional publicity for a project or for a client.

- The *Cutting Edge.*[1]

- An assortment of brochures and information on finished projects.

- Special arrangements with architectural firms in other locations to provide the basis for a variety of desirable joint ventures.

RNL participated in a number of market segments, which it identified as follows, together with its view of the required approach.

Segment	Approach
Government	
City and county governments	Personal selling, political involvement.
School districts	Personal selling (professional educational knowledge required).
State government	Political involvement, written responses to RFPs (requests for proposals, from clients), personal selling.
Federal government	Personal selling, very detailed RFP response, no price competition in the proposal stage.
Private sector	Personal selling, social acquaintances, referrals, *Cutting Edge*, preliminary studies, price competition.
Semiprivate sector (includes utilities)	Personal selling, *Cutting Edge*, referrals, continuing relationships, some price competition.

Net fee income and allocation of marketing expenses by major segments is given in the following table. The general feeling at RNL was that there is a lapse of 6 to 18 months between the marketing effort itself and tangible results such as fee income.

---

[1] The *Cutting Edge* is an RNL publication designed to inform clients and prospects about new developments in architecture and planning and about significant RNL accomplishments (see Exhibit 13.3 for an example of an article on a typical issue).

EXHIBIT 13.3 **Example of an Article from the *Cutting Edge***

The Cutting Edge

Planning for Parking

The recent boom in downtown Denver office building has resulted in tremendous increases in population density in Denver's core, bringing corresponding increases in the number of vehicles and their related problems as well.

Auto storage, or parking, is one of the major resulting problems. Most building zoning requires parking sufficient to serve the building's needs. Even building sites not requiring parking are now providing parking space to remain competitive in the marketplace.

RNL's design for this above-grade parking structure at 1700 Grant aided in facilitating lease of the office building.

Parking solutions can range from a simple asphalt lot to a large multi-floor parking structure; the decision is based on many factors including site access, required number of spaces, land costs, budget and user convenience.

For many suburban sites, where land costs are sufficiently low to allow on-grade parking, design entails mainly the problems of circulation and landscaping. Circulation includes issues of easy site access and optimal efficient use of the site. Landscaping, including landforming, can visually screen automobiles and break up ugly seas of asphalt common to poorly designed developments.

At the opposite end of the parking spectrum are downtown sites where high land costs necessitate careful integration of parking into the building concept. This is often accomplished by building parking underground, below the main structure. Parking design, in this case, becomes a problem of integrating the circulation and the structure of the building above. While building underground eliminates the need for

acceptable outer appearance, the costs of excavation, mechanical ventilation, fire sprinklering and waterproofing make this one of the most expensive parking solutions.

Between on-grade parking and the underground structure is the above-grade detached or semi-detached parking structure. This solution is very common in areas of moderate land cost where convenience is the overriding factor.

Site conditions do much to generate the design of an above-grade parking structure, but where possible the following features should ideally be included:

1. Parking is in double loaded corridors, i.e. cars park on both sides of the circulation corridor to provide the most efficient ratio of parking to circulation area;

2. Parking at 90 degrees to circulation corridors rather than at angles, once again the most efficient use of space;

3. Access to different garage levels provided by ramping the parking floors, efficiently combining vertical circulation and parking;

4. A precast prestressed concrete structure (this structure economically provides long spans needed to eliminate columns which would interfere with parking circulation and the fireproof concrete members have a low maintenance surface that can be left exposed);

5. Classification as an "open parking garage" under the building code, meaning that the structure has openings in the walls of the building providing natural ventilation and eliminating the need for expensive mechanical ventilation of exhaust fumes;

6. A building exterior in a precast concrete finish, allowing the designer to combine structure and exterior skin into one low cost element.

RNL recently completed work on the $20,000,000 1700 Grant Office Building for Wickliff & Company. The inclusion of a 415 car parking garage in the 1700 Grant project provided one of the amenities necessary for successful leasing in a very depressed leasing market.

A Publication of **RNL**/Inception ● by Richard T. Anderson ● Vol. II No. I ● 1576 Sherman Street Denver, Co. 80203 (303) 832-5599

	1982		1983		1984 (estimated)		1985 (estimated)	
	Net Fee	**Marketing Expense**	**Net Fee**	**Marketing Expense**	**Net Fee**	**Marketing Expense**	**Net Fee**	**Marketing Expense**
Government	$ 800	$104	$1,220	$101	$1,012	$150	$1,200	$140
Private	1,376	162	1,261	140	1,200	195	1,616	220
Semiprivate	88	11	118	24	100	25	140	30
Interiors	828	40	670	30	918	100	1,235	110
Urban design	95	20	31	10	170	30	220	40
Total	$3,187	$337	$3,300	$305	$3,400	$500	$4,411	$540

Note: All amounts are in thousands.

Salient aspects of budgeted marketing expense for 1985, by segment, were:

1. *Government.* Heavy emphasis on increased trips to Omaha (a key Corps of Engineers location), Washington, and other out-of-state, as well as in-state, locations plus considerable emphasis on participation in municipal conferences.

2. *Private.* Personal contact at local, state, and regional levels with corporations, banks, developers, and contractors plus local promotion through Chamber of Commerce, clubs, VIP lunches, *Cutting Edge,* promotion materials, and initiation of an advertising and public relations effort.

3. *Semiprivate.* Increased level of personal contact and promotional effort.

4. *Interiors.* Major allocation of salary and expenses of a new full-time marketing person to improve direct sales locally plus other promotional support.

5. *Urban design.* Some early success indicates that land developers and urban renewal authorities are the most likely clients. Planned marketing expense is primarily for personal contact.

Additional marketing efforts being given serious consideration included:

- A more structured marketing organization with more specific assignments.

- Increased visibility for the firm through general media and trade journals; paid or other (e.g., public relations).

- Appearances on special programs and offering special seminars.

- Use of more sophisticated selling tools such as videotapes and automated slide presentations.

- Increased training in client relations/selling for project managers and other staff.

- Hiring a professionally trained marketing manager.

- Determining how the national firms market (i.e., copy the competition).

- Expansion of debriefing conferences with successful and unsuccessful clients.

- Use of a focus group to develop effective sales points for RNL.

- Training a marketing MBA in architecture versus training an architect in marketing.

RNL Clients

RNL described its clients as

1. Having a long history of growing expectations with respect to detail, completeness, counseling, and cost control.
2. Mandating the minimization of construction problems, including changes, overruns, and delays.
3. Having an increased concern for peer approval at the completion of a project.
4. Having an increased desire to understand and be a part of the design process.

Extensive interviews of clients by independent market researchers showed very favorable impressions about RNL. Terms used to describe the firm included:

- Best and largest architectural service in Denver.
- Innovative yet practical.
- Designs large projects for "who's who in Denver."
- Long-term resident of the business community.
- Lots of expertise.
- Designs artistic yet functional buildings.

RNL's use of computer-aided design systems was seen as a definite competitive edge. Others mentioned RNL's extra services, such as interior systems, as a plus, although only 35 percent of those interviewed were aware that RNL offered this service. In general, most clients felt that RNL had a competitive edge with regard to timeliness, productivity, and cost consciousness.

Two major ways that new clients heard about RNL were identified. One was the contact RNL made on its own initiative when it heard of a possible project. The other was through personal references. All those interviewed felt advertising played a minor role, and in fact, several indicated they had questions about an architectural firm that advertises.

Clients who selected RNL identified the following as playing a role in their decision:

- Tours of RNL's facilities.
- Monthly receipt of *Cutting Edge*.
- Low-key selling style.
- RNL's ability to focus on their needs.
- Thoroughness in researching customer needs and overall proposal preparation and presentation.
- RNL's overall reputation in the community.
- Belief that RNL would produce good, solid (not flashy) results.

Clients who did not select RNL identified the following reasons for their decision:

- RNL had less experience and specialization in their particular industry.
- Decided to stay with the architectural firm used previously.
- Decided to go with a firm that has more national status.
- Other presentations had more "pizazz."

Overall, clients' perceptions of RNL were very positive. There was less than complete understanding of the scope of RNL services, but its current approach to clients received good marks.

Marketing Issues at RNL: Some Views of Middle Management

Richard von Luhrte joined RNL in 1979, following extensive experience with other firms in Chicago and Denver. In 1984, he led the firm's urban design effort on major projects, served as a project manager, and participated actively in marketing. He came to RNL because the firm "fits my image." He preferred larger firms that have extensive and complementary skills. He commented on marketing as follows:

> RNL has a lot going for it. We have a higher overhead rate, but with most clients, you can sell our competence and turn this into an advantage. I think RNL is perceived as a quality firm, but customers are also concerned that we will gold-plate a job. I'd like to be able to go gold plate or inexpensive as the circumstances dictate. But it's hard to convince a customer that we can do this.
>
> For many of our clients continuity is important, and we need to convey that there will be continuity beyond the founders. RNL has done well as a provider of "all things for all people," and our diversification helps us ride through periods of economic downturn. On the other hand, we lose some jobs because we're not specialized. For instance, we haven't done well in the downtown developer market. We're starting to do more, but if we had targeted the shopping center business we could have had seven or eight jobs by now. One way to operate would be to jump on a trend and ride it until the downturn and then move into something else.
>
> There's always the conflict between specialization and fun. We try to stay diversified, but we ought to be anticipating the next boom. At the same time, there's always the problem of overhead. In this business you can't carry very much, particularly in slow times.
>
> I like the marketing part of the work, but there's a limit on how much of it I can, or should, do. Plus, I think it's important to try to match our people with our clients in terms of age and interests, which means we need to have lots of people involved in the marketing effort.
>
> Oral presentations are an important part of marketing, and we make a lot of them. You have to make them interesting, and there has to be a sense of trying for the "close." On the other hand, I think that the presentation is not what wins the job, although a poor presentation can lose it for you. It's important that the presentation conveys a sense of enthusiasm and that we really want the job.

As comptroller, Jane Washington was involved extensively in the firm's discussions about its marketing efforts. As she described the situation:

There is little question in my mind that the people at the top are committed to developing a marketing orientation at RNL. But our objectives still aren't clear. For instance, we still haven't decided what would be a good mix of architecture, interiors, and planning. Interiors is a stepchild to some. On the other hand, it is a very profitable part of our business. But it's not easy to develop a nice neat set of objectives for a firm like this. Two years ago we had a seminar to develop a mission statement, but we still don't have one. This isn't a criticism. Rather, it's an indication of the difficulty of getting agreement on objectives in a firm of creative professionals.

One problem is that our approach to marketing has been reactive rather than proactive. Our biggest marketing expenditure is proposal preparation, and we have tended to respond to RFPs as they come in, without screening them for fit with targeted segments. From a budget standpoint we have not really allocated marketing dollars to particular people or segments, except in a pro forma kind of way. As a result, no one person is responsible for what is a very large total expenditure.

Another problem is that we don't have precise information about our marketing expenditures or the profitability of individual jobs. It would be impractical to track expenditures on the 500–1,000 proposals we make a year, but we could set up a system that tracks marketing expenditures in, say, 10 segments. This would at least let individuals see what kind of money we're spending for marketing, and where. We also could change from the present system, which basically measures performance in terms of variation from dollar budget, to one that reports on the profitability of individual jobs. I've done some studies on the profitability of our major product lines, but those don't tie to any one individual's performance.

Rita Mitchell, who has an MS in library science and information systems, joined RNL in 1981. Originally her assignment focused on organizing marketing records and various marketing information resources. In her new role as new business development coordinator, she had a broader set of responsibilities. According to Rita:

We definitely need some policies about marketing, and these ought to spell out a marketing process. In my present job, I think I can help the board synthesize market information and so help to develop a marketing plan.

I do a lot of market research based on secondary data. For instance, we have access to Dialog and a number of other online databases, using our PC. Based on this research, and our own in-house competence, I think I can do some good market anticipation. The problem is what to do with this kind of information. If we move too fast, based on signals about a new market, there is obviously the risk of being wrong. On the other hand, if we wait until the signals are unmistakably clear, they will be clear to everyone else, and we will lose the opportunity to establish a preeminent position.

With respect to individual RFPs, our decision on which job to quote is still highly subjective. We try to estimate our chances of getting the job, and we talk about its fit with our other work, but we don't have much hard data or policy to guide us. We don't, for instance, have a good sense of other RFPs that are in the pipeline and how the mix of the jobs we're quoting and the resulting work fits with our present work in progress. The Marketing Committee [consisting of John Rogers, Vic Langhart, Phil Goedert, Rich von Luhrte, Dick Shiffer, Rita Mitchell, and occasionally, Bob Johnson] brings lots of experience and personal knowledge to bear on this, but it's not a precise process.

We have a number of sources of information about new construction projects: the *Commerce Business Daily* [a federal government publication], the *Daily Journal* [which reports on local government construction], the Western Press Clipping Bureau, Colorado trade journals, and so forth. Monitoring these is a major activity, and then we have the problem of deciding which projects fit RNL.

Bob Johnson, a project manager and member of the Marketing Committee, commented:

> The way the system works now, we have four board members and 12 project managers, most of whom can pursue new business. They bring these opportunities before the Marketing Committee, but it doesn't really have the clout to say no. As a result, people can really go off on their own. I'd like to see the committee flex its muscles a little more on what jobs we go after. But there's a problem with committing to just a few market segments. Right now we're involved in something like 30 segments. If we're wrong on one, it's not a big deal. But if we were committed to just a few, then a mistake could have really serious consequences.
>
> For many of us, however, the major problem is managing the transfer of ownership and control to a broader set of individuals. Currently the prospective owners don't really have a forum for what they'd like the company to be. My personal preference would be to go after corporate headquarters, high-tech firms, speculative office buildings, and high-quality interiors. But there probably isn't agreement on this.

Marketing Issues: The Views of the Founders

Vic Langhart started his practice of architecture in 1954 and has taught design in the Architecture Department of the University of Colorado. He was instrumental in developing new services at RNL, including Interplan and SMS, and was heavily involved in training of the next level of management. In 1984, he supervised day-to-day operations and also served as president of Interplan and SMS. Looking to the future, Vic observed:

> Our toughest issue is dealing with the rate of change in the profession today. It's probably fair to say there are too many architects today. But this is a profession of highly idealistic people, many of whom feel their contribution to a better world is more important than dollars of income, and so will stay in the field at "starvation wages." We wrestle with the question of "profession or business?" but competition is now a fact of life for us. The oil boom of the 1970s in Denver triggered an inrush of national firms. Many have stayed on, and we now have a situation where one of the largest national firms is competing for a small job in Durango. We're also starting to see more direct price competition. Digital Equipment recently prequalified eight firms, selected five to submit proposals that demonstrated understanding of the assignment, and asked for a separate envelope containing the price.
>
> Our tradition at RNL has been one of quality. I think we're the "Mercedes" of the business, and in the long haul, an RNL customer will be better off economically. A lot of things contribute to this—our Interplan concept, for instance—but the key differentiation factor is our on-site-planning approach.
>
> In 1966–1968, we were almost 100 percent in education. Then I heard that they were closing some maternity wards, and we decided to diversify. Today we have a good list of products, ranging from commercial buildings to labs and vehicle maintenance facilities. In most areas, the only people who can beat us are the superspecialists, and

even then there's a question. Our diversification has kept our minds free to come up with creative approaches. At Beaver Creek, for example, I think we came up with a better approach to condominium design than the specialists. Plus, we can call in special expertise if it's necessary.

Over the past several years we've had a number of offers to merge into national or other firms. We decided, however, to become employee owned. Our basic notion was that RNL should be an organization that provides its employees a long-time career opportunity. This is not easy in an industry that is characterized by high turnover. Less than 10 percent of architectural firms have figured out how to do it. But we're now at 35 percent employee ownership.

I'm personally enthusiastic about Interplan. It has tremendous potential to impact our customers. In Seattle, for instance, a bank came to us for a simple expansion. Our Interplan approach, however, led to a totally different set of concepts.

We've had some discussion about expansion. Colorado Springs is a possibility, for instance. But there would be problems of keeping RNL concepts and our culture. We work hard to develop and disseminate an RNL culture. For example, we have lots of meetings, although John and I sometimes disagree about how much time should be spent in meetings. A third of our business comes from interiors, and there is as much difference between interior designers and architects as there is between architects and mechanical engineers.

In somewhat similar vein, John Rogers commented:

In the 1960s, RNL was primarily in the business of designing schools. We were really experts in that market. But then the boom in school construction came to an end, and we moved into other areas—first into banks and commercial buildings. We got started with Mountain Bell, an important relationship for us that continues today. We did assignments for mining companies and laboratories. In the late 1960s, no one knew how to use computers to manage office space problems, and we moved in that direction, which led to the formation of Interplan. We moved into local and state design work. One of our showcase assignments is the Colorado State Judicial/Heritage Center.

In the 1980s, we started to move into federal and military work, and this now represents a significant portion of our business.

We have done some developer work, but this is a tough market. It has a strong "bottom line orientation," and developers want sharp focus and expertise.

As we grow larger we find it difficult to maintain a close client relationship. The client wants to know who will work on the assignment, but some of our staff members are not good at the people side of the business.

Currently we're still doing lots of "one of a kind" work. Our assignment for the expansion of the *Rocky Mountain News* building, our design of a condominium lodge at Beaver Creek, and our design of a developer building at the Denver Tech Center are all in this category. A common theme, however, is our "on-site" design process. This is a process by which we make sure that the client is involved in the design from the start and that we are really tuned in to his requirements. I see this as one of our real competitive advantages. But I'm still concerned that we may be trying to spread ourselves too thin. Plus, there's no question that there is an increased tendency to specialization: "shopping center architects," for example.

We need to become better marketers, but we have to make sure that we don't lose sight of what has made us the leading architectural firm in Denver: service and client orientation.

Microsoft Corporation: The Introduction of Microsoft Works

In July 1987, Bruce Jacobsen, the product manager for Microsoft Works for the IBM® PC and Compatibles (Works), and Ida Cole, the director of Microsoft's International Products Group, were preparing for a presentation to Microsoft's country managers. Works was a new, integrated software product that included a spreadsheet, word processor, graphics program, database, and communications program. The country managers were the chief operating officers of Microsoft's international subsidiaries. The purpose of the presentation was to outline Works' design and tentative positioning strategy and to ask for questions and suggestions from the field.

The upcoming meeting was an important one for Works. In 1986, over 41 percent of Microsoft's sales dollars were to countries outside the United States. It was critical to win the support of the country managers for the marketing strategy to increase the chances of the new product's success.

Cole and Jacobsen were aware that two issues were likely to fuel a lively debate during the meeting. The first involved requests to modify the design of Works. Microsoft's strategy was for a standard version of Works to meet a set of common needs around the world. That philosophy allowed for limited "localization," whereby the program and the documentation were translated into local languages, and small changes were made to accommodate local conventions for currency, time and date formats, and so on. However, the programs that provided spreadsheet, word processing, and other functions remained unchanged. Several country managers had asked

Source: This case prepared by Assistant Professor Thomas J. Kosnik as the basis for class discussion rather than to illustrate either effective or ineffective handling of an administrative situation. Certain information has been disguised. Copyright © 1987 by the President and Fellows of Harvard College. Harvard Business School Case 588-028.

for features to meet the needs of their markets that would require redesign of Works' programs. Microsoft had to decide how to respond to the requests.

The second issue was Works' product positioning strategy. Jacobsen was planning to position Works as an easy-to-learn, easy-to-sell product for the home and small business market. Ida Cole believed that the U.S. positioning strategy might not be appropriate in a number of countries.

Jacobsen sent an electronic message to Jabe Blumenthal, the program manager and designer for Works, inviting him to drop in on the discussion. Then he turned to Ida Cole.

"Well, Ida, what are we going to say to the country managers?"

The Worldwide Market for Microcomputer Software

The microcomputer software industry emerged in the United States during the mid-1970s, as a number of enterprising individuals left more conventional pursuits to develop programs for the first generation of microcomputers. Bill Gates, chairman of Microsoft, was among those industry pioneers. As a freshman at Harvard University, Gates developed a BASIC programming language for micros. He dropped out of Harvard to found Microsoft in 1975.

Microcomputer Software Categories

By 1987, most observers divided the fledgling industry into different segments, based on the products sold. The first category was *systems software*. One group of systems software products included operating systems, such as Microsoft's Disk Operating System (MS-DOS). Operating systems provided a layer of communication between individual software programs and the computer itself. Another type of systems software included programming languages, such as BASIC, PASCAL, and COBOL. Such high-level languages were used to write programs to perform functions for the computer user.

The second software category was *application software*. It included horizontal applications and vertical applications. Horizontal application software performed broad functions that were used by different customers for a variety of tasks. Microsoft Works and Lotus 1-2-3® were examples of horizontal applications. Vertical applications performed a narrower set of functions to support a specific set of tasks. Examples included accounting software for law firms and sales force management systems.

In 1986, the microcomputer software industry was over $5 billion in retail sales, with 14,000 companies offering over 27,000 different products around the world. Industry observers divided the $5 billion total into sales of $250 million for systems software, $2.25 billion for horizontal applications, and $2.5 billion for vertical application software.

Leading Competitors in the Microcomputer Software Market

Microcomputer software was sold both by hardware companies, such as IBM and Apple, and by "independent" software companies whose products ran on a variety of computer hardware. The leading independent microcomputer software companies in

EXHIBIT 14.1   **Leading Independent Microcomputer Software Vendors (sales dollars in millions)**

Company Name	Worldwide Sales in 1986[a]	Name(s) of a Few Leading Products	Category of Software Products[b]
Lotus Development Corp.	$283	1-2-3 Symphony Jazz	GP spreadsheet GP integrated GP integrated
Microsoft Corp.	$260	DOS Excel Microsoft Word	SS operating system GP spreadsheet GP word processor
Ashton-Tate	$203	DBase III Framework Multimate	GP database GP integrated GP word processor
Word Perfect	$ 52	WordPerfect Wordperfect Executive	GP word processor GP integrated
Autodesk	$ 50	Autocad CAD Camera	SP computer assisted design products
Borland	$ 38	SideKick TurboPascal	GP organizer SS language
Micropro	$ 36	Wordstar Wordstar 2000	GP word processor GP word processor
Digital Research	$ 26	CP/M GEM	SS operating system SS operating environment
Software Publishing	$ 26	PFS: Write PFS: File First Choice	GP word processor GP database GP integrated

[a]Sales based on the period from January 1 to December 31, 1986. In the first half of 1987, Microsoft sales exceeded Lotus Development Corporation's sales.

[b]GP = General purpose application software; SP = special purpose; SS = system software.

1986 are shown in Exhibit 14.1. All of the largest microcomputer software companies were headquartered in the United States. However, two of Microsoft's largest competitors were aggressively expanding their international sales. Twenty-four percent of Lotus Development Corporation's 1986 sales were outside the United States, compared with 14 percent a year earlier. Ashton-Tate's international sales comprised 20 percent of its 1986 total.

Two companies were the most likely to compete with a product like Works on the IBM PC. Software Publishing, which had dominated the market for easy-to-learn inexpensive products with its PFS series, had recently introduced an integrated product called First Choice. It was priced at $179, and included word processing, spreadsheet, communications, and limited database functions for the first-time computer user. Some industry watchers predicted that Software Publishing would have an improved version of the product ready for release by the autumn of 1987. Borland, which had a reputation for clever, easy-to-use products at very low prices, marketed a best-selling product called Sidekick for $59, to support telephone lists, light calculations, and other tasks. It was rumored that Borland might enhance Sidekick to compete with Works.

Microsoft Corporation

Overall Leadership

Microsoft was a leader in the micro software industry. The company chairman, Bill Gates, was a programmer-turned-entrepreneur whose vision for Microsoft was "to make the software that will permit there to be a computer on every desk and in every home." His hard-driving style pervaded the company. Microsoft's president, Jon Swirley, a former executive at Tandy Corporation (Radio Shack), brought a wealth of experience about marketing of microcomputer products to the top management team. Both men were hands-on managers who delegated responsibility but demanded outstanding performance and attention to detail.

Much of Microsoft's success had come through timing and skill in managing alliances with leading hardware manufacturers. One example of timing had become an industry legend. In 1980, IBM approached Gates to have Microsoft design the operating system for the new personal computer it was planning. Gates first sent IBM to Digital Research, who already had an operating system. When IBM was rebuffed by Digital Research's attorney, it called Gates back, and he seized the opportunity. Microsoft's Disk Operating System became an industry standard. As other hardware manufacturers introduced PC clones, they turned to Microsoft to develop a version of MS-DOS for their machines. By 1986, Microsoft had supplied operating systems for over 300 different models of microcomputers.

Microsoft also made an early commitment to the emerging "second standard" in microcomputers, the Macintosh™ computer from Apple®. Several Microsoft application software products, including Word, Excel, and Works for the Macintosh, enjoyed a leadership position among Macintosh users.

International Marketing Strategy

Timing and hardware alliances were important facets of Microsoft's international marketing strategy as well. The company began its efforts in the international arena in 1982. Microsoft entered a number of countries with local language versions of its products a year or two before most of its competitors. In addition to being first with local language software, Microsoft formed alliances with leading computer companies in Europe and Asia. Through a series of Original Equipment Manufacturer (OEM) arrangements, the sales forces of hardware OEMs sold Microsoft products like Multiplan (spreadsheet) and Word (word processing) along with their microcomputers to large corporations in many countries.

As a result of early entry and strong OEM alliances, Microsoft's Word and Multiplan products were market leaders in a number of countries in Europe and Asia. In 1986, the International Division had over 350 employees, and international sales were over $106 million. However, that leadership position was being challenged by Lotus, which had recently introduced a local version of 1-2-3 in Japan and had 200 employees outside the United States and over $67 million in international sales in 1986.

Organization

Exhibit 14.2 shows part of Microsoft's corporate organization chart. In addition to serving as chairman, Bill Gates was also the acting vice president of Applications Software, the division where Bruce Jacobsen worked as a product manager. Gates's keen interest in the application software side of Microsoft's business had led him to assume that role until the right person could be found to fill the position. Bruce Jacobsen reported to Mike Slade, the Works group product manager, who reported to Jeff Raikes, the director of Applications Marketing, who in turn reported to Gates. However, the informal management style and heavy use of electronic mail in decision making led to a great deal of direct communication between product managers, like Jacobsen, and Bill Gates and Jon Swirley.

Exhibit 14.3 shows the organization of the International Division. Jeremy Butler had responsibility for International. Ida Cole reported to Butler, as did three other directors responsible for international operations in Europe, Asia, and Intercontinental (the rest of the world).

Financial Performance

Exhibit 14.4 contains a five-year summary of Microsoft's financial performance. The company's growth and earnings record had made it a favorite of many Wall Street analysts. Its 1986 return on sales was the highest of any company in the *Datamation 100*, an annual review of the largest companies in the computer hardware and software industries. In the first half of 1987, Microsoft's sales surpassed Lotus Development Corporation's, making it the largest microcomputer software company in the world. Microsoft's 1986 sales by product line were: systems software and languages = 53 percent; applications software = 37 percent; hardware and books = 10 percent.

Segmenting the Software Market

At Microsoft, four dimensions were considered in analyzing market segments for software products: the computer hardware environment, the usage situation, the level of the customer's needs, and the country/language.

Segmenting by Computer Hardware Environment

Microsoft developed application software products to meet the needs of customers who bought the most popular "standard" types of computer hardware. The first major standard in IBM-compatible microcomputer technology was established with the introduction of the IBM PC in 1981 and extended with the more powerful IBM AT in 1984. A number of companies around the world introduced PC compatible computers—also known as "PC clones"—that used the same software and functioned the same way as the IBM PC but offered slight enhancements and lower prices. These "clone makers" moved even more quickly to imitate the IBM AT.

The average price of a PC-compatible dropped from almost $3,000 in 1983 to below $1,000 in 1987. IBM lowered its prices as well, but continued to lose market share to the "act-alike" vendors. Exhibit 14.5 shows unit sales from IBM and the clone makers. In 1987, IBM introduced the Personal System 2 (PS/2) family—a second

EXHIBIT 14.2 **Microsoft's Corporate Organization Chart**

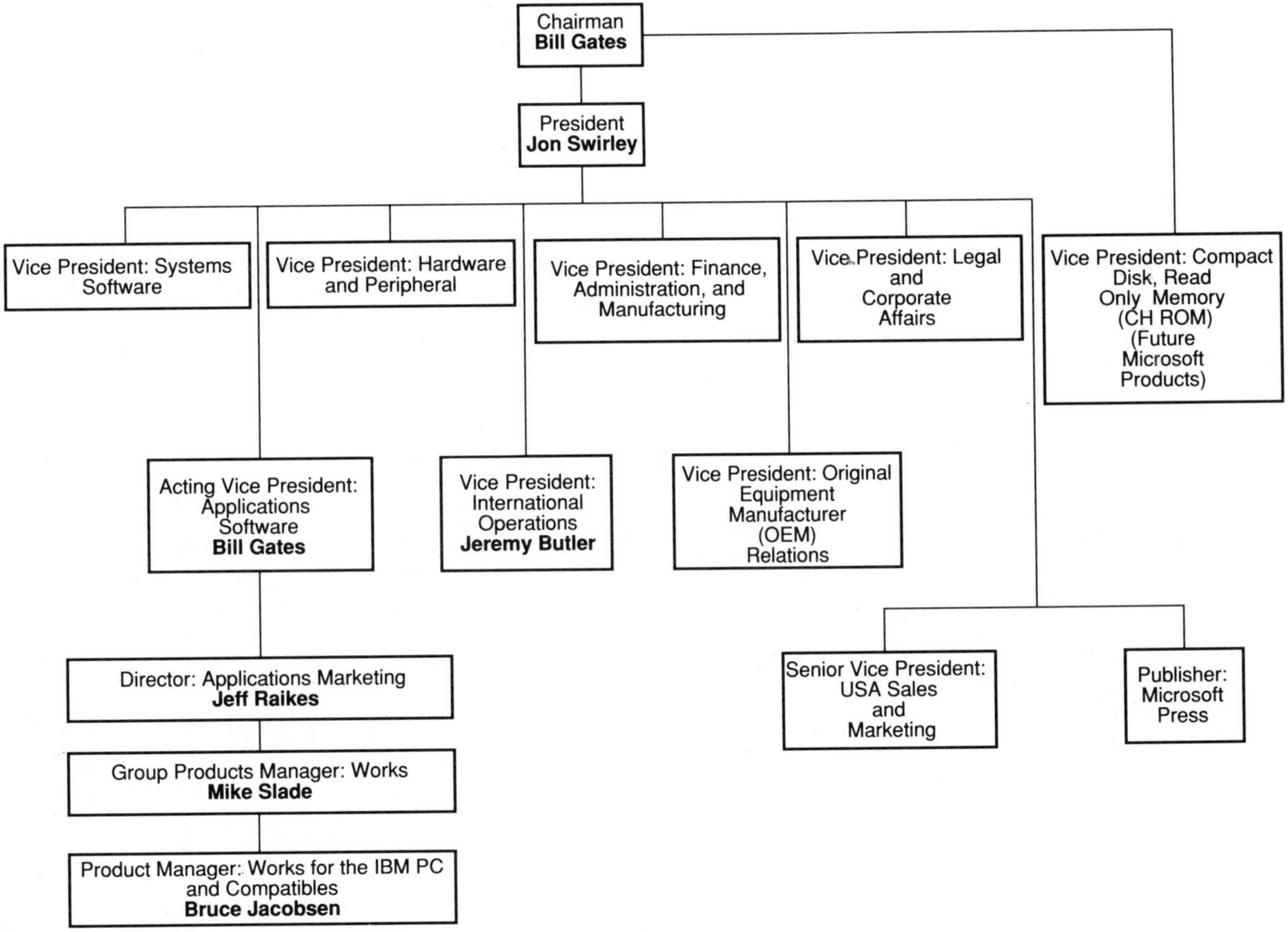

Chairman
Bill Gates

President
Jon Swirley

Vice President: Systems Software

Vice President: Hardware and Peripheral

Acting Vice President: Applications Software
Bill Gates

Vice President: International Operations
Jeremy Butler

Vice President: Finance, Administration, and Manufacturing

Vice President: Original Equipment Manufacturer (OEM) Relations

Vice President: Legal and Corporate Affairs

Vice President: Compact Disk, Read Only Memory (CH ROM) (Future Microsoft Products)

Senior Vice President: USA Sales and Marketing

Publisher: Microsoft Press

Director: Applications Marketing
Jeff Raikes

Group Products Manager: Works
Mike Slade

Product Manager: Works for the IBM PC and Compatibles
Bruce Jacobsen

Source: Microsoft Coporation internal records.

EXHIBIT 14.3   Organization Chart for Microsoft's International Operations

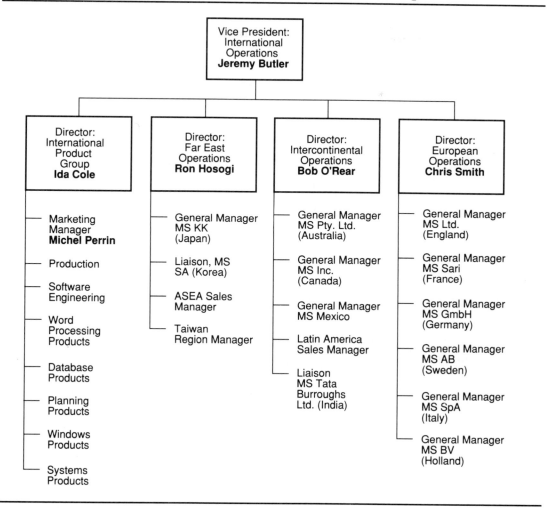

Source: Microsoft Corporation internal records.

generation of IBM machines with greater power and graphic capabilities that had the potential to overthrow the standards it had created with the IBM PC and AT.

Although Microsoft Works was technically capable of running on both the old and new generations of IBM computers, its primary target hardware was any IBM PC, or PC-compatible. The more mature, "low-end" IBM-compatible hardware was selected for Works because simple inexpensive software was needed for the millions of customers who were planning to purchase inexpensive machines for use in homes and small businesses. Other Microsoft products, including Word (word processing) and

EXHIBIT 14.4   **A Summary of Microsoft's Financial Performance: 1983–1987***

	1983	1984	1985	1986	1987
Net revenues	$50,065	$97,479	$140,417	$197,514	$345,890
Cost of revenues	15,773	22,900	30,447	40,862	73,854
Gross margin	34,292	74,579	109,970	156,652	272,036
Research and development	7,021	10,665	17,108	20,523	38,076
Sales/marketing	11,916	26,027	42,512	57,668	85,070
General and administrative	4,698	8,784	9,443	17,555	22,003
Income from operations	10,657	29,103	40,907	60,906	126,887
Nonoperating income (loss)	407	(1,073)	1,936	5,078	8,638
Stock option bonus					(14,187)
Income before tax	11,064	28,030	42,843	65,984	121,338
Income tax	4,577	12,150	18,742	26,730	49,460
Net income	$ 6,487	$15,880	$ 24,101	$ 39,254	$ 71,878
Total assets	$24,328	$47,637	$ 65,064	$170,739	$287,754
Stockholders' equity	$14,639	$30,712	$ 54,440	$139,332	$239,105
Earnings per share	$0.15	$0.35	$0.52	$0.78	$1.30
Number of employees	367	608	910	1,153	1,816

*Microsoft's fiscal year ran from July 1 to June 30.

Source: Microsoft Corporation financial statements.

EXHIBIT 14.5   **Unit Sales of IBM PC Compatible Microcomputers in Two Technology Families (in thousands of units)**

Type of Technology	1981	1982	1983	1984	1985	1986
U.S. Market Only						
IBM PC & XT	35	190	590	1,553	1,287	1,009
PC compatibles from clone makers	0	2	108	367	839	1,270
Total PC compatible	35	192	698	1,920	2,126	2,279
IBM AT				22	261	384
AT compatibles from clone makers					132	490
Total AT compatible	0	0	0	22	393	874
Worldwide Market (includes U.S.)						
IBM PC & XT	35	195	670	1,855	1,961	1,538
PC compatibles from clone makers		2	113	427	1,069	1,610
Total PC compatible	35	197	783	2,282	3,030	3,148
IBM AT				22	330	572
AT compatibles from clone makers					151	641
Total AT compatible	0	0	0	22	481	1,213

Source: International Data Corporation reports on the microcomputer market.

EXHIBIT 14.6   Forecast Sales of Low-end IBM-Compatible Microcomputers in Selected Countries (thousands of units)

Country	1986 Population (in 000)	1986 Estimated Unit Sales	1987 Forecast Unit Sales	1988 Forecast Unit Sales
U.S.A.	240,856	2,279	2,000	1,500
England	56,458	170	225	220
Canada	25,625	106	120	110
Australia/New Zealand	19,098	34	45	40
France	55,239	139	160	155
West Germany	60,734	136	145	120
Italy	57,226	83	115	130
Netherlands	14,536	46	60	55
Portugal	10,095	2	5	10
Sweden	8,357	39	45	40
Spain	39,075	16	30	50
Japan	121,042	50	50	30
Total	708,701	3,100	3,000	2,460

Note: The figures above included IBM PCs, XTs, and computers from other manufacturers that were compatible with those IBM microcomputers. They do NOT include IBM ATs, IBM PS/2s, or computers from other manufacturers that were compatible with those IBM microcomputers.

Sources: A variety of International Data Corporation (IDC) market research studies from 1986 and 1987. Data have been disguised.

Excel (spreadsheet) were targeted at the purchasers of AT-compatibles and PS/2 computers.

Exhibit 14.6 is a forecast of the unit sales of low-end IBM machines and PC clones in selected country markets. There was considerable controversy about the potential impact of the new IBM PS/2 computers on the sales of the older models of IBM-compatible PCs. Some experts speculated that the market for the less-powerful models would decline, as customers migrated to newer easier-to-use models. Others argued that most new computer users would purchase the older less-expensive products, because in most situations the benefits of the new technology were not worth the cost. The debate heightened uncertainty about future growth of the older IBM products, PC-clones, and the software that ran on them.

Segmenting by Usage Situation

Microsoft, following most commercial market research reports, identified four major segments by customer usage of microcomputer products: business/professional, home/hobby, scientific/technical, and education.

The business/professional segment consisted of people who used microcomputers for a variety of functions in organizations. While the specialized applications depended on the industry in which a company operated, the general applications of word processing, spreadsheet, graphics, database, and communications were used in most businesses to provide automated support for office functions. Within Microsoft, the business professional market was further divided into large and small organizations. Large companies tended to have extensive data processing capabilities, more formal buying procedures for computer products, and more sophisticated requirements for computer support. Small businesses tended to have few, if any, employees with data processing expertise, a less-structured buying process, and simpler needs.

The home/hobby segment was composed of individuals and families who used a computer for practical and recreational purposes in the home. Customers in the home/hobby segment tended to buy smaller less-expensive computer systems than did those in the business professional marketplace.

The scientific/technical segment consisted of scientists and engineers who used computers for tasks that ranged from analysis of laboratory experiments to computer aided design (CAD) and computer aided engineering (CAE). Members of this segment often needed powerful, expensive computer hardware for special scientific programs. They also used word processing, spreadsheet, database, graphics, and communication software.

The education segment included students, teachers, and administrators in schools, colleges, and universities. Administrators used microcomputers for planning and fund-raising, and faculty were introducing computers into their curricula. Students used word processing, spreadsheet, and graphics for term papers, presentations, and examinations. Many customers in this segment needed simple, inexpensive computers, but some required the power and sophistication typically demanded in scientific/technical environments.

Segmenting by Customers' Depth and Clarity of Software Needs
Jeff Raikes divided the office productivity software market into "breadth customers" and "depth customers." Breadth customers were professionals or managers who did a little bit of everything and needed a combination of spreadsheet, word processing, database, graphics, and communications. They were likely to want low price and simplicity in software that supported those functions, as well as "integration," which provided the ability to move information between spreadsheets, databases, and word processing documents. Depth customers were specialists who made heavy use of at least one function, like writers using word processing or financial analysts using spreadsheets. They were likely to be less price-sensitive, more willing to learn a complex product, and driven by the need for power and sophistication to do all that they demanded.

Raikes believed that people buying low-end PC-compatibles in the future—especially first-time buyers—were likely to be breadth customers: "the kind of people who come into a store to buy a computer but aren't sure why." In his mind, Works was ideal for breadth customers, because it met a variety of needs at a relatively low price. Bill Gates agreed, calling Works "the macho integrated product for the first time user."

Segmenting by Country and Language
It was necessary to translate software into the local language to establish a significant presence in any particular country. At Microsoft, the process of creating a local-language version was called *localization*.

A major distinction existed between countries with languages based on an alphabet, like the United States or Western European countries, and those that used hieroglyphic symbols, like Japan and other Asian countries. One letter in the alphabet required a single byte of computer memory for storage purposes. However, a character in a language like Japanese Kanji required two bytes of computer memory. As a result of this difference, programs written in two-byte languages like Japanese had to be designed differently from those written in one-byte languages like English, French, and German.

Ida Cole stressed that there were differences among one-byte languages as well:

> German is 29 percent longer than English. That means it takes 29 percent more space to translate a phrase from English to German. As a result, messages in English that might fit on one line of an 80-character computer screen might be too long for the line when translated into German. That could change the way the screen looks to the users. Programs that might fit into one diskette in English might require two diskettes in German. If that happens, it requires writing a different users' manual, because German users need to insert different disks for various functions. The ripple effects can be enormous. Germany isn't alone. French is 10 percent longer than English, and there are problems in other languages, too. We in International try to get the program managers to think of these differences between languages when they first design a product so what the user sees on the screen or in the manual is essentially the same around the world.

Some at Microsoft believed that, other than translating into the native language, very little was needed for localization in various countries. Jeff Raikes asserted that "The office productivity market is pretty similar worldwide." However, many in Microsoft's International Division believed there were substantial differences between countries. Profiles of several European country-markets are summarized in Exhibit 14.7.

Differences in Hardware

Because "compatible" rarely meant "identical," the hardware sold by leading PC-clone manufacturers in various countries had implications for localization. For example, there were slight differences in the keyboard layouts to accommodate the use of non-English characters, such as tildes and accent marks. As a result, software documentation that showed a diagram of the keyboards from leading PC-clone manufacturers in France was different from the documentation for Italy, Holland, or Germany. The leading printers used in each country also varied, leading to slight differences in the set of printing programs (called printer drivers) and user manuals.

Differences in Microsoft's Competitive Position and Corporate Image

There also were differences in the relative position of competing software products in various countries. For example, in countries like Italy and Holland where Lotus 1-2-3 was the market share leader for spreadsheet software, Microsoft country managers wanted to label Works' spreadsheet columns with letters and rows with numbers, creating an "A1" reference number for the cell in the first row and column. That labeling made it easier for those familiar with 1-2-3 to use Works. However, in France and

EXHIBIT 14.7   **A Comparison of Market Conditions in Selected Country-Markets**

Comparative Criteria	France	Germany	Holland	Italy
Leading IBM-compatible hardware manufacturers, ranked roughly in descending order of 1986 unit sales of low-end PC clones	IBM Bull Goupil Olivetti	IBM Schneider/ Amstrad Olivetti Siemens	IBM Olivetti Tulip Phillips	Olivetti IBM Sperry Commodore

Estimated position of Microsoft products:
  Multiplan spreadsheet
  Microsoft Word
	
	Market leader
	Market leader
		
		Market leader
		Market leader
			
			In the top 4
			In the top 5
				
				In the top 3
				Tied for #2

Microsoft corporate advertising theme	"The software of the simple life"	"Software with a Future"	"Pioneers in Compatibility"	"Power and Simplicity Together"
Number of dealers surveyed reporting sales of Microsoft products to the following market segments:				
Public accounting	15	47	21	22
Banking	35	27	12	
Financial services	36	23	19	
Architecture	8	40	18	
Construction	38	50	14	
Engineering	29	47	20	
Medical/dental	5	44	8	
Legal	9	39	5	
Home	19	46	8	1
Other	66	52	15	4
Total number of dealers responding to the survey	71	70	32	27
How important is a low price for success of software like Works?	Somewhat important	Not very important	Very important	Very important

Sources: Information on leading hardware manufacturers is from International Data Corporation. All other information is from Microsoft internal records.

Germany, Microsoft's Multiplan was the leading spreadsheet product. Those countries wanted Works' cell in the first row and column to be labeled "R1 C1," making it easier for Multiplan users to learn Works.

Even in countries like France and Germany in which Microsoft products were market leaders, the positioning of Microsoft as a company—which might affect how customers perceived its products—was not the same. For example, in France, much had been made of the "ease of use" of Microsoft application products. French advertisements had a corporate "tag line" after the Microsoft name that roughly translated as "software for the simple life." A butterfly was displayed as the Microsoft logo in French ads.

In Germany, the Microsoft corporate tag line was "Software with a Future." According to International, the German customer was not worried about ease of learning so much as ensuring that the software would not become technologically obsolete as new generations of hardware made it possible for the software to become more powerful. Microsoft's corporate logo in Germany was a series of cartoons by the German poet Wilhelm Busch. The cartoons were quite popular in Germany but meant nothing to people in other countries who were unfamiliar with Busch's work.

Differences in the Importance of Target Market Segments

Data on the relative potential of market segments in various countries were difficult to obtain. Exhibit 14.7 contains the results of a survey of retail dealers of Microsoft software in France, Germany, Holland, and Italy. Each dealer was asked whether it sold a significant number of Microsoft office productivity products in each of 10 market segments.

Differences in Price Sensitivity

Some at Microsoft believed that there were national differences in price sensitivity. The suggested retail prices for localized versions of Microsoft products varied from 10 percent higher to 40 percent higher than the price of the U.S. version. England was the lowest, with a 10 percent increase. Holland was 15 percent higher, and Italy averaged 25 percent higher. France was 30 percent more and Germany 40 percent higher. Since Microsoft headquarters charged the same price per unit of software to each subsidiary, some speculated that the variation was due to country-by-country differences in the perceived relationship between price and quality. One European country manager explained: "In England, customers want the lowest possible price for software. They are always shopping for a bargain. In France and Germany, people look at software the way they do wine. If it doesn't cost a lot, it can't be good quality."

Others argued that the price differences arose because the channels of distribution varied by country. Price discounting of software occurred in countries that had a well-developed direct mail channel, or that had mass merchandisers (discount department stores) carrying computer software. For example, while Bruce Jacobsen was planning a recommended retail price of $195 for Works in the United States, he estimated that discounting activities due to direct mail software distributors was likely to drive the "street price" of the product to around $140. England had both a direct mail and a mass merchandiser channel, with some retailers offering computers at very low prices. International believed that the street price for Works in England might go as low as $110. In Germany, which had no direct mail distribution channel for software and a higher proportion of sales via an OEM channel to large companies, the street price was rarely more than 20 percent lower than the recommended retail price.

Other Differences among Countries

Some intercountry differences were the result of local habits and customs. For example, countries like France and Germany used the metric scale for distance, while England used feet and inches. This affected the spacing when printing text from a word processor or spreadsheet. The standard size of paper also changed from country to country. The formats for currencies and for time and date varied around the world.

National attitudes about copyright restrictions caused software copy protection to be essential in some countries to keep unauthorized pirating of software to an acceptable level. Microsoft did not use copy protection in the United States. The aggravation it caused customers and the added cost and quality problems it raised in the production process were a bigger headache than the loss of revenues from pirated copies. But some country managers demanded copy protection. One electronic mail message to Jacobsen said:

We may need a copy protection scheme applied for certain countries. We don't need it in Germany and Switzerland, and hopefully, we can talk France out of it. But Italy and South America will probably insist, as they would only sell one copy in each language otherwise.

While some cross-cultural differences required a change in the software itself, others affected the packaging and documentation. Mary Oksas, the localization manager for Works, recounted an example:

We were trying to come up with a good story line to use in the training manual for Works around the world. First the U.S. documentation team suggested a "health club" theme . . . figuring that the potential market for Works was young, affluent, and would probably be into fitness and health. That was before we told them that, in a number of European countries, dieting and health clubs have a very negative connotation. Then the U.S. team decided to go with a "stockbroker" theme, until we let them know that stock-brokers in London and in Japan don't perform exactly the same functions as their counterparts in the States. Now they are suggesting a travel agency or a pet shop theme, in hopes that attitudes about vacations and animals are pretty similar around the world. The jury's still out on that suggestion.

The trade-offs in viewing the target market segments for Works globally, rather than on a country-by-country basis, were significant. Establishing a worldwide standard product with only minor variations to accommodate national differences reduced the time required to develop localized versions of the software. In an industry where early entrants in a product category enjoyed a substantial advantage over latecomers, the benefits of reducing the localization timetable were potentially great. A global standard also reduced the cost and time needed to develop enhanced versions of a software product, which were typically rolled out every 12 to 18 months after the initial product launch.

On the other hand, if the standardized software did not meet the needs of a particular country, the product was unlikely to succeed in that market. Moreover, it generally took longer to design a global product than it did to develop a product for the U.S. market. The relentless pressure to launch a new product in the United States, either to preempt competition or to ensure availability during the heavy year-end buying season, often caused Microsoft development teams to resist requests for features that were important for global markets, but unnecessary for the United States.

Key Roles and Activities in the Development of Works

The Application Software Division
The U.S. version of Works was being developed through the cooperative efforts of Bruce Jacobsen, the product manager, responsible for marketing, Jabe Blumenthal, the program manager, responsible for product design, and Tony Cockburn, the development manager, who led the team of programmers who wrote the software. In addition, a team from User Education was responsible for developing the manuals and Computer Based Training (CBT) for Works.

The International Product Group

The International Product Group, located in Microsoft headquarters in Redmond, Washington, was responsible for creating localized versions of Works. Ida Cole maintained liaison with the country managers, provided information about Works, solicited their requests for product features, and developed the suggested international strategy for pricing, positioning, and advertising. Michel Perrin, Microsoft's international marketing manager, was responsible for coordinating the efforts of the marketing managers in the international subsidiaries, who reported directly to their respective country managers. Mary Oksas, Works' localization manager, ensured that the software, documentation, and computer based training (CBT) were translated into various languages, oversaw testing of the local language versions of the software, and designed the packaging for each country.

The International Product Group was planning to develop localized versions in seven non-English languages: French, German, Swedish, Italian, Dutch, Spanish, and Portuguese. The investment to localize Works was estimated at $84,000 per country, assuming that there were no major changes to the programs. Microsoft planned to charge the same price per unit ($68) to subsidiaries for localized versions of the product. Exhibit 14.8 is a forecast of unit sales and retail prices of Works in each country.

While the International Products Group was developing the localized versions of Works for Europe, Japan was responsible for its own localization. Technical complexities of the two-byte architecture and the unique issues in adapting products for the Japanese market led Microsoft to establish a separate group in the Japanese subsidiary to develop its own products and localize software developed in Redmond for Japan.

Country Managers in Microsoft's International Subsidiaries

Soon after his arrival at Microsoft, Bruce Jacobsen had been told by another product manager about how the international subsidiaries operated:

> The country managers are kings. They and the marketing managers who work for them exercise a lot of autonomy in most marketing decisions. For example, Microsoft Redmond typically recommends a worldwide retail selling price for a product and suggests a positioning strategy and communications theme. But the management in each subsidiary ultimately decides what price to charge, what distribution channels to use, what advertising to employ, and what market segments to attack.

When Jacobsen recounted the conversation to Ida Cole, she reminded him of the ways in which they really could have an impact:

> The country managers and their marketing managers are focused on tactical issues in their day-to-day operations. They are driven by the goals of selling existing Microsoft products. As a result, during a new product launch, they tend to rely on us to conduct market research, think about the longer-term issues, and present an overall marketing strategy. They won't go along with everything we suggest . . . . They'll use it as a starting point, and tell us the things that don't make sense based on the realities of their local markets.

EXHIBIT 14.8 **Forecast Monthly Sales of Works' English and Localized Versions**

Country	Forecast of Monthly Unit Sales of PC Works' English Version (1)	Forecast of Monthly Unit Sales of PC Works' Localized Version (1)	Forecast Suggested Retail Price Per Unit of Localized Version (2)
U.S.A.	6,000	0	$195
England	1,000	0	$215
Canada	500	0	$215
Australia/New Zealand	380	0	$215
France	0	650	$254
West Germany	200	500	$273
Italy	50	160	$244
Netherlands	80	200	$224
Portugal	25	80	$220
Sweden	100	200	$234
Spain	50	200	$234
	8,385	1,990	

Notes: For planning purposes, it was assumed that Microsoft subsidiaries' selling prices to the channels of distribution would be approximately 50 percent of the suggested retail prices in their respective countries.

Localized versions for the subsidiaries were manufactured in Ireland and sold to all subsidiaries for 35 percent of the U.S. suggested retail price.

Import tariffs were not considered in this analysis.

Sources: (1) Preliminary forecasts by country managers of Microsoft's international subsidiaries made in June 1987.
(2) Estimates by Microsoft International Product Support Group based on past experience with other products.

The Debate over the Design of Works

Microsoft planned to develop the U.S. version of Works, incorporating as many of the features required for other countries as possible, given limited programmer availability and project deadlines. The U.S. version would be launched in mid-September. One month later, after minor changes, the International English version would be released. That version was the baseline product that would be translated into different languages.

Microsoft had received requests from country managers for two additional features in Works. First, France and Germany wanted a software "toggle switch" that would let the customer choose whether Works' cell references appeared as "A1," like Lotus 1-2-3, or as "R1 C1," like Multiplan. This feature would let a customer decide whether he wanted the spreadsheet in Works to "look like" either Lotus 1-2-3 (A1) or Multiplan (R1 C1). That way, a person who used Lotus at the office and was buying a home computer could make Works look like 1-2-3, greatly reducing the time required to learn Works. A person who had used Multiplan at the office could choose to make Works spreadsheet look like Multiplan, thereby minimizing learning time. In the United States, where 1-2-3 had a dominant market share position and very few customers had seen Multiplan, Microsoft planned to make Works look like Lotus 1-2-3 (A1 format), and the toggle switch feature was not important. In Europe, where both Multiplan and 1-2-3 were widely used, the toggle switch might have particular value to customers.

Second, country managers had asked that additional programs be so written that Works files could be converted to the Multiplan file format. Conversion programs allowed the exchange of information between Works and other spreadsheet products. If a person made a spreadsheet using Multiplan at the office and wanted to bring it home to continue working on evenings or weekends, she could convert it to use on Works and then back again. Conversion programs also allowed a person with Works to share data with colleagues using Multiplan. Works originally was designed only to allow data exchange with Lotus 1-2-3. Like the toggle switch option, file conversion programs might be particularly useful in some European countries due to the widespread use of Multiplan.

If Microsoft incorporated the two changes in the U.S. version, the introduction of Works in the United States would be delayed by two months. The additional time was needed to develop documentation and CBT showing both the A1 and R1 C1 displays, and to write several new programs. It would still take one month to go from the U.S. to the International English version.

If the programmers developed the U.S. version without the two requested changes and then tried to add the features to the International version, a major redesign would be required. Substantial portions of the programs for the U.S. version would have to be rewritten, and the elapsed time required for the International version would increase from one month to five months.

Several country managers had informed Ida Cole that, without the toggle switch and conversion programs, Works was unlikely to be successful in its markets. They were also concerned that, without the changes, Works might even undermine the market position of Multiplan by promoting the Lotus 1-2-3 user interface and file formats.

However, Jabe Blumenthal argued strongly against changing the design because of the adverse effects of missing the target U.S. launch date. The introduction of Works was set for mid-September, which allowed retailers just enough time to order the product and train their people how to sell it before the end of October. That timetable was critical because November and December were a period of heavy buying activity for computer products, as the home market made purchases for Christmas and some businesses bought at the end of the year for tax reasons. Retailers were likely to resist or ignore a new product launch in the midst of their busiest season. Missing the September launch date also would increase the risk that Software Publishing's First Choice or a new product from Borland might establish a leadership position in the segment targeted for Works.

The labor and direct overhead cost of keeping the development team on Works was $50,000 per month. However, there was also an opportunity cost. A month spent on Works was a month that was unavailable for other software products, and programmers were in critically short supply. Assessing the impact of the decision on future sales was difficult, since unit sales forecasts for the United States were based on a September 15 launch date, and for the other countries assuming that Microsoft would make the two modifications.

Works' Positioning

Jacobsen was planning to position Works as an easy-to-learn, easy-to-sell, integrated solution to the productivity needs of "breadth users" in homes and small businesses who were buying their first computer. Tentative advertising plans were to use a Swiss Army knife as an internationally recognizable symbol of an easy-to use tool with multiple functions.

Microsoft had a family of application software designed to meet the needs of "depth users" and "breadth users" on IBM compatible computers and on the Apple Macintosh. Exhibit 14.9 identifies a few of those products. One of the challenges in positioning Works was to distinguish it from the other Microsoft products, thereby minimizing customer confusion and the risk that Works might cannibalize sales of other software.

In discussing Jacobsen's positioning, Ida Cole pointed out the concerns of several country managers. First, throughout most of the world, the home and small business market for IBM compatible machines were much smaller than in the United States, making his positioning difficult to execute on a global basis. Second, in European countries where Multiplan and Word were market leaders, the financial risk of cannibalization was greater than in the United States.

Plans for the Launch

Jacobsen was developing the details for an introductory U.S. marketing communications campaign with a price tag of $2.8 million and a target launch date of September 15. With a suggested list price of $195, trade margins averaging 50 percent of retail selling price and cost of goods just over $18, Microsoft's unit contribution for Works was approximately $79. Jacobsen was confident that the projected U.S. volume of 6,000 units a month would more than offset the costs of the introductory campaign.

Conclusion

As they continued working on the presentation, Jacobsen silently wondered how he should respond to country managers' suggestions about design changes to make Works more attractive for their local markets. He saw merit in both Blumenthal's and the country managers' arguments and knew he needed to formulate a position on that topic for the meeting. In addition, there might well be other requests for design modifications, and he and Ida Cole needed to develop an approach for handling them if they arose.

Jacobsen also pondered how, if at all, he could modify his product positioning for Works to make it more effective as the foundation for communications strategy for the product around the world.

Cole interrupted his reverie: "Earth to Bruce—let's put together a slide or two with our major recommendations and then brainstorm about the reactions we're likely to get from the country managers."

EXHIBIT 14.9   **Selected Products in the Microsoft Family of Software**

Product Name	Description	U.S. recommended retail selling price of the product on the		
		Apple Macintosh	IBM PC/XT/AT and Compatibles	IBM PS/2 and Compatibles
Products for depth users				
Multiplan	Sophisticated spreadsheet for quantitative analysis. Graphics available as a separate product. Key competitor: Lotus 1-2-3	$295	$195	N/A
Word	Sophisticated word processor Key competitor: Word Perfect	$395	$450	$450
Excel	New and very advanced product for spreadsheet, graphics, and data management Key competitor: Lotus 1-2-3	$395	$395 (only on IBM ATs and compatibles)	$395 (launch was planned for one month after Works')
Products for breadth users				
Works	Integrated, easy-to-use product for: —Spreadsheet —Word processing —Graphics —Data management —Communications. Key competitor: Software Publishing's First Choice	$295	$195	$195

Brand Pipe Company

Mr. Alan Buford, manager of the Brand Pipe Company, a division of the Arnol Corporation, was considering a directive he had just received from top management of the parent organization. He was told by Arnol management that he was to come up with a specific marketing strategy and plan to stop the losses of the division as soon as possible and to provide a base for continued growth in the future.

Company Background

Brand Pipe, located in the Puget Sound area of the state of Washington, was a plastic extruder serving the Pacific Northwest. The company began operations in the early 1950s and subsequently was acquired by Arnol Corporation, a large company in an unrelated field. Company sales were $1.8 million, making it the second-largest extruder in the Pacific Northwest. Profits however, had declined, and the company had operated at a loss for the past year and a half.

    The management staff at Brand Pipe consisted of Mr. Buford, who acted as both general manager and sales manager; Mr. George Timkin, the plant manager; Mr. Alan Britt, the plant engineer; and a plant foreman.

Industry Background

Thermoplastic pipe was made from four types of plastic resins: polyvinyl chloride (PVC), rubber-modified styrene (styrene), acrylonitrile butadiene styrene (ABS), and polyethylene (poly). The resins differ in chemical and physical characteristics, such as

Source: This case is produced with the permission of Dr. Stuart U. Rich, Professor of Marketing, and Director Emeritus, Forest Industries Management Center, College of Business Administration, University of Oregon, Eugene, Oregon.

resistance to acids and bases, strength, melting point, and ease of extrusion. These plastic resins were bought from the large national petrochemical suppliers.

Plastic pipe competed with iron, aluminum, and asbestos-cement pipe in the Northwest market. In comparison with the other materials, plastic pipe was considered superior in terms of cost, ease of installation and maintenance, and deterioration from environmental influences. Plastic pipe was considered inferior to the other materials in terms of crushability, strength, and melting temperature. Plastic pipe could not be extruded in sizes greater than ten inches in diameter and also had a high degree of thermal expansion that restricted its use in some applications.

A machine called an extruder was used to form plastic pipe by heating the resin to near its melting point, forcing the fluid mass through a die, and then cooling the formed pipe in a water bath. A relatively unsophisticated plant to manufacture plastic pipe could be built for approximately $150,000. In fact, one of the successful competitors in the ABS market in the Northwest, the PJ&J Company, had what was called a "backyard operation" and operated out of a converted garage.

The different resins could all be satisfactorily extruded on the same machine, with the possible exception of PVC, which required a stainless steel die instead of the usual mild steel die. All that is required to change resin type is to change the resin fed into the machine. A die change to make different-sized pipe is even simpler. The extruder can be left hot and the pressure relieved so that the die can be changed.

Brand Pipe Company Extruded Pipe

All four thermoplastic resins were being converted by Brand Pipe into plastic pipe ranging from one-half inch to eight inches in diameter. The final product has pressure ratings from 80 psi (pounds per square inch) to 600 psi. The company's pipe was of standard quality and was comparable to that produced by competing pipe extruders.

Brand Pipe Company had just completed capital expenditures for new resin-blending and pipe-extrusion equipment that executives described as "the most technically advanced in the industry." The company had a plant investment of over $2 million. In view of Brand Pipe's unprofitable operating performance, it was considered doubtful that the Arnol Corporation would agree to additional capital expenditure appropriations. Brand Pipe owned and operated four modern pipe-extruding machines as well as three older machines. Despite the modern production setup, a production problem arose from the firm's inability to maintain adequate control over pipe-wall thickness. Pipe production used 7 percent more resin material than was theoretically required to ensure a minimum pipe-wall thickness. The plant engineer was in charge of quality control, but, because of substantial workload, he had spent little time on the costly material waste problem.

Since corporate management imposed tight limits on finished goods inventories, Brand Pipe had aimed at minimizing inventories. Rush orders, which frequently could not be filled from inventory, necessitated daily extrusion machine changeovers. However, a relative cost study conducted by the plant engineer showed that Brand Pipe could conceivably hold a much larger finished goods inventory and still not reach the point where costs of holding inventory would exceed machine changeover costs.

Brand Pipe averaged seven machine changeovers per day, at an average loss to contribution to fixed overhead of $25 per changeover.

Plastic Pipe Market Segments

Brand Pipe Company produced some 200 separate pipe products of varying sizes and resin types to supply 11 market segments. Mr. Buford felt that, in order to use plant capacity to the utmost, Brand Pipe had to reach all of these end-use segments. Brand Pipe's sales volume was highest in water transportation markets for PVC and styrene pipe. The company's total pipe production by resin type (in pounds) was as follows:

Poly	450,000
PVC	3,871,000
ABS	769,000
Styrene	1,032,000
Total	6,122,000

Arnol Corporation market researchers had concluded that demand for plastic pipe would increase during the next five years in all market segments in the states served by Brand Pipe—that is, in Oregon, Washington, Idaho, and northern California. A summary analysis of each market segment follows, including current consumption estimates and five-year growth projections for Washington alone and for the four-state region including Washington.

Agricultural Irrigation

The agricultural irrigation segment was the largest-volume plastic pipe market in the Pacific Northwest. Plastic pipe, however, accounted for only 11 percent of all pipe used for agricultural irrigation. Newly developed plastic component systems, particularly plastic-component sprinkler irrigation systems, were replacing many open-ditch and metal pipe water transportation systems. Arnol market researchers, in describing growth potential for this plastic pipe market, stated that the "pendulum is swinging from metal to plastic pipe as the primary water transportation method." PVC resin pipe was used almost exclusively to supply this segment. Total plastic pipe consumption in Washington was 8.25 million pounds. Total for the four-state market area (Washington, Oregon, Idaho, and northern California) was 16.5 million pounds. Estimated growth for the next five years for Washington, as well as for the whole region, was 17 percent.[1]

Private Potable Water System Market

Building codes continued to favor copper and aluminum and to exclude plastic pipe from use for home water-supply systems. Although public utilities were utilizing PVC plastic pipe for public water systems, plumbing contractors shied away from using polyethylene pipe in private systems. Total plastic pipe consumption for Washington

---

[1] Growth figures are for the five-year period. They are *not* annual growth rates. Therefore, a five-year growth figure of 61 percent is equivalent to a 10 percent average annual growth rate.

was 145,000 pounds. For the Northwest region it was 350,000 pounds. No growth was forecast for the next five years.

Mobile Home Market

Most ABS plastic pipe sold to the mobile home market segment was used in plumbing fixtures. Most mobile home manufacturers sought to buy plastic fixtures on a national contract basis. It was a rare occasion when one of these national concerns purchased pipe from a local or regional extruder. Washington plastic pipe consumption was 130,000 pounds; regional consumption was 1.4 million pounds. A 90 percent growth figure was forecast for Washington, and 75 percent for the region.

Public Potable Water

Some public water utilities were using PVC plastic pipe for water service lines that connect households to main water distribution lines. Styrene pipe had given way in recent years to the stronger, less brittle, more inert PVC pipe. Washington consumption was slightly over 2 million pounds, and regional consumption over 5 million pounds. A 100 percent growth figure was projected for both the state and the region.

Industrial Market

Plastic pipe applications in processing, material supply, transfer, and waste disposal were severely limited in the industrial market segment. According to Mr. Buford, this was due to thermoplastic pipe's sensitivity to steam, sparks, and hot fluids. The most prominent industrial application was in copper mining, with minor applications in pulp and paper manufacturing, food processing, and seawater transfer. Total consumption in Washington was 600,000 pounds; for the region, slightly over 1 million pounds. Growth was projected at 45 percent for both the state and the region.

Turf Irrigation Market

Turf irrigation included applications such as public and private lawn-watering systems. Small-diameter PVC pipe was generally used by this market segment. Consumption in Washington was 3 million pounds; in the region it was 5.9 million. The projected five-year growth was 66 percent for Washington and 57 percent for the region.

Drain Waste and Vent Market

The drain waste and vent market was defined as all plumbing pipe running from and venting sinks, toilets, and drains to the structure drain. ABS pipe accounted for 86–90 percent of the market, with the remaining amount held by PVC. Plumbing unions had opposed the use of plastic pipe in favor of traditional materials, apparently because of the easy installation of plastic pipe with its resultant labor savings. Yet the unions claimed the traditional steel and iron pipes were superior. Consumption in Washington was slightly over 1 million pounds; regional consumption was 1.75 million pounds. Washington growth was projected at 27 percent; regional growth at 35 percent.

Conduit

Electric conduit was used primarily to protect and insulate electric power lines and telephone lines, both underground and in buildings. Competitive materials included the traditional aluminum metals. Major users in this market were large contractors and utilities that bought on a competitive bidding system. Consumption in Washington was 465,000 pounds; regional consumption was 1 million pounds. A 75 percent growth figure was projected for Washington, and 50 percent growth was forecast for the region.

Sewer and Outside Drain

The sewer and outside drain market segment used plastic pipe for connections from house to septic tanks and sewer systems, downspout drainage, water drainage, and septic tank drainage. The primary resins used were styrene and PVC. The major competitive materials were asbestos fibers, cast iron, and vitrified clay; however, they were generally competitive only in the large sizes used in a public sewer system. The FHA had recently approved plastic pipe for rural homes. Washington consumption was 1.4 million pounds, and regional consumption was 2.8 million pounds. A 90 percent growth figure was forecast for Washington, and 78 percent growth was predicted for the region.

Gas Transportation Market

In the gas transportation segment, plastic pipe was used to distribute low-pressure natural gas from major terminals through distribution mains to residences, businesses, and industrial users. Gas companies, which bought the pipe in large lots or on a yearly basis, had tested the plastic pipe and were not entirely pleased with the results. They favored the traditional steel pipe and the new epoxy-coated steel pipe that combined the inherent advantages of both plastic and steel. Washington consumption was 123,000 pounds; regional consumption, 300,000 pounds. Growth projection was marginal.

Water Well Service and Stock Water

Plastic pipe was used in rural areas to bring water from the individual farm wells into the home and to distribute it to outlying farm buildings to water livestock. The primary resins used were PVC and polyethylene. Washington consumption was 400,000 pounds, and regional consumption was 900,000 pounds. Relatively little growth was projected.

The four types of plastic pipe varied in their adaptability to use in the various markets just described. Adaptability depended on the physical attributes of the resin type as well as cost advantages needed for low-grade applications. PVC was the most versatile and was used in all market segments. Poly was suitable for use in all markets except sewer and outside drain, mobile homes, and drain waste and vent. ABS was adaptable for use in six of the eleven markets: public potable water, private potable water, turf irrigation, mobile homes, drain waste and vent, and gas transportation. Styrene was used for the most part in sewer and outside drain, drain waste and vent, and conduit markets.

Promotion and Sales

Brand Pipe used a limited amount of advertising in promoting its plastic pipe, preferring to rely on personal selling as its main promotional device. In the past the company had advertised in trade journals and in agriculturally oriented magazines such as *Pacific Farmer*. It also sponsored early-morning farm radio programs on local stations, and utilized the usual product information folders and catalogs.

Recently Brand Pipe had used a mailer soliciting inquiries on a "spike sprinkler" coupling for irrigation. The spike sprinkler was a device to position a sprinkler in the field, and it was considered a superior pipe coupling. The company had contracted for exclusive distribution of the coupling to be used with its pipe, but did not itself produce the device. Brand Pipe had mailed 1,000 of the product folders and had received 200 inquiries. Mr. Buford was enthusiastic about the response and planned to increase mailer promotion in the future.

The company salespeople were assigned by geographic area, and they called on pipe distributors and large end users in each area. They were responsible for sales of all company products in their respective areas. The three main sales areas were the Seattle–Puget Sound area, the Portland and eastern Oregon–eastern Washington area, and the southern Oregon–northern California area. Each of these areas was covered by one salesperson. In addition, Mr. Buford had a number of working contracts and made visits to major accounts. This was relatively simple because most of the major distributors were located within short distances of the division office.

In addition to the field salesperson, there was one in-house salesperson who handled small "drop-in" business, short-notice orders, and customers requiring a quote on an order of pipe. Often, a distributor would phone in an order, asking for a price quote and delivery at the end user's site the next day. If the company was not capable of meeting a price and delivery schedule, the customer would take that business elsewhere. The company tried its best to provide service on these accounts so that it could maintain plant capacity, even if it meant machine changeovers to produce the order.

Since the salespeople were assigned one to an area, they were responsible for missionary, maintenance, and service selling. They were compensated, according to corporate policy, by straight salary with no commissions paid for different product sales. They called on distributors and large end users and were expected to educate distributors on product knowledge and use and to handle field complaints. Often these complaints emanated from a do-it-yourself end user who had not followed the directions for joining pipe sections together correctly. At times the salespeople tried to stimulate sales by going to the end user and providing technical service such as product specification and pipe-system design.

Distribution

Brand Pipe sold the majority of its plastic pipe through distributors, with 20 percent of the accounts contributing 75 percent of gross revenue. Only in the case of large end users such as utilities and major contractors did the company try to sell directly. In such cases, the company paid the regular commission to the area distributor only if the distributor managed to learn of the sale and the distributor was of some importance to the company. Marketing terms were 2/10 net 30.

Pipe distributors, who were paid a commission of 5 to 10 percent of sales, performed several major functions: (1) they broke bulk and sold to many retailers in their area; (2) they used the pipe along with many other components in the piping systems that they installed, such as agricultural irrigation systems, plumbing systems, and turf irrigation systems; and (3) they provided financing and inventory service for their customers. Distributors held preparatory inventory in seasonal markets such as agricultural irrigation. In preparation for the seasonal demand, Brand Pipe would deposit "dated" shipments at the distributor's warehouse.

Pipe distributors in most market segments considered price to be the most important factor determining from whom they bought pipe. Most distributors agreed that one pipe was as good as another; they considered delivery service to be the next most important factor. They did not feel that technical service offered by the manufacturer was very important in their choice of suppliers. In fact, some distributors were very ambivalent about the usefulness of manufacturers' salespeople. They did not feel that technical service by the manufacturer was very important in the sale of pipe. Some felt that the best thing salespeople could do was stay out of the field. They disliked pipe salespeople's "muddying the water" at the end-user level and making promises to the end user that the distributor was unable or unwilling to fulfill. Other distributors, however, felt that pipe salespeople could and did help by providing product knowledge to the distributor salespeople. Under no circumstances did any of the distributors favor having pipe salespeople contact the end user.

Distributors generally viewed the price competition within the industry with disfavor. One reason was the lowered profit margin on sales of the pipe. Since distributors usually made a fixed percentage on sales, their income was reduced by lowered prices. Another reason was the distributors' concern that when they were making a bid on a system including plastic pipe, their competitors might get a more favorable quote on plastic pipe and therefore be able to quote a lower bid. The distributors wanted plastic pipe prices stabilized so that their bids could be based on their own competence and economic situation rather than on the pricing practices of the pipe manufacturers.

Although distributors disliked price competition, they were glad to see that Brand Pipe and other producers had lowered the price to the point where imported pipe was not a major source of market supply. Many were reluctant to handle shipload quantities of imported pipe with its resultant inventory and handling problems. They much preferred a convenient source of supply, which the local producers could provide.

Although some distributors had considered making their own plastic pipe, they did not at the time consider such production attractive. For the time being, they were content to buy pipe from suppliers. Brand Pipe had been a factor in this decision by improving service and by lowering prices.

In view of the continuing poor profit situation of his division, Mr. Buford had considered trying to integrate forward and capture the distributors' margin. One of the salespeople had felt that Brand Pipe salespeople could do as good a job selling plastic pipe to end users as the distributors did.

Transportation

Approximately 75 percent of Brand Pipe's annual volume was shipped via common carrier, with the remaining 25 percent being delivered by company-leased trucks or through factory "will-call" by customers. Because of competitors' practices, in most cases either Brand Pipe's shipments were prepaid to Northwest destinations or comparable freight allowances were made from gross sales price when pipe orders were picked up at the plant by customers. Because plastic pipe was so bulky, shipping costs averaged about 15 percent of the selling price. This meant that each competitor had a substantial advantage in selling in its own home market.

Pricing Policy

Mr. Buford looked over the profit summary report (see Exhibit 15.1) and wondered whether changes in the present pricing policy might lead to improvements in the profit picture of his division. The present policy of "meeting or beating the price offered by any other supplier" had been initiated earlier when the Japanese began exporting large quantities of plastic pipe to the Pacific Northwest. Because of lower raw material costs and a suspected dumping policy, they were pricing their products below those of local suppliers. Even though there were disadvantages in the sales agreements offered by the Japanese (such as order sizes of shipload quantities only), the Japanese were able to capture a significant portion of the market due to their low price.

The effects of the Japanese entry into the Pacific Northwest market were immediately felt by Brand Pipe, since the Japanese were marketing PVC—the major resin type produced by Brand Pipe. At that time, Mr. Buford reasoned that the size of the Pacific Northwest market could not accommodate another supplier of plastic pipe. He felt that steps must be taken immediately to drive the Japanese out of the Pacific Northwest.

To achieve this goal, Brand Pipe adopted its present pricing policy, thus forcing the Japanese to compete on terms other than price, such as speed of delivery, where the Japanese were at a strict disadvantage. Soon after this, other suppliers followed suit. The average price levels gradually eroded from $0.28 per pound down to $0.26 per pound. With the decreased price, the Japanese left the Pacific Northwest market, and Mr. Buford felt that they would not reenter it until the price came back to $0.28 per pound.

Recently, the Sierra Plastic Pipe plant had burned to the ground. This company had been the major supplier for southern Oregon and northern California. A number of the other suppliers including Brand Pipe increased their plant capacity in anticipation of taking over the accounts that they were sure Sierra would lose. To prevent the loss of its accounts, Sierra bought plastic pipe on the open market and was thus able to maintain its customers while its plant was being rebuilt. Because Sierra was able to remain in business, and because the growth of the Pacific Northwest market was not up to expectations, a considerable overcapacity on the part of all suppliers soon developed in the Pacific Northwest. This overcapacity was estimated at 30–40 percent, but some suppliers were continuing expansion.

EXHIBIT 15.1   **Profit Summary Report, per-Pound Basis**

	Poly	PVC	ABS	Styrene
Gross sales price	0.3625	0.2760	0.3648	0.2762
Less discounts, freight, and allowances	0.0710	0.0138	0.0378	0.0377
Net sales price	0.2915	0.2622	0.3270	0.2385
Less variable costs (raw materials and conversion)[a]	0.3050	0.2230	0.3392	0.2110
Direct margin (contribution to fixed costs)	−0.0135	0.0392	−0.0122	0.0275
Less fixed costs	0.0397	0.0375	0.0501	0.0314
Profit	−0.0532	0.0017	−0.0623	−0.0039

[a] *Case author's note:* For analysis purposes, treat conversion as *changeover costs* only. Other labor costs are included in the fixed cost figure.

Because of the overcapacity and the desire on the part of executives to maintain market share, Brand Pipe had continued its present pricing policy. It was reasoned by Mr. Buford that a reduction in price would increase market share, which would increase production and narrow the gap between plant capacity and the production level, thus minimizing fixed cost per unit.

In evaluating the present pricing policy, Mr. Buford came to two conclusions. First, the profit picture for his division was most likely quite similar to that of the other regional suppliers. Second, although the distributors enjoyed the low price that was resulting from the fierce price competition, they were unhappy with the volatility of the price levels that was also generated.

Competition

Domestic competition in Brand Pipe's marketing area came from six regional manufacturers and five to eight major national producers. The number of national producers varied because some of them moved in and out of the Northwest market, depending on economic conditions. The regional manufacturers had about 75 percent of the market, while the larger national firms and a few import firms controlled the rest. Three of the regional firms controlled 60 percent of the Northwest market. Sierra Plastics was a leader, although Brand Pipe and Tamarack Pipe closely followed. The three companies produced essentially the same products.

Tamarack Pipe was within 50 miles of Brand Pipe's plant and was a strong competitor in the Portland, Oregon, market and the Puget Sound market. Due to its location in southern Oregon, Sierra Plastics had a strong competitive position in the southern Oregon–northern California market, resulting from its lower transportation cost in this area compared with those of Brand Pipe and Tamarack.

Brand Pipe had tried to differentiate its product in the past, but had met with limited success. In an attempt at differentiation, Brand Pipe had changed the color of its PVC pipe from gray to white. Other competitors, especially the nationals, had made some progress in differentiating their products. Babbitt Corporation, a national supplier of pipe and piping systems to industry, had added plastic pipe to its product line and advertised in such national periodicals as *Chemical Engineering*. Babbitt was very strong in the industrial segment of the market. Cable Company had distinguished its pipe by application to sump pump installations and had a virtual monopoly in this specialized application. PJ&J in northern California was the chief supplier of ABS pipe in the Pacific Northwest, primarily through being the least expensive marketer. For example, Brand Pipe was able to buy PJ&J pipe and resell it for less than it would cost to produce comparable pipe.

In recent months, Brand Pipe salespeople had reported that Tamarack had begun to concentrate more on the agricultural irrigation market, while Sierra was concentrating on being the primary supplier of plastic pipe for conduit. Even though this latter market was small, it was anticipated to mushroom when the housing market resumed its growth. The large national firms had concentrated on the mobile home industry and appeared to have the greatest number of manufacturers, since contracts were negotiated on a countrywide basis.

The large national manufacturers were either owned by or affiliated with national petrochemical companies. These companies usually adjusted to the prevailing market conditions and were a stabilizing influence on the market.

The competitive conditions that had prevailed in the Northwest had depressed the financial conditions of some of the smaller independent firms, and it was not known how much longer they would continue operations. The larger independent firms, although experiencing losses, were as well financed as Brand Pipe and were still battling for increased market share.

Conclusion

Mr. Buford realized that a number of changes were needed in many parts of his company's marketing program. He saw that some of these changes were interrelated; for example, decisions on pricing strategy might have an important impact on product policy, and vice versa. Certain decisions had to be made very soon if the company's profit position were to be improved, whereas other decisions could be postponed for a while.

Mr. Buford felt that his planning task was made more difficult by the limited size of the management staff in his division. Although the parent corporation provided help in market research and some coaching in general planning procedures, the actual planning and strategy determination was Mr. Buford's responsibility. Because of the need to keep division overhead expenses down to a minimum, Mr. Buford knew that no additional management staff could be hired at the present time.

As he walked into his office, pondering what to do first in the way of planning, his phone rang and the in-house salesperson asked him to okay a price quote on a drop shipment for the next day. Mr. Buford okayed the quote, and then sat down muttering, "How can I find time to plan for the months and years ahead when daily operating problems demand so much of my time?"

Lectron Corporation

The Lectron Corporation was founded in the early 1970s by William Patton to develop new electrical products for industrial and commercial markets. Prior to founding Lectron, Mr. Patton was executive vice president of a leading electrical products manufacturing company and had 20 years' successful experience in the industry.

After two years of extensive research and development at a cost of approximately $300,000, the Lectron control was developed. Although the product was being marketed primarily as a motor control, the general design of this unit is suitable for many electrical switching applications, including temperature controls, lighting controls, and as a motor control. During the development stage, sales were minimal and usually to selected industries for special applications which served to prove the product under normal operating conditions.

Recently Mr. Patton has shifted his emphasis from development and field testing to consideration of how best to market the product with limited funds. The product, by all estimates, fits a market need, is technically sound and priced competitively, and has superior performance characteristics, yet it is far from reaching its full market potential, estimated to be in the millions of dollars. As a result, a great deal of planning is being done to identify the type of marketing program that would lead to increased sales growth and the "take off" stage in the product life cycle.

Product

The Lectron motor control was a completely solid-state device: that is, it was totally electronic and had no mechanical moving parts. Its design was well tested and used only top quality components, such as those manufactured by RCA and Westinghouse.

This case was prepared by Professor David McConaughy of the University of Southern California. Reprinted by permission.

It met appropriate National Electrical Manufacturers Association standards and was the first such device approved for switching applications by Underwriter's Laboratory, a safety and circuit certification company. Underwriter's approvals are accepted and often required by state and industry safety departments and insurance companies.

The primary function of the Lectron control was to provide a "soft start," that is, to reduce the heavy current inrush and starting torque of an electric motor. By avoiding the high initial current flow and torque, the following benefits occurred:

1. Reduced starting power requirements.
2. Reduced line voltage drop during motor starts.
3. Reduced possibility of damage to the motor and equipment that it drives.
4. Reduced thermal and electrical stress on motor and electrical circuits.

The Lectron control was more trouble-free, provided smoother operation, was quieter, operated in a wider range of environments, and was less expensive than alternative "soft-start" equipment. Because of its solid-state design, the Lectron control did not cause the electromagnetic interference that was common with mechanical types of switching, and thus it reduced "electromagnetic pollution," which was of growing concern to the FCC. Exhibits 16.1 and 16.2 show the product and an example of the relevant data and benefits. Exhibit 16.3 gives the background of a highly successful application on a Coast Guard cutter which created a great deal of interest in the marine industry and received widespread publicity in new product and new application sections of trade publications.

Competition

At the time, there was no direct competition, and the Lectron control was the only effective solid-state product on the market. This probably will change, as many solid-state control circuits were being developed and published by component manufacturers and the Institute of Electrical Engineers. However, Mr. Patton does hold several comprehensive patents on the Lectron circuit. Electromechanical starters that provided a similar function produced by GE, Westinghouse, Allen-Bradley, and other firms were, of course, competition because they were an accepted method of "soft-start" control. Of these, the principal control being used was the auto-transformer. While this device limited initial power surge, it made a jerky shift to each power level as the current was increased. This jerky movement had a high burn-out risk compared to the Lectron control, which was smooth throughout the entire starting cycle. Other "soft-start" controls were the part winding starter, which may require a specially designed (thus costly) motor, and the primary resistor starter, which mechanically switched an electrical resistor bank in series with the motor as it was started. Exhibit 16.4 gives a brief comparison among the costs and features of the various starting devices. Exhibit 16.10 describes these different devices.

EXHIBIT 16.1   **The Lectron Control**

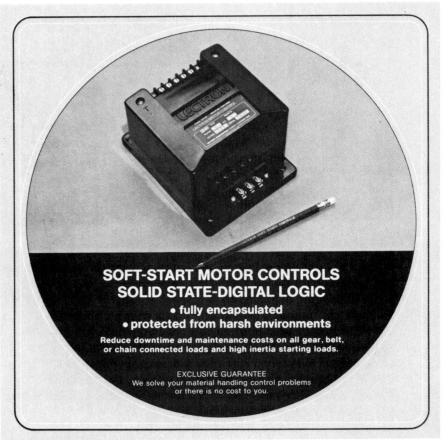

Market Potential

The exact market potential for Lectron control was unknown because it could be used in a large number of industrial equipment and electrical control applications. The total market for motor and related controls of all types was in excess of $1 billion a year with the relevant control market perhaps as large as $800 million a year.

EXHIBIT 16.2 **The Lectron Control: Features and Applications**

Lectron Soft-Start Controls

General Description:

Lectron soft-start controls are general-purpose devices for remote, automatic, or manual starting of three phase squirrel cage induction motors.

Starting characteristics, both torque and acceleration, are readily adjustable by access to simple adjustment screws through the top of the control module.

Switching options include low voltage, three wire momentary start/stop, 110 low voltage on/off or by contactor for reversing or dual speed operation.

The low voltage digital logic design, encompassing state of the art technology, insures perfect balance, reliability, long life, and easy interface with other control systems.

Applications:

☐ Conveyor lines, both high-speed and heavy duty.
☐ Bridge cranes and monorail systems.
☐ Stackers, balancers, unloaders, etc.
☐ Centrifugal blowers and pumps.
☐ Other high-inertia starting loads.
☐ Any belt, gear, or chain connected load.

Features:

Adjustable starting torque—limits inrush and mechanical shock.
☐ Adjustable rate of acceleration—1 to 30 seconds— standard (other by request).
☐ Noiseless, maintenance-free operation.
Fully encapsulated affected by difficult environmental conditions.
Eliminates switching transients common to electromechanical devices—the prime cause of motor failure.
Smooth, stepless transition from start to full-on.
☐ Compact size—lightweight.
☐ Guaranteed performance.

EXHIBIT 16.3   **Case History: Solid State, Reduced Voltage Motor Controls Give the Coast Guard a Low-Cost Cure for Electronic Failure**

Environment:

Coast Guard Cutter Point Carrew, operating out of the Eleventh Coast Guard District

Problem:

The addition of electrical and electronic equipment on ocean-going vessels, generally, and small craft, particularly, has taxed the generator and distribution system beyond its capacity to supply constant voltage. The condition becomes critical on start up of three-phase induction motors.

The voltage drop on normal starting of a three-horsepower motor reduced line voltage below the tolerance of electronic equipment such as radar, thus creating a potential hazard and, at best, an interruption in communications.

Test Duration:

Device installed June 14, 1972, and still operating as of this date, November 24, 1972.

Solution:

Repeated tests using the Lectron motor control showed no visible effect on the radar performance. There was no detectable radio interference on AM and FM receivers. The test installation was considered 100 percent satisfactory and seems an attractive cure for electronic failure caused by voltage fluctuations that exist on many cutters and boats. It appears more cost-effective than the alternatives of individual voltage regulators and rewiring to provide a separate, quiet ship's distribution system.

Comparative Cost:

	Autotransformer Reduced Voltage Starter	Lectron Solid-State Control
Material Cost (Note)	$1,100	$265
Installation Cost	$100 (est)	$20
Weight	80 lbs (est)	3.5 lbs
Volume	7060 cu in.	64 cu in.
Moving Parts	17	0

Note: The Autotransformer consisted of a total replacement of existing controls, whereas, the Lectron device was a retrofit unit installed within and compatible with the existing system.

Comparative Performance:

	Before Installation	After Installation
Bus Volts (steady state)	450 Volts	450 Volts
Bus Volts—max drop	20 Volts	5 Volts
Current Starting Surge	28 Amps	8 Amps
Current—Steady State	4.3 Amps	4.3 Amps

The material contained herein was furnished by the United States Coast Guard, Eleventh Coast Guard District. It should not be considered as Coast Guard approval nor a recommendation of the Lectron Solid State Motor Control.

EXHIBIT 16.4   **Comparison among Features and Prices for Selected 10-Horsepower Motor Starters**

Type of Control	Type of Start	Size	Weight	List Price	Comments
Magnetic starter	On-Off Only	12″ × 7″ × 6″	15 pounds	$ 162	Switches full power only.
Primary resistor	Stepped-Smooth	29″ × 18″ × 10″	120 pounds	$ 839	Low efficiency.
Autotransformer	Stepped-Smooth	35″ × 24″ × 12″	450 pounds	$1,139	Most widely used reduced voltage starter.
Part winding	Stepped-Smooth	21″ × 14″ × 7″	100 pounds	$ 448	Requires special motor with winding taps.
Star-Delta	One-Step Start	35″ × 35″ × 12″	210 pounds	$ 695	Three-phase motors only.
Lectron	Continuous-Smooth	12″ × 10″ × 5¾″	15 pounds	$ 875	Solid-state—no moving parts.

Source: Company records.

To aid in market planning, Mr. Patton collected available market data and developed a list of potential industrial applications where he felt that the Lectron control offered distinct advantages. Exhibit 16.5 lists the value of shipments of switchgear and control apparatus. Exhibit 16.6 lists the shipment of selected industries where the Lectron control could be used, and Exhibit 16.7 is a list of possible applications.

While the demand and shipments for industry equipment were clearly derived from capital investment plans of industry, even when such spending declined, the demand for labor-saving devices and motors rarely declined. Thus, Mr. Patton thought that general economic conditions should not affect the need for the Lectron control very much. On the other hand, developing a marketing program to sell to an industry having rapid growth, such as the pump and compressor industry (due to energy-related capital expansion and the growth of food processing), mining, and pulp and paper mills, might produce built-in growth once the Lectron control was adopted.

Current Lectron customers seem unrelated by product or industry and usually purchase the Lectron control for very limited and unusual applications where no other starter would work. Two major crane-manufacturing companies were in the process of testing the Lectron control, and Mr. Patton hoped to sell 2,000 to 3,000 units in this market. Several brewing and bottling companies had successfully tested the Lectron device to control pumping operations and had expressed great enthusiasm for the product, although no formal commitments from either of these markets had yet been forthcoming. At a volume of 2,000 units, the manufacturing margin was estimated to be about 75 percent.

In addition to his own efforts, Mr. Patton used six sales representatives in the major industrial areas of the country. Most orders, however, ended up being placed directly with the company as a result of several press releases describing the Lectron control, or as a result of Mr. Patton's work with selected customers. Orders were typically for

EXHIBIT 16.5   **Value of Shipments of Selected Switchgear and Control Apparatus 1974**

SIC	Product	Number of Producing Companies	Shipments (Mil$)	Growth 1973–74
3613 701	Magnetic Control Circuit Relays	56	$256.5	9.3%
3613 704	Starter Accessories, overload relays	25	17.2	3.6%
3622 012	A.C. full voltage starters 600 volts or less	42	182.9	27.4%
3622 013	A.C. contractors 600 volts or less	30	37.5	–6.0%
3622 011	A.C. reduced voltage controls	19	25.2	NA
3622 015	Synchronous motor starters	6	NA	NA
3622 016	Motor control centers	55	145.1	54.0%
3622 018	Starters and contractors for motors over 600 volts	21	37.3	33.2%
3622 081	Rheostats and resistors	17	20.1	39.6%
3622 097	All other general industry devices	48	268.1	28.5%
3622 045	Marine and navy auxiliary controls and accessories	18	27.0	.4%
3622 048	Metal mill, crane, and hoist controls, constant and adjustable voltage	30	66.3	11.6%
3622 049	Definite purpose contractors and starters for refrigeration and air conditioning	9	23.5	NA

Source: U.S. Department of Commerce.

one or only a few controls and were shipped by United Parcel Service after being built to order by the small production department.

Marketing Strategy

After five years of directing his attention to problems of product development and manufacturing, Mr. Patton has become increasingly aware of the need for a comprehensive marketing plan if Lectron is to reach its full business potential. He was not sure that his sales representatives were effective in developing new markets, although his sales cost was only 8 percent with this approach. Company-employed salespersons would be more committed to sell the product, except that they are expensive, and Mr. Patton was not sure which companies and market areas to direct them to. Exhibit 16.8 lists some typical sales costs, but Mr. Patton recognized that selling costs were higher in major metropolitan areas, such as New York, Chicago, and San Francisco, where costs were 40 to 60 percent higher than average. In the smaller cities of the Southeast, such as Greenville, near the textile industry, costs were 15 to 20 percent below average.

Mr. Patton has also developed a list of possible trade publications where Lectron advertising might be placed. Before he does any advertising, he wonders if he should get wholesale distribution so that customers can get local service and delivery of the product. He was not strongly in favor of distribution through wholesalers, as his earlier experience with electrical wholesalers led him to the conclusion that (1) wholesalers didn't make an effort to push the product, (2) wholesalers carry too many other

EXHIBIT 16.6   **Selected Industry Data**

Industry Category	SIC	1975 Shipments (Mil$)	Establishments	Average Annual Growth Rate 1967–75		Major Producing Areas
				Shipments	Exports	
Pumps and compressors	3561 3563	$4,700	643	10.8%	15.6%	North Central Northeast
Material-handling equipment	3534 3535 3536 3537	$3,720	1,250	5.7%	17.9%	Middle Atlantic North Central Western
Mining machinery	3532	$1,550	240	14.5%	16.4%	Pennsylvania West Virginia Ohio
Oil machinery	3533	$3,250	314	20.6%	28.6%	Texas Oklahoma California Louisiana
Food products machinery	3551	$1,745	675	10.8%	16.1%	North Central California New York
Textile machinery	3552	$ 845	578	1.8%	12.7%	Northeast Southeast
Switchgear	3613	$2,760	898	5.0%	NA	NA
Motors and generators	3621	$3,125	775	4.0%	NA	NA
Industrial controls	3622	$2,093	1,173	6.0%	NA	NA
Shipbuilding	3731	$4,710	455	8.6%	NA	Great Lakes, East, West, and Gulf Coasts

Source: U.S. Department of Commerce.

products, and (3) wholesalers really lacked the technical knowledge to understand potential applications. It seemed to him that some form of personal selling would be required, and if this were done properly, perhaps he might not have to advertise until he could better afford it, as the costs for advertising in many trade publications seemed quite high. Exhibit 16.9 lists the publications Mr. Patton was considering.

Mr. Patton had identified three possible marketing strategies he felt had some promise for success:

1. Sell product concept to electrical design engineers and OEM equipment manufacturers and encourage them to specify the Lectron control, include it with their products, or at least recommend it to their customers.

2. Sell control services by selling the control, including wiring and connecting equipment, to end users of equipment or possibly to OEMs.

3. Sell control to manufacturing and maintenance buyers to solve a specific application problem or to reduce maintenance and breakage.

EXHIBIT 16.7   **Potential Applications**

Blowers
Centrifugal
Constant Pressure

Brick Plants
Augers
Conveyors
Dry Pans
Pug Mills

By-Product Coke Plants
Door Machines
Leveler Rams
Pusher Bars
Valve Reversing Machines

Cement Mills
Conveyors
Crushers
Dryers—Rotary
Elevators
Grinders, Pulverizers
Kilns

Coal Mines
Car Hauls
Conveyors
Cutters
Fans
Hoists—Slope
Hoists—Vertical
Jugs
Picking Tables
Rotary Car Dumpers
Shaker Screens

Compressors
Constant Speed
Varying Speed
   Centrifugal
   Plunger Type

Cranes—General Purpose
Hoist
Bridge or Trolley—Sleeve
Bearing
Bridge or Trolley—Roller
Bearing

Concrete Mixers

Flour Mills
Line Shafting

Food Plants
Butter Churns
Dough Mixers

Hoists
Mine Hoists—Slope
Mine Hoists—Vertical
Contractors Hoist
Winch

Larry Car

Lift Bridges

Machine Tools
Bending Rolls
Boring Mills
Bull Dozers
Drills
Gear Cutters
Grinders
Hobbing Machines
Lathes
Milling Machines
Presses
Punches
Saws
Shapers

Material Handling
Coal and Ore Bridges
   Holding
   Closing
   Trolley
   Bridge

Metal Mining
Ball, Rod, or Tube Mills
Car Dumpers—Rotary
Converters—Copper
Conveyors
Crushers
Tilting Furnace

Paper Mills
Beaters
Calendars

Pipe Working
Cutting and Threading
Expanding and Flanging

Power Plants
Clinker Grinders
Coal Crushers
Conveyors—Belt
Conveyors—Screw
Pulverized Fuel Feeders
Pulverizers, Ball Type
Pulverizers, Centrifugal Type
Stokers

Pumps
Centrifugal
Plunger

Rubber Mills
Calendars
Crackers
Mixing Mills
Washers

Steel Mills
Accumulators
Casting Machines—Pig
Charging Machines
   Bridge
   Peel Revolving
   Trolley
Coiling Machines
Conveyors
Converters—Metal
Cranes
   Hoist
   Bridge and Trolleys,
      Sleeve Bearing
   Bridge Trolleys, Roller Bearing
Crushers
Furnace Doors
Gas Valves
Gas Washers

Hot Metal Mixers
Ingot Buggy
Kick Off
Levelers
Manipulator Fingers
Pickling Machine
Pliers—Slab
Racks
Reelers
Saws—Hot or Cold
Screw Downs
Shears
Shuffle Bars
Side Guards
Sizing Rolls
Slab Buggy
Soaking Pit Covers
Straighteners
Tables
   Approach
   Roll
   Shear Approach
   Lift
   Main Roll
   Transfer
   Tilting Furnaces
   Wiring Stranding
   Machines

Textiles
Weaving
Knitting
Throwing
Winding
Tufting

Wood Working Plants
Boring Machines
Lathe
Mortiser
Moulder
Planers
Power Trimmer and Mitre
Sanders
Saws
Shapers
Shingle Machines

Other possible market considerations were selling to government agencies, such as the Coast Guard, or other manufacturers of controls, even though there seemed to be little interest among the major manufacturers. Also, Mr. Patton wondered if he might be more successful if he sold the complete control package including possibly the motor rather than just the control alone.

EXHIBIT 16.8 Productivity and Costs for Selected Types of Salespersons

Type of Salesperson	Metropolitan Area			Suburban Area	
	Average Direct Cost	Calls per Year	Cost per Call	Calls per Year	Cost per Call
Account representative—calls on already established customers; selling is low key with minimal pressure to develop new business.	$23,500	1,195	$20	598	$39
Detail salesperson—performs promotional activities and introduces new products; actual sale is ultimately made through a wholesaler.	$20,500	1,912	$11	1,195	$17
Sales engineer—sells products where technical know-how and technical aspects are important to sale; experience in identifying and solving customers' problems is required.	$29,750	1,030	$29	665	$45
Industrial products salesperson—sells a tangible product to industrial or commercial purchasers; a high degree of technical knowledge is not required.	$25,000	1,673	$15	956	$26
Intangibles/service salesperson—must be able to sell effectively intangible benefits such as design services or application concepts.	$24,250	2,153	$11	1,195	$20

Source: *Sales and Marketing* magazine, February 9, 1976.

As Mr. Patton cleared a space on his desk he wondered to himself if Thomas Edison and other pioneers in the electrical industry had gone through this process.

He then carefully began considering how to choose an appropriate marketing strategy that would hasten the success of the Lectron control.

EXHIBIT 16.9 **Cost and Circulation Data on Selected Trade Publications**

Magazine	Circulation	Cost of B & W Page	Comments
Automation	90,223	$2,280	Production engineering emphasis; trade-show issues.
Control Engineering	70,627	$1,925	Instrumentation and automatic control emphasis.
Design News	123,189	$2,760	Design engineer's idea magazine.
Electrical Apparatus	15,031	$ 750	Magazine of electromechanical operation and maintenance, edited for the after-market.
Electrical Contractor	40,004	$1,350	Electrical construction and maintenance industry.
Electrical Construction and Maintenance	70,521	$2,295	
Electrical Equipment	75,060	$3,053	Edited for electrical and electromechanical engineers who research, design, and install electrical or electromechanical products.
Electrified Industry	32,600	$1,110	Edited for electrically responsible engineers; covers automation, electric controls, material handling, and electrical maintenance.
Electrical Wholesaling	16,114	$1,350	Controlled circulation to electrical distributors; sourcebook of electrical wholesaling, marketing, and selling.
Factory	91,086	$2,590	General interest manufacturing magazine.
Food Processing	56,031	$1,420	New product reports, case histories; covers processing equipment, material handling, etc.
Industrial Equipment News	142,735	$7,915	What's new in equipment, parts, and materials; covers literature and catalogs that are available.
Industrial Maintenance and Plant Operation	105,581	$3,390	News tabloid magazine for those responsible for maintenance and operation of industrial plants.
Machine Design	127,419	$2,554	
Marine Engineering/Log	22,490	$ 800	Covers new developments in marine engineering and naval construction.
Materials Handling Engineering	76,733	$2,090	Technical magazine for material-handling, packaging, and shipping specialists.
New Equipment Digest	139,120	$2,340	Covers equipment materials, processes, and design literature and catalogs.
Pit and Quarry	22,242	$1,085	Directed to management who specify and buy equipment, supplies, and services for mining, quarrying, and processing nonmetallic minerals.
Purchasing	74,498	$2,385	News magazine for industrial buyers.

Source: Standard Rate and Data Service, June 24, 1976.

EXHIBIT 16.10 **Starting Devices: Product Description**

Auto-Transformer Control

Auto-transformer-type starters are the most widely used reduced voltage starter because of their efficiency and flexibility. All power taken from the line, except transformer losses, is transmitted to the motor to accelerate the load. Taps on the transformer allow adjustment of the starting torque and inrush to meet the requirements of most applications. The following characteristics are produced by the three voltage taps:

Tap	Starting Torque % Locked Torque	Line Inrush % Locked Ampere
50%	25%	28%
65%	42%	45%
80%	64%	57%

Part Winding Controls

Part winding starting provides convenient economical one-step acceleration at reduced current where the power company specifies a maximum, or limits the increments of current drawn from the line. These starters can be used with standard dual-voltage motors on the lower voltage and with special part winding motors designed for any voltage. When used with standard dual-voltage motors, it should be established that the torque produced by the first half-winding will accelerate the load sufficiently so as not to produce a second undesirable inrush when the second half-winding is connected to the line. Most motors will produce a starting torque equal to between $\frac{1}{2}$ to $\frac{2}{3}$ of NEMA standard values with half of the winding energized and draw about $\frac{2}{3}$ of normal line current inrush.

Primary Resistor

Primary-resistor-type starters, sometimes known as "cushion-type" starters, will reduce the motor torque and starting inrush current to produce a smooth, cushioned acceleration with closed transition. Although not as efficient as other methods of reduced voltage starting, primary-resistor-type starters are ideally suited to applications such as conveyors, textile machines, or other delicate machinery where reduction of starting torque is of prime consideration. Starters through size 5 will limit inrush to approximately 80 percent of lock rotor current and starting torque to approximately 64 percent of locked torque. Larger sizes are custom designed to the application.

Star-Delta Control

Star-Delta-type starters have been applied extensively to industrial air-conditioning installations because they are particularly applicable to starting motors driving high inertia loads with resulting long acceleration times. They are not, however, limited to this application. When six- or twelve-lead delta-connected motors are started star-connected, approximately 58 percent of full-line voltage is applied to each winding, and the motor develops 33 percent of normal locked rotor current from the line. When the motor has accelerated, it is reconnected for normal delta operation.

Multicon, Incorporated (A)

John E. Clark, Executive Vice President of Multicon, shook his head and smiled as he walked off the second tee. His ball had hooked badly into the trees and high rough on the left side of the second hole, and his next shot would be a difficult one. "There's no doubt about it," he said, "As little as I have played, I can't just come out and put the ball in the fairway. This is only the second time I've been out this year, but I guess that I can't complain . . . . Business has been so hectic since the 'split' that I just haven't had time to work on my game."

Clark referred to the split that had removed Multicon from divisional status as part of Murphy Controls Company over a year before. "We're still completing the move to become an independent company now," said Clark, eyeing his golfball and measuring the approach to the green with a harsh stare. "As a matter of fact, there are some shifts in ownership and organization that are going to take place shortly, and they will really put us in a position to move!" Falling silent, Clark hesitated momentarily considering which club to use for his next swing. His hand paused briefly on his pitching wedge, the correct club for simply playing his ball back to the fairway, but quickly settled on his two-iron. Undaunted by the brow of the hill over which his ball would have to rise or the trees it would have to negotiate on its way to the green some 200 yards distant, Clark slashed at the ball.

"Our biggest difficulty, other than financing, of course, is a strategic issue. It is an extremely complex situation," commented Clark as he walked greenward. "Multicon has made a good name for itself as a 'systems house' putting together 'turn-key' robotics installations for manufacturing concerns. But, we are good at both general-purpose

Source: This case was prepared by Dr. David W. Rosenthal, Associate Professor of Marketing at Miami University, Oxford, Ohio, as a basis for class discussion rather than to illustrate appropriate or inappropriate handling of administrative situations. Certain data have been disguised.

robotics, and vision systems." Clark's second shot had rattled into the trees to the right of the green, and he now had an almost impossible shot just to put his ball on the green and keep it there. "The question facing us now is, should we continue in robotics or should we specialize in vision systems?" Clark's third shot rolled quickly down the sloping green, past the hole and off into the fringe some 25 feet away.

Speaking as he lined up his lengthy putt, Clark noted, "The big advantage of staying with robotics is that we have developed some great expertise in a variety of applications. That's 'money in the bank.' At the same time, vision systems are really state-of-the-art, and there are only a few companies in the country that have our knowledge and proven abilities in that area. We'd be awfully hard to touch in a couple of years." Clark settled himself over his putt, stroked the ball, and watched motionless as it "broke" to his right and settled some 18 inches from the hole. After his "tap-in" for a bogey five, Clark commented, "Guess I'll have to settle for bogey . . . . My practice time is unlikely to get any better for the foreseeable future."

Company Development

Multicon had begun in mid-1982 as a division of Murphy Controls Company. Murphy Controls Company was a small, Cincinnati-based distributor of industrial control devices. At that time, it was apparent that the programmable controls distributed by the company lent themselves to networking with industrial microcomputers, and that an increasing need for appropriate software was developing. The Multicon Division was formed to improve Murphy's position in this business.

John E. Clark, then a regional manager with Automatix, a Boston-based firm in robotics and machine vision, was hired to manage the new division with help from Roscoe C. Forche, a member of the Murphy Controls engineering staff.

"I won't say that those were the 'good old days,' because they weren't," said Forche. "Business was tight; the economy was lousy. We were right in the depths of the recession, and capital expenditures on machinery were at a low point. Start-up problems were the rule rather than the exception. Still, we had a good base to work from, and we knew for certain that the market would improve."

In the twelve-month period ended December 31, 1983, the Division had achieved sales of $929,000 and an after-tax profit of $71,000. Multicon was created as of January 1, 1984, to take over the operations of the division. In calendar year 1984, Multicon generated sales of $1,903,000 and an after-tax profit of $58,000. Additional financial information may be found in Exhibits 17.1–17.3.

The executives of Multicon expected the company to generate billings of $3.21 million in the calendar year 1985, based on existing bookings and as a result of an evaluation of outstanding proposals. The company currently held a $450,000 line of credit with local banks and anticipated additional capital requirements of $150,000 plus an increase in bank debt to cover up to a total of $850,000 in working capital. The company was expected to generate a pretax profit of $287,000 for 1985 if sufficient working capital could be secured, but despite the excellent record of growth, local banks were not enthusiastic about increasing the company's debt position.

EXHIBIT 17.1   **Comparative Income Statement**

	1983	1984
Sales	$928,921	$1,903,349
Cost of sales:		
Materials	$626,015	NA
Program development	81,332	NA
	$707,347	$1,513,768
Gross profit on sales	$221,574	$ 389,581
Operating expenses:		
Wages and benefits	$ 62,175	$ 152,402
Travel and sales promotion	23,173	72,323
Shop expense	8,755	NA
Depreciation, rent, insurance	12,511	20,968
Utilities and telephone	6,918	11,343
Supplies	NA	13,782
Interest	NA	21,754
Other	14,195	32,547
	$127,727	$ 324,119
Income before provision for federal income taxes	$ 93,847	$ 65,462
Provision for federal income taxes	$ 23,289	$ 7,200
Net Income	$ 70,558	$ 58,262

Organization

By June 1985 the Multicon organization had grown to include 17 people. Ronald P. Barker, 44, was the president and chief executive officer of both Murphy Controls Company and Multicon. At Multicon his duties principally related to overall supervision and increasingly to finances. John E. Clark, 31, was executive vice president and was responsible for all marketing, engineering, manufacturing, and administrative activities. Increasingly, Clark found himself in the role of CEO as Barker retreated to managing the parent company, Murphy Controls Company.

The engineering functions of the business were overseen as a whole by Randall C. Forche, 31, from his position as vice president of engineering. Forche controlled all technical matters in all functional areas of the firm, reporting to Clark in a staff relationship. Also reporting to Clark were Terrell Zielesnick, Manager of Applications Engineering, and Geoff D. Plum, Manager of Project Engineering. Generally, Zielesnick was responsible for the sales development engineering while Plum was responsible for the design and actual building of the systems. An organization chart and brief biographies of the officers are shown in Exhibits 17.4 and 17.5.

Products

Multicon operated in computer aided manufacturing (CAM) in two principal markets, machine vision and industrial robots. The company has acted as a "systems house"

EXHIBIT 17.2   **Balance Sheet—Calendar Year 1984**

Assets

Current assets:

Cash	$ 746
Accounts receivable, net	253,102
Receivables from affiliate	49,668
Inventories	192,741
Costs & profits in excess of billings on uncompleted contracts	263,692
Other	346
Total current assets	$760,295
Property and equipment:	
Furniture and fixtures	$ 47,652
Shop equipment	4,928
Leasehold improvements	3,725
Automobile	8,865
	$ 65,170
Less—Accumulated depreciation	8,770
	$ 56,400
Deferred organization costs, net	$ 8,989
Total assets	$825,684

Liabilities and Shareholders' Equity

Current liabilities:

Note payable	$110,000
Trade accounts payable	364,944
Accrued payroll and other	30,625
Advance payments from customers	62,822
Deferred income taxes	12,600
Total current liabilities	$580,991
Shareholders' equity:	
Common stock, no par value, 100,000 shares authorized, 60,000 shares issued and outstanding, stated at	$ 500
Paid-in capital	186,231
Retained earnings	57,962
	$244,693
Total liabilities and shareholders' equity	$825,684

connecting a variety of manufacturers with end users. The term "value added reseller" was also used to describe the types of activities conducted by Multicon.

Clark described Multicon's business as being similar to that of a good stereo salesperson. " When a customer visits a good stereo salesperson, they are asked about their needs, the amount of money they wish to spend, the types of music they listen to, and how they wish to listen. Perhaps even the type of furniture and housing they have can play a role. Having gained an understanding of the client's needs, the salesperson, using his knowledge of the available equipment in the market, can help to pick out the most appropriate kind of speakers, a turntable from another manufacturer, an amplifier from a third company, and so forth."

EXHIBIT 17.3   **Statement of Changes in Financial Position for the Year Ended December 31, 1984**

Sources of Cash:

Operations

Net income	$ 58,262
Expenses not requiring an outlay of cash-deferred income taxes	12,600
Depreciation and amortization	8,169
Cash provided by operations	$ 79,031

Increase in

Note payable	$ 85,000
Trade accounts payable	262,293
Accrued payroll and other	30,625
Advance payments from customers	62,822
Total sources of cash	$519,771

Uses of Cash:

Additions to property and equipment	$ 53,046
Deferred organizational costs	6,754
Dividends paid	300

Increase in

Trade accounts receivable	156,281
Receivables from affiliate	72,957
Inventories	254,341
Other	346
Total uses of cash	$544,025
Decrease in cash	$(24,254)
Cash, beginning of period	25,000
Cash, end of period	$ 746

"A systems house brings together the best robotic or vision components for a particular job, writes programming to enable the assembled components to do the work, develops instructions and training for the users, installs the equipment, and troubleshoots the whole thing until it is running smoothly. In short, a manufacturer who wishes to install a robotic assembly would make use of a systems house to hand over an operational set of equipment, 'turn-key' system."

The Multicon company provided one-, two-, and three-dimensional vision systems for machine guidance, part sorting, inspection, and gauging. Integrating hardware from the major vision systems manufacturers with application engineering, software, optics, lighting, and peripheral devices, the company offered operational systems for industrial users. As of June, 1985 the company had successfully installed more than 25 vision systems. Primary suppliers of vision systems to Multicon were Automatix Autovision Systems and Opcon 20/20 Systems.

In the industrial robot area, Multicon had focused efforts on assembly, sophisticated parts handling, and special processes. The company offered turnkey robot cells including hardware, software, and peripherals such as end of arm tooling, sensor

EXHIBIT 17.4   **Organization Chart, June 1985**

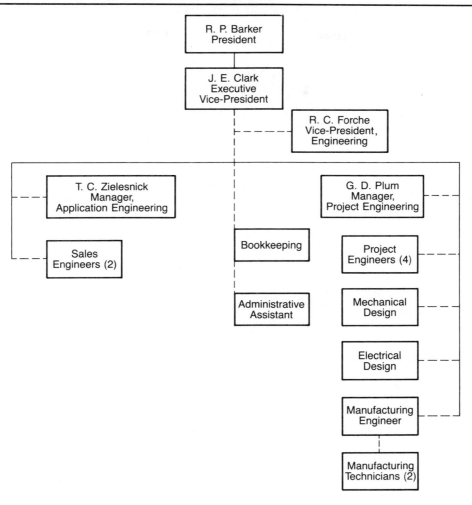

integration, parts delivery systems, and controls. Multicon was a designated Systems Application Center for Hitachi America and as a Systems Integrator Reseller for Cincinnati Milacron.

The company had designed and installed a number of systems for a broad spectrum of applications, including a vision system for the high speed inspection of consumer products packaging, labeling and content; a machine vision system with custom optics and lighting to inspect for casting flaws in the bores of machined parts; a machine vision system for the detection of weld seams in rolled steel; and robot cells for the loading of lead fittings into the die cavity of injection molding machines.

EXHIBIT 17.5 **Executive Biographies**

John E. Clark

Cofounder and Executive Vice President
Age 32
BBA Marketing, University of Cincinnati, Cincinnati, Ohio, 1976
1976–1980 Sales engineering positions with Honeywell and Texas Instruments
1980–1982 Regional Manager, Automatix, Inc., a Boston-based start-up company in the field of machine vision and robotics
1982–1983 Manager, Multicon division of Murphy Controls Company
1984–present Executive Vice President, Multicon, Inc.
Charter member of Robotics International and the Machine Vision Association of Society of Management Engineers (SME).

Roscoe C. Forche

Cofounder, and Vice President Engineering
Age 31
BS and MS, University of Cincinnati, Cincinnati, Ohio, 1975 and 1977
1978–1982 Sales Engineer and Manager Technical Services, Murphy Controls Company
1982–1983 Chief Engineer, Multicon Division of Murphy Controls Company
1984–present Vice President Engineering, Multicon, Inc.
Charter member of Robotics International and Machine Vision Association of SME.

Geoff D. Plum

Manager, Project Engineering
Age 35
BSC and MBA, University of Louisville, Louisville, Kentucky, 1973 and 1980
1968–1980 General Electric Company, various positions including manufacturing engineer, production supervisor, and advanced manufacturing engineer
1980–1985 Cincinnati Milacron, Industrial Robot Division, Supervisor of Application Development
1985–present Multicon, Inc., Manager, Project Engineering
Charter member of Robotics International of SME.

Terrell Zielesnick

Manager, Applications Engineering
Age 35
BSEE, Ohio State University, Columbus, Ohio, 1977
MBA, University of Cincinnati, Cincinnati, Ohio, 1985
1976–1980 Goodyear Atomic Corporation, Electrical and Project Engineer
1980–1981 Ziel-Blossom and Associates, Electrical Engineer
1981–1984 Crouse Hinds Company, Supervisor, Applications Engineering
1984–present Multicon, Inc., Manager, Applications Engineering
Member of the Institute of Electrical and Electronic Engineers
Member of Robotics International of SME
Registered Professional Engineer, Ohio.

Operations

Multicon sales took place on a project basis. Sales leads came from direct contact, trade-show activities, presentations to industry associations, and referrals from manufacturers and customers. John Clark oversaw the sales activities of the two individuals who called on prospective customers, and he made sales calls himself as well.

Once a customer contact had been established, the Multicon executives and engineers took great pains to determine that the prospective customer had a definite and viable need for a robotic or machine vision system, and that Multicon possessed the expertise to deliver an operational solution. It was often required that samples of the customer's product be made available and that engineering documentation be provided.

As Terrell Zielesnick, who provided presale engineering support, noted, "The worst thing that can happen is for a customer to have a misconception about his needs and our capabilities. If a clear problem is not defined, we won't attempt to develop a proposal. It is not uncommon to find 'customers' who are simply looking for a free education or who have heard about this newfangled robotics stuff and figure that it is about time to jump into it. It takes us a long time and a lot of effort to develop a well-reasoned proposal to solve a specific problem. We can't afford to waste our energies on too many unaccepted proposals. Besides, the well-defined projects are difficult enough!"

Generally, a Multicon sales engineer visited the prospective customer's site and attempted to further qualify the project by reviewing its technical and commercial content. He attempted to determine whether it was a project Multicon was competent to do, whether the project was funded, who the competition might be, and why the customer wanted to do the project. The particulars were then reviewed by Clark and Zielesnick, who authorized further development and a feasibility study, possibly including a customer-funded demonstration.

Pricing was the responsibility of the marketing group, headed by John Clark. Once a proposal was written, it was submitted for review to a committee composed of Clark, Forche, Zielesnick, and Plum. Proposals were not submitted to a customer before approval by that group. Once a proposal was accepted, the project was transferred to the engineering and production departments. Typically, a project manager was appointed who "shepherded" the project through engineering, design, and production. The final step in the process consisted of a demonstration and acceptance by the customer at the Multicon facility. Multicon employees then followed the project into the customer's location for installation, start-up, testing, and training.

As a value added remarketer, Multicon marked up the price of the hardware that it sold as part of its systems. While the actual markups varied from supplier to supplier and even from product to product, the company set 30 percent as a target markup. Increasingly, however, robotics hardware was being marked up only an average of about 15 percent, while vision systems hardware continued to average roughly 30 percent. Considerable downward pressure appeared to be building on robotics equipment prices. In the installation of most systems, testing, software development controls, training and set-up costs added from half to twice the cost of the hardware alone. These labor-intensive functions were difficult to estimate and added considerable risk to the pricing process. Should a particular job be quoted at too large a price, the customer would be unlikely to contract for the system, but if the price were too low, difficulties in the engineering or applications process could actually result in a loss for Multicon.

The Robotics Industry

In 1985 the robotics industry was in a state of rapid change. Technological advances during the previous ten years and growing capability to apply the benefits brought by robotic automation had brought the industry to a new level of sophistication. Even the definition of an industrial robot had changed dramatically in just a few years. While old definitions had focused on the ability of a robot to accomplish "3-D tasks" (Dumb, Dirty, and Dangerous) to the advantage of human workers, the new definition focused on flexibility. In 1985, the Robotic Industries Association (RIA) defined an industrial robot as "a reprogrammable, multifunctional manipulator designed to move material, parts, tools or specialized devices through variable programmed motions for the performance of a variety of tasks."

While industrial robots had been invented some 25 years before, the real growth in installation and use of robots in industry had only begun in the early 1980s. At that time, industry analysts eagerly developed forecasts for market growth reaching yearly sales of $2 billion by 1990. Individual companies predicted their own sales to be as high as $1 billion by 1990 and loudly proclaimed their projections to the press.

By 1985, however, it had become obvious that the industry had not grown at the pace predicted earlier. A variety of reasons were commonly cited as constraints to the adoption of robots, primary among them: the economic recession of the early 1980s, unrealistic expectations about the capabilities of robots brought on by popular movies such as *Star Wars,* lack of government support in the form of tax incentives for installation, and labor demands for maintaining employment levels. Actual installations and sales figures for the industry are shown in Exhibits 17.6 and 17.7.

The purchase and installation of a robotic manufacturing cell was often an emotional one, stemming from a variety of fears. Industry sources countered these fears by referring to the following points: (1) most current robot installations involved the selection of a robot over another form of equipment, not to replace a person; (2) robots in factories generally performed the hazardous, boring, demoralizing and repetitive tasks that allowed workers to be removed from dangerous environments; (3) the increased productivity offered by robots could pave the way to a shorter work week, higher pay, and better working conditions; and (4) higher productivity could mean fewer jobs lost to overseas manufacturers in competitive industries.

Industry analysts and participants had anticipated that after the economic recession ended, there would be an industry "shakeout" reducing the number of competitors in the market. The shakeout had not yet occurred in June 1985, but there were indications that many companies were on the brink of insolvency. John Clark described the situation: "We're also starting to see, not the demise of the industry, but that the industry troubles are starting to have an effect. Only three years ago, everybody forecasted the industry as being just absolutely successful, with high growth rates, good profitability—and every major company wanted in. GE got into it; Westinghouse got into it; and Caterpillar bought into Advanced Robotics. GM bought into GM-Fanuc (GMF). Just this year, Ford bought into American Robotics. Everybody thought it was just nirvana."

But now, in 1985, the headaches are starting to show. Outside of GMF, whose numbers are suspect because they're part of GM and you can't get a handle on them, everybody's losing money. *Everybody's* losing money. I think that's starting to have its toll. People look at GE, you know, as an illustration of the problems in the industry. They had huge corporate resources, a lot of commitment, big hoopla, and they have not been a major factor in the market . . . . And they've been in it for four or five years.

EXHIBIT 17.6   **Shipments by U.S.-based Robot Suppliers**

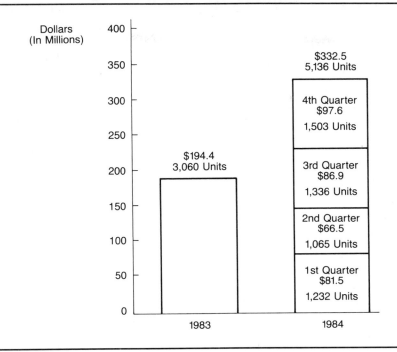

One of the main problems with the industry today is that in 1980 everybody believed the forecasts. In 1980, numbers were banging around like you wouldn't believe. The problem is that because everyone believed the forecasts, they built to capacity and staffed to meet that inflated view of demand. Now the industry is plagued by overcapacity. Many companies went so far as to buy inventory, almost on specula- tion. Now they have literally hundreds of robots stuck in warehouses. They have to sell them off cheap, and I think that generates a lot of pressure. A guy is running a profit cen- ter, and he's getting killed by having this inventory tie up his capital. I think that's part of the crash coming, the reductions in pricing, just to correct the initial forecast errors.

The shakeout's started. I think the economy's as good as it's going to get for a couple more years. And I think that, if anything, from a capital-equipment standpoint, it may even be on the downside. GMF's market presence in automotive goods, which is the biggest user of robotics to date, is being felt by the rest of the robot community. And I think, if you put those two things together, people've been living on high hopes for a little bit too long and the reality is starting to close them down. Some people are just plain running out of money.

The robotics industry was characterized in two ways, by the applications for which robots were purchased and by the companies who manufactured (or assembled) the robots. The major industry applications had been in the automotive industry, primarily in the area of spot welding. Estimates ranged as high as 60 percent of industry sales

EXHIBIT 17.7   **U.S. Robot Population (Installed Base)**

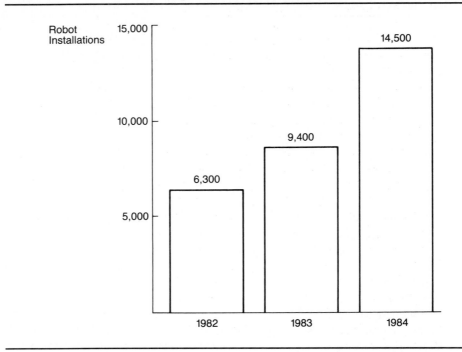

going to automotive spot-welding applications. Other automotive applications in-cluded: arc welding, materials handling, painting, stamping, and metal working. Automotive applications as a whole were estimated to account for as much as 80 percent of robot sales. Other applications included parts manufacturing, injection molding, and materials handling. A list of major U.S. robotics firms and their estimated market shares for 1983 and 1984 is shown in Exhibit 17.8.

The Machine Vision Industry

Machine visions systems ranged in complexity from simple television camera–computer hookups to sophisticated laser-based, three-dimensional robotic controls. The basic concept of a vision system was to "digitalize" an image, providing a source of data for a computer software package to interpret. In simple terms, a television camera would take a digital picture of a brightly lit scene, breaking the image into thousands of individual points or cells called "pixels." Each pixel would be assigned a numeric value between 0 and 63, according to the pixel's level of brightness or darkness. A microcomputer attached to the system would then be capable of interpreting the numeric data from the image, according to a set of programmed instructions.

EXHIBIT 17.8   **U.S. Robot Manufacturers: Estimated Share of Market, 1983–1984**

	Share of Market	
Manufacturer	**1983**	**1984**
Cincinnati Milacron	17%	17–20%
Westinghouse/Unimation	15%	6–7%
GMF Robotics	9%	30–35%
DeVilbiss	9%	4%
Automatix	7%	7%
Others	43%	27–36%

A simple illustration of an application might be a vision system to determine whether an assembly line had a part on it at a given location. The vision system would "view" the location, registering a constant level of brightness when no part was present. As a part was delivered to that point, the level of brightness would change, causing a change in the numeric value of the pixels in the image, allowing the computer to recognize that a part had arrived.

Similar to the early predictions regarding the robotics industry, estimations of market size and growth in the machine vision area varied widely during 1985. Estimates of the 1984 machine vision market ranged from $40 million to $80 million and from 50 to 120 companies participating. Estimates for market growth ranged from 50 percent per year to an optimistic doubling each year, yielding market size projections of $1 billion by 1990. The range of market projections is illustrated in Exhibit 17.9.

The machine vision market in 1985 was dominated by a group of five companies controlling up to 80 percent of the sales in the area. The remainder of the market was divided among many smaller firms. The market was characterized by many small "start-up" companies with limited product lines and capabilities. The five major companies and their estimated 1985 market shares are shown in Exhibit 17.10.

John Clark described the market, "There is no barrier to entry. None. Any halfway bright person could go to Digital Equipment Company and buy an O.E.M. computer, say, for about $5,000 and from any number of companies buy an interface board that lets a camera "talk" to the computer, and go to any video store and buy an off-the-shelf camera that's used for security surveillance or something, put it all in a cabinet that costs a couple hundred bucks, and he's got a vision system. It doesn't do much, and it's not very sophisticated, but he's a player in the market! That is what is happening right now. The market is just full of "mom and pop" companies, little guys with a garage. It's a mess."

The purchase of a vision system was often less emotional than the purchase of a robot. While considerable publicity had surrounded the issue of job displacement with robots, little pressure had been felt by the vision industry. Vision systems purchase decisions tended to be made at lower levels of management than were robot purchase

EXHIBIT 17.9   **Machine Vision Industry Market Estimates, 1985**

	Market Estimate	
Year	Companies	Dollars
1980	30	NA
1981	NA	NA
1982	NA	NA
1983	NA	$35M–$84M
1984	50–120	$75M–$80M
1985	150	$150M
**		
1987		$480M
**		
1989		$455M
1990		$800M–$1B

NA: Not available, M = million, B = billion

EXHIBIT 17.10   **Machine Vision Industry: Estimated Market Shares by Company, 1985**

Company	Estimated Share
Automatix	20–22%
View Engineering	20–22%
Machine Vision International (MVI)	14–15%
General Electric	5–10%
Diffracto	8–10%
Others	21–33%

decisions, because plant managers apparently did not require the same reassurance of upper management support as they did with robot installations.

Zielesnick suggested that purchasers of vision systems were less sensitive because the systems often did the job better than the currently used processes: "A good example is label inspection. Picture dishwashing-liquid bottles coming by. You are sitting in a chair in front of a conveyor, and the bottles are coming by at the rate of five a second, 300 a minute. On the other side of the conveyor is a mirror, and your job is to look both at the front of the bottle, and in the mirror, at the back of the bottle. You are supposed to identify those bottles that have torn labels or labels that are misplaced by more than a sixteenth of an inch. That's a lousy job, and you probably aren't doing it very well."

Competition in the vision systems market focused on product characteristics, particularly computing speed and power, developing software packages and decision logic, and developing expertise in on-site engineering elements such as lighting, lenses, and so forth. Increasingly, manufacturers of vision systems were relying on systems houses for programming and on-site engineering functions in the channel of distribution.

The Current Decision: Interview with John Clark

The thing that makes our strategic decision so difficult is that we have some compelling reasons to stay with robotics, and at the same time, we have strong reasons to go with vision systems. With our resources, I'm not sure that we can afford to do both . . . at least, not well.

Robotics

Currently our sales are roughly 60 percent robotics and 40 percent vision. A robot system is worth anywhere from $60,000 to $120,000 in sales to us on the average. A vision system can go anywhere from $20,000 to $200,000 with an average installed price of about $75,000. When we started the year, we were shooting for 40 percent robotics and 60 percent vision, but it just hasn't worked out that way. With a small company like ours, a single large order can make a dramatic shift.

Our position in the robotics industry is at once a problem and an advantage. We are one of a number, probably less than 100, of systems houses in the country. In terms of skills and experience, that number falls to about 50. But, that number is growing, and the robot manufacturers are encouraging it. We are software and controls oriented, but other systems houses are positioned at the metal-fabricating end of the business. They can actually design a system and build the conveyors to actually create a production line. Our stated policy is that we don't want to get into metal working. We have a good skill set, and we have good people, but we will be competing with companies that can provide the metal side, too.

Another problem with the robotics business is the margins. The robot manufacturers aren't giving us the margins that we need right now. Fifteen percent is typical. If you look at a robot cell that cost $100,000 installed, there is probably a $60,000 robot in there. At 15 percent, that generates a nice volume, but it is actually a cash burden. We actually have to go out and buy that piece of equipment. If we have to carry it for 90 or 120 days while we put all the pieces together, program it, put it into the customer's plant, and start it up . . . all before we get paid; that 15-percent margin almost doesn't cut it. That may change. We are trying to force the robot manufacturers to change, but I just don't know.

Robotics is very, very service oriented. There is nothing wrong with that, but the big leverage comes from having a product to sell. Our role in the robotics business is strictly service; design engineering, drafting, mechanical engineering, electrical engineering, training, and start-up. There is no proprietary product that Multicon will own. When you place a robot cell, sure you gain the expertise and knowledge of that application, but the next placement, even for the same application, will require a completely new set of services. You can't just plug it in . . . . There's no "product" opportunity there.

On the positive side, the robot market is growing at 50 or 60 percent per year, and it will continue for a lot of years. We are in a very, very good start-up service. The market is more mature than the vision market, so we think that a robot is easier to sell than a vision system right now. The industry has already gone through the pains of education and establishing its worth. Our overall marketing costs are lower in robots than in vision. Further, we have a good name in the business, and we have great expertise.

A key to success for us has been our people. We've got good access to robotics engineers, and there is a shortage of robotics and machine vision engineers in the marketplace. Still, we have been able to hire key people, and we will be able to attract more, particularly in robotics.

Machine Vision

We are early, early in the machine vision cycle or phase of development. We are one of a very, very select few machine vision systems houses in the country. There may be three or four people like us, but I've only identified one. I'm sure that there are others, but there aren't many. Because of that, we can establish a very strong market identity, and that is very important.

We have established some good relationships, probably stronger relationships with our machine vision vendors than we have with our robot vendors. They are embracing us just a little bit tighter for a whole variety of reasons, but that is a definite plus.

Probably the major advantage for vision is that it gives us the opportunity to become product driven. There are real opportunities to develop proprietary packages based around a piece of machine vision hardware that becomes "a product" out in the market. Our first is a label-inspection package. The consumer-products packaging community doesn't want to buy a vision system for label inspection, they want to buy something to inspect labels, and they want the vision system to be 'transparent.' They don't want to have to fool with it. Their product comes through the test space; a good product is passed through, and a bad product is kicked out. We have a standard system that will do that with standard design, standard manufacture, standard software, and standard lighting. We'll still have to customize it a little, but we can tell a customer that we can or cannot do the job in about an hour.

Machine vision is a higher risk going in than robotics for every project. The initial contact on a new application is riskier from our standpoint. We may look at it; we may evaluate it and say that we can do it. Our assumptions and evaluations may not be as accurate in vision. It's easier to be off, and at that point, we are pumping a lot of unforeseen resources to finish a commitment made to the customer. That is a risk.

A big problem in machine vision is that it is difficult for us to find people to work on it. It is a skill that is not in the market, so you kind of have to "home grow" it. There is a significant cost in finding people and in training them to contribute. We should be hiring people six months to a year before we really need them. We need to invest the $50,000 to $70,000 per head in educational costs to get them up the learning curve. Right now, that is a problem for us.

Another major concern is that the machine vision manufacturers won't always be willing to rely on service groups like us. As they get more sophisticated in their applications software, it will become much easier to tell the vision system to do something. Users won't need a systems house to design, program, and install a system. It is the old "user friendly" issue. The more the manufacturers invest in research, the less important our role as just an applier will become.

Conclusion

Clark smiled as he stood over his golf ball on the right side of the fairway on the par-five eleventh hole. For one of the few times today, he had driven the ball straight and long. Looking toward the green, he reached for his three-wood. Despite the long distance to the green and the pond guarding the approach, Clark intended to take the risky shot rather than "laying up" with an iron. After taking a practice swing, he addressed the ball and smoothly stroked what had to be his best shot of the day.

"Well, we'll see," laughed Clark, replacing his club in his bag. The result of the shot was not visible as the pond was out of sight over a ridge in the fairway and the green was too far to see a ball clearly. "There are only so many opportunities, and you have to do the best with them that you can!"

Ethical Dilemmas in Business Marketing

Individuals in marketing and sales positions are frequently confronted by ethical problems and dilemmas. The scenarios presented below were real situations faced by individuals during their first year on the job after graduation from college. After reading each scenario you should decide what action you would have taken.

1. I presently sell a line of industrial compressors to customers and the standard sales pitch indicates that they are the best for the money available in the market. Unfortunately, I also know that this isn't true. However, they make up 40 percent of my line and I cannot successfully make my quota without selling at least $85,000 worth per month. It's probably okay, because all salespersons say theirs are the best.
Would you take the same selling approach?

2. My field sales manager drinks excessively and has accompanied me on sales calls hung over and smelling of alcohol. This behavior does not enhance my professional reputation with my customers or the company. I have decided not to say anything, as the field sales manager writes my review and can dramatically influence my success or failure in this, my first selling assignment.
Would you report the sales manager to upper level management?

3. I am working for a large company which is heavily involved in defense contracts. I have recently been transferred to a new division that builds nuclear weapons. These are weapons of which the public is not aware and of which I do not personally approve. However, our work is entirely legal and classified top secret.

These scenarios were developed by Professor John B. Gifford and Jan Willem Bol, Miami University. They were part of a study of the ethical problems recent business school graduates faced on their first job.

I have decided to stay with the company because I find my work challenging and I am not directly involved with any phase of the actual nuclear component of the project.

If you had similar attitudes, would you stay with the company?

4. I recently had the opportunity to buy a new IBM XT computer, printer, and software for $1000 from our MIS Director. He apparently received these items "free" with a large computer order for the company. I would be doing mostly work for the company at home on the computer. I decided to accept his offer and paid him $1000 cash.

   What action would you have taken?

5. After a business dinner with an important client in California, he implied that he wanted to go out and "do the town" plus . . . . Although I wasn't sure what the "plus" might involve, there was a 50/50 chance he wanted an affair on the side. I said I was tired, and retired alone for the evening. I also lost the account which had been a 90 percent sure thing.

   What action would you have taken?

6. By coincidence, your salesperson and your distributor are both pitching your product to the same prospect. The distributor, however, does not know this yet. You know that when he finds out he will offer a competitor's product that will most certainly undercut your price. Your salesperson is totally dependent on commission.

   Should you ask your salesperson to back off?

7. A buyer for a large government institution (a good prospect with potentially high volume) offers you information about the sealed bids of competitors. You know the practice is questionable, but he is a good friend and no one is likely to find out. Besides, you are below quota, and need the commission badly.

   Will you accept his offer?

8. An industrial customer has indicated that our lubricants were priced about 5 percent higher than those being offered by our competition. He indicated that if I would drop my price $7\frac{1}{2}$ percent, he would cancel his order with our competition and buy from me. This will mean a $1,400 commission for me personally. I agreed.

   What action would you have taken?

9. As an industrial salesperson, you are in the office of a prospect to provide a verbal price on a project. You and your sales manager have determined that a specific price is the right price for your organization and you believe you will win the contract. However, as the prospect walks out of his office you see a copy of your competitor's proposal on his desk with a substantially lower price. You will need to give him your price now, as he walks back into the room.

   Will you change your price?

10. I have a set quota of goods that I must sell every month. Sometimes it becomes necessary to overstock my customers in order to meet my quota. Most of the customers are not very sophisticated, and don't even know how much inventory they should carry.

    Is this an appropriate sales tactic?

NAME INDEX

SUBJECT INDEX

Abbott Laboratories Hospital Products Division, and decision support system, 132
ABI/Inform, 143
Accessibility, and market segment evaluation, 161
Accessory equipment, foundation goods, 21
Account behavior spectrum, and customer characteristics, 76–77
Accounting firms, marketing savvy, 340
Accounting performance analysis, 128
Action system, 100
Activities, and marketing control systems, **524**
Activity based cost system, 537
Administration
  channel, 381–389
  and large firm purchasing, 35
  price, 439–441
  sales, 503–510
Advantage, competitive
  assessing, 218–225
  country specific, 244–247, 256, 258, 266
  sources of,
    business marketing firm, 220–222
    multidomestic versus global, 257
Advertisement
  Anderson Consulting, information technology, 529
  business-to-business ads, 453, 455
  close-supplier relationship, 69
  cost, 470–471
  creating awareness, 456–457
  CSX, benefits to users, 466
  decision model, 459
  and derived demand, 7
  Digital Equipment and end-use application, 167
  direct mail 471–474
  effectiveness, 475–478
  Federal Mogul distribution system, 409
  formal, 49
  Hewlett-Packard and dealers, 485
  IBM, commitment to service, 328
  Intel, 24
  Kodak, business-to-business market, 494
  new media, 470
  physical characteristics of, 467–468
  role in business marketing strategy, 452–458
  sales efficiency and effectiveness, 454–456
  Stanley Vidmar, 454, 455
  Sun Microsystems and price/performance theme, 425
  Texas Instruments, digital signal processor, 313–314
  TRW corporate image campaign, 457
  Xerox, 15
  and quality, 276
Advertising Age, 468
Advertising expenditures, 460–464, 470–471
  objective-task method for estimating, 461–462
  rule-of-thumb methods for estimating, 460–461
Advertising media, 468–475
  business publications, 468–470

cost allocation for, 470–471
direct mail, 471–474
frequency and scheduling, 471
selection of, 475
telemarketing, 474–475
Advertising message, 464–468, 486
  basing appeal on benefits, 465–466
  and perception, 464–465
Advertising objectives, 458–460
  creative strategy statement for, 460
  target audience for, 460
  written, 458–459
ADVISOR project, 463
Advisory councils, dealer, 385
Advisory support, 22
Afton Industries, (Case Study), 656–659
Agreement, cultural variation of, 99
Air-conditioning systems, four microsegments, 173–174
Alcoa, 68
Alfred P. Sloan Foundation, 306
Always-a share customer, 77–78
American Hospital Association, 127
Anderson Consulting, information technology achievements, 529
Annual plan control, 533
Annual Survey of Manufacturers, 140
APICS News, 469
Apple Computer
  business-to-business ads, 453
  and derived demand, 6
  and market segmentation, 160
Assignment process, and SIC codes, 135
AT&T, 101
  business-to-business ads, 453
  R&D investments, 232
Atlas Corporation, service responsiveness, 171
Attention, selective, 116
Attitude, "be something", 346
Attraction, as power, 112
Australia, trade barriers, 355
Auto industry
  buyers and supply chain, 13
  sales to, 141
  seating market, 141
  worldwide competitive pricing, 429
Autonomous strategic behavior, 301–305
  compared with induced behavior, 301
  illustrated, 303–305
  project endorsement, 305
  project initiation, 303–305

Backward integration, 223
Balance of payments, service exports, 355
Ball bearings, demand and usage factor, 190–191
Barriers
  to success, 317–318
  trade, 355–356
  trading zones, 250, 261
Basebook, 141
Basic industries, and SIC system, 134–135
Baxter, international markets, 244
"Be something" attitude, 346

Beckman Instruments
  global message leveraging, 473
  and marketing intelligence, 126–128
Behavior
  organizational buying, 53, 95–96, 491–493
  purchasing, 57–58
  strategic, 300–305
Beliefs, and market driven organizations, 217–218
Benchmarking, 161–162
Benefits
  advertising message, 465
  direct mail, 472
  lease, 446
  market segmentation, 163, 169
  product, 421–422
Beta Pharmaceuticals: Pennsylvania Distribution system, (Case Study), 628–633
  background, 629–631
  consultants' findings and plans, 631
  subsystem, 632–633
Bidding
  competitive, 442–445
  models, 445
  strategy, 444–445
Bindicator, and market potential index, 185
Blue Ribbon Commission on Defense Management, 47
Boeing
  international markets, 177, 244
  product line, 280
  R&D investments, 232
Borland International, 464
Bottom-up forecasting, 197–198
Boyle Machine & Supply Co., profile, 365
Brake shoes, transportation system, 413
Brand Pipe Company, (Case Study), 694–703
  background, 694–696
  competition, 702–703
  distribution, 699–700
  market segments, 696–698
  pricing policy, 701–702
  promotion and sales, 699
  transportation, 701
Breadth of technologies, 311
Break-even analysis, 433, 434
Bribery, global business practices, 254
Brokers, 371, 390
Budgets
  advertisement, 461, 462
  trade show, 483–484
Buildings and land rights, 21
Bundling service, **346–347**
Business-level strategy, 226
Business marketer
  and customer commitment, 78–79
  and new task buying, 72
  and purchasing problems, 75–76
  required adaptations, 70
  and value analysis, 86–87
  and vendor analysis, 91
Business marketing
  computer-assisted salesperson, 209